DOCUMENTS RELATING TO THE NORTH WEST COMPANY

Originally Published as
Champlain Society Publication XXII

A Facsimile Edition by
GREENWOOD PRESS, PUBLISHERS
NEW YORK   1968

First Greenwood reprinting, 1968

LIBRARY OF CONGRESS catalogue card number: 68-28610

This work has been printed on long-life paper and conforms to the standards developed under the sponsorship of the Council on Library Resources.

Originally published as
Champlaign Society Publication XXII

Printed in the United States of America

SIMON McTAVISH
From a painting in the McCord National Museum, Montreal

DOCUMENTS RELATING TO THE NORTH WEST COMPANY

EDITED

WITH INTRODUCTION, NOTES, AND APPENDICES

BY

W. STEWART WALLACE, M.A.

TORONTO
THE CHAMPLAIN SOCIETY
1934

PREFACE

THE materials in print with regard to the history of the North West Company have hitherto been fragmentary. Apart from the scattered journals or narratives of individual fur-traders, they have been limited in the main to the agreements of 1802 and 1804, printed in L. R. Masson's *Bourgeois de la Compagnie du Nord-Ouest*, and some additional documents, published during recent years in the *Canadian Historical Review*. It has been my good fortune to find in Hudson's Bay House in London and in the Sulpician Library in Montreal, as well as elsewhere, other documents of importance relating to the North West Company (such as the minutes of the Company at Grand Portage and Fort William from 1801 to 1814); and it has seemed to me worth while to bring together in this volume the chief materials, both published and unpublished, which are now available with regard to what may be described as the constitutional history of the Company.

For the rare privilege of access to the vast wealth of material in the archives of Hudson's Bay House in London, and for permisson to reproduce in this volume the documents from Hudson's Bay House bearing on the history of the North West Company, I have to acknowledge here my great debt to the Governor and Committee of the Hudson's Bay Company. Without this permission (which is acknowledged in the case of each document here reproduced) the present volume could not have been undertaken. I should be remiss in my duty also if I did not here confess my indebtedness to the officers of the Company, especially the secretary, Mr. J. Chadwick Brooks, and the archivist, Mr. R. G. Leveson Gower, whose patience with and kindness toward me during the happy weeks which I spent in Hudson's Bay House could not have been exceeded.

The annotation of these documents has presented a problem. The frequency with which the individual names appeared in them, especially in the various agreements and minutes, would have necessitated innumerable cross-references, had the notes regarding them appeared as foot-notes. It was deemed better therefore to throw these biographical notes into an appendix, arranged alphabetically, in such a way as to provide a sort of biographical dictionary of the Nor' Westers. Into these brief biographies has gone a good deal of original research. In some cases I have been so fortunate as to get track of the descendants, and to obtain from them information which would otherwise, perhaps, have been lost. In other cases, I have succeeded, thanks to the good offices of my friend Mr. E.-Z. Massicotte, in finding crucial information of a documentary character in the magnificent collection of archival material under his care in the Old Court House at Montreal. In many cases, I have been kindly permitted to draw upon the biographical material relating to servants of the Hudson's Bay Company collected by Mr. R. G. Leveson Gower in Hudson's Bay House in London. Frequently, the material contained in the biographical sketches has been drawn from a dozen different sources; and it has not been possible, naturally, to indicate the source of each item of information. But

PREFACE

where the information contained in a sketch has been derived chiefly from one source, I have as a rule indicated my indebtedness to my informant. Where I have omitted to acknowledge any indebtedness, I hope that those who have been kind enough to help me will forgive the omission, and accept the general assurance of my thanks. To mention everyone, indeed, who has kindly helped me, sometimes by a mere hint, to track down the biographical details of which I was in search, would be to transform this preface into a catalogue.

I must not omit, however, to express my gratitude to Professor George M. Wrong, Professor H. A. Innis, and Mr. J. B. Tyrrell, who have been so long-suffering as to read part of the volume in galley-proof, and to give me the benefit of their criticism.

W. S. W.

CONTENTS

	PAGE
PREFACE — — — — — — — — —	vii
HISTORICAL INTRODUCTION — — — — — —	1

DOCUMENTS

1. EXTRACT FROM A LETTER OF ANDREW GRAHAM, MASTER AT YORK FORT, TO THE GOVERNOR AND COMMITTEE OF THE HUDSON'S BAY COMPANY, DATED YORK FORT, AUGUST 26, 1772 — — — — — 39

2. EXTRACTS FROM MATTHEW COCKING'S JOURNAL OF OCCURRENCES AND TRANSACTIONS AT CUMBERLAND HOUSE, 1775-6 — — — 44

3. EXTRACT FROM MATTHEW COCKING'S JOURNAL OF THE MOST REMARKABLE TRANSACTIONS AND OCCURRENCES AT CUMBERLAND HOUSE, 1776-7 — — — — — — — — — 46

4. LETTERS OF SIMON MCTAVISH AND JAMES BANNERMAN, 1774-9 — 47

5. REPORT FROM CHARLES GRANT TO GENERAL HALDIMAND ON THE FUR TRADE, APRIL 24, 1780 — — — — — — — 62

6. LETTER OF BENJAMIN FROBISHER TO ADAM MABANE, DATED MONTREAL, APRIL 19, 1784 — — — — — — — 66

7. LETTER OF BENJAMIN AND JOSEPH FROBISHER TO GENERAL HALDIMAND, DATED OCTOBER 4. 1784 — — — — — — 70

8. LETTER OF SIMON MCTAVISH TO JOSEPH FROBISHER, DATED APRIL, 1787 — — — — — — — — — — 75

9. ARTICLES OF AGREEMENT BETWEEN SIMON MCTAVISH AND JOSEPH FROBISHER, NOVEMBER, 1787 — — — — — — 77

10. DEED OF ASSIGNMENT OF GREGORY AND MCLEOD, 1788 — — 82

11. NORTH WEST COMPANY AGREEMENT, 1790 — — — — — 84

12. DOCUMENTS RELATING TO THE ENGAGEMENT OF JEAN BAPTISTE CADOT, JR., WITH THE NORTH WEST COMPANY, 1795 — — — 90

13. AGREEMENT OF MCTAVISH, FROBISHER AND COMPANY, 1799, WITH STATEMENT OF ACCOUNTS — — — — — — — 94

CONTENTS

		PAGE
14.	The Agreement of the North West Company at Grand Portage, July 5, 1802	108
15.	Agreement among the Partners of the XY Company, dated October 24, 1803	125
16.	Last Will and Testament of Simon McTavish, dated July 2, 1804	134
17.	The Agreement of the North West Company at Montreal, November 5, 1804	143
18.	Agreement of Sir A. Mackenzie & Co., November 9, 1804	157
19.	Minutes of the Meetings of the North West Company at Grand Portage and Fort William, 1801-1807, with Supplementary Agreements	170
20.	Minutes of the Transactions of the North West Company at Fort William, 1807-1814	246
21.	Articles of Agreement of McTavish, McGillivray and Co., 1811	292
22.	Draft of Agreement of McTavish, McGillivrays & Co. 1814	295
23.	Letter from W. McGillivray, to J. G. McTavish, dated Fort William, July 15, 1820	317
24.	Extracts from Colin Robertson's Correspondence Book, 1817-22	318
25.	Index to Indenture of March 26, 1821, made between the Governor & Co. of Hudson's Bay and Messrs W. McGillivray, S. McGillivray, and Edward Ellice	321
26.	Extract from Hudson's Bay Company minute book, March 21, 1821; Proceedings at a General Court relating to the Amalgamation with the North West Company	327
27.	Letter of William McGillivray to the Rev. John Strachan	327
28.	Extracts from Simon McGillivray's "Preliminary Explanation of the Accounts and Statements submitted to the Creditors", Montreal, 16th Jan. 1826	329
29.	Extract from Letter of Thomas Thain to the Wintering Partners of the late North West Co., London, February 25, 1826	334
30.	Letter of Governor Simpson to the Governor and Committee of the Hudson's Bay Co., dated at Montreal, April 26, 1826	334

		PAGE
31.	A Letter from Simon McGillivray, Esq. to the Creditors of the Firms of McTavish, McGillivrays and Co. and McGillivrays, Thain and Co. of Montreal, in the Province of Lower Canada; dated London, 26th February, 1827. With an Appendix, containing Statements in Explanation of the Circumstances under which the Insolvency of these Firms was Declared at Montreal, on the 27th of December, 1825	353
32.	Letter to Simon M'Gillivray, Esq. in Answer to one Addressed by Him to the Creditors of the Late Firms of M'Tavish, M'Gillivrays & Co. and M'Gillivrays, Thain & Co. dated London, 26th of February, 1826, by Henry Mackenzie, late Partner of the Former Firm	387
Appendix A: A Biographical Dictionary of the Nor'-Westers		425
Appendix B: A Select Bibliography		506
Index		515

LIST OF ILLUSTRATIONS

SIMON McTAVISH	*Frontispiece*
WILLIAM McGILLIVRAY	*Opposite p. 12*
JOHN OGILVY	*Opposite p. 16*
WILLIAM McKAY	*Opposite p. 22*
SIMON McGILLIVRAY	*Opposite p. 30*

HISTORICAL INTRODUCTION

THE rise and fall of the North West Company is one of the most dramatic episodes in the economic history of North America. Beginning as a pool or syndicate formed by a few bold adventurers who had penetrated to the fur-bearing regions of the Canadian North West in the early days of British rule, it developed into an organization which was one of the first examples of "big business" in the New World. Within the brief space of fifty years, its wintering partners opened up the whole of the North West from Lake Superior to the Pacific Ocean, and from the sources of the Mississippi to the Arctic Sea; and despite the competition of the ancient and powerful Hudson's Bay Company, invested by royal charter with exclusive rights over the watershed of Hudson Bay, it made good its sway over this vast empire. Its wilderness headquarters, at Fort William on Lake Superior, became, during the height of the season, a teeming town of over three thousand persons; and Montreal, its financial headquarters, was a metropolis of fur-trade magnates. Its partners came to occupy seats in the legislatures and councils of Canada, and even of Great Britain; and it was said (perhaps without justification) that they dominated the government of Canada.

Then the Fates intervened. In 1811, the Earl of Selkirk, who had acquired a controlling interest in the Hudson's Bay Company, obtained a grant of territory in the valley of the Red River; and on the banks of this river he founded a colony which cut across the North

West Company's line of communications. The result was a life-and-death struggle between the North West Company and the Hudson's Bay Company for supremacy in the West which culminated in the ruin of the Nor'-Westers. In 1821, the North West Company was driven to accept absorption in the Hudson's Bay Company; and in 1825, the firm of McTavish, McGillivrays and Company, which had been the virtual directorate of the North West Company, closed its doors. The fur-trade was diverted from Montreal to Hudson Bay; and Montreal lost its primacy as the *entrepôt* of the fur-trade. The canoe route from Montreal to Athabaska became deserted, and almost forgotten. Fort William sank into a half-ruinous post of third-rate importance; and in 1839, Washington Irving was able to write the epitaph of the Nor' Westers in this famous sentence: "The feudal state of Fort William is at an end; its council chamber is silent and desolate; its banquet-hall no longer echoes to the auld-world ditty; the lords of the lakes and the forests are all passed away."

It is not possible within the scope of this introduction to narrate in detail the history of the North West Company. That theme would require a volume in itself. All that is possible here is to sketch in outline the fortunes of the Company, in such a way as to provide a background for the documents that follow.

The western fur-trade had its beginnings during the later days of French rule in Canada, under the La Vérendryes and their successors; but the Seven Years' War and the Conspiracy of Pontiac interrupted the trade, and it was not until after 1763 that it was revived. The first trader to penetrate to the Saskatchewan after the British conquest appears to have been a French Canadian, known to the Hudson's Bay men as "Franceway", who had been in the west during the French régime, and who went past Lake Winnipeg in 1766, or possibly in 1765. He was followed by James Finlay, who wintered on the Saskatchewan, at what came to be known as Finlay's House, in 1768-9, and by Thomas Corry, who spent the winters 1771-2 and 1772-3 on the Saskatchewan. Thereafter the trade was opened up by an ever-increasing number of adventurers. The year 1772 saw in the North West not only Corry, but also "Franceway", Barthélemi Blondeau, and William Bruce; and the year 1773 saw the arrival of Joseph and Thomas Frobisher. In 1774, upwards of sixty canoes "came inland from the Grand Portage" (according to the statement of Samuel Hearne at Cumberland House), and among the masters of these canoes were several new arrivals, notably James Tute, Charles Paterson, William Holmes, and Peter Pangman. Peter Pond and Alexander Henry made their first appearance in the West in 1775; Booty Graves, Charles McCormick, and Nicholas Montour in 1776 and 1777; Venant St. Germain, Patrick Small, and Robert Grant, among others, in 1778-9.[1]

The business connections of these traders are not always clear. "Franceway" appears to have been outfitted by Isaac Todd and James McGill of Montreal; but James Finlay and William Bruce seem to have been trading on their own account. From an early date, however, there was apparent a strong tendency toward combinations of traders, brought about, no doubt, by the risks and long credits that the trade entailed. From Andrew Graham's report to Hudson's Bay House in 1772,

[1]For an account of these early expeditions to the West, see W. S. Wallace, *The pedlars from Quebec* (Canadian historical review, 1932).

it is clear that Thomas Corry was merely the spearhead of a group of traders which included Thomas Walker at Quebec, Maurice Blondeau at Montreal, George McBeath and Isaac Todd at Michilimackinac, and John Askin at Emissions, near Sault Ste. Marie. When Alexander Henry reached Grand Portage in 1775 he "found the traders in a state of extreme reciprocal hostility, each pursuing his interests in such a manner as might most injure his neighbours";[1] and on reaching Cumberland House he joined his stock with that of the Frobisher brothers, and decided to winter with them, in order to reduce the evils of competition. Other traders did likewise, though these early pools were but temporary affairs and did not always end happily. In the spring of 1776, Matthew Cocking writes in his journal at Cumberland House, "I am informed that the Master Pedlers up above are at present at Variance, and some of them parted stocks. One in particular[2] is tenting, and Trades without the Stockades."

Just when the original nucleus of the North West Company was formed, it is almost impossible to determine. It may have been the group which was behind Franceway and Corry in the years 1765-71; and certainly some of this group were afterwards heavily interested in the North West Company. On the other hand, it may have been some later combination. Certainly, by 1775 the signs of concentration were clear to behold. In that year a single licence was granted to James McGill, Benjamin Frobisher, and Maurice Blondeau for twelve canoes, with seventy-eight men, to go to Grand Portage

---

[1] Alexander Henry, *Travels and adventures in Canada and the Indian territories*, Ed. by J. Bain (Toronto, 1901), p. 235.
[2] This, as appears later in the journal, was Peter Pangman.

HISTORICAL INTRODUCTION 5

and beyond; and when the various groups of traders reached the West, a union of interests took place on the Saskatchewan at least. Alexander Henry gives a clear account of this pool of 1775:

> "Four different interests were struggling for the trade of the Saskatchiwaine, but, fortunately they had this year agreed to join their stock, and when the season was over, to divide the skins and meat. This arrangement was beneficial to the merchants; but not directly so to the Indians, who, having no other place to resort to, nearer than Hudson's Bay, or Cumberland House, paid greater prices than if a competition had subsisted."[1]

This combination was confined, it is apparent, to the West, and lasted only for the winter; but it was almost immediately reflected in a pooling of interests in Michilimackinac and Montreal. Lawrence Ermatinger, one of the small independent merchants trading to the North West, some of whose papers are in the Public Archives of Canada, refers to "the North West Company" in a letter dated November 28, 1776,[2] and Patrick Sinclair, the lieutenant-governor of Michilimackinac, writing in 1780, referred to "the North West Company" as "sending an embassy to Congress in '76"[3]—a reference the meaning of which is obscure, but which proves beyond question the existence of some sort of organization or association of the North West traders at that early date. By 1778, we find John Askin at Michilimackinac addressing letters to the "Gentlemen of the N. W. Co. at Montreal" (by whom he seems to mean McGill, Frobisher, and Paterson), writing to Joseph Frobisher and John McGill at Grand Portage as those designated "to transact the business of the N. W. Co. this season", and referring to "the Great

---
[1] Alexander Henry, *Travels and adventures in Canada and the Indian territories*, Ed. by J. Bain (Toronto, 1901), p. 320.
[2] H. A. Innis, *The fur trade in Canada* (New Haven, 1930), p. 211.
[3] Can. Archives, *Haldimand Papers*, B. 217, p. 468.

Company" in a letter to Todd and McGill at Montreal.[1]

By 1779 the union of interests in the North West was completed by the formation of a sixteen-share concern, or association of partnerships, the composition of which is described in a report on the Indian trade made by Charles Grant to Sir Frederick Haldimand, the governor of Canada, on April 24, 1780. As Sir Alexander Mackenzie put it, the traders to the North West "joined their stock together, and made one common interest." The sixteen shares were, according to Grant's report, divided as follows:

"Todd & McGill	2 shares
"Ben & Jos. Frobisher	2 do.
"McGill & Paterson	2 do.
"McTavish & Co.	2 do.
"Holmes & Grant	2 do.
"Wadden & Co.	2 do.
"Ross & Co.	2 do.
"Oakes & Co.	2 do."

Since this list affords us the first full and definite information regarding the composition of the North West Company in its earlier stages, it calls for annotation. Todd and McGill was the partnership of Isaac Todd and James McGill, both of whom played an outstanding part in the business life of Montreal from the earliest days of British rule until the death of McGill in 1813 and of Todd in 1815. Benjamin and Joseph Frobisher were brothers, natives of Yorkshire in England, who, with their younger brother Thomas, were engaged in the western fur-trade from 1764 until the death of Joseph, the last surviving brother, in 1810. McGill and Paterson were John McGill, the brother of James McGill, who died in 1797, and Charles Paterson, who was drowned in Lake Michi-

[1] M. M. Quaife, *The John Askin Papers*, vol. I (Detroit, 1928), pp. 83-160, *passim*.

gan in 1788. These three houses were closely associated, and might indeed be regarded as almost one. McTavish and Co. was a house established in Montreal in 1774 by a young Scotsman named Simon McTavish, of whom more anon. His first partner had been James Bannerman, the captain of one of the early sailing vessels on the Great Lakes, with whom he had engaged in the forwarding business; but in 1779, Bannerman had returned to England, and the other member of McTavish and Co. in 1779 would appear to have been Patrick Small, a young Scotsman of good family who had been introduced into the fur-trade through the friendship between McTavish and Small's great-uncle, General John Small, afterwards the lieutenant-governor of Guernsey. Holmes and Grant were William Holmes, whom we have already met on the Saskatchewan, and Robert Grant, one of the numerous Grants in the fur-trade at the end of the eighteenth century, the relationships of whom constitute one of the major puzzles of the trade. Wadden and Ço. was a firm formed by Jean Etienne Wadden or Wadin, a Swiss merchant who settled in Montreal soon after the Conquest, and who was murdered in the North West in 1782, and Venant St. Germain, a French Canadian. McBeath and Co. was composed of George McBeath, a merchant who was prominent at Michilimackinac from 1768 to 1782, and Peter Pond, an American trader, who was one of the most daring pioneers of the fur-trade in the West. Ross and Co. was the business name of John Ross, a small trader, who was murdered by Peter Pond's men in the West in 1787; and Oakes and Co. was a partnership between Forrest Oakes, an English merchant who settled in Montreal in 1761, and was well-connected in England, and his brother-in-law, Lawrence Ermatinger, a Swiss merchant, some of whose descendants played a famous part in the fur-trade.

The statement has been made that the agreement of 1779 lasted for only one year, and that in 1780 it was renewed for a period of three years; but that at the end of two years it was broken.[1] Possibly the breach of the agreement was connected with quarrels which led to the murder of Wadden at Lac la Ronge in March, 1782, by Pond's men. However this may be, it is certain that in 1783 a new agreement was made, which resulted in a radical reorganization of the trade, and the elimination, not only of some of the smaller traders, but also some of those traders who had been earliest in the North West and had held a large proportion of the shares in the pool of 1779. Though we lack a list of the partners who composed the North West Company of 1783, Professor H. A. Innis has, by dint of a brilliant piece of reconstruction,[2] compiled the following conjectural list of the shares held in this Company:

Partners	Shares
Simon McTavish	3
B. and J. Frobisher	3
George McBeath	2
Robert Grant	2
Patrick Small	2
Nicholas Montour	2
Peter Pond	1
William Holmes	1
	16

This list, which must be approximately correct, reveals two interesting and important facts. In the first case, it

[1] *Some account of the trade carried on by the North West Company* (Report of the Public Archives, Canada, 1926, pp. 60-61.)

[2] H. A. Innis, *The North West Company* (Canadian historical review, 1927, pp. 309-10).

is clear that the smaller traders have been dropped. Wadden was dead, and his partner, Venant St. Germain, now sinks into the category of an employee. John Ross becomes a free trader, and is later killed. Forrest Oakes and Lawrence Ermatinger fade about 1783 from sight. On the other hand, Isaac Todd, James and John McGill, and Charles Paterson—some of the most important names in the agreement of 1779—also disappear. For this there can be only one explanation. During the years 1780-82 there is the closest co-operation between Todd, the McGills, and Paterson on the one hand, and the Frobishers and McTavish on the other. Charles Paterson gives security for McTavish in the fur-trade licences of 1782, and James McGill gives security for the Frobishers. After 1783, moreover, there is the clearest evidence that the relations between the Frobishers and McTavish, on the one hand, and Todd and the McGills, on the other, were most amicable. The obvious explanation is that in 1783 there was an agreement—possibly a gentleman's agreement—whereby Todd, the McGills, and Paterson agreed to withdraw from the North West, and confine themselves to Lake Michigan and the Mississippi, while McTavish and the Frobishers agreed to withdraw from the "South West trade" and confine themselves to the North West. This conjecture is supported by the fact that about 1785 the first Mackinac Company was formed, with Todd and McGill as backers and outfitters, and with Charles Paterson as director of the trade in the upper Mississippi. The south-western trade at that time was twice as large as the north-western; and it is probable that James McGill, who believed that the American Revolution would not seriously affect the south-western trade, thought that he had made a good bargain. But actually the south-western trade was already on the wane; and the north-western trade was only at the beginning of its development.

In these arrangements, one may perhaps be permitted to detect the fine Italian hand of Simon McTavish, who was destined to become the guiding spirit of the North West Company. McTavish was a young Scotsman from Invernessshire, who had come to America about 1770, and had embarked in the fur-trade from Albany. He had wintered in Detroit as early as 1773, and perhaps earlier. His was possibly one of the four interests mentioned by Alexander Henry as being on the Saskatchewan in 1775; and we know definitely that from 1775 to 1779 he was engaged in the North West trade, in partnership with James Bannerman. Certainly, he was an important member of the pool of 1779. From the letters which he wrote during those years, which have been preserved, one gets a quite different impression of him from that conveyed by Masson in his *Bourgeois de la Compagnie du Nord-Ouest*, where he is depicted as the autocratic and over-bearing "Marquis" or "Premier" of the fur-trade. In these early years he appears to have been a young man who loved "good wine, good oysters, and pretty girls", and was possessed of a charming sense of humour; and there are signs also of that generous and kindly spirit which is so evident in his last will and testament. But, whatever his private character, there is no doubt that he was possessed of a first-class mind for business. When the Quebec Act annexed to Canada in 1774 the Indian countries, he promptly moved his headquarters to Montreal; and during the difficult period of the American Revolution he continued to carry on the fur-trade with conspicuous success. Though he had not, so far as we know, been west of Grand Portage, his uncanny prescience had taught him that the future of the fur-trade was in the far North West; and it is a legitimate inference that he had something to do with the redistribution of interests in 1783.

The idea underlying the reorganization of 1783 was that of a monopoly. Having divided the field between the members of the pool of 1779, McTavish and his partners in the agreement of 1783 hoped, apparently, that they would be able to make the country north-west of Lake Superior their own preserve. For the moment, however, this hope proved illusory. From the beginning the North West Company, as reorganized in 1783, was called upon to face severe competition from a firm of Montreal merchants who had long been interested in the North West trade, but who had been excluded from the association formed in 1783. This was the firm of Gregory, McLeod, and Company. Over the earlier history of this firm, as over so much else in the history of the fur-trade, some obscurity rests. The firm seems to have been formed in 1773, when James Finlay, the pioneer of 1768, entered into partnership with a young Englishman named John Gregory; and from 1773 to 1783 the canoes of Finlay and Gregory figure annually in the fur-trade licence returns. It was in the service of this firm that the young Alexander Mackenzie entered upon his apprenticeship in the fur-trade about 1779. In 1783, Finlay retired from active participation in the fur-trade, to become in his later days inspector of chimneys in Montreal; and Gregory took into partnership a Detroit trader named Normand McLeod. Gregory, McLeod and Company succeeded in 1783 in enlisting the services of several western traders, notably Peter Pangman and John

Ross, who had been excluded from the North West Company; and for four years they provided the North West Company with a very lively opposition.

The details of the struggle between the North West Company and Gregory, McLeod and Company are locked in the limbo of the unknown; but it is clear that the struggle was acute. "After the severest struggle ever known in that part of the world", wrote Sir Alexander Mackenzie later, "and suffering every oppression that a jealous and rival spirit could instigate; after the murder of one of our partners, the laming of another, and the narrow escape of one of our clerks, who received a bullet through his powder horn, in the execution of his duty, they were compelled to allow us a share of the trade."[1] The partner who was murdered was John Ross, who had been one of the members of the pool of 1779. During the winter of 1786-7 Ross, representing the opposition, and Peter Pond, who had after some hesitation joined the North West Company, found themselves facing each other in the Athabaska country; and during the winter Ross was shot and killed in a scuffle with Pond's men. This, the second murder in the West with which Pond had been connected, brought about his retirement from the western fur-trade; and it brought about also a union between the North West Company and Gregory, McLeod and Company. The news of Ross's death was brought down to Grand Portage in the summer of 1787 by Roderick McKenzie, the cousin of Alexander Mackenzie, and William McGillivray, the nephew of Simon McTavish; and it produced such an effect that it was decided on the spot to unite the interests of the rival companies, lest the death of Ross might lead to reprisals. Two of

[1] A. Mackenzie, *Voyages from Montreal* (London, 1801), pp. xix-xx.

WILLIAM McGILLIVRAY
From a painting in the McCord National Museum, Montreal

HISTORICAL INTRODUCTION

Pond's men were arrested, and brought down all the way to Quebec for trial; but the evidence against them was insufficient, and they were acquitted.

Before the union of the North West Company and Gregory, McLeod and Company took place, however, and before even the news of Ross's murder reached Grand Portage, Simon McTavish had made another move in that triumphal progress which was to place him at the head of the North West Company. On April 14, 1787, Benjamin Frobisher died in Montreal, thus breaking up that triumvirate of brothers which had for over ten years carried on the business of the house of Frobisher at Montreal, at Grand Portage, and in the interior. A few days later Simon McTavish addressed to Joseph Frobisher the letter, reproduced on pages 75-7, in which he proposed that he and the Frobishers should unite forces.

This proposal was not immediately put into effect (though it is probable that Joseph Frobisher gave it a favourable reception), for shortly after making the proposal, McTavish left for the summer meeting of the partners of the North West Company at Grand Portage; and here he found himself suddenly called upon to arrange for the absorption in the North West Company of the partners of Gregory, McLeod and Company. The North West agreement of 1783-4 had still two years to run; but this was perforce superseded in 1787 by a new agreement, which was to run for five years, and in which the partners of Gregory, McLeod and Company were included.

The North West Company of 1787 was reorganized on the basis of twenty shares, instead of sixteen. Of these four were assigned to the surviving partners of Gregory, McLeod, and Company—one each to John Gregory, Normand McLeod, Peter Pangman, and Alexander Mackenzie. Peter Pond and William Holmes each retained their single shares, though Pond disposed of his a year or two later to William McGillivray. George McBeath, who had fallen on evil days, appears to have sold one of his shares to Simon McTavish, but kept the other; and Patrick Small, Nicholas Montour, and Robert Grant all continued to hold two shares. This left seven shares for Simon McTavish and Joseph Frobisher; and of these it is evident that Simon McTavish held four. When, therefore, Joseph Frobisher accepted McTavish's proposal in November, 1787, and the firm of McTavish, Frobisher and Company was formed, the new firm had already a dominant interest in the North West Company, for they controlled not only their own seven shares, but also the four shares held by Patrick Small and Nicholas Montour, the first of whom was McTavish's lieutenant, and the second of whom was Frobisher's.

Within the brief space of eight years, therefore, Simon McTavish had risen from the position of being a comparatively undistinguished member of a sixteen-share pool to being the senior partner in a firm which dominated a merger of all the rival interests of the North West. That he achieved this result by means of his own efforts, no one can contend. He was not responsible for the death of John Ross or for that of Benjamin Frobisher; but it is evident that he knew how to turn events to his own advantage, and to this extent he may be regarded as the architect of his own success.

The dominating position of McTavish, Frobisher and Company in the North West Company was confirmed and strengthened by the North West agreement of 1790, which was to come into effect in 1792. The first article of this agreement laid down that "McTavish, Frobisher and Coy. shall do all the business of this concern at Montreal"; and the fourth article provided that McTavish, Frobisher and Company should be represented at the annual meeting at Grand Portage, in the event of Simon McTavish not being able to attend, by John Gregory and Daniel Sutherland, the latter of whom was apparently brought into the North West Company as a friend of Simon McTavish. This agreement was to last until 1799; but in 1795 a new agreement was made, of the details of which we know little, since no copy of it appears to have survived. We know, however, that the number of shares in the North West Company was increased from twenty to forty-six, thus permitting the introduction of a number of new partners, though the firm of McTavish, Frobisher and Company retained a controlling interest. We know also that it was agreed that the "agents" who were now to represent McTavish, Frobisher and Company at Grand Portage were to be William McGillivray and Alexander Mackenzie, who had been made partners of the firm in 1795. John Gregory was also made a partner in McTavish, Frobisher and Company about 1795, but he henceforth occupied a more or less dormant position; and Daniel Sutherland, having served his purpose as the personal representative of Simon McTavish, retired from the North West Company altogether, to become later a partner in the XY Company. These re-arrangements put the finishing touches to the dominating position held by McTavish, Frobisher and Company in the fur-trade. Not only did the firm do all the buying and selling for the North West Company, but it controlled a majority of the shares in the Company, and the "agents" who met the wintering partners at Grand Portage were chosen from among its partners. To describe McTavish, Frobisher and Company as the virtual directorate of the North West Company after 1795 would not be far from the truth.

During the years from 1787 to 1795 the North West Company prospered exceedingly, to such an extent that during these years a number of the wintering partners of the Company—notably, Patrick Small, Nicholas Montour, Peter Pangman, Robert Grant, and William Thorburn—were able to retire in affluence, some to estates in Scotland, and some to seigniories in Lower Canada. This was the time also of the Company's most striking contribution to geographical discovery, when Alexander Mackenzie explored to its mouth in 1789 the Mackenzie River, and reached the Pacific Ocean in 1793.

During this period the North West Company encountered almost no opposition from Grand Portage. In 1793, it is true, David Grant, "an old experienced trader" who had been a clerk of the Frobishers, together with Peter Grant and some others, attempted to set up an opposition on the Saskatchewan and Red Rivers; but their attempt was crushed, by means destined to become traditional in the fur-trade. David Grant died in Montreal in 1797, a ruined man; and Peter Grant was compelled to seek re-employment in the North West Company.

About 1797, however, opposition of a more formidable character developed from two different sources. One of these was the Montreal firm of Forsyth, Richardson and Company. This was a subsidiary of the London firm of Phyn, Ellice and Company,[1] which had long been engaged

---

[1]For an account of the history of this firm, see R. H. Fleming, *Phyn, Ellice and Company of Schenectady* (Contributions to Canadian Economics, 1932, pp. 7-41).

JOHN OGILVY

From a painting in the McCord National Museum, Montreal

in the fur-trade from Detroit and Michilimackinac. The other was the Montreal firm of Parker, Gerrard and Ogilvy,[1] which had also been long engaged in the fur-trade, and had even before 1797 invaded the North West Company's preserves about Lake Superior. Both these firms were obliged to turn to the North West trade by the handing over in 1796 to the United States of the western lake-posts, including Detroit and Michilimackinac. On October 28, 1798, Forsyth, Richardson and Company joined forces with the Detroit firm of Leith, Jamieson and Company; and the new organization was frankly named "the New North West Company". For a year or two a triangular struggle went on in the North West; but in 1800 a union was brought about among the opponents of the North West Company through the inclusion in the New North West Company of John Ogilvy, of Parker, Gerrard and Ogilvy, and John Mure, of Quebec. To this new organization came now to be applied popularly the name "XY Company". Finally, in 1802, the New North West Company received a powerful adhesion in the person of Sir Alexander Mackenzie. Mackenzie, it will be remembered, belonged originally to the "Little Company" of 1783-7, and it is possible that he never became reconciled to the policies of the North West Company. Certainly, after his return from his epoch-making dash to the Pacific in 1793, he became dissatisfied with the attitude of his partners toward his work; and about 1798 he had a serious disagreement with his fellow-agent, William McGillivray. In 1799 he withdrew from the North West Company, and went to England, where

[1] Some account of the history of the firm will be found in A. Shortt, *Founders of Canadian banking: The Honourable George Moffatt* (Journal of the Canadian Bankers' Association, January, 1925, pp. 177-90).

he published his *Travels*, and won international fame and a knighthood at the hands of George the Third. It is probable that he gave some sort of support to the New North West Company from the beginning, for a nephew who bore his name was one of the original wintering partners of the Company in 1798, and another relative, George Moffatt, entered the employ of Parker, Gerrard and Ogilvy about 1800; but in 1802 Mackenzie, on his return from England, definitely joined the New North West Company as a partner. He immediately took a leading part in it; and in 1803 he reorganized it under the name of "Sir Alexander Mackenzie and Company".

The New North West Company proved a serious competitor with the old. It appears to have had at its command a capital not less than that of its opponents; and it was only in the field that it was weaker. Mackenzie appears to have tried to detach from the North West Company some of its more experienced traders, such as his cousin Roderick; but he was unsuccessful, and, apart from himself, most of the wintering partners of the New North West Company were young and inexperienced. Some of them, indeed, such as James Leith and John Haldane, were youths imported directly from Scotland. On the other hand, we know that by 1800 there was already some dissension between McTavish, Frobisher and Company and the wintering partners of the North West Company; and the conflict between the rival organizations in the West does not seem to have been conducted with the bitterness that had marked previous conflicts. Our knowledge of the details of the struggle is derived in the main from only a few stray journals which have survived;[1] but, if we may judge from

[1] See particularly the journals of Thomas Verchères de Boucherville (who

HISTORICAL INTRODUCTION

them, little blood seems to have been spilt, and occasionally the rival traders were on fairly amicable terms.

It was on the financial side that the struggle had its most serious repercussions. Competition reduced the profits of the fur-trade to such an extent that both the old company and the new were losing money. The Indians were being debauched, and important fur-bearing areas began to show signs of exhaustion. Simon McTavish, however, was not the sort of man to submit idly to the threat against his supremacy. He had overcome opposition too often to yield to it now. He introduced new economies into the trade, and he sought new areas to exploit. In 1800 he sent his nephew, Duncan McGillivray, on an abortive expedition to try to open up the fur-trade on the Pacific slope; and in 1802 he actually sent an expedition, under Alexander Fraser, to Hudson Bay, to try to break the monopoly of the Hudson's Bay Company. He obtained also the lease of "the King's posts" on the St. Lawrence. It is probable that his traditional reputation as harsh and overbearing, and his nickname of "Le Marquis", date from this period. Had he lived, it is interesting to speculate on the outcome of the struggle. But in the summer of 1804, while still a comparatively young man, he was carried off by what appeared at first a trifling illness, just as he was in the midst of building, with his profits from the fur-trade, a magnificent mansion on the mountain at Montreal.

Immediately after the death of Simon McTavish, the forces working toward union made themselves felt; and on November 5, 1804, the New North West Company

was a clerk in the XY Company), Jean Baptiste Perrault, Daniel Williams Harmon, Archibald Norman McLeod, and Hugh Faries, and the autobiography of John McDonald of Garth.

was absorbed in the old, on terms which, if fair, were severe. Sir Alexander Mackenzie "was excluded from any interference" in the fur-trade; and the business of the amalgamation was still to be conducted by McTavish, Frobisher and Company. The wintering partners of the New North West Company, however, were absorbed by the combined organization, and were given shares in it; and the New North West Company, as a whole, was given a quarter interest in the trade. The North West Company's agreement of 1795 had expired in 1802, and had been superseded by an agreement which had increased the number of shares from forty-eight to ninety-six, the object of this being apparently to strengthen the interests of the Company in the interior by giving partnerships to a large number of senior clerks. But this agreement was in 1804 superseded by a new agreement, under which the number of shares was increased to one hundred; and of these, by means of the retirement of a number of shares and other readjustments, twenty-five were set aside for the New North West Company. In order to protect their interests, "the XY people" were given the right of nominating an agent to represent them at Kaministiquia (or, as it was soon to be known, Fort William), which had in 1803 taken the place of Grand Portage as the wilderness headquarters of the Company; but this provision did not prove wholly effective, and (as we shall see) "the XY people" suffered the common fate of minority shareholders, despite the fact that Sir Alexander Mackenzie devoted much thought to organizing their interests under the firm name of Sir Alexander Mackenzie and Company.[1]

The decade that followed the union of the XY Com-

[1] See R. H. Fleming, *The origin of "Sir Alexander Mackenzie and Company"* (Canadian historical review, 1928, pp. 137-55).

pany with the North West Company saw the North West Company's greatest period of expansion and success. On Simon McTavish's death, the direction of the Company passed into the hands of his nephew, William McGillivray. McGillivray, who had been the first English clerk engaged by the Company in 1784, and who had been the chief "agent" of the Company since the defection of Alexander Mackenzie in 1798, may not have had the genius for business possessed by his uncle, but he had had a long experience in the North West trade, and he proceeded to surround himself with practical fur-traders, who understood the conditions that they faced. His brother, Duncan McGillivray, who (like himself) had served a long apprenticeship in the West, and Roderick McKenzie, the cousin and correspondent of Sir Alexander Mackenzie, had been admitted to partnership in the firm of McTavish, Frobisher and Company in 1800, after the retirement of Joseph Frobisher in 1798; and gradually the older members of the firm disappeared. John Gregory returned to private life in 1806, and James Hallowell, who had been brought into the firm for financial reasons in 1787, had retired even earlier than this. Hallowell's sons, William and James, continued to be members of the firm until they were forced out in 1814; and in 1811, Simon McGillivray, the youngest brother of William McGillivray, who was lame and who had been a partner in the London supply house of McTavish, Fraser and Company, was brought into the firm. But in 1806, when the name of the firm was changed to McTavish, McGillivrays and Company, it was strengthened by the addition to it of two such veteran winterers as Angus Shaw and Archibald Norman McLeod.

Under such direction the North West Company pushed

out to "new fields and pastures green". In 1807, David Thompson, a wintering partner who has been described as "the greatest land geographer the British race has produced", crossed the Rockies, and opened up the fur-trade on the Pacific slope; and in 1808, Simon Fraser (the fourth of that name to be connected with the North West Company) followed to its mouth the river which still bears his name. For a time it looked as though the North West Company was to be forced to meet on the Pacific slope the competition of the Pacific Fur Company of John Jacob Astor, which in 1810 founded Fort Astoria at the mouth of the Columbia; but in 1813, after the outbreak of the War of 1812, Fort Astoria was handed over to the Nor'-Westers, and the North West Company thereupon fell heir to the whole of the fur-trade on the Pacific slope. In the prosecution of this trade, the Company embarked upon a policy of maritime expansion. The Company's vessels sailed from England for the Columbia by way of Cape Horn, and from the Columbia they carried some of the furs of the Pacific slope to the markets of China.[1]

During this period the North West Company crushed, with ruthless efficiency, all competition from Canada. Interlopers and free traders were discouraged by means which, if not actually illegal, bordered on illegality. Lord Selkirk, in his *Sketch of the British fur-trade in North America*, has provided us with some interesting illustrations of the means employed. One of these illustrations will suffice:

"In the year 1801, Mr. Dominic Rousseau of Montreal, sent a canoe and four or five men, under the charge of Mr. Hervieu, his clerk, to Lake

---

[1] See Marion O'Neil, *The maritime activities of the North West Company* (Washington historical quarterly, 1930, pp. 243-67).

WILLIAM McKAY

From a painting in the possession of Mrs. H. M. Blaiklock, Montreal

Superior, with an assortment of goods, calculating that he should dispose of them to advantage among the servants of the North-West Company, during their annual assemblage at the Grand Portage on Lake Superior. Small as this adventure was, it excited the jealousy of the North-West Company. Hervieu pitched his tent, and opened his shop, at a distance of about a gun-shot from their fort, or trading post; but it was not long before he was accosted by some of the partners, and particularly by Mr. Duncan M'Gillivray, who peremptorily ordered him to quit the place telling him, that he had no right to come there. . . . . . .

"In the year 1806, Mr. Rousseau again attempted a trading adventure to the Indian country. He entered into partnership with a Mr. Delorme, whom he dispatched from Montreal with two canoes loaded with goods for the interior. Mr. Delorme proceeded as far as Lake Superior, and, in order to avoid collision, he there took the old route by the Grand Portage, which the North-West Company had then abandoned. When he had advanced a few days' journey through the intricate and difficult country beyond Lake Superior, he was overtaken by Mr. Alexander M'Kay, a partner of the North-West Company, with a number of men, who went forward along the route, by which Mr. Delorme was to advance, and proceeded to fell trees across the road, at the portages, and on all the narrow creeks by which they were to pass. They soon accomplished such a complete obstruction, that Mr. Delorme with his small party, found it impossible to open a passage for his loaded canoes. His adventure being thus entirely frustrated, he left his goods, and made his retreat with his men only. On his arrival at Fort William, the trading-post of the North-West Company, he found Mr. M'Gillivray, by whose direction these obstructions had been made. To him Delorme presented the keys of the packages which he had left, and remonstrated on the unjustifiable manner in which he had been treated; but his appeal was fruitless. Finding that no redress could otherwise be obtained, Mr. Rousseau brought an action of damages against the Company; but the case did not come to trial, a compromise having been offered and accepted. The North-West Company agreed to pay for the goods which Delorme had left beyond the Grand Portage, at the invoice price as valued at Montreal. By this, Mr. Rousseau lost all the wages of the men, and other expenses he had incurred in the outfit, but he thought it advisable to accept the compensation, however inadequate, rather than trust to the chance of obtaining justice in the courts of law."

Such methods of meeting competition in the fur-trade were not new, nor did they cease with the disappearance of the North West Company, as may be seen by anyone who cares to read John McLean's *Notes of a twenty-five years' service in the Hudson's Bay Territories*; but it was perhaps at this period that these methods reached their highest degree of effectiveness. The "ancient North West spirit" was marked by a most admirable courage and fortitude; but it was capable on occasion of a decided form of *Schrecklichkeit*.

From the beginning the Nor'-Westers had been at war with the Hudson's Bay Company. The Hudson's Bay Company runners who penetrated into the interior in 1767 had carried printed dodgers warning the "Canada pedlars" against interfering with the Company's trade, and the "Canada pedlars" had paid no attention to these warnings. But the warfare thus begun had seldom become acute. The Hudson's Bay Company had never attempted to assert in the courts the exclusive trading privileges in Rupert's Land conferred on them by their charter; and their servants had seldom ventured to interfere with the Nor'-Westers. There had been clashes, but in these, as a rule, the Hudson's Bay men had come off second best. It was not to be expected that poorly-paid employees would be able to meet the competition of the bold adventurers who were themselves partners in the North West Company. The Nor'-Westers did not deny to the Hudson's Bay men whatever share the latter could get of the fur-trade in the watershed of Hudson Bay, though they came to regard the Athabaska country as their own special preserve; but the Hudson's Bay men apparently regarded the competition of the Nor'-Westers as a necessary evil, except near the forts on Hudson Bay itself. The North West Company advanced, indeed, the claim that the exclusive rights granted to the Hudson's Bay Company in the watershed of Hudson Bay were invalid; but the Hudson's Bay Company never thought it worth while to bring their claim to an issue. Shortly before his death Simon McTavish conceived the idea of securing a controlling interest in the Hudson's Bay Company, and thus bringing about a merger of the two companies, but for reasons that are obscure, this project, which would have changed materially the course of events, fell through.

Only after 1811 did the struggle become acute. It was in that year the Earl of Selkirk, the youthful Scottish peer who had obtained a controlling interest in the Hudson's Bay Company, and who had conceived the rather wild scheme of planting a colony of Scottish crofters on the banks of the Red River, obtained a grant of forty-five millions of acres in the valley of the Red River. On this he proceeded to found a settlement, near the site of the present city of Winnipeg, which lay across the line of communications of the North West Company. This was something that the North West Company was not prepared to tolerate, for it struck at the very existence of their trade. How Lord Selkirk ever imagined they would submit tamely to this threat, it is difficult to conceive. They promptly resolved to break up the Selkirk settlement. Twice they drove the settlers from their homes; and on June 19, 1816, there took place a pitched battle at Seven Oaks, near the Red River settlement, between the Hudson's Bay men and the half-breed partisans of the North West Company, that resulted in the massacre of Robert Semple, the governor of Selkirk's colony, and twenty of his men. When news of this affair reached Lord Selkirk, he was on his way to the Red River with a force of mercenary soldiers; and he promptly seized the North West Company's headquarters at Fort William, arrested several of the partners of the Company, and sent them back to Canada for trial.

26 HISTORICAL INTRODUCTION

It is not within the scope of this introduction to attempt to describe the struggle that took place during the years 1811-20, both in the West and in the law courts, between Lord Selkirk and the Nor'-Westers—a struggle that gave rise to a veritable avalanche of controversial literature.[1] To describe the contest even in a superficial way would require an amount of space disproportionate to the scale of this sketch, as well as the repetition of a story already fully told by other writers. All that is necessary here is to point to the results of the struggle.

On the face of things, the North West Company did not come out of the contest badly. Despite Lord Selkirk's powerful connections, and the strength of his legal position, with the Hudson's Bay Company's charter behind him, the North West Company won most of the lawsuits arising from the dispute (partly, it was said, because of the strong influence which the Company was able to exert on the government of Upper and Lower Canada); and in 1820, Lord Selkirk, worn out by the struggle, died in the south of France, whither he had gone to recover his health, a disappointed and apparently beaten man. But in reality the Nor'-Westers had won a Pyrrhic victory. Lord Selkirk had not only interrupted seriously the routine of their trade, but he had roused the Hudson's Bay Company to an activity in competition which they had never heretofore shown. He enlisted in the service of the Hudson's Bay Company a number of former servants of the North West Company, men of aggressive temper such as John Clarke and Colin Robertson; and these had carried the war into Africa. In 1816,

[1] For a bibliography of the Selkirk controversy, see the *Canadian historical review*, 1932, pp. 45-50.

the Hudson's Bay Company invaded the Athabaska country, which had hitherto been regarded as the special preserve of the Nor'-Westers; and elsewhere the Hudson's Bay Company roused itself to redoubled efforts. It had always had the advantage of lower costs, since the cost of transporting goods to the interior from Hudson Bay had been half that of transporting them from Montreal; but the ineffective competition which the Hudson's Bay Company's servants had offered had rendered this difference in costs largely nugatory. Now, however, strenuous opposition from Hudson Bay cut the North West Company's profits to zero or minus. Add to this the cost of the expensive litigation imposed upon the Company by the legal struggle with Lord Selkirk, and it will be seen that the contest involved the North West Company in heavy losses. Up to 1814 the Company had been prosperous; but the probability is that, if an accurate accounting had been kept of its operations from 1814 to 1821 (which was, apparently, not done), these would have revealed the fact that it was plunging into bankruptcy. It should be explained that the North West Company had this defect in its financial structure that it did not have, like most modern incorporated companies, a reserve fund, but distributed its profits after each annual venture. Indeed, many of its younger partners were in debt to it, since it had advanced to them the price of their shares. It will be seen, therefore, that the North West Company was ill equipped to meet a prolonged struggle such as was imposed on it by Lord Selkirk.

Just when the partners of the North West Company, and in particular the partners of McTavish, McGillivrays and Company, began to realize that they were headed toward insolvency, it is difficult to determine. Though

William and Simon McGillivray, as well as Thomas Thain (who became a partner of McTavish, McGillivrays and Company in 1813, and took charge of their accounts), received large advances from McTavish, McGillivrays and Company, there is evidence that the Company held back payments that they had contracted to make. Sir Alexander Mackenzie, before his death in 1820, complained that he had not received a farthing of the moneys owing to him; and in 1830 his widow obtained in the courts an award of £10,000, representing, in part, payments owing to her husband at this period. When the agreement constituting McTavish, McGillivrays and Company came to an end in 1822, the firm was not wound up (a fact sufficiently significant), but the firm of McGillivrays, Thain and Company was formed for the purpose of taking over its assets and liabilities. When both these firms became insolvent in 1825, it was found that their accounts were in hopeless confusion. The statement was made by Simon McGillivray that their books were balanced in 1821; but one may be permitted to doubt whether the balance-sheet struck at this time represented the true state of affairs.

It seems clear, however, that the financial condition of the North West Company dawned upon the majority of the wintering partners only at the annual meeting at Fort William in 1820. For many years, it is true, there had been discontent among the winterers. Simon McTavish had complained about their attitude toward the "agents" as early as 1800; and in 1808, Daniel McKenzie had dubbed his fellow-partners "McGillivray's geese". But it was only in 1820 that this discontent came to a head. By that time the majority of the partners who met at Fort William had come to realize that the affairs of the Company were in a parlous condition, and that only by a union of the North West and Hudson's Bay companies could the suicidal strife between them be brought to an end. They delegated two of their number, Dr. John McLoughlin and Angus Bethune, to proceed to London to attempt to negotiate a union; and in November, 1820, McLoughlin and Bethune actually sailed for London from New York, together with Colin Robertson, a former Nor'-Wester who had enlisted in the service of the Hudson's Bay Company, and to whose letters we are indebted for much of our knowledge of the negotiations that followed.

Meanwhile, however, other influences were at work. The British government was perturbed by the long-continued disturbances in what were called "the Indian countries of North America"; and the colonial secretary, Lord Bathurst, appealed to Edward Ellice, of the firm of Inglis, Ellice and Company, which was a supply house both for Sir Alexander Mackenzie and Company and for McTavish, McGillivrays and Company, in the hope that he might be able to bring about a union of the Hudson's Bay and North West interests. Ellice was an admirable person for this purpose: he had been a strong partisan of the North West Company, but he was a rising man in the Whig party, and having married the sister of Earl Grey in 1809, and having been elected member for Coventry in the House of Commons in 1818, was likely to carry weight with the Governor and Committee of the Hudson's Bay Company. At the same time, William and Simon McGillivray, having had their hands forced by the wintering partners, became convinced that in union lay the only solution of their difficulties; and the end of 1820 found them also in London, ready to enter into negotiations with Hudson's Bay House.

In these circumstances, the Governor and Committee of the Hudson's Bay Company occupied a strong position. They signified their willingness to discuss union; but they were able to play the wintering partners off against the agents of the North West Company, and indeed to dictate their own terms. After an amusing triangular negotiation, they declined to deal only with the wintering partners, since they feared that if they did so the McGillivrays and Ellice might set up a new opposition; and the agreement finally made was between the Governor and Committee of the Hudson's Bay Company on the one hand, and William McGillivray, Simon McGillivray, and Edward Ellice on the other hand, "on behalf of themselves and the North West Company of Montreal". It is usual to describe the union brought about in 1821 as an amalgamation of the two companies, but it is more accurately described as an absorption of the North West Company into the Hudson's Bay Company. Trade was to be carried on under the name and charter of the Hudson's Bay Company, which was now granted a monopoly; and the wintering partners of the North West Company were commissioned, by deed poll, chief factors and chief traders of the Hudson's Bay Company. As for McTavish, McGillivrays and Company, it ceased to perform the function of "agents" in the fur-trade; and it became merely the headquarters of the Montreal district. It is true that the two parties to the agreement were to find an equal share of capital, and to divide equally the profits and losses thereon; and that there was set up a joint board "for consulting and advising on the management of the fur-trade". But this board was purely advisory, executive authority being centred in the Governor

SIMON McGILLIVRAY
From a painting in the Masonic Temple, Toronto

and Committee of the Hudson's Bay Company; and in any case, a majority of the members of the board were appointed by the Hudson's Bay Company. In 1821, for instance, the Hudson's Bay Company were represented by J. Berens, jr., J. H. Pelly, A. Colville, and N. Garry, whereas the Nor'-Westers were represented only by William and Simon McGillivray and John Fraser, of McTavish, Fraser and Company in London. Annual changes were made in the composition of the board; and in 1824, John Fraser was replaced by Edward Ellice. But the proportion of Hudson's Bay men and Nor'-Westers remained constant.

In the summer of 1821, Nicholas Garry and Simon McGillivray went to America to put the union agreement into effect; and in August, 1821, they met the wintering partners at Fort William, in what was destined to be the last annual parliament of the North West Company. From the diary of Nicholas Garry, which has been preserved,[1] it is clear that relations between Garry and Simon McGillivray became decidedly strained. But all difficulties were finally smoothed over; the wintering partners received their commissions as officers of the Hudson's Bay Company, and went off to their wintering grounds; and the North West Company passed into history.

The story, however, does not end here. The union agreement of 1821 was to run for twenty-one years; and the assumption has been general that it provided a permanent basis for the union of the interests of the two companies. Such, however, was very far from being the case. The agreement had been in force barely three

---

[1] See *Diary of Nicholas Garry, deputy-governor of the Hudson's Bay Company, 1822-3* (Transactions of the Royal Society of Canada, 2nd series, vol. vi, sect. ii, pp. 73-204).

years when it was, by common consent, abrogated; and a new arrangement substituted. By this arrangement, William McGillivray, Simon McGillivray, and Edward Ellice were given substantial blocks of stock in the Hudson's Bay Company, in lieu of the shares of profit assigned them by the agreement of 1821; and the joint board for consulting and advising on the management of the fur-trade passed out of existence. The McGillivrays became merely private shareholders in the Hudson's Bay Company, without any voice in its direction; and only Edward Ellice was given a place on the committee or directorate of the Company. It was stipulated, moreover, that the McGillivrays and Ellice should stand between the Hudson's Bay Company and any claims made against the North West Company or McTavish, McGillivrays and Company; and they were required to set aside, out of the stock allotted to them, shares to the amount of £50,000 for meeting such claims.

It is not difficult to discern the reasons lying behind this new arrangement. The joint advisory board had been set up in 1821 partly, no doubt, in order to spare the feelings of the McGillivrays, and partly in order to ensure the smooth absorption of the Nor'-Westers into the Hudson's Bay Company. By 1824, thanks to the wise measures of George Simpson, the new Governor of the Company's territories in North America, the second of these objects had been achieved; and the need for the joint advisory board, which had probably not proved a very effective instrument of administration in any case, had passed away. On the other hand, the affairs of the McGillivrays had probably reached a point where it was dangerous to consider their feelings any longer. Henry McKenzie, one of the partners of McTavish, McGillivrays and Company, had protested against the high-handed action of the McGillivrays in agreeing to the union of 1821 without consulting their partners, and was threatening action in the courts. At the same time the financial affairs of the firm were evidently approaching a crisis. Early in 1824, Simon McGillivray was so embarrassed financially that he was compelled to sell at auction in London his valuable collection of paintings. In these circumstances, it seemed, no doubt, only common prudence for the Hudson's Bay Company to protect itself against possible litigation, and incidentally to throw the McGillivrays to the wolves.

The event proved the wisdom of this course. In August, 1825, Thomas Thain, who was in charge of the office of McTavish, McGillivrays and Company and McGillivrays, Thain and Company in Montreal, and was at the same time resident agent of the Hudson's Bay Company for the Montreal district, suddenly left Montreal for Great Britain, in a manner which gave the impression that he was absconding; and on his arrival in England he succumbed to an attack of mental illness which made necessary his removal to an insane asylum. Shortly afterwards, on October 16, 1825, William McGillivray, who had been in ill-health for some time, died; and Simon McGillivray was compelled to come out to Montreal, at a time when he could ill afford to leave his affairs in England, to attempt to straighten the affairs of the Montreal office. He found the books of McTavish, McGillivrays and Company locked in Thomas Thain's private rooms, and gave up all hopes of balancing them; but he promptly met the creditors of McTavish, McGillivrays and Company, and placed the whole of his personal fortune, as well as that of his brother, at their disposal. He was not able, however, to get his creditors to agree upon the course of action he proposed, and he was compelled to place his affairs in the hands of trustees, leaving Pierre de Rocheblave in temporary charge of the Montreal office. Not until 1830 did Simon McGillivray's trustees receive from Edward Ellice the sum of £110,000 to meet his liabilities; and even then his creditors received only ten shillings in the pound. But by this time Simon McGillivray had passed out of the picture. In 1829 his penniless condition compelled him to accept an appointment as a gold commissioner in South America; and he was obliged to leave his nieces, the daughters of William McGillivray, in destitute circumstances in London. Such was the fall of the proud house of McTavish, McGillivrays and Company, who had been only a few brief years before uncrowned rulers of nearly half a continent.

It was fortunate that Edward Ellice, who now stood between the Hudson's Bay Company and the hungry creditors of the North West Company, was a man of great wealth; for litigation over the debts of the North West Company went on for many years. In Hudson's Bay House in London there are preserved numerous legal documents labelled "North West Company Partners' Trust". These are the documents which tell the story of how the claims of the creditors of the North West Company were finally satisfied; and the last of the documents bears the date of 1851.

The story of the Nor'-Westers, though not without its darker pages, is a brilliant chapter in the history of Canada. No braver or more picturesque band of adventurers ever put it to the touch, to gain or lose it all. Some of them were French-Canadian traders and *voyageurs*, the sons of those who had followed La Vérendrye to the rivers and prairies of the West in the dying days of the French régime. Others were American frontiersmen who had served their apprenticeship in the fur-trade in the valleys of the Ohio and the Mississippi. Most of them were Scottish Highlanders, the sons of those who had come to Canada in Wolfe's army or as United Empire Loyalists in the American Revolution. The number of them who were connected with that gallant regiment, the 78th or Fraser's Highlanders, is remarkable; and it is no less remarkable that the numerous Frasers, McTavishes, and McGillivrays, who played such an important part in the history of the North West Company, nearly all came from Lord Lovat's estates. The names of the North West Company partners sound like a roll-call of the clans at Culloden. These men were hardy, courageous, shrewd, and proud. They spent a good part of their lives travelling incredible distances in birch-bark canoes, shooting rapids, or navigating inland seas. They were wrecked and drowned. They suffered hunger and starvation. They were robbed and murdered by the Indians, and sometimes by one another. They fell the victims of smallpox, syphilis, and rum. Yet they conquered half a continent, and they built up a commercial empire, the like of which North America at least has never seen.

It is one of the ironies of history that this gallant enterprise should have been brought to nought through a compatriot of those Scots who formed its backbone. Lord Selkirk may deserve the credit for establishing in the Canadian West the first colony of real settlers; but he deserves just as well the opprobrium of having ruined the first great industry that Canadians, by means of fortitude and foresight, had developed. The fall of the North West Company, for which Lord Selkirk was mainly responsible, was a blow to both Canada and its commercial centre, Montreal. It meant that the fur-trade was diverted from Montreal to Hudson Bay. It meant that large numbers of Canadian people, who had relied on the fur-trade for their livelihood, were robbed of their means of support. It meant the end of that picturesque group of fur-trade magnates who had made Montreal famous for its hospitality. Within an unbelievably short time, this element disappeared from the life of Montreal, and took refuge in small towns in Upper and Lower Canada, where the cost of living was more in line with their diminished incomes; and now, after only a little more than a century, it is difficult to find in Montreal more than a handful of those in whose veins runs the blood of "the lords of the lakes and the forests".

DOCUMENTS RELATING TO THE NORTH WEST COMPANY

DOCUMENTS RELATING TO THE NORTH WEST COMPANY

1. Extract from a Letter of Andrew Graham, Master at York Fort, to the Governor and Committee of the Hudson's Bay Company, dated York Fort, August 26, 1772.[1]

[*Hudson's Bay House, Letters from York Fort, v. 6, ff. 327/330.*]

York Fort August 26th. 1772.

Honourable Gentlemen....

The Situation of your Affairs in this Country is very unpromising, I have not been Indolent, I have gained certain Information of what is doing Inland, & think it my Duty to lay before you the success of my Enquiry. Your Trade at York Fort & Severn is greatly diminished, the Keskochewan Indians Who are the Support of it being intercepted by the Canadian Pedlars who are yearly Gaining fresh Influence over them by supplying them with Goods Inland. The Indians resort thither in the Winter for Ammunition & the whole body of the Natives build their Canoes not far distant from the residence of the Traders to whom they resort to Purchase Ammunition & other Articles in the Spring & finding they can procure Tobacco & other Necessarys so near & being kept in Liquor, every Inducement to visit the Company's Factorys is forgot, & the prime ffurrs are picked out & traded, the refuse is tied up & brought down to us by the Leading Indians & their followers: of such as these is Your Honours' Trade composed;

[1]This letter provides the earliest evidence which has hitherto come to light regarding the concentration of interests among the "Canada pedlars". It is reproduced by permission of the Governor and Committee of the Hudson's Bay Company.

the Wolves are seldom taken by the Canadians. After they were all gone there was very little Coat & Parchment Beaver & no Martins but thirty four Canoes of Indians coming down the North River gave a fine help out being well gooded both in Quality & Quantity amongst which a large Parcell of Split Cats which they Purchase from the Western Archithinues two of whom came with them. I shewed them how to Case & Stretch them, & they promised to bring them so & tell their Countrymen.

I received two Letters from Thomas Corry but returned no Answer to either, not thinking myself at Liberty without Permission from the Honourable Board. Wappenassew the Indian mentioned in Corry's Letters is a Person of Prime Consideration with the Natives & his Influence is very extensive, he came to York Fort in 1755 & continued with us until two Years ago, when the Canadians who have great need of his Assistance to promote their Trade & protect their Persons, tried every means to attach him to their Service, & they have succeeded. He lives in their House all the Winter, dines at Table with the Master, & his family are Cloathed with Cloth & no favour is refused, In return he induces the Indians to resort thither, he Convoys the large Canoes up & down to Michillimackinac & in great Measure prevents the numerous Tribes through which they are obliged to pass, from molesting them.

On the 11th of July, John Cole came down hither with three Canoes of Indians he was Servant to Thomas Corry but left him on Account of Ill usage, & came to York Fort in hopes to be employed; he is a strong, tall, able Man, speaks the English, French, & Indian Languages, was formerly one of the Battoe Men, & has travelled over a large extent of Ground from Bristol in New-Jersey, but never was at Quebeck or Montreal, talks very sensible, & can write a little, & very much belov[d]. by the Natives; from him I got the foll[g]. Particulars. The Company (mentioned in Corry's Letters) consists of Mess[rs]. Blandeau at Montreal & Keshew his Brother, George McBeath, Tod, & Thomas Corry at Michillimackinac, John Erskine[1] at Emissions, 9 Miles above that Fort; & another French Gent[n]. Name unknown, They all have much influence over the Natives. Particularly Corry & Erskine, the latter for-

[1] John Askin.

THE NORTH WEST COMPANY 41

merly was a great Fur trader above Albany Town, where he became Bankrupt, & afterwards came to Canada where he carries on a large Trade, not less than 500 packs of Furrs annually, when mustered from all Parts.

The Goods are fitted out from Quebeck by one Justice Walker,[1] (the same Person who in the Year 1765 was Assaulted, & had his nose slit, & his Ears cut off;) from thence they are forwarded to Mr. Blandeau at Montreal who sends them up to Fort Michillimackinac where Major Rogers formerly Commanded leaving this place (where two Companies of the Royal Americans under the command of Capt[n]. Turnbull are stationed) they are sent in large Canoes made of Birch Rind & Cedar seven fathoms long with Seven men in each thro' Lake Superior up to the great carrying place, which requires 10 days to carry their goods across, & are then embarked in Canoes of half the former dimensions, & proceed by Rivers to the Rainey Lake, or Lake Liprè, where Francis & Mishel Buoy two Brothers reside who are old standing Traders to the Southward & have great Command over the Indians; having passed that, they proceed to the Woody Lake, and up Winnepeg River to Winnepeg Lake, little Sea or what we commonly call the Great Lake, (as You will see mentioned in the Indian sketch) which requires between twenty & forty days to pass thro' to a large fall at the entrance of the River De Pane (i.e. Keskachewan River) which leads to the Cedar Lake where Corry traded this Year, & is two Days Journey below Basquea.

In this long Journey they have 113 carrying places, & pass thro' different Nations of Indians who are often very unruly unless their extravag[t]. demands are complied with. Corry has a decent kind of a House, Stockaded round, he brought with him thirty Men including himself & Pilot, & seven are left to take care of the House, & goods which remained undisposed of, until the arrival of Erskine this fall, who succeeds & intends to build a proper house, the Servants are sent out amongst the Indians to inform them where they have put up, & to induce them to come into Trade, sev[l]. tribes unknown at your Factorys have left their former Country, & drawn nigher the Canadian Settlements for the

---

[1]Thomas Walker. See A. L. Burt, *The mystery of Walker's ear* (Canadian Historical Review, 1922).

conveniency of Trade, in short the Pedlars being on the Spot, & the Indians in want of Ammunition &c. certainly will be detrimental to your Affairs, this Information entirely agrees with the report of Bat & Primo[1] who were coming down hither with 160 Canoes, but were met in the River De Pane by other Indians who told them that the Canadians were at the Cedar Lake, & had Plenty of Goods & Spirituous Liquors, upon which they wheeled off to go thither notwithstanding all the Arguments of our Men to perswade them to the contrary.

The Indians that did come down never offered to deny having traded their prime Furrs with Canadians but seemed to Manifest an Uncommon Indifference about coming down, & when trading I overheared them say to each other, "Purchase only this or that Article as for the rest we can get them Yonder".

Corry & Erskine are desirous of getting Primo and Bat with them, not that they want their Service, but because they draw the Natives, for I firmly believe they are Assiduous in your Service, but (as John Cole & Primo says) nothing will do but the making of a Settlement Inland.

The great Encouragm.t I gave the Indians has reduced the overplus. I maturely considered the matter & did for the best, I sent Wappenassew & several others some Tobacco with strict orders to come down next Year, I am of opinion, they will obey me, if Erskine's New England Rum does not prevail.

The Number of Year's I have been acquainted with York Fort & the attention with which I have viewed Your Honours' Affairs, I hope will warrant the offering of my Sentiments on this occasion.

It appears to me that the only way of increasing the Furr Trade is to have an Inland Settlement to supply the Natives with Necessarys, Ammunition Tobacco & Brandy would be the Principal Articles, without the latter the Indians would not resort to Your House if they could procure it else where. In an undertaking of this kind Your Honours have many advantages over the Pedlars, Your distance would be small in comparison to theirs (John Cole declared that he would engage to conduct large loaded Canoes up to the River de Pane in forty Days, the Indians in light Canoes

---

[1]Isaac Batt and Louis Primeau, two servants of the Hudson's Bay Company.

go in thirteen Days with fine Weather) the falls & carrying places are far less Numerous, no Natives to pass thro' but such as annually take Debt at the Fact^y. & are in friendship with us; The Brazile Tobacco would be strong enticement to the Indians, & the largeness of the Company's Standard seems likely to deter the Canadians from pursuing a traffick which must be carried on under many disadvantages.

I have entertained John Cole in your Service for three Years at 12^{Li}. pr. Annum, & given him leave to bring down next Year a fellow Servant of his, named Bove, a Canadian, a good able Man who resides amongst the Natives, so if Your Honours should think proper to adapt a Measure of this Nature those Men with Primo & Bat will serve to initiate others. Cole desired me to inform the Board, that they would find him no bad Man, & that he would do his utmost for their Interest. He says 14 Men would be sufficient & I am certain the Natives would give Assistance the Master at York Fort must push it up with a willingness, & a Master of the Undertaking, must be a Young, lively Person, that will continue some Years in your Service, I know no Person that would Answer so well as Messrs. Hearne at Churchill & Mr. Hutchins at York Fort. John Cole told me that it must be carried on the same manner as the Canadian Pedlars, in large Birch Rind Canoes, two of which I have ordered down next Year.

The Canadians are chosen Men inured to hardships & fatigue, under which most of Your Present Servants would sink, A Man in the Canadian Service who cannot carry two Packs of eighty Lbs. each, one & an half League losses his trip that is his Wages. But time & Practice would make it easy, & even a few Canadians may be got who would be thankful of Your Honours Service. John Cole informed me that the traders above in their Discourse concerning the Little North (meaning Hudson's Bay) wondered that we lay along the Sea & did not penetrate Inland.

I have often reflected that the Accounts given us by Men sent Inland were incoherent & unintelligible, I thought therefore that a sensible Person might Answer the Purpose much better, & make many observations which may be of Utility, & mentioning my Sentiments to Mr. Cocking, he readily offered himself for any Service to promote Your Interest. I have therefore sent him Inland with a Leading Indian, he will give a rational Account of

Things, & endeavour to find the Longitude & Latitude of Places having been instructed therein by Messrs. Falconer & Lockey, at the same time his Rank at the Factory, will make him more respected by the Natives, & induce them to pay a regard to what he says.

....

.... Let me then have cause to bless Your Goodness. Which will ever bind me to be
> Honble. Sirs
>> Your Grateful & obliged
>>> Humble Servant

ANDREW GRAHAM

Endorsed.
YF 1772. Mr. Andrew Graham
Letter from him Dated 26th August
treating on the C^{os}. affairs—his
observations on the advances made
by the Pedlars, with his thoughts
of the most probable means to circumvent
them—begs for leave to send home a
Child—and to Pay the Balance due to him.

2. EXTRACTS FROM MATTHEW COCKING'S JOURNAL OF OCCURRENCES AND TRANSACTIONS AT CUMBERLAND HOUSE, 1775-6.[1]

[Hudson's Bay House.]

1776
Jany 22d.
MONDAY Wind S.W. Clear Weather, very sharp. Henry with his two Men set off on their way to the Upper Settlement & Frobisher with his Men on their return to the Beaver Lake. These Pedlers seemed to be very polite rather upon the extreme, owing to their intercourse with the French Canadians; indeed the common

---

[1] The version of Matthew Cocking's journal edited by L. J. Burpee in the *Transactions* of the Royal Society of Canada, 3rd series, vol. ii, sect. ii, is a very much abbreviated and garbled version of the original journal, from which a great deal of interest to the historian of the fur-trade has been omitted. The present extracts are reproduced by permission of the Governor and Committee of the Hudson's Bay Company.

Men seem to affect a kind of fulsome finesse in their Beheaviour to each other, much above their Situation. Our Conversation ran chiefly on indifferent Matters, but sometimes flagging, kept up with Accounts of their own Affairs, much of no consequence; but the chief, that French Laws having been established in Canada last April they suspect the Pedling Business will be confined to few hands as in the French time, and consequently that the present Quantities of Furrs Yearly carried down will be much deminished tho' the Proffits accrueing will be much greater in proportion. That at present the Traders most of them carry on the Business seperately, being supplied with Men & Goods from Montreal; But being so Numerous several of them are obliged often to reside in one Place, when to prevent Confusion the Goods are laid in one common Stock for the time, and one Person takes the Direction of the whole, each Trader receiving his proportion of Furrs according to his Stock. That the Traders are Yearly increasing, and this Year no less than sixty Canoes with Goods came from the Grand Carrying Place: by this means the Proffits, considering the great adventures in coming here to Trade are reduced to near as low an Ebb as the Missisipi Trade, and the minds of the Natives are continually corrupting by the seperate Interest of the Traders who use very ungenerous methods with each other. They were very free in their observations on some of their fellow Traders &c. The pedler Bruce who was in the little Sea Lake as mentioned in my last Years Journal, and in my former Journal to be at Basquio, Is it seems at present below the large Sea Lake. These Pedlers giving as a reason for his shifting so often that his severe method of treating the Natives prevents his residing twice in one Place The Pedler Franceway who has been many Years Trading in these Parts being superanuted is retired.

[May] 17th.
FRIDAY Calm Weather most part clear, in the Evening Cloudy with lightening and distant Thunder. The Indians went away. They seemed to be much pleased with their Treatment and renewed their Promises made Yesterday. I am informed that the Master Pedlers up above are at present at Variance and have some of them parted Stocks, one in particularlar [sic] is Tenting & Trades without the Stockades.

3. EXTRACT FROM MATTHEW COCKING'S JOURNAL OF THE MOST REMARKABLE TRANSACTIONS AND OCCURRENCES AT CUMBERLAND HOUSE, 1776-7.

[*Hudson's Bay House.*]

1777.
February 7th

FRIDAY Wind variable clear Weather. Last night Robert Longmore & Malchom Ross arrived from Inland bringing four Sledge Loads of Furrs, hauled by Dogs. They tell me that they came from Mekisew Wachy /ie/ Eagle Hill/ mentioned in my first inland Journal/ When the Indians they left /chiefly Assinnee Poetuck/ are pounding Buffalo, that they set off from there forty Days ago, but having to wait to provide Sledges & Snow Shoes on the Road detained them much. They say that there is so little Snow on the Ground where they came from that the Indians had not yet then occasion for Snow Shoes or Sledges. That an Indian did set off to accompany them Here, But when they came to the upper Pedlers House He Traded a little Provision which was all that belonged to Him and then left them to turn Back. However the Pedlers gave our Men a little Supply of Provision and were otherwise very kind. Robert Longmore & Malchom Ross accordingly proceeded by themselves, keeping the River all the way, and passed the lower House, where one Master with Isaac Batt and a few Men are residing; These have hardly any Goods left, what few they had being chiefly Expended. Robert Longmore informs me; that there are several Indians Above, who propose some to go to York Fort & others to come Here to Trade next Summer; But that many notwithstanding have been, and others are continually going down to the Pedlers with Furrs and Provisions; And there are many of the Pedlers Men interspersed through the Natives who Trade and collect all the Furrs they can. He says that the Pedlers at first had three Settlements, and there was great Emulation between them in endeavouring to undersell each other, by which means they hurt themselves much; the reason was, that some who had a Difference with their fellow Traders last Spring refused to join Stocks, But however these finding the Inconvenience of their acting seperately and through Perswasions used by others they consented to Join, and accordingly they all sent up to the

Upper Settlement, except one Master with a few Goods who was Stationed at the lower House, as before mentioned.

4. LETTERS OF SIMON McTAVISH AND JAMES BANNERMAN, 1774-9.[1]
[*Edgar Papers, Detroit Public Library.*]

New York   December 24th 1774

Dear William—I executed your Commission, for as I did not go to Quebec I wrote to M[r] Lees & made your appology agreeable to your desire. I staid three Weeks at Montreal where I was treated with a great deal of hospitality by the people in general.

Your friend Isaac Todd has his hands full of the publick business, being one of those delegated by the Merchants of Montreal to prepare two Petitions, One to His Majesty, & the other to the Common Council of London, begging the repeal of the Canada Bill, which is so justly looked on by them with horror—Their present Governour, (the first contriver & great promoter of this Evil) is universally detested. I apprehend this Bill will be of infinite hurt to our Trade, for shou'd it be repealed in the first Session of the New Parliament we will not have the News before July or Aug[t], & in the mean time, what are we to do for Rum? As we will not be allowed to bring up any from Schenectady—But in case it shou'd not be repealed at all, we must inevitably break off our Connexion with this Province & have our Supplies from Canada—Goods are now 25 p C[t] higher than before the commencement of the present disturbances, notwithstanding all the reproach the Congress threatens those with, who will raise their prices.—I am afraid Indian Trade will be at a stand Next Year for want of Amunition, as His Majesty (who is certainly damnably frightned) has Issued a proclamation prohibiting the exportation of firearms or any kind of Amunition from Great Britain for 6 Months; this has already raised Powder to £16 P Cw[t] & it will be 20£ before the expiration of two Months, so husband well what you may have on hand of that, & all other Articles.

[6]These letters are introduced here because of the light they throw on the character and the early operations of Simon McTavish, to whose organizing genius the North West Company largely owed its development.

Woe be to you! if you don't write me all the News by the Express. Viz[t] who is married or likely to be soon, What the present Topick of Conversation is over the Ladies Scandle Broth in the afternoons, the Disputes & Jealousys Subsisting between them about precedency, at the Assemblys &[c] (as Sure I am, there are many, or Detroit is much altered) & the State of Partys this Winter —in short, I expect to hear of all your proceedings from you.

For my part, I am now here, in the land of good cheer viz good Wine, good Oysters, & pretty Girls: tho' people in general discourage all kind of dissipation, thereby conce [seal] ith the Association of the Congress—On this. Account, we have no plays; & decency prevents my dancing, as I rec[d] the news of my Fathers death at Niagara, my black coat serves now Saturday & Sunday.

I saw the Charming Miss M[c]A.....n at Albany without any of those Surprising emotions we hear of in romance on the meeting of lovers—My taste must certainly [be] depraved, for I asure you she is greatly improved since she left Detroit

I paid my respects to our intended Governess at Montreal, was I her husband, I would certainly be jealous of you, for she [is] eternally talking of you, I made her very uneasy by telling her the man that had her sheep had run away to the Post, & had made away with them

James Rinkin came from Albany with me, he is return[e]d some days ago, & intends to Winter with your Brother's Family.

Remember me to all friends, particularly Our Mess Mates I need not wish you a Merry Christmass for I dare say youll make it so. for my own part, I'll go very solmly to Church & Detroit shall be remembered in my prayers, as I believe few of you pray for youselves

I saw two Country men of yours hanged yesterday. *alass poor Ireland!*

—Believe me yours very Sincerely
SIMON M[c]TAVISH

Michillimackinac May 12th 1776

Dear Billy Inclosed you will find M[r] Lyons's Sales of your Rum & State of your Acc[t] with him Ballance £194. 2/0 which he has promised to pay me here—I made no delay in endeavouring to find out from him if the Rum was realy sold or not, but he had time enough to consider of the answer he wou'd return me. As Finchley & Tremble walkd a dozen Miles by Land & so got here two days before me, & told of the rise of Liquors &c^a at Detroit.

Now give me leave to Congratulate myself on my safe arrival here which, after having been buffetted about by the Ice in the Streights for five days & being obliged to return into the Rivers mouth by a Storm when we were 50 Miles on our way, & my happy escape from—I am afraid to say it but you may guess. I say, after all these matters I look upon it as a happy event.

The folks here were a little surprised by our News, for they were entirely in the dark about the great matters transacted since last Summer in Canada I believe we Exagerated some matters to increase their Wonder. If the Yankeys don't kill you before Bannerman comes away & that you are not Handcuffed, send me a little News, if any has transpired since I came away but I need not question it, Detroit is not such a Barren soil. Comp^{ts} to all Friends—

I am Yours Sincerely   SIMON M^{c}TAVISH

Addressed: To Mr William Edgar Merch^t Detroit
Endorsed: Simon McTavishs Letter 12th May 1776.

Michilimackinac June 9th 1776

Dear William The Felicity arrived this morning when I rec^d your favour which has confirmed the intelligence we have had from Montreal of Montgomerys death &c^a—The only person who has arrived from that place is a Brother of Legras' who left Montreal the 22d April & came here with Goddard Who has been at Niagara in May & came from there the most part of the way by Land—it seems that some of the Montreal Merchants has been at the Congress in the Spring to Sollicit permission to go on with their Business up this way as usual, & were told that Commissarys were to be appointed at Montreal to give Passes, & to regulate the Trade, until such time as they shoud arrive, there is none allowed to bring up Goods nor to come themselves, so that we are in the dark entirely about whats transacting in Canada. Nor is it likely that we shall have any goods up this Summer unless the dispute between England & the Collonies are settled soon, or that the Continental Troops do recover possession of Canada—which the Friends of Government possitively affirm they must soon accomplish, as Cap[t] Forbes of this Reg[t] who commands at Osswegatchie was to have set off for Montreal with a *Party* from his Garrison to drive the Yankeys out of Montreal—& Goddard has gone to La Bey with one of the officers from this Fort to beat up for Indian Volunteers who are to join Col° Butler with the five Nations And then drive the Rebels entirely out of the Province I give you joy of your Victory over the T—ys in the Rum Store affair, may your Party alway prevail! I shall set off in a few days for the Grand Portage & then in all probability shall pay you a visit at Detroit till which time God bless you—

SIMON M[c]TAVISH

Comp[ts] to all Friends

June 10th

As the Angelica did not go yesterday I have an opportunity of maintaining Old Eddlestens good opinion still by sending him three Bandanae Hand[fs] I promised him at Detroit, & I did not think to deliver him then nor shou'd I have now thought of it if I had not heard that he has been upbraiding me with my breach of promise after I was gone—pray deliver them to him with my Comp[ts]—I make no doubt but you will do all lies in your power for our Interest in case any of the people indebted to us comes in, I request you will look after Gouin if he shou'd come or send in —probably the death of his Father may induce him to come—if Lorrain comes in, or sends us the Ballance due on his Note, please to disc[t] that he ought to pay Interest, as Lorrain Equipd Marian last year, I wou'd not be surprised shou'd he propose some Terms on his Acc[t]—I took on his debt to be so desperate that cou'd a half or even less, be secured I wou'd willingly be off with him— I am very sorry to hear that game . . . has not behaved as he ought on your Acc[t]—I am little Surprised that Boyle has not even wrote us. I wou'd not easily Suspect him of any Sinister Views to do us an injustice but I wou'd be glad you may look after him—you see how free we make with your time, but be aSured it is from our Opinion of your Friendship, & that we wish to have an Opportunity

to do you a service to convince you we wou'd not be backward—
Remember us to all friends—

Lyons we guess from the behaviour of his Partner [*one word illegible*] Montreals refusing his Bills last year, will & were every one he owes here in Peltry, so mu[*seal*] for you

Mr William Edgar

Mackina June 10th 1776

Mr Edgar   There was a Pair of Gold Sleeve Buttons left in the Drawer of the Counter, M^r McTavish sold them to a French Man at this place, please to send them up when an opportunity offers Compt^{mts} to Mr Macomb tell him the Rascal Ainse wont take the Vessel. wherefor we think proper to put her up to sale in order to ascertain the damages, and that as their is little to do for the Felicity we have thought proper to send Capt Wright to the Saulte in the Perriauger, he will probably be here in ten days, since yesterday a Canoe arrived from St Marys the owner of her says the Indians from that Quarter Stopt at the Sault being afraid that application would be made to them to join the others who are going to Montreal—I believe McBeath will be a widower in a short time, his wife has been Sick ever since her arrival   McTavish will leave this for the Portage soon—The time of my return to Detroit depends on many circumstances however we are happy in having you to look after our affairs—Sugar & Indian Corn are in great plenty at this place—

Dear Sir believe me your Friend & wellwisher

JA^s BANNERMAN

Mr Willm Edgar

Addressed: To Mr William Edgar Merch^t Detroit

Dear Sir, I forgot a Barometer with Mr Ettleston as the Person it belongs to will be here in a few days I beg it may be sent up by the 1st opportunity   If Pierre Reaume pays the 1,000 Flour send it up in Bags, we have reason to expect Flour from Knaggs for his Acc^t which if he pays let it be also sent up.   I left Iron with Thibault for a Pix Ax as soon as it is made you'll please to deliver it to Ettleston. If you can get either Flour or Corn from those who owe us, take it and send it here—If Mr Meldrum will let us have his Grease at what he once offer'd it viz 1/4 take it, you may even give him 1^d or 2^d more provided it can be here before the 10th of July—The people from the Missisipi have had bad Success—an Expedition of Indians will leave this in a few days for Montreal —for any other news I refer you to M^r McTavishs Letter whatsoever may occur relative to Trade shall be communicated to you as it Occurs—People here are more moderate than at Detroit, tho I believe no less affcted to the Cause of Gov^t My C^{pts} to Mr Fleming Ja^s Abbott & Wife not forgetting Robin—and as many more as you please

JAMES BANNERMAN

Addressed: To Mr William Edgar Merc^{ht} Detroit
Endorsed: McTavish and Bannarmans Letters 10th June 1776

Michilimackinac June 23^d 1776

Mr Willm Edgar There are seven Canoes arrived from Mont^l and we have News frome there so late as the 15th of May, it is confidently believ'd here that the Continental Troops are gone from Canada. Mr Henry and others from Albany bought to the Amount of £15,000 St^g in Merchandise, which they sent from Montreal in Sleds to Albany. So that Indian Goods are very scarce in Canada. All the Powder ab^t 900 Barrels was last Fall Started overboard into the River, As there has no Canoes arriv'd since the 12th Ins^t its imagin'd they wait for Powder from Quebec—

I have seen the London Sale of the Hudsons Bay Co. Peleteries, by which it seems fine Peleteries support their prices, Beaver indeed sold higher than last year. we can't yet judge how Leather has sold, nor is there any one yet arriv'd from Montreal who seems inclin'd to purchase.

Should Boyle or Heron profer their peleteries to us, you may allow them as good prices as others give, the reasons why we would take Peleteries rather than Bills you already know. M^r McTavish went to the Portage the 12th Ins^t—tell Mr Macomb that he may expect the Felicity in a few days after the welcome, I shall write him if upon enquiry I may be able to learn what has become of his Goods that arriv'd in Quebec last Fall. my opinion at present is that the Vessel was not permitted to pass Quebec, On a Supposition that no Corn or Flour would have been permittd to leave Detroit, The Traders from Mont^l furnish'd themselves with Provisions necessary for their People, neither Guillon, or Solomon are yet arrived here,

Compt^s To all Friends
Your Most Hum^{bl} Servt
JAMES BANNERMAN

People from the Missesipe are mostly arrivd, Fagan is not yet come, I'm afraid he'll play Abbott & Co a Slippery trick,

Since writing the above we have receiv'd an acc^t of our Perriaugees arrival from the Grand Portage at the Saute of St Maries; she left the Portage the 9th Ins^t, no body was then arriv'd from their wintering Ground, so that we cannot guess what success people have had in the North, McTavish will go from St Maries to the Portage in the Perriaugee, for which place I imagine she has already saild.

Michilimackinac July 26th 1776

Dear Wm The 21st Inst I received a Letter from the Portage, McTavish found Bruce there on his Arrival, he had done very little, Pond out of 2 Canoes had only made 10 Packs, Greaves was not arrived nor any News of him, our affairs in that Quarter will turn badly out, tho we are not singularly unfortunate

I beg you would get our Packs at Detroit press'd, you have only to count the Number of Plies in each Pack of Deer Skins. I do not expect McTavish till ab^t the 15th of August & untill he arrives I cannot come down

The latest news from Montreal is the 26th Ultimo. I suppose Allan Patterson is ere now arrivd at Detroit from Montreal for Gods sake miss no opportunity of Dunning for we have had so bad success here & in the North, that we shall be pinchd to satisfy our Creditors I have purchased at this place Goods &c to the Am^t of £3,000 a great part of which must be paid this year. I

intend to be concerned in some Little adventures on Lake Superior, if but a little peletries can be got from that place they will be valuable. I have got a Surfeit of Detroit & the damnd Ouabache— If any Letters are arrivd for us please to forw^d them

Your much oblig^d H Serv

Ja^s Bannerman

Addressed: To Mr William Edgar Merch^t Detroit
Endorsed: James Bannerman Letter 26 July 1776

Dear Willm I learn that the rascal Gouin has had the Effrontery to come in without bringing the few Packs with him, & I'am afraid he intends to give the little he has to Sterling, for Gods sake try (if it is not yet too late) to get security from him that he will deliver his peleteries to us, or if he has any property about Detroit or Else where get it secured

I shall write him a few lines by this opportuny [sic] & I beg you would use your utmost endeavors with him, I know it is a very disagreeable task, but it is what one friend must do for another —I have a part of your payment from Lyons secure, & I believe there is no danger from him, I write Forsith pressing him to pay you, for the Reasons you will see by his Letter, which I leave open for your perusal—

I send you the list of packs sent p^r the Felicity, they are neither weigh'd nor press'd—I beg you may get the Raccoons & small Furrs press'd as soon as possible, I doubt not but there will be Letters from Alex^r Ellice for us, if they are come to hand please to forward them.

Try if possible to get money to pay Thos Williams & Fleming, I would not like to give them Dfts—I expect McTavish will be in ab^t the middle of Augt I cannot pretend to leave this before his arrival or before I have particular Intelligence from him, No news yet from the Portage which is very odd

If you have time and can find men I wish you would get our Stable or Store plaister'd and, made water tight.

I make no doubt but the Govr will leave the House before the middle of next month, when in all probability we shall have Occassion for it—this you will please to signify to him

If you have the Flour ready you may send it, if not ready give yourself no unecessary trouble because I think there is as much of that Article as will Sell

Never had poor Devil more trouble than I have had with the Jews and their Contracts, I had sold the most of the provisions to Capt Depeyster at a very low rate, and am now obliged to buy dear to replace the Quantity sold. Nobody expected Solomon up, and indeed by justice I was not obliged to furnish him any as he was not here himself nor any person for him to receive the Corn and Flour the time agreed on, but two or three Scoundrels on the Jury tird the others out, and I was obliged to give him half the Quantity promised in his first Agreement, I never will for the future be concerned in Contracts of any kind—

There are several letters here from Montreal dated the 26th Ultimo, In a Pacquet from Porteous enclosed to me, came several letters amongst the rest one for Macomb & one for Fleming so that they will inform you of all the news I know—

we are to have no Goods this Year (tant mieux) our friend Alexander the Coppersmith is at the Bottom of this dissapointment . . he is a person too base to give me any sort of pain—If Boyle & Heron come in before we get down endeavor to settle with them. it is time Greaverat should think of settling for him self & Brother. I imagine it would suit him better to give Peleteries than money or Df^{ts} Peltrys are a dangerous Speculation this year, I'm inform'd that Deers skins of any kind & Raccoons were of no value at London by any of the Sales & that the best kind of Peleteries fell greatly by the last Sales, owing its said to the Acc^t of Montgomerys having faild in his attempt on Quebec—

I'm afraid I have been taken in this Summer, I imagined no Goods would have come up, wherefor I made large purchases of Goods, provisions, & Liquors by which I'm afraid I shall lose considerably

Your Humble Servt
JAMES BANNERM [*seal*]

If Gouin is not at Detroit do not send him the Letter & indeed if there is not some appearance of getting Justice of him I believe it will be better not to deliver it all

Michilimackinac Augt 15th 1776

Dear Billy   The 10th Ins^t I arrived from the Grand Portage and read your letter of News to Bannerman the most of which Coroberates with what Intelligence we had by the Grand River

I am sorry that we may shake hands upon our success in getting in Our Ouabach debts; Mr Gouin is certainly a d——d Rascal. Some Arrangements I made at the Grand Portage oblige me to go down to morrow by the Grand River in C^o with McBeath, I shall probably be up by Osswyatchee by the beginning of October. If I can dispose of our Peltrys to my Satisfaction, if not, hurra for England—

Our bad Success at Detroit, has been in some measure made up by my Jaunt to the Carrying place. We can say with a heart felt Satisfaction, that this Fall we can pay every one their own.

It is not prudent to Animadvert upon publick affairs at present, and I can be but a bad judge having had no later News than the 1st July from Montreal all I'll say, is that I sincerely wish for a Speedy reconciliation, the old Toast, & I believe wish of every good man. Bannerman has received paym^t from Lyons for your Acc^t and will settle it with you on his arrival at Detroit, if I can render you any Services on the Communication forwarding any Goods or Packs that may be on the way, or otherwise, when I am coming back, send me your directions to Niagara.

Do you never make a Mistake in a morning and walk in to your right hand Neighbor to talk Politicks as usual.

Our old Friend & mess mate John Porteous is arrived in Montreal, We had a letter from him, I believe he intends to sett up business there, perhaps to be concern'd with P & E—

There are some letters for us from Blackburne &c^a that must have been forwarded this Spring from Montreal your way, that I wish to have a peep at, at present, you may tell S. Fleming, I can't say whether we have got the £20,000 prize or not, not even if the Tickets have been purchased on our Acc^t Remember me to all Friends, McBeath desires to join me in Comp^{ts} to the Doctor & Fleming.

Believe me Dear William Your Sincere wellwisher & Hble Servt

S<small>IMON</small> M^cT<small>AVISH</small>

Mr William Edgar

Montreal September 22^d 1776

Dear Billy Yesterday favour'd me with the receipt of your letter, for once you have guess'd right, for I am going home with all our Packs on our own risque, you will say (and very justly too) that this is playing high, especially as Peltries have sold so well here. Fortune has proved so kind a Mistress to me for some years past that perhaps I am too Sanguine; and the Jade may now Jilt me effectually by lowering the Prices of Furrs at home—at any rate I am determin'd to Venture.

I am very sensible of the treatment we have met with last year from our London Friends—but I shall put it out of their power to use me so for time to come.

I wish the D——l had Mr Wiggins for preventing you from coming here, I flatter'd myself all along my way down the Grand River with having the pleasure of talking over a great many Matters with you at this place; its true, there are a good many Detroiters here, but then they are not my intimates, and we hold but little discourse together. I Congratulate you on your Success in keeping the *Court* in our part of the Town, tho' I dare say Collin Andrews wou'd be as well pleased you wou'd let your lodger go further from his Stoop.

Todd & I bids *bon jour* to one another when we meet & thats all, I have purchas'd the few things I send up from Mr Kay who was concern'd with Paterson.

Your Goods were on the way up before I arrived here, & I dare say you will get them up in time to dispose of great part of them this Fall. This goes by Macnamara who sets off today—I shall write you by McBeath in the mean time I remain

Your Sincere Wellwisher—& Humble Servt

I beg my Comp^{ts} to
Doctor Anthon &
Flem^g
Mr William Edgar

Simon McTavish

Montreal Octr 4th 1776

Dear William I was just now Debating with myself whether nor not I shoud send you the whole Sheet or only the half, & now I know I will be at a loss for matter to fill up even that

I am so perplexd between the plague of sending away the Boats & receiving & Shipping Our Packs that I have but little time to say much—I wrote you before that I was going home & you know my principal reasons for so doing. Our Vessel will sail from here the 10th a fine jolly fellow our Capt is and was it not for some Ladies we are to take in at Quebec (Who will doubtless be *Spewing* on us this stormy Season) I woud Promise myself much Satisfaction from the jaunt. John Porteous Ben Frobisher & several others are to be my fellow passengers—John & I will not forget to Toast our Detroit Friend^s in a bumper now & then. McBeath Macomb &c^a can explain the Term of Swindling to you, and give you a history of the Wonderfull exploits of our Armys & Fleets in this Province since their Arrival—(Not a Rebel to be seen from this to Point Fair *already*) I refer you to them for the Current News of this place which you'll find very trifling—I shall often wish next Winter that I cou'd convey myself to Detroit to pass an evening with some Friends—You must not forget to send me a Picture of the times there in the Spring, I apply to you as I know you paint well.

Don't you think I will be able to swagger & strutt with Johnny Robison When I'll come from London! I believe I shall, it must give a man an Air of importance to have been there, & it leaves a person of a fruitfull genious scope to tell many fine Storys of himself which none of you poor Bearskin catchers can Contradict— To be serious with you I am damnably afraid I shall repent of my Jaunt, if Peltrys fall I shall have great reason, for we Ship £15,000 in Peltrys which might have been pretty well sold here— Apropo' Sage Billy how came you to keep your Packs at Detroit this year! I realy think you are to blame, the Market now is not bad, & no one knows what it may be next yea[r] I wish it may turn out well for you—

The beggars benison to you William.

S M^{c}TAVISH

Addressed: To—Mr William Edgar Merch^t Detroit
Endorsed: Simon McTavish's Letter 4th Oct^{br} 1776

Detroit May 20th 1777

Dear Sir I returned from Niagara the 11th Inst^t Stedman was sailed for Oswegatchie before my arrival at F^t Slosser. I was obliged to promise that last years Carriage should be paid for at the rate of 6/p^r 112^w their was no Alternative, our Goods must have remained at Niagara, as Capt Lernoult refused interfering in the matter, & hinted that such Steps had been taken by Col^l Caldwel in favor of John Stedman as would entirely frustrate all we had done or could do in the matter, the Goods stored at Niagara were in bad Condition, we have lost of our Cargo above £90 sterling first cost of Dry Articles—besides Liquors & many Articles missing, which I take for granted are Stolen

I found a Box of Candles of your Mark which James Renkin has taken in charge—

I hope your Voyage will be successful on your own part, tho I dare not flatter myself with any great expectation from that Quarter, but I'm convinced you will do every thing in your power for our Interests. Our affairs here are at present in the charge of Mr Williams, & I beg that on your return you would aid him or Trimble all in your power—I wrote McTavish from Niagara when I acquaintd him with your Jaunt to the Country of Knaves, he will no doubt write you by the first opportunity after his Arrival —I have advised him to arrange matters in such a manner as to be able if possible to quit these Countries in the Fall 78. against which time (if not sooner) I hope these troubles will be over. I shall expect to hear from you from time to time & beg you would communicate any thing material that may occur relative to our Affairs, There are about fifty Dutch Men and others from the frontiers arrived at Niagara in the course of last Fall & this Spring, but they are the least capable of giving any rational Acc^t how affairs are situated down the Country of any people I ever saw. by what they say the unhappy people below experience more hardship from the want of Salt than from that of any other necessary of life— believe me dear Billy the hardships sustaind from the wanton & unbridled fury of party rage thro out America can be but faintly conceived by us at a distance. Be it your business & mine to sympathise with the miseries incident to the unhappy state of the Country—I only wait for a wind to set off for Mackina, from thence as soon as possible to the Grand Portage. Capt Robison & his family were well he & Mrs Robison desired to be remembered to you. I inquired of a Hartman what part Robt Ellice had acted in these times, & find that on acc^t of his attachment to Gov^t he was obliged to leave Schenectady with a passport to Philadelphia & instead of going there he went to New York from thence to England   Charles Morrison remains neutral so far as it is possible for a man to do.   C Martin went to Ireland—Campbell House & property remains inviolate contrary to a report propagated here with an intention to ingratiate the Author or Authors with the great people   Voici toutes mes Nouvelles

Soyons Amis comme a l'ordinaire

JAMES BANNERMAN

Dear Billy   I rec^d your Laconick Epistle—of the 13th Jan^y—I expected a longer one   I must confess surely, there wou'd be no treason in telling poor Simon how your dances, & party work among the Ladies went on & you know how dearly I love a little scandle   I give Sampson joy with all my Soul—& am so little envious that I rejoice at the happiness he must have in finding himself a Father—kiss the mother for me & tell her I sincerely congratulate her on an event of so much consequence to her future happiness—as it must cement the Conjugal tie—I'm sure Fleming will be doatingly fond of her & his Son.

We have had a continual round of dissipation here, dancing Clubs drinking &c ^{a}& yet I do not like the place—tho' I have taken my share of all the Amusements it affords.   I believe, as we advance in Life we are more difficult to be pleased—this is rather a Melancholly reflection—but I begin to experience the truth of it—perhaps its owing to my not having a Sweetheart for I was always like a fish out of water when not in Love

I hope my Friend Billy has some favour'd she to pass his Evenings with—pray whats become of poor Charlotte—she was dying you told me last Summer—send me half a sheet of News to Michill^a by the first Vessel next Spring as I shall call there on my way to the Portage & I shall put it to the Credit of our Epistolary Acc^t.

God bless you! may you keep your health & make a Sufficiency of money to quit Detroit & live else where at your ease—

believe me Yours Sincerely

SIMON M^{c}TAVISH

March 9th 1778
Mr Wm Edgar—

THE NORTH WEST COMPANY

Montreal 22^d April 1779—

Dear William I just now received your favor of the 15th February, wherein you doubted whether it would reach me before I left Montreal, I assure you that it is doubtful when Passes for the Upper Country will be granted or whether any will be granted. The Governor has been pleased to signify that he will not grant a single Licence till he has further intelligence from Detroit and whether he will or not depends I believe on the nature of that intelligence—

You are pleased to think I would have been happier at Detroit than here last winter, it may be so, but believe me I am much reconciled to the Society, tho not to the climate of Montreal I have been much troubled with a Vertigo all Winter, & even now I have some slight attacks of it, my best respects to Monsr Le Commissaire & sa Dame, tell him I pray God defend him from all Bilious Winds, and imaginary Evils wishing him at same time as much hapiness as this world, with a belle Dame & un Enfant ou deux par an, can afford

I hope for the pleasure of seeing you here this Fall. The little news we have here is so ill founded & circumstantial that I put no dependance upon, ni le pour, ni le contre, we have the Kings speech at the meeting of Parliament the 27th November, Whereby it appears Trade in most of its branches had been protected & great Reprisals made on the Enemy, we have yet no Intelligence of the Arrival of the Fur Fleet tho their are reasons to induce people to think it went safe, Compliments to Abbot & his wife—to Meldrum, Trimble, Mr Williams, &ca &ca—N.B. James Rinkin is not among these vague Characters of &ca^s.

Believe me your most Sincere Well wisher

JAMES BANNERMAN

Mr William Edgar
Endorsed: James Bannermans letter 22^d April 1779

Montreal Octr 14th 1779

Dear Sir I embrace this opportunity by Mr Abbot to acquaint you that I expected a Letter from you this Summer by some of the many opportunities that must have offered—

I presume you have found it worth your while to prosecute the Trade at Detroit as from your favor last winter I inferred that You would not reassume business at that Post—So You & your amorous Competitor C Barber have broke the heart of the once admired Miss Gouin, The Passion is contagious at Detroit, "Where its operations are in general singular, & some times whimsical". I shall only instance the marriage of the 2 Sisters which took place merely from Spite to Finchley & two or three other poor *Devils who wanted to dance with the* Girls   I beg my Compliments to M^r & Mrs Fleming & cela sans badiner, You are now approaching towards the amorous period of Life, whence I flatter my self with soon hailing you Le Maris si non Le Pere de Famille—pray how do party matters go at Detroit—above or below par, does a Recollection of the party squables ci devant so prevalent at Your place vex you or not, for my part I regard them in retrospect in the same manner I do my childish amusements—

I mean to leave this the 18th & have bespoke a Passage for England, what I may in future is left to chance which (in my opinion) exceeds prevoyance my best respect to all Friends particularly Ja^s Rinkin, & Roche de Boute alias Capt Barber, & believe me in sincerity

    Your Friend & well wisher

                              JA^s BANNERMAN

5. REPORT FROM CHARLES GRANT TO GENERAL HALDIMAND ON THE FUR TRADE, APRIL 24, 1780.

[*Public Archives of Canada, Series B, v. 99, p. 110.*]

SIR,—In Conformity to Your Excellency's request, I made every inquiry in my power concerning the trade carried on between the mercantile people of this Province and the Savages of the Upper Countries, but the time since you spoke to me on that head being short to collect all the intelligence I wanted, I am not yet furnished with information sufficient to lay every branch of that trade before Your Excellency so full and clear as I would wish. However, such knowledge as I have acquired of that business is as follows, and submitted to Your Excellency's consideration to

THE NORTH WEST COMPANY 63

grant passes for carrying on the current year's trade, as you may judge consistent with the welfare of commerce and the safety of the Province.

At all times the trade to the Upper Countries has been considered the staple trade of this Province, but of late years it has been greatly augmented, in so much that it may be reckoned one year with another to have produced an annual return to Great Britain in Furrs to the amount of £200,000 Ster., which is an object deserving of all the encouragement and protection which Government can with propriety give to that trade.

The Indian Trade by every communication is carried on at great expense, labour and risk of both men and property; every year furnishes instances of the loss of men and goods by accident or otherwise. It is not therefore to be expected that the traders in general are men of substance; indeed few of them are able to purchase with ready money such goods as they want for their trade. They are consequently indebted from year to year, until a return is made in Furrs, to the merchants of Quebec and Montreal who are importers of goods from England and furnish them on credit. In this manner the Upper Country Trade is chiefly carried on by men of low circumstances, destitute of every means to pay their debts when their trade fails; and if it should be under great restraints, or obstructed a few years, the consequences would prove ruinous to the commercial part of this Province and very hurtful to the merchants of London, shippers of goods to this country, besides the loss of so valuable a branch of trade in Great Britain.

In these troublesome times the least stop to the Indian Trade might be productive of very bad effects, even among the Savages who are at present our friends or neuter, who on seeing no supply of goods would immediately change sides and join the enemies of Government under pretence that the rebels had got the better of us, and that we had it not in our power to supply them any more. All the property in the upper Countries in such a case would become an easy prey to their resentment; and the lives of all His Majesty's Subjects, doing business in these Countries at the time of a rupture of this nature, might probably fall a sacrifice to the fury and rage of disappointed uncivilized barbarians.

I am informed that of late years from ninety to one hundred canoes have annually been employed in the Indian Trade from

Montreal by the communication of the great river to Michillimakinak, Lakes Huron and Michigan, LaBay and the North West; but this particular may be better ascertained from the Registers Office, where I imagine not only the number of canoes but the names of the men employed in that trade and the places of their destination is recorded. Without access to that office it is impossible to be exact in these points. From the different posts above mentioned comes at least one half the Furrs annually exported from Canada, one fourth is supposed to come from Niagara, Detroit and their environs and one fourth is said to be produced at the lower posts and inhabited parts of the Province.

I do not know how many canoes may be wanted this year for the Trade of Michillimakinak and its dependencies, but I imagine a greater number than usual is absolutely necessary, because they will have to carry from Montreal all the provisions requisite for that Trade which was mostly furnished in former years from Detroit, and carried from thence to Michilimakinak in vessels of burthen, by which means a great deal of expense was saved in carriage. As to the danger of goods sent by the Grand River to the North West, or LaBay falling into the hands of the Rebels, or being carried to them by disaffected persons, I am told it is hardly possible to be effected, the communication being so difficult of access and the distance so great, that the carriage of goods conveyed by that route would cost much more than they can by any means be worth. In this I shall insert the average value of a canoe load of goods, at the time of departure from Montreal, at Michilimackinac and at the Grand Portage. From that it may be judged how far it is practicable to carry on any commerce with the enemies to Great Britain by LaBay, even by disaffected persons from Lake Michigan goods may be carried to the Rebels, but at very great expense, labour and risk, the access through that channel being also difficult and a great way to go, though not so far as the former. For my part I am not at present perfectly acquainted with the routes or distances to give a distinct account of them, therefore I refer to the maps of these countries from which that particular will be better ascertained.

A canoe load of goods is reckoned at Montreal, worth in dry goods to the amount of £300 first sterling cost in England, with 50 per cent. charges thereon makes £450; besides that, every canoe carries about 200 gallons of rum and wine, which I suppose worth £50 more, so that every canoe on departure from that place may be said worth £500 currency of this Province. The charges of all sorts included together from Montreal to Michilimakinac £160, and from thence to the Grand Portage £90, so it appears that each canoe at Michilimackinac is worth £660 currency; every canoe is navigated by eight men for the purpose of transporting the goods only and when men go up to winter they commonly carry ten.

Considering the great number of people in this Province immediately interested in the Indian trade, it is hardly possible to suppose but there may be amongst them some disaffected men, but the major part of them I sincerely believe are sure friends to Government and it would be hard the whole community should suffer for the sake of a few bad men, since regulations and laws are, or may be made sufficiently severe to prevent in a great measure, or altogether every effort that may be made to convey goods to the enemy, and if any person whatever should attempt designedly to violate such regulations, as are made for the welfare and safety of the whole the law ought to be put in execution against him with the utmost rigour, on conviction of guilt and the offender never should be forgiven offences committed against the Publick in general. This I know to be the wish of every honest man within the circle of my own acquaintance, and I daresay it is the same with every well meaning man throughout the Province, for it is evident that severe laws never were made for the Government of good men, but for the purpose of securing good conduct and behaviour among such as require it, and however rigorous the laws may be, in such times as the present they can neither affect nor offend any person, but such as may have some views to transgress them.

As to that part of the Trade carried on over Lake Ontario and Erie, I am not well versed in it, therefore shall say nothing more on that head than what I have heard from the best authority, that is, that improper preferences have been given in transporting goods to Niagara and Detroit, by which means it is represented that the Trade of these countries has fallen into a few hands, to the great detriment of many honest men, equally good subjects and to the additional expense of government being obliged to purchase what may be wanted for public service from a few individuals probably for enormous prices whereas if the Trade was more general every purchaser of goods would be less liable to imposition.

Last year the passes for the Indian goods were given out so late, that it was impossible to forward goods to the places of destination, especially in the North-West. For that reason those concerned in that quarter joined their stock together and made one common interest of the whole, as it continues at present in the hands of the different persons or companies as mentioned at foot of this. The canoes for the North West are commonly the first sent off and indeed the earlier all the canoes bound up the Grand River goes off the better, because most of the men that navigate them can be back in time to cut the harvest and do other needful services.

I have the honour to be with great respect,
Your Excellency's most obedient
and most humble servant,

QUEBEC, 24th April, 1780.   CHAS. GRANT

Todd & McGill	2 shares	
Ben & Jos. Frobisher	2 do	
McGill & Paterson	2 do	
McTavish & Co.	2 do	The North West is divided into sixteen shares all which form but one Company at this time.
Holmes & Grant	2 do	
Wadden & Co.	2 do	
McBeath & Co.	2 do	
Ross & Co.	1 do	
Oakes & Co.	1 do	

6: LETTER OF BENJAMIN FROBISHER TO ADAM MABANE,[1] DATED MONTREAL, APRIL 19, 1784.

[*Public Archives of Canada, Series B, v. 75—2, p. 75.*]

Montreal, 19th April, 1784.

SIR,—When you was at Montreal your time was so much

[1] Adam Mabane (1734-1792), a member of the Executive Council of Quebec. See Mrs. F. C. Warren and the Hon. E. Fabre-Surveyer, *From surgeon's mate to chief justice: Adam Mabane* (Trans. Roy. Soc. Can., 1930).

employed in matters of Public Concern, that I had not the opportunity I wished for to enquire your sentiments on the ambiguous sence of the late Treaty of Peace, respecting the Line of Boundary between this Province and the United States, from Lake Superior to the Westward; with regard to which I must remark that there is no such thing as a Long Lake as expressed in the Treaty, the only communication from Lake Superior is by that tract of land known by the name of the Grand Portage, which leads to a very small river on the west side, that derives its source from an adjacent lake, and from thence to the extent of Lake la pluie about one hundred leagues. It is not, as described a Long Lake, but is rather a Chain of Lakes, few of which have any visible inlet or communication with each other, which occasions in that short distance upwards of forty carrying places, so that we are at a loss to know from the Tenor of the Treaty where the line is intended to be drawn, and anxiously wish to be informed about it, that we may not without previous notice and sufficient time given to withdraw our property, be deprived of the only communication from this Province to the North West. Indeed for my own part I apprehend a survey of the Carrying Place and the Country adjacent will be highly necessary to ascertain and fix unalterably the Line in that Quarter, while on the other hand it will give us time to discover another passage if such a thing exists, whereby we may in all events leave that branch of the Fur Trade to this Province.

The Gentlemen who are engaged in it have ever since the year 1776, carried it on under all the disadvantages inseparable from a state of War, occasioned by the high advance on goods and heavy Insurance, notwithstanding which the natives have been every year amply supplied. Posts that the French were unacquainted with have been discovered, and neither industry nor expense have been spared to extend it and prepare for the return of peace, in hopes that it would enable them in some degree to recover the incredible losses they have sustained, but so far from that they have everything to fear from the line of Boundary to be fixed in that Quarter, unwilling however to relinquish a Business in which they have so long persevered, and animated with that spirit natural to men who can Boast of having brought it, to its present Value & Extent, I have the pleasure to acquaint you that the Proprietors have formed themselves into a Company for the Term of Five years, of which my Brother Mr. Joseph & myself, from the great Interest we held in it, & our long Experience, are named the Directors. The supplies for the present year are accordingly prepared, and ready to be sent off early the next Month, a state of which so far as is required we have delivered to Mr. Davison the Deputy Secretary here, directing him to apply for the Pass the Company requires, which is for Twenty Eight Canoes, valued at £20,000 Currency, and hope there can be no objection on the part of His Excellency the Governor to Grant it.

This large supply, added to the property the Company have already in that Country demands their utmost attention; They do not know how soon they may be deprived of the immediate and at present the only Communication from Lake Superior, and on that account they intend at their own Expense unless Government prefer to undertake it, to discover if possible another passage, that will in all Events fall within the British line, in which they may avail themselves in case of need—Such an undertaking must prove an arduous one, and be attended with great Expence, while their success will remain very uncertain, on which account the Company are induced to hope, that if it is discovered it will be granted to them in full right for a Certain term of years, not less than seven, as a reward for their Public Spirit, and the advantages that will result in this Province from the discovery; in the meantime should the Upper Posts be given up, we are Convinced His Excellency will give such orders as may appear to him necessary for the Company's Protection, and effectually prevent any Persons from the United States penetrating into Lake Superior, until the Line of Boundary in that Quarter is surveyed, and unalterably fixed, that their Property may not be exposed nor the present Communication in the least degree interrupted untill they are legally entitled to take possession and if by that Time no other Passage is discovered, they even hope in that case, it may be stipulated for the Carrying place, and the Communication to the Extent of their Territory on Lake Du Bois to remain equally free for both parties, which from the great Superiority we have over them in that Business will almost effectually Secure it to this Province; and this demand may be insisted on with great propriety from the Carrying Places to that Extent laying equally on both sides the Line, so that it would be impossible to penetrate into that Country without encroaching upon each other; besides there is no Furr trade within their limits in that Quarter, but what the Company, or any other from this Country would gladly relinquish, and of Course their Views if they are well informed of the Country cannot be to benefit themselves but to distress others who have better prospects.

If ever this Country see the fatal moment of giving up the Upper Posts, probably others may be Established in different places on the opposite side of the Line in which Case if Government thinks Lake Superior and the Countries with which it communicates worthy of notice, permit me to give you my opinion, which may be of some use, untill a Survey is made, especially at this Time when the Settlement of the Loyalists and others are under Consideration —That is to have a Post so as to Command the Entrance into Lake Superior, either below the Falls of St. Mary's or above them, with regard to the former I cannot point out any particular spot suitable for the purpose, but with respect to the latter I can speak with some certainty—I mean the Place called Point aux Pins where Mr. Baxter who was sent out from England some years ago in search of Copper Mines fixed his residence. It is situate on the East side about two leagues above the Falls on a narrow Channell that Commands in the most effectual manner the entrance into Lake Superior, it has the advantage of a fine Bason formed by the Point where vessels lay in Deep Water within a few yards of the shore equally secure in Winter as in Summer. The Land above the Point is Sandy, but backwards I have been informed it is very good, and Capable of raising Grain of different kinds, nor is there any risque of being disturbed by the Natives, they are too few in number and would be more inclined to Court the Friendship of those that may be settled there than to distress them. All the Indian Corn such a settlement could raise for many years, would be taken from them at a high price by those who frequent Lake Superior in preference to that of getting it from Detroit, and on the other hand a very slender stock of Provisions added to the Fishing they would be possessed of at the Falls for seven months in the year would enable them to live Comfortably untill their Lands were stocked, and in a state of Cultivation.

Such a Settlement would prove of public utility, and in the Course of a few years give an oppty to continue those searches on the North Side that were begun by the French, and recently by Mr. Baxter, the former were obliged to relinquish their prospects from the only Vessel they had on the Lake being Lost about the Time this Country was Conquered, and the latter chiefly from the high price of labour & Provisions.

I beg leave to recommend the Contents of this Letter to your most serious Consideration, requesting you will communicate it to His Excellency when oppy. offers or if more agreeable I will write to Major Mathews on such matters as you may point out, to be laid before Him, in the mean Time I request you will favor me with your Sentiments and remain with great respect & Esteem

dear Sir

your most obed & very hble sert.

BENJN. FROBISHER

The Honble. ADAM MABANE, Esq.

7: LETTER OF BENJAMIN AND JOSEPH FROBISHER TO GENERAL HALDIMAND, DATED OCTOBER 4, 1784.

[*Public Archives of Canada, Series Q, v. 24-2, p. 409.*]

Montreal, 4th October, 1784.

SIR,—We beg to lay before your Excellency for your Consideration the enclosed Memorial on the subject of the trade to the North-West; to which we request your Excellency will permit us to add a few remarks respecting the rise and progress of that Business at different periods, since the Conquest of this Country, and state to your Excellency the nature and extent of it, and the Advantages which will Arise, not only to the Proprietors, but to this Province in general, from a well regulated System in conducting it.

The first adventurer went from Michilimakinak in the year 1765. The Indians of Lake La Pluye having then been long destitute of Goods, stop't and plundered his Canoes, and would not suffer him to proceed further. He attempted it again the year following, and met with the same bad Fortune. Another attempt was made in the year 1767; they left Goods at Lake Pluye to be traded with the Natives, who permitted them to proceed with the remainder; and the Canoes penetrated beyond Lake Ouinipique.

From this period the Trade of that Country was attempted by other Adventurers with various success, and we were among the number in the year 1769, when we formed a connection with Messrs. Todd & McGill of Montreal, for the purpose of carrying on the Business, but the Indians of Lake La pluye, still ungovernable and rapacious, plundered our Canoes, and would not suffer any part of our Goods to be sent further. Before we could be acquainted with this misfortune, our Goods for the year following were at the Grand Portage, and we were then too far engaged to hesitate for a moment. A second attempt was made in which we were more successful. Our Canoes reached Lake Bourbon, and thenceforward we were determined to persevere. Taught however by experience that separate Interests were the Bane of that Trade we lost no time to form with those Gentlemen, and some others, a Company, and having men of Conduct and Abilities to conduct it in the Interior Country, the Indians were soon abundantly supplied and being at the same time well treated, New Posts were discovered as early as the year 1774, which to the French were totally unknown: And had we not been interrupted by new adventurers, the public in the course of a few years would have been well acquainted with the value and extent of that Country, of which even at this time, our knowledge is very imperfect. These Adventurers consulting their own Interest only, without the least regard to the management of the Natives, and the general welfare of the Trade; soon occasioned such disorder, that those who had the most substantial prospects, lost no time to withdraw their property, since which this Business tho' not altogether neglected, has been carried on under great disadvantages occasioned by a variety of Interests, sometimes partially, and at other times totally unconnected with each other; insomuch that at the latter end of the year 1782, those who had persevered were no more than Twelve in number, and being convinced by long experience, of the advantages that would arise from a general Connection, not only calculated to secure and promote their mutual Interests, but also to guard against any encroachments of the United States on the line of Boundary, as ceded to them by treaty from Lake Superior to Lake du Bois—They entered upon and concluded Articles of Agreement, under the title of the North-West Company, of which we were named the Directors, dividing it into sixteen shares; of which each proprietor holds a certain number proportionate to the Interest he then had in the Country. And to prove to the world, that they have no Views but what are directed to extend that Business, and promote the Commercial Interest of the Province, it is expressly ordered in the Thirty-second Article that their Agreement for the purpose of carrying on a Trade to the North-West, shall be registered at the Secretaries Office for this Province at Quebec, for the Inspection of the public.

Their first object was to prepare the necessary supplies and provide against any interruption to their business from the United States, by discovering another passage from Lake Superior to the river Ouinipique, at least 40 Leagues distant from the American line, at the Lake of the Woods, to secure at all events a Communication with the North-West. Having every reason to expect from the line to be drawn as explained in the late treaty of Peace, that they would soon be dispossessed of the Grand Portage, situated at the North-West extremity of Lake Superior, which is the only part of that Country where there is a possibility of getting to the Water Communication which leads to Lake du Bois, and thenceforward to every part of the Country beyond it; from which Your Excellency will perceive the Grand Portage is the Key to that part of British America; and should the United States be put in possession before another passage is discovered, that valuable Branch of the Furr Trade must be forever lost to this Province. Urged by these reasons the Company lost no time in procuring the best information of the Country; and early in June last, they actually sent off from the North side of Lake Superior a Canoe with Provisions only, navigated by six Canadians under the direction of Mr. Edward Umfreville, who has been Eleven Years in the Service of the Hudson's Bay Company and Mr. Venance St. Germain; both of them men who speak the Language of the Natives and who are in other respects very well qualified to execute the Company's intentions.

Their Instructions were to proceed to Lake Alempigon and thence in a West direction by the best Road for the Transportation of Goods in Canoes to the River Ouinipique at, or as near as may be to the Portage de L'Isle, and by Letters received from them at Lake Alempigon 30th June, it appears they had met with innumerable difficulties from the want of Indian Guides, but they had then one who had undertaken to conduct them to Lake

THE NORTH WEST COMPANY 73

Sturgeon and they express'd the most sanguine hopes of getting forward from thence to the River Ouinipique. The Company have no accounts of them since that period, and as all their Canoes are now returned from the Grand Portage, they cannot until the next year give your Excellency any further information concerning this discovery.

The Inland Navigation from Montreal, by which the North-West business is carried on, is perhaps the most extensive of any in the known World, but is only practicable for Canoes on account of the great number of Carrying places. To give your Excellency some Idea of which, there are upwards of ninety from Montreal to Lake du Bois only, and many of them very long ones.

Two setts of men are employed in this business, making together upwards of 500; one half of which are occupied in the transport of Goods from Montreal to the Grand Portage, in Canoes of about Four Tons Burthen, Navigated by 8 to 10 men, and the other half are employed to take such goods forward to every Post in the interior Country to the extent of 1,000 to 2,000 miles and upwards, from Lake Superior, in Canoes of about one and a-half Ton Burthen, made expressly for the inland service, and navigated by 4 to 5 men only, according to the places of their destination.

The large Canoes from Montreal always set off early in May, and as the Provisions they take with them are consumed by the time they reach Michilimakinac, they are necessitated to call there, merely to take in an additional Supply, not only for themselves but also for the use of the Canoes intended for the Interior Country and the Consumption of their servants at the Grand Portage, but as these Canoes are not capable of carrying the whole of such Provisions it thence becomes necessary to have a Vessel or Boats upon Lake Superior for that Transport only, and the utmost dispatch is required that everything may be ready in point of time to send off their supplies for the Interior Country, for which purpose the Goods, Provisions and everything else required for the Outfits of the year, must be at the Grand Portage early in July; for the carrying place being at least Ten Miles in length, Fifteen days are commonly spent in this Service, which is performed by the Canoemen, who usually leave the west end from the 15th July to the 1st August, according to the distance of the places they are intended for.

Their general loading is two-thirds Goods and one-third Provisions, which not being sufficient for their subsistence until they reach winter Quarters, they must and always do, depend on the Natives they occasionally meet on the Road for an Additional Supply; and when this fails which is sometimes the case they are exposed to every misery that it is possible to survive, and equally so in returning from the Interior Country, as in the Spring provisions are generally more Scanty. In winter Quarters, however, they are at ease, and commonly in plenty, which only can reconcile them to that manner of life, and make them forget their Sufferings in their Annual Voyage to and from the Grand Portage.

We have taken the liberty to mention these matters so minutely to your Excellency to demonstrate how precarious that business is, and to show the impossibility of carrying it on to any extent in opposite Interests, without manifest ruin to some of the parties concerned and the destruction of the Trade. While on the contrary, by a well regulated System in that long and precarious chain of connections which a Company alone can establish and execute, every Advantage may be derived for discovery and improvement.

The present Company have accordingly adopted the most proper measures to answer those ends, and have entered upon the Business with a determined Spirit, to supply the Natives plentifully with every necessary they require which is the only sure means to extend it and to obtain a perfect knowledge of the Country, so far as it may be done without interfering with the Commercial rights of the Hudson's Bay Company, which on all occasions they will carefully avoid.

The property the Company have already in that Country, exclusive of their Houses and Stores, and the different Posts, as appears by the settlement of their Accounts this present year Amounts to the sum of £25,303.3.6 Currency; and their Outfits for the next Spring which will be sent from Montreal as soon as the Navigation is open, will not fall much short of that sum so that the Company will have an Interest at the Grand Portage in July next of about £50,000, original Cost, in Furrs, to be sent to Montreal by the return of their Canoes, and in goods for the Interior Country, from which your Excellency may judge of what may be expected from that Trade, when in our power by an exclusive Right for Ten Years to explore the Country and extend it.

We beg your Excellency's pardon for troubling you with this

long detail, we have done it merely to give your Excellency the best information respecting a Trade which, is hardly known, and still less understood, except by those who have been in that Country, requesting your Excellency will take this letter in support of their Memorial, into your consideration, and extend to the Company your Favour and Protection, to obtain for them An Exclusive Right to the Trade of the North-West, on the Conditions stated in the Prayer of their said Memorial to Your Excellency.

We have the Honour to be with the utmost respect in behalf of the North-West Company,
>Your Excellency's,
>>Most obedt. and
>>>Most hbl. servts.,
>>>>BENJN. & JOS. FROBISHER

To His Excellency,
>General HALDIMAND,
>>Quebec.

8: LETTER OF SIMON McTAVISH TO JOSEPH FROBISHER, DATED APRIL, 1787.

[*Letter Book of Joseph Frobisher, McGill University Library.*]

>Montreal April 1787.

Mr. Joseph Frobisher.

Dear Joe,
Ever since the death of my worthy friend, your Brother, I have been considering in what manner our business in the N.W. can be best managed, so as to keep up our present influence and interest in that country; for we may be well assured, the late unfortunate event, will encourage those who wish to support Gregory in a Perseverance of the present opposition which I am afraid may be done with success in the end unless we take the most effectual steps to prevent it.

Our present concern is drawing near a close and it is natural for the different parties to be now looking forward beyond the term of it; your being alone, will render it impossible for you to attend to the business here and above, so as to engage to renew the present concern, on the same Footing, the consequence would be a division, and getting into different companies, by which means we should be weakened and loose every advantage, we now have over others in that trade. I am also much in the same Predicament with you; I should be at a loss to attend the outfits and other business here, and go every year to the Portage, which is unavoidable for any person largely interested in that country, we at present hold between us near one-half the concern, after deducting Montour & Small's proportions in our shares; and I see no means so likely to support our consequence in that country as to join our Fortunes and names in a general copartnership, one half each, to continue while we find mutual satisfaction in it; in which case I presume we may still keep our present shares in any future concern, which we shall form, and have the supplying the company altogether which I think we shall be equal to as I intend at all events to withdraw out of the Michilimackinac Business when the General Store is at an end, and should Montour & Small or either of them quit the Business we could get the Patersons[1] into that country in their Place. Blackwood[2] wishes to give up supplying Holmes & Grant and Forsyth will dispose of McBeath's 2/16ths both which will be our Interest to buy.

By your remaining here the summer you can have your affairs so arranged that the connexion may take place in the Fall and begin with next year's outfit; as for my matters they are so easily seen into that I can at any time join.

As we are supplied from Home by two Houses which we have reason to esteem we would continue the business, one-half with each. for we should have occasion for the credit allowed by both, to carry on the business on an extensive scale, as we do now, and

[1]Charles and Allan Paterson. Charles Paterson, who was one of the early traders on the Saskatchewan, was drowned in Lake Michigan in 1788. His brother Allan then retired from the fur-trade, married a daughter of the Hon. John Munro (a member of the first Legislative Council of Upper Canada), and settled down in the "new settlements" on the north bank of the St. Lawrence.

[2]John Blackwood (d. 1819), of Quebec, afterwards (1813-19) a member of the Legislative Council of Quebec, who married in 1793 the widow of Charles Grant, the author of the report on fur-trade made in 1780 to General Haldimand. He must be distinguished from the John Blackwood, a merchant of Montreal, who died in 1815, and was apparently not related to him.

all our own capitals beside, for which reason I would think it prudent to confine ourselves entirely to the N.W. which we can attend to well enough, by one of us, going up every summer. But previous to any connexion of the kind taking place, it will be right we should give every information to one another, necessary to show how we stand with the world, as far as can be at present ascertained.

I wish you to consider this matter well and let me have your opinion, I have put my thoughts on paper on purpose to give you an opportunity of weighing all the circumstances.

Yours

S. McTavish

9: Articles of Agreement between Simon McTavish and Joseph Frobisher, November, 1787.

[*W. Dummer Powell Collection, Quebec Papers, v. 75, pp. 154-7, Public Reference Library, Toronto.*]

Articles of Agreement indented, had, made, agreed and concluded upon at Montreal in the Province of Quebec this . . . day of November in the year of our Lord One Thousand Seven hundred and eighty seven Between Simon McTavish and Joseph Frobisher both of Montreal aforesaid Merchants.

Whereas the mutual Interest of the said Simon McTavish and Joseph Frobisher requires that the Trade now carried on by the said parties severaly with certain Adventurers in a joint Account of Trade with the Indians on the North West Frontiers of the said Province under the name and designation of the Northwest Company, should hereafter be carried on jointly to the mutual Profit and Loss of the said Simon McTavish and Joseph Frobisher.

First It is therefore agreed, that the said Simon McTavish and Joseph Frobisher do become and hereby declare themselves Copartners in Trade under the Firm and Designation of McTavish and Frobisher for five years from this date.

Secondly That Whereas the said Simon McTavish and Joseph Frobisher are at present severaly engaged in divers distinct and separate concerns in Trade which if continued might prove prejudicial to the interest of the said intended mutual concern It is agreed that from and after the date of the presents no business whatsoever shall be undertaken or carried on by either of the said parties severaly, unless it be to support and close as soon as conveniently may be done, the several Concerns or Adventures in Trade in which the said Simon McTavish individualy or the said Joseph Frobisher as one of the late Firm of Benjamin and Joseph Frobisher may be actualy engaged at present.

3dly That from and after the date of these presents no further support be given by the said Simon McTavish or the said Joseph Frobisher to any concern they or either of them may be engaged in but with the consent of the other signified in writing and submitted by the Party giving such Consent.

4th That the original Stock of the said Copartnership shall consist of Eleven sixteenth shares of the trading Capital of the Adventure to the North West in Company now valued at 16960.9.1½ and in Goods not placed in the said adventure to the amount of 2821.0.1½.

5 That each Partner shall take Credit with the Copartnership for such Sums as on his Individual Account shall come into the stock of the said Copartnership and shall be allowed Interest on all such Sums from the date of such Credit.

6 That the Stock of the said Copartnership shall be subject to the payment of the sums specified in a schedule hereunto annexed marked A, after payment whereof neither of the said Copartners shall be at liberty to draw from the remaining Stock of the said Copartnership in any one year pending the same, more than the sum of Five hundred pounds for his personal Account, any Sum or Sums received or to be received by the said Copartnership on Account of such individual Copartner to the Contrary notwithstanding.

7 That the business of the said Copartnership at Montreal shall be carried on at the Counting House and in the Stores and Vaults of the said Joseph Frobisher, and that in the Month of January of each year it shall be agreed upon and settled in writing by the said intended Copartnership what Allowance shall be made to the said Joseph Frobisher for Rent, Clerks Wages and other extra Expences for the Current year.

8 That neither of the said Copartners shall become Security for

any other Person in any sum whatsoever without the consent of the other Partner in writing under Seal or indorsed on the Articles of Copartnership.

9 That the Books of Account and all papers belonging to the Copartnership shall at all times be free and open to the Inspection of either Copartner.

10 That in the Month of October in One thousand Seven Hundred and Ninety two preceeding the period for the expiration of the said Copartnership, the said Copartners or one of them shall give to the other notice in writing that he will not continue or extend the Duration of the said Copartnership beyond the said period, otherwise the said Copartnership shall continue in full force as to all its liens on the parties untill fourteen Months after such notice shall be given.

11 That after such notice shall be given by either of the said Copartners to the other of his Intention to conclude the said Copartnership after the Expiration of five years from the day of the date hereof, A state of the Copartnership Affairs shall be made out as accurately and Expeditiously as possible and if no other amicable arrangement can be had between the parties within six months after such notice, Either of the said Copartners offering the largest sum of Money to the other for that purpose shall be at liberty to make his Election of taking or resigning to the other the whole of the Concern and Interest of the said Company or Copartnership at such Evaluation as the said Parties may agree upon or, as in Case of Difference between them, two friends chosen by the Copartners or an umpire chosen by such friends may fix upon such Concern or Interest. And that such Friends or, in Case of Difference such Umpire, shall establish the mode of payment and Security to be given by the party acquiring such Concern or Interest to the Party resigning the same.

12 That all disputes between the said Copartners arising in the affairs of the said Copartnership shall be referred to the Award and Arbitrament of two Merchants, one to be chosen by each of the said Copartners or to the Umpirage of such Merchant as the said Arbitrators may in Case of Difference elect to determine between them.

13 That in the Event of the Death of either of the said Copartners within the five years of fixed Duration of this Copartnership, the surviving partner may at his option continue the same to

the end of the said Term of five years, admitting the legal representative of his deceased Partner to the same Rights and priviledges as were enjoyed by his deceased Partner.

And for the due observance of the aforesaid Articles of Agreement the said Simon McTavish and Joseph Frobisher do hereby respectively bind themselves, and each of them himself, his heirs, Executors and Administrators under the penalty in case of Contravention, of such Damages as may be awarded by Arbitrators agreeable to the Proceedure of the article above recited.

In Witness whereof the said Simon McTavish and Joseph Frobisher have severaly and interchangeably executed these presents by subscribing their names and affixing their Seals respectively to this present writing indented and to the Counterpart thereof at Montreal aforesaid the day and year of use herein above written—Sealed & witnessed
in presence of—

Schedule A. containing Detail of Sums of Money payable out of the Stock of the Copartnership of McTavish and Frobisher referred to in the Sixth Article of the annexed Agreement.

To Louis Chatelan	on demand	197.18.10
To Pierre Laurent	do	94.17.
To Charles Boyer Junior	do	106.
To David Grant	do	204. 5.
To Venance St Germain	do	24.15.
To Ed. Umphreville	do	47. 2.10
To Nicolas Montour	do	3149.11
To Brickwood Pattle & Co	do	3764 8 5¼
Total		7588 18 1¼
To Joseph Frobisher 1789		554. 1.8¼
To Do 1790		554. 1. 8¼
To Do 1791		554. 1. 8¼
To Dyer Allan & Co on demand		10530. 6. 1
		Hfx Cy. £19781. 9. 3
11/16ths—24669.15.1		16960. 9. 1½
		2821. 0. 1½

THE NORTH WEST COMPANY 81

the amount in Goods to form a stock equal to the Demands upon it but the goods Mr McT has to appropriate to that purpose are the Inventory of sundries delivered into the N.W. Store 2227.7.10¼ his 5/16ths Interest in goods remaining in Sd Store after the outfit of this Spring & Inventory amounting to £838.12.11½ Total 3066.0.9¾.

McTavish & Frobisher
Dr Ben & Joseph Frobisher
                    To Sundries
Viz

Louis Chatelan	197.18.10
Pierre Laurente	94.17
Francois La France	46. 7. 1
Charles Boyer Junior	106.
David Grant	204. 5
Venance St Germaine	24.15
Ed. Umphreville	47. 2.10
Nich. Montour	
Balance due him this Day 2324. 5. 5½	
Am't his 1/3ᵈ profit on the adventure for 1786 should the furs shipped this fall am't 825. 5. 6½ their valuation	
	3149.11. 0
	3870.16. 9
[Less Francois La France, 46.7.1]	3824. 9. 8

Sir

The above are accounts to be assumed by Mr. McTavish, except that of Fran. La France 46.7.1 which is effaced; you will please to take notice that the Amt 825.5.6½ due Montour is only conditionaly; the first sum 2324.5.5½ positive.

                            Your hble. Sevt.
                            J. HALLOWELL

10: Deed of Assignment of Gregory and McLeod, 1788.

[Notarial Archives, Montreal, Beek 403.]

Before the underwritten Notaries Residing in the City of Montreal in the Province of Quebec duly admitted and Sworn Personally came and Appeared John Gregory, and Normand McLeod of the same place Merchants and Co-partners in Trade, and their Trustees, Robert Ellice and Company, Richard Dobie and Edward William Gray for and in the behalf of others the Creditors of the said Gregory and McLeod of the One Part, John Richardson for and in the name of the Co-partnership of Robert Ellice & Company of the Second part, and Joseph Frobisher for and in the name of the Co-partnership of MacTavish, Frobisher and Company and for the North West Company of the Third Part. Which said Parties declared to have made and agreed upon the Covenants and agreements herein after mentioned (to wit) Whereas by an agreement concluded on the Thirteenth day of December One thousand seven hundred and Eighty Six before François Le Guay Notary Public between John Gregory & Normand McLeod aforesaid of the one part, and Robert Ellice and Company, Richard Dobie and Edward William Gray with the other Creditors of said Gregory & McLeod of the other part, the said Robert Ellice and Company, Richard Dobie and Edward William Gray were appointed Trustees of said Gregory & McLeod for certain purposes therein mentioned; and amongst others to receive and divide the Returns pro rata amongst the Creditors and Whereas since that agreement an Arrangement has taken place between the said Gregory and McLeod on one part and Simon McTavish & Joseph Frobisher & Company in behalf of themselves and others concerned with them in the North West Company on the other part by which arrangement the said Gregory and McLeod are to Receive one-fifth of the General Returns with an Addition or deduction such as the Property of each party in the interior country as per Inventories to be taken for that purpose may Require And Whereas the Division of the North West Furrs, would not only be attended with considerable expences to the concerned, but might if they were not carefully & judiciously Receipted, occasion prejudice to one of the Parties besides depreciating the value of the smaller parcel if Shipt afterwards to England, it being Generally found that the larger the Quantity the more beneficial the Sale And as from the present alarming Prospects it might injure the Interested exceedingly to push the disposal here, under the disadvantage of a deficiency of Purchasers arising from Recent losses or Scarcity of Money.

Therefore to obviate all which inconveniences and to insure as much as possible every chance of benefit to the said Gregory and McLeod and their Creditors It is hereby Agreed upon between the said Gregory & McLeod and their Creditors & Trustees, Robert Ellice & Co. & McTavish, Frobisher & Co. for the North West Co. in manner as follows Viz The said Gregory & McLeod and their Trustees in behalf of themselves and the Creditors aforementioned in General consent and agree to the said One-fifth belonging to Gregory and McLeod of the North West Company returns, being delivered & rendered to the order of Robert Ellice and Coy in England on the Conditions after expressed, The said McTavish, Frobisher & Coy for the North West Company, engage and oblige themselves to hold said undivided fifth share of the Return subject to the order of said Robert Ellice & Co. for the purpose of being consigned to their Correspondents in England for Sale, and also engage to Bale up said Share free of any Commission or expences Except Baling and what extra Store Rent they may by reason of said extraordinary quantity of Furrs, which they are to be Reimbursed for by Robert Ellice & Co. And the said Robert Ellice & Coy agree to Receive and Ship to England, said Gregory & McLeod's undivided fifth share of the North West Coy Returns for this Year on the following Conditions. Viz. A Valuation of said Furrs to be made here by three Persons, one of which to be chosen by Gregory & McLeod & their Trustees and the other by Robert Ellice & Compy if these disagree they are to appoint a third. At that Valuation Robert Ellice & Comy will Receive them in the first Instance as a payment on account of their supplies to the Estate of Gregory and McLeod and the obligation of paying to the Trustees in the Fall what the said Valuation may exceed their Claim and to Account for the profit that may arise on the Sales, after deduction from the neat proceeds the charges of Baling, Entry and Shipping with River Freight (if any is paid) or any unforseen unavoidable expences on them they may pay with consent of the Trustees. The Creditors engaging to refund what they may fall short of such Valuation either immediately its being known, or out of the future dividends, with Interest And as the Estate is to have the chance of benefit or loss on the Sales, Robert Ellice and Company are to be allowed any interest accruing on their Account, for the difference of time that may arise between the usual time of Selling Furrs here, and that of the Neat Proceeds of these coming to their credit in England deducting therefrom the time that would elapse on an average between Receipt of a Bill of Exchange here on common usance and its payment in England.

For the said Partners have so agreed upon and [it] is the true Intent and Meaning of these presents anything therein contained to the Contrary Notwithstanding and For the true performance thereof the said Partners did and do hereby bind themselves the one to the other. Thus done and passed at Montreal in the Province aforesaid on the Tenth day of May in the Year of our Lord one thousand and seven hundred and eighty eight and Signed by the said Parties after being duly Read by us Notaries.

We the Creditors do Approve and Accept of this Agreement

ALEXANDER HENRY
R. CRUICKSHANK

JOHN GREGORY
NORMD MACLEOD
ROBERT ELLICE & Co.
RICHARD DOBIE
EDW. WM. GRAY
JOHN RICHARDSON
JOS. FROBISHER

BEEK
Not. Pub.
1788

11: NORTH WEST COMPANY AGREEMENT, 1790.

[*Archives of the Quebec Seminary.*]

ARTICLES of agreement entered into at the Grand Portage between McTavish Frobisher & Coy, Nicholas Montour, Robert Grant, Patrick Small, William McGillivray, Daniel Sutherland, John Gregory, Peter Pangman, and Alexander Mackenzie, for the purpose of carrying on a Trade on their joint Accounts, to that part of the Indian Country commonly called the North West, or elsewhere as the Parties may hereafter agree; to be divided into twenty shares of which McTavish Frobisher & Coy are to hold six twentieths, Nich^s Montour two twentieths, Robert Grant two twentieths, Pat Small two twentieths, Will McGillivray one twentieth, Daniel Sutherland one twentieth, John Gregory, two twentieths, Peter Pangman two twentieths, and Alex. Mackenzie, two twentieths, in all profits and loss arising from thence; to commence with the first outfit for the year 1792, and to continue there after for the full and complete term of seven years.

Article first,
That McTavish, Frobisher & Coy, shall do all the business of this concern at Montreal and import the goods necessary for the supplies, charging 5 per cent at the bottom of the invoice, and interest from the time they fall due in England, at the rate of 5 per cent p. annum, with 4 per cent on the amount of the whole outfit, at the close of each year, the goods, men, wages, provisions, (wherever they may be purchased), cash disbursements, etc, to be included, and interest at 6 per cent p. annum on all advances, imports excepted.

Second.
That the furs shall be shiped to England by McTavish Frobisher & Coy on account of this concern, for which they are to be allowed a commission of one half p. cent on the amount. The neat proceeds whereof are to be credited each individual of the company in proportion to the share or shares, he or they hold, so soon as they are carried to the credit of McTavish Frobisher & Coy in England.

Third.
That Mr Montour & Mr Pangman shall winter and transact the Company's businessat Forts des Prairies, Mr Small, Mr McGillivray & Mr MacKenzie, shall winter and transact the business at the English River, and Mr Robt Grant shall winter and transact the business at the Red River; subject however to such changes, as the majority of the Concern present in the summer at this place, shall think most for their interest. But that two of the parties may winter below, each year, in rotation, or as they may agree amongst themselves, upon paying the salary of an able clerk each, to take their places, and to return the year following to their stations, cases

of sickness only excepted: Or otherwise to relinquish the one half of what share, or shares, he or they may hold in the concern in favor of such deserving clerk or clerks, as he or they so relinquishing may judge proper, provided they are such as are approved of by the Company; if not, to be settled by ballot; and the person or persons so retiring may retain the other half of his or their share or shares in the concern, without any attendance to the business: it is further understood, and agreed to by the parties who may so relinquish, that the clerks in whose favor they resign shall have the shares on the same principle, as the property is at present calculated to cost at the different posts.

Fourth.

That for the conducting of the business, one of the house of McTavish Frobisher & Coy, John Gregory and Daniel Sutherland, shall come up annually to this place, unless Mr McTavish's presence in England, shall be found more for the interest of this concern, in which case, the former are to be exempted. And as it is thought necessary for the interest of the present North West concern, that Mr McTavish should go to England this autumn, that the parties belonging to that concern, subscribing to this agreement, give their assent thereto, on condition of McTavish Frobisher & Co'y making over to Daniel Sutherland one of their twentieth shares, for the two remaining years of said concern, in order to give him weight, to represent their interest in assisting Mr Gregory to manage the Company's affairs here.

Fifth.

In case of the death of any of the parties hereto, before the expiration of this agreement, his or their executor, or executors, may nominate another person, in his or their place to be approved of by the concern; who shall in every respect conform to this agreement.

Sixth.

If all the parties herein, choose to retire from the business at the expiration of this agreement, a small assortment of goods shall nevertheless be sent to the Portage, if judged necessary, but not otherwise, in order to realize, and bring to final close in the most advantageous manner, the remaining business of this adventure, and whatever the clerks, guides, and canoemen, may be then indebted, shall be considered as debts due to this concern, and not otherwise.

Seventh.

The contracting parties most solemnly declare that in the respective departments, in which they may be employed in the management of this business, they will keep faithful and exact accounts of all and every part of their transactions, so far as they are able, and will oblige all clerks and others under their direction to do the same, and further, they shall use every exertion, within the reach of the industry and abilities to promote on every occasion the interest of this concern.

Eighth.

That as all the parties hereto, have or may have other concerns in trade, in no wise connected with this business, and the present agreement being solely for the purpose of carrying on a joint adventure to the North West; in order therefor to prevent any of the parties from being involved, or in any manner responsible for one another, it is stipulated, and provided, that on no pretence whatever, shall any of the parties sign for, or contract debts for account, or in the name of any of the other parties, without a special power for that purpose.

Ninth.

All persons of what denomination soever, whether principals, or others, who winter in the interior country, or elsewhere, shall deliver, or send to the Portage annually, an exact account of the goods, or other property they had remaining, as also of the peltries and canoemen, they may have left in the country, and as far as they are able, shall produce faithful accounts of their transactions, and the expenditure of the goods, comitted to their care the preceding year. The principals who winter, as well as those who come up from Montreal (while on the voyage, and at this place) shall be allowed their personal necessaries, out of the common stock of the concern, and no more, every thing exceeding this limitation, they are required to keep an account of, and either send or bring the same to the portage annually, in order that it may be charged to their accounts.

Tenth.

All difficulties that may arise in conducting this business shall be decided by the votes of twelve shares, which, in such case shall be considered as unanimous in every matter of what nature soever, and the contending party or parties, shall be obliged to submit to it; but in any case where the votes are under twelve, it shall be left to the arbitration and decision of four desinterested persons, men conversant in this business, who, if they cannot agree, shall chose an umpire, and the award signed by such five persons, or any three of them, shall be binding to all parties.

Eleventh.

All persons interested in this concern, shall not upon any account, enter into any new engagements, during the term of this agreement, to the detriment of this concern. This article shall be equally binding upon any one of the concern, who disposes of their share to any other person.

Twelfth.

In case this agreement is disolved at the end of seven years, and that all the parties choose to continue in this business, on their separate account, or otherwise, without renewing this concern, in such case, all the goods remaining on hand, clerks, guides and canoemen, who are indebted to the company, whether at the Grand Portage, or in the interior Country, shall be equally divided, according to the different shares. The forts, buildings, and fixed property at the Grand Portage, to be sold in four lots, at public sale, to the highest bidder, and those in the interior country, to be sold in like manner, in single lots, for each post.

Thirteenth.

That whenever either of the parties become worth more money than what it requires to carry on their proportion of the outfits; if left in the hands of Messrs McTavish, Frobisher & Coy, they are only to be allowed interest on the surplus at the rate of five per cent per annum.

Fourteenth.

That the accounts of each years outfit, shall be made up in november, after the goods are forwarded from Montreal, and accounts current with each of the parties to be signed and interchanged yearly.

Fifteenth.

That Mr MacKenzie shall pay to George McBeath a premium of three hundred and fifty pounds current money of the province of Quebec, over and above the stock that will remain on hand in the name of George McBeath in spring 1792, at the prices agreed upon by the article third, upon his relinquishing all pretentions to any interest in the concern, and, that Mr Gregory and Mr Pangman, shall satisfy Normand McLeod and William Holmes, for the good will of the shares, which they hold in the present North west concern, and which form two of their shares in the new concern.

Sixteenth.

That whereas it is judged necessary by the parties hereunto subscribing, to have no witnesses to this agreement, it is nevertheless hereby, most expressly understood, and solemnly declared, to be equally valid, and binding on all parties, in every respect, as if the same had been duly executed in form by a notary public, any law or usage to the contrary notwithstanding.

Seventeenth.

For the true performance of all and every part of the foregoing articles, each party binds himself unto the others, in the penal sum of five hundred pounds, current money of the province of Quebec, for every twentieth share, to be paid by the party failing to the party observing, or willing to observe, the same.

In witness whereof we have hereunto set our hand and seals at the Grand Portage, this twenty fourth day of July one thousand seven hundred and ninety.

    McTavish Frobisher & Co.
    Nicholas Montour
    Robert Grant
    Pat: Small
    Will. McGillivray
    D. Sutherland
    John Gregory
   {John Gregory by power of attorney for
    Peter Pangman
    Alex. MacKenzie

12: DOCUMENTS RELATING TO THE ENGAGEMENT OF JEAN BAPTISTE CADOT, JR., WITH THE NORTH WEST COMPANY, 1795.[1]

[*Public Archives of Canada.*]

Monsieur Jean Bapt. Cadott fils.

Au Sault St. Marie le 18 aout 1795

Monsieur

Comme Je vous ai Proposer de vous Engager dans la Service de la Compagnie de Nord Ouest Si Sa vous Convient pour l'espace de Trois Anné, Je peut vous promettre Cent Cinquante Louis p Anné et Fournir des Hard &c Comme les Autres Messieurs dans la Service du dit Compagnie et Ce que vous Prenderay pour votre Compte vous Sera Charger Egalement Comme eus et le Bled et Farine que vous aurez Besoin pour Subsister Monsieur votre Pere et Sa Famille vous Seront Charger le Meme Prix du Detroit avec les Poches et Port. Je Sera flattir de Recevoir une Lettre de vous par Mons. McGillivray ou MacKenzie qui Passeront a la fin de Ce Mois.

Je Suis Monsieur
votre tres Hble Serviteur
JOHN GREGORY

En presence des temoins sousignés fut present Monsr. J. Bte. Cadotte lequel s'engage volontairement par ces presents à la Compagnie du Nord Ouest pour hyverner Trois Années en qualité de Comis et ira dans un des Postes ou ils Jugeront a propos pour leurs Commerce, executera ponctuellement toutes les Ordres qui lui seront données par les dits Sieurs ou toutes autres representants ou Agent de la dite Compagnie s'il arrivoit qu'il y'ait quelque personne contre la dite Societé le dit Sieur J. Bte. Cadotte fera son possible pour faire echoir ses Voisins dans leurs entreprises autant qu'il sera en son pouvoir—En un mot ferat tout ce qu'un bon et loyal Comis doit et est obligé de faire sans laisser le service n'y abandonner leurs Interêt jusqu'au tems limité Cette Engagement ainsi faite pour prix et somme de Trois Mil six Cens Livres encien

[1] These documents illustrate the sort of agreement into which the North West Company entered at this period with traders who were not merely clerks nor yet partners, but were independent traders under contract with the Company.

cour de la province de Quebec par Année, et une Equipment comme les autres Messieurs dans le dit service, et ce qu'il pourra prendre sur son Compte lui sera chargez comme à eux, et le Blèd et Farine qu'il pourra avoir besoin pour faire subsister Monsr. son pere et sa famille lui sera chargez le meme prix du Detroit avec les Paches et le Post.—

Le terme de cette engagement à commencer quand le premier Canot de la Compagnie du Nord Ouest arrivera ici de Montreal le printems prochain et de continuer Jusqu'a son arrivé ici L'Automne Mil sept Cens quatre vingt dix Neuf.—

Faite au Sault de St. Marie le 2d Septr. 1795.

Temoins   W. McGillivray Agent pour le Compy. N. West.
Cuthbert Grant
John Welles   J. Btte. Cadotte Junr.

ARTICLES OF AGREEMENT had, made, concluded & agreed upon at the Grand Portage this twenty-fifth day of July in the Year of Our Lord One thousand Seven hundred & Ninety Six, Between William McGillivray & Alexander McKenzie Esquires, Agents acting for & on behalf of the North West Compy of the one Part, & Jean Baptiste Cadotte Gentleman on the other Part.—

WHEREAS by certain Articles of Agreement bearing date at the Sault de Ste Marie the Second day of Septr. last the said J. Baptiste Cadotte became bound & obligated to serve the said North West Compy in the Capacity of Clerk for the term of Three Years; & WHEREAS from the high opinion entertained of the integrity and ability of the said Jean Baptiste Cadotte & for other good causes & purposes; The Parties to these Presents, have mutually consented & agreed to open an adventure or Trade to the Indian Country on their Joint Account and risk, to commence after the day & date of these Presents, and to continue for & during the Space of Five Years: Be it known therefore by these presents that the beforementioned Agreement shall for the present cease & have no Effect—and instead thereof, they the said Parties, have chosen, concluded, and agreed upon the Terms, Conditions & Stipulations herein Aftermentioned.

That is to say.—

Article 1st

    The said North West Compy by their said Agents agree to furnish, fit out & Provide at this Place or the Fond du Lac, all such goods as the said Jean Baptiste Cadotte may require for the said Trade or Adventure; say a yearly Assortment of Merchandize not exceeding Six Canoes Load such as are usually required for this Country (the quantity however to be augmented or diminished as may hereafter be mutually agreed upon) at & for the following Rates and Prices Viz.—Dry Goods at an advance of Forty Per Cent on the Current Prices of Montreal; Tobacco, Amunition, Iron Works, Soap & such like goods at an advance of Seventy five Per Cent on the Prices aforesaid; Liquor & Provisions (from Montreal) such as Rum, Beef, Pork, Butter &c. &c. at One hundred Per Cent on the Prices Aforesaid; Freight of Provisions from Detroit at eighteen Livres (Montl. money) Pr. Piece; ditto from Michilimackinac at Twelve Livres Pr. Piece.—

Article 2nd

    The North West Compy by their Agents, shall in their own Name engage such Clerks, Interpreters & Men as may be required for this Concern and all Engagements otherwise made, shall be in the Name of the North West Company & upon the following Terms; Viz.—Advances made to Men from Montreal shall be chargeable without deduction, but those Men who shall be hired in this Country & who shall (at the Time of engaging) be already indebted to the said North West Company: such debts shall be only Taken and Assumed by this Concern at half the amount or valuation of the debt, no debt whatsoever shall be reckoned upon or so Taken for more than (or over & above) the Sum of Eight hundred Livres: this clause to be reciprocal in as much, that the North West Company shall receive back the debts of this Concern upon the same Principle & footing: Not that it is meant hereby, nor can it be so understood, that any such debtors can or Should avail themselves by this Arrangement, but that the full Original amount shall become the right & Property & be at the disposal of the Party holding them.—

Article 3rd

    The said Jean Baptiste Cadotte doth promise, covenant &

agree to & with the said North West Company & Agents aforesaid that he will Trade, vend, Sell & barter all such goods as shall be so furnished & provided, in the best and most advantageous manner, for & on the joint account of them, the said Parties; That he shall keep regular & fair account of all his Transactions (for which he shall be allowed his personal necessaries out of the common Stock) subjecting himself nevertheless (and all those who shall or may be employed under him) to the following reservations, limitations and restrictions; First, the said Trade or adventure shall be confined to certain boundaries, to Wit, the Lac Rouge & its dependencies, beginning at the little River Auinuipique, comprehending the Lac des Sangsue—Red cedar Lake, said Lac Rouge & extending as far as the River, that discharges itself into the Great Red River: Second, Reciprocal,—The Parties to these Presents shall neither of them, on any pretence whatsoever, meddle or interfere with the Trade or traffick of, or belonging to the respective Posts of the other; by decoying or debauching the Indians in the habit of Trading at one Post to that of another; Nor shall either Party injure or attempt to wrong the Other, by trading Furrs, giving or withdrawing Credits to, or from Indians belonging to each others Posts or otherwise: For it is hereby mutually agreed upon, that in case of default, the Party so transgressing, shall forfeit to the other all such Furs so Traded or Taken & shall likewise incur any Penalty that disinterested Persons may allow.—

Article 4th

And the said North West Company agree to receive from the said Jean Baptiste Cadotte, either at this place or Fond du Lac all such Furs & Peltries as shall proceed from the said Adventure, at regular, fair & Stated Prices, which prices shall be fixed upon by the Parties themselves Yearly at the time of making the Outfit; Those for the Present year shall be as follows; Viz. Beaver at Nine Livres 70 Pound Otters twenty livres each Marten, four Livres, Fisher Six livres each Minks fifty Sols each, Bears twenty four livres each, Cubs twelve livres each, Raccoons forty five sols each, Cased Cats sixteen livres each, Foxes ten livres each, Deer Skins two livres pr. pound, and all real summer Peltries half these prices only;

& and in proportion for other years: The amount of which Furrs & Peltries shall be placed to the Credit of said Adventure each & every year, in the Month of November next after the delivery of the same.—

Article 5th

And lastly it is Stipulated & mutually agreed upon between the said Parties, that as from the high prices at which Goods & provisions are sold for this year at Montreal, that there may arise a loss upon the first Outfit; The said North West Company by their Agents aforesaid Promise and agree that they only shall sustain & take upon themselves (and shall hold free the said Jean Baptiste Cadotte) from any such Loss that shall or may Arise, that is to say, upon the first Years adventure only; And that because it is moreover agreed upon that at the expiration of that Period it shall and may be lawful for the said Jean Baptiste Cadotte to make his choice or election either to recede from or take up this present Agreement, or to enter upon resume & abide by the first aforementioned Agreement: Then Shall this, or the other; become void & null & of no Effect, and one only remain in force, any thing herein mentioned to the contrary in any wise Notwithstanding.

IN WITNESS whereof the Parties have hereunto set their hands & Seals at the Grand Portage Aforesaid, the Day and date first above Written.—

| Signed Sealed and delivered in Presence of.— A. N. McLeod Richard Wm Barr | J Btte Cadotte W McGillivray Alex Mackenzie |

13: Agreement of McTavish, Frobisher and Company, 1799, with Statement of Accounts.[1]

[*Hudson's Bay House.*]

ARTICLES OF AGREEMENT had made and concluded upon at Montreal in the Province of Lower Canada this second Day of

[1] Reproduced by permission of the Governor and Committee of the Hudson's Bay Company.

THE NORTH WEST COMPANY

December in the Year of our Lord One Thousand Seven Hundred and ninety nine, by and between Simon McTavish, John Gregory, William McGillivray, Duncan McGillivray, and William Hallowell all of Montreal aforesaid—Whereas the said Simon McTavish, Joseph Frobisher, James Hallowell, John Gregory, and William McGillivray were by Articles of Partnership bearing date at Montreal the twenty eighth Day of September One Thousand Seven Hundred and Ninety three Co-Partners and joint Traders residing and carrying on Trade at to and from Montreal aforesaid under the Firm of McTavish Frobisher & Company for a term of years as therein is more fully set forth—and were also Co-partners and joint Traders with John Fraser residing and carrying on Trade at to and from London in the Kingdom of Great Britain under the Firm of McTavish Fraser & Company which said first mentioned Firm or Trading House of McTavish Frobisher & Co were also the Equippers of and Agents to a certain other Company (herein after mentioned) carrying on Trade to the Interior part of the Indian Country—commonly called and known by the Name or Firm of the North West Company, all which Concerns are more fully expressed and explained by the said Articles of Co-partnership bearing date on the twenty eighth Day of September One Thousand Seven Hundred and Ninety three as aforesaid reference being thereunto had. And whereas by Articles of Agreement bearing date the fourth Day of November One Thousand Seven Hundred and Ninety five the said Simon McTavish, Joseph Frobisher, John Gregory and William McGillivray did admit Alexander Mackenzie to be a Co-partner jointly with them, generally in all and singular their said connections and Concerns in Trade as aforesaid—And whereas the said James Hallowell on the thirtieth day of November One Thousand Seven Hundred and Ninety five and the said Joseph Frobisher on the first day of May One Thousand Seven Hundred and Ninety eight did respectively by amicable arrangements with their said Partners retire from and relinquish all the said Trade connections and Concerns so carried on and conducted as aforesaid. And whereas by Articles of Agreement bearing date the thirtieth Day of October One Thousand Seven Hundred and Ninety five, the said Simon McTavish, John Gregory and William McGillivray did enter into a Concern with Sundry other Persons therein named by the name and description of the North West Company (before mentioned) for a term of years yet unexpired, that is to say from the Outfit of the year One Thousand seven Hundred and Ninety Nine to the returns of the Outfit of the Year One Thousand eight Hundred and five of which the Persons composing the present House of McTavish Frobisher & Co held and hold fifteen Shares as by said Agreement reference being thereunto had will more fully appear And whereas the said late House or Firm of McTavish Frobisher & Co did also by articles of Co-partnership bearing Date the twenty first Day of June One Thousand Seven Hundred and Ninety Nine enter into a Trading Concern with James Caldwell and Simon Fraser of Albany for a term of Years also unexpired under the Firm of Caldwell Fraser & Company of which said Concern the present House or Firm of McTavish Frobisher & Co are Interested and hold one full third Share or part as by said Articles will also more fully appear And whereas the period of duration as well as of the first recited Original Co-partnership as of the said also before recited Articles of Agreement under which the said Alexander Mackenzie was admitted a Co-partner did expire on the thirtieth Day of November last and did then finally cease and determine whereby the said Parties being totally disengaged and at full liberty to make any such further and other connections in Trade as to them might seem convenient Now be it known that the said first above mentioned Parties Viz^t Simon McTavish, John Gregory, William McGillivray, Duncan McGillivray and William Hallowell having a full and competent knowledge of all the before recited circumstances have and do hereby agree to and with each other, and to and with their and each of their Heirs Executors and Administrators in manner and form following that is to say vizt

Article 1st

That the said Simon McTavish, John Gregory, William McGillivray, Duncan McGillivray and William Hallowell shall and will and do hereby consent and agree to become from this Day Co-partners and joint Traders under the name or Firm of McTavish Frobisher & Company, generally in every branch of Trade hitherto carried on by the former House or Firm of McTavish Frobisher & Company or that shall or may hereafter be agreed upon by and between them, conformable to the

THE NORTH WEST COMPANY

respective rates or Proportion of Interest herein after mentioned.

Article 2nd

That the said Co-partnership shall continue and be in force for a period of Seven Years to be computed from the first day of December Instant that is to say until the first Day of December which will be in the Year of our Lord One Thousand eight Hundred and Six.

Article 3rd

That the said Co-partnership Interest and Concern shall be divided into Ten equal Shares or Parts of which the said Parties to these Presents shall have receive and enjoy to his and their own proper use or uses as follows vizt

Simon McTavish...........Four Shares
John Gregory..............Two Shares
William McGillivray.......Two Shares } Ten Shares
Duncan McGillivray.......One Share
William Hallowell.........One Share

of all the clear and Nett Profit, benefit and advantage, which from time to time during the said Co-partnership shall arise or may accrue by the Management of the said joint Trade or the encrease or Improvement thereof, and that all Charges Debts Losses or other Contingencies which may arise grow or become due to be paid by reason of the said joint Trade, shall during the said Co-partnership be paid sustained, borne and defrayed, and be deducted and satisfied before any dividend according to the said Parties Interest or Share therein as above said.

Article 4th

It is further hereby agreed by and between the Parties to these Presents that whereas they intend to continue to carry on Trade in the City of London (as carried on and conducted by the said former Firm of McTavish Fraser & Co) that their proportion of Interest respectively therein shall be, and is hereby stipulated to be conformable to the preceeding Article, Subject nevertheless to the proviso following vizt that if John Fraser of London herein before mentioned, shall agree to associate himself with the said Parties and become a Partner with them in their said intended Trading House in London, that then the same shall be carried on and conducted for the same period of Seven Years to be computed as before said under the Firm of McTavish Fraser & C° and that they the said Parties shall and do hereby agree to allow in that case to the proper use of the said John Fraser one full third Share of the Profits and advantages arising therefrom, he to be subject to the same proportion of Loss that may arise or accrue therefrom; and shall over and above his said third share be entitled to have and receive out of the clear and Nett Profits of the said Concern for his Labour Care and dilligence therein an Annual allowance of Five Hundred Pounds Sterling during the said Co-Partnership.

Article 5th

And whereas in order to prevent any doubts or disputes that may arise in the future management of the said business relating to the Debts and Credits of the Trade heretofore carried on under the said beforementioned Firm of McTavish Frobisher & Co Now these Presents Witness that the said Parties hereto have and do hereby agree to and with each other and to and with each of their Heirs Executors and Administrators that the Balance Sheet or Schedule of the Debts and Credits of the said late Firm of McTavish Frobisher & C° hereto annexed signed by the said Parties and making a part hereof shall be and is hereby assumed and undertaken by them respectively in the manner therein and thereby particularly expressed, by which they consent and agree to be bound liable and responsible and not otherwise.

Article 6th

It is hereby further agreed by and between the said Parties that for the purpose of conducting their said business to the best advantage and until they shall see proper to change and alter the same that the said Simon McTavish shall Superintend the Correspondence and Finance department, the said John Gregory the Outfits Packing and Shipping Concerns, and the said William and Duncan McGillivray the Agency for con-

THE NORTH WEST COMPANY

ducting the business of the North West Company as well on the Communication from hence as at the Grand Portage as Stipulated in the Agreement between the House of McTavish Frobisher & Company and the said North West Company That the said William Hallowell shall reside constantly in Montreal for the more effectually managing the Compting-House department, that he keep the Books of Account himself with the assistance of such Clerks as may be judged necessary during the said Co-partnership, and that he the said William Hallowell shall and will (if deemed necessary by the Majority of the Partners at the expiration of this Concern) continue to reside in Montreal for One Year after the expiration of this Concern and keep himself so far disengaged from any other pursuit as to enable him to wind up settle and close the affairs of the said Concern and joint Trade, which he hereby consents and engages to do and fullfil, and in satisfaction of his care and dilligence therein it is hereby agreed that the said William Hallowell shall be entitled to have and receive for his said services during the said Year the Sum of Five Hundred Pounds Currency

Article 7th

Whereas it is the intention of the said Simon McTavish to retire from this Country and to reside and settle in London (so soon as it may be considered that his presence in Canada can be dispensed with without prejudice to the said establishment and Concerns) in which case said William McGillivray will be required to assist in Superintending the business at Montreal, It is therefore hereby further Covenanted and Agreed that the said William McGillivray be authorized to treat conclude and agree with any of the Persons composing the North West Company (who may be judged most fit and acceptable) to become a joint Partner with them in the present House or Firm of McTavish Frobisher & Company and in the different branches of Trade by them carried on, whose department shall be to succeed in assisting and managing that part of the business herein before allotted to William and Duncan McGillivray jointly; And the said William McGillivray is also hereby further authorized to make such arrangements for that purpose with the said Person as he may judge most for the advantage of the Concerned, but not to allow him the said Person so to be admitted as aforesaid a greater proportion or Share than one eleventh part of the whole Interest of their said Trade; And in the event of the said Simon McTavish retiring as aforesaid It is hereby Stipulated Covenanted and Agreed that his Interest in the present established Concern, shall (at the period of closing or balancing the Books that year he shall so retire) diminish or change, that is to say, from four tenth Shares of the whole to three tenth Shares or parts only, which tenth Share so to be given up shall fall into the House generally in proportion to the respective Interests of the Parties therein.

Article 8th

Provided allways and it is hereby expressly agreed conditioned and concluded by and between the said Parties to these presents and it is the true intent and meaning hereof that if either of the said Parties to these presents, or the Person hereafter to be admitted a Party hereto as aforesaid, shall happen to depart this life before the said term of Seven Years, shall by course of time run out and be expired, that then and in that case the Interest of the said deceased shall cease and terminate on closing or balancing the Books of the said Concern on the thirtieth Day of November of the same year save and except the said John Gregory whose Heirs it is expressly Covenanted and Agreed shall be entitled to participate in the Profit or Loss arising from one of the Fifteen Shares, say one of the Fifteen Fortysixths, of that branch of their Trade which they hold by Agreement with the North West Company until the expiration of that Concern in the year of our Lord One Thousand eight Hundred and Six; but it is also expressly agreed by these Presents that in case of the decease of either the said Simon McTavish, John Gregory or William McGillivray previous to the expiration hereof as aforesaid that then and in that case the Interest of the said Duncan McGillivray shall encrease and be equal to the Share or proportion of either of them the said John Gregory or William McGillivray or the Survivor of them for the remaining period of the Concern.

THE NORTH WEST COMPANY

Article 9th

Whereas there are Sundry Adventures Engagements and Contracts entered into prior to this date by the late Firm of McTavish Frobisher & Company the event of which is not yet ascertained or known, but in the Issue of which Alexander Mackenzie late a Partner in said House may pretend or claim an Interest; Now it is the true intent and meaning hereof and of the said Parties to these Presents that in case the said Alexander Mackenzie his Heirs or Assigns shall or may establish a legal Claim or demand therein and thereto or to any part of the Advantages and Profits arising therefrom, or in case the said Simon McTavish, John Gregory and William McGillivray may in order to facilitate an Amicable Settlement with the said Alexander Mackenzie consent and agree to admit him to any proportion of such Interest or advantage without legal discussion (which they the said Simon McTavish John Gregory and William McGillivray are hereby Specially authorized to do) that then and in that Case the same shall be equally borne and Sustained generally by the said Parties according to their beforementioned proportions or Interests in the said Concern, any Specific appropriation thereof heretofore contemplated notwithstanding.

Article 10th

It is also hereby further Covenanted that each and every of the said Parties shall be entitled to have and receive at and after the rate of Six per Cent annually for all such Sum or Capital as may appear at their Credit in the Books of the said Concern.

Article 11th

It is also hereby expressly agreed and the said Parties to these presents hereby Specially bind and oblige themselves their Heirs and Executors each to the other and to their and each of their Heirs Executors and Administrators that in case of the decease of either of them the said Parties previous to the expiration of the present Concern and Co-partnership, his or their Heirs or Executors shall not be entitled to claim or demand of the Survivors for one Year thereafter more than the legal

Interest of such Capital as (on closing the Books of that year) he may appear to possess or be at his Credit (if so much of the said Term should remain unexpired) at which period if there should happen to be four Years remaining unexpired of said Term, one fourth only of the said Capital and Interest shall or may be exacted, and if three years only remain unexpired then one third of the same may be claimed and exacted and in either case the remaining Nett Sum with the Interest shall be divided and paid in equal annual payments thereafter during the remainder of the unexpired Term; but if it should so happen that there should remain but one year unexpired then the whole of the said Capital and Interest shall and may be demanded Claimed and exacted at the close of the Concern.

In Witness whereof the said parties to these Presents have hereunto and to four other parts hereof interchangeably set their Hands and Seals at Montreal aforesaid the Day Month and Year first above written.

Signed, Sealed and delivered
  in the presence of
    T. WALKER
    JOHN K. WELLES

SIMON MCTAVISH
JOHN GREGORY
W. MCGILLIVRAY
WM. HALLOWELL
DUNCAN MCGILLIVRAY

Memorandum. Whereas the Parties to the foregoing Articles have determined that Roderick Mackenzie, at present a Partner, and holding two forty sixth shares in the North West Company, is a proper Person to assist in the management of their Concerns at the Grand Portage, conformable to the provision made in the Seventh of said Articles, they hereby admit him a Partner in their House on the following Conditions.

That he shall return to the Grand Portage this Spring and pass the succeeding Winter in the Interior as a Wintering Partner: On his return to the Grand Portage in the Summer of the Year One Thousand eight hundred and one he shall avail himself of his privilige of resigning One of his forty sixth Shares to the North West Company, and retire from Wintering in the Indian Country: His remaining One forty sixth Share in said Company shall become the property of the House of McTavish Frobisher & C° with all the Profits that may thence accrue from the Outfit of the present Year One Thousand eight Hundred and during the whole Term of the foregoing Articles of Agreement: That he shall act as an Agent in Conducting the business of the North West Company as well on the communication from hence as at the Grand Portage as stipulated in the Agreement between McTavish Frobisher & C° and the North West Company.

On the above Conditions, Simon McTavish, John Gregory, William McGillivray, Duncan McGillivray, and William Hallowell, the Parties at present composing the House of McTavish Frobisher & C°, do agree to admit the said Roderick Mackenzie as a Partner in their said House, that his Interest therein shall be One Eleventh of the whole, comprehending all the Interest of the House in Europe or Elsewhere; That it shall commence on the closing of their Books on the thirtieth Day of November One Thousand eight hundred and continue to the end of the Term of the foregoing Articles: That in case the said Roderick Mackenzie should die before the expiration of said Term, his general Interest in the House shall end with the close of the Books on the thirtieth day of November next following, but the One forty sixth Share brought by him into the House shall revert to his legal representatives with all the profits accruing from the Outfit that may have been made in the year such an Event may happen.

We have maturely Considered the Terms and Conditions of this Memorandum, Accept and Approve of the same, and hereby Bind Ourselves, that is, Simon McTavish, John Gregory, William McGillivray, Duncan McGillivray, and William Hallowell, On the One Part, and Roderick Mackenzie on the Other Part, our Heirs and Executors each to the other and to their and each of their Heirs and Executors to the full accomplishment of the same.

In Witness whereof We have hereunto set our hands and Seals this Nineteenth Day of April in the Year of our Lord One Thousand eight hundred.

Signed, Sealed
and delivered in
the presence of
    JAMES HALLOWELL
    JAMES HALLOWELL Jun*r*

ROD. MACKENZIE
SIMON MCTAVISH
JOHN GREGORY
W MCGILLIVRAY
DUNCAN MCGILLIVRAY
WM HALLOWELL

DOCUMENTS RELATING TO

Dr The New Firm of McTAVISH FROBISHER & CO (established under the Articles of Copartnership hereunto annexed)—in Account Current with THE OLD FIRM OF McTAVISH FROBISHER & CO— **Cr**

1799 30th November		£	s	d	1799 30th November		£	s	d
	To Sundries whose Accounts they assume vizt					By Sundries whose Accounts they undertake to pay vizt			
"	Edward Edwards	28	18	6	"	Voyageurs Fund	804	16	6½
"	Thomas Walker	76	15	1½	"	Tousst Le Sieur	294	16	7½
"	Peter Grant	1514	15	8½	"	Simon Fraser Senr	1821	1	9½
"	Alexr McLeod	542	8	11	"	John Delisle	28	14	10
"	Duncan McGillivray	445	"	8	"	Joseph Dufaux	80	1	"½
"	Merchandize for amount Inventory	49	"	8	"	Benaiah Gibb	9	13	4½
"	Peter Laurie	361	15	5½	"	Simon Fraser N.W.	3962	7	1
"	Richd Cartwright	"	10	"	"	James Hallowell Junr	206	19	9½
"	J. C. Stewart	4	1	3	"	Joseph St Germain	106	13	9
"	Hugh Finlay	217	2	4	"	Robert Thompson	2573	19	10½
"	James Grant	32	10	"	"	Wm Thorburn	128	5	4½
"	Adventure to Detroit Inventory	434	7	6	"	Venant St Germain	79	4	7½
"	James Woolrich	1161	15	10	"	Cuth. Grant	4562	7	8½
"	Eneas Cameron	834	12	9	"	Noel & Shorts	60	3	"
"	Archd N. McLeod	2923	1	8	"	John Murray & Son	8	12	8
"	John Bell & Co	170	"	"	"	Richd Dobie	85	9	6½
"	Adventure from New York Inventory	2308	"	3	"	Duncan Fisher	3	"	4
"	Daniel McKenzie	356	13	9	"	Estates G&S—amount due to Pat. Small	882	11	1
"	Charges on Merchandize Stationary	80	"	4½	"	Errol Boyd	99	17	3
"	Alexr Fraser	1355	1	8	"	Alexr Henry	13	16	2½
"	William Mackay	229	11	10½	"	John Miln	695	11	8½
					"	John Grant	12	14	8
					"	The Daughters of the late Simon Fraser	"	5	4

THE NORTH WEST COMPANY

		£	s	d
"	John Young	540	12	"¼
"	Adventure pr the America	17964	11	3
"	James Caldwell	26	16	"
"	Mrs Goddard	3	4	8
"	Share late James Finlay's	3741	2	2½
"	Interest 1800	371	15	10
"	Alexr McDougall	2306	7	9
"	Robert Cruickshank	11	17	4
"	Tousst Pothier	458	12	10
"	Isaac Todd	7	5	"
"	John Grant of Kingston	9	17	3
"	Angus Shaw	4316	9	9¼
"	Alexr McDonell	5	7	1
"	Share late Simon Fraser's	3579	10	5¼
"	Archd McDonald	15	"	"
"	N. West Co 1799	300	"	"
"	Adventure of Teas to Detroit	440	2	9
"	Cash	72	12	2½
"	Projected Adventure to China	18075	6	10½
"	Angus McIntosh	11573	8	2
"	Rodk Mackenzie	1021	11	5½
"	Rum—Inventory	4547	8	7
"	Caldwell Fraser & Co	3277	9	7½
"	N. West Co 1800	42432	8	11½
"	Richd Donovan	366	14	"
"	Burns & Woolsey	448	11	11
"	John Finlay	2447	10	1
"	Dond McTavish	2630	19	3
Amt. Debit Carried forward £		132392	"	9¼

		£	s	d
"	Capt Thos Fraser	368	17	3
"	Seton Maitland & Co	8281	9	6¼
"	William Lindsay	42	16	6
"	Pierre Belleau	86	"	10
"	William Robertson	5086	5	5
"	Nicholas Montour	48	11	3½
"	John Watson	178	9	11½
"	William McGillivray	15533	1	7
"	George Kittson	37	7	11
"	John Gregory	7850	8	10
"	George Selby	99	11	4
"	Louis Chastelain	296	1	7
"	J & A McGill	323	18	3¾
"	J. Bte Desmarrais	362	10	"
"	Simon McTavish	67284	8	11½
"	William Hallowell	4772	9	8½
"	James Finlay	2966	18	11
"	Alex Mackenzie	22504	16	6½
"	James Hallowell	8693	1	10
"	Joseph Frobisher	33739	9	7½
"	Bills	8533	18	4½
"	McTavish Fraser & Co	97220	1	7¼
"	Commissions	86	19	4
Amt. Credit Carried forward £		302804	18	11

106 DOCUMENTS RELATING TO

The New Firm of McTavish Frobisher & Co in a/c with The Old Firm of McTavish Frobisher & Co

Dr					Cr
1799 30th November	To amount Debit brought from the other side	£132392 " 9¼	1799 30th November	By amount Credit brought from the other side	£302804 18 11
	" John McDonald	2599 17 3			
	" Charles Chaboillez Junr	2657 5 8			
	" John McDonell	2736 13 4			
	" Share late Cuth. Grant's	2648 " "			
	" Fifteen Shares in N. West Outfit 1799	39719 19 7½			
		£182753 16 7¾			
	The foregoing Accounts amounting to One Hundred and Eighty Two Thousand Seven Hundred and Fifty three Pounds Sixteen Shillings and Seven Pence three Farthings are assumed by the New Firm of McTavish Frobisher & Co absolutely and without reserve.				
	To Adventure to China 1793 £117 3 7				
	" Adventure to China 1795 62 0 4				
	" Adventure to China pr the Warley & Hindostan 1239 2				
	" Suspended Accounts being amount paid Blackwood & King as a compromise for				

Liberties	336	6	7	10	
" Consignts to McTavish Fraser & Co 1799	8387	14		3	
" Adventure to China pr the Walpole	795	13			
			119784	7	4¾
The last Seven Accounts amounting to One Hundred and Nineteen Thousand Seven Hundred and Eighty four Pounds Seven Shillings and four Pence three farthings, are assumed by the New Firm of McTavish Frobisher & Co for the purpose of conducting the business relative thereto; But on the Account, and risk, of the Parties to the Old Firm of McTavish Frobisher & Co, as they respectively stood, interested and engaged.					
To Balance due by the Old Firm to the New Firm of McTavish Frobisher & Co			266	14	10½
Currency			£ 302804	18	11
Currency			£ 302804	18	11

Montreal 30th November 1799.

Simon McTavish　　**Duncan McGillivray**
John Gregory　　　 **Wm Hallowell**
Wm McGillivray

14: THE AGREEMENT OF THE NORTH WEST COMPANY AT GRAND PORTAGE, JULY 5, 1802.[1]

[*Reprinted from L. R. Masson*, Les Bourgeois de la Compagnie du Nord-Ouest, *deuxième série (Quebec, 1890), pp. 459-481.*]

WHEREAS by certain articles of agreement made and entered into at Montreal, in the Province of Lower-Canada, on the thirtieth day of October, one thousand seven hundred and ninety five, by and between Simon McTavish, Joseph Frobisher, John Gregory and William McGillivray, these composing the Firm of McTavish, Frobisher & Co, of Montreal aforesaid, merchants and co-partners, and Angus Shaw, Roderic McKenzie, Cuthbert Grant, Alexander McLeod and William Thorburn, these represented by Alexander McKenzie their Agent and Attorney, a Joint Concern or trade to that part of the Indian Country commonly called the North-West was agreed to be carried on, the said parties and others to be admitted Partners therein under the said Articles of Agreement on their joint account and risk for a certain term or number or years, that is to say to commence with the first Outfit of the year one thousand seven hundred and ninety nine, and to terminate with the returns of the Outfit of the year one thousand eight hundred and five, the said Concern to consist of forty six shares and to be regulated and carried on under the different terms, stipulations and conditions in the said Articles of Agreement mentioned and contained;

AND WHEREAS, under and in virtue of the said Agreement, the following Persons now carrying on trade to the said Indian Country as Partners, under the name or Firm of the NORTH-WEST COMPANY, that is to say the said Simon McTavish, John Gregory, William McGillivray and Duncan McGillivray, William Hallowell and Roderic McKenzie, now composing the said House or Firm of McTavish, Frobisher & Co; Angus Shaw, the said Roderic McKenzie, Alexander McLeod, Wm. Thorburn, Daniel McKenzie, Wm. McKay, John McDonald, Donald McTavish, John McDonell,

[1] The original of this agreement, or a copy of it, was in the possession of the Hon. L. R. Masson when he published in 1889-90 his *Bourgeois de la Compagnie du Nort-Ouest*; but is not to be found, I am informed, in the Masson Papers now in the Public Archives of Canada, and I have not been able to ascertain its present whereabouts.

Archibald Normand McLeod, Alexander McDougall, Charles Chaboillez, John Sayer, Peter Grant, Alex. Fraser, Eneas Cameron, John Finlay, Duncan Cameron, James Hughes, Alex. McKay, Hugh McGillis, Alex. Henry, J. Bte. Cadotte, John McGillivray, James McKenzie and Simon Fraser conceiving it essentially necessary to alter and change the aforesaid articles of agreement and to form a more regular solid permanent system for the Government and Regulations of the various rights and interests of the Parties concerned in the said trade and commerce, in order thereby and by a mutual confidence and good understanding to unite and consolidate their interests in such manner as to render all attempts which now are or hereafter may be made by other Persons to injure them in their said trade and commerce fruitless and ineffectual, and above all to preserve and secure to the said Parties concerned, their heirs and assigns the many benefits and advantages which, by their united labours and exertions in the said Indian Country, they have become entitled to reap and receive in the further continuance of the said trade and commerce and particularly from the enlarged plan of carrying on the same and the increased number of outfits and other expenses which have become necessary for that purpose and which must eventually be productive of greater advantages and emoluments to the parties concerned;

THESE PRESENTS THEREFORE WITNESS that the said Simon McTavish, John Gregory, Wm McGillivray, Duncan McGillivray, Wm Hallowell and Rod McKenzie, now composing the said House or Firm of McTavish, Frobisher and Company, of Montreal, aforesaid merchants; Angus Shaw, Daniel McKenzie, Wm McKay, John McDonald, Donald McTavish, John McDonell, Arch. N. McLeod, Alex. McDougall, Chs Chaboillez, John Sayer, Peter Grant, Alex. Fraser, Eneas Cameron, John Finlay, Duncan Cameron, Js. Hughes, Alex. McKay, Hugh McGillis, Alex. Henry, John McGillivray, James McKenzie, and Simon Fraser, do hereby consent and agree that from and after the first day of December of the year one thousand eight hundred and two, the aforesaid articles of agreement of the thirtieth day of October one thousand seven hundred and ninety five, be and the same and every part thereof is hereby declared to be rescinded and annulled in so far as the rights and interests of the said Parties to these presents are or may be thereby affected or bound and the said Parties to these presents do hereby mutually consent and promise and agree to carry to the interior part of the said Indian Country commonly called the "North-West", and to all and every other part and place where they shall see fit a trade and commerce in furs and peltries and other commodities on their joint account and risk as copartners, under the Name and Firm of the North-West Company to be governed and carried on under the following Rules and Regulations.

ARTICLE 1

That the present copartnership or concern shall commence with the outfit of the year one thousand eight hundred and three and shall continue remain and be carried on for the space and term of twenty years hereafter, ending with the returns of the outfit of the year one thousand eight hundred and twenty-two by and between the said Partners to these presents and the survivors of them and others to be admitted Partners under the present agreement.

ARTICLE 2

That the present concern shall consist of ninety two shares to be divided held and enjoyed by and amongst the said Parties to these presents, and others to be hereafter admitted as Partners therein in manner following that is to say the said Simon McTavish, John Gregory, Wm. McGillivray, Dun. McGillivray, Wm. Hallowell and Rod. McKenzie, now composing the said House or Firm of McTavish Frobisher and Company or whatever persons the said House may be composed of during the present concern shall have hold and retain thirty shares, John McDonald two shares, Donald McTavish two shares, John McDonell two shares, Arch. N. McLeod two shares, Chs. Chaboillez two shares, John Sayer two shares, Peter Grant two shares, Alexander Fraser two shares, Eneas Cameron two shares, John Finlay two shares, Dun. Cameron two shares, Jas. Hughes two shares, Alex. McKay two shares, Hugh McGillis two shares, Alex. Henry two shares, Alex. McDougall two shares, John McGillivray two shares, Jas. McKenzie two shares, and Simon Fraser two shares, making in all seventy six shares (1) and that the remaining sixteen shares not appropriated shall be disposed of to such person or persons as may hereafter be admitted into the present concern as a Partner or Partners therein or otherwise as the said Parties to these presents or their assigns being Partners in the said concern shall judge fit, and that until the said shares not appropriated or others hereafter to become vacant shall be disposed of the profits and advantages arising therefrom shall be equally divided among the existing Partners for the time being in proportion to the number of shares they hold in the concern who shall be liable to the risk and losses that may be sustained or thereby.

ARTICLE 3

It is stipulated and agreed by and between the said Parties to these presents that the Persons who now or at any time hereafter during the period of the present concern shall or may compose the said House of McTavish Frobisher and Company, at Montreal aforesaid shall and they are hereby exclusively authorized and empowered during the said period to direct conduct and manage the affairs of the said North-West Company at Montreal for and on account of the whole, to import all the necessary goods merchandizes and commodities fit and necessary for carrying on the aforesaid trade and commerce to hire and employ all Clerks, Interpreters and engagés from time to time as shall be necessary and requisite for carrying on the said business to make all advances for Liquors Provisions and other necessary articles of the same kind which shall be charged at the current market price at Montreal, for which said advances and trouble the said McTavish Frobisher and C° shall be allowed by the said Concern a Charge of four per cent on the amount of the whole outfit at the close of each year and interest on the goods imported at the rate of five per cent per annum from the time they fall due in England to the thirthieth day of November of the year the outfit is made in, from and after which period the said McTavish Frobisher and Company shall be allowed interest at the rate of six per cent upon the said goods so imported until the same shall be paid and satisfied. That the said House of McTavish Frobisher and Company shall also be allowed interest at the rate of six per cent on all cash advances which may be by them considered necessary or expedient to be made for the use and benefit of the Concern it being understood that the said McTavish Frobisher and Company shall and will on their parts credit and allow for all in their hands belonging to any of the Partners under the present agreement interest at the rate of six per cent per annum. And in as much as the said House of McTavish Frobisher and C° must necessarily keep up the present number of Partners therein for the performance of the several duties they are hereby become bound to fulfill for and on behalf of the said North-West Company and in order also to avoid all doubts and difficulties which might arise in case of a change of all or any of the Partners of the said House during the present Concern, It is therefore stipulated and agreed that every new Partner coming into the said House of McTavish Frobisher and Co and being thereby admited to any right, share or interest in the Present Concern shall be specially held and bound in and by this agreement admitting him a Partner in the House, to the observance of all every the different clauses and stipulations mentioned and contained in the present agreement in the same manner as the present Partners in the said House are hereby held and bound, in which case every new partner so coming into the said House during the period of the Present Concern shall be by the said Concern held and considered as entitled to all the benefits and advantages and bound to all duties and obligations contained in this agreement as if he had been present and signed and executed the same as one of the Partners now composing the said House.

ARTICLE 4

That the Furs Peltries or other produce or returns of the aforesaid trade and commerce shall be shipped to England or wherelse it may be thought fit by the said house of McTavish Frobisher and Co, on the account and for the mutual benefit and advantage of the whole Concern for which trouble the said House shall be allowed a commission one half per cent on the whole amount of all that is sent to England and two and a half per cent on whatever part of such returns as may be sold and disposed of in the United States of America or sent that way to a market in any other country.—And that the neat proceeds of the said furs peltries or other produce and returns of the said trade shall be credited to each Individual of the Concern according to his share and proportion therein as soon as the same shall be placed to the credit of the said House of McTavish Frobisher and Co.

ARTICLE 5

That two at least of the Partners of the said House of McTavish Frobisher and C° for the time being shall annually go to the Grand Portage for the purpose of conducting managing and carrying on the business of the concern on the communication to and at the Grand Portage as heretofore practised by the agents of the North-West Company. That the said partners shall assume and be stiled Agents of the North West Company and shall be aided and assisted in all occasions by the Wintering Partners whose duty it shall also be to attend in a particular manner to the Business of their respective Departments.

ARTICLE 6

That the account of each year's outfit shall be regularly closed after the outfit is made by the said House of McTavish Frobisher and Co. and one set of accounts current shall be by them annually forwarded to the Grand Portage one set to Temiscamingue and to any other of the Departments when the Parties concerned cannot conveniently attend at the Grand Portage to be by the said Parties signed and interchanged and any of the said Parties having any objection to the said accounts shall be bound to deliver in the same in writing within ten days after such account shall have been presented to him otherwise the said accounts shall be taken and considered as approved of by every such Party as fully and sufficiently as if he had signed the same.

ARTICLE 7

That a meeting or meetings if necessary of the Partners as conveniently can attend shall be annually held in the month of June or July at the Grand Portage at which meeting the Partners who cannot attend may be represented by their attornies who shall be entitled to vote for them in order to deliberate and determine upon all such matters and things as to them shall seem fit and proper to be done and executed and performed in and about the trade and commerce aforesaid and the interests thereof, and the majority of the Partners present or represented at the said meeting are hereby authorized and empowered to settle and determine all differences and difficulties among the Partners and all matters respecting the said trade and commerce or which by reason of the views, speculations and interests of the said concern becoming more extended may at any time hereafter be found necessary to be regulated, also to make such other and further Rules and Regulations (not being contrary to any Article of this Agreement) for the better managing and carrying on the said trade and commerce in future as they shall see fit. That every share in the said Concern shall be entitled to a vote of which fifty two shall be required and considered as a legal majority at the said meeting for deciding and determining upon all matters submitted to their consideration, and in all cases where the above number of fifty-two votes cannot be obtained by reason of the absence of Partners of shares unappropriated or otherwise, the legal majority shall in that case consist of the number of votes given and received that shall bear a proportion to all the appropriated shares at the time as fifty-two is to ninety-two. And it is hereby expressly convenanted stipulated and agreed that all and every the Rules, Regulations and decisions made and determined and resolved on by such majority in all the aforesaid cases shall be as effectual and binding upon all the Parties concerned, as well as those absent as those present at such meetings, as if herein specially expressed and provided for, and the said Parties and every one of them do hereby consent promise and agree to submit thereto and to execute and perform all things therein and thereby determined without opposition or delay.

ARTICLE 8

That the arrangements of all the Forts and Posts to be occupied by the said Concern with their establishment the wintering residence of the Partners of the Clerks and others and all matters incident thereto, shall be fixed, determined and appointed and generally directed and conducted by the majority of the Concern present at such arrangements.

ARTICLE 9

That the number of Wintering Partners to be allowed to go down to Montreal each year shall be regulated at the annual meeting of the Partners at the Grand Portage according to circumstances and agreeable to a list establishing the order of rotation which shall be made out at the commencement of this Concern

THE NORTH WEST COMPANY 115

by a majority of the Parties hereto or as they shall otherwise agree amongst themselves, provided that such number so to go to Montreal do not exceed five in any case whatever.—And it is hereby expressly stipulated and agreed that in case the Partner or Partners so going to Montreal shall neglect or refuse to return the ensuing Spring to fulfill the duties allotted to him or them by the Partners conducting the Business at Montreal without offering some good and sufficient reason or excuse of the validity of which the said annual meeting shall judge the said annual meeting may and they are hereby authorized to determine whether such Partner or Partners ought to be deprived of all his or their right and interest in the said Concern or of any and what part thereof and for what length of time, or in such other manner to determine respecting the same as to the said annual meeting shall appear just and reasonable according to the circumstances of the case—and in every case when the said annual meeting shall think fit to order and determine that any such Partner or Partners by reason of his or their conduct in the premises ought to be deprived of all his or their share in the Concern the same shall be held and considered as forfeited and lost to every such Partner or Partners and shall case and determine from the close of the outfit sent into the Country at the time such Partner or Partners was or were so permitted to go down to Montreal if not otherwise determined by the said annual meeting—and the share or shares of every such Partner or Partners shall at from and after the period they shall have been declared to have become forfeited by the said meeting revert to and be vested in the said Concern who are hereby empowered and authorized to appropriate and dispose of all and every such share or shares rights and interests to such other Person or Persons as they shall think fit.

ARTICLE 10

And to the end that a frugal distribution of the property and effects of the said Concern may be observed, it is hereby expressly understood and agreed that all and every of the said Parties to these presents or the Persons under them or any of them who shall winter in the Indian Country shall deliver or send to the Grand Portage every year and oftener if convenient and requisite a true faithful and exact account and Inventory of all the goods, provisions and other effects they or either of them may have remaining on hand as well as of the Peltries, debts due by the Indians and canoemen they or either of them may have left in the country with just and true accounts of the expedition of goods committed to their respective charge and direction, it being the intention that neither of the Parties who winter in the Indian Country or who come from Montreal to the Grand Portage on the business of the concern shall be allowed while there out of the common stock more than their personal necessaries but that whatever shall be expended by them or either of them exceeding this limitation shall be placed to the account of him or them making such expenditures.

ARTICLE 11

AND WHEREAS from the remote situation of many of the said Parties in the Indian Country their distance from each other and the possibility of any or either of them conducting himself or themselves in such a manner as render himself or themselves unworthy by their improper conduct of continuing a Partner in the said concern, it is therefore expressly agreed on and is the will and intention of the said Parties to these Presents that when such misconduct or neglect shall be prov'd to the satisfaction of the majority of the annual meeting of the concern herein before established every such Party or Parties so misconducting or misbehaving himself or themselves shall and may upon the determination of the said annual meeting in every such case be expelled from the said Concern and his or their share and interest therein shall thereupon cease and determine and shall revert to and be vested in the said Concern who are hereby authorized to appropriate and dispose of every such share as their own property in such manner as they shall see fit reserving however to the said annual meeting the right and power to determine otherwise as to the share and interest aforesaid of every such Party so misconducting or misbehaving himself as circumstances may require.

ARTICLE 12

The present agreement being intended for the purpose of carrying a trade and commerce in and to all and every part and parts

THE NORTH WEST COMPANY

of the Interior Country or where else it may be thought fit for the benefit of all the Parties concerned, and whereas some or all of the said Parties now is or are or hereafter may be concerned or interested in some other trade or business, It is therefore hereby expressly stipulated covenanted and agreed by and between the said Parties to these Presents that they shall not nor shall any or either of them become bound or responsible the one for the other nor shall the act or undertaking of any one or more of them bind or oblige the others nor shall any of the said Parties not being the Agents and legal Attornies of the said Concern have any power or authority to make or execute any agreement contract any debt or debts for, on account or in the name of the said Concern or any of the Partners thereof without a special power to that purpose first had and obtained.

ARTICLE 13

It being incompatible with the nature of this agreement and the trade to be carried on under it that all or any of the said Parties to these presents should engage in or undertake any trade Business or Concern to the detriment of the interest of the present Company and Copartnership or that can or may in any manner injure, hurt or interfere with the trade views or speculations thereof, It is therefore mutually covenanted and agreed by and between the said Parties to these presents that they shall not nor shall any or either or them during the period of the present Concern either jointly or individually enter into or engage in any trade Business or Commerce carried on or to be carried on in or to any part of the said Indian Country commonly called the North-West or its Dependencies or into any other posts places, or situations where the said Concern at the time of the commencement of this agreement or at any time during the continuance thereof shall or may carry on any trade or commerce, nor shall any of the said Parties directly or indirectly counsel advise assist or be concerned or interested in any trade business or commerce carried or to be carried on by other person or persons in the said Indian Country or at the said posts or places or their dependencies aforesaid, under the Penalty of FIVE THOUSAND POUNDS for each ninety second share held by the party failed or contravening this special clause and agreement, to be paid by him to the other Partners of the said Concern who shall or may conform hereto. And it is further stipulated and agreed by these presents that if any of the said Parties hereto or any other Person or Persons to be hereafter a Partner or Partners in this Concern shall at any time retire from or sell and dispose of his or their share and interest in the said Concern or forfeit or be deprived of his or their share therein under any of the articles of this agreement, every such party Person or Persons shall nevertheless be equally held and bound to the oberservance of this article and in case of contradiction thereto equally liable to the penalty of Five thousand pounds as if he or they had continued a partner or partners.

ARTICLE 14

AND WHEREAS it is intended and necessary that the consent of the Parties concerned should be had and taken in all matters touching the arrangements to be made with Partners withdrawing from the said Concern or assigning their interest therein as also for the admitting and receiving fit and proper persons as Partners in the said Concern instituting or defending suits settling and composing differences making and entering into agreements signing all necessary acts and deeds and doing other necessary matters and things touching and regarding the said Concern and the interest thereof in all cases when all or any of the matters aforesaid shall not have been regulated and determined at any of the meetings of the said Concern held at the Grand Portage as hereinbefore established and also for carrying into effect when necessary the Resolutions passed and adopted at such meetings: IT IS THEREFORE hereby stipulated and agreed that the said Simon McTavish John Gregory Wm. McGillivray Duncan McGillivray William Hallowell and Roderic McKenzie be and they or any two of them are hereby named constituted and appointed the Attornies of the said Concern for all the above purposes for and during the period of its continuance or until expressly revoked by the aforesaid annual meeting at the Grand Portage as hereinafter mentioned and not otherwise.—And it is further stipulated and agreed that a Power of Attorney from the said Parties to these Presents and from all and every other Person or

THE NORTH WEST COMPANY 119

Persons who shall or may at any time hereafter be admitted a Partner or Partners in the said Concern be made and executed in due form of law to the said Simon McTavish John Gregory William McGillivray Duncan McGillivray William Hallowell and Roderic McKenzie as Attornies as aforesaid, giving to them or any two of them as aforesaid full power for all the above purposes and for doing and performing all such other matters and things which to them or any two of them as aforesaid shall appear for the benefit and advantage of the Parties concerned and when a more special power from the said Parties to that effect might be requisite and necessary.—And whenever it shall become necessary to appoint other Attornies in the room and stead of all or any of those hereinbefore named either by reason of their decease their retiring from the Concern or otherwise, it is stipulated and agreed that the Partners in the same House of McTavish Frobisher and Co. being Partners in this Concern shall always have the preference— It is however hereby understood and agreed that in case the said McTavish Frobisher and Co shall at any time make an improper use of the powers hereby conferred on them as Attornies as aforesaid it shall be in the power of the said annual meeting at the Grand Portage by a majority of voices to alter or change the same or substitute other powers in their stead according to circumstances and as in the opinion of such annual meeting shall seem most advantageous for the benefit of the Concern.

ARTICLE 15

AND WHEREAS it may happen that before the time limited for the expiration of the present Concern some of the Partners may die or retire therefrom or others be admitted as Partners therein, IT IS THEREFORE hereby expressly stipulated and agreed that such change or alteration in the persons of the Partners shall in nowise dissolve alter or change the present Partnership and Concern which shall nevertheless continue and be carried on as the same Partnership and Concern under the Rules and Regulations contained in this agreement until the expiration thereof at the time hereinbefore limited.

ARTICLE 16

AND WHEREAS great difficulties might arise by continuing and extending the share and interest of a deceased Partner in the

Concern and all the rights and privileges he holds under it to his heirs or legal representatives on account of their not being Parties to his agreement, their distant places of Residence and consequent inconvenience that might arise in their being represented at the meetings of the Concern, to avoid all which delays and difficulties. IT IS HEREBY stipulated and agreed that upon the death of any of the Partners in the said Concern his share and interest therein shall cease and determine and the same shall from after his decease revert to and become the property of the Concern to be by them used and disposed of as they shall see fit; but in order that such heirs or legal representatives may enjoy in some measure the Benefits of the care industry and exertions of such deceased Partner in the said Concern, It is hereby stipulated that the heirs or legal representatives of such deceased Partner shall, for and during the space of seven years from and after his decease if the concern do not sooner determine, be entitled to demand have and receive of and from the Concern (to be accounted for and paid to such heirs and legal representatives by the said McTavish Frobisher & Co., as acting for the said Concern) an equivalent to one half of the share and interest such deceased Partner held in the Concern, being the same right which a retired Partner is entitled to claim and receive as hereinafter is mentioned. And the heirs and representatives of such deceased Partner, by taking and receiving such equivalent, shall be severally held and bound to the observance of all every the articles of this agreement respecting the doing assisting or being concerned in any matter or thing which may tend to the damage loss or injury of the Concern, and in case of contravention thereto he shall be deprived of all further benefit and interest to him or them out of the said Concern.

ARTICLE 17

Whenever any of the Parties to the Presents or others who may hereafter be admitted Partners in the present Concern may be desirous of retiring from the business of the Concern they shall and are hereby permitted to do so in the following manner and upon the following terms and conditions that is to say:— That the Partner now holding four ninety second shares under the present agreement shall and he is hereby permitted to retire from taking an active part in the Concern whenever he shall think fit and is hereby allowed to have and receive from the said Concern an equivalent of two of the said shares for and during the space of seven years from and after his so retiring if the present Concern shall so long continue and without any duty being attached to the interest he shall so receive. That the Partners who held one forty sixth share under the aforesaid agreement of the thirtieth day of October one thousand seven hundred and ninety-five and who now hold two ninety second shares under the present agreement shall and they are hereby permitted, two each year in rotation as their names stand in the agreement, to retire from taking an active part in the Concern upon giving one year's notice of such intention and shall have and receive from the said Concern an equivalent to one of the said shares for and during the space of seven years from and after so retiring if the present Concern shall so long continue but without being liable to any of the duties thereof. That Persons admitted as Partners under an assignment made to them of any of the aforesaid vacant fourteen shares or others who may hereafter be admitted as Partners in consequence of some of the existing Partners in the Concern having retired therefrom, or shares therein having become vacant, shall and they are hereby permitted to retire from the Concern two each year in rotation as they shall have been admitted into the same after having wintered three years in the Interior Country as Partners and upon their giving one year's notice as aforesaid of their intention to retire, and not otherwise. That all Partners shall be permitted in manner as above stated without holding or retaining any share or interest as aforesaid in the Concern from and after the period of their retiring whenever they shall think fit. That upon any Partners retiring from the Concern his proportion of all the goods in the Indian Country shall be accounted for to him by the said Concern agreeable to the following method which has been hitherto followed and observed in similar cases by the Persons heretofore concerned in the aforesaid trade and commerce, that is to say: The goods at the Grand Portage shall be accounted for at the rate of twenty-five per cent on the Montreal costs and advances, those at every other post in the North-West, except English River and parts beyond, at the rate of fifty-seven per cent on the cost and advances of the Grand Portage, those of the English River and Posts beyond it at the rate of ninety per cent on the cost and advances of the Grand Portage; And as the present concern have in view to extend their posts to other and more distant parts of the North-West, towards the Rocky Mountains and beyond them, the charge on goods at all such Posts shall be regulated according to the expense of sending them thither when known. It is however understood and agreed that whenever it shall be found from experience that the expense of carrying goods to the Grand Portage or into the Indian Country or Interior Country shall increase or diminish, a new tarif shall be made out accordingly it being the intention that young men succeeding to shares shall pay no more for such goods than their true cost. That all debts due by Guides, Men or Interpreters shall be accounted for at one third of their amount, the debts of the Clerks at their full value and it is expressly consented and agreed as a rule to be followed that all the forts and buildings at Grand Portage and in the Interior Country vessels boats cattle and all other property of and belonging to the said Concern upon the communication shall be accounted for conformable to the prices of value affixed to the same by the majority of the Concern the preceding year in the inventories made thereof; For all which said property or proportion of such retiring Partner therein the said Concern shall not be bound to account until one year after the account thereof shall be closed. That every Partner so retiring from the Concern is hereby considered to be subject to the same observance of and compliance with all the matters rules and regulations herein contained touching and concerning the said trade and commerce and in case of contravention thereto equally liable to the Penalties herein expressed as if he still continued an active Partner. That every Partner retiring from the Concern, except those who shall by misconduct or otherwise forfeit their shares and interest therein which thereupon revert to and become the property of the Concern as herein before mentioned, shall release assign and make over to the remaining Partners in the Concern or their Attornies herein before named for the benefit and behoof of the whole or to such person or persons as shall with the consent of the said Concern have been agreed to be admitted a Partner or Partners therein in the room or place such retiring Partner then holds or may be entitled to hold in the said Concern reserving to him the right to demand and receive of and from the said Concern for and during the space of seven years from and after the time of his so retiring if the Concern shall so long continue and be accounted for and paid to him by the said McTavish Frobisher and Company an equivalent to one half of the net produce if the shares and interest be held in the said Concern at the time of his retiring therefrom. And in case any partner should be desirous to sell and dispose of the interest he shall be entitled to have and receive from the said Concern after he shall have retired therefrom as aforesaid, he shall be permitted so to do provided such sale may be made to any of the Partners in the Concern who upon giving notice of their purchase shall be considered as vested in all the rights and interests and shall be permitted to have and enjoy the same in the same manner as such retired Partners could or might have done.

ARTICLE 18

That every Person hereafter to be admitted a Partner in this Concern shall be accepted and approved of by the other Partners or their Attornies named and appointed under this agreement and the said Partners or their said Attornies (or a Retiring Partner when it shall have been so agreed) shall thereupon by an Act in due form transfer assign and make over to every such person so to be admitted a Partner all such share and shares with the rights profits and advantages arising or to arise therefrom as it may have been agreed, such Persons shall have hold and enjoy in the said Concern, in and by which act every such Person shall bind and oblige himself to the performance and observance of all every the matter and things mentioned and contained in this agreement under the penalties therein expressed as full and effectually to all intents and purposes as if such Person had been a Party to these presents and signed the same.

ARTICLE 19

That all engagements and undertakings made and entered into by the Partners of the former North-West Company trading together under the aforesaid agreement of the thirtieth day of October one thousand seven hundred and ninety five touching the aforesaid trade and commerce shall be assumed allowed and confirmed by the present Concern and by them be carried into force effect as if made and entered into by the Parties to these Presents.

ARTICLE 20

[*Omitted.*]

ARTICLE 21

That whenever the Grand Portage is mentioned in this agreement it is understood to mean that Place of *Rendez-vous* for conducting and managing the general Business of the Concern in Summer, but should the Parties concerned determine and agree among themselves to remove and change such place of *Rendez-vous* from the Grand Portage to any other Place on Lake Superior more convenient for the purposes aforesaid the name of such shall be taken and considered as applying in the same manner to all the purposes of this agreement and being synonimous to the Grand Portage.

ARTICLE 22

And lastly it is stipulated and agreed that the present agreement shall be deposited with and remain in the hands of the Attornies of the said Concern hereby named and appointed and that every person having an interest therein shall be entitled to have free access thereto and communication thereof at all times when required.

IN WITNESS whereof the said Parties to these presents have hereunto set their respective hands and seals at the Grand Portage aforesaid this fifth day of July in the year of Our Lord one thousand eight hundred and two.

Signed,

Simon McTavish,	(L. S.)	Wm. Hallowell,	(L. S.)
Jno. Gregory,	"	Wm. McKay,	"
Wm. McGillivray,	"	John McDonald,	"
Dun'n McGillivray,	"	Arch'd McLeod,	"
John Sayer,	"	Alex. MacDougall,	"
Jas. McKenzie,	"	Alex. McKay,	"

SIM'N FRASER,	"	JOHN MCGILLIVRAY, "
CHAS. CHABOILLEZ,	"	R'D MCKENZIE, "
DAN. MCTAVISH,	"	JAMES HUGHES, "
PETER GRANT,	"	ENEAS CAMERON, "
DUN. CAMERON,	"	DAN. MCKENZIE, "
H. MCGILLIS,	"	ANG. SHAW, "
ALEX. HENRY,	"	JOHN FINLAY, "
ALEX. FRASER,	"	JOHN MCDONELL. "

Signed sealed and delivered, no stamp being used nor by law required, by the within named Parties in Presence of us.

(Signed,) J. C. STUART,
" JOHN K. WELLES.

15: AGREEMENT AMONG THE PARTNERS OF THE XY COMPANY, DATED OCTOBER 24, 1803.

[*Notarial Records, Old Court House, Montreal.*]

24th October 1803

ARTICLES of Agreement and Copartnership between Sir Alexander Mackenzie, William Parker, Samuel Gerrard, John Ogilvy, Thomas Yeoward, George Gillespie, John Gillespie and John Mure.

Before the subscribing Public Notaries for the province of Lower Canada, residing in the City of Montreal in the said province. Personally appeared and were present Sir Alexander Mackenzie Knight of said Montreal merchant of the first part; William Parker, Samuel Gerrard, John Ogilvy, Thomas Yeoward and George Gillespie, all of the same place, merchants of the second part; John Gillespie of the City of London, merchant, by the said George Gillespie his attorney by procuration of the third part; and John Mure of the City of Quebec in the said province, merchant by the said John Ogilvy his attorney by procuration of the fourth part; which said parties declared unto us the said Notaries, to have mutually agreed in manner and form, and for the purposes hereinafter contained as follows that is to say, The said parties for the assurance, trust and confidence which each of them hath and doth repose in the other have concluded and agreed to become copartners and joint-traders together, in the trade and business of merchants, as well in North America as in the United Kingdoms of Great Britain and Ireland, and in such other places where the said parties shall think fit to trade and merchandize for their benefit, advantage and profit; the said copartnership to commence in London on the tenth day of March now next ensuing, and in Quebec and Montreal on the first Day of May now next ensuing, and to continue for the space and term of three years to be computed from those periods upon the terms and conditions, and in the proportions and manner following, that is to say, the trade or business so carrying on by the said parties or any of them at Montreal during the said term, shall be carried on under the present existing firm of Parker Gerrard Ogilvy and Company for the joint account and interest of all the parties hereto, and the trade or business to be carried on in London, or any part of the United Kingdoms of Great Britain and Ireland, shall be carried on for the joint account and interest of all the parties hereto, under the firm of Sir Alexander Mackenzie Gillespie Parker and Company; the trade or business also to be carried on at Quebec, shall be carried on under the name of John Mure, and the trade or business to be carried on at Michilimakinac, shall be carried on under the name of George Gillespie, both for the joint account and interest of the parties hereto.

First.—It is agreed that all the trade and business that shall be carried on by the said parties, from and after the periods herein above limited for the commencement of this joint concern, shall be divided into eight equal parts or shares, and the said Sir Alexander Mackenzie, William Parker, Samuel Gerrard, John Ogilvy, Thomas Yeoward, George Gillespie, John Gillespie and John Mure, shall each have receive and be entitled to one equal and full eighth part or share of all the gains and profits arising from all the said joint trade or business so intended to be carried on in Montreal, Quebec, Michilimakinac and the United Kingdoms of Great Britain and Ireland as aforesaid; and each of them shall in like manner bear, pay and defray one equal eighth part or share of all the losses that may happen during the term of their said joint trade or business, as well as one eighth part or share of all charges and expences that shall or may arise or be incurred on account of the said trade or business during the said term: and for the better promoting the interest and advantage of the said joint concern the said John Gillespie shall reside in Great Britain during the term of the said trade or business there with the advice and assistance of Sir Alexander Mackenzie, William Parker or any other of the parties present to manage do and transact all matters and affairs relative to the business of the said copartnership, the said William Parker shall also reside in England or be at liberty to go where the business of the said copartnership may require and Samuel Gerrard, John Ogilvy and Thomas Yeoward in like manner and for the same purposes, do oblige themselves to reside in Montreal, and John Mure also doth oblige himself to do and transact all the business of the said copartnership at Quebec, and George Gillespie doth oblige himself to go to Michilimakinac annually, to transact and manage the business to be carried on there and in Upper Canada, for the benefit and on behalf of the said copartnership.

Second.—It is hereby agreed for the end and purpose of carrying on the said joint trade and business, that the said Sir Alexander Mackenzie shall on his part put in a certain stock agreed upon by and between the parties hereto, on which capital so to be supplied and brought in by him, he shall receive interest at the rate of six per cent. per annum, and whereas the said John Gillespie, William Parker, Samuel Gerrard, John Ogilvy, John Mure, George Gillespie and Thomas Yeoward, have for some time past carried on trade for their joint account in England, Quebec, Montreal, Michilimakinac and Upper Canada by reason whereof they have a certain stock of goods on hand as also sundry outstanding debts and sums of money due them in those places; now the parties hereto do hereby agree to take for their joint account such goods so remaining on hand at the commencement of the present copartnership at the rate of sixteen per cent. advance on the sterling cost, and such articles as do not come under that Description, as liquors &c. shall be taken at a reasonable and moderate valuation: and it is further agreed that the said outstanding debts and sums of money shall be brought into this joint concern, and to be by them assumed on deducting therefrom ten thousand pounds currency, as an indemnity for the loss that may accrue by dubious and bad debts: and the amount of the said goods, and the balances due the said Parker Gerrard Ogilvy and Company on the said outstanding debts, after making the deduction aforesaid, and discharging the debts due by them shall be applied to the credit of the accounts of the said John Gillespie, William Parker, Samuel Gerrard, John Ogilvy, John Mure, George Gillespie and Thomas Yeoward in the proportions that may be respectively due them bearing interest at six per cent. per annum from the first of May next.

Third.—It is hereby covenanted and agreed, that Sir Alexander Mackenzie, John Ogilvy and John Mure, now and heretofore carrying on a joint concern to the Indian Country commonly called the North West with other persons not parties hereto, shall and are hereby allowed to continue in such joint trade or concern, and the same to carry on in such manner as to them may appear proper for their seperate benefit and interest, or as a majority of the parties, trading to the said North West Country may agree, they voting against any proposal prejudicial to this copartnership; and they shall not by any act or deed of either of them do or transact any matter or things whereby the joint effects engagements or trade of this copartnership shall be in any manner prejudiced or disposed of and it is also understood that Sir Alexander Mackenzie and John Ogilvy are at liberty to go wherever their North West concerns may call them, any thing herein contained to the contrary notwithstanding: and it is hereby expressly agreed that the parties hereto except as above mentioned are not to be concerned as partners in the trade to the said Indian Country, nor are they to receive any profit, or be subject to any losses that have arisen or may arise therefrom: and in consideration of the said joint and seperate trade to be carried on by the said Sir Alexander Mackenzie, John Ogilvy and John Mure, it is further agreed that they shall allow to this copartnership each and every of them, a sum equal to one twenty fourth share of the net profits of this concern on the expiration thereof which said sum shall be carried to the debit of their respective accounts, and to the credit of the stock of this copartnership, to be afterwards divided amongst the parties hereto, in eighths or equal shares.

Fourth.—It is hereby covenanted and agreed by and between the parties hereto that neither of them shall be concerned in any trade of business separate from the within mentioned partnership upon any pretence whatever during the term thereof save and except as above admitted by this agreement.

Fifth.—It is also agreed that neither of the said parties shall during this copartnership without the consent of the others first had and obtained enter into any deed, bond or judgment, or otherwise become bound or charged as bail or surety, or give any promisory or other notes, or accept any bill or bills of exchange for himself and partners without their knowledge or consent, for any person or persons whomsoever, by means whereof either in America or Europe the said joint stock or trade or the monies goods merchandize debts profits or effects which shall be in due or belonging to the said copartnership, shall or may be prejudiced, attached, seised or taken in execution, but such transactions bills and notes are hereby excepted as are given by the parties above nominated to reside and transact the business of this concern in England, with a view to the interest of the general concern: and it is further covenanted and agreed upon that, if any of the parties hereto doth in any manner bind himself and partners contrary to the true and full intent and meaning of this article, such party shall and hereby obliges himself to quit and resign his interest and share of and in this concern if so required by the majority of the parties hereto, on their consenting to pay him in four annual payments his capital and a fair and just proportion of the net profits that had previous to such infringement of this article arisen out of the joint trade of this concern, the first of which payments shall become due and payable on the day of his exclusion.

Sixth.—All expences such as the rent of stores and counting houses, clerks salaries, and all expences of travelling by land and by sea on the business of the said joint concern as also all other reasonable charges and expences attending or incident to the said business, shall be borne paid sustained and made good by the said parties in the proportions aforesaid, and an extra allowance shall be made to John Ogilvy, Thomas Yeoward and George Gillespie of three hundred pounds currency per annum, and to John Mure of one hundred and fifty pounds per annum for extra house keeping expences occasioned by the business of this concern, and such reasonable and moderate extra expences as may be incurred by house keeping in London on account of this concern, shall also be borne by the parties hereto in the proportions aforesaid.

Seventh.—And it is hereby agreed by and between the parties hereto that it shall and may be lawful to and for each of them to take out of the said joint stock a reasonable sum for their private and particular expenses, and for no other purpose whatsoever, which said sum shall be charged to each of their private accounts with the partnership, and shall not exceed the annual interest of their respective capitals.

Eighth.—And it is hereby covenanted and agreed by and between the said parties, that John Gillespie and William Parker in London, Samuel Gerrard and Thomas Yeoward in Montreal, John Mure at Quebec and George Gillespie at Michilimakinac, shall and will provide and keep, or cause to be provided and kept, such and so many books as shall be necessary, wherein they shall fairly write and enter, or cause to be written and entered, the just and true particulars of all monies received and paid and of all goods, wares merchandize or commodities that shall be consigned, accepted, imported, exported, bought, sold and received in or delivered out, and of all debts contracted, and of all other matters, affairs or things, any ways relative or necessary, or conducing to the manifesting the true affairs, state and condition of the said joint trade or business of this copartnership: and that the same books, together with all papers and writings touching the said joint trade of this copartnership, shall as well during its term as afterwards, remain open and extant, and be kept in some convenient part of the counting house or place of trade where each of the said parties may have free access thereto, without any hindrance of the other of them, his executors or administrators, and the books of account of the said joint trade, so intended to be carried on shall be finally balanced in London on the tenth Day of March, and in Montreal on the first day of May of each and every year, and faithful copies of the balance sheets shall be signed and exchanged between the said parties, by the first safe and prudent conveyance that shall offer next thereafter: the private accounts also of the parties residing in England with the house in Montreal shall be transmitted them annually.

Ninth.—It is agreed that all transactions, bargains, purchases sales or other matters, relative to the trade of the said joint concern when one or more of the parties does not approve thereof shall be decided by the majority of the votes of the parties present.

Tenth.—It is hereby covenanted and agreed that if any one of the parties hereto wishes to retire from this concern at the expiration of the term limited for its duration, such person so retiring shall and doth hereby oblige himself to leave at interest his capital, and the profits that may become due and payable to him out of the joint trade of this copartnership, in the hands of the parties who may agree to continue and carry on the said trade provided they constitute a majority of the parties hereto; and his said capital and share of profits, with legal interest, when ascertained, shall be paid to him, his executors or administrators, by the said parties so continuing in copartnership, in five equal payments, the first of which shall not become due and payable until six months after the term of three years limited for the duration of this copartnership, and the remainder in four successive annual and equal payments.

Eleventh.—And it is also agreed that if a majority of the parties to this Act shall at the expiration of this concern see fit and advisable to continue the trade thereof, and for good and sufficient reasons require the parties constituting a minority to retire therefrom, the said minority, or such part of them so required to retire, shall quit the copartnership, on condition that the majority do truly and justly pay him or them, his or their capital and the share of profits, he or they may be entitled to from this concern, in three annual payments, the first of which payments shall commence on the day of his or their exclusion therefrom; it is however understood by and between the parties hereto that the said Sir Alexander Mackenzie shall in such case be paid the capital he puts into this concern, three months after the expiration thereof, and his share of profits in the manner and at such periods, as the other parties hereto may be entitled to have and receive their respective profits, and the said partnership stock of goods when any one or more of the parties hereto, retires from this copartnership conformable to this and the preceding article of this agreement, shall be valued at twenty per cent. advance on the sterling cost if in time of war, and at fifteen per cent. advance on the sterling cost if in time of peace, and such other articles as do not come under the above description shall be valued at a fair and moderate rate, and the outstanding debts of this copartnership on one or more of the parties retiring therefrom conformable to this and the tenth article

—shall be estimated immediately on their retiring as aforesaid at such value as the majority of the parties hereto may agree, with right of reference to arbitrators to be chosen in manner as herein mentioned if not satisfactory to the retiring party or parties; and the same shall be the mode of estimation of the goods, effects and outstanding debts in case of the death of any of the parties hereto during the period of this concern.

Twelfth.—It is also agreed that if the parties hereto find it necessary and convenient to purchase a house and stores, for the purpose of carrying on the joint trade and business of this concern the majority of the parties continuing and agreeing to continue it for their joint account, after the term limited for its duration, shall and are hereby bound and permitted to assume the same at the cost and charges thereon, as may appear by the books of account of the said copartnership.

Thirteenth.—In case of the death of either of the said parties during the said term of three years, no benefit of survivorship shall be had or taken by the surviving partners, but the said joint trade or business shall be carried on by the surviving partners for the benefit of themselves or the executors or administrators of the deceased partner or partners, on under and subject to the same terms and conditions as are herein expressed and contained, until the next general balancing day, when the interest of the executors or administrators of such partner or partners in the said joint trade or business shall cease as to a share of profits or risk of losses on any new transaction that may take place in the course of the said business after such last mentioned general balancing day, but the share or interest of such deceased partner or partners, being clearly, fairly and equitably ascertained, as to his or their proportion of the stock of monies and goods on hand, as of the outstanding debts due to the said joint concern, the same part, share and interest of such deceased partner or partners, shall be permitted and suffered to remain in the hands of surviving partners upon interest at and after the rate of six per cent. per annum payable half yearly, until the end and expiration of the said partnership term of three years, after which the same shall be paid off and discharged by the said surviving partners in five equal and successive annual payments, the first of which shall take place twelve months after the expiration of this copartnership, and at the end of this concern, true, faithful, correct and just accounts shall be taken of all the remaining partnership estate and effects of every kind and description as well in America as in Europe, and such accounts shall with all possible speed be signed by all the surviving partners and transmitted without delay by the first safe conveyance, by the either to the other, so that the whole and final state of the said partnership or joint trade may then be distinctly known; and they the surviving partners shall use their best and utmost endeavors to sell, collect, receive, get in and realize the same, so that the whole remaining partnership concerns, may as soon as possible be wound up and closed after the expiration of the said partnership; and such partnership estate property and effects, shall when and as the same shall from time to time be sold, collected, got in and realized, be divided between and among the said parties to these presents, their respective executors, administrators or assigns in the shares and proportions hereinbefore mentioned, in such fair and equitable way as may then be agreed upon by and between the parties hereto; and they the said parties do hereby covenant and agree for themselves, their respective executors and administrators, to join in any power or authority whatsoever that may be requisite to enable each other to recover the part or share of the outstanding debts due to the said partnership that may be allotted to them respectively upon such division as aforesaid, to and for the use of the party to whom the same may have been allotted: and in case any disputes or differences shall arise between the said parties, their respective executors or administrators touching or concerning the said joint trade or business, or any of the accounts, transactions or dealings relative thereto, or the construction of these presents, or any covenant, clause or matter herein contained, the same shall be finally determined, settled and adjusted by the award and determination of three disinterested persons, merchants, to be chosen in manner hereafter mentioned or of the majority of them, so as such award or determination shall be made and delivered in writing under the hands and seals of the said arbitrators or the majority of them to the parties in difference their executors or administrators, or such of them as shall desire the same, within six calendar months next after the date of the bond of reference, and shall be made a rule of Court of King's Bench for this district:

and it is hereby agreed such arbitrators shall be nominated and chosen in manner following, that is to say, one of them shall be chosen by each of the parties in difference, their executors or administrators respectively, and the other one by the two arbitrators that shall be first nominated.

And lastly for the due and true performance of all and singular the covenants, clauses and agreements herein contained, the said parties to these presents bind themselves their respective heirs, executors and administrators, the either to the other in the penal sum of ten thousand pounds current money of this province, formly by these presents. For thus &c—notwithstanding &c. promising &c. Obliging &c. Renouncing &c.

Done and passed at Montreal aforesaid, the twenty fourth Day of October in the year of our Lord one thousand eight hundred and three, in the forenoon, and signed by the said parties with us the said notaries on the original minute to remain of record in the Office of Jonathan Abraham Gray one of the said subscribing notaries, after having been Duly read according to Law:—the words expunged &c. one marginal note approved.—

      Alex. Mackenzie
      Wm. Parker
      Saml. Gerrard
      John Ogilvy
      Thomas Yeoward
      George Gillespie
      George Gillespie attorney by procuration of John Gillespie
      John Ogilvy attor^y. by procuration of John Mure

Thos. Barron   J. A. Gray not: pub:
 N. P.

16: Last Will and Testament of Simon McTavish, dated July 2, 1804.

    [*Somerset House, London.*]

I, Simon McTavish, now of the city of Montreal in the province of Lower Canada, Esqr., do make and declare this to be my last will and testament. I desire and request that all my just debts may be paid and fully satisfied, after which I hereby devise, bequeath, and dispose of all and singular my estate, property, and effects, in manner following,—that is to say, whereas in and by my marriage contract with my wife Margaret McTavish, bearing date at Montreal aforesaid, the first day of October, one thousand seven hundred and ninety-three, it is stipulated and agreed that after my death she shall receive, have, hold and enjoy during her natural life an annual rent or annuity out of my estate of three hundred pounds current money of this province, now my will is that over and above the said sum of three hundred pounds my said wife shall after my decease as aforesaid have and receive out of my said estate an additional sum of nine hundred pounds per annum during her natural life, making to her in all an annual rent or annuity of twelve hundred pounds current money aforesaid, and my executors hereinafter named are requested and charged to secure to my said wife out of the first assets that shall come to their hands out of my said property and estate a sufficient sum of money to be by them employed either in the purchase of real property or in some other sufficient manner, so as to raise and secure to my said wife the aforesaid sum or annuity of Twelve hundred pounds. I likewise give and bequeath to my said wife the free use and occupation of my present dwelling house in the city of Montreal, with its appurtenances, free of all charge and incumbrance during her lifetime; and after her decease the same shall revert and belong to my residuary legatees. I further give to my said wife all my household furniture and plate, one pair of horses, a four-wheeled carriage and a calash, also all the trinkets, cloathes, and wearing apparel I possess in this province.

It is my will and desire that until my children are of an age to be removed to England for their education, they shall remain under the care and management of my said wife, to whom a further allowance of fifty pounds per annum shall be made for the board of each of the said children, and as to whatever other necessaries may be requisite for the said children or either of them, the same shall be furnished and supplied out of their respective fortunes and legacies, I hereinafter bequeath to them, and each of them, that the majority of my executors in this country shall determine. When any of my said children is of a proper age to be removed to England for their education, with which determination my said wife must acquiesce, to each of my two daughters Mary and Anne I give and bequeath the sum of Ten thousand pounds sterling money of Great Britain to be by my said executors vested in the British Funds or some other Good Security, as soon as my property and estate can be realized and withdrawn from the trade and commerce in which I am now concerned in this country, that the interest arising from the two last mentioned legacies so vested and secured as aforesaid shall accumulate for the benefit and behoof of my said two daughters respectively, except such part thereof as shall be necessary for their maintenance and education as aforesaid, which said interest, with the aforesaid principal sums of Ten thousand pounds shall be paid to each of my said daughters on the day of their marriage, provided such marriage be made with the consent of the majority of my said executors, or when they shall have respectively attained the age of majority, whichever shall first happen and in case of the death of any one of my said daughters before she shall be so married or shall have attained the age of majority, the legacy hereby given and bequeathed to her shall revert and be paid to the survivors.

To my son Simon I give and bequeath the sum of Twenty thousand pounds sterling money to be secured and paid to him in the same manner as the two last before mentioned legacies are directed to be paid and secured to my two said daughters, and in case of the decease of the said Simon before he attains the age of majority or without lawful issue, then the legacy hereby made to him shall revert and be paid to my residuary legatees hereinafter named, and should my said wife hereafter bear any child or children to me, I give and bequeath to every such child or children the sum of Ten thousand pounds like sterling money to be secured, paid, and applied in the same manner as the aforesaid legacies to my other children.

To each of the two sons of my deceased brother Alexander by his wife Marjory, now or lately at Colledge at Aberdeen in Scotland, I give and bequeath the sum of Two thousand pounds sterling money aforesaid to be paid to each of them on his attaining the age of majority, that the said sum of money shall in the meantime be placed out at interest, which shall be applied towards educating them in a proper manner, and in case either of them shall die before he attains the age of majority, then my will is that the survivor of them shall have and receive the legacy of the deceased, and I hereby nominate and appoint as Trustees and Trustee to superintend the education of my said nephews, Simon Fraser of ffaralin, Esqr., Sheriff of the county of Inverness, and the Rev. Mr Peter Grant, minister of the Gospel at [*illegible*] in the said county, and the survivor of them, whom I request to accept of this charge, and I hereby give and bequeath to the said Simon Fraser and Peter Grant the sum of Thirty pounds sterling money each, to purchase a ring or other trinket as a mark of my friendship for them.

I give and bequeath to each of my nephews, William McGillivray and Duncan McGillivray, a sum of one thousand pounds like sterling money. To their brother Simon and each of their sisters I give and bequeath the sum of five hundred pounds like sterling money. I give and bequeath to each and every of the surviving children of my late sister Elizabeth Fraser, wife of Hugh Fraser of Bright Money, Esquire, the sum of five hundred pounds like sterling money. I give and bequeath to each and every of the surviving children of my late uncle Duncan McTavish by his lawful wife the sum of three hundred pounds like sterling money. I give and bequeath to Magdalene McGillivray, wife of William McGillivray, the sum of One thousand pounds current money of this province. I give and bequeath to Angus Shaw, Esqr., now at Quebec, the sum of One thousand pounds like current money of this province. I give and bequeath to Donald McTavish, now a partner in the North West Company, and to each and every his surviving brothers and sisters, children of the deceased Alexander McTavish, my uncle, the sum of Three hundred pounds sterling money aforesaid. I give and bequeath to each and every the surviving children of my deceased uncle Donald McTavish the sum of three hundred pounds like sterling money. To my godson Joseph Frobisher, son of my friend and late partner, Joseph Frobisher of Montreal aforesaid, Esqr., I give and bequeath the sum of five thousand pounds current money aforesaid, to be secured on interest by my executors, the said interest to accumulate and to be paid to my said godson on his attaining the age of majority, together with the principal. To my godson John Fraser, son of my partner John Fraser, Esqr., of London, I give and bequeath the sum of one thousand pounds sterling money aforesaid. To my sister-in-law Rachel McKenzie I give and bequeath the sum of one thousand pounds current money aforesaid. To my sister Marjory, now in Scotland, I give and bequeath an annuity of fifty pounds sterling money to be paid to her yearly and every year during her natural life, and my desire is that this legacy be under the particular direction of my brother-in-law Hugh Fraser of Brightmoney hereinbefore named as a Trustee by me, for this purpose specially named and appointed. To my Father-in-law Charles Chaboillez, late of Montreal aforesaid, Esqr., I give and bequeath an annual rent or annuity of one hundred and fifty pounds current money aforesaid, to be paid to him yearly and every year by my Executors, during his natural life, and I likewise acquit and discharge him of and from all claims and demands whatsoever I now have against him for monies I have heretofore advanced to him. I give and bequeath to the said Hugh Fraser of Brightmoney, Esqr., and to my said nephews William McGillivray and Duncan McGillivray a sum of One thousand pounds sterling money aforesaid, to be by them and the survivors and survivor of them held in trust for the special use, purpose, and interest of applying the interest thereof yearly and every year in assisting such of my poor relations in Scotland as I may have neglected to provide for by this my last will and testament.

I give and bequeath to the surviving children of William Kay, late of Montreal, aforesaid, merchant, deceased, the sum of One thousand pounds current money aforesaid, as I am doubtful whether I was justly entitled to the amount of the judgment rendered in my favor in the Court of Appeals in this province against the Estate of the said late William Kay, respecting the property of the late David McCrae.

I give and bequeath to my friend Dr George Selby the sum of two hundred pounds current money aforesaid as a mark of my esteem and regard, and to William Selby his son I give and bequeath the sum of five hundred pounds like current money.

I give and bequeath to each of the two Religious Communities of Nuns in this city, commonly called the Hospital General or Grey Sisters and Hotel Dieu, the sum of one thousand pounds current money aforesaid, being convinced that the said communities are of great public benefit and deserving attention.

I give and bequeath to my cousin Simon Fraser, senior, late of Quebec, now in Scotland, an annuity of Two hundred pounds sterling money aforesaid, to be paid to him yearly and every year out of my estate during his lifetime. I give and bequeath to my god-daughter Maria Sutherland, daughter of Daniel and Margaret Sutherland of this city, the sum of five hundred pounds current money aforesaid, to be paid to her on the day of her marriage or when she shall attain the age of majority, whichever shall first happen, that in the meantime the interest upon this legacy shall be paid yearly to the said Margaret Sutherland, her Mother, towards defraying the expence of her Education, and in case the said Maria shall die before she becomes entitled to receive this legacy, my will then is that the same shall go and be paid to the said Margaret Sutherland, her mother. I give and bequeath to Joseph Frobisher, Esqr., the sum of one hundred guineas as a mark of my friendship and regard. I give and bequeath to my friend and partner, John Gregory, one hundred pounds, and to William Hallowell a like sum of one hundred pounds current money aforesaid. I give and bequeath to James Reid of Montreal aforesaid, Esqr., the sum of one hundred pounds current money aforesaid. I give and bequeath to Harry McKenzie, now at Terrebonne, one hundred pounds current money aforesaid. I give and bequeath to Alexander Grant, son of Commodore Grant, and now at school at Quebec, the sum of one thousand pounds current money aforesaid, to be secured, paid, and applied in such manner as my executors shall see fit. I give and bequeath to Madame Doty an annual rent or allowance of twelve pounds to be paid to her yearly during her lifetime. I give and bequeath to Miss Charlotte Chaboillez, my sister-in-law, an annual rent or allowance of twenty pounds and to be paid to her yearly during her lifetime. I give and bequeath to my nephew Simon McGillivray, besides the sum hereinbefore mentioned, the additional sum of four thousand pounds current money aforesaid.

To my servants, Joseph Church, Pierre Fournier, I give and bequeath ten guineas each. I give and bequeath to John McTavish, now at the King's Posts, the sum of five hundred pounds current money aforesaid; and it is my will and desire that none of the foregoing legacies exceeding one hundred guineas be paid out of my estate until seven years at least after my decease, unless sufficient monies for that purpose shall have been realized therefrom without loss or inconvenience to the concern or concerns in which I am now a partner, and as to all the rest and residue of my estate, property, and effects whatsoever and wheresoever or of what nature and kind soever, whereof or wherein I shall be in any wise possessed or interested at the time of my decease, I give, devise, and bequeath the same and every part thereof to my son William and to his heirs forever, to be by him held and enjoyed as soon as he shall have attained the age of majority, and in the meantime that the same be held and enjoyed by my said executors in trust for him, and in case of the death of the said William before he attains the age of majority I then give, devise, and bequeath all the aforesaid rest and residue of my said estate, property, and effects to my said son Simon, and to his heirs forever, subject to be held in trust by my said executors in trust for him until he shall attain the age of majority, and in case of the death of my said son Simon before he attains the age of majority, I then give, devise, and bequeath all the aforesaid rest and residue of my estate, property, and effects to my said daughters Mary and Anne and to their heirs, to be equally divided between them, share and share alike, and in case of the death of either before she attains the age of majority or without issue of her body lawfully begotten, that the whole shall go to the survivor and to her heirs forever, save and except as to the estate of Dunardary in the shire of Argyle in Scotland, which I purchased some time ago from Niel Malcolm, Esquire, and also the lot of ground and appurtenances which I lately purchased near the Mountain of Montreal aforesaid, it being my will and intention that the said estate and lot of ground and appurtenances shall be taken, held, and enjoyed by the male line of my family, in manner as hereinafter limited—that is to say, I give and bequeath the said estate of Dunardary and all and singular its rights and appurtenances, and also the lot or parcel of ground belonging to me near the said Mountain, with all the improvements thereon and appurtenances thereunto belonging, to my said son William, and to his heirs male forever, but until my said son shall attain the age of majority, my will is that my said executors do hold and possess the same in trust for him, and in case of the death of my said son William without heirs male of his body lawfully begotten, I give, devise, and bequeath the said estate of

THE NORTH WEST COMPANY 141

Dunardary and lot of ground aforesaid of my said son Simon, and to his heirs male forever, subject however to be held and enjoyed by my said executors in trust for my said son Simon until he shall attain the age of majority, and in case of the death of my said son Simon without heirs male of his body lawfully begotten, then I give, devise, and bequeath the said estate and lot of ground and all and every the appurtenances aforesaid, to John McTavish, the oldest of my nephews, son of my late Brother Alexander, and to the heirs male of his body lawfully begotten, and for want or in default of such heirs of the said John McTavish, then I give, devise, and bequeath the said estate and lot of ground to the younger son of my said late Brother Alexander, who I believe is named Alexander, or by whatever other name he is called or known, and to the heirs of his body lawfully begotten, and for want or in default of such heirs of the said Alexander, then I give, devise, and bequeath the said estate of Dunardary and the lot of ground aforesaid to my said nephew William McGillivray and to heirs male of his body lawfully begotten, and for want or in default of such heirs of the said William McGillivray, then I give, devise, and bequeath the said estate and lot of ground to my nephew Duncan McGillivray and to the heirs male of his body lawfully begotten, and for want or in default of such heirs, I give, devise, and bequeath the said estate and lot of ground to my said other nephew, Simon McGillivray and to his heirs forever, provided always that in the aforesaid limitations to the succession and right of claiming and holding the said estate of Dunardary and lot of ground aforesaid, the oldest of the male line shall always succeed alone to the whole of the said estate and lot of ground, and that the same shall not be liable to any division among younger heirs, and provided also that such of the persons hereinbefore named, or their heirs, or any or either of them, as shall or may under the limitations hereinbefore contained be entitled to claim, hold, and enjoy the said estate and lot of ground who are not named McTavish shall be held bound, in order to entitle him or them to claim, hold, and enjoy the same, to assume, take, and bear the name of McTavish, and also my arms, and on default of any of the said persons complying herewith, the said estate and lot of ground shall thereupon be transferred to and vested in the next Heir to the person so refusing according to the limitations aforesaid, who shall be thereupon entitled to claim, have, hold, and enjoy the said estate and lot of ground in the same manner as if the person or heir so refusing as aforesaid had never existed or deceased, upon such next surviving Heir bearing my name and arms as aforesaid, and in case all my said children should die before they are entitled to receive and have the several legacies hereinbefore given, devised, and bequeathed to them and each of them, I then give, devise, and bequeath all the aforesaid rest and residue of my said estate, property, and effects, save and except the said estate of Dunardary and lot of ground aforesaid, which shall be held and taken agreeable to the limitations hereinbefore contained and not otherwise, to my said nephew, John McTavish and in case of his death before he attains the age of majority, then to my other nephew, Alexander McTavish, and to his Heirs, or by whatever other name he may be called or known, being the younger son of my late brother Alexander, and in case of the death of my said nephew Alexander or younger son of my said late brother Alexander, before he attains the age of majority, then to my said nephews William McGillivray, Duncan McGillivray, and Simon McGillivray, equally among them and their respective heirs, share and share alike.

And for the execution of this my last will and testament and the due performance of all and singular the matters and things hereinbefore mentioned and contained, I hereby nominate and appoint my said nephews, William McGillivray and Duncan McGillivray, and said Joseph Frobisher, Esqr., my partner John Fraser of London, Esqr., my brother-in-law Hugh Fraser of Brightmoney, Esqr., my friend Isaac Todd of Montreal, Esqr., and the said James Reid, Esqr., and the survivors and survivor of them my executors and executor, hereby giving power to them and every of them to remain vested and seized of all and singular the estate, property, and effects by me now bequeathed and devised, for the purposes contained in this my last will and testament, and to hold and exercise the Trust now hereby reposed in them and each of them over and beyond the year and day limited by the laws of this province, willing and entrusting that their power under the present last will and testament and their Trust aforesaid shall not cease or determine until all and every the dispositions, provisions, and appointments hereinbefore mentioned and contained shall have been fully paid, satisfied, and complied with;

and my will also is that whenever it shall appear useful or necessary for the benefit of my estate, the said Executors and the survivors and survivor of them shall and may sell and dispose of such parts of my real property (save and except the said estate of Dunardary and lot of ground aforesaid) as to the majority of my said executors shall seem meet and circumstances may require.

I hereby revoke and annul all other wills and testaments and codicils thereto by me at any time heretofore made. In witness whereof I have to this my last will and testament contained on this and the twelve preceding pages of paper set my hand and seal at Montreal aforesaid this second day of July one thousand eight hundred and four.

SIMON McTAVISH

Witnesses { SIMON FRASER, Bout de l'Isle de Montreal
WM. GILMOUR
LEWIS CHARLES

Proved in London on Oct. 17, 1804, by the oath of Duncan McGillivray and John Fraser, Esqrs.

17: THE AGREEMENT OF THE NORTH WEST COMPANY AT MONTREAL, NOVEMBER 5, 1804.[1]

[*Reprinted from* L. R. MASSON, Les Bourgeois de la Compagnie du Nord-Ouest, *deuxième serie (Quebec, 1890), pp. 482-499.*]

THIS AGREEMENT made and executed at Montreal in the District of Montreal in the Province of Lower Canada this fifth day of November in the year of Our Lord one thousand eight hundred and four by and between John Gregory, William MacGillivray, Duncan McGillivray, William Hallowell and Roderic McKenzie being the Partners now composing the House of Mc-

[1] The original of this agreement, or a copy of it, was in the possession of the Hon. L. R. Masson when he published in 1889-90 his *Bourgeois de la Compagnie du Nord-Ouest*; but it is not to be found, I am informed, in the Masson Papers now in the Public Archives of Canada, and I have not been able to ascertain its present whereabouts.

Tavish Frobisher and Company of Montreal aforesaid, the said Duncan MacGillivray being in this behalf represented by the said William MacGillivray his Attorney; and Angus Shaw, Daniel McKenzie, William McKay, John MacDonald, Donald McTavish, John McDonell, Archibald Normand McLeod, Alexander MacDougall, Charles Chaboillez, John Sayer, Peter Grant, Alexander Fraser, Eneas Cameron, John Finlay, Duncan Cameron, James Hughes, Alexander MacKay, Hugh McGillis, Alexander Henry, John MacGillivray, James McKenzie, Simon Fraser, John Duncan Campbell, David Thompson and John Thomson by the said John Gregory and William MacGillivray their Agents and Attornies duly authorised, the said Persons hereinbefore named being the Partners now composing the Company or Concern trading to the North-West or Indian Country and distinguished by the name of the Old North-West Company, OF THE ONE PART, and Sir Alexander MacKenzie, Thomas Forsyth, John Richardson and John Forsyth the last three trading in Montreal aforesaid under the Firm of Forsyth Richardson and Company, the said John Richardson and John Forsyth for themselves in their own persons, and the said Thomas Forsyth being represented by them the said Richardson and John Forsyth, his Attornies; Alexander Ellice, John Inglis and James Forsyth of London, Merchants, trading under the Firm of Phyn Inglis & Company by the said John Richardson and John Forsyth their Attornies, John O'Gilvie of Montreal aforesaid Merchant, John Mure of Quebec Merchant by the said John O'Gilvie his Attorney; Pierre Rocheblave, Alexander McKenzie, John MacDonald, James Leith, and John Wills, the last five being wintering Partners and represented by Sir Alexander McKenzie their Attorney; John Haldane another wintering Partner represented by the said John Forsyth his Attorney and the said Thomas Forsyth (represented as aforesaid) John Richardson and John Forsyth, as Trustees and assignees of the Estate of the late Firm of Leith Jamieson & Company, and Thomas Thain of Montreal aforesaid, all of whom are Partners in the said North-West or Indian Country distinguished by the name of the New North-West Company OF THE OTHER PART.

WITNESSETH, that the said Parties to these Presents now and heretofore trading to the said North-West Country in opposition to each other being desirous to put an end to said opposition and to avoid the waste of property attending thereon and to carry on the said trade in a more advantageous manner DO for this purpose consent and agree to coalesce and join their respective interests and to make the following stipulations and arrangements in that behalf.

ARTICLE I

That the said Parties to these Presents shall and do hereby coalesce and join their said respective interests in the trade and commerce aforesaid which joint interest and concern will commence with the Outfit of the year one thousand eight hundred and five and shall continue to be carried on during the period limited by the articles of agreement of the said Old Company bearing date the fifth day of July one thousand eight hundred and two, that is to say, for eighteen years yet to come. That the present Coalition and joint Concern shall be carried on under the name or Firm of the North-West Company and shall include as well the trade commonly carried on in and to the said North-West Country by both the said companies, as the trade carried on at all the other Posts or places now occupied by the said Old Company.

ARTICLE II

That the said Old Company shall hold and possess three fourths of the said joint concern and the said New Company shall hold and possess one fourth thereof and when the number of shares of the said joint concern shall be increased to one hundred, the said Old Company shall hold seventy-five of such shares and the said New Company twenty-five, in all profits and losses that shall occur in the said joint trade and concern.—That the said Old and New Company shall each divide their respective shares and proportions aforesaid in the said joint concern unto and amongst their individual members in such a manner as they shall see fit;—It is however hereby understood and agreed that the said New Company or their representatives shall and do transfer and secure to each of their six Wintering Partners in the Interior Country one hundredth share of the whole of the said joint concern, and shall allow and pay to the said Wintering Partners and their Successors the same advantages and emoluments as shall be   and paid by the said joint concern to such Wintering Partners of the said Old Company as do now hold one ninety second share therein, and which ninety second share will by the present agreement become one hundredth share in the said joint concern.

ARTICLE III

That the Partners of the said New Company and their Representatives shall hold and possess their said one fourth part or twenty-five shares in the said joint concern for and during the continuation of the present agreement and no such part or share as may become vacant by the death of any of the Partners in the said New Company or otherwise shall revert or belong to the said joint concern, but the same shall be preserved and retained by the said New Company or such Persons as shall become Partners in their Concern under such conditions and arrangements respecting purchases transfers and division of shares amongst themselves as they shall see fit; Upon condition however of being bound to fulfill and observe every engagement and stipulation which the present Partners of the said New Company have become and now are bound and liable to fulfill and observe by these presents agreeable to the forms and Rules established in this behalf by the said articles of agreement of the said Old North-West Company bearing date the fifth day of July one thousand eight hundred and two (except in so far as the same are altered or modified by this agreement) and to all such other Rules and Regulations as shall be made by the said joint concern. It is however understood and agreed by and between the said Parties to these presents that in case of a vacancy by death or otherwise in any of the said six shares hereby reserved by the said New Company for their said six Wintering Partners such vacant shares shall revert and belong to the said joint concern and be by them disposed of and filled up as they shall see fit, and it is further understood and agreed by and between the said Parties that the share and interest which the late Firm of Leith Jamieson and Company held in the said New Company shall at the expiration of the firts outfit of the said joint concern be transferable to such of the Partners of the said New Company as shall agree to purchase the same.

ARTICLE IV

That the said New Company shall be entitled to and have and

receive one fourth part or share of all the commissions and advantages that shall or may   or arise from the said joint concern, first deducting from the amount of the whole the actual expenses of the General Establishment for transacting the Business of the said joint Concern.

ARTICLE V

That it being the intention of the said New Company at the expiration of their agreement bearing date the twentieth day of October of the year one thousand seven hundred and ninety-eight to put their said six Wintering Partners upon the same footing in every respect as Wintering Partners of the said Old Company who now hold one ninety second share and which will become one hundredth share of the said joint concern when the number of the shares thereof will be increased to one hundred as aforesaid. It is therefore stipulated and agreed that when the present agreement shall next summer at the Grand Portage or other place of Depot on Lake Superior be notified to the said Wintering Partners, they shall be bound to declare their acceptance thereof or their intention of retiring therefrom at the expiration of the aforesaid agreement of the twentieth day of October one thousand seven hundred and ninety-eight and in case the six Wintering Partners or any of them shall decline to accept and acquiesce in the present agreement it is further stipulated and agreed that the said New Company shall have a right to fill up the vacancies that may happen by said refusal or retirement of all or any of the six Wintering Partners by such of any of their deserving Clerks as they shall see fit. It is however understood and agreed that after the said vacancies shall have been filled up by the said New Company the said Old Company shall have the right to appoint to, and fill up the three next vacancies that shall happen in the shares of the Wintering Partners of the said joint concern, the said Old Company having promised the same; which vacant shares being filled up as aforesaid, all other vacancies which shall or may happen in the wintering shares of the said joint concern shall be regulated and filled up according to length of service and merit without distinction or partiality resulting from the Person or Persons to be appointed having been a Clerk or Clerks either to the said Old or New Company.—AND it is further understood and agreed that in case of any of the said six Wintering Partners shall refuse to accept any share under the present agreement as aforesaid, he shall not in that case be exonerated or discharged from his debts or engagement by him entered into, or to which he may be liable as a Partner of the said New Company but under the express condition of binding himself not to interfer directly or indirectly in the trade carried on or to be carried on by the said joint concern within the limits hereinafter described under the same restrictions and penalties as retiring Partners of the said Old Company are liable to under their aforesaid articles of agreement of the fifth day of July one thousand eight hundred and two.

ARTICLE VI

That although the said New Company are by the present agreement limited to one fourth part of the said joint trade to be carried on from Canada into the Interior Country yet should circumstances arise in the course of events that should enable the said Joint Company to obtain a participation in the general trade and rights of the Hudson Bay Company or the whole thereof by purchase then and in that case it is hereby covenanted and agreed that the members who shall then represent the said New Company shall not be hereby precluded from negociating with the representatives of the said Old Company for a more extensive participation in said Joint Concern which thereby shall or may be formed or extended and for such Quantum hereof as shall be agreed upon; But it is understood that any permission which may be obtained from the said Hudson Bay Company for a partial transit of merchandize or returns through their Territories shall not be considered as forming a ground for the Negociation of such increased participation; And it is also understood that the said New Company shall sustain no part of the Expenses which have been occasioned by the late adventure made by the said Old Company to the Hudson Bay Territory by Sea; But in case a permission shall have been obtained by the negociation which the said Duncan McGillivray has been instructed to carry on with the Hudson Bay Company for such a transit, then the expenses of the said Adventure shall be fairly stated and a fourth part thereof be supported by the said New Company, who shall also sustain and pay a proportion of the consideration which may have been agreed to be given for such permission of transit and shall also be bound to fulfil the conditions of such agreement as may have been made by the said Duncan McGillivray in that behalf. That the said New Company shall not in any case be liable to the expenses or consequences of any law suit which the said Hudson Bay Company may institute by reason of the trespass they may conceive to have been committed upon their Territory or Rights by the said New Company, or be bound to take part in any future adventure by sea to Hudson's Bay unless the Permission of that Company shall be first had and obtained.

ARTICLE VII

That one fourth part of all the goods wares and merchandize required for the purposes of the said joint trade shall be imported by the Agents of the said New Company from their correspondences in London and one undivided fourth part of the returns or exports of the said joint trade shall be consigned to the Correspondents of the New Company by their said Agents, and in no case shall there be a division of the said returns or exports between the said Old and New Companies previous to the sale thereof. That the whole of the Imports and Exports relative to the said joint trade shall always be on the account and risk thereof although imported from or consigned to distinct or different Houses. And the said Correspondents shall also effect the insurance upon the goods wares and merchandizes furnished by them and upon the consignments made to them as aforesaid. That at the request of the joint Agents of the said Old and New Companies each of them shall furnish a due proportion of capital and cash advances necessary for providing supplies and carrying on the said joint trade, which cash advances on the part of the said Old Company shall be furnished and paid by the House of McTavish Frobisher and Company and on the part of the said New Company shall be furnished and paid by the House of Forsyth Richardson and Company. That the proceeds of the returns of the said joint trade when realized shall be accounted for and divided or remitted and paid in the proportions above mentioned as the case may require.

ARTICLE VIII

That the aforesaid Articles of agreement of the said Old Company bearing date the fifth day of July one thousand eight hundred and two (a copy of which is hereunto annexed) shall be binding on each and every of the Partners of the said New Company and their Successors and all others to be admitted Partners in the said joint concern in the same manner as if the said articles were inserted at length and formed part of the present agreement except in so far as they are altered or modified in and by this Present Agreement.

ARTICLE IX

That the said New Company shall appoint and furnish two Agents being Partners of the said New Company and of the said joint concern to represent them and to be employed in such branch or branches of the exclusive department of the said joint concern at Montreal as shall be found expedient and necessary, one of which said Agents shall go annually to the place of depot on Lake Superior, whenever the same shall be fixed, to participate with the Agents of the Old Company in the joint management of the outfits and other business and arrangements of the said joint concern, and which Agent of the said New Company shall be considered the Attorney of the Partners of the said New Company Wintering Partners thereof excepted, unless when such Agent acts by special power from any of the said Wintering Partners then absent and there vote for the said Partners accordingly. That such of the said Wintering Partners of the said New Company as may be present at the meetings of the said joint concern at the said place of depot, shall personally vote, and such Partner who may be absent may appoint as his Attorney any other Partner of the said joint concern as he shall think fit and the Wintering Partners of the said Old Company may do the like. That the said Agents of the said New Company shall act the one for the other as circumstances may require and when both of them are at Montreal one of them shall be considered as the acting Agent in the Department allotted to him and the other shall give assistance in that department when the same shall be required; And it is understood that such other Agent when at Montreal after the accounts of each year from the Upper Country are settled shall take all necessary information and do every thing that may be requisite or useful in and about the Business to be done at the depot aforesaid the ensuing season.

ARTICLE X

The said New Company hereby nominate and appoint as their said agents the said John Ogilvie and Thomas Thain who shall continue and remain as such and during the space of five years from the day of the date hereof and it is understood and agreed that exclusive of the Agent of the said New Company who shall go to the place of depot on Lake Superior for the Business of the said joint concern the said New Company shall and may the next ensuing Season if they see fit send up any other of their Partners to settle the Business of the said New Company and to consolidate the joint concern by delivering and receiving the property of the said two companies, which being effected the duties of such other Partner shall cease.

ARTICLE XI

In the event of a vacancy in one or other of the Agencies of the said New Company during the said five years by death or the retiring of the said Agents or either of them from the said joint concern, or in case at the expiration of the said five years the said two Agents or either of them shall decline to continue as Agents or Agent as aforesaid of the said New Company, the Partners of the said New Company shall and may in such cases and in every other vacancy that may afterwards happen in the said Agencies nominate and appoint any other fit and proper Person or Persons as Agent or Agents as aforesaid being Partners of the said joint concern.

ARTICLE XII

That all goods at Montreal shall be taken at cost and charges and the goods in the inventories and Indian Credits at the different Posts in the Interior Country belonging to each of the Old and New Companies (those remaining at Hudson's Bay included) shall be received and taken by the said joint concern at the evaluation made according to the tarif of advance of the said Old Company now in all and the debts due by Winterers of the said Old and New Companies shall be assumed by the said joint concern according to the mode of evaluing the same by the said Old Company. That the Forts and buildings the vessels on the Lakes Superior,

Huron and Erie, comprehending three eighths of the Schooner Nancy, shall be taken by the said joint concern upon a fair principle of evaluation to be agreed upon;—and all contracts and agreements made and entered into by either of the said Old and New Company shall be assumed and fulfilled by the said joint Company according to the true spirit and import of every such contract and agreement.

ARTICLE XIII

That the Business of forwarding the goods, wares and merchandizes of the said joint concern at Kingston and Niagara shall be conducted and carried on by the correspondents of the said Old and New Company jointly without any division being made of the said goods wares and merchandises and the said correspondents shall participate in the profits and advantages arising from the said forwarding business in the proportion of the interests of the said Old and New Company in the said joint concern. That at Sandwich, Angus MacIntosh the present agent of the said Old Company shall be continued as the agent of the said joint concern, but the correspondents of the New Company shall supply the proportion of provisions required for the said joint concern upon the same terms and conditions and of like quantities as those supplied by the said Angus MacIntosh while agent as aforesaid.

ARTICLE XIV

That the Tobacco to be imported from the United States for the said joint concern shall be ordered proportionably from the respective correspondents of the said Old and New Company.

ARTICLE XV

That the mode of settling and determining all questions touching and regarding the said joint concern at the meetings thereof to be held at the place of depot on Lake Superior shall be according to the Rules and Regulations established by the aforesaid agreement of the said Old Company, reference being had to the increased number of shares into which the said joint concern will by the present agreement become divided, and every power which shall be given for the commencing and conducting of suits, or for other purposes at Montreal shall include the names of the Agents of the said New Company.

ARTICLE XVI

That all the Wintering Partners of the said Old and New Company, or those who may become Partners of the present Joint Concern, shall have an equal right and privilege of coming down to Montreal in rotation according to a rule to be agreed upon.

ARTICLE XVII

That no trade or business shall be undertaken or carried on by the said joint concern but what is properly understood to be the FUR TRADE or necessarily depending thereon without the express consent and acquiescence of the Representatives or Agents of the said New Company, except the Fisheries carried on at the different posts below Quebec, now leased by the said Old Company.

ARTICLE XVIII

That each of the said Parties to these presents shall, as soon as conveniently may be, make up an account of their advances for the said joint trade for the year one thousand eight hundred and five, and of which regular entries shall be made accordingly.

ARTICLE XIX

That the Inventories of the goods and debts at the respective posts of the said Old and New Companies in the Interior Country shall be received and taken in the state they are produced at the said place of General Depot the next summer, those at the other depots, Lake Lapluie included and on the communication, shall be considered as definitive but all the others shall be verified in the Interior Country when taken in the Fall of the year one thousand eight hundred and five; And the respective Parties to these Presents shall not be bound to each other for the amount of such Inventories until the thirtieth day of November one thousand eight hundred and six.

ARTICLE XX

[Omitted]

XXI

And it is hereby understood and agreed that none of the Parties to these presents nor any Person or Persons who may hereafter become a Partner or Partners of the said Joint Concern shall directly or indirectly carry on or be concerned in any separate trade at any of the posts or places now occupied or that may be hereafter occupied and traded to by the said Concern, nor sell or supply goods or furnish aid and support to any Person or Persons trading to the same posts or places with the said Joint Company under the penalties contained in the aforesaid articles of agreements of the said Old Company bearing date the said fifth day of July, one thousand eight hundred and two. It is however well understood and agreed that the selling of Goods and furnishing supplies by any Partner or Partners of the said Joint Company to any Person or Persons trading to or at any Posts or Places the waters whereof fall into the Mississippi or any other part or place to the Southward of Lake Superior reckoned from the mouth of the River St. Louis shall not be considered as a breach of the present agreement and no penalty shall attach on or be incurred by the Partners or Partner who may have so sold goods and furnished such aid supplies, but no goods shall be sold by any Partner or Partners of the said Joint Concern to be taken or carried into the Interior of the said North West Country by the route of the said River St. Louis and if any Person or Persons who may have purchased goods or received supplies and aid from any Partner or Partners of the said Joint Concern shall without the consent of such Partner or Partners go into the said Interior Country by the route of the said River St. Louis or by the Mississippi, Missouri, or any other indirect route, and trade to any post or place occupied by the said Joint Company or where they may carry on trade at the time provided the same be to the Northward of the above described limits, then and in such case the Agents of the said Joint Concern shall give notice thereof in writing to such Partner or Partners, whereby he or they shall be required to desist from selling goods to equipping supplying aiding or supporting such Person or Persons so trading as aforesaid in, to, or at the same places with the said Joint Company and in opposition to their interests. And in case such Partner or Partners of the said Joint Concern shall after such notice given and requisition made still persist to furnish Goods and afford supplies support and aid to such person or persons so continuing his or their said trade such Partner or Partners shall then be considered to have committed a breach of the present agreement and be liable to all the penalties aforesaid.

AND FINALLY it is agreed that the said Parties to These Presents have hereby negociated and coalesced upon principles of equality and reciprocity of rights excepting as to the Quantum of interest with the influence resulting therefrom and the modifications thereof which the present agreement may be fairly construed to introduce, such principles shall be resorted to in clearing up or settling any difference of opinion should such hereafter arise upon the true construction or import of any of the articles of this Agreement.

IN WITNESS whereof the said Parties to these presents have to two parts hereof set and subscribed their names and affixed their seals at Montreal aforesaid, the day and year first above written.

ALEX. McKENZIE.
THOMAS FORSYTH, by JOHN RICHARDSON and JOHN FORSYTH, his atts.
JOHN RICHARDSON.
JOHN FORSYTH.
ALEX. ELLICE, by JOHN RICHARDSON and JOHN FORSYTH, his atts.
JOHN HALDANE, by JOHN RICHARDSON snd JOHN FORSYTH, his atts.
THOM'S FORSYTH, by JOHN RICHARDSON and JOHN FORSYTH, his atts.
JOHN RICHARDSON, } Trustees and assignees of the Estate of the
JOHN FORSYTH,   } late firm of Leith, Jamieson & Co.
JOHN INGLIS, by JOHN RICHARDSON and JOHN FORSYTH, his atts.
JAMES FORSYTH, by JOHN RICHARDSON and JOHN FORSYTH, his atts.
JOHN OGILVIE.
JOHN MURE, by JOHN OGILVIE, his atty.
P. DE ROCHEBLAVE, by ALEX. MACKENZIE, his atty.
ALEX. MACKENZIE, by ALEX. MACKENZIE, his atty.
JOHN MACDONALD, by ALEX. MACKENZIE, his atty.

James Leith, by Alex. MacKenzie, his atty.
John Wills, by Alex. MacKenzie, his atty.
John Finlay, by John Gregory & Wm MacGillivray, his atts.
Duncan Cameron, by John Gregory & Wm MacGillivray, his atts.
James Hughes, by John Gregory & Wm MacGillivray, his atts.
Alex. McKay, by John Gregory & Wm MacGillivray, his atts.
Hugh McGillis, by John Gregory & Wm MacGillivray, his atts.
Alex. Henry, by John Gregory & Wm MacGillivray, his atts.
John MacGillivray, by John Gregory & Wm MacGillivray, his atts.
James MacKenzie, by John Gregory & Wm MacGillivray, his atts.
Simon Fraser, by John Gregory & Wm MacGillivray, his atts.
John D. Campbell, by John Gregory & Wm MacGillivray, his atts.
D. Thompson, by John Gregory & Wm MacGillivray, his atts.
John Thomson, by John Gregory & Wm MacGillivray, his atts.
John Gregory.
Wm MacGillivray.
Duncan MacGillivray, by Wm MacGillivray, his atty.
Wm Hallowell.
Rod. McKenzie.
Angus Shaw, by John Gregory & Wm MacGillivray, his atts.
Dl. McKenzie, by John Gregory & Wm MacGillivray, his atts.
Wm. McKay, by John Gregory & Wm MacGillivray, his atts.
John McDonald, by John Gregory & Wm MacGillivray, his atts.
Donald McTavish, by John Gregory & Wm MacGillivray, his atts.
John McDonell, by John Gregory & Wm MacGillivray, his atts.
Arch. N. McLeod, by John Gregory & Wm MacGillivray, his atts.
Alex. MacDougal, by John Gregory & Wm MacGillivray, his atts.
Chs Chaboillez, by John Gregory & Wm MacGillivray, his atts.

JOHN SAYER, by JOHN GREGORY & WM MACGILLIVRAY, his atts.
PETER GRANT, by JOHN GREGORY & WM MACGILLIVRAY, his atts.
ALEX. FRASER, by JOHN GREGORY and WM MACGILLIVRAY, his atts.
ENEAS CAMERON, by JOHN GREGORY & WM MACGILLIVRAY, his atts.

Signed and sealed and delivered in the presence of

EDW'D WM GRAY
FRED'K W. ERMATINGER

18: AGREEMENT OF SIR A. MACKENZIE & CO., NOVEMBER 9, 1804[1]

[*Hudson's Bay House.*]

ARTICLES of agreement had made and fully agreed upon the ninth day of November in the year of our Lord one thousand eight hundred and four by and between Sir Alexander McKenzie, Thomas Forsyth, John Richardson and John Forsyth, the last three trading in Montreal aforesaid, under the Firm of Forsyth Richardson & Company the said John Richardson and John Forsyth for themselves in their own persons, and the said Thomas Forsyth being represented by them the said John Richardson and John Forsyth his attornies, Alexander Ellice, John Inglis, and James Forsyth of London merchants, trading under the firm of Phyn Inglis and Company, by the said John Richardson, and John Forsyth their Attornies, John Ogilvy of Montreal aforesaid merchant, John Mure of Quebec merchant by the said John Ogilvy his Attorney, Pierre Rocheblave, Alexander McKenzie, John McDonell, James Leith and John Wills, the last five being Wintering partners and represented by the said Sir Alexander McKenzie their Attorney, John Haldane another wintering partner represented by the said John Richardson and John Forsyth his Attornies, and the said Thomas Forsyth (represented as aforesaid) John Richardson and John Forsyth, as Trustees and assignees of the Estate of the late Firm of Leith, Jameson and Company and Thomas Thain of Montreal

[1]Reproduced by permission of the Governor and Committee of the Hudson's Bay Company.

aforesaid, all of whom the latter excepted are partners in the Company at present trading to the said North West or Indian Country, distinguished by the name of the New North West Company.

Whereas articles of agreement or partnership for carrying on Trade to the Interior of the North west Country, were on the twentieth day of October one thousand seven hundred and ninety eight, entered into by and between the said **Forsyth Richardson & Company, Leith Jameson & Company, Alexander McKenzie, George Sharp and John McDonald, Pierre Rocheblave, Daniel Sutherland and François Beaubien** (the latter of whom and George Sharp by death ceased to be partners) and to which persons at different times were joined as partners, the said **Phyn Inglis & Company, John Ogilvy, John Mure, James Leith, Sir Alexander McKenzie, John Haldane, and John Wills,** which last named persons assumed and carried on their said trade to the North west, under the Firm of Sir Alexander McKenzie & Company, but were commonly called and known by the name of the New North West Company; and which said Articles of Agreement were made and intended to continue to the first day of May One thousand eight hundred and six. And whereas circumstances having rendered it expedient and proper that a coalition should take place with the other company trading to the North West commonly called the old North West Company. An agreement to carry the said Coalition into effect between the said old & new North West Companies hath on the part of the said Old & New Companies been, at Montreal on the fifth day of November Instant, entered into and executed accordingly. And whereas it is necessary and proper, in consequence of the formation of the said Joint Company, that the parties to these presents, being partners of the said new Company and who are by the said joint agreement, collectively entitled to one fourth in the Trade to be carried on by the said Joint Company, should for their own guidance and to settle their said fourth in the said joint concern amongst themselves, make such agreement as to them seemeth just and equitable. Now therefore these Presents witness that they the said parties in consideration of the Premises have mutually consented and agreed and do hereby mutually consent and agree to the several Articles, Matters and things following, that is to say,—

Article 1st

That the agreement at present subsisting as above said under the firm of Sir Alexander M'Kenzie & Company (excepting as to the partners hereafter mentioned) shall not end on the said first day of May 1806; But is hereby Covenanted and agreed that the same shall be continued and extended from the said 1st day of May 1806 for and during the space of Seventeen years after or until the expiration of the agreement entered into on the said 5th day of November Instant by the said coallesced or Joint Company, which will end with the Returns of the Outfit of the year 1822, conformable with the articles of agreement of the said Old Company, to which the partners of the said New Company have by their said joint agreement accorded, with certain alterations and modifications, which have been made thereto in consequence of the said joint agreement; and it is, however, hereby understood and agreed that although the existing articles of agreement of the said 20th day of October 1798 are continued as aforesaid, yet the principles of that agreement shall only govern the parties to these Presents up to the return of the Outfit of the year 1805 inclusive, and that all profits and losses and all incidental expenses are to be shared or borne in conformity to the said agreement of the 20th day of October 1798, by the Parties thereto in the same manner that the said parties have heretofore practised, used and put the same in execution; and in as much as the change of circumstances and the said coallition and formation of the said joint Company have rendered a new agreement absolutely necessary. It is Covenanted and agreed that from and after the Returns of the Outfit of the said year 1805, the said Old agreement of the 20th Day of October 1798, shall be considered as superceded and ended, and the principles of the present agreement during the continuation thereof as aforesaid shall be resorted to and govern the parties to these Presents.

Article 2nd

That the Interests of the late firm of Leith Jameson & Company and Daniel Sutherland in the said agreement of the 20th day of October 1798, shall cease and end with the expiration thereof on the said 1st day of May 1806, or with the return of the outfit of the said year 1805.

Article 3rd

That in as much as by the said Joint agreement of the said Old North West Company the said New Co. (including the shares of the above mentioned Partners who are to retire on the 1st day of May 1806) are to have, hold, possess and enjoy one fourth of the said joint concern as aforesaid; and which joint concern by the said agreement, it is covenanted shall, as soon as conveniently may be divided into one hundred shares or parts; It is hereby understood, covenanted and agreed, that the six wintering partners of the said Firm of Sir Alexander McKenzie & Co. who are named in the said joint articles of agreement, to wit, Alexander McKenzie, John McDonald, Pierre Rocheblave, James Leith, John Haldane and John Wills, or those who may succeed to them and become partners of the said joint concern, shall, commencing with the Outfit of the year 1806 (provided they do acede and agree to this and the said joint agreement) each and every of them shall, have, hold, and enjoy one hundredth share or part in the said Joint Concern, upon the same footing and under the like conditions, advantages, profits, and losses and subject to the same Rules, Regulations, Penalties, servitudes and burthens in every respect as the wintering partners of the said Old Company, who now hold one ninety second shares therein and who will hold one hundredth shares in the said joint Concern when that concern shall be divided into that number of shares.

Art. 4th

That as by the said joint articles of agreement the partners composing or who may compose the said New Company in the said joint concern to be replaced by the said New Company in case of a vacancy as in the said joint articles of agreement is stipulated. And in as much as the said John Ogilvy and Thomas Thain have been nominated and appointed in the said joint articles of agreement, as the Agents of the said New Company, with an obligation upon them to act in that situation for at least the term of five years, one of whom is annually to go to the general depot or Rendezvous on Lake Superior and to act for each other, if Circumstances require it,—It is agreed that as a consideration for the Services of the said Agents, or as long as they shall continue to act in that situation, and discharge the duties thereof and incident thereto they shall

THE NORTH WEST COMPANY 161

severally have hold and enjoy—That is to say—the said John Ogilvy, two hundredth shares, and the said Thomas Thain one hundredth share in the said joint concern when divided in the manner mentioned in the preceding Articles, and the said Thomas Thain in addition to such Share shall be entitled to receive annually, Two hundred pounds Currency.

Article 5th

That as under the said agreement of the 20th day of October 1798, the said six wintering partners, namely, Alexander McKenzie, John McDonald, Pierre Rocheblave, James Leith, John Haldane, and John Wills, hold each a share and Daniel Sutherland a wintering partner's share and Sir Alexr. McKenzie, by his said agreement of accession to the last mentioned agreement, two wintering partners' shares, upon which shares a very extensive loss hath arisen—It is, under a review of all the circumstances, considered proper that the said persons in respect to the said wintering shares, being nine shares in all, should at the expiration of the said agreement of the 20th day of October 1798 as aforesaid be exonerated and discharged from all the losses that at the period of such expiration shall have arisen, or be incurred during the period of the agreement, and they are hereby discharged accordingly. Provided always and it is hereby agreed and understood that the said six wintering partners (the said Sir Alexander McKenzie having already accepted thereof) shall have it in their power to accept or accede to the said Joint Agreement and to this present agreement, or to decline becoming a partner of the said Joint Concern or a party to these presents; which acceptation or refusal the said partners will be bound to declare upon the said joint agreement and these presents being communicated to them, and in case any of the wintering partners should decline accepting the said joint agreement and these presents and becoming parties thereto and hereto, such person or persons so declining shall not in any respect be considered as exonerated and discharged from such losses, or any part thereof, until he or they shall come under an obligation with sufficient penalties not to interfere or be concerned directly nor indirectly in trade, to any part of the North West Country, within the limits described in the said joint agreement, for and during the term of the said Old N.W. Co.'s agreement, being for 18 Years yet to come including the Outfit of 1805; and in case of a breach of such obligation the claim and demand for the said losses against the person or persons committing such breach shall in no manner be considered as exonerated or discharged from his or their proportion of the losses aforesaid; but the claim therefore shall be considered in its full force against the party or parties so committing such breach.

Art. 6th

That as the said Daniel Sutherland, after the expiration of the said agreement of the 20th day of October 1798, is to retire and have no participation in the said joint concern—It is agreed that in consideration of his so retiring, in addition to his being exonerated from his proportion of losses aforesaid that attach and attend on his said Wintering Share, he shall be entitled to demand have and receive of and from the said New Co. annually for five years to be computed from the said 1st day of May 1806, the sum of £200 Currency, the last payment whereof shall be made on the 1st day of May 1811 without he the said D. Sutherland being required to render any services to the said joint Company, from the said 1st day of May 1806. But it is understood and agreed that the above exoneration, discharge and allowance, is made to the said Daniel Sutherland upon condition that he shall come under the same obligations and restrictions respecting non-interference in the said trade to the North West Company as is expressed in the preceding Article in regard to wintering partners, and not otherwise.

Article 7th

That in order to afford and provide for the means of such exoneration and discharge from the losses of the before mentioned partners in respect to the said nine wintering shares and the said allowance of £200 Currency, for five years to the said D. Sutherland, as well as an annual allowance of £200 Currency, to the said Thomas Thain before mentioned,—It is hereby agreed that the said Phyn, Inglis & Co. and their successors, the said Sir Alexander McKenzie and his successors, the said Forsyth, Richardson & Co. and their successors and the said John Ogilvy and John Mure and their successors shall respectively bear, sustain, and be chargeable each with one fourth thereof; and in consideration of their being so chargeable with the said losses and the payment of the allowances they shall respectively be entitled to and shall each (the said John Ogilvy and John Mure as one) hold a one hundredth share in the said concern, as an indemnity in part for their said undertaking, and for the residue of such indemnity, each of the said parties shall be entitled to and shall receive a fourth part of the general quarter part of all the Commissions and advantages that may accrue, arise, or be derived from the said Joint Company or concern stipulated in the said joint agreement to belong to and appertain to the said New North West Co.; subject, however, to the payment of the said New Co.'s proportion of the expences of the general Establishment for conducting the said joint business.

Art. 8th

That as the late Firm of Leith, Jameson & Co., from the deaths which have happened amongst the partners of the said firm and the impractibility of their heirs furnishing a proportion or portion of Capital to the said joint concern and also from the necessity of closing the affairs of the said firm, as speedily as circumstances will permit, that firm or its representatives cannot become and continue parties to the said joint or extended agreement; nor hold any interest in the said joint concern, after the returns of the Outfit of the said year 1805. It is agreed that the three shares of the said firm of Leith Jameson & Co., at the expiration of the agreement to which they were parties, to wit, on the 1st day of May 1806, shall be sold, transferred, and conveyed and the same together with all the rights and privileges acquired to the said firm of Leith Jameson & Co. by the said joint agre^t., are hereby sold, transferred and conveyed by the said Forsyth Richardson & Co., the Trustees and assignees, to the said firm as aforesaid in manner following, that is to say, to the said Phyn Inglis & Co. one of the shares of the said firm of Leith Jameson & Co., and to the said Forsyth Richardson & Co. another of the shares, and to Sir Alexander McKenzie their remaining share, being all money shares, which sales and transfer shall entitle the said purchasers and transferees respectively to hold each one hundredth share in the said joint concern, commencing with the Outfit of 1806, exclusive of the other money and indemnity shares they respectively hold and possess in the said joint concern; and in consideration of the said sale and transfer, the said purchasers do hereby respectively promise and oblige themselves to pay in London, on the 1st day of August 1806 to the order of the Trustees of the said late firm of Leith Jameson & Co., the sum of £2500 Currency converted into stirling money at par, being the capital put into the said New Co., by the said Leith Jameson & Co. and which the representatives of the said late firm are desirous of withdrawing without incurring any further risk of loss, beyond the returns of the Outfit of the said year 1805; and which sums the said purchasers respectively agree to pay even in case the said capital should be nearly or entirely exhausted and lost.

Art. 9th

That exclusive of the six shares herein before enumerated to be held by the said six wintering partners, of the three shares to be held by the said Agents and of the four (4) indemnity shares to be held as before mentioned, by the said Phyn, Inglis & Co., Sir Alexander McKenzie, Forsyth Richardson & Co. and John Ogilvy & John Mure, there remains twelve money shares (including the three above mentioned shares sold for the benefit of the said firm of Leith Jameson & Co.) being each one hundredth share in the said joint concern; which 12 money shares shall be held as such in manner following, that is to say, by Phyn Inglis & Co., three of such shares, by the said Sir Alexander McKenzie, Three of such shares, by the said Forsyth Richardson & Co., Four of such shares, by the said John Ogilvy & John Mure, two of such shares, so that the whole of the twenty-five shares belonging to the said New Co. in the said joint Concern, in virtue of the said joint agreement shall be held and possessed by the different partners of the said New Co. who shall be entitled to all the profits and advantages of their respective shares and liable to all the losses that may accrue thereon. The said shares to be held respectively by the said parties as stated in the following general distribution, or Recapitulation thereof, that is to say,

Phyn Inglis & Co........	3	money & 1	indemnity share	4	shares
Sir Alexander McKenzie..	3	" & 1	"	"	4	"
Forsyth Richardson & Co..	4	" & 1	"	"	5	"
John Ogilvy & John Mure.	2	" & 1	"	"	3	"

THE NORTH WEST COMPANY

John Ogilvy	2 agent's share		2 shares
Thomas Thain	1 " "		1 "
Alexander McKenzie	1 Wintering share		1 "
John McDonald	1 " "		1 "
Pierre Rocheblave	1 " "		1 "
James Leith	1 " "		1 "
John Haldane	1 " "		1 "
John Wills	1 " "		1 "

25 shares

Art. 10th

That it is hereby agreed that the partners of the said New Co. or the said Firm of Sir Alexander McKenzie & Co. and their representatives, shall have the right of making such arrangements amongst each other respecting the purchases, sales, and transfers of the said money or indemnity shares as they shall see fit, during the continuation of the said Joint Concern; and it is also agreed that in the event of the death of any of the partner or partners, holding money or indemnity shares, the benefits, profits, and losses thereon shall accrue to the Heirs or representatives of the deceased partner or partners, provided always that the said Heirs or Representatives shall conform to and fulfill all and every the Stipulations, covenants, and conditions, contained in this agreement and the said joint agreement entered into as aforesaid with the said Old Co., and to which they (as the representative or representatives of a partner or partners) shall be as liable as the deceased partner or partners was or were, when living, and a party to these presents, in as full and ample a manner as if he or they, had signed the present agreement and the said joint agreement; and be liable also to all the Rules, Regulations, Articles, penalties of the said Old Co.'s agreement, in so far as the same is confirmed by and makes part of the said Joint agreement. But it is understood that the said Heir or Heirs of deceased partners, holding money or indemnity shares, shall have the power and be at liberty to sell and dispose of the same to any other person or persons who shall be approved of by the said surviving partners of the said New Co. However, it is agreed and understood, that the said Surviving partner or any of them shall have a preferable right to become the purchaser or purchasers of such share or shares, to become vacant by death as aforesaid, and have the refusal thereof, upon the same terms and conditions, that the said Heirs or representatives could sell the said share or shares to any other person or persons whatever. And it is hereby covenanted and agreed that in no case whatever, shall a sale be made of any share or shares to any person or persons whatsoever without subjecting the purchaser or purchasers of such share or shares, to all the Rules, regulations, Covenants, agreements, obligations, and penalties, of whatever nature or kind soever, to which the said partner or partners, from whom the said share or shares was or were divided, was or were liable and subject to, at the time of his or their deaths, in consequence of his or their holding the said share or shares in the said joint concern. And it is also covenanted and agreed that the said six wintering shares, hed by the said six wintering partners, shall in case of death, and in every other respect be subject to all and every the rules, regulations and servitudes and be governed in the same manner as the shares of wintering partners of the said Old Co. are by the Rules and regulations in that behalf already made and entered into by the said Old Company's agent acceded to by the said Joint Agreement or Coalition.

Art. 11th

That in consideration that the advances made by the said Ho. of Phyn, Inglis & Co. of London, to the said New Co., have been very heavy,—It is agreed that they shall continue to transact all the business in London stipulated by the said Joint agreement, dated the said 5th day of November instant, to be transacted by the correspondents of the said New Co. provided that they shall do such business upon as favourable terms as any other established Ho. in London shall do business for the Canada; and that the goods imported from them, shall be chargeable by the said New Co. to the joint Concern, upon like terms as prescribed by the said Articles of agreement of the Old Company.

Art. 12th

That the Sd. partners holding the Sd. 12 money shares, under this agreement, do hereby covenant, promise and agree, that on the first day of January which will be in the year of our Lord 1810, there shall be paid by them in London, for each of their said shares, to the said Phyn, Inglis & Co. such a sum as shall then be requisite to make the Balance, at the Credit of the account of each of the said partners in the Books of Sir Alexander MacKenzie & Co. amount to the sum of £2500 Currency, converted into sterling at par, for each of the said money shares, so held by every such partner, by which means a stock or Capital of £30000 Currency will then become deposited, for carrying on the said New Co.'s proportion of the business of the said Joint Concern. But interest shall be allowed on the said sum so deposited, and the said deposit or Stock shall not be with drawn, before the end of the said Joint Concern, it being understood that the said Phyn, Inglis & Co. shall continue to do the business of the said New Co. in London during the term of this Agreement. It is however Agreed that the surplus, which shall be at the Credit of any of the said partners over and above the said Capital of £30000 Currency, after the same shall have been made up and desposited as aforesaid, shall annually be paid by the said Phyn, Inglis & Co. to any and all the Sd. partners, so entitled to such surplus, upon an order or draft for that purpose, signed by the said agents of the said New Co., who shall annually previously to the granting such order or draft make out and transmit to the said Phyn, Inglis & Co. a full and complete statement of the affairs of the said New Co. and of such surplus. And it is agreed and understood that each partner or partner's account in the Books of the said New Co. shall be debited with or credited by interest as the case may be according to the legal rate of interest in this Province. And it is agreed that the wintering partners of the Sd. New Co. shall in respect to monies resulting from their shares, be on the same footing, as the wintering partners of the Old Co. are or shall be; yet it is understood that wintering partners who may come down to Montreal in rotation shall there receive a reasonable sum to defray their Expenses, and what shall be advanced to them, by the agents of the said New Co. out of its Funds, to be chargeable to the accounts of the wintering partners receiving such sums.

Art. 13th

That the agents of the said New Co. or firm of Sir Alex[r]. MacKenzie & Co., shall be guided by the majority of the votes of the partners thereof as herein after mentioned; and the said agents shall keep regular Books distinct from those of the Joint Co. in order to enter and be enabled to exhibit what concerns the separate interests of the said firm in respect to the partners thereof and their accounts with their Correspondents in London, and they shall annually on the 30th day of November make out and render statements of the Outfits of the said Joint Co. and of the Concerns of the said New Co. and the accounts of the partners thereof. It being understood that the wintering partners of the said New Co. shall annually be furnished with accounts in the manner practised in respect to the wintering partners of the said Old Co. and in all matters that concern the business of the said Sir Alexander MacKenzie & Co. none other [than] the said John Ogilvy and Thomas Thain their said Agents and their successors as agents, are exclusively authorized to sign [for] the said firm of Sir Alexander MacKenzie & Co.

Art. 14th

That the partners in the said New Co. holding money, indemnity or agents' shares under this Agreement, and those who may hereafter hold such shares, shall vote at Montreal in proportion to the shares they hold (reckoning every share a vote) and all questions on which differences of opinion shall there arise touching the management of the said Joint Co. or the interest of the said New Co., shall be decided by a majority of the votes held by the partners present, who may hold money, indemnity, or agents' shares, who may vote in their own right or as attornies to absentees holding shares of the like description, such majority shall be reckoned by the number of shares then voting. Partners holding money, indemnity, and agents' shares, who may be absent from Montreal, shall give a power to some partner of the said New Co., who may be present at Montreal to vote for him or them, and in the event of such absent partner or partners not giving such power he or they shall be as much bound by the decision of the partners present, as those who may be represented, as if he or they had been present and had personally voted, it being the fault of such partner or partners, if he or they are not represented. And the Agent of the said New Co. at the depot or Rendezvous on Lake Superior shall always vote as the attorney of the partners of the said New Co., who are not wintering partners, and he may also represent any wintering partner who shall see fit to appoint him as their attorney by a special power. And it is further agreed and understood by the parties hereto, that the said Sir Alexander MacKenzie may, after the 30th day of November 1809 transfer and make over, one of his said money shares to Alexander Dowie his Nephew, if he thinks fit so to do. In Witness whereof the said parties to These Presents have hereunto subscribed their names and affixed their Seals, at Montreal, the day and year first above written.

Signed, Sealed, and delivered
in the presence of
(Signed) T. A. Turner
" Will. Ireland

(Signed) John Wills by
 Alex. McKenzie his att. (L.S.)
" John Haldane by
 John Richardson his att. "
" & John Forsyth, his do "
" Thomas Forsyth by
 John Richardson }
 & John Forsyth } his att. "
" Thomas Forsyth by } Trustees
 John Richardson & } of the
 John Forsyth } Estate of
  his att. } Leith
" John Richardson } Jameson
" John Forsyth } & Co.
      (L.S.)
" Thomas Thain   (L.S.)

(Signed) Alex. MacKenzie (L.S.)
" Thomas Forsyth by
 John Richardson & }
 John Forsyth } his att. "
" John Richardson "
" John Forsyth "
" Alex. Ellice by
 John Richardson & }
 John Forsyth } his att. "
" John Inglis by
 John Richardson & }
 John Forsyth } his att. "
" James Forsyth by
 John Richardson & }
 John Forsyth } his att. "
" John Ogilvy "
" John Mure by
 John Ogilvy his att.
" Alex. McKenzie by
 Alex. McKenzie his att. "
" John Mcdonald by
 Alex. McKenzie his att. "
" James Leith by
 Alex^r. McKenzie his att. "

Whereas the parties holding money and indemnity shares in the foregoing agreement have on the 19th day of July last, at the Grand Portage, entered into a separate agreement with the wintering partners named in the said foregoing agreement; It is hereby covenanted and agreed that the fifth article of the said foregoing agreement, in as far as the same respects the exonerating and discharging the said wintering partners, is hereby rescinded and annulled; and that the said agreement entered into as aforesaid at the Grand Portage and bearing date the 19th day of July last shall be taken as the rule and followed and observed in all things whatsoever respecting the said wintering partners.

In witness whereof the parties to these presents have hereunto set their Hands and affixed their Seals, at Montreal this 19th day of October in the year of our Lord 1805.

Signed, Sealed and delivered
   in the presence of
(Signed) Thos. A. Turner
      "   W. Ireland

Signed by every Individual & representation of foregoing page which See.

19: Minutes of the Meetings of the North West Company at Grand Portage and Fort William, 1801-1807, with Supplementary Agreements.[1]

[*Bâby Collection, Sulpician Library, Montreal.*]

At a meeting of the North West Company, held at the Grand Portage the 30th June 1801—

    Present Simon McTavish
                Willm McGillivray
                Angus Shaw
                Roderick Mackenzie
                Alexander McLeod
                Daniel McKenzie
                William MacKay
                John Mcdonald
                Donald McTavish

[1] The manuscript volume containing these minutes and supplementary agreements was found among the papers of Samuel Gerrard, one of the trustees appointed by Simon McGillivray in 1826 to administer the affairs of McTavish, McGillivrays and Company, and of McGillivrays, Thain and Company. The volume is apparently a copy of the original, and must have gone to Samuel Gerrard with other documents relating to the North West Company, which have since disappeared.

THE NORTH WEST COMPANY 171

    John Mcdonell
    Archd Norman McLeod
    Peter Grant
    John Sayer &
    Charles Chaboillez

It was unanimously Resolved—that the Gentlemen whose names follow should be admitted Partners of the North West Company for one Forty sixth share each, their Interest in the same to Commence with the Outfit of the Year 1802 vizt

    Hugh McGillis
    Alexander Henry
    Jean Bte Cadotte
    John McGillivray
    James McKenzie &
    Simon Fraser

Provided they formally accept the same—

    Signed Simon McTavish
     " Wm McGillivray
     " Angus Shaw
     " Alexr McLeod
     " Roderic McKenzie
     " Daniel McKenzie
     " William McKay
     " John Sayer
     " Daniel McTavish
     " Peter Grant
     " John Mcdonald
     " Archd Norman McLeod
     " John Mcdonell
     " Charles Chaboillez &
A New Copy   " Rod: McKenzie for ⎫
 J. C. Stewart   John Finlay ⎭

WHEREAS by the 21st Article of the present North West Companys Agreement it is stipulated that any Partner of the North West Company upon conducting himself in a manner unworthy of his situation should be expelled the same, And whereas it is notorious that many of the Clerks and Interpreters at present in the Companys Service are frequently guilty of Drunkeness & thereby rendered incapable of performing this duties they owe to the Concern—to prevent therefore this (*greatest of Evils*) from gaining Ground and, if possible, *to root it out altogether:*—It is resolved.—

That henceforward any Partner of the Concern who can be proved by undoubted Evidence, to have been in the Wintering Ground from Liquor rendered incapable of Conducting his Business—shall be subject to the Penalties of the above Article of the North West Agreement—And any Clerk or Interpreter found guilty of this Vice in the Wintering Grounds or along the road shall forfeit his Wages for the Current year, and it shall be incumbent on all the Gentlemen of the Concern to report the Conduct of such People as are within their Districts every Summer at this Place.

Grand portage 30th June 1801

Signed Simon McTavish
Wm. McGillivray
Angus Shaw
Roderick McKenzie
Alexander McLeod
John Sayer
Donald McTavish
Charles Chabiollez

a true Copy
J. C. Stewart

Daniel Mackenzie
William McKay
Peter Grant
A. N. McLeod
John Mcdonell
John Mcdonald

We hereby accept of the Shares alotted to us by virtue of the Resolve passed this day, and having perused the North West Agreement bearing date the 30th October 1795 and since ratified and Confirmed—bind ourselves strictly to observe the same with all the Clauses Conditions and Penalties thereof, holding ourselves bound as fully and amply to all intents and purposes as if Partners subscribing to the Original Agreement above referred to

Witness
    J. C. Stewart
Signd H. Mackenzie

Grand portage 30th June 1801
Signed H. McGillis
Alexr Henry
J. Bte Cadotte
John MacGillivray

The proprietors of the }
North West Co.
Gentlemen

Grand portage 4th July 1801

By the 11th Article of the North West Company's existing Agreement, it is Stipulated and agreed, that during the term of the present Concern, any partner holding Two Forty-sixths Shares in Said Company may retire from all attendance on the Business on relinquishing one forty Sixth Share thereof to the Concern; and as it is my intention to avail myself of Such Clause, I hereby Resign and Relinquish in favor of said Company one forty Sixth Share of the two I hold by the present existing Agreement, reserving to myself the eventual profit that may arise on my remaining forty Sixth Share until the end of the now existing Concern—I remain

Gentlemen
Your Obedient humble Serv[t].
(Signed) Rod. Mackenzie

WHEREAS it was unanimously determined upon by all the Partners of the West Company present at the place in the month of July last, that McTavish Frobisher & Company should purchase the Stock of the King's domains or Tadousac Posts for this Concern at the Ensuing Sale, and that Angus Shaw, one of the said Partners should take upon himself the management thereof. And whereas in consequence of, and conformable to the above determination the said McTavish Frobisher & Company have purchased the Lease aforesaid for the Term of Twenty years from the first of October next ensuing one eight hundred and two, for the sum of one thousand and Twenty Five Pounds Currency per annum, and further to consolidate and secure unmolested the Trade thereof, did also purchase the Lease of the private Seignory of Mille vaches belonging to Peter Stuart Esquire of Quebec and others for the Sum of Three hundred Pounds per annum for the same length of time.

It is now resolved that the said purchases and arrangements is hereby approved of and assumed by the North West Company, and that the said Angus Shaw Shall undertake the Superintendence and Control of the Company's Agents for the manner with the Partners conducting Departments in the North West/take the management thereof, for which purpose he will make the City of Quebec his place of Residence making an annual Tour every summer /or when ever his presence is required/of the Posts that now are, or may be established for the further extension and benefit of the said Trade. He to retain his full Share and Interest in the North West Company to all intents and purposes as if a wintering partner conducting a Department in the north west. And to enable him to defray the Expence that will necessarily attend the hiring proper Stores for the business at Quebec, or other casual expenditures—McTavish Frobisher and Company hereby agree to relinquish in favor of the said Angus Shaw the Commission they are entitled to, on the Outfit and Revenue of the said department—

It is also resolved that in case of the retiring or death of the said Angus Shaw before the Expiration of this Concern, then a legal majority of this Concern to appoint such other person as to them appears the most fit and proper for the Station, Such Person being a wintering partner of the North West Company, to whom after such appointment, said McTavish Frobisher and Company agree to give up the Commissions in like manner as they do to Angus Shaw, in order to Defray the Expenses of Storage and a Clerk.—Grand portage the 6th day of July 1802

(Signed) (Signed)
  Wm. McGillivray for self &   Duncan Cameron
  McTavish Frobisher & Co   William McGillivray
  Alex: McLeod   for Aneas Cameron
  Donald McTavish   William McGillivray
  John Mcdonnell   for Wm. Thorburn
  Archd. Nor: McLeod   Rod: McKenzie
  John Sayer   for Peter Grant

THE NORTH WEST COMPANY 175

John Finlay	Duncan McGillivray ⎫
James Hughes	for Alexr. Fraser ⎬
Duncan Cameron	Duncan McGillivray ⎫
H. McGillis	for Ch: Chaboillez ⎬
Alex^r. Henry	Wm. McKay
J. B^{te}. Cadotte	Wm. McKay ⎫
John McGillivray	for Alex. McKay ⎬

   J. C. Stewart witness ⎫ Signed
   J. G. McTavish do ⎬

a True Copy ⎫
H. Mackenzie ⎬

WHEREAS in the 10th Article of the Agreement of the North West Company bearing date the 5th July 1802 it is stipulated and agreed upon that a list of the Wintering Partners shall be made out to establish the order of Rotation in which the said partners shall be allowed to go to Montreal, and that the said Concern shall decide yearly what number can be spared from the business; which number in any case whatever, is not to exceed Five.

It is therefore resolved conformable to the above Agreement that the wintering Partners Shall be allowed to go down in the following order Viz

  William Mackay
  Arch^d. Nor: McLeod
  Peter Grant
  Daniel Mackenzie
  John Mcdonald
  John Sayer
  John Mcdonald
  John Finlay
  Charles Chaboillez
  Duncan Cameron
  James Hughes
  Alexander McKay
  Hugh McGillis
  Alexander Henry
  Jean Baptiste Cadotte
  John McGillivray
  James McKenzie
  Simon Fraser

In Witness whereof the Partners present have hereunto set their hands at the Grand portage this 10th of July 1802

    (Signed) William Mackay
      " Archd. Nor: Macleod
      " Donald Mactavish
      " John Sayer
      " John Macdonell
      " John Finlay
      " Duncan Cameron
      " James Hughes
      " H. McGillis
      " Alexr. Henry
      " J. Bte. Cadotte
      " John McGillivray
      " McTavish Frobisher & Co

Witnesses
 J. C. Stewart } Signed
 J. G. McTavish }

A true Copy }
H. Mackenzie }

CONVENTIONS faites entre les Agents de la Compagnie du Nord Ouest soussignés, & Michel Cadotte, pour le Commerce de la pointe Chaguamigon, de la Rivière des Sauteux, & de lac des Courte oreilles, pour l'espace de trois années, à commencer par l'Envoye de l'année 1803 et à conclure avec l'Envoye de l'année 1805. Les Conditions telles qui suivent—Savoir—

Premiere—Que la dite Compagnie du Nord Ouest et le dit Michel Cadotte seront de moitié en tous Profits ou Pertes qui pourront resulter de ce Commerce.

Seconde—Que les Marchandises, Boissons, & Vivres—Comis et Hommes proprises, pour cette Société seront fournis et Engagés par la dite Compagnie du Nord Ouest, à la raison de quarante per Cent sur les prix de Montreal pour les Marchandises sèches—Soixante-Quinze per Cent sur les prix de Montreal pour l'amunition, et le Tabac, & pour les Boissons, Graisse, Provisions, et les Ferrailles Cent per Cent sur les dites prix. La farine et le bled qu'il faut, aux prix des Inventaires de la dite Compagnie du Nord Ouest.

Troisième—Que les hommes montant de Montreal & qui y'ont reçus des avances, seront reçus par cette Société, et le montant de leurs avances mis à Compte sans en rien deduire —toutes les autres avances faites par la dite Compagnie seront mises à Compte à la raison d'une moitié pourvû que telle moitié n'excede pas la somme de Mil livres ancien Cours, & quand cette Société les rendra à la Compagnie ce sera aux mêmes conditions.

Quatrième—Que les Castors & Pelletries appartenants à la dite Société seront reçus par la dite Societé du Nord Ouest aux prix suivantes—étant Cours Ancien—Savoir—

Les Castors........................ 11 la livre
Martres....................... @ 5
Pecans........................ " 6
Loutres....................... " 20
Visons .... " 3
Loupserviers.................... " 10
Rats Musquées................. " 15
Peaux d'ours................... " 60
   "   d'oursons................. " 30
   "   en parchement............ " 12
   "   des Chevreuils............ " 4.10

Le Sucre 15 sols la livre, et la Gomme 12 sols la livre, & bien entendu que ces peaux soient de recette, & que toutes pelletries d'Eté ou vicié seront à demi-prix.

Cinquième—Que les Marchandises et les autres effets qui pourront y avoir de reste chaqu'année après la traite faite, seront mis à l'avoir du Compte de cette Societé avec les Retours aux prix de ces Conventions, & que les Comptes seront reglés et signés une fois par année.

Sixième—Que le dit Michel Cadotte s'oblige de ne pas envoyer ou faire aucune Traite avec les Sauvages des Postes occupés par la dite Compagnie du Nord Ouest—hormis que des Gens opposés à la dite Compagnie dans leur commerces et qui pourrons être ses voisins soient pour aller en derouine ou autrement faire tort aux dits Postes—alors et dans ce cas Monr Cadotte ferra son possible pour leur nuire.

Septième—Il est convenu entre les Parties soussignés que—si les Peaux d'ours et oursons diminuent en valeur d'ici au bout de deus ans—alors que les prix seront reglés en conscience à proportion des prix de Londre—Mais pour deux envoyés il n'y aura aucun Changement—

Huitième—Que les Parties soussignés—c'est à dire, William McGillivray and Duncan McGillivray agents de la dite Compagnie du Nord Ouest d'un part, & Michel Cadotte de l'autre part, se lient & s'obligent les uns aux autres de suivre fidellement ces conventions pendant le tems specifié en toutes ces articles sous les Peines d'une Somme de trois cens Livres cours actuel, que le parti manquant payera un parti qui suivra ces Conventions. Fois de quel Les Soussignés ont passé et signé cette acte de convention à Kamanitiquiâ ce sixième Jour de Juillet l'an Mil huit Cent et Trois.

Michel Cadotte

Temoins
H. Mackenzie   W. McGillivray ⎱ Agents
J. C. Stewart   D. McGillivray ⎰ of N.W. Co.

Vu que l'acte ci dessu doit echoer avec l'Envoye de l'an 1805 & que les deux Partis veulent la renouveller pour un terme de trois années consecutifs, à commencer avec l'Envoye de l'an mil huit cent & six, et à finir avec celle de Mil huit cent & huit.—Il est arretté, par ces presents, que le dit Convention sera aux *mêmes conditions* que l'acte ci dessus, à l'exception de la seconde article, que sera changer en ce qui suit, Scavoir:—la Marchandises sèches seront à *trente trois & un tier* pour cent, de benefice, sur le pris de Montreal—la poudre—tabac & ferailles à *soixante et quinze* pour cent; et la plomb, vivres, & boissons à cent per cent de Benefice sur même prix—datté à Kamanitiquia l'an Mil huit Cent & cinq le cinq de Juillet & ont signés en presence des temoins

Michel Cadotte

Temoins   W. McGillivray ⎱ Agents
John Pickel, Junr   D. McGillivray ⎰ N.W. Co.

THE NORTH WEST COMPANY 179

Know all men by these Presents that whereas Simon MacTavish, John Gregory, William McGillivray, Duncan McGillivray, William Hallowell, and Roderick McKenzie, Angus Shaw, Donald MacTavish, John Macdonell, Archibald Norman MacLeod, Alexander Macdougall, Charles Chaboillez, John Sayer, Peter Grant, Alexander Fraser, Duncan Cameron, John Finlay, James Hughes, Hugh MacGilles, Alexander Henry, Jean Baptiste Cadotte, John McGillivray, William MacKay, John Macdonald, Duncan Cameron, Alexander MacKay, James McKenzie and Simon Fraser.

Have made and entered into certain Articles of Copartnership for Carrying on a Trade and Commerce in the North West or Indian Country and other Places bearing even date with these Presents—and whereas it is in and by the said articles of Copartnership amongst other things Stipulated and agreed that the Several Parties thereto shall make, and execute a Power of attorney in due form of Law to the said Simon McTavish, John Gregory, William McGillivray, Duncan McGillivray, William Hallowell, and Roderick MacKenzie for the Purpose thereon Contained.

Now know Ye, that the said Angus Shaw, Donald McTavish, John Macdonell, Archibald Norman MacLeod, Alexander Macdougall, Charles Chaboillez, John Sayer, Peter Grant, Alexander Fraser, Aeneas Cameron, John Finlay, James Hughes, Hugh McGilles, Alexander Henry, Jean Baptiste Cadotte, John McGillivray, William MacKay, John Macdonald, Duncan Cameron, Alexander MacKay, James MacKenzie and Simon Fraser.

Have and each of them hath made, Constituted, and appointed, and by these Presents Do and each of them doth make Constitute and appoint the said Simon MacTavish, John Gregory, William McGillivray, Duncan McGillivray, William Hallowell and Roderick MacKenzie, or any two of them of whom the said Simon MacTavish, John Gregory, William McGillivray Duncan McGillivray William Hallowell and Roderick McKenzie shall be one, their Lawful attornies and attorney for the said Constituents, and in their name or names, and to and for their use as Copartners under the aforesaid articles of Agreement, to ask, demand, sue for, recover and receive, all and every such sum and sums of Money, Goods, effects, debts, and demands whatsoever which now are or hereafter may become due by any person or persons whatsoever unto the said Constituents or Copartners as aforesaid and in default of Payment and satisfaction thereof to have, use and take all Lawful ways and means in the name or names of the said Constituents for the recovery thereof by a suit or suits at Law, attachment, arrest or otherwise, to submit the same to Arbitration, and enter into all necessary Bonds to that Effect—Also to Compound and agree for the same, as the said attornies or either of them shall see meet and Case require—and upon receipt and recovery of all or any the said Debts, dues, Sum or Sums of Money, Goods and Effects or any of them, or any part thereof Sufficient acquittances and discharges for the same for the said Constituents and every of them as Copartners as aforesaid to make and give.

As also for the said Constituents and in their name and behalf as Copartners as aforesaid to accede and agree to the retiring and withdrawing of any Partner or Partners from the aforesaid Copartnership and Concern, who may be desirous to retire from the same, upon the terms and Conditions Expressed in the aforesaid articles of agreement or upon such other terms and Conditions as to the said attornies or any two of them as herein before Expressed shall appear advantageous to the said Concern, and to Procure, Receive and Receipt from every such Partner so retiring a sufficient Transfer and assignment in writing of all his Right share and Interest in the said Concern, meant and intended to be made over thereto, agreeable to the aforesaid article of Agreement, and if need be, to appear as Parties on such assignment and for and on behalf of the said Constituents to sign and accept the same.

Also for the said Constituents and in their name and behalf as Copartners as aforesaid, to make and Conclude any bargain, Agreement, Purchase, Sale or other thing touching and Concerning the said Company and Copartnership or the Property thereof as the said attornies or any two of them as herein before Expressed May Conceive to be for the Benefit and advantage of the said Concern and for them the said Constituents and in their name and behalf as Copartners as aforesaid and when the Case may require to Carry into force and Effect all, every, or any of the Resolves made and passed at any of the meetings of the said Concern annually held at the Grand Portage, and to that Effect and whenever the same may be necessary in any of the aforesaid instances, to sign, Seal, execute, and deliver in due form of Law all and every Act Deed and Convention or agreement the said attornies or either of them, Shall or may in the name and behalf aforesaid make, Conclude, and Agree upon, with any person or persons whatsoever in and about the Premises.

And also in Case any loss injury or damage Shall be done or Occasioned to the said Concern or the Interests thereof by any Person or Persons whatsoever, then for the said Constituents and in their name and behalf aforesaid to institute a suit or suits against such person or persons for all such Loss injury or damage, and the same to Carry on and Prosecute until full and entire Satisfaction shall be had and obtained in that behalf, to agree and Compound touching the same, and to give all necessary discharges when Satisfied, and in General to do execute and perform all and every such further and other Lawful and Reasonable acts and Deeds matters and things whatsoever needful and requisite for the several Purposes herein before mentioned as fully and Effectually to all intents and Purposes as the said Constituents or either of them might or could do if Personally Present. The said Constituents hereby willing and intending that the Present power of attorney shall have all the force and Effect meant and intended in and by the aforesaid articles of Copartnership and to Continue and remain until an Express Revocation thereof in Writing signified to the said attornies—and for the better Carrying into Effect all and every the matters herein before mentioned and Contained the said Constituents in their name and Capacity aforesaid Do hereby authorize and empower the said Simon MacTavish, John Gregory, William McGillivray, Duncan McGillivray, William Hallowell, and Roderick MacKenzie to nominate and appoint one or more attorney or attornies under them for the Purposes aforesaid, Ratifying and hereby Promising to ratify allow and Confirm all and whatsoever the said attorneys or any two of them as herein before Expressed shall Lawfully do or cause to be done in and about the Premises by Virtue of these Presents—In witness whereof the said Constituents have hereunto set their Hands and Seals at the Grand Portage the Sixth day of July one Thousand Eight Hundred and two

	Signed Angus Shaw	Jn. McGillivray
Signed sealed	Angus Shaw for	William McKay
& Delivered in	Alexr. Macdougall	William McKay for
Presence of	Donald McTavish	Alexr. McKay
J. C. Stewart	Jno. Macdonell	Duncan Cameron
J. G. MacTavish	A. N. McLeod	Jno. MacDonald
John K. Welles	Jno. Sayer	James McKenzie
	Jno. Finlay	Simon Fraser
	James Hughes	
	Hugh McGillis	
	Alexr. Henry	
	Jean Bte Cadotte	

AT A MEETING of the Proprietors of the North West Company held at Kaminitiquia the 9th day of July 1803

Present William McGillivray   Jno. Sayer
         Duncan McGillivray   James MacKenzie
         William MacKay   Simon Fraser &
         A. N. MacLeod   Duncan Cameron
         Jno. Macdonald

It was Resolved that Mr. David Thomson now in the Companys service at Athabasca be, and he is hereby nominated and appointed to two ninety second Shares in said Company formed by the Agreement enter'd into the 5th day of July 1802—Provided he accepts and Satisfies the same and all its Clauses; his Interest in the same to Commence with the Outfit of the year one Thousand Eight Hundred and four—

	Signed	William McGillivray
Witness	"	Duncan McGillivray
J. C. Stewart	"	William McKay
Jno. K. Welles	"	A. N. McLeod
	"	Jno. Macdonald
	"	Jno. Sayer
	"	James McKenzie
a true Copy	"	Simon Fraser &
J. C. Mackenzie	"	Duncan Cameron

WHEREAS by certain articles of Agreement entered into at the Grand Portage on the fifth day of July one thousand Eight hundred and two, a society or Concern was formed and Constituted under the name and denomination of the North West Compy, to Commence with the Outfit of the year one thousand Eight hundred and three, and to be Composed of certain Persons Parties thereto, and others to be admitted Partners therein and to be conducted, regulated and Carried on under the terms Conditions and stipulations mentioned and Contained in said agreement.

And whereas by the twelfth article of said Agreement, it is stipulated "That from the remote situation of many of the said Parties, their distance from each other, and the Consequent possibility of any or either of them conducting him or themselves in such a manner as to injure the said Concern or its Interest, or otherwise, to render him or themselves unworthy by other improper Conduct of Continuing a partner in the Concern. It is therefore expressly agreed upon, and it is the will and intention of the said Parties to these Present, that when such misconduct or Neglect shall appear evident and Satisfactorily proved to the majority therein before established of the said Concern, and be by them so expressed to the Party or Parties so neglecting or misconducting themselves, he or they may in every such case be expelled from the said Company or Concern and his or their Interest therein shall thereupon cease and determine, and the same shall revert to, and become vested in the said Concern who are hereby authorised to appropriate and dispose of the same in such manner as they shall see fit". And whereas Jean Baptiste Cadotte one of the said Parties to the aforesaid agreement, holding two ninety Second Shares by virtue thereof, in said Concern, Has conducted himself improperly by neglecting his duty and indulging in drunkenness and Riot since the period of the Commencement of the said Copartnership or Concern, whereby he has render'd Himself unworthy and unfit to Continue any Longer a Partner therein. It is therefore unanimously Resolved at a meeting of the Proprietors of the North West

Compy held at Kaminitiquia on the nineteenth day of July one thousand Eight Hundred and three.

   Present William McGillivray Charles Chaboillez
       Duncan McGillivray Peter Grant
       William McKay   Duncan Cameron
       Donald MacTavish   Hugh MacGilles &
       John Macdonald   Alexr. Henry
       A. N. MacLeod

That conformable to the said article Twelfth, the said Jean Baptiste Cadotte be, and, he is, hereby deprived of his said Two ninety second Shares, and he is hereby expelled from the said North West Company and deprived of every Share and Interest therein as fully and effectually as if he had never been a Partner or signed the said Agreement. In Witness the said Parties have hereunto set their Hands and Seals this nineteenth day of July in the year one thousand eight Hundred and three at Kam^a

          Signed William McGillivray
Signed Sealed and   Duncan McGillivray
Delivered in Presence of   William McKay
 Jno K. Welles   Dond McTavish
 J. C. Stewart   Jno. Macdonald
              A. N. McLeod
              Charles Chaboillez
              Peter Grant
              Duncan Cameron
              Hugh McGilles &
              Alexr. Henry

KNOW all men by these Presents, that we William McKay, Donald McTavish, John Macdonald, Archibald Norman McLeod, Charles Chaboillez, Peter Grant, Duncan Cameron, Hugh McGilles and Alexander Henry, Proprietors in the Company or Concern trading to the North West or Indian Country under the name or denomination of the North West Company having taken into Consideration the conduct of Jean Baptist Cadotte one of our Partners in the said Concern holding two ninety second Shares thereof, find it to have been highly improper and inconsistent with his duty and with the Character of a Partner of the North West Company, he having during the last Winter indulged himself in drunkenness and Riot to the great loss and injury of the said Concern.

And whereas by articles of Agreement bearing date the fifth day of July one Thousand Eight Hundred and two by which the said Company is Constituted and appointed, it is expressly Stipulated and agreed upon in the twelfth article thereof that any Partner conducting himself improperly, neglecting his duty or being guilty of other unworthy Conduct, shall be deprived of his Shares and Interest in the said Concern and expelled from the same, by a Majority of the Partners present at any of the Annual Meetings of the Concern held at the Grand Portage or else where, provided such misconduct or neglect shall appear evident and Satisfactorily proved to said Majority, And whereas it does appear evident and satisfactorily proved to us the said William MacKay, Donald MacTavish, John Macdonald, Archibald Norman McLeod, Charles Chaboillez, Peter Grant, Duncan Cameron, Hugh McGilles and Alexander Henry—being all the Wintering Partners present and forming a legal Majority of the Concern, that the said Jean Bte Cadotte has Conducted himself improperly: It is therefore unanimously Resolved the He is unworthy and unfit to Continue any longer in the said Concern or to enjoy any benefit or advantage therefrom and that the said Jean Baptiste Cadotte Conformable to the said Article twelfth in the aforesaid Articles of Agreement, be, and he is hereby deprived of his said two ninety second Shares, and of every right and Interest whatsoever in said Concern, and that he be, and he is hereby expelled from the same, in such manner that every title Interest or Expectation he may held therein may cease and determine from this Period, as fully and Effectually as if he had never been a Partner in the said Concern or never signed the said Agreement—and whereas the said Jean Baptiste Cadotte (Notwithstanding his Scandalous Conduct) May thro' resentment or the instigation of others, be incited to sue or Prosecute the said North West Company or its Agents at Montreal for damages or for a Continuation of his Shares therein.—Now Know ye that We the said William McKay, Donald McTavish, John Macdonald, A. N. McLeod, Charles Chaboillez, Peter Grant, Duncan

Cameron, Hugh MacGilles, and Alexander Henry Have made, named authorized and appointed and by these Presents Do make, name—authorize, and appoint Simon MacTavish Jno Gregory William McGillivray, Duncan McGillivray, William Hallowell and Roderick MacKenzie under the firm of McTavish Frobisher & Coy, our Partners and Agents in the said Concern at Montreal or any two of them, our attornies for us and in our behalf and for themselves as Partners to ratify and Confirm our said Resolve—expelling the said Jean Baptiste Cadotte and to expel— and cause to be expelled in any necessary form of Law the said Jean Baptiste Cadotte from the aforesaid Concern and deprive him as aforesaid of every Share, Right and Interest and expectation therein as Effectually as if the said Jean Bapte Cadotte never had been a Partner in the same and any deed, act or Instrument for this purpose requisite or necessary for us and in our names to sign, seal, Execute, and deliver us, and for our Acts and Deeds, and do or perform every matter and thing which shall be found necessary or requisite for us to Sign, Execute, and deliver, do or Perform in order to Carry into force and effect the said Resolve expelling the said Jean Baptiste Cadotte as aforesaid as fully and Effectually to all intents and purposes as we ourselves might or could do, if personally Present at Montreal—Hereby ratifying, allowing and Confirming all and whatsoever our said attornies for us and for themselves as Partners shall do or Cause to be done in the premises by Virtue of these Presents.

In Witness whereof we have hereunto Set our Hands and Seals at Kaminitiquia this nineteenth day of July in the year of our Lord one Thousand Eight Hundred and three.

	Signed	William MacKay
Signed Sealed and	"	Donald McTavish
delivered in Presence of	"	Jno. Macdonald
Jno. K. Welles signed	"	A. N. MacLeod
J. C. Stewart	"	Charles Chaboillez
	"	Peter Grant
	"	Duncan Cameron
	"	Hugh McGilles &
	"	Alexr. Henry

WHEREAS by Article twenty first of the North West Companys agreement bearing date the thirtieth day of October one Thousand Seven hundred and ninety five, it is Stipulated and agreed, That any Partner or Partners conducting him or themselves in such manner as to injure the Concern established by said agreement or the Interest thereof or otherwise rendering himself or themselves unworthy by other improper Conduct of Continuing a Partner in the same: It is expressly agreed upon that when such Conduct or Neglect shall appear evident and Satisfactorily proved to the Majority of the said Concern, and shall be by them so expressed to the Party or Parties so neglecting or misconducting themselves, He or they may in such case be expelled from the said Company or Concern, and his or their Interest shall thereupon cease and determine, and revert to and become the Property of the Concern.—And whereas at a meeting of the North West Company held at the Grand Portage on the thirtieth of June one Thousand Eight Hundred and one. It was unanimously agreed upon and Resolved that Jean Baptiste Cadotte, then Clerk to the Concern, should be admitted a Partner to hold one forty sixth Share in said North West Company, provided he should formally accept the same.—And whereas the said Jean Bapte Cadotte did on the same day formally Accept the said one forty sixth share, binding himself Strictly to the observance of all Clauses Conditions and Penalties Contained in Said Agreement bearing date the thirtieth day of October one Thousand Seven Hundred and ninety five in as full and ample a Manner as if he had been a Party thereof Originally and had Subscribed his name to the same.—And whereas at a meeting of the North West Compy held at Kaminitiquia on the nineteenth day of July one Thousand Eight Hundred and three to take into Consideration The affairs of the Concern. It does appear evident and satisfactorily proved to the Parties Present (whose name are subscribed underneath) that the said Jean Bapte Cadotte has conducted himself improperly and by neglecting his duty last Winter has caused a severe loss to the Concern, whereby he has rendered himself unworthy of Confidence and of Continuing any longer a Partner in the Said Company—It is thereby Resolved Conformable to the said Article twenty first of said Agreement entered into on the Thirtieth day of October one Thousand Seven

Hundred and ninety five, and afterwards ratified and Confirmed, that the said Jean Bapte Cadotte be, and he is hereby deprived of his Share, and expelled from the Concern, and that his Interest therein shall cease and Determine with the return of the Outfit of the year one Thousand Eight Hundred and two and shall revert to, and become the Property of the Concern, to be by them disposed of as they shall see fit.

In Witness whereof the Parties present have hereto set their Hands and Seals at Kam[a] this nineteenth day of July one Thousand Eight Hundred and three

Signed Sealed and Delivered in the Presence of Jno K. Welles J. C. Stewart } Sd	Signed William McGillivray for self & McTavish Frobisher & Co	15
	Duncan McGillivray	
	William McKay	1
	Peter Grant	1
	A. N. MacLeod	1
	Dond McTavish	1
	Duncan Cameron	1
	Charles Chaboillez	1
	Hugh McGilles	1
	Jno Macdonald	1
	Alexr Henry	1
	Jno McDonald for Jas Hughes	1
	A. N. McLeod for Jno Finlay	1

Votes 26

KNOW all men by these Presents, whereas Simon MacTavish, John Gregory, William McGillivray, Duncan McGillivray, William Hallowell and Roderick McKenzie, Composing the firm of McTavish Frobisher & Coy, Angus Shaw, Daniel MacKenzie, William MacKay, Donald MacTavish, John Macdonald, Archibald Norman McLeod, John Macdonald, Alexander Macdougall, Charles Chaboillez, John Sayer, Peter Grant, Alexander Fraser, Aneas Cameron, John Finlay, Duncan Cameron, James Hughes, Hugh McGilles, Alexander Henry, John McGillivray, Alexander MacKay, James McKenzie, and Simon Fraser, now carrying on Trade and Com-

THE NORTH WEST COMPANY 189

merce to the North West or Indian Country and other places as Copartners under the name and designation of the North West Company, under certain articles of Agreement for that Purpose made and entered into bearing date at the Grand Portage the fifth day of July one thousand eight hundred and two. And whereas the said Company having Confidence in the integrity and abilities of John Duncan Campbell heretofore one of their Clerks, and being desirous of admitting him as a Partner in the said Company and Concern for one of the Shares therein now Vacant, and unappropriated under the Terms and Conditions in the said articles of Agreement mentioned and Contained—Now Know Ye that the said William McGillivray, Duncan MacGillivray, William MacKay, Donald MacTavish, A. N. McLeod, John Macdonald, Charles Chaboillez, Peter Grant, Duncan Cameron, Hugh MeGilles, and Alexr Henry, being present and the said William McGillivray and Duncan McGillivray as Attornies for and on behalf of the said Simon McTavish, John Gregory, William Hallowell, Roderick MacKenzie, Angus Shaw, Daniel MacKenzie, John Macdonell, Alexander Macdougall, John Sayer, Alexander Fraser, Aneas Cameron, John Finlay, James Hughes, John McGillivray, Alexander MacKay, James MacKenzie, and Simon Fraser, being absent from this Place, have sold, assigned, and made over, and by these Presents, do sell, assign, and make over to the said John Duncan Campbell, Now present and accepting, one full and equal ninety second Share in the aforesaid Company and Concern, beginning with the Outfit for the Year one thousand Eight Hundred and four being half of the Forty sixth share vacanted by Alexander MacLeod, on his Retiring last year under the North West Companys Agreement bearing date the Thirtieth day of October one Thousand Seven Hundred ninety and Five, and one of the ninety second Shares declined by said Alexr MacLeod in the Present Agreement dated the fifth day of July 1802) with all and every the right, benefits, and advantages, arising or to arise therefrom—To have and to Hold the said ninety second Share in the aforesaid Company or Concern, and all other the Premises hereby Resolved and assigned unto the said John Duncan Campbell, agreeable to the Terms and Conditions of the aforesaid articles of Agreement dated the fifth day of July one Thousand Eight Hundred and two, as fully and Effectually to all intents and Purposes, as any of the before named Persons, being Partners in said Concern, now hold, exercise and enjoy their respective shares therein.—And whereas the said John Duncan Campbell by Virtue of this assignment hath become Partner in the aforesaid Company and Concern but not having been a Party to the aforesaid Articles of Agreement under and by virtue of which the said Company and Concern is constituted and Carried on, and this assignment made, and being desirous and willing in every respect to Conform and Comply with all and every the said Articles of Agreement which he now declares to have read and Perused, and to be therewith fully satisfied and Consenting thereto for that Purpose hath, and hereby doth bind and oblige himself Strictly to observe, comply with and submit to all and every the Clauses Stipulations, Penalties and obligations in the aforesaid articles of agreement mentioned and contained and every rule and regulations made or to be made, under and by Virtue thereof respecting the said Trade and Commerce as fully and effectually to all intents and Purposes as if the said John Duncan Campbell had been a Party thereto, had and with the Other Partners therein named signed and Subscribed the same, willing and intending that these Presents shall have the same force and effect.

In witness whereof the said Parties to these Presents have to two Parts thereof interchangeable set their Hands & Seals at Kaminitiquia this twenty second day of July one Thousand Eight Hundred and three.

	Signed	John Duncan Campbell
Signed Sealed and Delivd	"	William McGillivray
in Presence of	"	Duncan McGillivray
J. C. Stewart	"	William McKay
H. MacKenzie	"	Donald MacTavish
	"	A. N. McLeod
	"	Jno Macdonald
	"	Charles Chaboillez
	"	Peter Grant
		Duncan Cameron
		Hugh McGilles
		Alexr Henry

KNOW all men by these Presents, that whereas John Duncan

Campbell hath by an Act bearing even date with these Presents been admitted a Partner for one ninety second Share in the Company and Concern now carried on to the North West or Indian Country, by Simon MacTavish, John Gregory, William McGillivray, Duncan McGillivray, William Hallowell and Roderick MacKenzie, Composing the firm of McTavish Frobisher & Co, Angus Shaw, Daniel MacKenzie, William MacKay, Donald MacTavish, John Macdonell, Archibald Norman McLeod, John Macdonald, Alexander Macdougall, Charles Chaboillez, John Sayer, Peter Grant, Alexr Fraser, Aeneas Cameron, John Finlay, Duncan Cameron, James Hughes, Hugh McGilles, Alexander Henry, John McGillivray, James MacKenzie and Simon Fraser, under the name and designation of the North West Company, under certain Articles of Copartnership for that Purpose made and entered into bearing date the fifth day of July one thousand Eight hundred and two, and whereas in and by the said Articles of Agreement or Copartnership, it is amongst other things Stipulated and agreed, that every new Partner coming into the Concern shall make and execute a Power of Attorney in due form of Law to Simon MacTavish, John Gregory, William McGillivray, Duncan McGillivray, William Hallowell, and Roderick MacKenzie, for the Purpose therein contained. Now Know Ye that the said John Duncan Campbell hath made Constituted and appointed, & by these Presents doth make, Constitute and appoint the said Simon MacTavish, John Gregory, William McGillivray, Duncan McGillivray, William Hallowell, and Roderick McKenzie, or any two of them, of whom the said Simon MacTavish, John Gregory, William McGillivray, Duncan McGillivray, William Hallowell and Roderick McKenzie, shall be one, his Lawful attornies and attorney for the said Constituent, and in his name, and to and for his use as Copartner under the aforesaid Articles of Agreement, to ask demand, sue for Recover and receive all and every such sum and sums of Money, Goods, Effects debts and demands whatsoever which now are or may hereafter become due by any Person or Persons whatsoever unto the said John Duncan Campbell as Partner as aforesaid; And in default of Payment, and satisfaction thereof to have, use and take all Lawful ways and means in the name of the said John Duncan Campbell for the recovery thereof by a suit or suits at Law, attachment, arrest or otherwise, to submit the same to arbitration, and enter into all necessary bonds to that effect, also to Compound and agree for the same, as the said attornies or either of them shall see, meet, and the case require, and upon receipt and recovery of all or any the said Debts, dues, sum or sums of Money, Goods and Effects or any of them, or any part thereof. Sufficient acquittances, and discharges, for the same for the said John Duncan Campbell, as Copartner as aforesaid to make and give. As also for the said John Duncan Campbell and in his name, and behalf as Copartner as aforesaid to accede and agree to the Retiring and withdrawing of any Partner or Partners from the aforesaid Copartnership and Concern, who may be desirous to retire from the same, upon the Terms and Conditions expressed in the aforesaid articles of Agreement, or upon such other Terms and Conditions as to the said attornies or any two of them as herein before Expressed, shall appear advantageous to the said Concern, and to Procure, receive and accept from every such Partner so retiring a sufficient Transfer and assignment in writing of all his rights share and Interest in the said Concern, mean and intended to be made overthereto agreeable to the aforesaid Articles of Agreement, and if need be, to appear as Parties in Such assignment, and for and on behalf of the said Said John Duncan Campbell—to sign and accept the same.

Also for the said John Duncan Campbell and in his name and behalf as Copartner as aforesaid to make and Conclude any Bargain, Agreement, Purchase, Sale or other thing touching and Concerning the said Company and Copartnership or the Property thereof as the said attornies or any two of them as herein before Expressed may conceive to be for the benefit and advantage of the said Concern and for him the said John Duncan Campbell and in his name, and behalf as Copartner, as aforesaid, and when the case may require to carry into force and Effect all, every, or any of the Resolves made, and passed at any meeting of the Partners of the said Concern held annually at Kaminitiquia, and to Effect and whenever the same may be necessary in any of the aforesaid instances, to sign, seal, execute, and deliver in due form of Law all and every Act deed, Convention or agreement the said attornies or either of them, shall or may in the name and behalf aforesaid, make, Conclude, and agree upon with any Person or Persons whatsoever in and about the Premises.—And also in case any loss, injury or damage, shall be done, or Occasioned to the said Concern or the Interest thereof by any Person or Persons whatsoever, then for the said John Duncan Campbell and in his name and behalf aforesaid to institute, a suit or suits against such Person or Persons for all such less, injury or damage and the same to Carry on and Prosecute until full and entire satisfaction shall be had and obtained, on that behalf to agree and Compound touching the same, and to give all and necessary discharges when satisfied—and in general to do execute, and Perform all and every such further and other Lawful and reasonable acts, and deeds matters and things whatsoever needful and requisite for the several Purposes herein before mentioned as fully and Effectually to all intents and Purposes as the said John Duncan Campbell might or could do if Personally present.

The said John Duncan Campbell hereby willing and intending that the Present Power of attorney shall have all the force and Effect meant, and intended in and by the aforesaid Articles of Agreement, and to Continue and remain until an express revocation thereof in writing signified to the said Attorneys—And for the better Carrying into effect all and every the matters herein before mentioned and Contained the said John Duncan Campbell in his name and Capacity aforesaid doth hereby authorize and empower the said Simon MacTavish, John Gregory, William McGillivray, Duncan MacGillivray, William Hallowell and Roderick McKenzie to nominate and appoint one or more attorney or attornies under them for the purpose aforesaid—Ratifying, and hereby Promising to ratify allow and Confirm all and whatsoever the said attornies or any two of them as herein before expressed shall Lawfully do or cause to be done in and about the Premises by Virtue of these Presents.

In witness whereof the said John Duncan Campbell hath hereunto Set his Hand and Seal at Kam^a this twenty second day of July one Thousand Eight Hundred and three.

Signed John Duncan Campbell

Signed Sealed and Delivered
in Presence of
J. C. Stewart } Signed
H. MacKenzie

WHEREAS the great sacrifices occasioned by the Opposition carrying on against the North West Company for five years successively and other causes, have considerably diminished the profits on the shares, and seems to point out the necessity of adopting every measure by the concerned, that can tend to retrench expenses and introduce a system of Economy throughout the Country. And as it appears essential to the adoption of this system that certain regulations should be fixed upon, respecting the management of different Branches of the business in future—the Freight and Transport of their property and Canoes and the proper distribution of their Engagés going into and coming out from the Wintering Posts, becomes a matter of the greatest importance. The undersigned Proprietors therefore, at a general Meeting held at Kamanitiquia the fourth and afterwards the tenth day of July One thousand eight hundred and four, after due consideration have come to the following Resolves.—

1st That the practice of making use of Light Canoes by Proprietors be entirely abolished throughout the North West departments.

2d That every Proprietor shall attend his Canoes in Person *in going in to and coming out* from the Wintering Grounds.

3d That no Proprietor shall have a less Load in his Canoe than Eight pieces *under the regular Load of the Canoes of his Brigade*, this to make room for his Baggage.

4th That no Proprietor shall have more than one Man, over and above the number that are in his loaded Canoes.

And as the want of punctuality in acting up to the above restrictions and regulations, must be attended with great & unnecessary expence to the Company—Any Proprietor failing to conform thereto, shall forfeit to the Concern the sum of Fifty pounds for every extra Man he may take into his Canoe either in going in, or in coming out and the sum of ten pounds for every piece of Goods he may have in his Canoe less than the number above specified.—It being however necessary that the Companys Agents at Kamanitiquia should be informed as early as possible every Spring of the occurrences at the different departments after the departure of the Winter Express. It is resolved, that one light Canoe shall be appropriated to this purpose which shall collect all the letters the Proprietors may have to forward from their respective Quarters—for which purpose they will have such Papers as they wish to send in readiness on the road when the Canoe passes, And as one of the Proprietors of the Athabasca department should come annually to Kamanitiquia—it is thought necessary and proper that the Light Canoe shall come from that department only, it being otherways out of the power of such Proprietor to come out in time

                      Signed   W McGillivray
Witness J. C. Stewart   Rod McKenzie
   "   John Pickel   W McKay
                                       James Hughes
                                       Archd No: McLeod
                                       Charles Chaboillez
                                       David Thompson
                                       Alex Henry
                                       Alexander Fraser
                                     Duncan Cameron
                                     John Mcdonald
                                     Dond McTavish
                                     John McGillivray
                                     H MacGillies
                                     John Duncan Campbell

WHEREAS by the seventeenth Article of the North West Agreement bearing date at the Grand portage the fifth day of July One thousand eight hundred and two, It is stipulated and agreed upon that whenever it is found from experience, that the expence of transporting Goods from Montreal to the place of Rendezvous, and from thence to the Posts in the Interior shall have encreased or diminished,—it shall be in the power of the Concern to change and alter the same according to the true expence and Cost of the Transport of such Goods:—And it appearing to the Concern by correct calculation that the present Freight and advance are inadequate to form the just value of Goods at the place of Rendezvous and in the Posts of the Interior:—The undersigned Proprietors, forming a legal majority of the North West Company; At a meeting held at Kamanitiquia the tenth day of July in the year of Lord one thousand eight hundred and four—have come to the following determination.—Resolved Unanimously, that the Property belonging to this Concern shall henceforth be valued, at all the Posts and settlements of the Company in the North West, and on Lake Superior, according to, and at the rates of Advance or percentage of *The Tariff or Schedule* hereunto annexed, and not otherwise; The said evaluation and advance to commence with the Inventories assumed by, and composing part of the present Outfit 1804 and henceforward to be continued.—All Proprietors (and by their Orders) persons having Goods in charge to class or assort their Inventories conformable to said Schedule

(Signed) by the Parties as above:

Witnessed as above

KNOW all Men by these presents, Whereas Simon McTavish, John Gregory, William McGillivray, Duncan McGillivray, William Hallowell and Roderic McKenzie, composing the firm of McTavish Frobisher and Company and Angus Shaw, Daniel McKenzie, William McKay, John Mcdonald, Donald McTavish, John Mcdonald, Donald McTavish, John Mcdonell, Archibald Norman McLeod, Alexander Mcdougall, Charles Chaboillez, John Sayer, Peter Grant, Alexander Fraser, Aneas Cameron, John Finlay, Duncan Cameron, James Hughes, Alexander McKay, Hugh McGillies, Alexander Henry, John McGillivray, James McKenzie, Simon Fraser and John Duncan Campbell now carrying on Trade and Commerce to the North West or Indian Country and other places as Copartners under the name and designation of the North West Company under certain Articles of Agreement for that purpose made and entered into bearing date at the Grand portage the fifth day of July one thousand eight hundred and two; and whereas the said Company having confidence in the Integrity and abilities of David Thompson heretofore one of their Clerks and being desirous of admitting him as a Partner in the said Company and Concern for two of the shares therein now vacant and unappropriated under the terms & conditions in the said Article of Agreement mentioned and contained Now Know ye that the said William McGillivray Roderic McKenzie William McKay John Mcdonald, Donald McTavish, Archibald Norman McLeod, Charles Chaboillez, Alexander Fraser, Duncan Cameron James Hughes Hugh McGillies

Tariff or Schedule referred to in the annexed Resolve of the North West Company.

At Batchiwina, Michipicoton and the Pic, Twenty per cent advance on the Cost at Montreal of all Goods as imported, *without distinction of Pieces*: At Kamanitiquiâ, Twenty three per cent advance on the Montreal Cost of all Goods without reserve.

	To the Fond du Lac Department	To the Nipigon department and dependencies	To Lac La Pluie—Lac Ouinipique—Upper & Lower Red River & Fort Dauphin	To Forts des Prairies or the Rivière Opas departments	To the English River and dependencies	To the Upper Athabasca River	To Athabasca & Dependencies	
On dry Goods comprehending Bales, Cassettes, Cases Guns—Knives, Hats; and Baskets of Kettles	26	45	45	60	65	70	80	per cent advance on the Cost and Advance to Kamanitiquiâ of the different classes of Goods as per Margin.
On Tobacco	65	105	105	150	155	175	210	
On Gunpowder	53	90	90	125	130	140	170	
On High Wines	130	210	210	305	310	350	420	
On Shot & Ball	167	375	375	350	360	400	490	
On Iron Works	105	130	130	165	170	190	230	
N:B the foregoing Goods assorted, average	55	87	87	112	113	123	130	
And the average Freight of each Piece indiscriminately is	£4.10/	£7.10/	£7.10/	£10.15/	£11./	£12.5/	£14.16/	per cent on the Cost & Advance above specified Halifax Currency

Alexander Henry John McGillivray and John Duncan Campbell, being present, and the said William McGillivray and Roderic McKenzie as Attorneys for and on behalf of the said Simon McTavish John Gregory Duncan McGillivray, William Hallowell, Angus Shaw, Daniel McKenzie, John Mcdonell, Alexander Mcdougall, John Sayer, Peter Grant, Aneas Cameron, John Finlay, Alexander McKay, James McKenzie and Simon Fraser being absent from this place, have sold, assigned and made over and by these presents, do sell, assign and make over to the said David Thompson, now present and accepting, two full and equal Ninety-second shares in the aforesaid Company and Concern, beginning with the Outfit for the present year one thousand eight hundred and four (being the two ninety second Shares that became vacant by the expulsion of Jean Baptiste Cadotte by virtue of a certain Instrument of the Concern bearing date at this place the nineteenth day of July one thousand eight hundred and three) with all and every the rights benefits and advantages arising or to arise therefrom, to have and to hold the said two ninety second shares in the aforesaid Company or Concern and all other the premeses hereby resolved and assigned unto the said David Thompson, agreeable to the terms and Conditions of the aforesaid Articles of Agreement dated the fifth day of July One thousand eight hundred and two, as fully and effectually to all interests and purposes, as any of the before named Persons, being Partners in the said Concern, now hold exercise and enjoy their respective shares therein. And whereas the said David Thompson by virtue of this assignment hath become a Partner in the aforesaid Company and Concern, but not having been a Party to the aforesaid Articles of Agreement under and by virtue of which the said Company and Concern is constituted and carried on and this assignment made, and being desirous and willing in every respect to conform to and comply with all and every the said Articles of Agreement which he now declares to have read and perused and to be therewith fully satisfied and consenting thereto, for that purpose hath and hereby doth bind and oblige himself strictly to observe, comply with, and submit to all and every the clauses stipulations penalties and obligations in the aforesaid Articles of Agreement mentioned and contained and every rule and regulation made, or to be made, under and by virtue thereof respecting the said Trade and Commerce,

THE NORTH WEST COMPANY

as fully and effectually, to all intents and purposes as if the said David Thompson had been a Party thereto, and had with the other Partners therein named Signed and subscribed the same, willing and intending that these presents shall have the same force and effect. In Witness whereof the said Parties to these presents have to two parts thereof interchangeable set their hands and Seal at Kamanitiquia this tenth day of July in the year of our Lord one thousand eight hundred and four.

		Signed—Wm Gillivray	LS
Signed sealed and delivered in the presence of		" Roderic McKenzie	"
		" Wm McKay	"
J. C. Stewart		" John Mcdonald	"
John Pickel		" Dond McTavish	"
& counter-		" Arch No: McLeod	"
Signed, also		" Charles Chaboillez Junr	"
Wm Gillivray (LS)	as & pro-	" Alexr Fraser	"
Rod McKenzie(")	curation	" James Hughes	"
	from, and	" Duncan Cameron	"
as Attorneys for		" H MacGilles	"
Simon McTavish	LS	" Alexr Henry	"
John Gregory	"	" John McGillivray	"
Duncan McGillivray	"	" John Duncan Campbell	"
Willm Hallowell	"	" David Thompson	"
Angus Shaw	"		
Danl McKenzie	"		
John Mcdonell	"		
Alexr Mcdougall	"		
John Sayer	"		
Peter Grant	"		
Æneas Cameron	"		
John Finlay	"		
Alexr McKay	"		
James McKenzie	"		
Simon Fraser	"		

KNOW all men by these Presents, That Whereas David Thompson hath, by an act bearing even date with these Presents, been admitted a Partner for Two Ninety second Shares in the Company and Concern now carried into the North West or Indian Country by Simon McTavish, John Gregory, William McGillivray, Duncan MacGillivray, William Hallowell and Roderick MacKenzie. Composing the Firm of MacTavish Frobisher And Company, and Angus Shaw, Daniel McKenzie, William MacKay, John Macdonald, Donald MacTavish, John Macdonell, Archibald Norman MacLeod, Alexander Macdougall, Charles Chaboillez, John Sayer, Peter Grant, Alexander Fraser, Æneas Cameron, John Finlay, Duncan Cameron, James Hughes, Alexander MacKay, Hugh MacGillis, Alexander Henry, John MacGillivray, James Mackenzie, Simon Fraser and John Duncan Campbell—now carrying on Trade and Commerce to the North West or Indian Country, under the Name and designation of the NW Company, under certain articles of Copartnership for that purpose made and entered into bearing Date the fifth Day of July One Thousand Eight Hundred and Two, and whereas in and by the said articles of agreement or Copartnership, it is amongst other Things stipulated and agreed, that every new Partner, coming into the Concern shall make and execute a power of attorney in due form of Law to Simon MacTavish, John Gregory, William MacGillivray, Duncan MacGillivray, William Hallowell, and Roderick MacKenzie for the Purposes therein Contained. Now Know Ye, that the said David Thompson, Hath made, constituted and appointed, and by these Presents doth make, constitute and appoint the said Simon MacTavish, John Gregory, William MacGillivray, Duncan MacGillivray, William Hallowell and Roderick MacKenzie, or any Two of them of whom the said Simon MacTavish, John Gregory, William MacGillivray, Duncan MacGillivray, William Hallowell and Roderick MacKenzie shall be one, his Lawful attornies, and attorney for the said Constituent; and in his name, and to and for his use, as Copartners under the aforesaid articles of agreement, to ask, demand, sue for, recover and receive, all and every such sum and sums of money, Goods, Effects, Debts, and Demands whatsoever, which now are, or may hereafter become due by any Person or Persons whatsoever unto the said David Thompson—as Partner, as aforesaid, and in Default of payment, and satisfaction thereof to have, use, and take all Lawful ways and means in the name of the said David Thompson for the recovery thereof by a Suit or Suits at Law, attachment, arrest, or otherwise to submit the same to Arbitration, and enter into all necessary Bonds to that effect, also to compound and agree for the same as the said attornies, or either of them shall see meet, and the case require and upon receipt and recovery, of all or any the said Debts, dues, sum or sums of money, Goods, and effects, or any of them, or any part thereof, sufficient acquittances and discharges, for the same, for the said David Thompson as Copartner as aforesaid to make and Give—As also for the said David Thompson, and in his Name and behalf as Copartner as aforesaid to accede and agree to the retiring and with drawing of any Partner or Partners from the aforesaid Copartnership and Concern who may be desirous to retire from the same, upon the Terms and Conditions expressed in the aforesaid articles of agreement or upon such other Terms and Conditions, as to the said attornies or any two of them as herein before expressed, shall appear advantageous to the said Concern and to procure, receive, secure, and accept from every such Partners so retiring a sufficient Transfer and assignment in Writing of all his Rights, share and Interest in the Said Concern, meant and intended to be made over thereto—agreeable to the aforesaid articles of agreement and if need be, to appear as Parties in such assignment and for and on behalf of the said David Thompson—to sign & accept the same—

Also for the said David Thompson, and in his name and behalf as copartner as aforesaid, to make and Conclude any Bargain agreement Purchase sale or other Things touching and Concerning the said Company and Copartnership or the Property thereof as the said attornies, or any two of them as herein before expressed may conceive to be for the Benefit and advantage of the said Concern, and for him the said David Thompson And in his name, and behalf as copartner as aforesaid and when the case may re-require to and any into Force and effectual, every, or any of the Resolves made, and passed at any meeting of the Partners of the said Concern held annually at Kamanitiquia, and to effect. And whenever the same may be necessary in any of the aforesaid Instances to sign, seal, execute and deliver in due form of Law all and every act, deed, convention and agreement, the said attornies or either of them shall or may in the name and behalf aforesaid, make, conclude—and agree upon with any Person or Persons whatsoever in and about the Premises, and also in case any Loss injury, or damage, shall be done or occasioned to the said Concern or the Interest thereof by any Person or Persons whatsoever therefor the said David Thompson and in his name and behalf aforesaid to institute a suit or suits against such Person or Persons for all such Loss Injury of damage and the same to carry on and prosecute until full and entire satisfaction shall be had and obtained on that behalf to agree and compound touching the Same And to give all and necessary discharges when satisfied, And in general to do execute, and perform all and every such further and other Lawful and reasonable acts, and Deeds, matters & things whatsoever, needful and requisite for the several Purposes herein before mentioned as fully and effectually to all intents and Purposes as the same David Thompson might or could do if personally present. The said David Thompson hereby willing and intending that the present Power of attorney shall have all the Force and effect meant And intended, in and by the aforesaid articles of agreement and to continue And remain until an express revocation thereof in Writing signified to the said attornies.—And for the better carrying into effect all and every the matters herein before mentioned And Contained, the said David Thompson in his name and Capacity aforesaid doth hereby authorise & impower the dsai Simon MacTavish John Gregory, William MacGillivray, Duncan MacGillivray, William Hallowell and Roderick MacKenzie to Nominate and appoint one or more attorney or attornies under them for the Purpose aforesaid, Ratifying and hereby promising to ratify, allow and confirm all and whatsoever the said attornies or any Two of them as herein before expressed shall Lawfully do or cause to be done in and about the Premises by Virtue of these Present.

In witness whereof the said David Thompson hath hereunto set his Hand and Seal at Kamanitiquia this Tenth Day of July One Thousand Eight Hundred and Four

Signed sealed and delivered
   in the presence of
    J. C. Stewart
    John Pickel

signed David Thompson

RESOLVE fixing the advance of Goods for Clerks in the Interior passed 1805. It is understood that henceforth, the Prices of Goods at the Places of Rendezvous—say Kamanitiquia & Lac La Pluie

THE NORTH WEST COMPANY 203

to every Clerk or other who—by their agreement have the Goods at Diminish'd Prices—shall be as follows—
100 per Cent to be charged on the cost of Goods at Montreal for the risk, trouble & Freight attending bringing such Goods from Montreal to the place of Rendezvous—And 50 per Cent on the above Prices from the Place of Rendezvous to the different Departments & Posts in every part of the interior Country—to all Clerks, who have an opportunity of purchasing goods, at the Place of General Rendezvous—but 100 per Cent only on the Montreal Prices shall be the Cost of Goods to those who remain to pass the Summer in Land, or, who do not order things from the place of Rendezvous by their Friends—
No Clerk on any Pretence whatever shall be allowed to carry on Traffic with men or others, it being understood they only purchase such articles as are absolutely required for their own use—
The allowance of 20£ to Partners & Clerks in lieu of equipments—having (from being so general) become an abuse—& Consequently attended with Loss & inconvenience. It is understood the custom shall henceforth cease & determine—except to such Clerks as are by express agreement settled with Otherwise—

AT A MEETING of the proprietors of the North West Company held at Kamanistiquia on the 6th Day of July 1805—to consider of the present State of the Negotiation with the Hudsons Bay Company, for obtaining a transit for their property thro' Hudson Bay to the North West or interior Country: And also to decide on the proper Measures to be adopted for bringing the Said Negociation to a favorable conclusion; It was resolved that (as it appears that the Said Hudsons Bay Company are not disposed to grant such a transit, without Compensation, or as they themselves express it 'without sufficient indemnity & security' to be given on the part of the North West Company,) the Agents of the concern shall be & they are hereby authorized & directed to offer to the Said Hudsons Bay Company—a sum not exceeding Two thousand pounds sterling (or there about,) a Year, for such transit, for a period to be agreed upon—providing they consent that the North West Company, Shall establish a free communication with the interior Country, by Nelson or Hayes' Rivers, without being Subject to any interference or molestation whatever; And as the object is of importance, the Agents of the Concern are also directed & Authorized (as an additional advantage to the Hudsons Bay Company) to propose withdrawing the posts of the North West Company from East Main & Moose River, & to agree to relinquish in future the whole trade of the Coast of Hudsons Bay to themselves, reserving only the right of establishing as the Concern may see fit, the Communication with the inland Country by York Factory, that their property may be carried backward & forward without hindrance or obstruction, on the part of the Hudsons Bay Company.

And it is also resolved that should the above proposals be accepted, or should any Amicable Arrangement be effected, (without which the Concern must relinquish their present views in Hudsons Bay) the said Agents are directed to take, without loss of time the proper measures for commencing the necessary operation in the Bay.

In Witness Whereof the parties present have hereto set their hand, place and date above stated—

Signed—William McGillivray
" Roderick McKenzie
" Duncan McGillivray
" Daniel McKenzie
" William McKay
" John McDonald
" A. Norman McLeod
" Hugh McGillis
" Alexander Henry
" Duncan Cameron
" Alexr Fraser
" Alexr McKay
" John Duncan Campbell
" John McGillivray
" Thomas Thain
" James Leith
" John Haldane
" Chs. Chaboillez
" John Sayer
" John McDonell

THE NORTH WEST COMPANY

AT A MEETING of the proprietors of the North West Company held at Kamanistiquia on the 5th day of July 1805 to take into consideration the services, & Claims of their Clerks: It was unanimously resolved that Archibald McLellan, Ranald Cameron, & C. O. Ermatinger should be the first Clerks provided for—And that in consideration of their services & the expectations which they have at different times received from the Concern, & also to stimulate them to continue their zeal & good conduct in the discharge of their duty—that they be forthwith informed, that it is the intention of the Concern to assign over to them respectively one share or hundredth part of the North West Company for the Outfit of the Year 1808, providing they be disposed to receive the Same on the Conditions contained in the North West Company's agreement, bearing date the 5th July 1802—and providing also that their Conduct in the interior Should Continue to meet the approbation of their Employers—

In Witness whereof the proprietors present have hereto set their hands this 5th day of July 1805 above stated—

Signed William McGillivray
" Duncan McGillivray
" Roderick McKenzie
" Daniel McKenzie
" William McKay
" John McDonald
" A. Norman McLeod
" Hugh McGillis
" Alexander Henry
" Duncan Cameron
" Alexander Fraser
" John Duncan Campbell
" Alexander McKay
" John McGillivray
" Charles Chaboillez
" John McDonell
" John Sayer

AT A MEETING of the proprietors of the North West Company held at Kamanistiquia on the 6th day of July 1805 to take into consideration the best mode of carrying into effect the Coalition Agreement, but more particularly that part of it which regards the extension of the Concern from Ninety two to One hundred shares—the following resolutions were agreed upon vizt—Whereas by the said Agreement bearing date at Montreal the 5th day of November 1804, it is stipulated & agreed upon in the 2nd Article thereof, that until the North West Company, be encreased from 92 to a 100 Shares, the Old Company shall account to the New Company, Yearly, for one fourth part of all profits or losses arising from the Concern, but when such extension or increase of Shares shall have taken place, it is stipulated & agreed upon, that Twenty five out of the Hundred Shares shall be assigned over to the said new Company in lieu of the said fourth part—And Whereas the following shares shall be at the disposal of the Concern for the Outfit next ensuing vizt—Two Ninety Seconds to be relinquished by each of the following Gentlemen at the Close of the present Outfit vizt Roderick McKenzie, Alexander McLeod, William Thorburn, Simon Fraser, James Finlay & Cuthbert Grant: And one Ninety Second Share relinquished by Peter Grant & John Finlay, respectively forming in all fourteen vacant Shares. And Whereas it is necessary & expedient for carrying the above article into effect, that Eight new Shares, should be created in addition to the above said Ninety two Shares, forming in all one Hundred Shares, to constitute in future the North West Company, which said 8 new Shares added to the said 14 vacant Shares will make 22 Vacant Shares to be disposed of & appropriated as the Concern may see fit & proper. And Whereas it is very desirable to carry the above Article 2nd into effect as soon as possible, according to the true intent & Meaning of it, it is therefore proposed to reserve the said 22 Vacant Shares for this purpose, but as three Shares are still wanting to complete the Number required—the agents of the Company as a mark of their good will & disinterestedness to the Wintering partners, have presented the Concern with three of the Shares holden by McTavish Frobisher & Co. (to be returned out of the first Vacant Shares falling in to the Concern as is more fully explained & set forth in a letter of the 5th instant) which will Enable the Concern to execute the Said Second Article for the Outfit of 1806—by assigning Over to the New Company 25 hundredth Shares, instead of the fourth part to which they are in the interim entitled—

It is therefore resolved that the said 8 new Shares be And they are hereby created, and added to the 92 Shares of which the Concern at present Consists, forming in all One Hundred Shares, to constitute in future the North West Company, and the said 100 Shares & each of them shall be held & enjoyed under all the Clauses, Conditions, & Stipulations, mentioned & set forth in the North West Company's agreement dated the 5th July 1802, And that in every Case & question touching the Said agreement the said 100 Shares & each of them shall be considered as synonimous with the said 92 Shares, in as much as regards the rights & privileges of the respective parties holding the same—it being understood that with the said Outfit of 1806, every such 92d Shall in future become a Hundredth, of all profits & losses arising to the Concern. And it is further resolved that the said Vacant Twenty five Shares or hundredth parts, being equal to one fourth part of the Concern, shall be relinquished, & they are hereby assigned & made Over to the said New Company, according to the tenor of the said Coalition Agreement to be held & enjoyed by them as is therein set forth—

In Witness Whereof the proprietors present have hereto set their hand, place & date above Stated—

(Signed)	William McGillivray	⎫
"	Duncan McGillivray	⎬ 30
"	Roderick McKenzie	⎭
"	William McKay	2
"	John McDonald	2
"	A. Norman McLeod	2
"	Hugh McGillis	2
"	Alexr Henry	2
"	Duncan Cameron	2
"	John McGillivray	2
"	Alexr Fraser	2
"	John Duncan Campbell	1
"	Alexr McKay	2
"	Charles Chaboillez	2
"	John McDonell	2
"	John Sayer	2

Shares 55

Rotation

In the year 1799 The Partners by mutual agreement drew Lots for their Rotations they were accordingly fixt in the following Manner—Three to go to Montreal each year—

Angus Shaw Alexr McLeod Alexr Fraser	first year—or	1800
Peter Grant William McKay Daniel McKenzie	second year—	1801
John McDonald John Sayer A. N. McLeod	third year—	1802
Donald McTavish John Finlay John McDonell	fourth year—	1803
& Charles Chaboillez		1804

This List of names comprehends all the Wintering Partners of the NWCo. in 1799 except Mr. Roderick McKenzie

And it was carried by a majority of Votes that this Rotation should commence with the year 1800 only—notwithstanding which decision Mr. Roderick McKenzie was permitted to go down in Rotation in 1799—

On forming the new agreement the 5th July 1802 a new List was made by resolve—the Partners were accordingly placed in the following order for Rotation (The agreement giving a Power to the Annual Meeting at the places of Rendezvous to declare what number of Partners shall go to Montreal in One Year)

William McKay	Donald McTavish
Arch: N. McLeod	John McDonald
Peter Grant	John Sayer
Daniel McKenzie	John McDonell

THE NORTH WEST COMPANY

John Finlay	Alexr Henry
Chs Chaboillez	John McGillivray
Duncan Cameron	James McKenzie
James Hughes	&
Alexr McKay	Simon Fraser—
Hugh McGillis	

Alexander Fraser went to Montreal in Rotation according to the first List in 1801—

And was employed in the year 1802 & 1803 as a Partner assisting the Company's Concerns in the Kings Posts & Hudsons Bay he returned to the North West in 1804—

In 1802 William McKay & A. N. McLeod having declared their Intentions of availing themselves of their Right to go down that year—they were requested to Winter—the Company having absolute occasion for their services—therefore their staying ought not to be of any disadvantage to them—

William McKay was again prevailed upon in 1803 to Winter on a plea of necessity & could not avail himself of his Rotation until 1804—none of the other Partners made application to the Company in 1802 or 1803 (except Mr. Daniel McKenzie who is stated to have intended going down to Montreal in Rotation in 1803 but at the request of Mr Roderick McKenzie one of the agents, agreed to Winter, therefore his name comes in with those who actually went in 1803) On a view of all these considerations the following list of Rotation is made out where the rights of all Parties are attended to—& on a supposition that each went down regularly as they had a right—In future it is considered that six Wintering Partners may be spared each year instead of five—

1802	William McKay
	A. N. McLeod
	*Peter Grant
1803	Daniel McKenzie
	John McDonald
1804	Donald McTavish
	*John Finlay

*those marked thus have retired

1805   John Sayer
       John McDonell
       Chs Chaboillez
       Duncan Cameron
       Alexr McKay

1806   James Hughes
       Alexr Fraser
       Hugh McGillis
       Alexr Henry
       John McGillivray#   #Note—Mr Rochblave has
       James McKenzie   gone down on Mr McGillivray's
1807   Simon Fraser   rotation—   D M G—
       Wm McKay   Kamia 19th Augt 1806
       A. N. McLeod
       Daniel McKenzie
       John McDonald
       Donald McTavish

1808   David Thompson   Alexr McKenzie   James Leith
       John Duncan Campbell John McDonald   John Haldane
       John Thompson   John Wills
       Pierre Rocheblave & his Partners by seniority

The undersigned Proprietors present at Kamanistiquia the 8th July 1805 after due consideration & examination of the foregoing Statement & List of Rotation, approve & Confirm the same—It is therefore (to prevent doubt & difficulty in future) Resolved, that the Rotation of Partners be regulated accordingly.—

Sign'd William McGillivray for self &   John McGillivray
        McTavish Frobisher & Co   Duncan Cameron
        Daniel McKenzie   Alexr Fraser
        William McKay   John Duncan Campbell
        John McDonald   Alexander McKay
        A. N. McLeod   Charles Chaboillez
        Hugh McGillis   John McDonell
        Alexr Henry   John Sayer

AT A MEETING of the Proprietors of the North West Co held at Kamanistiquia the 14 July 1806, to take into consideration the affairs of the Concern—It was suggested that the number of women and Children in the Country was a heavy burthen to the Concern & that some remedy ought to be applied to check so great an evil, at least if nothing effectual could be done to suppress it entirely.—It was therefore resolved that every practicable means should be used throughout the Country to reduce by degrees the number of women maintained by the Company, that for this purpose, no Man whatever, either Partner, Clerk, or Engagé, belonging to the Concern shall henceforth take or suffer to be taken, under any pretence whatsoever, any woman or maid from any of the tribes of Indians now known or who may hereafter become known in this Country to live with him after the fashion of the North West, that is to say, to live with him within the Company's Houses or Forts & be maintained at the expence of the Concern.

Resolved that each proprietor respectively shall be answerable for the conduct of all the people in his department, and that they shall be answerable to him for every offence committed against this resolve, and for the more strict observance thereof resolved that every proprietor who shall transgress against this resolve or suffer any other person or persons within his immediate charge or direction to transgress it—shall be subject to the penalty of One Hundred Pounds Hx. Cy. for every offence so committed to be forfeited to the rest of the Concern.—It is however understood that taken the Daughter of a white Man after the fashion of the Country, should be considered no violation of this resolve.

In witness whereof the parties present have hereto set their hands, place and date above written

Signed, Duncan McGillivray   Duncan Cameron
         Rod: McKenzie   John Haldane
         Thos Thain   P^re Rocheblave
         John McDonald   James Leith
         Dond McTavish   Alexr McKay
         John McDonell   David Thompson
         A. N. McLeod   James Leith
         James Hughes   John Haldane
         David Thompson   Wm McKay
         H. McGillis

RESOLVE for appointing Mr. James McKenzie to winter on the Kings Posts.

Whereas from the great number of Proprietors now in this Country, it is impossible to place them all to advantage in the North West Departments, And whereas the business of the Concern extends to other Departments out of the North West, which ought not to be neglected, and which it is conceived would be essentially benefitted by the presence of a Partner. And whereas the Kings Posts Department is of this number, the present manager of it Mr. Shaw having it only in his power to visit the Posts annually, while the business at Quebec and along the Communication chiefly engages his attention & prevents him from paying sufficient regard to the Trade of the interior Country.

It was therefore resolved at a meeting of the North West Company held at Kamanistiquia on the 4th July 1806, that Mr. James McKenzie now going to Montreal on his rotation, should be appointed, and he is accordingly appointed, to Winter next year at the Kings Posts and there to remain until the Concern shall otherwise determine—it being understood that he shall confine himself to the various duties of a wintering Partner, without releasing Mr. Shaw from any part of his present Duties.

In witness whereof the parties present have hereto set their hands this 14 day of July 1806 in Kamanistiquia.

Signed H. McGillis	Signed D. McGillivray
P. Rocheblave	R. McKenzie
James Leith	Thos Thain
John Haldane	John McDonald
Wm McKay	Dond McTavish
D: Thompson	John McDonell
Alexr McKay	A. N. McLeod
	Duncan Cameron
	James Hughes

THE NORTH WEST COMPANY

Athabasca Department

Wages of Devants[1] 600r., Do of Govn[s2] 600r and of Milieux 400r.

Equipments

of Bouts[3]	of Milieux
1 Blanket 3 pr	1 Blanket 3 pr
1 " 2½ "	1 " 2½ "
2 pr Leggins	2 pr Leggins
2 Bracelets	2 Shirts
2 Shirts	2 Bracelets
2 Handfrs	2 Handfrs
4 Canots Tobc	3 Canots Tobc
3 La: Knives	2 Large Knives
3 small Do	2 small Do
½d Beads	
¼d Vermillion	

English and Rat River Departments—Wages and Equipment the same as the Athabasca

Rocky Mountains F.P.

Wages and Equipments as above—except that the Milieux have 50r more wages—or 450r.

Upper Forts des Prairies

Bouts 500r Wages, Milieux 400r & the E: River Equipt.

Lower Forts des Prairies

Bouts 450r Wages—Milieux 350 Wages & Com: Equipt vizt

Bouts	Milieux
1 Blanket 3 pr	the same Equipt except
1 " 2½ "	1 Canots Tobc less than the Bouts
2 Shirts	
2 Bracelets	
2 pr Leggins	
4 Canots Tobc	

[1] Bowsmen.
[2] Steersmen.
[3] Bowsmen and Steersmen.

It is understood that the Men of Cumberland House may if necessary have something more—but not exceeding 50r.

Fort Dauphin
Bouts from 400r-450r & Milieux 300r or 350r wages and Common Equipment

Upper Red River
Bouts from 400r-500r Wages, Milieux 300r-350r and Common Equipment

Lower Red River
Bouts from 400r-450r Wages & Milieux 300r and Common Equipment

Lake Ouinipque
Bouts from 50r-500r & Milieux 350-400r Wages and Common Equipment

Lake La Pluie
Bouts 450r Wages—Milieux 300r-350r and Common Equipment

Lac des Isles
Bouts 350r Wages & Milieux 400r
Com: Equipt

Monontague
Bouts from 400r to 450r Wages & Milieux 300r-350r
Com: Equipment

Lake Nipigon
Bouts 400r-450r Wages & Milieux 300r-350r
Com: Equipment

Athabasca River Department
Bouts 700r Wages & Milieux 500r
and E: River Equipment

THE NORTH WEST COMPANY

Fond du Lac Department
from 400r-500r Wages & Comn Equipment

Folle Avoine Country
from 350r-400r Wages & Com: Equipment

Riviere de Montreal
from 400r-450r Wages & Com: Equipment

It having been found that much confusion and irregularity had arisen in the Wages & Equipment of Men throughout the Country, to the great loss and injury of the Concern. It was resolved at a meeting of the N West Co. held at Kama on the 15th day of July 1806. that the Wages & Equipment of the different Departments shall be regulated as above.

Signed, Duncan McGillivray
Rod: McKenzie
Thos Thain
Wm McKay
Dond McTavish
John McDonell
Duncan Cameron
James Hughes
H. McGillis
David Thompson
Alexr McKay
James Leith
John Haldane

At a meeting of the NW.Co at Kamanistiquia this 15th day of July 1806, it was resolved and, is hereby resolved that the present Agents of the NWCo shall hereafter be denominated Directors of the NWCo and all future agents of or for the NWCo shall and will be denominated Directors of the NWCo with the same individual Powers and no more as they had or might have had as Agents of or for the NWCo.

McGillis	— 1	1 Signed	A: N: McLeod
Mr. Chaboillez	— 2	2	John McDonell
Mr. McDonald	— 3	3	John McDonald
Alexr McKenzie	— 4	4	Dond McTavish
Daniel McKenzie	— 5	5	John Haldan
Alexr Henry	— 6	6	Du Cameron
John McGillivray	— 7	7	H McGillis
James McKenzie	— 8	8	Pr Rocheblave
Simon Fraser	— 9	9	Wm McKay
John Thompson	—10	10	David Thompson
Æ. Cameron	—11	11	James Leith
A. McDougal	—12	12	James Hughes
?	—13	13	Dun: McGillivray
Alexr Fraser	—14	14	Rod: McKenzie ⎫ Agents
J. Sayer	—15	15	Thos: Thain ⎭
		16	Alexr McKay

Whereas it appears that much inconvenience and many unpleasant consequences arise from the practice of suffering Men to bring *pacquettons* out of the Country on the Company's Canoes—And whereas such practice is in various ways contrary to the Interest of the Concern & even to the terms of the Mens Engagements; It was therefore resolved at a meeting of the North West Co held at Kamanistiquia on the 17 day of July 1806 That hereafter no man whatsoever shall be suffered to embark on the Company's Canoes or bring out of the interior Country or Wintering Ground to this place yearly more than two Buffaloe Robes or two dressed skins or one of each on any pretence whatever nor will it be permitted one Man to bring out any Leather for another under the penalty of 50 livres N.W.Cy.—And whereas it appears that many winterers have of late & particularly this year found means to bring out a considerable quantity of Furs & *Peltries*, with which they carry on an unlawful traffic in the Camp with petty Traders & Montreal Men—It was therefore also resolved that hereafter no Man whatsoever under engagements to the Company shall be permitted on any pretence whatever to bring out of the wintering ground, or to this place any furs or peltries whatsoever, under the penalty of forfeiting his wages—And for the one observance of these regulations every Proprietor is hereby directed to apprize his Men accordingly, that they may not plead ignorance of this resolve. In witness whereof the parties present have hereto set their hands place & date above written.

Signed—John McDonald
Dond McTavish
Dun: McGillivray
Rod: McKenzie
Thomas Thain
Wm McKay
Dond McTavish
John McDonell
Dun: Cameron
James Hughes
H McGillis
David Thompson
Alexr McKay
John Haldan
James Leith

WHEREAS several Measures have been suggested in the course of this summer for introducing more regularity into the business, & for enforcing a more strict system of economy throughout the Country—And whereas when any such measure appeared practicable to its full extent, a resolve was accordingly passed to enforce it hereafter as a case to the Concern, but when only practicable to a certain extent, & depending for its execution on the discretion and judgment of individuals—It was determined by the Concern that it should be carried into effect as much as possible without passing a positive rule, because a resolve should be only applied in Cases of certainty and should never be violated.

1st—And whereas in conformity with this principle, the practice of making transfers of Money between the Men was taken into consideration by the Concern, and was found to be a source of great loss & inconvenience. It was therefore agreed upon that this practice should in future be discontinued, except on this ground where the Concern shall decide on the propriety of such transfer: And at Lac La Pluie where the Person conducting the Athabasca business shall have a similar privilege of deciding on the propriety of transfers; but in all Cases the practice of making transfers shall be as much as possible restricted, but it is understood nevertheless that a monied Man may transfer any sum to a Man who is in debt.

2d—And whereas much confusion and irregularity has hitherto prevailed in the mode of supplying the Gentn in the Country with the articles of Tea Coffee &c. to prevent which in future it was agreed & understood by the parties present, that this matter should be regulated as follows vizt.

Proprietors..........6lb Tea 4lb Coffee & 4lb Chocolate

Principal Clerks in charge of Posts } 2lb Do 1lb Do & 1lb Do

Inferior Clerks Wintering with others } 1lb Do

The above quantities are intended as the Winters supply, and are independant of the consumption at this place and of the usual allowance carried off in Cases & Baskets but it is understood that neither Interpreters or Guides are entitled to any provision of this kind, they being generally fed at the tables of their masters.

In witness whereof the parties present have hereto set their names this 23d July 1806 at—Kamanistiquia.

Signed Alexr McKay David Thompson James Leith John Haldane	Signed Dun: McGillivray Rod: McKenzie Thos Thain Wm McKay Dond McTavish John McDonell Dun: Cameron James Hughes H. McGillis

Memo to regulate the Winter Express.

The Express to leave the Peace River on the 3d Jany 1807
Ditto   "   " Fort Augustus.......24 " Do
Ditto   "   " Isle a la Crosse.......12 " Do

By this means the Athabasca & English River Express will enter at Fort Vermillion on the 30 Jany or thereabouts.

THE NORTH WEST COMPANY

The Express to leave Fort Vermillion on the 1st Feby 1807
Ditto " " Fort S Louis........14 " Do
Ditto " " Riv: qui Appelle.....28 " Do
Ditto " " Mr. Henry's.........10 March
And soon without delay to Kam^a where it ought to arrive early in April.

The principal Points on which information will be desirable, are the appearance of returns. Mens Engagements, Arrangements of Posts—Expectations of Grease & Provisions &c &c with every kind of general information & remarks regarding the state of the Country.

Signed D: McGillivray
23d July 1806

Arrangement of Departments for 1806

Athabasca					
Daniel McKenzie	Prop:		Jos. Monin	Int:	
A N McLeod	"		J. B. La Prise	"	
Simon Fraser	"		Charles Martin	"	
John Thomson	"		D: Holmes	"	
Alex: McKenzie	"		Paul Boucher	"	
Peter Dease—	Clerk		Pierre Blondin—	Guide	
Edwd Smith	"		Pierre Delorme	"	
Peter Fraser	"		*Atha: River*		
Geo Keith	"		John McGillivray—Prop:		
Saml Black	"		Sim: McGillivray—Clerk		
Chas Grant	"		Alexr Stewart	"	
Andrew McKenzie	"		Jasp: Hawes—	Int:	
Fred: Goedeke	"		*English River*		
Alex: Henry Junr	"		Dond McTavish—Prop:		
Wm Mackintosh	"		J. D. Campbell	"	
A: M: McLeod	"		Robt Henry—	Clerk	
F. W: Wentzel	"		Colin Robertson	"	
Jas McDonell	"		Jos. Larocque	"	
Archd McGillivray	"		Jos. McGillivray	"	
John Stewart	"		John Forbes	"	& Int:
Michl Andrews—	Int:		Ls. Versailles	"	& "
J B: Brunosh	"		Colin Campbell	"	
Joachim Cardinal	"		James Keith	"	
J. B. La Fleur Sen S	"		Pat: Small	"	
J B. La Fleur Jun	"		Jos M. Paul—	Guide	
L. Brousseau	"		Jos. Cartier	"	
F. Lamisette	"				

Rat River

John Wills—Prop:
Wm Conolly— Clerk
D: Campbell "
Jac: Chastelain—Int:

Forts des Prairies

John McDonald— Prop: NW
John McDonald " AMKC
James Hughes "
David Thompson "
Rich: Montour—Clerk
W: Smith "
Jas MacMillan "
John Rowand "
D. W: Harmon "
Pierre Perra "
M: Quesnel "
F: McDonald "
Jac: Raphael " & Int:
Frans Duncan— Int:
Pre Gerome "
Jos. Cardinal "
Jos. Primeau— "
Jos. Rocque "
A. Duplessis "
Chas Le Claire—Guide
Ls Durand "

Upper Red River

John McDonell—Prop:
F: A: Larocque— Clerk
Chas McKenzie "
Dond Chisholm "
James Caldwell "
Fr Capois " & Int:
F. Denianais— Int:
Paul Tranquil "
Jos. Azure Guide
J. B. Sansregret "

Lower Red River

A. Henry— Prop:
M: Cotterell Clerk
Louis Dorion "
Wm Henry "
Alex Wilkie "

Tousst Veaudrie—Guide
J. B. Robillard "

Fort Dauphin

Chas Chaboillez— Prop:
Angus McGillis— Clerk
Allan McDonell "
Cuth: Cumming "
Jos. Collin—Int:
Jos. Halcro— Clerk
B: Frobisher "
W: Hamilton "
Chs Hamilton "
Nich: Ducharme—Guide

Lac Ouinipique

William McKay—Prop:
C. O. Ermatinger— Clerk
Alex: Farquharson "
Alex: Campbell "
John McPhail "
Geo. Nelson "
Ls Minecker "
Dom: Ducharme "
Angus Bethune "
Paul La Croix "
Jos. Lorin— Int:
Fr Richard Senr "
Fr Richard Junr "
Ant: Morriseau "
Jos. Durocher— Guide
Chas La Marche "

Nipigon

Dun: Cameron—Prop:
J. D. Cameron— Clerk
Rod: McKenzie "
R. D. Fraser "
J. Munro "
John Pritchard "
Rod Morrisson "
Chas Bruce Int:
Pierre Dumas "
Ls Dupuis "
J. B. Sauvé "
Isaac Bourguignon "
Jos. Monin—Guide

THE NORTH WEST COMPANY

Monontagué
John Haldane—Prop:
Æ. McDonell— Clerk
Alexr McDonell "
John Severight "
Aulay McAulay "
Nichs Landry—Int:
Louis Vallé—Guide

Lac La Pluie
A. McLellan— Clerk
Thos McMurray "
Wm McCrae "
Hugh Faries "
Ls Guimond "
Chas Chaloux—Guide & Int:
Richard Prichets— Int:
Louis Galliard "

Fond du Lac
Hugh McGillis—Prop:
Dond McKenzie—Clerk
James Grant "
E: Roussain "
Wm Morisson "
G. H. Monk "
Pre Chicoine "
Touss. Laronde "
Amable Durocher " & Int:
Alexr Clark "
E: Harrison "
B: Beaudrie—Int:
Vincent Roy " & P Cotte
F. Boucher "
G: Martel "

Folle Avoine
James Leith—Prop:
Su: La Mar— Clerk
J. McBean "
Jos. La Garde— Int:
Jos. S Germain "

Montreal River
Rand Cameron— Clerk
J. W. Dease "
Chs Gauthier "
Jean Barnett " & R Rasicott

Mil Lac
Jac: Adhemard—Clerk

Pointe
Mich: Cadotte
Mich: Cadotte— Clerk
Mich: Cadotte Ju. "
Leon S Germain "
J. B. Corbin "

Lac des Puis
Dr McLauchlan "

Kama
N McKenzie "
Jas. Tait "

Pic
Henry Munro "
Wm Harris "
Philo Lewis "

Michipicoton
Ber: S Germain }
Leon Chenier }
Dond McIntosh—Clerk
John Robertson "

Sault
Robert Logan "

to Watch De Lorme
Alexr McKay—Prop:
J. C. Sayer—Clerk
Ant: Vallé— Guide
Jos. Laverdiere "

Kama 30 July 1806

Abstract of Canoes for 1806.

Montreal Canoes for L L P....17
Athabasca   "   6
                                    — 23

Athabasca River............... 6
Eng: River.................... 7
Rat River..................... 3
Up. & L. Forts des Prairies...... 11
Fort Dauphin.................. 5
Up: Red River................. 5
Lower Red River.............. 6
Lake Ouinipic................. 10
Lac La Pluie.................. 5
Mil Lac & Lac des Puis......... 2
Nipigon....................... 10
Monontagué................... 6
to watch Delorme.............. 2
                                 ———
                                 101

Fond du Lac }
Folle Avoine } 14
Point......... 4   }.......... 22   the whole comprehended in
Montreal River. 4   9 Boats & 2 Canoes—
       —22

Total 123

Kama 30th July 1806.

BE IT KNOWN to all men, and it is hereby made Known that we the subscribing Parties to these Presents do recind, recall and revoke our deed of July the sixth one Thousand Eight Hundred and two granting Powers to and Constituting the House of McTavish Frobisher & Co our full and Lawfull attorney to act for us and Contract, buy, sell, engage and do every & all Kinds of business in which we are Concerned or interested, and we do hereby revoke, recall and recind all such Power or Powers of attorney formerly granted to the said House of McTavish Frobisher & Co or the People Composing that House and all and every such Power or Powers, are by these Presents revoked, recalled, recinded and annulled in due form and according to the rules stipulations and provisions made in the said Deed or Power or Powers for the Express and Special Purpose, and we moreover hereby and by these Presents, reserve to ourselves the right and privilege of acceding to or rejecting any future agreement, Plans, Speculation or Engagement made and Entered into on or in behalf of ourselves individually, or the North West Co Collectively on the faith of our said Power of Attorney. In testimony whereof we the Subscribing Parties being Partners of the North West Company having hereunto set our hands this tenth day of July one Thousand Eight Hundred and Seven.

Signed Wm McKay   Alexr Henry
  "   Daniel MacKenzie   Jno Macdonald
  "   D McTavish   Jno Macdonell
  "   A N. McLeod   Duncan Cameron
  "   H McGillis
  "   Jno McGillivray
  "   Alexr McKay

At a meeting of the Wintering Partners of the North West Company at Kamanistiquia this twelfth day of July one thousand Eight hundred and Seven—They found it necessary that one of the said wintering Partners should be appointed to act for the North West Company and Transact their business at Detroit and Michilimackinac or St Josephs, and impressed with the belief of the Propriety of such appointment, the said wintering Partners of the North West Company reserve to themselves the Privilege and power of acceding to or rejecting any Agreement or Contract made or Entered into with any person or Persons on or in behalf of said North West Company for any space of time exceeding one Year, untill their right to make such appointment shall be ascertained.

At the same meeting time and place it was also agreed that should the agents refuse to grant the Specified number of Six Copies of the General Accounts, we think it our Duty to insist, and lay in our Claims to Six Copies of the Said Accounts—

And in testimony hereof we the wintering Partners Composing said meeting hereunto set our hands

Signed Jno McGillivray   Archd N McLeod
P Rocheblave   A N McLeod for A McKenzie
D McTavish for self &   and Simon Fraser
Jno D Campbell   D McTavish for D Thompson
Jno MacDonald   and Jno Wills
James Leith   Jno Macdonell
Jno Haldane   Alexr MacKay
D Cameron   H McGillis
D McKenzie   Alex Henry
Wm MacKay
Jno Macdonald

THIS AGREEMENT made and executed at Montreal in the Province of lower Canada this Thirty first day of December in the Year One thousand Eight hundred and Six by and between William McGillivray Duncan McGillivray, William Hallowel and Roderic McKenzie—Jno Ogilvie and Thomas Thain Agents and Attornies of the North West Company on the one part, Josiah Bleakley Jacques Giasson, George Gillespie, Toussaint Pothier and David Mitchell Junior Agents and Attornies of the Michilimackinac Company of the Other Part.

Whereas by the Articles of Copartnership and Agreement of the said Michilimackinac Compy bearing even date with these presents, it is amongst other things stipulated and agreed, that in order to establish and cultivate that good understanding which ought to subsist between the said North West Company and the said Michilimackinac Company it becomes essential and necessary to form a line of boundary between them as Correct as may be, in the Countries, places, and Situations, where they respectively carry on Trade, and to make such other Provisions as may prevent a Collision of their Interests, or other misunderstanding between them, to effect which, the said Michilimackinac Company did empower and authorise their said Agents to enter into an Agreement with the said Agents of the North West Company and to make every necessary Stipulation in this behalf in manner as in the said Articles of Agreement particularly mentioned and Expressed.

Now these presents witness that in persuance of the said Articles of Agreement and by Virtue of the Authority therein Contained the said North West Company and the said Michilimackinac Company Represented by their respective Agents as aforesaid, do hereby Covenant promise and agree, the one with the other, in Manner following that is to say, First, that the said North West Co shall not outfit or carry on any Trade at any of the Posts on the south side of Lake Superior from Saint Maries to the Point Chaguamigon, the said Posts inclusive.—That the said North West Company shall also relinquish the Trade of the Interior Posts of *Lac des Flambeaux, Riviere des Saulteux, and dependencies*, and the Folle Avoine Country. That they shall not extend the Posts of *Lac du Sable* further down the Mississipi than the discharge of that Lake into the Mississipi, but if other Traders should establish Posts in the space between the Riviere Aile de Corbeau and Lake du sable then the said two Companies may do the same on the joint account.—That the said North West Compy shall establish no Posts on the Grand Red River higher up than the Entrance of the Chayenne River into the said Red River and shall not Trade with the Scioux Nation. That the said North West Company shall not establish any Posts beyond the height of land dividing the waters of the *quini de Loutre*. Secondly—That the said Michilimackinac Company shall not form any establishment nor make any Outfit nor carry on Trade in any manner on the North side of Lake Superior beyond the said North West Companys establishment at Saint Maries inclusive. That the said Michilimackinac Company shall not establish any Posts between the Point Chaguamigon and the Mouth of the River St Louis or Fond du Lac, but Passing up the River Brulé or route to the Folle avoine Country shall not be Considered as infringing this Agreement That the said Michilimackinac Company shall not establish any Posts higher up the Mississipi than the Entrance of the River *Aile de Corbeau* and that River or the direct water Communication from the Mississipi to the quini de Loutre shall be the boundary between the said Companies to the Height of Land at quini de Loutre. That the said Michilimackinac Company shall not establish any Posts for Trade on the Red River nor navigate that River, unless for the purposes of gaining the River Commonly called the Riviere des Scioux, on which River at the height of land or as high up as the head of the Navigation thereof, they shall be permitted to establish a Post. That the said Michilimackinac Company do hereby Agree not to approach nearer the Lac du sable from the Folle Avoine Country, than the said North West Company's Posts established in the Year one thousand Eight hundred and five.—That it is hereby expressly stipulated and Agreed that the said two Companies shall not interfere directly or indirectly with the Trading and establishments of each other wherever they come in Contact nor shall the one give any Aid or assistance to any opponent of the other—And it is also understood and Agreed that in order to maintain proper Subordination among the Servants and Men—neither Party shall encourage receive or harbour Deserters from the service of the other and that Mutual and reciprocal Aid and assistance be given by the one Company to the other in case of such desertion and for all necessary Purposes.—That the said Michilimackinac Company shall establish any Posts for Trade on the River St Maurice nor in any Part of the Grand River or Temiscamingue to the entrance of the French River into Lake Huron. That the said Michilimackinac Company shall assume the Contract entered into by the said North West Company and Michel Cadotte and shall also supply Goods to Jean Bapte Nolin and John Johnston at Saint Maries on terms not higher than those persons are now Supplied by the North West Co Provided the said Persons shall Continue to Pay regularly for such Supplies, and also on Conditions that they shall not draw the Indians from the Posts of Batchewina nor interfere with that or any other of the N W Cos Posts but this Agreement to supply Goods to the said Jean Bte Nolin and John Johnston shall not be obligatory for more than three Years from the day of the date thereof.—That the said Michilimackinac Company will agree to assume and do hereby assume all Engagements that the said North West Company may have made with Clerks and Men at the inland Posts given up and included within the said Boundary line, excepting the North West Companys old Apprentices, who shall not be bound to remain with the Michilimackinac Co unless they chuse it.—That debts due by Men to the said North West Company within the above Boundary line shall be Accounted for to them by the said Michilimackinac Company at one third of their Amount. Debts due by clerks shall be accounted for in the like manner as goods but not to exceed Fifty pounds Currency for any one of them.—And the Goods of the said North West Company at the said last mentioned Posts shall in like manner be Accounted for at the rate of Eighty per Cent on the Sterling cost of Goods usually sold by advance and Prix forte Articles in proportion the whole to be Payable on the 1st day of October next.—And it is hereby stipulated and agreed by and between the Parties to these Presents, that should any Ambiguity doubt question or Controversy at any time hereafter arise or happen between the said North West Company and the said Michilimackinac Company respectively represented by the Agents aforesaid Parties hereto, touching the said Boundary line which hath in good faith, been established and fixed, between the said two Companies or any matter or things relative thereto, and the said Parties or Companies cannot of themselves, Agree and Determine the same, then and in such case, the said Parties and the Partners or Agents of the said respective Companies, for the time being, shall and will forthwith commit the hearing and determination of any such Ambiguity, doubt, or question or Controversy to such indifferent men being Merchants, as shall be named by the said Parties, that is to say, one to be named by the said Agents or Agents for the time being of the said North West Company and the other by the said Agents or Agents for the time being of the said Michilimackinac Company and in case such two Persons cannot Agree and determine the matters so to them referred, within one Month, after such reference, than such Arbitrators shall name and appoint a third Person and that the award of the said Arbitrators and third Person or of any two of them to be made and Communicated to the said Parties, within one Month after the appointment of such third Person shall be final and Conclusive.—And the said Parties to these presents for and on behalf of the said respective Companies as agents thereto, and on behalf of their respective successors and legal Representatives do hereby consent promise and agree to stand to, perform, and Comply with all and whatever shall be determined by the said Arbitrators and third Person or any two of them. And that neither of the said Parties to these presents nor any or either of them nor any Agents or Agents, Partner or Partners for the time being, either of the said North West Company or of the said Michilimackinac Company or the legal Representatives of any or either of them, shall commence or bring any Action or suit or seek any remedy either at Law or Equity to be relieved on the Premises before such Ambiguity doubt question or Controversy shall be put to Reference aforesaid—And it is Particularly understood and Agreed upon that altho the North West Company and Michilimackinac Company are herein only mentioned, Yet that each and every of the Partners of both the said Companies as well after as before retirement therefrom shall during the Continuance of this Agreement that is to say for and during the space of *Ten Years*, from the day of the date thereof or during the Continuance of the said Michilimackinac Company be, and hereby is, and are respectively and Reciprocally bound to each other, and to the whole not to interfere in the Trade of the other Company.—Provided—always that Partners of the Michilimackinac Company after retiring therefrom altho continuing to hold a share therein as stipulated in their Agreement shall not be excluded thereby from their Trading or making Outfits to the River St Maurice and Ottawa nor shall any of the Partners of the said Michilimackinac Compy be considered as Contravening this Agreement if during its Continuance they or either of them shall in their individual Capacities sell Goods to Persons who afterwards trade the same in the said Rivers.—And for the due Performance of all and singular the matters and things herein contained and stipulated and agreed, the said Parties hereto, Agents and Attornies as aforesaid for themselves and as representing the said North West Compy and the said Michilimackinac Company do, and doth hereby bind and oblige themselves and every of them and all and every Partner and Partners of the said North West Company and the said Michilimackinac Compy in the Penal Sum of Five Thousand pounds to be paid by the Party or Persons infringing, breaking or Controverting the Present Agreement to the Party or Persons maintaining, observing and upholding the same.

For thus in good faith it hath been agreed upon by and between the said Parties who have to two Parts hereof set their Hands and seals the day and Year first above written one Part to remain in the hands of the said Agents of the North West Company and the other Part in the hands of the said Agents of the Michilimackinac Company.

	Signed Wm McGillivray
Signed Sealed and ⎫	D McGillivray
Delivered in Presence of ⎭	Wm Hallowell
Signed David Ross	Rod MacKenzie
Jas Reid	Jno Ogilvie
	Thos Thain
	Jos: Bleakley
	Jac: Giasson
	Geo Gillespie
	Tousst Pothier
	David Mitchell Junr

KNOW all men by these presents; Whereas William McGillivray Wm Hallowell and Roderic MacKenzie being the Partners now Composing the House of McTavish McGillivrays and Compy, Angus Shaw, Daniel MacKenzie, William MacKay, Jno Macdonald, Donald McTavish, A N McLeod, Jno Macdonell, Alexr McDougall, Charles Chaboillez, Jno Sayer, Peter Grant, Alexr Fraser, Hugh McGillis, Jno Finlay, Duncan Cameron, James Hughes, Alext McKay, Alexr Henry, Jno McGillivray, James MacKenzie, Simon Fraser, J. D. Campbell, David Thompson, Jno Thomson, Eneas Cameron, Sir Alexr MacKenzie, Thomas Forsyth, Jno Richardson, John Forsyth, Alexr Ellice, Jno Ingles, James Forsyth, Jno Ogilvy, John Mure, Pierre Rocheblave, Alexr MacKenzie, John Macdonald, James Leith, John Wills, Jno Haldane, Thomas Forsyth, Jno Richardson and Jno Forsyth as Trustees and assignees to the Estate of the late Firm of Leith Jameson & Compy and Thomas Thain, now Carrying on Trade and Commerce to the North West, or Indian Country, and other Places, as Copartners, under the name and designation of the North West Compy Under certain Articles of Agreement for that purpose made and Entered into, bearing date at Montreal the fifth day of November one Thousand Eight hundred and four.—And whereas the said Company having Confidence in the Integrity and ability of Kenneth MacKenzie heretofore one of their Clerks, and being desirous of admitting as a Partner in the said Company and Concern for one satisfied and Consented thereto, for that purpose hath and hereby Share, being that Vacant by Jno Finlay deed of Assignment dated at Montreal one thousand eight hundred and five, under the Terms and Conditions in the said Articles of Agreement Mentioned and Contained—Now know Ye that the said William McGillivray, William Hallowell, Roderic MacKenzie, Angus Shaw, Daniel MacKenzie, William MacKay, Jno Macdonald, Donald McTavish, A N McLeod, Jno McDonell, Alexr McDougall, Charles Chaboillez, Jno Sayer, Peter Grant, Alexr Fraser, Hugh McGillis, Jno Finlay, Duncan Cameron, James Hughes, Alexr MacKay, Alexr Henry, Jno McGillivray, James MacKenzie, Simon Fraser, Jno Duncan Campbell, David Thompson, Jno Thomson, Eneas Cameron, Sir Alexr MacKenzie, Thomas Forsyth, John Richardson, John Forsyth, Alexr Ellis, Jno Inglis, James Forsyth, Jno Ogilvy, Jno Mure, Pierre Rocheblave, Alexr MacKenzie, John Macdonald, James Leith, Jno Wills, Jno Haldane, Thomas Forsyth, Jno Richardson and Jno Forsyth, Trustees and assignees to the Estate of the late Firm of Leith Jameson & Co, and Thomas Thain, Either present or by their Attornies.—Have sold consigned and made over to the said Kenneth MacKenzie, Now present and accepting one full and Equal Share in the said Concern, being the Above mentioned Share assigned by Jno Finlay, beginning with the Outfit of the present Year one Thousand Eight hundred and Eight with all and every the rights benefits and advantages arising or to arise therefrom, To have and to hold the said one full share in the aforesaid Company or Concern and all other the Premises, hereby resolved and assigned unto the said Kenneth McKenzie Agreeable to the terms and Conditions of the aforesaid Articles of Agreement dated the fifth day of Novr one thousand Eight hundred and four, as fully and effectually to all Intents and purposes, as any of the aforesaid named persons, being Partners in the said Concern, Now hold, exercise, and enjoy their respective Shares therein.—And Whereas the said Kenneth MacKenzie by virtue of this Agreement hath become a partner in the aforesaid Company and Concern, but not having been a party to the aforesaid Articles of Agreement under and by virtue of which the said Company and Concern, is Constituted and Carried on, and this assignment made; and being Desirous and willing in every respect to Conform to and Comply with all and every the said Articles of Agreement, which he now Declares to have read and perused, and to be therewith fully doth bind and oblige himself Strictly to observe, Comply with and Submit to, All and every the clauses Stipulating, penalties, and obligations in the aforesaid Articles of Agreement, Mentioned and Contained, and every rule and regulation made or to be made, under and by virtue thereof, respecting the Said Trade and Commerce, as fully and Effectually to all Intents and purposes, as if the said Kenneth MacKenzie had been a party thereto, and had with the other Partners therein named, Signed and Subscribed the same, willing and Intending, that these presents Shall have the Same force and Effect.—In Witness Whereof the said parties, to these presents have to two parts thereof interchanged Set their Hands and Seals at Fort William in the district of Kamanistiquia this fifth day of July in the Year of our Lord one thousand Eight hundred and Eight—Angus Shaw Inserted on the Margin before signed—

Alexr McKenzie by T Thain Atty
Thomas Forsyth ditto
Jno Richardson "
Jno Forsyth "
Alexr Ellice "
Jno Inglis "
James Forsyth "
Jno Ogilvy "
Jno Mure "
Thomas Forsyth ⎫
John Richardson ⎬ Trustees and assignees to the Estate of the late Firm Leith Jameson & Co
Jno Forsyth ⎭
    by Thos Thain their Atty
James Leith
John Haldane
John Wills
Thomas Thain
Kenneth MacKenzie
Signed Sealed and Delivered
in presence of Alexr Dowie
                Geo Moffatt

William McGillivray for self and McTavish McGillivray & Co—
Daniel MacKenzie
Wm MacKay
Jno McDonald
Donald McTavish
A N McLeod
Duncan Cameron
James Hughes
Hugh McGillis
Jno McGillivray
J. D. Campbell
David Thompson by D McTavish Atty
Angus Shaw by Wm McGillivray Atty
Eneas Cameron by Ditto
Peter Grant " do
Jno Finlay " do
Simon Fraser " A N McLeod
Pierre Rocheblave   do

Copy

KNOW all Men by these presents; whereas William McGillivray, William Hallowell and Roderic MacKenzie [*illegible*] being the Partners now Composing the House of McTavish McGillivrays & Company,—Angus Shaw, Daniel MacKenzie, William MacKay, John Macdonald, Donald McTavish, Archd Norman McLeod, John Macdonell, Alexander Macdougall, Charles Chaboillez, John Sayer, Peter Grant, Alexr Fraser, Hugh McGillis, John Finlay, Duncan Cameron, James Hughes, Alexander MacKay, Alexr Henry, John McGillivray, James McKenzie, Simon Fraser, John Duncan Campbell, David Thompson, John Thomson, Eneas Cameron, Sir Alexr MacKenzie, Thomas Forsyth, John Richardson, John Forsyth, Alexr Ellice, John Inglis, James Forsyth, John Ogilvy, Jno Mure, Pierre Rocheblave, Alexr MacKenzie, Jno Macdonald, James Leith, John Wills, John Haldane, Thomas Forsyth, Jno Richardson and John Forsyth as Trustees and assignees to the Estate of the late Firm of Leith Jameson & Compy and Thomas Thain.—Now Carrying on Trade and Commerce to the North West or Indian Country and other Places as Copartners, under the name and Designation of the North West Company, Under certain Articles of Agreement for that Purpose made and Entered into bearing date at Montreal the fifth day of November one Thousand Eight hundred and four.—And Whereas the Said Company having Confidence in the Integrity and abilities of Archibald McLellan heretofore one of their Clerks, and being Desirous of Admitting him as a partner in the said Company and Concern, for one Share being that Vacant by Peter Grant deed of assignment dated at Montreal

one thousand Eight hundred and five, under the Terms and Conditions in the said Articles of Agreement Mentioned and Contained—Now Know Ye that the said William McGillivray, William Hallowell, Rod MacKenzie, Angus Shaw, Daniel MacKenzie, William MacKay, John McDonald, Donald McTavish, Archibald Norman McLeod, John McDonell, Alexr McDougall, Charles Chaboillez, John Sayer, Peter Grant, Alexr Fraser, Hugh McGillis, Jno Finlay, Duncan Cameron, James Hughes, Alexander MacKay, Alexr Henry, Jno McGillivray, James MacKenzie, Simon Fraser, J Duncan Campbell, David Thompson, Jno Thomson, Eneas Cameron, Sir Alexr MacKenzie, Thomas Forsyth, Jno Richardson,

Jno Forsyth, Alexr Ellice, Jno Inglis, James Forsyth, John Ogilvie, Jno Mure, Pierre Rocheblave, Alexr MacKenzie, Jno Macdonald, James Leith, Jno Wills, Jno Haldane, Thomas Forsyth, Jno Richardson, and Jno Forsyth as Trustees and assignees to the Estate of the late Firm of Leith Jameson and Compy and Thomas Thain, either present or by their Attornies. Have Sold assigned and made over to the said Archibald McLellan, Now present and accepting one full and Equal Share in the said Concern, being the above mentioned Share assigned by Peter Grant, beginning with the Outfit for the present Year one Thousand Eight hundred and Eight, with all and every the rights Benefits and Advantages arising or to arise therefrom.

To have and to hold the said one full Share in the aforesaid Company or Concern, and all other the premises, hereby resolved and assigned unto the said Archibald McLellan Agreeable to the Terms and Conditions of the aforesaid Articles of Agreement dated the fifth day of November one thousand Eight and four, as fully and Effectually to all Intents and purposes, as any of the before named Persons being Partners in the said Concern, Now hold Exercise, and enjoy these Respective Shares therein.— And whereas the said Archibald McLellan by Virtue of this assignment hath become a partner in the aforesaid Company and Concern, but not having been a party to the aforesaid Articles of Agreement under and by Virtue of which the said Company and Concern is Constituted and Carried on, and this assignment made; And being Desirous and willing in every respect to Conform to and Comply with all and Every the said Articles of Agreement, Which he now declares to have read and perused, and to be therewith fully satisfied and Consented thereto, for that purpose hath and hereby doth Bind and oblige himself strictly to observe, comply with, and submit to all and every the Clauses Stipulations and penalties and obligations in the aforesaid Articles of Agreement Mentioned and Contained, and every rule and regulation made or to be made under and by Virtue thereof.—Respecting the said Trade and Commerce, as fully and effectually to all Intents and purposes, as if the said Archibald McLellan had been a party thereto, and had with the other partners therein named, Signed and Subscribed the same, willing and intending that these presents shall have the same force and Effect.—In Witness whereof the said Parties, to these presents, have to two parts thereof interchangeable set their Hands and Seals at Fort William in the District of Kamanistiquia this Sixth day of July in the of Our Lord one thousand Eight and Eight.

Signed

Alexr Mackenzie by Thos Thain	Atty	William McGillivray for self and McTavish McGillivrays & Co
Thomas Forsyth	ditto	Daniel MacKenzie
Jno Richardson	ditto	Wm MacKay
Jno Forsyth	ditto	Jno McDonald
Alexr Ellice	ditto	Donald McTavish
Jno Inglis	"	A N McLeod
James Forsyth	"	Duncan Cameron
Jno Ogilvy	"	James Hughes
Jno Mure	"	Hugh McGillis
Thomas Forsyth ⎫	Trustees &	Jno McGillivray
Jno Richardson ⎬	assignees to	J D. Campbell
Jno Forsyth ⎭	the Estate of the late Firm of Leith Jameson & Co by Thos Thain	David Thompson by D McTavish
		A Shaw by Wm McGillivray
		Eneas Cameron by Do
		Peter Grant by Do
		Jno Finlay by Do
James Leith		Simon Fraser ⎫ by A N
Jno Haldane		Pierre Rocheblave ⎬ McLeod
Jno Wills		
Thomas Thain		

Signed by Archibald McLellan at Lac La Pluie 16th July 1808

    Witnesses   J G McTavish
                   Andrew MacKenzie
                            Copy
                            K McK.

KNOW all men by these presents Whereas William McGillivray William Hallowell and Roderic McKenzie, being the partners now Composing the House of McTavish McGillivray & Co Angus Shaw, Daniel MacKenzie, William MacKay, Jno Macdonald, Donald McTavish, Archd Norman McLeod, Jno McDonell, Alexr McDougall, Charles Chaboillez, Jno Sayer, Peter Grant, Alexr Fraser, Hugh McGillis Jno Finlay, Duncan Cameron, James Hughes, Alexr MacKay, Alexr Henry, Jno McGillivray, James MacKenzie, Simon Fraser, J Duncan Campbell, David Thompson, Jno Thomson, Eneas Cameron, Sir Alexander MacKenzie, Thomas Forsyth, Jno Richardson, Jno Forsyth, Alexr Ellice, Jno Inglis, James Forsyth, Jno Ogilvy, Jno Mure, Pierre Rocheblave, Alexr MacKenzie, Jno Macdonald, James Leith, Jno Wills, Jno Haldane, Thomas Forsyth, John Richardson and Jno Forsyth as Trustees and assignees to the Estate of the late Firm of Leith Jameson & Co, Thomas Thain, Kenneth MacKenzie and Archibald McLellan, now carrying on Trade and Commerce to the North West or Indian Country, and other places as Copartners, under the name and Designation of the North West Compy, under certain Articles of Agreement for that purpose made and entered into, bearing date at Montreal the fifth day of November one thousand Eight hundred and four.—And whereas the said Company having Confidence in the Integrity and abilities of Ronald Cameron heretofore one of their Clerks, and being Desirous of admitting him as a Partner in the said Company and Concern for one Share, being that Vacant by Mr Jno Sayer deed of assignment dated at Montreal one Thousand Eight hundred and Seven, under the Terms and Conditions in the said Articles of Agreement Mentioned and Contained, Now Know Ye that the said William McGillivray, William Hallowell, Roderic MacKenzie, Angus Shaw, Daniel MacKenzie, William McKay, Jno Macdonald, Donald McTavish, Archd Norman McLeod, Jno Macdonell, Alexr McDougall, Charles Chaboillez, Jno Sayer, Peter Grant, Alexr Fraser, Hugh McGillis, Jno Finlay, Duncan Cameron, James Hughes, Alexr MacKay, Alexr Henry, Jno McGillivray, James McKenzie, Simon Fraser, J Duncan Campbell, David Thompson, Jno Thomson, Eneas Cameron, Sir Alexr MacKenzie, Thomas Forsyth, Jno Richardson, Jno Forsyth, Alexr Ellice, Jno Ingles, James Forsyth, Jno Ogilvy, John Mure, Pierre Rocheblave, Alexr MacKenzie, Jno McDonald, James Leith, Jno Wills, Jno Haldane, Thomas Forsyth, Jno

Richardson and Jno Forsyth as Trustees and assignees to the Estate of the late Firm of Leith Jameson & Compy, Thomas Thain, Kenneth McKenzie and Archibald McLellan, either present or by their Attornies, Have sold assigned and made over to the said Ronald Cameron Now present and accepting one full and Equal Share in the said Concern, being the above mentioned Share assigned by Jno Sayer, beginning with the Outfit for the present Year one thousand Eight hundred and Eight with all and every the rights benefits and advantages arising or to arise therefrom.—To have and to hold the said one full share in the aforesaid Company or Concern, and all other the presents, hereby resolved and assigned unto the said Ronald Cameron, Agreeable to the Terms and Conditions of the aforesaid Articles of Agreement dated the fifth day of November one thousand Eight hundred and four, as fully and effectually to all intents and Purposes, as any of the before named persons, being Partners in the said Concern, now hold exercise, and enjoy their respective Shares therein.—And whereas the said Ronald Cameron by Virtue of this assignment hath become a Partner in the aforesaid Company and Concern, but not having been a party to the aforesaid Articles of Agreement under and by Virtue of which the said Company and Concern, is Constituted and Carried on and this Assignment made, And being Desirous and Willing in every respect to Conform to and Comply with, all and every the said Articles of Agreement, which he now Declares to have read and perused, and to be therewith fully satisfied and Consented thereto, for that purpose hath and hereby doth bind and oblige himself Strictly to observe, Comply with, and Submit to, all and every the clauses Stipulations and penalties and obligations in the aforesaid Articles of Agreement mentioned and Contained, and any rule and regulation made or to be made, under and by Virtue thereof—respecting the said Trade and Commerce, as fully and effectually to all Intents and purposes, as if the said Ronald Cameron had been a party thereto, and had with the other Partners therein named, Signed and subscribed the same, willing and intending that these Presents shall have the same force and Effect.—In Witness whereof the said Parties to these presents, have to two parts thereof interchangeable set their Hands and Seals at Fort William in the District of Kamanistiquia this Twenty third day of July in the Year of our Lord one Thousand Eight Hundred and Eight.

       Signed Rod MacKenzie for self & McTavish
           McGillivs & Co
           Daniel MacKenzie
Witnesses   Duncan Cameron
  Alexr Dowie   Jno Macdonell
  Geo Moffatt   H MacGillis
           Charles Chaboillez
           Thomas Thain for all the Parties of
             Sir A MacKenzie & Co
           Jno McDonald
           James Leith
           Jno Haldane
           Thomas Thain
           Kenneth MacKenzie
           Ronald Cameron

         Copy
         KMcK

WHEREAS by the Sixteen Article of the old North West Agreement bearing date at the Grand Portage the fifth day of July one thousand Eight hundred and two; said Article forming part of the General Agreement entered into at Montreal the fifth day of November one Thousand Eight hundred and four.—It was Stipulated and Agreed upon by the Contracting parties that upon the death of any of the Wintering Partners in the said Concern, His Share and Interest should cease and determine; but that the Heirs or Legal Representatives of such Deceased Partner should for and during the space of Seven Years from his Decease, be entitled to demand and receive from said Concern an Equivalent to one half of the Share or Interest such Deceased Partner held in the Concern,—And it having been represented by the Wintering Partners that by the Construction now put on the above Article, the Interest of a deceased Partner must sustain Injury, if after the Importation of the Goods intended for the Concern the ensuing Year at his risk, his full share in such goods should not be continued, until they are disposed of for the General Account.—In order therefore to afford every advantage to the Estate of a deceased Partner—It is now Agreed upon by the undersigned Wintering Partners of the North West Compy—and assented to by the Agents present, but without meaning to pledge the remainder of the Concern to a Concurrence in the Measure—that upon the Death of any of the Wintering Partners in the said Company, his Share and Interest shall cease; but that his Heirs or Legal Representatives of such deceased Partner shall for and during the next Year Ensuing, after his Decease, be entitled to claim and receive an Equivalent to the full share he held in the Concern,—And be further entitled to Demand and receive from the said North West Co and the Agents thereof, for and during the space of Six Years thereafter (if the Concern should so long continue) an Equivalent to one half of the Share or Interest such Deceased Partner held in the Concern.

In all cases strictly Conforming to all the rules & Regulations Stipulated for in the above Article of Agreement and securing inviolably the principles laid down in the same, from which this Resolve is not in the least meant or understood to Deviate. Fort William 14th July 1808

  Signed William McGillivray for self & McTavish McGs & Co
      Daniel MacKenzie
      William MacKay
      Jno Macdonald
      Donald McTavish
      Jno Macdonell
      Charles Chaboillez
      Duncan Cameron
      James Hughes
      Alexr MacKay
      Hugh McGillis
      Jno McGillivray
      J D. Campbell
      Alexr MacKenzie
      James Leith
      Jno Haldane
      Jno Wills
      Thomas Thain for self & Sir A McKenzie & Co
Copy   K MacKenzie
 KMcK Jno MacDonald

THE NORTH WEST COMPANY

WHEREAS a Concern or Company has been formed at Montreal by Forsyth Richardson & Co and McTavish McGillivray's & Co (with Authority to Admit other Associates) for carrying on Trade to the Indian Country from Michilimackinac, under the Firm of the Montreal Michilimackinac Company; and another Concern or Company has been formed at New York by Jno Jacob Astor and others, under the Firm of the American Fur Company, also for the purpose of Carrying on Trade to the Indian Country; And whereas experience has proved, that the people, supplying Materials for carrying on that Trade are best procured in part from and through Canada, and in part from and through the State of New York, Consequently an opposition between Companies so circumstanced, would be productive of certain loss to both, whilst a Reciprocal Communication of the advantages arising out of the locality would assure a Material benefit to each. It is therefore hereby concluded and agreed upon by and between William McGillivray of Montreal Merchant now at New York in the State of New York, for and on behalf of all those Concerned or that may become Concerned in the Montreal Michilimackinac Compy, and John Jacob Astor of New York Merchant, now at the same place, for and on behalf of all those Concerned, or that may become Concerned in the American Fur Company as follows viz.

ARTICLE 1ST

That for five Years from the first of April next all Outputs to be made for the Trade to the Interior Country from Michilimackinac, Commencing with the Outfit of the Year 1811, all Supplies of whatsoever Kind which shall be requisite for the said Trade, shall be furnished by each of the Companies aforesaid in equal proportions and from such places where the same can be procured to most advantage, whether England, Canada, or the United States.

ARTICLE 2D

That the Montreal Company shall Import by Quebec their proportion of Goods from England, and the American Fur Company shall import their proportion by New York, so as that one half of the Amount of the value of Goods, imported shall be by Quebec and the other half by New York, unless from Political events or other causes, it shall hereafter be found for Mutual benefit to vary the proportion—And the Montreal Company shall furnish all such Articles as will be required from Canada, and the American Fur Company all such Articles as it may be found necessary to have from the United States.—And for the supplies so imported and so procured or furnished, no more shall be charged by each Company than the Actual cost and charges, (Interest inclusive when such accrues) which they respectively shall have paid or become liable for, either in the first instance or in forwarding the same their ultimate destination. It being understood and hereby agreed, that each Company shall furnish to the other its due proportion and in due season, from time to time of all the Monies needful for the fulfilment of Engagements made or to be made as Occasions require, for the said supplies from Canada and the United States, as well as for the Cash advances which in the Course of the said Trade to be carried on therefrom shall become expedient and necessary Keeping always in view the principle of Equalising from time to time as nearly as may be the Respective Advances of each Company in their due proportions until that the Annual general Equalization herein after mentioned can take place.

Article 3d

And whereas certain Merchandize, Goods and Effects are remaining at Montreal, St Joseph and Michilimackinac being the remainder of the stock of the late Michilimackinac Company— And whereas the Montreal Company have purchased six sixteenths of said Goods, it is agreed that the said Purchase shall be for account of the present Concern at the price and terms purchased, And the American Fur Company shall also be interested in the remaining ten Sixteenths parts of said Goods, and shall Account for their proportion of Interest to the Montreal Company—viz The Goods at Montreal shall be taken at First cost and charges at the price at which Goods of Equal Quality will be shipped this Year from England and Payable the first day of January next, and those in the Upper Country at the Inventory price of the late Michilimackinac Company and payable on the first day of October 1812, and Debts due by Clerks and Engages shall be assumed by this Concern at such valuation as the Agents shall Judge fair to both parties, and in case of a disagreement they shall call a distinguished person to decide the Amount to be paid, that is to say, the proportion of the American Fur Company on the first of October next—It being understood however that the assumption of Debts here alluded to are of such persons only as shall be deemed necessary to be employed by this Concern for this Concern for the future.

Article 4th

That on the Arrival at Michilimackinac of the Goods and supplies so furnished by each Company the same (to avoid the ruinous consequences of opposition in the Interior) shall not be treated apart but shall be put together and the needful Outfits or supplies to Traders made therefrom, to which each Company shall Contribute an equal proportion as well as of every expence and advance needful for or incident to Equipments or Outfits to the Indian Country.

Article 5th

That this Concern shall annually send two Agents one of which to be appointed by each Company, with proper assistants to Michilimackinac to do the Business thereof, as well in respect to the Equipments or Outfits and receiving payments or returns therefrom and Sending the same down, as in respect to Keeping and settling the requisite Accounts and Transacting whatsoever else may Concern the trade; and the said Agents shall in the Month of October or earlier in each year furnish to each Company Lists or Schedules of the Supplies which they shall consider needful for the Outfit of the succeeding season, distinguishing therein such Articles as are to be provided from England, Canada, and the States Respectively: And no Agent shall receive for his salary or services more than the Sum of Two Thousand Dollars per annum—and his Expenses payd while on Actual duty for the Concern absent from Montreal or New York on the business of this Concern.

Article 6th

That all Returns from the Trade shall belong to each Concern in Equal proportions, and be sent undivided to such places as shall be considered best for the disposal of the same to most Advantage, and each Company shall observe its undivided share or proportion in each Article until sold, when the Nett proceeds thereof shall be divided, but if in the opinion of John Jacob Astor it shall be thought best that the Major part of the returns shall be sent to New York, not exceeding in the whole Amount two thirds of the Returns, the same shall be sent and sold or Shipped by the American Fur Company who are to be allowed two and one half per Cent Commission on the Amount, in Consideration of the said Mr. Jacob Astors Attention to the Superintending in the assortment, disposing and shipping of the same.

Article 7th

That Returns sent to Canada shall be disposed of by the Montreal Company, and Returns sent to the United States shall be disposed of by the American Fur Company, and the Nett proceeds Reciprocally accounted for by the one to the other in their Respective propositions, but no Commission shall be allowed thereon, other than Amounts mentioned in the foregoing Article to the American Fur Company, nor any Charge made beyond the Actual expenses disbursed.

Article 8th

That Shipments to England upon Account of the Companies, shall be consigned without Division of the Articles shipped to MacTavish Fraser & Co and to Inglis Ellice and Co, and the Nett proceeds thereof credited according to the respective Interests of the Companies therein—And Shipments elsewhere shall be consigned as may at the time be thought most advantageous for the Concern.

Article 9th

That there shall be establishments or Agencies provided at Montreal and New-York for Carrying on the Trade to the Indian Country hereby contemplated—That such Establishments shall be formed upon as economical principles as the case will admit of, And the Acting Agent of each Company at Montreal and New York, shall be the Agents as above mentioned who are to go up

Annually to Michilimackinac:—And in order to prevent unnecessary expences as far as may be, and to give to each Company an Interest that each branch of the business, shall be done in the place best adapted to it the Expences of the said Establishments respectively (according to an estimate or scale to be Agreed upon) shall be Reciprocally borne in the proportions that each Company shall have in the Trade.

Article 10

That Regular Books shall be Kept by Each Establishment at Montreal and New York, and General Accounts shall be stated therefrom, and rendered by the one Company to the other up to the 31st of December in each Year, at which period a general Equalization in the due proportions of all advances (when not already made) shall take place, Comprehending Interest where the same shall accrue thereon.

Article 11

To remove all causes of Collision with the Company Trading from Canada called the North West Company, it is hereby agreed that the Companies who are parties hereto, shall on no Account trade nor Equip any person to Trade after the Outfit of the Year 1811 with Indians beyond the Territorial Limits of the United States, unless to such part of Lake Huron as shall not be within the limits of any Trading Post, at present Established by the said North West Compy—Provided always that the said North West Co, shall also agree on their part not to trade nor Equip any person to trade after the said Outfit of the Year 1811 with Indians within the Territorial limits of the United States, nor beyond the limits of any Trading post near Lake Huron now Actually Established by the said Company. It being however understood, that for the Outfit 1811, each compy is to Conform itself to the Restrictions agreed upon between the North West Company and the said late Michilimackinac Company.

Article 12

And whereas the Factories established and supported at a heavy expence by the United States, for Trading with Indians may be withdrawn, it is therefore understood and hereby agreed upon, by and between the parties hereto, that in such case, the proportion of Shares herein before Established for each of the Companies, shall be altered in so far, that the Montreal Company shall only furnish one third part of all supplies and receive one third of all Returns and payments, & the American Fur Company, in such case shall furnish two third parts of all Supplies and receive two third parts of all Returns and payments and every disbursement and receipt of whatsoever Kind Shall in the like Case be in such new proportion; but the present Agreement is to remain in full force in all respects excepting as to such alteration of the proportions in the Event of such withdrawal of the said Factories.

Article 13

That on the Receipt of the Returns which shall arise from the Outfit to be made in the Year 1815—or sooner if the present Agreement shall by common consent of the parties thereto be annulled, then every thing in which the said two Companies shall have an Interest, whether consisting of Furs and Skins, Merchandise or other Effects, or debts due by traders or other Persons shall either be divided in Kind in the proportions above said, so as to be as nearly as possible of like proportional value or shall be put into the hands of Agents to be sold or realised for the common benefit, and the proceeds then divided, or the same shall be sold at public Auction to the highest bidder, who shall give sufficient security for duly complying with the Conditions of payment which shall have been Agreed upon to regulate such sale.

Article 14th

It is hereby expressly Agreed upon by and between the Parties hereto, that the North West Company shall after the present deliver up to this Concern all and every Post of Trade or Trading house, which they at present Occupy within the Territories or Limits of the United States of America and shall not hold any separate Interest in Trade with any other person or persons other than the present Concern in the Indian Country within the Territories of the United States of America, nor furnish any person or persons with Goods for the Purpose aforesaid—And it is Further declared and agreed upon that the Limits within which the Trade of this Concern shall be carried on has no application whatsoever to any Country beyond the Ridge of the Rocky Mountains, nor the River Mississipie nor to the North west Coast or in the Pacific *Ocean*, any thing herein contained to the Contrary notwithstanding.

Article 15

As both the parties to these presents have ordered Supplies of Goods for the Indian Trade from England and other places:—It is hereby understood that such supplies of whatsoever Kind or nature they may be, shall be received into the stock of this Concern and Accounted for by the one party to the other, as forming part of the Outfit 1811, without any advantage to the party so providing, than if such Supplies had been ordered by the Joint Concern.

Article 16th

It is hereby declared and agreed upon that the Business in Contemplation and to be carried on by this Concern shall be conducted under the Firm of the South West Fur Company, and shall so Continue for the full end and term of Five Years next to come or five Complete Outfits.

In witness whereof the parties to these presents have hereunto set their Hands and Seals at New York the twenty Eight day of January 1811.

Sealed and Delivered in presence of Signed David Hardenbrook	Signed { Jno Jacob Astor for and on behalf of the American Fur Compy Wm McGillivray for McTavish McGilli^s & Co and for and on behalf of Forsyth Richardson & Co and the North West Company

246 DOCUMENTS RELATING TO

20: MINUTES OF THE TRANSACTIONS OF THE NORTH WEST COMPANY AT FORT WILLIAM, 1807-1814.[1]

[*Hudson's Bay House.*]

The North West Company having met on the 10th July 1807 to concert the arrangement of the Departments for the Current year—the following distribution of the Wintering Gentlemen was unanimously agreed upon—

Athabasca
    Mr McLeod
    " Thompson
    " Fraser
    " Rocheblave
    " McKenzie

Atha' River
    Mr McGillivray

English River
    Mr M'Tavish
    " Campbell

Rat River
    Mr Wills

Fort des Prairies
    Mr M'Donald
    " Hughes
    " Thompson

Fort Dauphin
    Mr M'Donald

Up: Red River
    Mr M'Donell

Lower Red River
    Mr Henry

Fond du Lac
    Mr M'Gillis

[1] These minutes, which are reproduced by permission of the Governor and Committee of the Hudson's Bay Company, are in a manuscript book, preserved in Hudson's Bay House, which is apparently an original record. The minutes for 1807 are in the handwriting of Duncan McGillivray, those for 1808 and 1809 in that of Thomas Thain, those for 1810 in that of Angus Shaw, and those for 1811 to 1814 in that of William McGillivray. The book would appear to have been left in Hudson's Bay House by William McGillivray after the union of 1821. What has happened to the book containing the minutes from 1815 to 1821 is a matter of conjecture. It would seem probable that it too was deposited in Hudson's Bay House after 1821; but if so, it has disappeared. It may have been retained by William McGillivray while he was acting as a member of the advisory board on the fur-trade in 1821-4, or it may have been removed later in connection with one of the litigations which followed the failure of McTavish, McGillivrays and Co. in 1825.

Lake Ouinipique
    Mr Cameron
	Pic
	    Mr Chaboillez

River Ouinipique
    Mr A. McKay
	Michipicotan
	    Mr Leith

Lac des Isles
    Mr Ranald Cameron
	Lac La pluie
	    Mr McLellan

Monontague
    Mr Haldane
	Kamanistiquia
	    Mr Kenneth McKenzie

The Proprietors having Met on the 11th July 1807 Mr D. M'G on the part of the Agents, brought a charge of irregularity against Mr Sayer for absenting himself from his post on two different occasions, contrary to the opinion of the said Agent, and unmindful of the interest of the Concern.—In the course of a desultory conversation the general opinion seemed to be that the charge was not without foundation, but the object of it being absent it was considered hard to condemn him unheard. At length an expedient was suggested which for the present rendered any further discussion unnecessary; the Agents were authorized to make the following proposition to Mr Sayer on the part of the Concern, and they were directed to acquaint him that should he decline the same, he must come up to this place next year to resume his former situation of a Wintering Partner.

1st Mr Sayer to retire from the North West Company as an Active Partner, but to retain one half his interest therein for 7 years, on the conditions set forth in the Agreement. The other half of his present interest to be relinquished by him & assigned over to the Concern to be disposed of as they should think fit.

2d In consideration of such retiring & relinguishment as above said—The North West Co to assign over to Mr Sayer & to his Heirs forever, all their right and title to the farm at the Chats in the Grand River, together with the buildings Cattle &c thereon, in as full and ample a manner as they themselves hold the Above property; reserving only therefrom the Goods and other Articles usually intended for the Indian Trade. And should Mr Sayer be disposed to continue to Trade with the Natives on his own account he will be at liberty so to do, providing he does not interfere in any manner whatsoever with the Trade of the Posts belonging to the North West Co.

Mr Alexander McKay proposed that should Mr Sayer decline the above proposal he himself should have the preference of accepting it, which was unanimously agreed to, & consequently, should the said Mr Sayer decline the proposal, Mr A. McKay is considered as having accepted of it on the aforesaid conditions.

A long conversation then followed relative to the St Maurice & Kings Posts Departments, and the Wintering partners unanimously desired that the Outfit of the former should be in future so limited as to secure the Concern from loss,—that River being considered merely as a barrier to defend the borders of the neighbouring posts, and the Outfit thereto to be adapted to this purpose only.—With respect to the latter Department it was observed that the Stock employed in it was far too great compared with the profits; The Vessels Men & Boats employed in the fishing were freely descanted upon, and this part of the business was entirely disapproved of by the Wintering Gentn as being too expensive & perhaps ill-understood consequently they proposed that the Fishing along the whole Coast, with all the Vessels boats tackle &c employed therein should be disposed of to the best advantage, and that the Managers of that quarter should in future direct their attention exclusively to the Indian Trade alone, being the true & only Legitimate business of the NWCo. To all these proposals the Agents without hesitation gave their assent, & promised to take the necessary measures accordingly on their arrival at Montl.

July 13th.

The Wintering partners having objected that their Summer Accounts of each year should be charged to them respectively on the 30th Novr following—contrary to former custom—it was agreed that should the accounts hereafter be settled in that way— they should not be liable to pay any interest on such accounts for the next ensuing year.

The term 'Agents' having been objected to as being too frequently used, to the exclusion of what were considered more appropriate terms—It was agreed upon, that hereafter, the term 'Agents or Directors' should only be used as it was formerly applied to the House of M'T. Frobisher & Co & not otherwise.

July 13th Contd

The Partners of the Old Concern having taken into consideration, a claim made by the Wintering Partners of A. M. K Co, for retaining half their Share or interest in the Concern for 7 years after retiring from the Country, similarly to the provision made in such cases for the said partners of the old Concern; It was determined, that tho' the contracting parties to the N West Agreement of 1802, did not intend that such provision should be made for partners to be afterwards admitted into the Concern on One Share—yet it appeared necessary & proper that they (Partners holding one Share) should be entitled to such advantage—And as an Act of liberality & justice worthy of the Concern, it was unanimously resolved that such partners should hereafter hold or retain one half their share & interest, for the same time & in the same manner as is provided for in the said Agreement in behalf of the partners holding two Shares.

This determination was accordingly announced to the Wintering partners of A. M. K. Co, at which they expressed their satisfaction.

20th July—

A Meeting took place to decide on the relative claims of Mr Kenneth McKenzie & Mr Robert Henry (both Clerks to the Concern) to be promoted to the first vacant Share to be disposed of. The following Gentn gave their suffrages in favor of Mr McKenzie.—Messrs William McKay, Daniel McKenzie, M'Donell —A McKay—Rocheblave, M'Donald MKCo Leith & Haldane; And Messrs M'Tavish M'Donald Cameron—Henry, M'Gillis, & John McGillivray, declared for Mr Henry—by which it appeared that the majority of the Wintering Partners themselves, (independent of the interest of the Agents) was in favor of Mr McKenzie —It is Accordingly Agreed upon that Mr Kenneth McKenzie should be the first Clerk in the Company's service to be promoted to a share—And also that Mr Robert Henry should be the second person provided for, which is accordingly resolved.

The Wintering partners having proposed that the name of this place should be changed & that of Fort William substituted in its stead as being more simple and appropriate the Agents gave their assent and the name 'Kamanistiquia' is accordingly discontinued & abolished for ever & that of Fort William is adopted in its place.

The Agents having attentively perused this and the forgoing nine pages, said that they contain a correct and brief account of the principal transactions of the North West Co during the current Season—In witness whereof the said Agents have thereto set their hands this 31st July 1807 at Fort William aforesaid.

Duncan McGillivray
Rod Mackenzie } Agents N,W,Co,
Thomas Thain

MINUTES of the Deliberations and Transactions of The North West Company assembled at Fort William, at their regular Annual Meetings from the 3d to the 9th July 1808—Present at the Meetings, and at each of them by themselves or Attornies, Partners holding Eighty five Shares or Votes.

The State of the Inventories of the Interior, and other Stock belonging to the Concern being taken into consideration, and an ample discussion having taken place on the Subject, the following Points were decided Viz.

That the Advance charged on Goods remaining in the Interior was too high, the Expences of transport at present not being so Extravagant, as when the Calculations fixing this Advance were made, however correct at that time.

That in the present State of the Country, and the order of things brought about, in consequence of the Junction Agreement, the sum charged to the Inventories for Indian Credits was too much and ought to be diminished, as tending to create a false Stock —That the Forts, and Buildings all over the Interior Country and at Saint Marys, were rated too high in the Accounts, and which also was keeping up a false Stock.

That it was very desirable the present heavy Inventories and Stock of Goods on hand should be reduced, as far as the Safety of the Concern can admit of it, and that every measure tending to this object should be adopted by the Agents and Wintering Partners.

The above principles having been unanimously agreed to— Messrs Roderick McKenzie, Thain, McTavish, Duncan Cameron, & Haldane were appointed a Committee to investigate these

Serious Objects, & report to the Meeting the result, which was as follows; That having the proper Documents & Materials before them, are of Opinion, after mature Consideration, that the following alterations in the present System of carrying on the business in the Interior will ultimately tend to the Interest of the Concern.

In Athabasca, less Canoes being required to take in the Goods, than to take out the Packs, an equal proportion of the Expence ought to be deducted from the Outfit, and laid on the Returns, say One fifth.

We consider Athabaska River in the same light with Athabaska Department.

The Transport of Stores, such as flour Sugar, Beeff Pork &c being of the same Inconveniency with Powder, High Wines &c, we think the freight ought to be the same.

Outfits made in the Interior to distant posts such as Mackenzies River, New Caledonia from Athabaska and the Columbia from Fort de Prairies, requiring new Setts of Men and Incurring additional Expences, ought to be valued accordingly.

The present Amount allowed in the Inventories for Buildings is too high and ought to be reduced gradually, say Seven per Cent per Annum deduction.

Balance due by Indians at the taking of the Inventories in the Spring, we consider bad Stock—However as Indians of distant quarters & Chippewayans must be encouraged to work, by giving them Advances, we think some Allowance necessary—To Athabaska, and English River say One Shilling & Sixpence H. per Skin, provided that the Credits in Athabaska Department do not exceed Fifteen Hundred Pounds, nor those of the English River Department Five Hundred Pounds—The Old Amount exceeding this Sum to be reduced to this Standard in two Years, that is to say, One half of the deductions this Year, and the other half the next. The Iroquois Credits in the Athabaska & Athabaska River Departs to be valued as heretofore say One Dollar per Skin—It is understood that the Indian Credits at Michipicotton and the Pic, shall not exceed Twelve hundred Skins each, which are considered worth Half a dollar per Skin—All other Indian Credits to the Westward of St Marys are considered good for nothing, and of course not be placed upon the Inventories—The Credits due at Temiskamingue not to exceed in value Twelve hundred Pounds Currency—Those of the other posts in the lower Departments, abating the King's Posts, we consider good for nothing.

For the Articles In Use, half their Value when new, to be considered sufficient.

The Expences attending Goods to Michipicotton and the Pic, being the same as those to Fort William, we think the Advance ought to be the same, say twenty three per Cent on the Montreal Cost.

All the different Departments of Nipigon to bear the same Advance.

Lac La Pluye to be considered apart from other Departs Fond du Lac Ditto—Ditto

Lac Ouinipique
River Ouinipique
Upper Red River
Lower Red River
Fort Dauphin
} These Departments being much about the same distance from here, & the Expences being nearly the same—the Advance on the Goods &c ought to be the same.

English River & Rat River to have a Tariff apart from the other departments

Athabaska Department to have a Tariff apart

Athabaska River　　　　ditto　　　　ditto

Athabaska Equipts at Lac La Pluye ditto—ditto

Upper & Lower Fort de Prairies to have a separate Tariff.

The Advance on Goods at the different departments, to be formed from the true Statement of Expence attending the Transport of the property to each.

It is considered proper, that a certain proportion of the Expence of transport should be laid on the Returns from the Interior—It is supposed that an average loading of a Canoe is about twenty packs—But making allowances for Proprietors, Clerks, and other Incumbrances, we reduce this number again to fifteen, which at the rate of forty Shillings per pack will make Thirty Pounds per Canoe, to be deducted from the Expences now laid on the Goods for Transport Into the Interior.

As a Guide for the Agents of the Company, in order to procure the necessary Supplies for each Year, we think the Heads of Departments, should give in as soon as possible after their Arrival at this place, the requisition for the following Year, subject however to the Inspection, and Control of the Council.

Fort William 7 July 1808

Signed
- Rodk McKenzie
- Thomas Thain
- Dond McTavish
- Duncan Cameron
- John Haldane

The Report having been approved of by the Meeting, but it requiring more time, to enter minutely into the necessary Calculations, on the rate of Transport &c &c than could now be spared, it was left to the Agents to complete after their Return to Montreal, and it was agreed that these principles, & new rates so to be ascertained, should be applied to the Inventories; to be assumed by the Concern of 1808, now the property of the Adventure of the Year 1807.

Having taken into consideration the nature of the Equipments for the Men, and such other Articles as it has been customary to supply them with, and it having been represented by the Wintering Partners, that the use of Rattan Capots gave rise to general dissatisfaction in the Country; It was agreed that the Importation of Rattans from England should be discontinued, and that Blue Cloth of a suitable quality should be substituted in its stead—Nevertheless as there is a quantity of Rattan on hand, the throwing aside of which would occasion a loss to the Company, that Rattan Capots should still be used for next year, but whatever remained after the supply of next Season, should be made into Indian Capots.

It was also agreed that the prices of Goods at Fort William to Clerks should be reduced to Sixty two & a half per Cent on the Montreal Advance, And the prices Inland to thirty three & one third per Cent on those at Fort William—this at all the Posts in the Interior—The Goods to Interpreters to be at One Hundred per Cent on Montreal prices at Fort William.

To do away Jealousies Amongst the Men, and other irregularities, and in order that all the Men should be supplied from the same Shop without distinction, it was fixed, that the Sales at Maillouxs' House should be confined entirely to Liquors and Provisions, and at the same prices with the Canteen in the Fort.

These Regulations having been determined upon, the follg Partners viz Messrs William McKay
>John McDonald Garth
>A N McLeod
>Alex McKenzie &
>John Wills

being those to go to Montreal this Year, having declared their Intentions, the Meeting proceeded to settle the Departments throughout the Country, and the following Arrangement was agreed to—

1	Athabaska Depart	Mr Donald McTavish
		Mr Rocheblave
		Mr Simon Fraser
		Mr John Thompson
2	English River Depart	Mr. J. D. Campbell
3	Athabaska River	Mr John McGillivray
4	Upper & Lower River Opus	Mr James Hughes
		Mr Alex Henry
5	Columbia	Mr David Thompson
6	Lac Ouinipique	Mr Dun. Cameron
7	Lac Lapluye	Mr A McLellan
8	Upper Red River	Mr John McDonell
9	Lower Red River	Mr D McKenzie
10	Monontaguay	Mr J Haldane
11	Fort Dauphin	Mr John McDonald
12	Lac des Isles	Mr R Cameron
13	The Pic	Mr C Chabouillez
14	Michipicotton	Mr J Leith
15	Fond du Lac	Mr H McGillis

Deeds of assignment were signed, admitting Messrs Keneth McKenzie & Archibald McLellan to be Partners of the Concern, conformable to former Resolves, their Interests commencing with Outfit 1808—Mr McKenzies Share, by Agreement with him to be burdened, with the Consideration allowed to Mr Ermatinger by the Concern last Year.

Mr Angus Shaw's resignation of two Shares was presented by Mr W McGillivray and received by the Meeting—His Interest in such two Shares to cease with the present Outfit of 1808.

THE NORTH WEST COMPANY 255

Mr James McKenzie having been appointed in 1806 by a Resolve of the Concern, a Wintering Partner for the Kings Posts & Mingan, and the Agents at Montreal having determined to make the general Outfits to the Posts from them instead of Quebec as heretofore; it was not judged necessary to appoint a Successor at Quebec to Mr Shaw; it being presumed the business will henceforth be done without such an Appointment—But as Mr McKenzies Situation must subject him to extra Expence in his occasional Visits to Quebec or Montreal, on the Business of the Company, it was understood that all such Expence should be defrayed by the Concern, and paid on Mr McKenzies presenting his Accounts to the Agents.

Statements of the Trade & Situation of the Lower Departments collected from the general Accounts of the Concern, and from the Information of the Gentlemen who have these Departments In charge, under the Control of the Agents, were laid before the Meeting by the Agents—and the Regulations adopted at the Conference held at Montreal for that purpose in May last, were considered to be the best means within reach for carrying on the Trade of these Departments in future.

On different occasions during the Sittings of the general Meeting, various discussions on the general Accounts of the Concern took place, and several points, not sufficiently understood were satisfactorily explained.

On a proposition of Mr Alex McKay to retire from the Concern, on being allowed the Sum of One thousand Pounds Currency—it was agreed to—and the papers necessary for closing the Transaction being exchanged—he retires, holding one of his two Shares for Seven Years, beginning with the Outfit of the present Year and ending with that of 1814—The above Sum of One thousand Pounds to be placed to his Credit on the Books at Montreal on the 30 November next, and to be paid at mutual convenience during the ensuing year, and within Twelve Months if required.

In case of Errors arising on settling the Accounts Current of the Departments, the Inventories and Mens Accounts, and in order to have a reference to certain documents on such occasions, It was agreed that a Correct Copy of the above Vouchers should be deposited every season, by the Gentlemen managing Departments, in the Office at Fort William.

The Agents represented the unfortunate Case of many Old Voyageurs lately discharged from the Companys Service, who have no means of Support—and too Old and Infirm to work in Lower Canada; and recommended some provision to be made for these objects of charity—It was therefore agreed that the Agents of the NWCo should have placed at their disposal on the general Account, a Sum not exceeding One hundred pounds Currency per Annum, for the above purpose, to be divided in such manner, as in their Judgment appeared best, but no Individual to receive more than Ten pounds Currency in One Year.

Some deviation from the Resolve respecting Light Canoes having this Year taken place, it was fully agreed to and understood, that such deviation should not on any account serve as a precedent, but that a Resolve which has produced so many good Effects should always be strictly adhered to.

The Wintering Partners having objected to any Barters Accounts of any kind being kept in the Stores at Montreal, on the ground that everything required by the North West Co should be ordered from England by the Agents, excepting such articles as were necessarily purchased in Canada—The Agents assented thereto, and it is understood that in future, when any thing that cannot possibly be dispensed with, is wanting, that such Article shall be purchased.

Mr McGillivray declared Mr Shaw to be one of the Partners of the Firm of M'Tavish McGillivrays & Co and of course an Agent of the North West Company.

At the earnest request of the Wintering Partners, the Agents, as Partners, but not by way of resolve, agreed that for reasons set forth in said Memorandum, the Estate of a deceased Wintering Partner should be entitled to claim and receive of the Company an equivalent to the full Share, such Deceased Partner held for One Year after such decease—And be further entitled according to Agreement, to have half such Share for Six Years thereafter—No person is pledged to such agent on the part of the Agents, but such as were present and subscribing.

Mr William McKay gave in his resignation according to the North West Agreement, and retires accordingly from the Concern. —The above Notes or Minutes on the twelve preceding pages, having been perused and revised by the Agents, they are found to be correct Statements of the transactions and determinations of the general Meeting—In Witness whereof the said Agents have hereunto set their hands at Fort William this 16th day of July 1808.

> W McGillivray
> Rod Mackenzie } Agents for N W Co
> Thomas Thain

On the 18th July, At a Meeting of the Proprietors, the Case of Mr Ranald Cameron was taken into consideration (The North West Co having, in July 1805 passed a Resolve for admitting the said Mr Cameron into the Concern, provided his conduct was approved of, after a certain time, by the Partners at large)—And it appearing to the Meeting that, nothing had occurred to invalidate his claim, to the Share promised him—It was determined unanimously that he should become a Partner for One Share—On the 24th July therefore, after having previously perused the Agreement and Resolves of the North West Company, Mr Ranald Cameron executed the Papers required for his admission, and becomes interested in the Outfit of the Year 1808.

The plan of sending to Montreal an early Brigade of Canoes, with the Furs of the Posts about Lake Superior, and such other Posts as are contiguous thereto, having this Year been adopted for the first time, it was determined to continue the same plan next Season; And it was understood that the Partners in charge of these Posts and Departments, should exert themselves, to have all the Beaver and Muskrats brought to Fort William in all June for this purpose.

On the 24th July a Statement of the Trade and number of Establishments in the Lac Ouinipique & Upper Red River Departments were laid before the Meeting—It appeared, that in the Winter of 1807/8, there had been Ten Canoes, and as many Posts and Masters in Lac Ouinipique Department—That five of these Posts only produced 32½ Packs in all—it was therefore determined, that these five Posts should be given up, & the remaining five only established—Say *Skabitchiwine, Bas de la Riviere, Riviere Cassé, Riviere au Tourte, & Les Dalles*, and that Mr Cameron should make his Arrangements accordingly.

Respecting the Upper Red River Department, it appeared that

Six Canoes, and as many Posts yielded but 133 Packs & 576 Bags Pemican; that four out of the Six posts, produced only 53 Packs, and 26 Bags Pemican; It was therefore decided, that these four posts should be abandoned, and that only the *Riviere qui Appelle*, and *Pine Fort* should be established for the ensuing year—Mr John McDonell was accordingly directed to make his Arrangements in conformity to the above determination—The above Notes or Minutes on the two preceding Pages, contain Statements of the transactions, and determinations of the general Meeting, from the 18th to the 24th July—In Witness whereof the Agents have hereunto set their hands at Fort William this 24th July 1808.

Rod Mackenzie } Agents for
Thomas Thain } NWCo

Archd N M'Leod went to Montreal in the year 1808, in lieu of Mr Simon Fraser who supposed it to be his year of Rotation which afterwards was found a mistake in both Parties in consequence of which Mr M'Leod is exonerated from any Penalty on that Account.—this was determined by the Concern at Fort William 11 July 1809.

WMG

Review of Rotations founded on a Resolve passed the 8th July 1805.[1]

1805   John Sayer—[Retired]
        John M'Donell—[Montreal]
        Charles Chabouillez
        Duncan Cameron—[Montreal]
        Alexr McKay—[Montreal]

1806   James Hughes
        Alexr Fraser—[Montreal]
        Hugh McGillis
        Alexr Henry
        John McGillivray—[P Rochblave went down in his place]
        James McKenzie—[Montreal]

[1] The annotations in square brackets in this list were entered in another hand after 1812.

1807 Simon Fraser
William McKay—[Montreal]
A. N. McLeod
Daniel McKenzie—[Montreal]
John M'Donald
Donald M'Tavish

1808 David Thompson—[retired in 1812]
J. D. Campbell ⎫ John M'Donald went down on account of
John Thomson ⎭ indisposition.—W. McG
Pierre Rochblave—[A. N. M'Leod went down]
Alexr McKenzie—[Montreal]
John M'Donald—[J. Wills went down in his place]

1809 James Leith—[Mr Simon Fraser in his place]
John Haldane
John Wills
John M'Donell
Charles Chabouillez
Duncan Cameron

1810 Alexr McKay—[retired Outfit 1808]
James Hughes
Alexr Fraser—[Montreal retired]
Hugh McGillies
Alexr Henry
John McGillivray
James McKenzie—[Rotation in his place]

1811 Simon Fraser
William McKay—[retired Outfit 1808]
A. N. McLeod—[retired Outfit 1809]
Daniel McKenzie
John M'Donald
Donald M'Tavish
Kenneth McKenzie—[James Hughes]

1812 Ar: McLellan
Ranald Cameron—[D McKenzie in his place]

David Thompson—[retired 1812]
J. D. Campbell
John Thompson—[K. MacKenzie]
Pierre Rochblave—[went to Montreal in his Rotation]

1813 Alexr McKenzie
John M'Donald
James Leith
John Haldane
John Wills
John M'Donell—[retired in 1812]

Fort William 24 July 1808

MINUTES of Deliberations and Transactions of the North West Company, assembled at their regular Annual Meeting at Fort William in the Month of July 1809—present in person or by Attornies, Partners holding Seventy five Votes or Shares.

The Arrangements of the Departments having been taken into consideration, the following Gentlemen were unanimously appointed for the Season viz

Department		Canoes

Athabaska Depart
  Mr Donald M'Tavish
  Mr P. Rochblave &
  Mr J. Thomson
	}	26 Canoes

English River Mr John M'Donell	}	7 "
Rat River & Lower English River Mr Daniel MacKenzie	}	4 "

Shaskatchiwane River
  Mr James Hughes
  Mr Alexr Henry
	}	10 "
		2 "

Columbia Mr David Thompson	}	5 "
Athabaska River Mr John McGillivray	}	— 54

THE NORTH WEST COMPANY 261

Lake Ouinipique & River Mr Duncan Cameron	....	6 Canoes
Upper Red River Mr John McDonald	....	5 "
Lower Red River Mr John Wills	....	3 "
Fort Dauphin Mr John McDonald	....	5 "
Lac La Pluye Mr Archd McLellan	....	3 "
Fond des Lacs Mr Hugh McGillis	....	x 3 Boats
Pic & River Mr Alexr MacKenzie	....	x 5 Canoes
Michipicotton Mr James Leith	....	
Monontague Mr John Haldane	....	5 Canoes
Lac des Isles (Interior of Nipigon) Mr Ranald Cameron	....	4 "
Fort William Mr Kenneth McKenzie		
Lac Nipigon Mr Rod: McKenzie (Clerk)	....	3 "

                                               34

        Brought forward................54

                                             88 Canoes

The following Gentlemen go to Montreal on Rotation viz
    Mr Simon Fraser
    Mr Charles Chabouillez &
    Mr J. D. Campbell

Charges of a very serious nature having been brought against Mr Chabouillez, respecting his Transactions at the Pic last Season, but the necessary Proofs not being in readiness; it is fully understood that such Evidence as the case may require, is to be produced next Summer either to substantiate those Charges, or do them away.

The Resolve of the 14th July 1806 (for preventing Partners from permitting Women to be taken from the Indians) having been infringed—the Parties so transgressing paid each One Hundred Pounds Currency as a fine—The Agents for apparently countenancing or giving leave to Mr Logan at St Marys, to take a Woman from the Indians; And Mr Daniel Mackenzie from Lower Red River for having permitted one of his Men to do the same.

Having taken into serious consideration the present State of the Concern, and all matters regarding the Same, as well the Arrangements in the Interior, as that under the immediate control of the Agents—Orders, Supplies, Contracts &c &c. The following principles were fixed and determined upon as Rules of Conduct for all Parties henceforth.

That the Trade hereafter to be carried on, to the district beyond the Rocky Mountains, known by the name of Columbia, shall be precisely on the same footing as the Trade to Athabaska—that is—that the Canoes for that quarter with the Returns shall come annually to Lac La Pluye, and there take the Outfit, as otherwise it would be attended with too great an Expence to the Compy.

That all the Orders for Goods from the North West Departments shall every year be inserted in a Scheme at Fort William, which Scheme the Agents are to take to Montreal together with the said Orders, to have the whole completed, when the Requisitions for the other Departments are ascertained, previous to making out the general Memorandum for England.

That all Agreements entered into by the Agents (except such as the general Agreements of the North West Company specifies, as immediately connected with the Routine of the Business) shall be at their responsibility until laid before the Annual Meeting and approved of.

That henceforth no more than One Years Supply of Corn, Grease and Gum, with about two thirds of a Years Supply of Flour and Sugar, shall be kept on hand And it is understood that, propositions for a Contract shall this Year be made at Detroit for three or five Years, provided the price of Flour can be fixed at twenty Shillings York Currency per 112 lb and the Hulled Corn, at or under Nine Shillings Yk per Minot.

It is fully understood that every Partner of the North West

Company has a Right to inspect the general Accounts and Vouchers relative to the general Concern.

That a Contract for High Wines shall be entered into by the Agents for three Years at Detroit or Queenston on account of the Concern, if to be fixed at a Reasonable rate, and a proper degree of Strength, with a Security that may be deemed Sufficient against a disappointment—It is however understood, that if High Wines from Lower Canada can be procured, they ought to have a preference generally.

On considering the present State of the Michilimakinac Company, and the probability of their Concern being dissolved, before the expiration of the Ten Years, for which their Agreement was made—It is fully understood, that in the event of such a Dissolution, all Agreements entered into between the North West Company, and that Body, are done away of course; and the North West Company will then remain, in regard to the Southern Trade, on the footing on which they are placed by the 21st Article of the North West Agreement of 1804.

If the Agents injure the Concern through bad Management, the Rest of the Concern have the same Right to redress from them, as against any others persons concerned, who may injure the general Interest.

It is understood that no more than two Light Canoes shall come up annually from Montreal for the convenience of the Agents and the Clerks, who must necessarily be brought up to assist in the management of the Business.

Whenever Mr McGillivray may come to Fort William, a third Light Canoe shall be provided for his Conveyance.

All Liquors and Provisions required for the Outfit shall be purchased by the Agents in future for the North West Company and on account of the whole Concern, when such articles are wanted, at the most reasonable Rates at which they can be procured, without any Advantage to them, except their Commissions on the Outfit.—This modification the Agents agree to, at the request of the Wintering Partners, without any Reference to the manner in which these articles have been usually charged.

Mr Alexr Henry having come out from Fort Des Prairies in a Light Canoe, leaving 16 packs Inland, contrary to the spirit of the existing Resolve regarding such matters—The Meeting took the case into consideration, and having heard Mr Henry's reasons viz: the necessity of sending two Canoes for Columbia, to the Bas de la Riviere, and an early Canoe for the River Opas, that Department being out of Goods; the requisition for which Supplies would have been too late by the ordinary Course—These reasons were deemed sufficient, and he was exonerated from the Penalty—but it is fully understood, that it is not to be considered as a precedent for the future—Fort William 18th July 1809

W McGillivray ⎱ Agents
Thomas Thain ⎰ NWCo

MINUTES of Deliberations and Transactions of the North West Company Assembled at their regular Annual Meeting at Fort William in the Month of July 1810 present in person or by Attorny. Partners holding Seventy Votes or Shares.

The Arrangements of the different Departments having been taken into Consideration. The following Gentlemen were Unanimously appointed for the Season Viz.—

Athabasca Dept

Mr Donald McTavish Mr John McGillivray Mr Simon Fraser	....	26 Canoes Messrs Colin & Richard Campbell
Athabasca River Mr John McDonell	....	5 do
U. English River Mr John D. Campbell Mr Robert Henry	....	7 do
Lower English River Mr Daniel McKenzie	....	3 do
Fort De Prairies Mr James Hughes Mr Alex Henry	....	11 do
Fort Dauphin Mr John McDonald	....	5 do
U. & Lower Red River Mr John McDonald Mr John Wills	....	7 do

THE NORTH WEST COMPANY 265

Lac Ouinipique Mr Duncan Cameron	}	5 do
		69 Canoes
Lake La Pluie Mr James Leith	}	4 do
Fond Du Lac Mr Hugh McGillis	}	4 Batteau
Monontague Mr John Haldane	}	8 Canoes
Lac Des Isle Mr Ranald Cameron	}	4 do
Pic Mr Pierre Rocheblave Michilipicoton Mr Archd McLellan Columbia Mr David Thompson Kings Posts Mr James McKenzie Fort William Mr Kenneth McKenzie	}	3 do
		Canoes 92 & Boats

Mr John Thompson Goes to Montreal in Rotation.

Fort William 18th July 1810
Angus Shaw } Agents per
Alexr McKenzie } NWCo

MINUTES of the deliberations and Transactions of the North West Company assembled at Fort William at their regular meetings in the month of July One Thousand Eight Hund[d] & Eleven—Partners present by themselves or by their attorneys, holding Seventy four Shares—or Votes.

11th July—The first meeting assembled for the purpose of taking into consideration the State of the Trade hitherto carried on across the Rocky Mountains by the Sources of the Shaskatchiwan River—and also to consider the propriety of adopting the new Plan proposed by Mr David Thompson, of carrying on that Trade in future by way of the Beaver & Athabasca Rivers.

After a full discussion it was determined that the Route newly proposed, and which Mr Thompson attempted last Winter to pass through—would be attended with more expence & difficulty than the old one, and that therefore the Trade should continue to be carried on by the Route of the Shaskatchiwane River.

It was also resolved that the outfit of this years should be increased to five Canoes, and that Mr Jn. McDonald should be appointed to the superintendency of the Expedition assisted by J. G. M'Tavish—and to have this with all haste—intending by this arrangement that Mr David Thompson should be left to prosecute his plans of discovery on the west side of the Rocky Mountains towards the Pacific.

13th July—The Meeting assembled and the Agents laid before them the following Papers vizt.

A series of correspondence with the Ministers of Governmt and with the Committee of Directors of the Honle East India Compy—relative to a licence solicited from the latter on the part of the North West Compy—to enable them to dispose of such Furs & Skins in China as they might collect in course of their intended Trade on the North West Coast of America.

The Agreement entered into with J J Astor Esq in Jany last relative to the South Trade, together with various Extracts relating to the line of Boundary established or to be established between Great Britain & the U. States by that fixed upon to divide the Trade of the North West Co from the Michilimakinac Trade—or South West Company.

A proposal made by the agents that the Concern should purchase some part of the Stock of the Hudsons Bay Company —to establish an influence in their Comittee in order to bring about the fixing a Boundary with them.

14th July—The Meeting assembled and took into consideration the merit and length of services of the Companys Clerks throughout the Departments and fixed a Rotation for Promotion on these Principles—Partners were named to various departments but the Wintering Proprietors not being all arrived—the further arrangement of the departments—was put off until their arrival.—Various other discussions took place without coming to any decision.

15th July—The Meeting assembled and Rough Drafts of the Resolves proposed to be entered into were read, Messrs Leith Wills & Haldane entered a Protest against the Boundary Line settled with Mr Astor—against the Companys entering into or participating in the South Trade—against the Steps to be taken by purchase of Hudsons Bay Stock or otherwise in order to bring about a Boundary line with the Hudsons Bay Co and against entering into the projected Trade from China to the North West Coast of America.—Mr Rocheblave gave in a Protest against the appointment of Mr Alexr McKenzie as agent for Sir Alexr McKenzie & Co—against the purchase of Hudsons Bay Stock—against the participation in the South Trade to be carried on by the South West Fur Company and against the Boundary Line established to divide that Trade from that of the Concern (if more than the present Department of Fond du Lac, as it now stands was given up or occupied by the said South West Co). Various explanations respecting the general North West Accnts were asked and given—and the Accnts signed.

It was settled, that in order to prevent the unnecessary accummulation of Goods—at this place—and at Montreal, that particular attention should be paid to the making out the orders for the Departments, and when such orders are entered in the general Scheme Book, that the Agents assisted by Mr Kenneth McKenzie should examine and regulate *the whole* by an average of the last three years at their discretion—adding a Contingent Column and the Goods to be divided accordingly.

Mr Hughes agreed to put off his Rotation until next year—the Concern thinking it proper he should for this year, return to the Shaskatchiwan River.

It was agreed that Mr J. Bte Cadotte, having since the year 1802—received from the Concern One Hundred Pounds currency per annum as a donation at their pleasure—the same be discontinued after the payment that shall take place in the year 1813—it having been considered that he holds the place of Indian Interpreter in Upper Canada, and is thereby enabled to support himself without the Companys assistance.

16th July—The following Resolves were signed—vizt—that to enable the agents of the N West Company to purchase on account of the Concern, Hudsons Bay Stock to the Amount of Fifteen thousd Pound Sterling, with a view of establishing an Influence in the Committee of the said Company—in order to establish a Boundary Line with them—in the Interior Country.

A Resolve for entering into adventure and a Trade from England, and China to the North West Coast of America—provided a suitable licence to that Effect is obtained from the East India Company.

A Resolve for Accepting *One third* of the Interest held by Forsyth Richardson & Co & M'Tavish McGillivray & Co in the Concern entered into With John Jacob Astor Esqr, Known by the name of the South West Fur Company—a Resolve ratifying and approving as much of the said agreement as relates to the Boundary line established between the North West & South West Trade, being that which shall be fixed by Treaty as a national Line of Boundary between Great Britain & the United States.

And a Resolve fixing the Periods at which promotions to Shares shall take place from among the Clerks—and a list of Rotation of the same for precedence.

On representing the State of the Voyageurs Fund, & the unavoidable pressure upon it from the distress among the Voyageurs the last two winters—The Concern agreed to give One Hundred Pounds Cy to that Fund for the support of the distressed objects depending on it.

The Consumption of Liquor in all the Trade carried on by the North West Company—was next examined, (at present estimated at 10,000 Gallons—including Spirits) in order to ascertain the least possible quantity that might be made to Answer should *the Saints in Parliament*—in their mistaken notions of Philanthropy—persist in the Intention of abolishing the use of that Article wholely in the Trade—and it is the general opinion that even one Half of the above quantity or 5000 Gallons if restricted to that small quantity, might still serve the Trade was it found advisable to make any offer

THE NORTH WEST COMPANY 269

of that kind to Parliament, in order to prevent its total prohibition.

20th July—The Proprietors whose presence was waited for in order to Arrange the Different Departments, being arrived The Meeting proceeded upon that Business and the following Arrangement of Partners was agreed upon—viz—

1—Athabasca............	John McGillivray Simon Fraser Robert Henry	} 3
2—English & Rat Rivers & Cumberland Ho	} ...... Daniel McKenzie J D. Campbell John Thomson	} 3
3—Shaskatchewan River......	James Hughes Alexr Henry	} 2
4—Columbia............	John M'Donald David Thompson	} 2
5—Athabasca River.........	John M'Donell	1
6—Fort Dauphin............	John M'Donald	1
7—Lac De la pluie..........	Duncan Cameron	1
8—Red River............	John Wills J. Leith	} 2
9—Monontague............	Jno Haldane	1
10—Pic....................	Pre Rocheblave	1
11—Michipicoten............	Archd McLellan	1
12—Fond du Lac............	Hugh McGillis	1
13—Lac Ouinipique..........	J D. Cameron Ck	
14—Lac des Isles............	Ranald Cameron	1
15—Ft William..............	Kenneth McKenzie	1
16—Lac Nipigon............	Rod: McKenzie Ck	
17—St Maries..............	Robert Logan	"

Proprietors 21

Mr Donald M'Tavish goes to Montreal on Rotation.
Fort William 20th July 1811

Angus Shaw } Agents per
Alexr McKenzie } NWCO

MINUTES of Deliberations & Transactions of the North West Co assembled at their Regular Annual Meeting at Fort William in the Month of July 1812 a large majority of the Partners being present at the same.

(Copied from the Hand writing of A N McLeod Esq)

July 18th—The Partners having met it was the general opinion that the management of Departments should be entered upon without longer delay—tho' Messrs D McKenzie, J D Campbell & Mr J Thompson & John McDonald are not yet arrived—The following Arrangement of Partners was agreed upon viz

1	—Athabasca	John McGillivray
		Simon Fraser
		Robert Henry
2d	—English River	J D Campbell
	Cumberland House	John Thomson
3d	—River Opas F des P	Alexr Henry
4th	—Columbia	John George McTavish Clk
5th	—Athabasca River	Alexr Stewart—Clk
6th	—Fort Dauphin	John McDonald or Mr Leith
7th	—Lac la Pluie	Duncan Cameron
8th	—Red River	John Wills
9th	—Monontague & Lac Nip	Rod: McKenzie—Clerk
		James Leith
10th	—Pic	John Haldane
11	—Michipicoten	Archd McLellan
12	—Fond du Lac	James Grant—Clk
13	—Lac Ouinipique	Dougald Cameron
14	—Lac des Isles	Ranald Cameron
15	—Fort William	Hugh McGillis
16	—St. Maries	Robert Logan.

The Provisional appointment of Mr Leith to the Fort Dauphin Department was on the supposition that Mr McDonald who is reported to be in bad Health, goes down—The following Gentlemen go down in Rotation viz John McDonald, John McDonell, James Hughes—David Thompson, Kenneth McKenzie, Pierre de Rocheblave and Daniel McKenzie.

Mr Donald McTavish is appointed to set out immediately & proceed in the Columbia Business by sailing from England for the South West Coast, as soon as possible & conduct that Business in conformity to the Resolve of the Company last Year.

The Wintering Partners do not wish to contribute any sum of money for the Superannuated Fund.

On Account of the Declaration of war by the Americans it was determined to send as many men as could be spared, without detriment to the Business, to L La Pleuie to help getting the Packs out in as much haste as possible, and Mr McLellan volunteered to go and conduct the same—at the same time to use his influence to send out as many Indians as could be induced, to accompany us for the safeguard of the Companys Furs to the *French River*. And that Mr James Grant should go to Fond du Lac on the same Business; that Mr Shaw with the Gentlemen going to Montreal, and as many more as could be spared, should set out in the *Invincible* with a supply of arms amunition & Provisions for St. Maries—then to act as circumstances may require.

Athabasca Express to start from Dunvegan on the 1t of December—as it is of great consequence, it should not miscarry this year.

Partners of the North West Company not present are requested to send out next year their opinions whether a Partner retiring has a right to the Profits of his whole Share or Shares of the outfit on which he retires—say he appears by himself or attorney at Fort William in 1812—is he entitled to the Profits of his whole Share of that outfit?[1]

Mr John McGillivray is expected to come to this place next year & transact the Athabasca Business at Lac la Pluie.

It was Determined the Agents should write to Mr John Stewart now at Athabasca, that he is appointed by Company to take charge of the Department of New Caledonia & combine his Plans & operations with the Gentlemen on the Columbia, & that Mr Stuart is to proceed next Spring as early as possible down to the Sea,

---

[1] The agreement is extremely clear on this point—a Partner must either Winter, or retire for one year in Rotation, to entitle him to hold his full share—appearing at Ft. Wm. is nothing to the purpose—he must either winter by appointment of the Concern—or relinquish (without a regular assignment) one half of his Interest in the Co.——W McG.

there to form a junction with Mr J. G. McTavish and meet the Ship intended to come to the Columbia.

A Resolve entered into that Mr David Thompson now going down on Rotation shall be allowed his full Share for three years after the outfit and one Hund^d Pounds besides—that he is to finish his Charts, Maps &c and deliver them to the Agents in that time, after which he is to [be] considred as a retired Partner, and enjoy the Profits of One Hundredth for Seven Years—the Hund^d p. pan^m is meant for compensation for making use of his own Instruments &c &c and for furnishing him with implements for drawing, writing &c.

It was agreed that all apprentices (whose Engagements are expired) should on their first Engagement, be hired for three Years, and that no one should exceed £80, 90—& £100 for the first second & third Year—This Rule not to be deviated from—It was also agreed that all Persons throughout the Country should be under (written) Engagement to the Company—N B. This does not include —or refer to the Freemen scattered over the Country.

Mr Leith takes charge of Monontague, Lake Nipigon &c & Mr John McDonald goes back to Fort Dauphin.

It was agreed upon by all the Partners that it was proper to [illegible] all the Departments how necessary it is [illegible] fourth of the whole Outfit in reserve to supp [illegible] in the Interior should circumstances prevent a supply from being sent by any way or any means—and as the Gentlemen at the Head of the Provision Departments think well of it, and promise to practice it, it is to be hoped, & expected that all others will conform themselves to it.

It was understood that when Mr Thompsons half Share falls into the Concern, it shall not be appropriated until the full Sum of Three Hundred Pounds is compensated for to the Company from the Emoluments to accrue from such Half Share.

MINUTES of the deliberations & discussions of the Annual Meeting held at Fort William in the month of July (9th to 16th) 1813— Present in Person or by attorneys 73 votes.

9th & 10th The Partners assembled to consider generally the State of the Country and the short Returns produced by all the Departments, a determination was taken to curtail as much as

THE NORTH WEST COMPANY 273

possible every unnecessary Expence in order to meet the present Scale of the Trade, accordingly after a strict investigation it was ascertained that numbers of men as well Clerks were now in the Employment whose services could be dispensed with vizt

Sault of St. Maries	3 men		
Michipicoton	2	1 Clk, 1 Intr	
Pic	4	"	"
Fond du Lac	8	"	3
Lac des Isles	9	1	"
Lac la Pluie	6	1 Canoe Maker	
Riviere Rouge	1	1	1
Upper & Lower Fort des Prairies	20	1	
Lac Ouinipique	10	2	1
Cumberland House & Rat River	6	1	
English River	5	1	
*Athabasca	35		
Athabasca River	5	1	
Fort Dauphin			

*Athabasca doubtful on account of the men engaged the number to be discharged depending on that circumstance—The Casualties in the Country were in all 15 men—and alltogether it was apparent that the Trade of this Year & until the Returns increased considerably beyond the present Standard could be carried on with 150 men less than were in the Country in 1812—Lists were given in of the number of men & Clerks in each Department & it was determined that each Partner should act upon the reduced Scale as already stated.

It was represented by the Agents that the Orders for Goods sent to England last Fall were calculated on the principle fixt upon at this place last Summer vizt (that Partners or Clerks at the Head of Departments should reserve *one quarter* of the outfits he brought into the Interior Country in 1812 to guard against the Misfortune of receiving no supplies this Year from Montreal which was probable on account of the war) and that in consequence the general Scheme had been reduced *one fourth* for this year (depending upon such a resource) & that by the order sent to England the next Scheme would be precisely the same as this provided the present was not infringed upon.

The Agents also represented that from the circumstances of the war no Provisions of any Kind could be depended upon for next year & neither Tobacco nor High Wines; it was therefore proposed & agreed to unamislously that the outfits of the present year should be so curtailed as to have for next Year such a quantity of Tobacco & High Wines as would afford a moderate supply for the Country without any aid from Canada.—An exact account of all the Provisions—Tobacco, High Wines & amunition on Hand, was at the same time laid before the meeting.

12th—Meeting assembled—the usual Questions being asked whether those Who had a right to Rotation this year were disposed to avail themselves of it, they all declined except Mr Archd McLellan who goes down in his turn.

Mr Alexr Henry having been appointed by the Agents at Montreal to take the place of Mr Hughes, in the charge & Conducting of the Canoe for the Columbia in Case of Mr Hughes' Health not permitting him to proceed according to his appointment to cross the Mountains, and on his meeting Mr Hughes at the Lac de la Riviere Ouinipique—he having declined, or at least not acting up to the Intentions of the said appointment, for reasons which were not deemed satisfactory—It was therefore considered essential to the Interests of the Concern that a Partner with two able Clerks should still proceed to the Columbia in order to strengthen the Party already sent accross the mountains, and Mr Henry was appointed for this Duty, (always provided that Mr Hughes does not previously go forward) and to be accompanied by Mr Alexr Stewart & Mr James Keith.—After this Arrangement the Departments of the Country were taken into consideration & filled up as follows vizt.

Athabasca	John McGillivray
	Simon Fraser
	Robert Henry
	George Keith
Upper English River	John Thomson
Lower ER & Cumberland House	J. D. Campbell
Shaskatchewan River	J. Hughes or Alexr Henry
	Pierre Rocheblave
Athabasca River	John Haldane

THE NORTH WEST COMPANY

Lac Ouinipique	J. D. Cameron
L La Pluie	Duncan Cameron
Lac des Isles	Ranald Cameron
Monontague & ⎫	James Leith
Lac Nipigon ⎭	Rod: McKenzie Clk
Pic	John McBean "
Michipicoton	Hugh McGillis
Fond du Lac	Daniel McKenzie
Red River	John Wills
Fort William	Kenneth McKenzie
Fort Dauphin	John McDonald

The Partners present being called upon to declare whether any irregularity existed in the Management of the Business (of the Departments) that they were acquainted with—It appeared, that Mr Archd McLellan took a few Bags of Flour & Corn last Fall out of the Depots at St Maries, altho' he had already received his quantity from the Agents—he proved however that he had left a larger quantity of Provisions in his Inventory, but nevertheless it was considered irregular as it is well understood that all Depots must be held untouched wherever they are placed by the Agents. That Mr Haldane received at the Pic a Clerk belonging to the Hudsons Bay Company who had left that Service—it did not appear that he was inticed to leave his employers, but he refused to return to his Duty; it being however attended with great inconvenience to the Concern & productive of no good it was the general opinion that none of the Hudsons Bay Servants should in future be received into any of the Companys Forts except in cases of Starvation—and on *no account* to be engaged to the N W Co.

It was remarked that the Corn for the Montreal Canoes (to serve as Provisions for them from St. Maries) not having been sent to the Sault in the first Trip of the Invincible, occasioned an additional Expense in sending it forward—which was caused either by the neglect of the Agents or of Mr McGillis who had wintered at Fort William—The Agents explained that the mistake arose from its having been supposed that the Vessel would not have sailed from Ft Wm before the arrival of some one of them in the Spring—such having been the understanding on account of the war.

Mr Ranald Cameron was found fault with for having left his Canoes too far behind in order to come out light by which means they lost time—he stated in explanation that it was customary for him to come before the Canoes in order to ascertain whether or not the Provisions put *en cache* were safe, & this year in particular—wishing to learn the news as it was important that the Canoes for Lac des Isles should be at Head quarters as early as possible—Mr Cameron is therefore in future to use all exertions for getting his people out early to which end his accompanying them to the Borders of Lake Superior will much contribute.

It appeard that from 80 to 100 Bags Corn & 40 Kegs Grease were left at Lac la Pluie last Fall after all the Canoes were passed on for the Interior—the whole of which was expended during the winter—Mr Duncan Cameron stated that his Men & the Indians were in a State of Starvation, & that he could not preserve the Corn without allowing them to perish, the Fish & all other means having entirely failed. The consumption however appeared very extraordinary & it was freely commented on—Mr Cameron was blamed for not sending out his Beaver Packs in preference to others early, it having always been understood that the Beaver from L la Pluie & all the other near Posts was to be sent down by the first Brigades to Montreal.

It appeared that great inattention here prevaild in Keeping & forwarding the Accounts of the Provisions delivred to the different Brigades in passing out & in at the Bas de la Riviere—no regular Returns made & too great a waste of Pemican & Grease at that Depot in general which requires a radical reform, no less it was considered than changing the Post & making the Depot of Provisions, where there is no Trading Post.

On examining the Transactions of the Red River it appeared that the Trade of the lower Part of it has been entirely lost & the Character of the Company in some degree, brought into contempt in the Eyes of the natives owing to the very small outfits left at the Falls & Red Pembina last Fall.

The Cause of the great diminution in the Returns of the English River having been enquired into it appeard that almost all the Chipewayans from that Country had gone to Athabasca last Fall & it being well known that the few native Kristineaux of that Country can make no Hunt adequate to the Outfit—it being in consequence essential to get the Chipewayans back, if possible from Athabasca—Mr John Thomson supposed to have a better knowledge of them, was appointed to the Upper English River—hence his changing with Mr J D Campbell.

The Gentlemen managing at Fort Dauphin & Athabasca River not being yet arrived—no investigation of the Transaction of those Departments were entered into nor of Athabasca except that the unfortunate occurrence in McKenzies River—(the Death of Mr Alexr Henry Junr & his Men)—was chiefly attributed to the Change which had been made in that Department last Fall—this however is matter of conjecture.

The quantity of Provisions usually furnished from the Shaskatchewan & Red Rivers, was investigated, as upon the reduced Scale of the Trade it does not require to be as large generally, but as it is not expected that in any case, either Corn or Flour from Canada can be procurd next year the following quantities of Pemican & Grease appears to be necessary for the purpose of the Trade next Season—exclusive of the quantity required for bringing out the Canoes of Fort des Prairies to Bas de la Riviere Ouinipique vizt.

Dept at Cumberland House—Pemican

Athabasca Canoes coming out	28		
Upper & Lower English Rr	11		
To Bas de la Riviere	39	Canoes at 2½	100
Athabasca Canoes going in	22		
English River	10		
	32	at 3	96
Fort des Prairies	12	at 2	24
To Cumberland House			5
Athabasca River		5 Canoes at 3	15
Guides &c &c			10
Tauraux[1]			250

[1] Buffalo hides made into sacks, containing about ninety pounds of pemmican.

278 DOCUMENTS RELATING TO

Provisions to be furnishd by the Red River

Canoes coming out to Lac la Pluie
Athabasca.........................28 at 2		56

Canoes out to F. William
English River......................11	
Lac Ouinipique..................... 3	
Fort des Prairies...................14	
Athabasca Rr...................... 5	
Red River......................... 6	
39 at 3½	137
L L Pluie Canoes (if no followers).....	10
	203

Canoes going in vizt
Athabasca........................21	
Atha River........................ 4	
E River...........................12	
Red River......................... 6	
Fort Dauphin...................... 5	
Lac Ouinipique.................... 4	
Fort des Prairies...................12	
—64 at 3	192
Carried forward.........395	

Red River Provisions to be furnished

Brought forwd 395	

Passing Canoes—Light Canoes—casualty from the Columbia
   —Expenses in Summer & to Guides, Clerks & retainers of
   all descriptions
	35

for 1814—Tauraux	430

It is expected that the Fort Dauphin Department will furnish its own Provisions all the way out, should it give more than is necessary for its own Canoes the extra quantity is to come in deduction of the quantity from the Red River.

Expenditure of Grease annually to be furnished by the Red River & River $^a/_c$ as.

Canoes from Fort William to L L Pluie
- Lac la Pluie.................... 4
- Red River..................... 6
- Fort Dauphin................. 5
- Fort des Prairies..............12
- Lac Ouinipique................ 4
- Atha' River................... 5
- English River.................12

—48 at ¼	12
Montreal Canoes to L L P........ 28	7
Nipigon Canoes from F W........10	10
Fond du lac..................... 5	5
Pic & Michipicoton..............	15
40 large Canoes with Packs down....	30
Summer Consumption at Ft Wm....	50
L L P. for consumption in Summer & for Montreal Canoes coming out	30
Bas de la Riviere................	30
Cumberland Ho & Posts adjacent...	20
St Maries Winter, & Winter at Fort Wm	25
Kegs.........................	234
Kegs Grease to be furnished Not found	234
Various contingencies to be provided for	20
Kegs Grease........................	254

of which 160 annually to be brought to Headqtrs

15th—Assignment of Shares were made conformable to a Resolve passed in July 1811, for admitting into the Concern as Partners— Messrs Alexr Stewart, J D Cameron, John Stuart, George Keith & John George M'Tavish—for each *One Hundredth* Share.

During the various discussions which took place the Resolves passed from time to time by different Majorities for the

Maintainance of order & the checking of extravagance in the different Departments of the Business were frequently referred to, and a determination was unanimously expressed to Keep them in full vigour—particularly in regard to light Canoes—and for the Sake of Showing a good Example, the Agents from Montreal it was understood were not to have more than twelve Working Men for their Canoes exclusive of Servants.

A List of Rotation was fixed for the four following years—and the present.[1]

    1813—Archd McLellan—[went down]
            John McDonald—F.D.
            James Leith
            John Haldane
            John Wills &—[Dead]
            Duncan Cameron
    1814—Hugh McGillis
            Alexr Henry—[dead]
            John McGillivray
            John McDonald—[went down Rotation]
            James McKenzie
            Donald McTavish—[dead]
    1815—Robert Henry—[went down]
            Simon Fraser
            Daniel McKenzie—[went down]
            James Hughes—[Rotation]
            J D. Campbell x—[to take rotation next yr]
            John Thomson x—[to take rotation   do]
    1816—Pierre De Rocheblave [Retired]
            Ronald Cameron—[Haldane]
            Alexr Stewart—[J McG]
            J D. Cameron—[Leith]
            John Stewart—[Rotation]
    1817—George Keith
            John George M'Tavish

As it is Mr Alexr Henrys turn of Rotation next Year—& as he cannot from his great distance from the place of Rendezvous, avail

---

[1] The annotations in square brackets in this list were entered later in another hand.

himself of it conveniently—it is therefore understood that he shall be entitled to his Rotation in any year he may come from the Columbia—in place of his Rotation of 1814.

16th The general Accounts were examined & the discount on Bills drawn in Canada in order to place the Nt Proceeds of the Fur Sales in England at the Disposal of the Agents in Montreal where they are bound to account for the same to the Concern, was objected to, and a Protest entered accordingly by all the Wintering Partners present—No other objection was made to the Accounts.— It was stated to them by the Agents that all the remainder of the Goods in which they were Interested in the S. W. Fur Company was to be disposed of this Season—or that orders had been given to that effect.

No more Gum required at Fort William, there being enough with what F du lac & the surrounding Posts will furnish of that Article to answer sufficiently all the purposes of the Concern.

The Winter Express of last year having been detained between the Red River Posts & Lac Ouinipique whereby the intelligence intended to have been communicated to the Agents, was lost—It was therefore determined that for the ensuing Winter no other Route shall be taken for its conveyance but the *old* way of Fond du lac—and Mr Wills engages (from the Red River) without fail, to send it forward, how soon he receives it, to the Posts of the above Department—in order that it may reach the Agents at St Maries.

The extraordinary proportion of Damaged & Staged Beaver brought out of the Country was strongly stated by the Agents to the Wintering Partners & the necessity of adopting some means for diminishing the quantity urged—The Partners were also requested to encourage the Hunting of all Animals whose Skins could be got in good Season.

A general Letter from a majority of the Concern having last year been adopted to such as were not present at the time at Head Quarters, declaring it to be the opinion—that considering the circumstances of the war, and the possibility of the Enemy overrunning Canada, it might be found impossible to bring up any part of the ensuing outfit from Montreal this Year—therefore it was strongly recommended that any Person having charge of a Post or Department, should reserve as a contingent to meet such an

Event—one full fourth of his Outfit.—It is found that this determination has been but very partially acted upon—One Post in Nipigon—Athabasca, & the English (upper) & Fort des Prairies come the nearest to it, but *none* complete—no other Department seems to have paid attention to the above recommendation—which strongly points out the necessity of Keeping such Goods as are in Reserve for future Contingencies, always at Head quarters.

Fort William 17th July 1813
Wm McGillivray ⎧Agents
⎨ per
⎩N W Co

NB
(Copies of the above transmitted to the Partners of the Co in the Columbia & at Athabasca.

MINUTES of the general Meeting of the North West Company held at Fort William in the month of July 1814—Partners present holding for themselves or as Attorneys for absentees—Eighty Votes.

Monday }
July 11th }   The Meeting assembled & the first Business introduced was the transactions in the Columbia last Winter & Fall, which underwent a full discussion, no material objection was made to the terms on which the Purchase from the Pacific Fur Company had been made, except as to the Payments, the near period at which they are fixed being considered highly advantageous to the Concern—as the time it would take to realize the Property in order to meet such payments did not seem to have been considered, and the manner in which the Bills are drawn—throwing a Loss of at least £3000 on the Concern owing to the rate of Exchange between Canada & England.—The Advantages derived from the Arrangement were deemed considerable, by means of it the Posts were supplied for the Winter which from the non arrival of the Vessels expected could not have done otherways—and it greatly facilitated the getting out of the Country our Competitors the American Fur Company—The Concern therefore assumed the Arrange-

ment—although entered into contrary to the spirit of a Special Article of the General Agreement, and passed a Resolve for a more strict observance of the same in future.—The Agreement entered with Mr Duncan McDougall for admitting him to an equivalent to *one* Share in the Concern until a Share is assigned to him, was also Sanctioned—The Communications received from the Gentlemen of the Columbia in regard to the State and resources of the Country, and the information convey'd thereby highly satisfactory.—The means of future support to the prosecution were discussed, & as far as the present State of uncertainty would permit, (in regard to the Vessels destined for the Columbia) a Plan formed for the purpose.

If a favourable connection could be made with an American House—it was the general opinion—it should be adopted for facilitating the Business in China.

Next the number of Clerks & Men in the different Departments & Posts were investigated & considered—and the following Statement of them appeared to be nearly correct, as they stood last year—It was determined that such as did not produce adequate Returns should be reduced as in the following Scale.

Years 1813—& 1814 vizt

Nipigon..
  1 Proprietor
  Clerks................ 4
  Engagees.............24
  Guide................ 1
  Interpreters.......... 1
              — 30

for 1814
  1 Proprietor
  Clerks................ 3
  Interpreters.......... 1
  Summer men............4
  Engagees..............17
              — 25

Michipicoton
  1 Proprietor..........
  Clerks................ 3
  Engagees.............16
              — 19

  1 Proprietor
  Clerks................ 3
  Engagees.............12
              — 15

1813

Shaskatchewan River
2 Proprietors
- Clerks.................. 4
- Guides................. 2
- Interpreters........... 7
- Engagees..............58
  — 71

Rat River & C. House
1 Proprietor
- Clerks................. 3
- Guide.................. 1
- Interpreters........... 1
- Canoe men including S. men }......36
  — 41

L L Pluie
1 Proprietor
- Clerks................. 2
- Interpreters........... 1
- Guide.................. 1
- Engagees...............16
  — 20

Athabasca River & Lesser Slave lake
1 Proprietor
- Clerks................. 1
- Interpreters........... 1
- Guide.................. 1
- Engagees...............27
  — 30

1814

2 Proprietors
- Clerks.................. 3
- Interpreters............ 3
- Guides.................. 2
- Engagees................47
- Summer Men............. 7
  — 63

N.B. The Rat River on account of the strong footing which the H Bay have in it & the great number of Posts remaining was left as last year, but it was considered there were too many men.

1 Proprietor
- Clerks.................. 1
- Interpreters............ 1
- Engagees................11
- Summer Men............. 2
  — 15

1 Proprietor
- Clerks..................
- Interpreters............ 1
- Engagees................21
- Guide................... 1
- Sumr Men including 7 Eng }...... 3
  — 26

THE NORTH WEST COMPANY

1813
At Rocky Mountain Portage
  Interpreter............ 1
  Horse Keeper.......... 1
  Hunters............... 2
  Engagees ⎱
  Young Indian ⎰ 2
  —
  6

English River
  1 Proprietor
  Clerks................ 3
  Interpreters.......... 3
  Guides................ 2
  Engagees..............37
  — 45

Fort Dauphin
  1 Proprietor
  Clerks................ 4
  Interpreters.......... 2
  Guides................ 1
  Engagees..............30
  —
  37

1814
N.B. This Establishment to be knocked up except a Couple of Careful men to be left at the Portage with Horses & Provisions to facilitate the Communication with the Columbia— This arrangement was given in charge to Mr McGillis & to be controld between him & Mr Keith.

1 Proprietor
  Clerks................ 3
  Interpreters.......... 2
  Guide................. 1
  Engagees..............36
  — 42

Should the H Bay Company send in any Forces to this Dept Mr McGillivray is to have a good Canot of Athabasca men to strengthen the Posts.

1 Proprietor
  Clerks................ 4
  Interpreters.......... 2
  Guide................. 1
  Engagees..............27
  — 34

It is contemplated to strengthen further this Department on Account of the Strong H B opposition.

1813

Red River

1 Proprietor	
Clerks	4
Guides	1
Engagees	26
Interpreters	3
Summer men	6
	— 40

Lac Ouinipique

1 Proprietor	
Clerks	2
Interpreter	1
Guide	1
Engagees	16
	— 20

St Maries

Clerks	1
Engagees	6
	— 7

Vessels

Captn	1
Sailors	6
	— 7

Fond du lac

1 Proprietor	
Clerks	4
Engagees	24
	— 28

1814

The Department to have an Extra Canoe and men with an additional Proprietor on account of the Interference of the H B Co—& new Colony. Eight of the men of this Depart to be discharged or sent away from the Post for misconduct at the time the Provisions were seized.

1 Proprietor	
Clerks	2
Interpreter	1
Engagees	14
	— 17

The Post to remain in its present state for 1814

To remain the same

1 Proprietor	
Clerks	3
Engagees	26
	— 29

THE NORTH WEST COMPANY

1813
Athabasca
  5 Proprietors
  Clerks.................. 13
  Interpreters............. 8
  Engagees...............*162
  　　　　　　　　　　　——
  　　　　　　　　　　　183

1814
  5 Proprietors
  Clerks..................12
  Engagees...............92
  Summer men...........31
  Interpreters............. 8
  　　　　　　　　　　　—143

NB. The Number of Men to be further reduced if any of the said men can be discharged at Lac la Pluie—as from the number to be taken next year from McKs River there will be more men coming out than are required

　　Present total
　　Hired.................95
　　Unhired..............28
　　Discharged.......... 8
　　Summer men..........31
　　　　　　　　　　——
　　　　　　　　　　*162

Fort William
  1 Proprietor
  Clerks................ 1
  Engagees............22
  　　　　　　　　　—
  　　　　　　　　　23

  1 Proprietor
  Clerks................. 1
  Engagees..............15
  　　　　　　　　　— 16

These were the arrangements as settled in the Council but it is probable some changes may be made for strengthening the Division Posts & those threatened by the Hudsons Bay Company.— One or two Clerks to be sent next Winter or Spring from Athabasca to the Columbia.

Partners appointed for Departments for 1814

Athabasca	John McGillivray
	Robert Henry
	John Stuart
	George Keith
	Ed Smith (1814)
Upper English River	John Thomson
Lower English River	J D Campbell
Shaskatchewan River	James Hughes
	John Haldane
Lac Ouinipique	J Dougal Cameron
Athabasca River	Hugh McGillis
Fort Dauphin	John McDonald
Red River	Duncan Cameron
	Alexr McDonell (1814)
Lac la Pluie	John McLaughlin (1814)
Fort William	Kenneth McKenzie
Lac des Isles	Ranald Cameron
Nipigon	James Leith
Michipicoton	Archd McLellan
Fond du Lac	Donald McKenzie
Pic	John McBean (Clk)
	James Grant "

In all 21—John McDonald (from the Columbia) & Pierre Rocheblave go down in Rotation—the first of these Gentlemen in his own right—Mr Rocheblave takes by permission, the Rotation of Mr Simon Fraser (from Athabasca) having intimated some wish of going down and being his Rotation is not yet placed, John Wills remained in land so ill that he is not expected to live he was last Winter at the Red River.

An Investigation of the Departments took place in order to check irregularities, and to ascertain whether or not the regulations of last Year had been attended to, & if the Goods in Depot had been taken care of.

St Maries —No accounts yet received, but daily expected by the Vessel to arrive from that place.

THE NORTH WEST COMPANY

Pic	—A great saving of Provisions and no mismanagement in other respects.
Fort William	—A great saving of Provisions and good Management—an Extra number of Men complained of at this place, it appearing that they were left as not being required by the other Departments.
Fond du Lac	—A Dependence had been placed on Mr D McKenzie to bring out some Provisions for the support of the general Stock at Head Quarters & he received for that purpose several Pks of Goods last year. which were not expended (with the exception of 1 Keg High Wines & 26 Powder) a disappointment expressed at not getting these Provisions. More particularly as it appears that 35 Kegs of follavoine remained at Leech Lake.
Nipigon	—One Clerk too many and the Post falling to nothing—If Dorion's Post is not more productive this Winter it is to be thrown up in the Spring—Mr Leith to bring out at all Events the Extra Clerk.
Lac la pluie	—Mr Duncan Cameron broke in upon the Depot of Goods at L L P (the Atha Goods) taking therefrom 5 Blankets & 1 Piece Shirts—contrary to a formal Resolution of the Concern—last year apprehending a Scarcity.
Fort Dauphin	—The Depot entire. It appears that this Department was too short of men to cope with the Hudsons Bay Compy.
Cumberland Ho	—The Depot broke in upon by Mr Campbell and 1 Keg of Powder taken out of it—Too many men left in land & the wages of several of them too high.
Bas de la Riviere	—It appears that the great complaint made against this Post last year for the waste of Stores of Provisions usually left there

for the Summer, has had a good effect—that due care has been taken of them, and the Business of the place conducted with more advantage to the Concern than formerly.

Shaskatchewan River—Depot entire & the Trade in good order.

Upper English River—Ditto—Ditto.

Athabasca —The too high wages given to Summer Men complained of—Mr Ed. Smith blamed in this respect.

Athabasca River —Mr Decoigne broke in upon a Depot taking therefrom two Pieces—and being in other respects reported to be extravagant has been ordered out & goes to Montreal—nothing otherwise against his Character.

A Resolve past in 1811 respecting the Clerks who should be brought into the Concern having been considered—It appeared that *One & One Half* Shares only are at the disposal of the Concern, although the Intention was to promote *five* Young Men to Shares & that such Expectations had been given to them.—The Propriety of Keeping faith with these Gentlemen was no question, & it was determined to give them equivalents to Shares by a general contribution from the Concern until Shares should become vacant; but in order to save from this Burden the Wintering Partners & particularly those who have only one Share and as being more gratifying to the Young Men—M'Tavish McGillivray & Company (with the assent of Mr A McKenzie &c) gave up *Three & One Half* Shares for the Young Men, to be replaced from the first Shares which should fall vacant.

A Resolve to this Effect was past & signd—together with assignments of Shares to Edward Smith, J. McLaughlin Alexr McDonell James Keith & Angus Bethune.

The Situation of the Concern in the Interior with the Hudsons Bay Company—and particularly the Violent & illegal seizure of all the Provisions which had been collected at the Red River—under the authority of a pretended Proclamation issued by Miles McDonell—agent to Lord Selkirk—for laying an Embargo on all Provisions which should be collected in that Department (The Red

River)—It appeared that he had taken from the Hudsons Bay Company 200 Bags of Pemican & insisted on having an equal Number from the North West Company—which being very properly refused he took measures for seizing the whole—in which he succeeded—The Servants of the N W Co being frightened with a Show of Hostility & high sounding words—and not being supported by those who had the Charge of the Department. These also thought proper to decline the aid voluntarily offered by the natives on the occasion. The Gentlemen of the neighboring Departments however assembled with their men & Mr Miles was very near paying dear for his temerity but being averse to commencing actual Hostility and wishing to know the Sentiments of the Concern at large in this extraordinary transaction, they entered into a compromise—that he should Keep 200 Bags & give up the remainder.—Thus the matter ended for the time—not, it must be confessed—not much to the Credit of the Concern—and in consequence of what past at the meeting it is not probable that a similar attempt will be equally successful—a full determination was taken to defend the Property at all Hazards, & all the Wintering men being assembled for this purpose the true state of the case was explained to them, and the impression it made, it is hoped will render it a dangerous service to any man who may presume to plunder them—a feast of 13 Pts of liquor & Provisions was given to them on the occasion.

The Men of Red River & four of those from Fort Dauphin who had ill behaved on the seizure of the Provisions were pointed out to the others & disgraced.—The Intentions of Miles McDonell and the Heads of the Hudson Bay Interests were evident. They Supposed the Communication with Canada cut off by the Events of the War last Campaine—and by depriving the Company of the Provisions collected in the Interior the People must have been starved and the Business totally stopped.

Mr McGillivray having stated to the Wintering Partners that it was the Intention of his House (M'T. M'Gs & co)—and Forsyth Richardson & co, to continue to Trade to the South—if such favorable terms were obtained at a Price with the United States as would afford protection to the Trade—either by a new Boundary line, or by rendering the Territory of the Indians neutral—or other favorable circumstances taking place—and expressing it to be the wish of the two Houses that the North West Co would agree to hold an equal Share with each of them respectively in the proposed Trade, which would much simplify it, & enable the holders to carry it on with much more economy than on a separate Establishment—They (the Wintering Partners) agreed to take one third of said Trade, if entered into, or a proportion equal to what either of the two Houses will hold.—And Mr McGillivray declaring for his Establishment & for that of Messrs F R & co that they should not object, but rather propose that Mr Rocheblave should be the Agent with proper aid & assistance for carrying on this Business.—The Concern also agreed to this arrangement.

Various explanations of the Accts were asked and given by the Agents—The Sale of Salmon at Quebec in 1813 was considered as having been made at an under value—and a large quantity of grease purchased from Mr Crawford at St Josephs without any necessity, but which appeared to have arisen from a misunderstanding—The Exchange was again objected to on which account the general accounts of the Concern were not signed.

These Arrangements & Discussions took place from the 11th to the 16th July Inclusive, and the Minutes (foregoing) contain a true Account of every circumstance of moment that occurred.

W McGillivray } Agents NWCo

21: ARTICLES OF AGREEMENT OF McTAVISH, McGILLIVRAY AND CO., 1811.[1]

[*Hudson's Bay House.*]

ARTICLES OF AGREEMENT entered into and concluded by and between William McGillivray, William Hallowell, Roderick McKenzie, Angus Shaw, James Hallowell Junior, and Archibald Normand McLeod, carrying on trade in Montreal and other parts of America under the name of Firm or McTavish McGillivrays & Co, and also in London under the name or Firm of McTavish Fraser & Co of the one part; and Simon McGillivray, one of the partners

[1] Reproduced by permission of the Governor and Committee of the Hudson's Bay Company.

of the said House of McTavish Fraser & Co in London, of the other part, vizt.

Whereas on the first day of December One Thousand Eight Hundred and Six Articles of Agreement were entered into at Montreal by and between William McGillivray, Duncan McGillivray, William Hallowell, Roderick McKenzie, Angus Shaw, and James Hallowell Junior for the purpose of carrying on Trade under the Firm of McTavish McGillivrays and Company, which article of Agreement were further modified, vizt—On the fourth day of May One Thousand Eight Hundred and Eight, after the decease of Duncan McGillivray, one of the said parties, in as much as related to the situation and Interests of the said Angus Shaw, as is more fully set forth in said Agreements; *And whereas* by Articles of Agreement bearing date the first day of December, One Thousand Eight Hundred and Eight, the said Archibald Normand McLeod was admitted a partner in the said House or Firm of McTavish McGillivrays and Company upon the terms and stipulation which are explained in said Agreement, *And Whereas* it is judged expedient that Simon McGillivray (now of London, merchant, and a partner in the said House or Firm of McTavish Fraser and Company) should also become a partner in the said House or Firm of McTavish McGillivrays and Company. *It is now determined*, and the said William McGillivray, William Hallowell, Roderick McKenzie, Angus Shaw, James Hallowell Junior, and Archibald Normand McLeod, being the parties composing the said House of McTavish McGillivrays and Company agree to admit him, the said Simon McGillivray, as a partner into the said Establishment, and to include his name in their Firm on the following Conditions, vizt.

That this Interest or Share in the said House of McTavish McGillivrays and Company shall commence on the first day of December, One Thousand Eight Hundred and Eleven, and terminate according to the Agreements above referred to, and that the said share in their profits or losses shall be equal to Two Ninths of the profits or losses which may be made by the House of McTavish Fraser and Company in London, being the share he now holds in that House, after which the remainder of the profits or losses of the said House of McTavish McGillivrays and Company shall be divided amongst the other partners of their Firm in the manner explained in the said Articles of Agreement of the first day of December One Thousand Eight Hundred and Eight.

That whereas Simon McGillivray now holds (as before stated) Two Ninth Shares in the profits or losses of the said House of McTavish Fraser and Company in London, It is understood, and he hereby agrees, in Consideration of the preceding stipulation, to throw into the general mass of profits or losses of the said McTavish McGillivrays and Company the profits or losses which he may incur in consequence of his holding the said share in the said House of McTavish Fraser and Company in London.

And that the said Simon McGillivray shall take an active part in the management of the said Establishment, and watch over its Interests wherever they may come under his view, whether in Great Britain or in Canada.

In witness whereof the parties to these Presents, have hereunto set their Hands and Seals.

Signed sealed and delivered by the within mentioned William McGillivray, William Hallowell, Angus Shaw, and Archibald Normand McLeod, at Montreal in the Province of Lower Canada, this twenty-third day of October, one Thousand Eight Hundred and Eleven In presence of

W. McGillivray
Wm. Hallowell
Angus Shaw
A. N. Macleod

    John McTavish
    James McQuhae

Signed sealed and delivered by the within named Roderick McKenzie at Terrebonne in the Province of Lower Canada this twenty-third day of October One Thousand Eight Hundred and Eleven, in presence of

Rod. Mackenzie

    Jno. McKenzie
    H. Mackenzie

Signed sealed and delivered by the within named James Hallowell Junior at Quebec in the Province of Lower Canada this twenty-third day of October One Thousand Eight Hundred and Eleven In presence of

Js Hallowell, Junr

    Jno. Blackwood
    D. McTavish

THE NORTH WEST COMPANY 295

Signed sealed and delivered at London this \
fourteenth day of March One Thousand
Eight Hundred and Twelve (being first } SIMON McGILLIVRAY
duly stamped) by the within named Simon
McGillivray in presence of /
    JOHN PERRY
    JOHN FRASER, JR

22: DRAFT OF AGREEMENT OF McTAVISH, McGILLIVRAYS & CO. 1814.[1]
    [*Sulpician Library, Montreal.*]

    ARTICLES of Agreement, had, made concluded and agreed upon at Montreal in the Province of Lower Canada this First Day of November in the year of our Lord One Thousand Eight hundred and Fourteen.—By and between the Honorable William McGillivray of Montreal aforesaid, Simon McGillivray of London Merchant now present at Montreal, Archibald Norman McLeod, Thomas Thain John McTavish and Henry MacKenzie all of Montreal aforesaid Merchants.

    Whereas by Articles of Agreement bearing date at Montreal aforesaid the second day of December of the year One Thousand seven hundred and Ninety nine, Simon McTavish late of Montreal aforesaid Esquire now deceased John Gregory of the same place Merchant, the said William McGillivray, Duncan McGillivray, late of Montreal aforesaid now deceased, and William Hallowell of the same place Merchant, entered into a Copartnership to carry on Trade as Merchants at to and from Montreal aforesaid under certain Stipulations and conditions as therein set forth for the space and term of Seven years under the name or firm of McTavish Frobisher & Company—And whereas by virtue of a reserve made in the said Articles of Agreement Roderick MacKenzie of Montreal aforesaid Merchant, was afterwards on the Nineteenth day of April of the year one Thousand Eight hundred admitted a Partner of the said House or firm of McTavish Frobisher & Company—And whereas under and by virtue of the Articles of Agreement of the

    [1]This document, which is in the Bâby Collection in the Sulpician Library, Montreal, probably came from the papers of Samuel Gerrard.

Northwest Company bearing the fifth day of July of the year one Thousand Eight hundred and two the said House or firm of McTavish Frobisher & Co. acquired and held therein thirty Ninety second parts or shares, which by a subsequent agreement between the Partners of the said Northwest company and certain other Traders commonly denominated the new North West Company, bearing date on the fifth day of November of the year one Thousand Eight hundred and four and commonly called the Coalition agreement were extended and held as thirty hundredth shares—And whereas by articles of agreement bearing date the Twenty fourth day of September of the year One Thousand Eight hundred and Five, a certain other Company or Concern was formed by the said McTavish Frobisher & Company and John Fraser of London Merchant, the said Simon McGillivray and John Fulloh of London, under the name or firm of McTavish, Fraser & Co: in which said last mentioned Concern the said McTavish Frobisher & Company held four Ninth parts on shares as set forth in the said Articles of Agreement.—And whereas on the sixth day of July of the year One Thousand Eight hundred and four, the said Simon McTavish died, from and after which time the said House or firm of McTavish Frobisher & Company was continued and the Affairs and business thereof managed and carried on by the other surviving Partners herein before named.—And whereas on the Thirty first day of May of the year one Thousand Eight hundred and Six the said John Gregory retired and withdrew from the said House or firm of McTavish Frobisher & Company by certain articles of Agreement bearing date on that day did for the considerations therein mentioned transfer assign and convey to the then surviving Partners herein before named all his right share and Interest in the Concerns of the said House or firm of McTavish frobisher & Co:—And whereas On the thirtieth day of November of the year One Thousand Eight Hundred and Six the said Copartnership of McTavish Frobisher & Company determined and expired—And Whereas by Articles of agreement bearing date at Montreal aforesaid on the first day of December next following the said William McGillivray Duncan McGillivray William Hallowell and Roderick Mackenzie did consent and agree to continue and carry on Trade as Copartners in all the business previously carried on by the said House or firm of McTavish Frobisher & Company and did accordingly form and enter into a new copartnership for the term of seven years to be carried on under the name or firm of McTavish, McGillivrays & Compy and under certain stipulations and conditions fully set forth in the aforesaid articles of Agreement, reference to which is here made—

And Whereas by further Articles of agreement of the said last mentioned date the said William McGillivray Duncan McGillivray William Hallowell and Roderic Mackenzie then constituting the said newly formed firm of McTavish McGillivrays & Company did receive and admit Angus Shaw of Quebec in the said Province Esquire and James Hallowell Junior of Montreal aforesaid Gentleman to become Partners thereof, and to hold certain Shares therein upon the Conditions and subject to the terms specified in the said further Articles of Agreement reference to which is here made—

And whereas among other Conditions in the said last mentioned articles of agreement it was stipulated that the said Angus Shaw should and he did accordingly assign transfer and make over to the said House of McTavish McGillivrays & Company all the right Share and Interest which he then held or was entitled to as an active Partner of the said Northwest Company consisting of *four* hundredth Shares therein, and also all the right interest benefits advantages or Commissions he the said Angus Shaw was entitled to claim from the said Northwest Company for managing the business of the Department of the Kings Posts & Mingan under a resolve of the said Company made at the Grand Portage and bearing the date the Sixth day of July of the year one Thousand Eight hundred and two; which said right shares Commission and advantages so previously held by him the said Angus Shaw and thus assigned to the said McTavish McGillivrays & Company were to be and were by them retained and enjoyed and equally divided and distributed unto and among the Partners of the said firm in proportion to their respective shares therein—And it was farther stipulated that the said Angus Shaw and James Hallowell Junior should not for a certain time be announced & declared publickly as Copartners of the said firm and that in the mean time the said Angus Shaw should attend to the duties of his Situation as an active Partner of the Northwest Company and to the Management of the said Departments of the Kings Posts and Mingan in the same manner as if the said last mentioned articles of agreement had not been made And Whereas on the Ninth Day of April of the year One Thousand Eight hundred and Eight the said Duncan McGillivray died, and it was considered expedient by the Surviving Partners of the said firm that the said Angus Shaw should be declared a Partner thereof, and having in consequence ceased to be considered an active Partner of the said Northwest Company he resigned to that concern two of the four shares which he had previously held there in as aforesaid and his other two shares there in remained and were held by the said firm of McTavish, McGillivray & Company for the general benefit thereof.—And Whereas by Articles of Agreement entered into by the surviving parties to the said last mentioned agreement, and bearing date at Montreal aforesaid on the fourth day of May of the year one Thousand Eight hundred and Eight it was further stipulated and agreed that if from any cause the said Angus Shaw should not continue to be a Partner of the said House of McTavish McGillivrays & Company at the period when their concern should come to be renewed after the expiration of their then present agreement then and in that case the said Angus Shaw should be entitled to claim and receive the said two shares he so held in the North West Company to him and his heirs for and during the space of Nine years further, that is to say till the year one Thousand Eight hundred and twenty two—

And whereas by articles of agreement bearing date at Montreal aforesaid the first day of December of the year one Thousand Eight hundred and Eight the said Archibald Normand McLeod was admitted a Partner in the said House or firm of McTavish, McGillivrays & Company upon the terms and conditions contained in the said agreement reference to which is herein made— And Whereas by a Letter bearing date at Montreal aforesaid on the fifth day of May of the year One Thousand Eight hundred and Eight the said then surviving Partners of the said firm of McTavish McGillivrays & Compy. did assign and make over to the said Simon McGillivray one of the four Ninth shares previously held by them in the said House or firm of McTavish Fraser & Company of London in addition to one Ninth share which he the said Simon McGillivray had previously held therein—And Whereas by Public notice inserted in the London Gazette of the 25th day of September of the year one Thousand Eight hundred and Ten the said John Fulloh withdrew and retired from the said House of firm of McTavish Fraser & Company, leaving the one Ninth share which he had held in the said House to be applied in payment of a debt due from him thereunto—And Whereas the said Partnership of McTavish Fraser & Company expired on the Thirty first of May of the year One Thousand Eight hundred and thirteen and the said one ninth share some time held by the said John Fulloh as aforesaid reverted to and became the Property of the said firm of McTavish McGillivrays & Company was understood and agreed to be virtually continued for the term of seven years from that date—And Whereas by articles of agreement bearing date at Montreal aforesaid on the Twenty third day of October of the year One Thousand Eight hundred and Eleven, and executed by the said Simon McGillivray in London on the fourteenth day of March of the year One Thousand Eight hundred and twelve it was agreed by and between the parties then composing the said firm of McTavish, McGillivrays & Company and the said Simon McGillivray, that he the said Simon McGillivray should become an active Partner of the said House of McTavish McGillivrays & Company and that his name should be included in that firm as well as in the said firm of McTavish Fraser & Company of London—and also that he the said Simon McGillivray should give into the general mass of the Profits or losses of the said firm of McTavish McGillivrays & Company the two Ninth Shares which he had previously held in the said firm of McTavish Fraser and Company as aforesaid—And Whereas in virtue of the retirement of the said John Fulloh and the accession of the said Simon McGillivray the said House or firm of McTavish McGillivrays and Company became possessed of and held Six ninth, or Two third shares of the Profits or Losses of the said firm of McTavish Fraser & Company, whereof the remaining third is held by the said John Fraser—And whereas in reference to the continuation and renewal of the said firm of McTavish, McGillivrays & Company here in after recited and set forth, and in order the more effectually to ensue the security of their Concerns during his present absence from London he the said Simon McGillivray did on the Twenty second day of July last past enter into an agreement on their behalf with the said John Fraser and his son John Fraser the younger, wherein it was stipulated and agreed that he the said John Fraser the younger is for the present declared and authorized to act in all matters as a Partner of the said House of firm of McTavish Fraser and Company And that from and after the Thirty first day of May of the year One Thousand Eight hundred and Sixteen he shall receive one Ninth share of the Profits and emoluments thereof being one of the Ninth shares Now held by the said renewed firm of McTavish McGillivray & Company, which said ninth share is hereby made over and assigned to him the said John Fraser the younger from and after the said specified time, and it was further stipulated in the said agreement that in the event of the death of the said John Fraser at any time before the expiration of the said Partnership of McTavish Fraser & Company (in which event the three Ninth shares now held by him will revert to the said renewed firm of McTavish McGillivrays and Company) then and in that case one of the said Ninth shares shall be made over and assigned to the said John Fraser the younger in addition to the Ninth share above specified, and so as to increase his share to two Ninth parts of the Profits and emoluments of the said firm of McTavish Fraser and Company upon the conditions and subject to the terms and stipulations specified in the said Agreement to which reference is here made.—And Whereas on the thirtieth day of November of the year one Thousand Eight Hundred and two the said House or firm of McTavish, Frobisher & Company did assign and transfer to the late Joseph Frobisher of Montreal aforesaid Esquire now deceased, for the benefit of his son Benjamin Joseph Frobisher one of the Forty Sixth Shares which they then held under the articles of agreement of the said Northwest Compy, to be held and enjoyed by the said Benjamin Joseph Frobisher during the period of that agreement—And Whereas on the Sixteenth day of December of the year One Thousand Eight hundred and Six the said House or firm of McTavish McGillivrays & Company did for the consideration of Five hundred Pounds Current Money of the said Province of Canada to be by them paid annually to the said Joseph Frobisher and after his death to the said Benjamin Joseph Frobisher during the term of their Partnership, and which sum or annuity has by them been paid, purchase back from them the said Joseph Frobisher and Benjamin Joseph Frobisher the said Forty sixth share, which in virtue of the said Coalition Agreement of the Northwest Company herein before mentioned has been previously extended and held as two hundredth shares and which two hundredth shares were thus restored to the Mass of Shares held by the said House or firm of McTavish Frobisher & Company and subsequently by the said House or firm of McTavish, McGillivrays & Company as aforesaid—And Whereas by a certain Construction of the said Coalition Agreement of the Northwest Company herein before mentioned the right of the said House or firm of McTavish McGillivrays & Co, to Five of the Thirty hundredth Shares held by them in virtue of that agreement became questioned and upon a reference to arbitration it was decided that one fourth part of the Profits arising from the said five shares did belong and should be paid over to the agents of Sir Alexander Mackenzie & Company the designation assumed by the said *New* Northwest Company, subsequent to the said Coalition Agreement of the Northwest Company unless the said five shares should be given up by the said House or firm of McTavish McGillivrays & Company, and assigned over to Wintering Partners of the said Northwest Company by a legal majority of that Concern—

And Whereas on the thirtieth day of November last past the said Copartnership of McTavish McGillivrays & Company determined and expired, and the several partial agreements between the said original Partners and the said Angus Shaw James Hallowell Junior Archibald Norman McLeod, and Simon McGillivray herein before mentioned likewise determined and expired—

And whereas on the first day of December last past the said William McGillivray acting for himself and by virtue of a Power of Attorney from the said Simon McGillivray, the said Archibald Normand McLeod, and the said John McTavish did enter into an provisional agreement of Copartnership for the term of Nine years from that date, to be carried on under the old name or firm of McTavish McGillivrays & Company and to continue and carry on trade as Copartners in all the aforesaid business heretofore carried on by the said late house or firm of McTavish McGillivrays & Co: and Whereas the said provisional agreement contained among other clauses a Stipulation for a more regular and ample agreement to be entered into with all convenient dispatch and to contain such additional Articles and conditions as the Parties therein concerned should deem fit and expedient,—And Whereas the said Henry Mackenzie did on the fourteenth day of May last past become a party to the said Provisional agreement and the said Thomas Thain hath also agreed to become a party thereto.

And Whereas it hath been proposed to Donald McTavish, a Partner of the said Northwest Company to become a party to this agreement on his return from the Columbia River, and upon Conditions herein after mentioned.

And Whereas by certain articles of agreement bearing date on the Eleventh day of May last past the said Roderick Mackenzie did in consideration of the sum of Ten Thousand Pounds Current Money aforesaid to be paid to him by the said new firm of McTavish McGillivrays & Co: in the manner and at the times in the said Agreement & specified, assign transfer and convey to the said new House or firm all his right share & Interest in the capital and concerns of the said late House or firm of McTavish McGillivrays & Compy. And Whereas the said Angus Shaw hath also in consideration of certain conditions herein after specified, agreed to assign transfer and convey to the said new House or firm all his right share and Interest in the Concerns of the said late House or firm of McTavish McGillivrays and Company.

And Whereas the said William Hallowell hath brought a demand, And intimated an intention to institute a Law suit, in order to obtain certain shares of the said Northwest Company which he claims in virtue of his supposed rights as a Partner of the said late House or firm of McTavish McGillivrays & Company or of the said Northwest Company, and which shares if he succeeds in obtaining them must come in diminution of the Mass of the said shares of the Northwest Company to be held by the said New House or firm.

And Whereas in the said Provisional Articles of agreement and in reference to the said five shares of the Northwest Company the right to which of the said late firm of McTavish McGillivrays and Company was questioned, and disputed, as herein before mentioned, and which were only partially retained by the said late firm, it was agreed and stipulated that the Partners of the said new House or firm who acted as agents of the Northwest Company for the Current year were empowered and authorized to assign over to such Clerks of the Northwest Company as the Annual Meeting of Proprietors might think proper to bring forward as Partners the aforesaid five shares thereby making an addition of five active

THE NORTH WEST COMPANY 303

Partners to the Northwest Company, in order thereby to evince the disinterestedness of the House and to cultivate a good understanding with the Wintering Partners of the Northwest Company— And Whereas the said agents have only lent the said shares to the Northwest Company to be now assigned over to the Clerks in rotation who had been previously nominated to succeed to shares, and to be returned to the House when shares shall hereafter fall into the disposal of the Northwest Company—And Whereas the said five shares do for the present come in diminution of the Mass of shares of the Northwest Company to be held by the said new House or firm—And any of the said shares which may hereafter be restored by the Northwest Company will come in addition thereto.—

Now these Presents Witness that the said William McGillivray Simon McGillivray Archibald Norman McLeod Thomas Thain John McTavish and Henry Mackenzie having a full and competent knowledge of all and every the aforesaid Covenants Contracts Agreements and transactions, and willing and intending to assume ratify confirm execute and perform the same and every part thereof—And to demand require and receive all and every the benefits and advantages arising or to arise then from, save and except as hereinafter specified and excepted.—

Do hereby consent and agree to continue and carry on trade as Copartners in all the aforesaid business heretofore carried on by the said late House or firm of McTavish McGillivrays & Company and by the said new House or firm since the formation of the same and all matters in which they were in any wise interested or concerned, and also in all other matters which the said Parties hereto may hereafter see fit to undertake or to be concerned in under the stipulations and conditions herein after set forth—that is to say.

Article 1st

That the said Copartnership shall continue and be in force for and during the space of Nine years to be reckoned and computed from the first day of December last past and shall be carried on under the name or firm of McTavish McGillivrays and Company.

Article 2nd

That the said Copartnership interest and concern shall be divided into Nineteen Shares, of which the said William McGillivray shall hold and retain four shares, the said Simon McGillivray three shares, the said Archibald Normand McLeod two shares, the said Thomas Thain two shares, the said John McTavish two shares, the said Henry Mackenzie two shares—The Emoluments of two shares are reserved to be assigned and made over to the said Angus Shaw in consideration of certain conditions contained in a supplementary agreement of this date and the remaining two shares are reserved for the said Donald McTavish, in the event of his acceding to the proposal made to him to become a party to this agreement, and until his determination upon this point shall be ascertained the Profits and Emoluments of the said two shares shall be carried to an account to be opened for that purpose in the Books of the said Concern; and in the event that the said Donald McTavish shall not accede and become a party to this agreement, then and in that case the amount of the said account and also the said two shares hereby reserved for him shall be rateably and in proportion divided among the other shares herein before specified, so that the said Copartnership interest and Concern shall in that case consist of and shall be divided into the seventeen shares hereinbefore enumerated, and it is understood and agreed that the interest held in virtue of all the said shares shall commence and be reckoned from the Commencement of this Copartnership concern on the first day of December last past.—

Art. 3rd

In addition to the two shares above specified and in consideration of the benefit expected to be derived by the Concern from the services and experience of the said Thomas Thain it is agreed to give to the said Thomas Thain a further compensation which shall annually be deducted as a charge upon the gross Balance of the Profit and Loss account before the same shall be appropriated or carried to the Credit of the stock account as hereinafter specified— that is to say—If the Net Balance of the Profit and Loss account shall be such as to give for each share as herein before enumerated the sum of One Thousand Pounds Current Money aforesaid or upwards then and in that case the additional compensation to the said Thomas Thain shall be five hundred Pounds: if the Net Produce of the Profit and Loss account shall be only five hundred Pounds or less than five hundred Pounds for each share as aforesaid then the additional compensation to the said Thomas Thain shall be Two hundred and Fifty Pounds; and if the net Balance of the Profit and loss account shall exceed Five Hundred Pounds and be less than One Thousand Pounds for each share as aforesaid, then and in that case the additional compensation to the said Thomas Thain shall be equal to half the produce of one of the said shares whereof he himself is to hold two as aforesaid, the said compensation to commence and be reckoned from the first day of Decr. next after the date hereof, and not to be allowed for the first year of the said Copartnership the same being now nearly elapsed.

Art. 4th

It is hereby agreed that the said Thomas Thain's becoming a Party to this agreement is not in any manner or point whatsoever to affect the rights of the said Sir Alexander Mackenzie & Company, of which Concern he is now an agent, and if he shall continue to act in that capacity he shall on all occasions be competent to represent that Concern hereafter in the same manner and with the same rights and privileges as heretofore.—

Art. 5th

It is hereby stipulated and agreed that the said William McGillivray shall conduct and manage the correspondence and finance department, and with such assistance as he may require from any of his said Partners shall superintend the general business of the Concern that the said Simon McGillivray shall return to London to conduct and manage the concerns of the House there in the same manner as heretofore; that the said Archibald Normand McLeod, Thomas Thain, and Donald McTavish (in the event of his becoming a party to this Agreement,) shall act and be employed in the business of agents of the Northwest Company, as well at Montreal as upon the communication, and at Fort William, or elsewhere according as the said Concern shall see fit to determine, that the said John McTavish shall keep the Books of accounts of the said Concern and in general as every thing in and about the Compting House Department with such Clerks and assistants as may be found necessary; and in the event of the said Concern finding it expedient hereafter to extend their transactions and to engage in any partial or occasional business distinct from that connected with the Northwest Company; that the said Henry Mackenzie shall conduct and manage the same in such manner as may be hereafter determined on, and that in the mean time the said Henry Mackenzie shall be employed in any Department of the said Concern in which his services may be considered most useful.

Art. 6th

The said William McGillivray reserves to himself the right, in case he shall at any time find that the affairs of the said concern will admit of his absence from Canada, so to absent himself accordingly; and in case of such absence being protracted beyond one season, or in case of the death of the said William McGillivray during the continuance of the said partnership, then and in either of these cases the said Simon McGillivray shall come to Montreal to assume the management of the finance and correspondence Department of the said concern; and it is generally agreed and expressly specified by and between the said Parties hereto, that save and except the said William McGillivray, and the said Thomas Thain, who so long as he shall continue to hold the situation of agent of the said Sir Alexander MacKenzie & Compy. shall be required to assume the management of any Department unless the same shall be in some manner connected with the agency of the Northwest Company in Canada or at Fort William it shall be at the option and disposal of the Majority of the said Concern to change the arrangement of Departments contained in the preceding article and to employ any of the said Partners and also the said Thomas Thain in the event of his relinquishing the said agency of Sir Alexander Mackenzie & Compy. in any manner or in any business which may be deemed most conducive to the general benefit of the concern, and whether the said business or employment shall be in Canada or in any other Country And each of the Parties hereunto binds himself under the penalty of half the Profits and emoluments from such time forward accuring upon his share of this concern to be by him forfeited to his said partners to undertake readily and to conduct diligently and faithfully such business or employment as the majority of the Concern may or shall thus prescribe to him.

Art. 7th

In order to prevent any misconception in regard to the relative Duties attached to the different Departments of the said Concern herein before specified and the time within which such duties ought to be performed it is hereby declared to be mutually understood and agreed by and between the parties hereto that the Partner having charge of the Stores shall be responsible for the different articles required for the various Outfits being duly prepared and dispatched from the stores at such time and in such manner as never to retard or impede the sending off of Boats or Canoes at such periods as the Interests of the Concern may require, and also for the various Invoices and packing accounts being regularly made out and completed in such time as not to interfere with or retard the dispatching of the first light Canoe in proper season; and further that the said Partner shall be responsible for having the Orders to be sent to England for goods completed and ready to despatch in each year on or before the Twentieth day of October. —That the other Partners intrusted with the management of the Northwest Agency shall be responsible for engaging the requisite number of Canoe Men during the proper season, dispatching the Canoes from LaChine and receiving the same on their return in the fall, assorting and baling the Furs and Peltries.—They shall also superintend and conduct the Temiscamingue and Grand River Departments during the proper season, and he or they who return from the general Rendezvous of the Northwest Company at Fort William or elsewhere in each season shall be responsible for delivering the Northwest Scheme for the following Outfit duly completed on or before the first day of October and all other requisite Papers relative to the business of the season on or before the first day of November in each year. The Partner who is intrusted with the care of the general Books of the Agents of the Northwest Company shall be responsible for their being duly and regularly Balanced and closed and for the due delivery of the usual statements of the business of the year extracted from these Books on or before the last day of December in each year; and the Partner who is intrusted with the management of the Books and accounts of the said concern or firm of McTavish McGillivrays & Company shall be responsible for such Books being regularly Balanced and closed within fifteen days after such statements extracted from the Northwest Books shall be delivered to him as aforesaid.

Art. 8th

Upon the accounts and Books of the said Concern being annually settled and closed as herein before specified the Net Balance of the account of Profit and Loss for the year shall be carried to a general stock account to be opened in the Books of the said Concern The said stock account shall accumulate by the addition of successive Profits, or shall be reduced by Losses if any should be sustained and shall remain undiminished and undivided until the end of the Concern, and until the property thereunto belonging shall be realized as hereinafter specified and provided, save and except in case of the death of any of the said Partners during the continuance of this agreement in which event the Balance of the Account of Profit and Loss at the annual Settlement of the Books next following the death of such Partner shall as usual be carried to the stock account in which such Partner was intrusted, and such stock account shall from thence forward be closed and shall receive no further increase unless from Profits which may accrue upon realizing Northwest Outfits or other adventures in which the Concern shall have been embarked before the death of such deceased Partner, and shall sustain no reduction or diminution unless from Losses or bad Debts in which such deceased Partner shall have been intrusted, and the amount or Balance of such stock account, subject only to these additions or deductions shall from such day of annual settlement next following the death of such Partner be credited with Interest at the rate of Six per centum per annum and shall so accumulate with compound Interest until the close and termination of this Concern or Partnership, when the share belonging to such Deceased Partner in the amount of such stock account shall be adjusted and paid to his legal representatives in such manner as herein after specified and provided for,—And at the annual settlement of the Books of the said concern next ensuing after the settlement first following after the death of such Partner the Balance of the Account of Profit and Loss shall be carried to a new stock account which shall be then opened for the benefit of the surviving Partners and which shall accumulate to the end of the Concern in the same manner as herein before provided and set forth in regard to the first stock account.—And so on, in case of the death of more Partners during the Continuance of this Concern, in the same manner as herein specified in case of the death of one Partner.

Art. 9th

In order to facilitate to the Concern the carrying on and conducting the various branches of business in which the same now is or hereafter may be engaged it is hereby agreed that the Capital now belonging to the said William McGillivray and held by the said Concern shall remain engaged therein and the said William McGillivray shall not be authorized to withdraw or require payment of the same so as to reduce the amount of the principal thereof below the sum of fifteen Thousand Pounds Current Money aforesaid— That the Capital belonging to the said Simon McGillivray now held by the said Concern, the Capital which he and the said John McTavish may hereafter receive from the payment of Legacies by the Executors of the said late Simon McTavish.—the Capital which the said Henry Mackenzie may derive from the winding up and realizing the Concerns of Mackenzie Oldham & Company and all other Concerns at Terrebonne in which he was intrusted—And the Capital which the said Donald McTavish may become entitled to upon his resigning his situation as an active Partner of the Northwest Company (in the event that he the said Donald McTavish shall become a party to this agreement) shall respectively remain engaged in this Concern until the Close thereof, or until the death of any of the said parties which case is hereinafter specially provided for; that an *Account of Capital* shall be opened for each of the said parties in the Books of the said Concern and the said sums respectively placed to the Credit of the said accounts. —That the said Parties shall be entitled to receive Interest on the said Sums at the rate of six per centum per annum or to leave the same to accumulate in their option, and that in addition to such Interest that the parties to this agreement shall be entitled to draw from the Concern in each year the following sums, and no more, in order to meet their personal expenses; that is to say the said Archibald Norman McLeod Eight hundred Pounds Current money aforesaid, & the said Thomas Thain, John McTavish, and Henry Mackenzie each Five hundred Pounds like Current money—

The said William McGillivray being possessed of the largest Capital in the said Concern, and the said Simon McGillivray so long as he shall remain in London are specially excepted from this restriction and authorized to draw from the Concern such sums as their expenses may require; and in the event that the said Simon McGillivray shall as herein before provided for, remove from London to Montreal and in the event that the said Donald McTavish shall become a party to this agreement, then and in either of these cases, the other Partners of the Concern shall determine what sum or sums they the said Simon McGillivray and Donald McTavish, or either of them, shall be allowed to draw annually from the said Concern for personal expenses as aforesaid—And all sums so drawn by any or either of the aforesaid Parties shall of course be charged to the account of each and shall accumulate with compound Interest at the rate of Six per centum per annum until the same shall be paid or cancelled by the division of Stock and realizing of Property belonging to the Concern as herein after specified and set forth.

Art. 10th

As it is considered desirable that at some definite period before the close of this Concern arrangements should be made for continuing the business to be carried on thereby, or for winding up the same and realizing the property and effects thereunto belonging. It is hereby agreed that at least two years before the termination of the present partnership, that is to say on or before the Thirtieth day of November of the year One Thousand Eight Hundred and Twenty the respective parties hereto, and the then survivors of them shall be competent to require each from the others a distinct and explicit avowal of their intention in regard to renewing and continuing articles of Partnership, or winding up the Concern, as the case may be and in the event that a majority of the Concern shall enter into arrangements for the renewal and continuance thereof then the new Concern to be formed by such majority shall be held answerable for all the Engagements of this Concern and shall assume and enter into the responsibility, rights and Interests of this Partnership in every other Concern which may be dependent thereon or in which it may be engaged or intrusted, And such new Concern to be formed by such Majority as aforesaid shall hold and remain possessed of all the Stock Property Merchandises Debts credits and effects belonging in which may belong to this Concern, until the same can be realized for the benefit of all parties concerned and the proceeds paid to the parties retiring, in manner and form following, that is to say—On the thirtieth day of November of the year One Thousand Eight Hundred and Twenty-two a general Inventory and account shall be taken and made of all the stock Monies Merchandizes debts credits and effects of or belonging to this Copartnership, also of all the debts and monies due by this Copartnership to any person or persons whatsoever (and a full clear and correct balance and statement of accounts shall be made out and such part of the aforesaid stock account or accounts as shall consist of Money, or funds already realized, shall be divided in proportional shares, according to the shares held in the said Concern, and such proportional Shares shall be carried to the Credit of the parties to whom the same shall respectively belong, then if the amount of such proportional shares of realized stock and the amount of the account of Capital which may previously stand at the Credit of such retiring Partner or Partners as aforesaid shall together exceed the amount at the Debit of such Partner or Partners for Monies drawn and Interest thereon as herein before specified so as to leave a clear realized Balance of Moneys belonging to such retiring Partners or Partner as aforesaid, then and in that case such retiring Partner or Partners shall be entitled to claim and demand payment thereof from such continued Partnership or new Concern within the Space of Twelve Months after the said termination of this Concern and such continued Concern or new Partnership shall be bound to make such payment accordingly; and such Continued Concern or new Partnership shall also be bound without charge or expense to such retiring Partners or Partner to realize divide account for and pay over to such retiring Partners or Partner all the remaining part of the stock Property and effects of this Concern to which such retiring Partners or Partner may be entitled as follows, that is—the Furs and Peltries which may have been shipp'd in the fall preceding such termination of this Concern, so soon as the same shall be sold and the Proceeds received the Outfit which may have been made to the Northwest in the season preceding such termination of this Concern, so soon as the Furs and Peltries obtained in return for the same can be regularly sent to the usual market or markets, sold, and the Proceeds received as aforesaid—The debts due to the Concern so soon as the same can be collected, or if more agreeable to the Parties such retiring Partners or Partner may assign his or their Interest in such Debts to the said continued Partnership or new Concern at a Valuation to be mutually agreed upon—The Goods which may have been imported or purchased during the season for any new or projected adventure or outfit to the Northwest or elsewhere shall be taken by such new Concern or Continued Partnership at Cost and Charges—and all other Property and effects belonging or which may belong to this Concern, such as Shipping, Buildings stores, Goods, Northwest Inventories, Indian debts, &Ca. &Ca.— shall be taken and retained by such new Concern or continued Partnership at a just and reasonable valuation, and in case of difficulty or difference of opinion, each of the said parties, that is to say, such new Concern or continued Partnership on the one part, and such retiring Partner of Partners, or any one of them on the other shall name and appoint a disinterested Merchant (with power if necessary or deemed by them requisite to call in an umpire) whose opinion and award in the premises shall be deemed conclusive; and the share to which such retiring Partner or Partners shall be entitled of such valuation or appraisement, shall be accounted and paid by such new Concern or continued partnership to such retiring Partner or partners within the space of Twelve Months after such valuation shall be agreed upon, or at such time as the said Arbitrators shall direct—

And in order to prevent any misconception in regard to what is meant by the term *a majority* of this Concern, it is hereby distinctly and explicitly declared that such Majority is to be decided by reckoning the number of shares, and not of individual Partners— And in the event that a Majority of this Concern shall not enter into arrangements for the renewal and continuance thereof as aforesaid, and that it shall become necessary to wind up and close the business and transactions of this Concern or Partnership; then and in that case it shall be the duty of the Partner or Partners usually employed in the Department of the Northwest agency, to go to the general rendezvous of the Northwest Company at Fort William or elsewhere, in the summer following the termination of this partnership. And to receive, convey to Montreal, assort, ship, consign and otherwise dispose of the returns to be then obtained for the outfit of the preceding year in the usual manner and for the general benefit of the Parties concerned—It shall be the duty of the Partner employed in conducting the Concerns of the said House or firm in London to receive sell realize and account for the Proceeds of such returns for the benefit of the Parties concerned in the usual manner—And it shall be the duty of the Partner employed in keeping the Books and accounts of this concern to remain at his post and to make up and exhibit just true and accurate accounts of the said returns so to be realized and of all other matters and transactions in which the Concern may remain intrusted for which several duties the said respective Partners shall receive an adequate compensation & at of the said property and returns and all other stock moneys Merchandizes debts Credits and effects whatsoever shall be realized wound up and disposed of in such manner as to the said Concern or a majority thereof shall seem fit, and in the decision and arrangements of such majority for such purpose the other parties concerned shall acquiesce, and the Proceeds of all such stock Merchandizes debts credits and effects whatsoever shall be with all practicable speed divided and paid over to the parties to whom the same shall respectively belong.

Art. 11th

It is hereby stipulated and agreed by and between the said Parties here to that the death or retiring of any Partner from this Concern or the admission of any active Partner or Partners there into shall not affect determine or change the Copartnership here by established nor the period of its duration, but that the same shall nevertheless be upheld continued and carried on under all the clauses conditions and stipulations in this agreement contained until the final conclusion and determination of the aforesaid term of Nine years—And in case of the death of any of the Partners in the present Concern during the continuance thereof—his share and Interest therein shall determine and cease on the next ensuing day of settlement of annual accounts which shall follow such event (which is hereby settled and regulated to be on the thirtieth day of November of every year) beyond which day the Interest of the Partner dying shall not be extended in any of the Affairs of the Concern save and except in such transactions as shall have taken place before the death of such Partner, the result of which at such next ensuing annual settlement of accounts may not be completely ascertained or realized—And further that on such annual settlement of Accounts next after the decease of such Partner a general and complete Inventory and statement of accounts shall be taken in the same manner as herein before agreed to be taken at the end of the Concern manifesting in a clear and satisfactory manner the true state and situation of the affairs of the said Concern for the time being, and exhibiting the true and exact share and proportion of—belonging to the said deceased partner of all the stock Capital and, profit in the said concern which share and proportion the surviving Partners shall be accountable for and bound to pay or cause to be paid to the legal representatives of such deceased Partner in manner following that is to say the heirs Executors or legal representatives of such deceased Partner shall be entitled to claim demand and receive from the surviving Partners during the past of the current year which may remain unexpired at the time of the decease of such Partner until the said day of annual settlement as aforesaid a sum of money proportionate to the whole sum which such Partner would be entitled to draw out of the Concern in the whole year as herein before mentioned and no more: the said heirs, Executors or legal representatives shall also be entitled to claim demand and receive from the said surviving Partners the Balance if any which shall appear at the Credit of the *Account of Capital* of such deceased Partner as herein before specified and described and the said surviving Partners shall be accountable for and bound to pay the same in annual Instalments of equal proportions thereof for each year which shall remain unexpired of this Partnership at the said day of annual settlement of accounts next following the decease of such Partner with Interest annually upon such part thereof as shall remain unpaid, so that the whole of such deceased Partner's *Account of Capital* shall be paid off before the termination of this Concern.—that the share of the *Stock Account* belonging to such deceased Partner shall remain in the hands of the survivors, during the period of the present Concern at the expiration whereof the same shall be divided and the said heirs Executors or legal representatives shall be entitled to claim demand and receive from the surviving Partners the share thereof to which the Estate of such deceased Partner shall be entitled in the same manner as herein before specified in regard to retiring Partners save and except that in the event of the whole of the stock account in which such deceased Partner was interested being realized and received by the surviving Partners before the Close of the Concern then and in that case the share thereof to which the Estate of such deceased Partners share be entitled shall be considered a debt to be positively paid by such surviving Partners within six Months after the close of this Concern and shall not depend upon the realization of the subsequent stock account or accounts in which such deceased Partner was not intrusted and in case of difficulty or difference of opinion between such heirs Executors or legal representatives and such surviving Partners the same shall be left to be decided by the arbitration of independent merchants as herein before specified in regard to retiring Partners.

Art. 12

It is Covenanted and agreed that none of the Parties hereto save and except the said William McGillivray and the said Simon McGillivray shall be competent to act as a Partner of the said House or firm of McTavish Fraser and Company, or in any manner to represent this Concern in England unless specially authorized and empowered so to do by a Majority of this Concern.

Art. 13th

And in order to prevent all disputes and difficulties touching the Debts and Credits of the said late House or firm of McTavish McGillivrays and Company in the management of the business of the present Concern, it is hereby stipulated and agreed by and between the said Parties hereto that the schedule of the said debts and Credits hereunto annexed and signed by the said Parties as making part hereof shall be and the same are hereby undertaken and assumed by the said parties as containing a true statement of all the said debts and Credits and for which they agree to be respectively bound and liable.

Art. 14

And whereas by the Articles of agreement of the said Northwest Company herein before referred to it is amongst other things stipulated and agreed that every new Partner admitted or received into the said House or firm of McTavish, Frobisher and Company, or into the business by them carried on as agents of the said North West Company by whatever other name or firm that house might be called or known shall be held and bound by the agreement admitting him a Partner to keep and observe all and singular the clauses stipulations and engagements in the said Articles of agreement contained respecting the trade commerce and speculations of the said Northwest Company under all the Penalties therein specified and set forth—And the said John McTavish and Henry Mackenzie having seen the said articles of agreement of the said Northwest Company do accept and approve thereof and do hereby each of them severally promise bind and oblige himself well and truly to fulfill comply with and observe the same and every part thereof in as far as regards the carrying on any trade, commerce or business or being therein concerned or interested either directly or indirectly to the prejudice of the Interests of the said North West Company during the period of their aforesaid agreements.

Art. 15th

Whereas there are sundry adventures and engagements entered into by the said late firm of McTavish McGillivrays & Company, and sundry shares by them held in the said North West Company to which the said William Hallowell pretends and claims an Interest as herein before mentioned. Now it is the true interest and meaning hereof and of the parties hereto that in case the said William Hallowell his heirs or assigns shall or may establish a legal claim or demand therein and thereto, or to any part of the advantages and Profits arising there from or in case a Majority of this Concern shall in order to facilitate an amicable settlement with the said William Hallowell consent and agree to admit him to any proportion of such Interest or advantage without legal discussion or in order to compound and terminate the same, that there and in either of these cases, each proportion so to be obtained by or granted to him the said William Hallowell together with the costs and expenses of resisting his claims shall be borne and sustained generally by the said Parties hereto according to their proportions or shares in this Concern as herein before mentioned any specific appropriation thereof here to fore contemplated or any individuals more specially implicated in the said claims or discussions notwithstanding.

Article 16th

Whereas the Profits and emoluments arising or to arise from Two Nineteenth Shares of this Concern as specified in article Second of this agreement, are in consideration of certain conditions contained in a supplementary agreement of this date assigned and made over to the said Angus Shaw as aforesaid, and as it might be doubtful from the purport of the said second Article whether the said shares were not liable to be increased in proportion to the shares held by the parties hereto in the event that the said Donald McTavish shall not become a party to this agreement. Now it is hereby declared to be understood and agreed by and between the parties hereto that no increase of benefit or greater interest in this Concern then the said two Nineteenth shares shall arise or accrue to the said Angus Shaw his heirs Executors or legal representatives from the said Donald McTavish not becoming a party to this agreement, or from the death or retiring of any of the present Partners in this Concern or of any other partner or partners who may hereafter be admitted thereinto, nor shall the same be subject to diminution in consequence of any future extension of shares or admission of partners into this Concern the true intent and meaning of the parties hereto being that the right interest and benefit to be derived by the said Angus Shaw from the Profits and emoluments of this Concern shall in no case whatever exceed or fall short of two nineteenth parts or shares of the whole.

23: Letter from W. McGillivray, to J. G. McTavish, dated Fort William, July 15, 1820.[1]

[*Hudson's Bay House.*]

My dear Sir,

I wrote you by Mr. Stuart acquainting you with the plan I had in view for your wintering—which I hope you will think well of—it is now decided—but the Doctor[2] (who feels very sore at being removed from this place) tried every means to defeat the plan, and he and those whom he got to join him, make themselves ridiculous.

---

[1] Reproduced by permission of the Governor and Committee of the Hudson's Bay Company.
[2] Dr. John McLoughlin.

As I expect to see you here, which is my wish—you must lose no time in coming out. Mr. McLeod starts to-morrow morning for Lac la pluie and will explain to you all particulars regarding the transactions of this place—which are now *set on Paper* at least.

The Doctor and Mr. Bethune go down on Rotation, and are to be appointed *Deputies* to negociate a new agreement. On this however two words are to be said before we quit the ground. The wintering Partners here must not consider themselves entirely the N.W.Co.

Mr. J. D. Campbell sent a formal message by D. McD. that he should not be appointed to any place, as he was to retire. Mr. C. Grant, it is presumed of course goes down—and Mr. Hughes goes. On the hopes of seeing you soon, I remain,

My dear Sir,
Faithfully yours,
W. McGillivray

J. G. McTavish, Esqr.

[P.S.] You should write to your friends in the Interior in any way you like, to send you Powers of Attorney next year to act for them. We are likely not to be unanimous in making a new agreement. The people here are a strange sett.

24: EXTRACTS FROM COLIN ROBERTSON'S CORRESPONDENCE BOOK, 1817-22.[1]

[*Hudson's Bay House.*]

New York, Nov. 1820.

Who do you think accompanies me to England in the ALBION but Messrs. McLaughlin and Bethune? The latter I found in the steam boat at Burlington, he wished to be very polite, but I kept him at a distance—the doctor I found at this place.

[1] Reproduced by permission of the Governor and Committee of the Hudson's Bay Company. These extracts are from a manuscript book containing copies of Colin Robertson's correspondence with an unnamed correspondent whom he addresses as "My dear M."

Packet Ship ALBION.

The cloth being withdrawn and the land in sight, the wine went about rather freely, when a subscription was set on foot for the stewards and other servants. Our friend the Doctor had put down his name, and I took up the pen for the same purpose, but perceiving Bethune writing I turned round to Abby Carriere—"Come, Abby, put down your name, I don't like to sign between two North Westers". "Never mind, Mr. R.," replied Monsr. Carriere, "remember our Saviour was crucified between two thieves." The Doctor was in a dreadful passion, but being an honest Catholic did not like to quarrel with one who stood so high in the Church.

London, Jany. 1821.

I know not what the Doctor is about, but the negociations have commenced. . . . The Receiver General [Caldwell][1] and his friend Mr. Edward Ellice called at my lodgings the other day, and I had a good deal of conversation with the latter. He talked a good deal of the influence of himself and friends, and as to the charter of the Company he seems to think it hung on his *nod*. He was very severe in his remarks on Messrs. McLaughlin and Bethune, and their powers of attorney, etc. . . . He took a fresh ground by observing that his friend Simon McGillivray was too prone for a negociation of this kind, that he would be happy to meet Mr. Colville half way. I replied I should have much pleasure in communicating his sentiments to Mr. C. . . . .

I was a good deal amused this morning in an interview I had with Mr. Colville, while relating how very severe Mr. Ellice had been, in his remarks on a Mr. McLoughlin, who accompanied me to England. "So—" says Mr. Colville, "McLaughlin's a stout fellow, Mr. Ellice will better take care of himself". "Then, you have seen Mr. McLaughlin, Sir?" This was rather an embarrassing question, & I immediately changed the subject—so that with all your caution, the Doctor is continually starting up before me at full length.

Mr. C. is willing to listen to any moderate proposition, but

[1] Sir John Caldwell, bart. (1775-1842), receiver-general of Lower Canada from 1810 to 1823.

seems to think, they must lower their terms, before any negociation can be entered into. He appears to have taken pretty high ground, which the present situation of our affairs in some measure authorises. . . .

Now, my good Sir, with regard to our friend the Doctor—he is too honourable a man to expose the actual state of the N.W.Co's affairs unless he makes an agreement for himself and friends which I understand he is averse to. . . . Messrs. Ellice & McGillivray talk as if the Bank of England was at their disposal, and when they come to touch on the business of the interior, they will be equally ostentatious in stating their advantages, so that when Mr. C. comes to weigh these matters, I would not at all be surprised but Simon makes a better bargain than he has a right to expect.

Boulogne. Jany, 1821.

I had a long conversation with Simon a few days previous to my departure from England, which I presume was premeditated on the part of Mr. Caldwell, as he popped in just as we had finished breakfast. The old story of the Grand Rapids was smoothed over, as a prelude to other matters, when my two voyaging companions were brought on the market, their powers of Atty, &c.—all of which Simon treated with the utmost contempt. . . . As for the eighteen powers of Attorney, it is very doubtful, my dear M., if all these gentlemen can be depended on. You may remember the powers Sir A. Mackenzie was possessed of when he made the break with Simon McTavish—but not one of them joined the standard of the Knight.[1] . . .

But you must not set me down as a McGillivray man, or attack my principles when I confess candidly, that I like Simon much better than his friend the Member of Parliament; there is a sort of highland pride and frankness about the little fellow that I don't dislike. He has no blarney about him. . . .

He seems bent on a union, and after all his claims and advantages are thrown out, he comes back to that point, and dwells upon it with more than ordinary pleasure.

[1]This sentence throws an interesting light on the withdrawal of Mackenzie from the North West Company in 1798, and his subsequent adhesion to the XY Company.

Paris, 25th Jany, 1821.
I had letters from London the other day reporting the negociations as being broken off by Simon, but I think he will return to the point, he was too eager in the pursuit to give up the chase.

Paris, 17th February, 1821.
By my last letters from London I learn that a reconciliation is nearly completed between the two companies. The whole trade is comprised under one concern to be carried on from the first of June next under the name and charter of the *H.B.Co.*—What a dreadful blow this must be to the Montreal agents.

Fort William, 12 July, 1821.
Let me hear no more of your nonconformist, for, with the exception of poor McLaughlin, there is not one of them who has a grain of real independence in their whole composition. Simon McGillivray has carried everything without even the semblance of opposition. The first day he opened the business, the second the Deed and Release was signed, and the third all was peace and harmony, except poor Bethune who was sent to Coventry the day of his arrival.

The wintering partners dissatisfied with the Union? Any terms would have been acceptable in the present state of their affairs. The half share caused a little murmur, which Mr. Simon smoothed down by a handsome dagger to one, a pair of pistols to another, and a bountiful shower of promises for the vacant factories.

25: INDEX TO INDENTURE OF MARCH 26, 1821, MADE BETWEEN THE GOVERNOR & CO. OF HUDSON'S BAY AND MESSRS W. MCGILLIVRAY, S. MCGILLIVRAY, AND EDWARD ELLICE.[1]

Folio
1. Recital of the North West Company's articles dated 5th Nov., 1804.

---

[1] Reproduced by permission of the Governor and Committee of the Hudson's Bay Company. The indenture itself is a document of over 10,000 words; and in view of the fact that it was superseded three years later by another agreement, it has been thought sufficient to reproduce here only the index to the indenture, which is, in effect, the indenture itself, stripped of legal verbiage.

2. That the Gov. & Co. & N. W. Co. agreed to unite their interests.
3. The parties covenant with each other.
4. That the trade heretofore carried on by both parties shall for 21 years, commencing with the outfit of 1821, and ending with the returns of the Outfit of 1841, be carried on by and in the name of the Gov. & Co. exclusively.
5. The Business in England to be transacted at the H. B. House in London.
6. The goods, provisions, and stores of both parties on hand on the 1st June, 1821, to form part of Capital, and Inventories to be made thereof and same valued at a certain tariff.
8. The trading goods and supplies shipped to Canada and Articles already ordered for the Outfit of 1821 to form further part of Capital and be valued at a Tariff &c.
9. The trading goods, &c., prepared for the North West Company as Outfit of 1821 to Temiscamingue and Lake Huron, Ottawa River and the Kings Posts to form further part of Capital.
10. All other trading goods which have been ordered by either party as part of Outfit of 1821 to form further part of Capital, and to be shipped, consigned, & delivered over to the Gov. & Co.
11. The Gov. & Co. to order such other goods as they may think proper for outfit.
12. In estimating goods, cost price only to be charged.
13. The debts owing by Indians to form further part of Capital, but no value to be allowed for them to either party.
14. Debts due from Traders Clerks &c to the extent of one year's Salary or wages to form further part of Capital.
15. Hudson's Bay House in London, with Furniture and Ships, to be valued and form further part of Capital.
16. The amounts of the respective valuations to be added together, so as to form two several sums total.
17. £5000 to be deducted from the amount of the Stock &c of the parties of the second part and added to the Amount of the Stock of the Gov. & Co. as a compromise in respect of certain Claims.
18. The difference between the two several sums to be brought

THE NORTH WEST COMPANY

into the Concern so as to make the Shares of Capital equal, with interest from the 1st June, 1821.

19. On or previous to 31st December, 1822, notice in writing of all the Depots, Stations &c of the N. W. Co. to be given to the Gov. & Co., and possession thereof delivered.
20. If parties of the second part refuse or fail to deliver such possession, all Interest payable in right of their share of Capital and profits may be retained by the Gov. & Co. until possession given.
21. The Depots, Stations &c from the 1st June, 1821, to be held as part of Capital Stock, but no value to be put thereon.
22. Gov. & Co. to be at liberty to pull down and destroy Depots &c.
23. A Board to be constituted for managing the Trade and two members to be named out of Committee and two persons to be named on part of parties of the second part.
24. Three members to constitute a quorum.
25. There shall be always one of those two Members who are to act on behalf of parties of the Second part to form such quorum, and a majority to be competent provided it includes one of such two members.
26. The powers and duties of the Board.
27. The parties of the second part to do all acts necessary for transferring the Indentures of all apprentices and engagements of Clerks, &c.
28. The Company are to perform all such Engagements as are Entered into with the said apprentices &c.
28. The Expences of the Establishments of the Governor and Company from and after the 1st June, 1821, to be paid out of the Concern.
29. Except expences which shall wholly relate to Colonization or any other Business separate from the Concern.
30. The clear gains to be divided into 100 Shares, Vizt. 20 to the Gov. & Co., 20 to the parties of the 2nd part, 40 to Chief Factors and Chief Traders.
31. If any loss on the 40 shares to be made good out of profits in the ensuing year. The 40 Shares to be appropriated according to a Deed Poll bearing even date therewith. 5 Shares to the said Gov. & Co., subject to an arrangement with the Repre-

sentatives of the late Earl of Selkirk. 5 other Shares to the said Simon McGillivray or Ellice as a compensation, &c, for which their receipts to be a discharge.

32. The remaining 10 shares, one moiety to the said Gov. & Co., and the other moiety to the said parties of the second part.

32. The Governor and Company to order such Outfits during the said Concern as they should think fit.

33. The Gov. & Co. to cause the furs to be consigned to England or elsewhere, and sell the same by public sale or private contract, and not to be answerable for default of Brokers, &c.

34. The Concern should be carried on in the name of the Governor and Company, but no commission charged for conducting the same. The Company may sell the Hudson's Bay House and purchase any other upon the like trusts.

35. The receipts of the Gov. & Co. or persons authorized by them to be good discharges.

35. Inventories of trading goods on the 1st June, 1822, or usual periods and every succeeding year to be made out and the same valued.

36. Debts due from Traders Clerks &c. to be included and valued at a fair Estimate, and Debts due from Indians to be included, but without any Valuation.

37. A general acct on the 1st June, 1823, and every succeeding 1st June to be made out and stated in the manner mentioned.

42. If the profits or losses not paid at the expiration of 14 days after the first June then with interest from the expiration of the said 14 days.

42. If the Gov. & Co. shall be in advance beyond their share of Capital, one half to be on demand brought by the parties of the Second part into the Concern with interest.

43. All Interest payable to the parties of the second part and twenty Shares of the profits may be retained by the Governor and Company for defraying deficiency in their Share of the Capital with interest.

44. The 10 Shares to belong one moiety to the Gov. & Co. and the other to the parties of the second part and to be invested to accumulate on certain trusts.

47. The Gov. & Co. to keep a proper set of books for the purposes of the trade.

47. The two Members of the Board who are to act on behalf of the parties of the second part to be at liberty to inspect all reports, correspondence, papers and accounts, and take copies or extracts from the Accounts.
48. The Chief Factors and one of the Governors or other person to be specially appointed to preside and form Council.
49. The Gov. & Co. to appoint two persons as Governors to preside at the Northern and Southern Factories.
49. To constitute a Council not less than seven Chief Traders in the Northern and three in the Southern District to be present besides the President.
49. In the absence of a Governor or President, or other cause, the persons that may have met may adjourn.
50. In case of death or absence of the Governor or other person specially appointed, the Senior Chief Factor of each district to preside, and if number to form Council cannot assemble then Chief Factors and Chief Traders may form a Council, and may adjourn from time to time.
51. Every member, whether Chief Factor or Chief Trader, to have one Vote, and a bare majority, with the concurrence of the President, sufficient; but for want of such concurrence majority of at least two-thirds to be requisite.
51. Neither party to the agreement to be concerned in any trade with the Indians.
54. The Hudson's Bay House to be taken by the Gov. & Co. at a valuation, and the depots, stations, &c., in America without any consideration.
55. The receipts of parties of the second part or of such of them as shall be in England to be a sufficient discharge.
56. In event of death, Bankruptcy or Insolvency, neither the share of the parties of the second part in the Capital or any monies payable by the Concern, other than the interest, profits, and dividends to be drawn out.
57. If parties of the second part refuse or fail to deliver up the Depots, Stores &c, the Governor and Company by notice in writing may determine the Concern.
58. The Gov. & Co. may grant any part of their Territory, if such

grant does not interfere with trade and such rights be reserved, and that the persons be restricted from carrying on trade.

59. The Gov. & Co. may at their own expence engage in any trade with the Colonists or other persons if same does not interfere with carrying on the said trade thereby agreed on.

60. The arrangement between the parties hereto not to vest in the Concern any other property than therein mentioned or under the Concern liable for any debts, goods &c that is therein mentioned.

61. Covenant by the parties of the second part that the Governor and Company shall peaceably hold the Depots &c and exclusively carry on the trade without interruption by the parties of the second part or any person interested in the North West Company.

62. That the parties of the second part will at all times indemnify the Gov. & Co. against all claims of any persons concerned in the North West Company who may not concur in the arrangements thereby agreed on and all losses and expences on that account.

63. That the parties of the 2nd part or any person interested in the North West Co. shall not oppose the rights granted by the Charter and will concur in any Application for defining such rights.

64. If any dispute to arise the same to be referred to three arbitrators, and that said arbitrators shall have power to dissolve the Concern.

65. That the reference shall be made a Rule of the Court of King's Bench.

66. Covenant for the Gov. & Co. that the trade during the Concern may be carried on through such parts of the Territory as is granted to the late Earl of Selkirk.

67. The Deed thereby entered into not to bind the Gov. & Co. or any members of the said Co. individually or in any other than their corporate capacity.

68. If all the parties of the second part shall not execute, all such as do shall be bound in like manner as if all had executed.

26: EXTRACT FROM HUDSON'S BAY COMPANY MINUTE BOOK, MARCH 21, 1821; PROCEEDINGS AT A GENERAL COURT RELATING TO THE AMALGAMATION WITH THE NORTH WEST COMPANY.[1]

¶The Governor laid before the Court a Draft of an Agreement proposed to be entered into between the Governor & Company of Adventurers of England trading into Hudson's Bay on the one part, and William McGillivray, Simon McGillivray, & Edward Ellice on the second part, on behalf of themselves and other Persons, Partners in an Association called the North West Company, by which Deed it was agreed to unite the whole Fur Trade carried on by the said parties into one Concern, to be from the 1st day of June next carried on solely by and in the name of the Hudson's Bay Company, & the said parties on the 2nd part to find an equal share of Capital and to divide the Profits & Losses as therein recited for the Term of Twenty one years. . . .

¶Resolved that this Meeting do sanction the Board of Directors in agreeing to the arrangements proposed to be entered into between this Company and Mr. William McGillivray, Mr. Simon McGillivray and Mr. Edward Ellice on behalf of themselves & the North West Company of Montreal, and do fully authorize the Committee to carry the same into effect. . . .

¶The Governor then laid before the Court a Deed for the Appropriation of Forty Shares of the Profit & Loss of the Trade, to be henceforth carried on by this Company, among certain Persons who shall conduct the business in Ruperts Land and in the interior of North America, and do fully authorize the Committee to carry the same into effect.

¶Resolved that the said Deed be a Bye Law of the Company.

27: LETTER OF WILLIAM MCGILLIVRAY TO THE REV. JOHN STRACHAN.
[*Ontario Bureau of Archives.*]

Fort William, 26 July, 1821.
My dear Sir,
 I avail myself of the opportunity of Mr. Alexr McDonell going

[1]Reproduced by permission of the Governor and Committee of the Hudson's Bay Company.

down by York, to tender you my devoirs.—I have been at this place since the 1st inst: settling a most important Business—the carrying into effect the various Deeds and Covenants entered into on the part of the North West Company in London with the Hudson Bay Company:—these arrangements are happily completed, and I part with my *old troops*—to meet them no more in discussions on the Indian trade—this parting I confess does not cause me much regret—I have worked hard & honestly for them, and I am satisfied that I have at least, done my duty. I have been an Agent or Director, since 1794—and Chief Superintendent since 1799, the management has not been easy, for we had many storms to weather from without, and some *derangement in the Household.* But thank God! the whole is closed with honor—and the trade will be productive if well managed, after the Country shall have been restored to order, which it will require a couple of years to effect,—thus the Fur trade is forever lost to Canada! the treaty of Ghent destroyed the Southern trade—still the Capital and exertions of a few individuals supported the Northern trade, under many disadvantages, against a Chartered Company, who brought their goods to the Indian Country at less than one half the Expence that ours cost us—but it would have been worse than folly, to have continued the contest further. We have made no submission—we met & negotiated on equal terms—and rating the N. W. Co. collectively—they hold now 55 out of 100 shares.

The Division of the Interest is this—The Hudsons Bay Company as Capitalists, hold 30 shares—the old agents of the N. W. Company 30 shares (these sixty shares supply the Capital, in equal proportions) & 40 Shares remain permanent in the Interior Country for the Wintering Partners—of these the Wintering Partners of the N. W. Co. have 25, & those of the H. B. Co. 15—the 40 Wintering Shares are divided into 85ths. The Partners are classed into Chief Factors & Chief traders—the former hold 2 85ths, the latter 1 85th,—but as the Factors retire, the traders take their places—and the vacancies that may occur after a certain time to be filled up from the Clerks—the Partners on retiring retain half their Interest from five to seven years, as the case may be,—the term of during is 21 years, commencing with the present year.

A Board of direction sits in London, composed of two members of the Hudson's Bay Committee, two members of our side (the Capitalists)—with the Governor & deputy Governor—This Board must regulate the trade, and until the Country is got into proper order—it is probable I must assume a charge of it—which for some little time will occasion my absence from Canada—

If it is any gratification to you to have this account of our general arrangements (and I am persuaded it will be) I know no man more entitled to it—I shall ever retain a just sense of your friendly and steady assistance throughout the contest which was well calculated to overwhelm us.—My own fortunes have been singular as connected with the N W Fur trade—I was the first English Clerk engaged in the Service of the N.W.Co. on its first Establishment in 1784, and I have put my Hand and Seal to the Instrument which closes its *career*—and *name* in 1821—

The loss of this trade to Montreal & the immediate district in its vicinity, will be severely felt among a certain class of the People—the yearly disbursements in cash from the office in Montreal to the people employed in various ways, as well as for provisions and stores, was not less than £40,000 pr annum—a large sum taken out of circulation—and combined with the present distressed state of the trade in the Province is matter of regret—the anti-northwesters of our City have got rid of us, but not exactly in the way they wished—But I am prosing—

My Brother Simon left this for York Fort in Hudsons Bay on the 21st—he is to inspect the Depots and Inventories of Property belonging to the H.B.Co. (to form part of the Stock)—and this duty performed, he will make the best of his [way] to Montreal—I think by way of Timiskamingue.

I beg my respectful regards to Mrs. Strachan, and am my dear Sir ever yours most faithfully

W. McGillivray

Honble & Revd ⎱
Dr. Strachan ⎰

28: Extracts from Simon McGillivray's "Preliminary Explanation of the Accounts and Statements submitted to the Creditors", Montreal, 16th Jan. 1826.[1]

[*Hudson's Bay House.*]

The firm of Sir Alexander Mackenzie & Co. consisted of certain

[1]Reproduced by permission of the Governor and Committee of the Hudson's Bay Company.

capitalists in Canada and in England who together with *six* Wintering Partners of the North West Company, held amongst them ¼ or twenty five of the Hundred Shares into which that concern was divided, whilst the other 3/4ths or 75/100ths were held by the firm of McTavish, McGillivray & Co. and by an indefinite number of Wintering Partners, being all of them for the time being, except the six beforementioned, and some of whom held two and some one share each, according to the time at which they had become Partners. Those who retired from the concern were also entitled to hold a moiety of their Interest therein for a term of years, and as such shares fell in by such retirement, or by death of Partners, the vacancies were filled up by electing new partners from amongst the Clerks, and for the shares of such new Partners, the firm of McTavish, McGillivray & Co. or in North West phraseology "the Agents" advanced the necessary capital, so that the young partners always began with a Debt to the Agents, the payment of which depended upon the subsequent produce of the share, and as the trade was productive rather of losses than of profits for some years, it will be seen that some of the young partners have got considerably indebted to the House.

The North West Company being thus, by its constitution, subject to changes of the parties interested in the trade of successive years, it was always necessary to open a new and separate set of Account Books for the transactions of each annual Outfit, and it was only at the close of the year, and after the Books of each such Outfit were settled and balanced, that the results were brought into the general Books of the Concern, or as they were technically called "the Agents' Books", which thus comprehended all the transactions of the North West Company, and from which the particular shares or interests belonging to McTavish, McGillivray & Co. and to Sir Alexander McKenzie & Co. and to the Wintering Partners were subsequently deduced and divided. The Process therefore necessarily depended in the first instance on the settlement of the accounts of the different outfits, which were made as follows, vizt.

The Proceeds of the Sales of the returns obtained from the trade, and the Inventories of Property, Goods, and effects, remaining from the trade, or otherwise belonging to the Company being added together, the sum was divided, and carried to the Credit of those Partners to whom the same belonged; whilst the Amount which

THE NORTH WEST COMPANY 331

has in the mean time been advanced to the succeeding Outfit, together with the amount of Inventories so transferred and credited to the Partners interested in the old Outfit, were all added together and the sum divided, and charged to the debit of those Partners who were interested in the New Outfit.

This explanation of the process whereby the Accounts of the North West Company were stated and carried on from one year to another, will tend to show how the settlement has been affected by the operation of my arrangement with the Hudson's Bay Company in 1821. By that arrangement it was agreed that the Property, Goods, Stores and Provisions in the possession of or belonging to the Hudson's Bay Company and the North West Company, in England, in Canada, and at the different Forts, Factories, Stations and trading Posts occupied or possessed by both parties—together with the supplies purchased or prepared for the trade of the Current Year—or in *North West language* the "Inventories" and "Outfits" belonging to both parties,—should be taken into account at a certain tariff of advance, varied according to circumstances, and that the amount should form part of the Capital Stock for carrying on the trade of the New Concern. The Indentures, Engagements, and Accounts of Clerks, Apprentices, and Servants, whether Dr. or Cr. were also subsequently transferred to the New Concern, who allowed a certain rate of valuation for servants Debts, &c., and when it is recollected that these trading Posts and Stations, at which such Inventories were to be taken, and such Balances or Debts to be settled extended all over the Northern part of this Continent from the Gulph of St. Lawrence to the Columbia River, and from the Canadian Lakes to the borders of the Arctic Sea, with different tariffs of advance; and different rates of Servants' wages, for each Department, it must be obvious that the actual labour of arranging and amalgamating all these various Accounts and statements into one consistent Mass, was of itself a task of no ordinary difficulty; to say nothing of the more delicate and still more difficult task of reconciling conflicting claims and statements, and bringing into good feeling and co-operation men betwixt whom such very serious differences had so recently subsisted. These matters occupied the attention of some Gentlemen at the Hudson's Bay House, and of my Brother and myself, almost incessantly during the winters of 1821/2 and 1822/3, during which we were both in London, nor was it until the 26th of March in the year 1823 that we at length struck a Balance of the Account of Capital, but still subject to some reference to accounts and interests in the Interior Country; and inasmuch as the process of obtaining an answer to one of these references, occupies a whole season, besides that answers are not always either satisfactory or even conclusive, it is perhaps not to be wondered at that some points of minor importance connected with servants' Accounts and Balances remain still unascertained. . . .

The Books of the firm have remain unbalanced, since the last Balance taken on the 30th of Novr., 1821, nor can the final Balance take place until after all these other accounts shall have been previously adjusted.

On the termination of that Partnership on the 30th of Novr. 1822, my Brother, myself, and Mr. Thain being appointed Agents in this Province, for superintending and managing therein the trade and concerns of the Hudson's Bay Company, it became necessary to assume some designation for that purpose, distinct from the Old firm, and accordingly the firm of McGillivray, Thain & Co. was devised; but no new Agreement or Articles of Partnership were entered into, or deemed requisite, the only business being to transact the business of the Hudson's Bay Agency, and to wind up and close the concerns of the Parnership of McTavish, McGillivray & Co. The transactions of the new firm were meant to be, and so far as I know they have been limited to these objects solely; and from what I see of them—for until very recently I myself had nothing to do with them—they appear to consist chiefly of payments and advances of money to various persons; the funds for which payments and advances have been provided partly by securities or new engagements given in Canada, but chiefly by means of Bills drawn on London, and which I have had to pay, as is more fully explained in my previous Memoranda. . . .

I believe Mr. Thain has made considerable progress towards the settlement of the unfortunate Montreal Accounts, but all the statements and papers connected with them, are now, as he himself informed me, locked up in his Room, together with his own private papers; and besides the reluctance which I feel in suffering that Room to be opened, or these papers to be examined so long as there is any prospect of his own return, I am persuaded that any attempt of mine, or of any other man, to extract any information from them, in their present state, would not only be a task of much difficulty, but might be an impediment to their ultimate settlement, and to the production of those clear and explicit (at least, if not satisfactory) statements which I still expect with confidence from Mr. Thain himself.

The fact is that Mr. Thain's confidence in his own powers and his disposition to take every trouble off the hands of other people, has all along induced him to undertake too much and to trust too much to the labour of his own hands.

He has been at the same time, so far as depended on the custody and settlement of Account—the managing Agent and Financier and Book-keeper of the North West Company, and of Sir Alexander McKenzie & Co. and the managing Partner and Financier of the firm of McGillivray, Thain & Co. besides sundry public avocations, and other demands upon his time. Among these various functions I particularly mention that of Book-Keeper, because although there has always been a regular Book-keeper on the Establishment of the House, and although the current transactions of receipts and payments, have always been regularly posted up, yet the General Arrangements which can alone show the results of these extensive transactions which I have described, have always been taken from Entries prepared by Mr. Thain himself, and therefore the actual Book-Keeper can only be held responsible for the technical accuracy of his disposal of the materials thus placed in his hands. . . .

Accounts of some of the most extensive and complicated transactions in which the House has been engaged, and of which Mr. Thain has had the sole charge, have been left much in arrears, and many of the Documents necessary for their elucidation are locked up amongst a mass of his private papers while the Accounts themselves and the Documents to which I have access, appear to me to be in such a state of confusion that it seems scarcely possible for any other man than Mr. Thain himself to clear them up satisfactorily.

29: Extract from Letter of Thomas Thain to the Wintering Partners of the late North West Co., London, February 25, 1826.[1]

[*Hudson's Bay House.*]

I sailed from Quebec on the 5th August, with a view of obtaining medical advice in the Country, to visit my relatives in Scotland, and also to adjust accounts connected with the late firm of Sir Alex. Mackenzie & Co. I was seized on the 15th Sept., the third day after my arrival with a most violent attack of Brain Fever, which brought me so low that my life was considered in very imminent danger. I have since had repeated relapses, and lately a very serious one, which has left me in that miserable, weak, nervous State that renders one totally unfit to attend to any kind of business, and I am now writing this letter contrary to the express instructions of my Physician....

Suffice it to say that I, until very lately, never had the most distant idea of being placed in a situation to require delay or probably a composition from any person to whom I was justly indebted.

30: Letter of Governor Simpson to the Governor and Committee of the Hudson's Bay Co., dated at Montreal, April 26, 1826.[2]

[*Hudson's Bay House.*]

Honbl. Sirs,

I arrived here on the 13th Inst., and found Mr. De Rocheblave in charge of the Honble. Compy's affairs, having been appointed thereto by Mr. McGillivray on his departure from hence for England in February last. Mr. De Rocheblave gave me immediate access to all documents connected with the business and readily furnished me with such information as he possessed (which altho' bounded in respects to many of the transactions from the circum-

---

[1]Reproduced by permission of the Governor and Committee of the Hudson's Bay Company.

[2]Reproduced by permission of the Governor and Committee of the Hudson's Bay Company.

stances of his being totally unconnected therewith for several years past) has been very useful to me in many of the arrangements made for the Conduct of the business for the ensuing Season. None of the commissioned gentlemen or clerks here appearing to me qualified to transact the business during my absence in the interior, I have considered it expedient to continue Mr. De Rocheblave in charge until my arrival in the Fall, which I trust your honours will approve, and from his habits of business and general character I have no question that his management will offer satisfaction . . . .

G. SIMPSON

31: A LETTER FROM SIMON MCGILLIVRAY, ESQ. TO THE CREDITORS OF THE FIRMS OF MCTAVISH, MCGILLIVRAYS AND CO. AND MCGILLIVRAYS, THAIN AND CO. OF MONTREAL, IN THE PROVINCE OF LOWER CANADA; DATED LONDON, 26TH FEBRUARY, 1827. WITH AN APPENDIX, CONTAINING STATEMENTS IN EXPLANATION OF THE CIRCUMSTANCES UNDER WHICH THE INSOLVENCY OF THESE FIRMS WAS DECLARED AT MONTREAL, ON THE 27TH OF DECEMBER, 1825.[1]

London, 26th February, 1827.

SIR,

I AM induced once more to trespass upon the attention of the Creditors of the Firms of M'Tavish, M'Gillivrays and Co., and M'Gillivrays, Thain and Co., of Montreal, in consequence of Letters which I have received by the last arrivals from New York; and in reply to which, it is fit that I should offer, both to those Creditors *who have* become parties to my Deed of Assignment, and to those *who have not*, this final explanation of the causes and the consequences of those delays which have arisen, and those impediments which have been interposed to the progress of my arrangements; in order that the *former* class of Creditors may understand to whom these delays, so injurious to *their* interests, are imputable, and to the end that the *latter* may at length be satisfied, if plain facts can satisfy them, that inasmuch as *each of them* has, to the extent of his claim, been the cause of injury to his own

[1]This letter was printed in London for private circulation by "B. McMillan, Bow-Street, Covent Garden, printer in ordinary to His Majesty" in 1827.

property, as well as that of others, the only course now left for them to follow, if guided by any regard for their own interest, is to endeavour to prevent the mischief which they have thus done, from extending further, and, if still possible, to prevent a large Estate, in which each of them has some interest, from being involved in irretrievable ruin.

Assuming, therefore, that you are already acquainted with the statements laid before the Creditors in Montreal, above a year ago, and the Deed of Assignment executed by me on the 2d of February, 1826, to which it had been well for themselves, if all the Creditors had assented with that promptitude which I had a right to expect, and which *I did* most confidently expect; assuming also, that you have seen my Circular Letter of the 25th of July last, I shall begin by observing, that it now appears, the statement of my transactions with the Bank of Montreal, contained in that Letter, and the appeal therein made to the Stockholders of the Bank, against the proceedings of a majority of the Directors, have at length produced their effect, and that the proceedings of the Directors have been over-ruled by an overwhelming majority of their constituents.

In that Letter, I only put it as a *supposition*, "whether these Directors could be actuated by any other feeling than a wish to "promote the interests of their Stockholders?"—and I suggested "the consideration, whether *this* was not one of those cases in which "the Stockholders themselves would be the most competent judges "of their own interests; especially if there should appear any cause "to suppose that any feeling of irritation, or animosity, or old "grudge, operating on the mind of any individual, against me or "my connexions, could have been mixed up in the recent resolutions "of a majority of the Directors?"—and under the extraordinary circumstances of a set of Directors seeking, if they could, to ruin the interests of a large body of Creditors, including, to a certain extent, those of their own constituents. I submitted, "that it "would be well for the Stockholders who had the largest interests "at stake, to make some inquiry into the composition of this "majority of Directors, and to consider what interests these "Directors, individually, might have in the Stock, and upon what "grounds or feelings they might have acted in their recent decision, "before that decision should finally be carried into effect."

As an illustration of these suppositions and observations, I am now induced to offer to the consideration of the Stockholders, a short Statement of the subsequent transactions which have taken place, and a brief view of the comparative amount of interests involved in this question.

Shortly after the dispatch of my Circular Letter already referred to, I received, through the Trustees at Montreal, a proposal from the Bank Directors, to withdraw the prosecution instituted against me by their Agents, on condition of receiving an immediate payment of about 12*s*. 6*d*. in the pound, on the balance due to the Bank, after the deduction of the Bank Stock belonging to my Firm, which, by the Charter, the Bank was indisputably entitled to retain for part payment of my Bills.

This proposition showed pretty clearly the opinion of the Directors themselves, as to the validity of their claim to a preference over the other Creditors, on any other ground than that of the compulsory process commenced against me by their Agents, and which was equally open to any other Creditor refusing to assent to my arrangements. It also showed, how little these Gentlemen were capable of appreciating the straight forward policy of a man who had at once declared every fact within his knowledge, and voluntarily surrendered every shilling of his means; who had therefore nothing further, either to explain or to concede, and who consequently had nothing to fear or to lose.

My answer was necessarily a decided rejection of this proposition, because I had not reserved the means of making separate arrangements with, or payments to, any Creditor. I stated at the same time, that if *all* the Creditors had executed my Deed of Release, and should *all concur* in making me a similar offer of an assignment of their claims for a payment of 12*s*. 6*d*. in the pound, with a reasonable time for paying the same; then, bad as times and prospects were, I might still succeed in an effort to obtain the support of friends who might be induced to join with me in incurring the risk and responsibility of accepting the same; but that, in the situation in which the Dissentient Creditors, and especially the Bank Directors, had placed me, I was precluded from entertaining the question of any partial arrangements whatsoever.

On receiving this answer, my Trustees again brought the subject under the consideration of the Bank Directors; and the majority now finding the attempt hopeless, to extort a preference over the other Creditors by compulsory proceedings, changed their ground, and all at once became particularly solicitous to promote, as they professed, the interests of the Creditors in general, by requiring a surrender of the security which I had, out of my own separate property, given to the Receiver-General of Upper Canada, and to Mr. Gerrard, for separate debts to the amount of 23,600*l*.; which debts, be it remembered, I am advised by Counsel, could, if no such security had been given, have been recovered in full out of my separate Estate, even under a Commission of Bankruptcy; and by securing which, therefore, I have in fact protected the Estate from Government Extents, and expensive litigation, and have not, in the slightest degree, impaired the rights or interests of any Creditor, or any class of Creditors. These considerations, as well as the circumstances stated, and the consequences suggested, in my Circular Letter, were represented to the Board by the Trustees, but without effect. The majority seemed determined not to be convinced or satisfied, without obtaining *some* concession; and, as a *sine quâ non*, they demanded that Mr. Gerrard, and the Representatives of Mr. Dunn, should surrender into the general mass of the Estate, the sum of 9000*l*. Hudson's-Bay Stock, which had been transferred to them for the security of the particular Debts already specified.

This was a demand, compliance with which did not in any manner depend upon *me*, because I had, with consent of the Creditors, parties to my Deed, and as thereby expressly authorized, transferred this stock, and divested myself of all power to resume any control over it; nor was it to be expected that the Gentlemen legally in possession of the same, should surrender it, on the unauthorized and illegal demand of this majority of Bank Directors. The Trustees accordingly, after wasting some time in fruitless negotiation, at length determined to resort to the measure which I had suggested some months before, and to appeal to the Stockholders against the majority of the Directors.

This majority consisted of only a superiority of *one vote* at the Board; and I shall hereafter shew what interest the individuals composing the same, had in the stock of the Bank, and in that claim against me, or rather against Messrs. Dunn and Gerrard, which they asserted with such extraordinary pertinacity. So eager and so determined, however, were *the leaders* of the majority on that point, that, regardless, as it should seem, of any interest or consideration, except the gratification of their own peculiar feelings, they endeavoured to prevent this appeal, and refused to concur in calling the general meeting of Stockholders, the requisition for which purpose required the signature of seven Directors; but *two* of the Gentlemen who had so far followed these leaders, appear *at this point* to have halted, and individually concurred in the proposed appeal to their constituents, although at the Board they still voted with the majority, of which they had previously formed a part.

Anticipating what would be the decision of the General Meeting, and on the pretext, which I am advised was unfounded and fallacious, that if a Commission of Bankruptcy should issue against me within twelve months of the date of my Deed of Assignment, it would be possible to deprive Messrs. Dunn and Gerrard of the 9000*l.* Hudson's Bay Stock, already mentioned, and to add the same to the mass of the Estate, the leaders of the party then proposed resolutions at the Board, to instruct the Bank Agents in London to proceed against me immediately, by suing out a Commission of Bankruptcy, so as to prevent, or to render nugatory, any reconsideration of their proceedings by the General Meeting. This attempt was first made *after* the publication of the requisition for the General Meeting, and being then unsuccessful, the attempt was repeated *on the* 15*th of December*, only thirteen days before the meeting of Stockholders; and so nearly was the object accomplished, that the question was lost only by the absence of one Director, and the casting vote of the President, the Board being equally divided.

In proposing to send such instructions, *one* material circumstance appears to have been overlooked; which is, that the validity of any Commission of Bankruptcy which their Agents, or which any other Creditor could sue out against me, would be extremely doubtful. If *I should determine*, as a refuge against any measure of personal annoyance, to seek the protection of the Commissioners of Bankruptcy, a *voluntary* declaration of insolvency would settle the question at once; but if, on the contrary, any of those Creditors should attempt to *drive* me into the Gazette, they must first *prove* an act of Bankruptcy against me; and if I should resist that proceeding (as in the event of the success of this attempt of the majority of the Bank Directors, I most assuredly would have done), then it would remain for the Lord Chancellor to decide, whether my Deed of Assignment, or any other of my transactions, was or was not an act of Bankruptcy.

It is therefore manifest, that even if the attempt had succeeded, it would have left the Bankruptcy still doubtful, unless *I* should chuse hereafter to resort to it as a voluntary proceeding; and that it would only have ensured *the certainty* of a suit in Chancery, whereof the ruinous consequences which must have ensued to the interests of the Creditors, have, in my Letter already referred to, been sufficiently stated; and these consequences appear to have been duly appreciated by the Stockholders, so soon as they had an opportunity of judging for themselves.

I shall now proceed to state a few facts, shewing the amount of interest in the question, which was held by the Bank generally, and in particular by the party whose temporary situation, as Directors, has enabled them to inflict such injury as they have done, upon the interests of other parties, and from whose over-zealous protection, those other parties, not excepting their own constituents, have had so narrow an escape.

The Debt of the Firm of M'Gillivrays, Thain and Co. to the Bank, consists of Bills drawn on London for 18,000*l*. sterling, or currency	£20,000 0 0
Damages in Canada, including all charges, 10 per cent.	2000 0 0
Total Debt	£22,000 0 0
In part of which, the Bank is entitled to retain the Stock belonging to the Firm and its Partners, consisting of 163 shares, on which the instalments paid, of 37*l*. 10*s*. each, amount to	6112 10 0
Balance—Actual Debt to the Bank of Montreal	£15,887 10 0
Or, in round numbers, say, currency 16,000*l*.	

The question on which the *last stand* was made by the majority of the Directors, was to deprive Messrs. Dunn and Gerrard of the 9000*l*. Hudson's-Bay Stock, transferred for their security, as already explained; and the *value* of this question to the Estate, will appear from the following calculation, viz.

The Debts of the House, according to Schedule A, Attached to my Deed of Assignment, and which, to the best of my knowkedge, is accurate, amounted to	£196,000
Balances due by the Firm in London, to Messrs. Burns, Pozer and Dunn, who have, on explanation, become parties to the Deed, about 15,000*l*. sterling, suppose currency	18,000
And I must *now* add the Balance due to the Bank of Montreal, as above	16,000
Making the total Debts under the Deed	£230,000
And if the Assets be estimated at 12*s*. 6*d*. in the pound, which, but for the proceedings of the Bank Directors, I should probably have been enabled to offer for them, they would amount to	£143,750
If the 9000*l*. Hudson's-Bay Stock, were to be added, estimating the price at 225 per cent., and exchange at 8 per cent. premium, it might increase the Assets by a sum of	24,300
Making the whole amount	£168,050
But in *that* event (supposing it possible), the Debts now secured by that Stock must be added to the above sum of	£230,000
Say, Receiver-General of Upper Canada — £12,600	
And Samuel Gerrard, Esq. — 11,000	23,600
Making (in that event) the whole Debts	£253,600
Upon which amount, a dividend of 12*s*. 6*d*. in the pound, would be	£158,500
And the amount of Assets as above, increased by the 9000*l*. Hudson's-Bay Stock, would be	168,050
The difference, therefore, would be	£9,550
And Ninepence in the pound, on 253,600*l*. is	9,510

Therefore, still on the supposition of the Estate paying 12*s*. 6*d*. in the pound, *the loss* of the Bank of Montreal would have been 7*s*. 6*d*. in the pound on 16,000*l*. currency, or 6000*l*.; and the *value* to the Bank, of the *point* on which so much stress has been laid, as to the 9000*l*. Hudson's-Bay Stock, would be at the utmost 9*d*. in the pound on the same sum, or 600*l*.

For the ill-advised, and really impracticable attempt to obtain which trifling advantage, in the face alike of justice, of equity, and of the interests of the Creditors, the Estate has already been deeply injured, even if the mischief should *now* end; and looking at the consequences which *may still ensue*, exclusive of the delay, the expense, the depreciation of property, and the increased difficulty of recovering debts, or adjusting claims, which have *already arisen* from the proceedings of the Directors, and their Agents in London, it really exceeds *my* power of calculation to estimate the extent of the injury, which, in utter disregard of all explanation, and with a perverse pertinacity, unequalled by any thing I have ever heard of in commercial transactions, these Gentlemen have inflicted upon the property of other persons, in which they themselves had so extremely trifling an interest.

The amount of that interest is easily estimated. The Capital Stock of the Bank of Montreal consists of 250,000*l*. in shares of 50*l*. each, on which calls to the amount of 37*l*. 10*s*. per share have been paid up: so that the actual capital paid up in money, is 187,500*l*. currency. And the number of shares is *five thousand*, *ten* of which, or a capital of 375*l*., or fifteen hundred dollars, constitutes a qualification for a Director. And it appears rather a singular circumstance, that of the *seven* Directors who formed the majority in these proceedings, *five* held only a bare qualification of *ten shares* each, or capital in the whole to the amount of 1875*l*.

The interest of *each* of these Gentlemen in the debt of my Firm to the Bank, was 32*l*. currency, or 128 dollars.

If the Estate paid 12*s*. 6*d*. in the pound, the *loss of each* of them would have been 12*l*. or 48 dollars.

And the *value to each of them*, of the question about the 9000*l*. Hudson's-Bay Stock, was exactly 1*l*. 4*s*., or $4\frac{80}{100}$ dollars.

So that it is evident those Directors had a very slight *personal interest* in the protection of that property which they have done so much to injure; and in reply to the argument by which I understand throughout these proceedings, the majority of the Directors attempted to justify their conduct, namely, that it was their duty to obtain as much as possible for their constituents, I will now state the decision of those constituents themselves, upon full consideration of the merits of the case; and notwithstanding the influence generally possessed by a body of Directors, over the opinions of the Proprietors, whose confidence it is always to be presumed they possess.

Of the five thousand shares which form the Capital Stock of the Bank, I have understood that a considerable portion is held by Citizens of the United States, who, according to the Charter, are precluded from voting at General Meetings; and I am informed, that of these Alien Stockholders, several of those most deeply interested (I have heard the names of Mr. Carroll of Maryland, and Mr. Brevoort of New York) wrote letters, which were produced at the recent meeting, disapproving of the proceedings of the Directors, while no such letters were produced from any Proprietors in the United States, approving the same.

I mention particularly the circumstance of the Stock so held by American Citizens, being unrepresented, in order to explain the fact, that the meeting was in reality one of the most numerously attended that has ever been held at the Bank, although the number of shares on which the votes were taken was under three thousand or about three-fifths of the whole capital; and as my Letters of the 25th and 27th of July, had been for some months in the hands of all the Stockholders, they had every opportunity to investigate *the facts*, and to arrive at a deliberate and dispassionate conclusion upon the *merits* of the case; so that their decision may be quoted as entitled to considerable weight, in the estimation of all persons who have any interest in the concerns of this unfortunate Estate.

These Letters were read to the Meeting, together with a Statement of the transaction, submitted on behalf of those Directors by whom the Meeting had been summoned, and from which Statement the following Extracts appear to me deserving of particular attention, viz.

1*st*, "When Messrs. Thomas Wilson and Co. had taken harsh "measures against Mr. M'Gillivray and Mr. Thain, the Solicitors "of that House stated, that '*it would be necessary to prove, on behalf* "'*of the Bank, not only that particular funds belonging to the Drawers* "'*of the Bills were directed to be appropriated for their payment, but that the parties authorized to administer those funds, had assented to such appropriation, in order to obtain success in the suit, and to ensure a final liquidation of the claim, either from those funds, or from the parties administering the same.*'"

2nd, "The means of proving these points are merely presumptive, and of themselves inadequate. With respect to the appropriation by the Drawers, we have nothing more explicit than what is contained in Mr. M'Gillivray's Letter of the 23d of January,* in which he says, '*I did not indeed expressly hypothecate or set aside any specific fund for the payment of these Bills*, nor did I deem any such measure necessary, because I had no doubt about all my Bills being duly honoured.'"

3rd, "In the Assignment, a specific fund is indeed named, but is charged merely with the Bills as a contingency; and neither in

*Before Messrs. Thomas Wilson and Co. commenced their proceedings, I had furnished them with a copy of this Letter of the 23d of January; and although the tone of unwarranted assumption and unfounded and injurious imputation in which they thought fit to address me in reply, prevented the possibility of *my* holding any further communication with them, yet Mr. Ellice, in his capacity of Trustee, gave to Mr. Wilson personally, and afterwards, at his request, to his Solicitor, explanations, in substance the same with those which I have since given to the Creditors and to the Stockholders. The Solicitor's opinion, as now disclosed by the Directors, appears to have been moderate and judicious; but I confess myself at a loss to understand upon what principle, under the circumstances stated, and with that opinion before them, Messrs. Thomas Wilson and Co. could have resorted, as they did, to compulsory process of the most offensive description, particularly as it regarded poor Thain, against whom, as well as against me, a Writ was taken out for 16,000*l.*, and who, notwithstanding the serious illness under which he was known to be suffering, and in the midst of that mental irritation which has since become aggravated into actual madness, must have been dragged to a prison, if I had not found two Friends who had sufficient confidence in us, to become answerable for him, as well as for myself, and each of whom was able to justify bail to the amount of 32,000*l.*

It is not now very material, nor is it my present purpose to inquire, what may have been the motive or the object of this summary proceedings, which it appears was adopted by the Agents without any instructions from their Principals;—whether it could have been, that personal offence was taken, or that any feeling of wounded self-importance required atonement, because a man in my unfortunate circumstances should presume, even in self-defence, to repel false and caluminous allegations, and to resist imperious demands, with which compliance was impossible; or whether it was merely an experiment, to try if any advantage could be obtained, or any concession extorted, by means of personal

"the Letter nor in the Assignment, do we find any thing explicit,
"peremptory, and irrevocable, respecting an appropriation of Stock
"to meet these Bills."

4*th*, "In the next place, the Drawers of the Bills, and the Ad-
"ministrators of the funds in England, have *not* intimated their
"consent to the appropriation, either by accepting the Bills, or
"by offering to secure the amount by the transfer of Stock on
"any terms."

After these Documents had been read, the first Resolution proposed (with certain reservations, entirely unimportant and unobjectionable, so far as I am concerned), was, "That in the "opinion of this Meeting, it is expedient, and the President of "the Corporation is hereby instructed without delay to accede to "the Assignment executed by Simon M'Gillivray, Esq. on the "2d of February last."

To which an Amendment was moved by Mr. *Leslie*, and secon-

annoyance:—but *it is* material to refer to the consequences which have ensued, and of which this proceeding has been in a great measure the cause.

Had it not been for the sake of supporting the measures already adopted by the Agents, and on the plea that it was impossible a House of respectability could be capable of acting so harshly, without *some ground* to justify their conduct, I am informed that the majority of the Directors could not at any time have been induced to concur in sanctioning their proceedings; and had it not been for the impression produced by the knowledge of my being prosecuted by the Agents, and of the Directors having refused to accept my Assignment, thereby setting an example to other Creditors, who had delayed, or who may have been doubtful about executing the Deed, and who may thus have been led to imagine that some benefit might be derived from pursuing a similar course—it is more than probable that every one of those Creditors would ere now have assented to my arrangements. In short, if it had not been for the consequences which can be distinctly traced to those proceedings of Messrs. Thomas Wilson and Co., I firmly believe that the difficulties, now perhaps inseparable, which have since arisen, and which are hereinafter stated, might have been prevented.

It is therefore not in complaint of any personal annoyance inflicted on myself, however unmerited I may consider it to have been, nor yet in impeachment of any proceeding authorized by law, that I offer these observations; but in vindication of my own Character, and in justification of the Statements which I produced, and the prospects which those statements warranted me in holding out to the Creditors, when my propositions for the Assignment of my Estate were first submitted to them, I now deem it requisite to explain, and to trace to their origin, the proceedings which have marred those prospects, by impeding, and rendering precarious, if not finally frustrating, every beneficial result of my arrangements.

ded by Mr. *Moffatt*—"That the Directors be instructed to take the "opinion of Counsel in London, as to the right of bringing back "to the general mass of the Estate, the payments made to Samuel "Gerrard, Esq. and to J. H. Dunn, Esq. or his Representatives, "or to any other person, on the eve of, or after Bankruptcy, and "to report the same to a General Meeting of Stockholders, to be "called for that purpose on the first Monday in July next."

Thus, instead of the high ground taken, and the arbitrary proceedings dictated by the leaders of the majority at the Board of Directors, in sanctioning prosecution, and attempting to sue out a Commission of Bankruptcy against me, they now resorted to *evasion* and *procrastination* of the question, the effect of which they probably knew would have been the same with that of the more open course of hostility previously pursued.

On putting the question, a division took place, and the votes of the Stockholders, and the shares of Stock held by the respective parties, were declared as follows, viz.

	Shares.	*Votes.*
For *immediately* acceding to my Assignment	2349	522
For *six months' postponement*	484	142
Majority	1865	380

This of itself appears sufficiently decisive, the minority holding only about one-fifth part of the Stock upon which votes were received; and if I could add the 315 shares held by Messrs. Carroll and Brevoort, and 163 shares held by myself and my late Firm, but in right of which my Trustees did not claim to vote, then the majority would be increased to 2343 shares, and the minority would be reduced to about one-sixth part of the Stock for which representatives were present.

In order, however, to see the remarkable unanimity of the *Stockholders* on the question thus referred to them, it may be well to analyze the composition of this minority a little further; and the information which I have received, enables me to show of whom it actually consisted, and what interest they held personally in the matter at issue.

The minority so holding 484 shares, consisted of the following classes and persons, viz.

THE NORTH WEST COMPANY

	Stock.		Value.
Three Directors—Messrs. *Leslie, Moffatt,* and *Porteous*— holding of the Bank Stock	40 shares	..	£1500 0 0
Two other Proprietors, holding	30 —	..	1125 0 0
Total, *actually present,* holders of	70 —	..	£2625 0 0
Partners and other connexions of Messrs. *Leslie* and *Moffatt,* whose Powers of Attorney were held by those Gentlemen	78 —	..	2925 0 0
An absent Proprietor, whose Power of Attorney was held by *one* of the above-mentioned "two other Proprietors"	45 —	..	1687 10 0
Minority so far	193 —	..	£7237 10 0
Besides the following, viz. *Peter Burnett,* Esq. who is in England, and whose Power was held by *Mr. Leslie*	111	..	4162 10 0
Estate of R. Patterson, of which *Mr. Moffatt* is the Administrator	180 —	..	6750 0 0
Making the whole	484		£18,150 0 0

I state the *two last sums* separately, because, from Mr. Burnett's own Letters to me, I have cause to believe that his Attorney voted in opposition to his opinion, as well as in disregard of his interest; and Mr. Moffatt being the representative of the Estate of R. Patterson, had the power of voting as he thought fit, without reference to the parties concerned, and without prejudice to any interest of his own.

Leaving out, therefore, these 291 shares, over which Messrs. Leslie and Moffatt had a temporary control, but in which they had no actual interest, it appears that the parties actually present and voting at the meeting, held 70 shares, or less than 1-70th of the whole Stock, and their absent connexions, whose powers they held, were possessed of 123 shares, or less than 1-40th, the whole party together holding 193 shares, or about 1-26th of the Capital of the Bank; and taking the Debt of my Firm, as before mentioned, at 16,000*l.* we shall find that

The interest of *the party* in that debt, was 1-26th, or - £615 8 0
If 12*s.* 6*d.* in the pound were paid, their loss would be - 230 16 0
And the value *to them*, of carrying the question upon which the ruin of the Estate was hazarded, could only, at the utmost, have been 9*d.* in the pound, or - 23 1 7

It was the same party who thus appear to have had so trifling an interest at stake, namely, Messrs. *Leslie*, *Moffatt* and *Porteous*, who had on all occasions led that majority of the Directors which dictated to the Board the proceedings hereinbefore detailed. Messrs. *Leslie* and *Porteous* were a majority of the Committee of three Directors sent to confer with my Trustees; and who reported to the Board, that the proceedings against me in England ought to be followed up; and it was *Mr. Moffatt* who, on *both the occasions* already mentioned, between the publication of the requisition for the General Court, and the holding of the same, brought forward at the Board of Directors the proposition to instruct their Agents to sue out a Commission of Bankruptcy against me, and so to prevent the possibility of any interposition by the General Court, for the protection of their own interests against the ruinous consequences of throwing my Estate into the Court of Chancery.

It thus appears, that *those three Directors* have, throughout these proceedings, been *the leaders* of the majority of the Board; and I admit that *I* have no right to impugn the conduct of either the *leaders* or the *followers*, in that respect; but I *have* a right to explain the transactions which have taken place, involving the interests of my Estate, and the injury which has been inflicted upon my Creditors. I speak of my *Estate and my Creditors*, rather than *myself*, because, as to any interests of my own, I am extremely doubtful whether it would not have been much more to my advantage, to have passed *at once* through the ordeal of a Commission of Bankruptcy, which, if *other Dissentient Creditors* shall follow the example of these Bank Directors, it may, after all, be impossible to avoid, rather than to remain, as I now do, with my arrangements for the benefit of the Creditors, and for my own release, still left in a state of suspense, by the indecision, or the prejudice, or the ignorance of their own interest, which has hitherto prevented some few of the Creditors from giving their assent to my Deed.

It may therefore be argued, that these Gentlemen (whatever may have been their intentions) have really, in trying to drive me into a Commission of Bankruptcy, been trying to do me an act of kindness; and I must do them the justice to say, that I have heard they disavow any feeling of personal hostility towards *me*. I have also been informed, that in the recent proceedings at the Bank, *other* persons were, more than myself, the object of that persevering hostility, which was directed in the first instance against me, only because it was *through me* that those other persons could alone be reached.

I have heard that this hostility was particularly aimed at *Mr. Gerrard*, the late President of the Bank, who is one of my Trustees; and I am induced to think this the more probable, from my own knowledge of the discussions and the feelings of parties at the Board, previous to the election of Directors in the year 1826, during a part of which discussions I was a Member of the Board, and in which the *leaders* and the *followers* of the party were (except a few changes arising from new elections) the same as in the recent proceedings against myself.

Now it is not necessary that I should set myself up as the advocate of Mr. Gerrard's administration, although it may have been, as I have always understood it was, an amendment upon that of his predecessor, without perhaps being in itself perfect, since perfection in such arrangements is seldom attained, otherwise than by progressive steps of improvement, arising from experience; and it should be recollected, that *banking* is still, *in Canada*, rather a matter of experiment, than an established or well-understood system. If, however, the *price* of the Stock, and the payment of *Dividends*, be any criterion of the prosperity of a banking concern, then the Stockholders will be the best judges of the comparison between the successive administrations which have regulated the transactions of the Montreal Bank; and if holding a large interest in the Stock, be any test of sincerity in promoting the prosperity of such an institution, then the comparison between Mr. Gerrard and at least *one* of the self-styled reformers of his system, is rather striking. At the commencement of the operations of the party, *for the benefit of the Stockholders*, by impeaching the conduct of Mr.

Gerrard as President, *he* was, as I am informed (and by referring to the Transfer Book, the fact may easily be ascertained), the holder of a very considerable sum of Bank Stock; while *Mr. Moffatt*, who was the mover on the occasion, had previously, as I understand, taken the precaution to sell out the whole of *his* Stock, except the mere qualification of *ten shares*. These proceedings against Mr. Gerrard were repeatedly defeated at the Board, but always brought forward again, because it seems to have been the practice of that party, that a question once decided, was not left at rest, but was always subject to be revived, whenever there might seem to be a chance of its being carried—by manœuvre or surprise—*per fas aut nefas*—if on any occasion *the party* could hope to muster a majority of the Board.

An instance of this practice has already been stated, in the *repeated* attempts to dictate to the Board of Directors, Resolutions which, it was supposed, would drive *me* into a Commission of Bankruptcy, without waiting for the decision of the general meeting of Proprietors, although summoned for the special purpose of giving that decision. In the case of *Mr. Gerrard*, through means of the departure from Montreal of some of his friends, and the introduction in their place of new Directors, in the election of whom, be it remembered, the Stockholders had no voice, because such vacancies between the annual elections, are filled up by the Board of Directors—through these means, and by the perseverance of the party against him, they finally succeeded *at the Board;* but at the succeeding annual *general meeting*, their proceedings, although nominally approved by *one* Resolution, were, *in fact*, rescinded and rendered nugatory by *another;* and thus, although not so signally as in the recent instance, the majority of the Directors was defeated by the decision of their constituents.

If, therefore, it should in courtesy or in charity be supposed, that in those repeated instances, the leaders of the party at the Board of Directors were in reality actuated by no other feeling than a stern sense of public duty, and a due regard to the interests of their constituents, then it must be admitted that they have been rather unfortunate in the decisions so repeatedly pronounced by those constituents upon their measures. If, on the contrary, however, it should appear to the Stockholders impossible not to draw the conclusion, that the *supposition*, with the quotation of which, from my Letter of the 25th of July, this Letter is commenced, was well founded—and from their decision, it would really appear they *have drawn* that conclusion—then, although it may to *them* be of slight importance, whether the mark aimed at by Messrs. Leslie, *Moffatt* and *Porteous*, was *Simon M'Gillivray* or any one else, yet I submit, *it is* of some importance to consider, whether in these proceedings, the trust delegated to the Directors has been made subservient to the gratification of party spirit or personal enmity, no matter against whom directed; and whether the concerns of an institution, conducted on such principles, are likely to prosper.

It appears to me perfectly demonstrated by the facts herein stated, that the interests of the Proprietors *have been* trifled with and sacrificed, by *a party* who had obtained a temporary ascendency in the management of the Bank, but who had scarcely any interest in its prosperity; and whether their conduct is to be imputed to ignorance, or prejudice, or obstinacy, or party spirit, I care not, but I think it quite impossible to imagine, that it could have proceeded merely from a due regard for the interests of those constituents whose benefit they professed to have principally in view.

The judgment of those constituents themselves, has been sufficiently pronounced by the decision of that General Meeting, at which it may almost literally be said, that *the party* stood alone, with all the Stockholders against them; and leaving to those Stockholders, as the parties chiefly interested, to consider whether they will apply any remedy, or adopt any precaution, to prevent the future mismanagement of their own concerns, I shall now return to the consideration of *yours* and *mine;* and the first inference which I would suggest—from the conclusion which appears to have been drawn by the Stockholders—and my chief reason for introducing so minute a detail of the proceedings which led to that conclusion—is the expectation, that it may produce some effect on those Creditors of my Firm, who have not yet executed my Deed of Assignment, and who may have been deterred from so doing, by the example of the Bank, and the hope of sharing in some imaginary benefit to be derived from refusing their assent to my arrangements.

Those Creditors, therefore, who may have been thus influenced by the example of the Bank, or the opinions of any individual

Directors, will now, I trust, be satisfied, so far as the same example, or the decision of the Bank Proprietors can satisfy them, that no benefit can be expected to arise to any party, either from a repetition of compulsory proceedings against me, or from a continuation of the state of suspense in which my arrangements for their own benefit now remain, waiting for their decision. The Bank Directors, and their Agents, as the holders of protested Bills of Exchange, drawn by myself, and payable in London, although they had no legal right to any preference over other Creditors, had yet undoubtedly greater facilities in suing out summary process, or in establishing summary proof of their claim, than any other Creditor can have; besides, that they had the opportunity of indulging any propensity which might prompt them to litigation, without being deterred by the consideration of expense, because *that*, as well as the injury inflicted on my Estate, would fail to be sustained, not by themselves, but by their constituents; and when, with all these facilities, and without any forbearance or mitigation in taking every advantage of them, these powerful men have failed in extorting any compromise or concession from me, is it likely that any other claimant can be more successful? On the contrary, is it not manifest, that when no compromise or concession *can* be made—and for the most conclusive reason, because *every thing* has been already conceded—it must be equally useless, so far as *I* am concerned, for any Creditor to resort further, either to coercive measures, or to experiments upon my endurance of a continued state of suspense?

In regard to the history of my unfortunate concerns in Canada, the large fortune which I voluntarily surrendered for the payment of the Debts of my Partners, and the arrangements which I suggested for the benefit of the Creditors, I have very little explanation or remark to offer, in addition to the Statements laid before them at Montreal in January 1826, and my Circular Letter of the 25th of July, already referred to. In order, therefore, to avoid occasion for repetition, as well as for the information of those Creditors residing at a distance from Montreal, who may not have had access to these Documents, I shall annex them as an Appendix to this Letter; and I am further induced to adopt this course, by the wish to give every person concerned, the opportunity of comparing with each other, the Statements which I have from time to time pro-

THE NORTH WEST COMPANY 353

duced, and of considering the effect and the benefit to themselves, of my voluntary propositions, as compared with the utmost advantage in the power of any party to extort by the most rigorous legal proceedings.

In Appendix C, page 13, I allude to *some* of the questions which, in the event of my having recourse, or being driven to a Commission of Bankruptcy, will inevitably cause delay, and litigation in the Court of Chancery; and several other intricate questions have since arisen, in addition to the intrinsic difficulty of which, and to the proverbial caution—not to say slowness—of that Judge for whose decision they must wait, there are circumstances connected with the state of the Law itself, which merit the most serious consideration of every party having any interest in these complicated concerns.

The Bankrupt Law of England has recently undergone considerable modification. The last Act, "to Amend the Laws relating to Bankrupts," (6 of Geo. IV. cap. 16), passed on the 2d of May, 1825, commences by repealing twenty-one former Acts of Parliament, from which certain clauses are then re-enacted as new provisions,—some with, some without amendments,—and other clauses are added; and the Act so framed, constitutes the present code of Bankrupt Law. Now, *one* consequence of this very recent alteration of the Law is, that there are yet few decisions on record, whereby, in intricate cases, to ascertain the operation of the *new Law;* and the *old Laws* being rescinded, the cases which had been decided under *them*, are no longer precedents. Acts of Parliament are sometimes obscure in their provisions, and imperfect in their construction; and until cases arise by which their operation may be construed, different Counsel may construe them differently, and it may remain doubtful which of the learned Gentlemen is right.

This appears to have been the case with some of the questions put to Counsel by Mr. Ellice and myself, on the one side, and by the Hudson's-Bay Company on the other. (See Appendix C, page 14). These questions, in fact, involve cases which have not yet been decided; and if the Creditors are to *wait*, and to *pay* for obtaining the decision of them, and so establishing precedents for other cases, then it must be obvious, that all hope of any beneficial result must be even more remote than I have formerly represented it to be.

In consequence of the opinion so given to the Hudson's-Bay Company, that my Assignment was, or may be held to have been, an act of Bankruptcy, and therefore that it would not be safe for the Company to transfer my Stock otherwise than under the sanction of a Court of Equity, the Governor and Committee have given me notice, that they will not permit the transfer of the Hudson's-Bay Stock standing in my Brother's name, and assigned by me to the Trustees. It is quite useless to remonstrate, or to argue on this subject, unless all the Creditors shall have become parties to my Deed; and in the mean time, the Stock is absolutely locked up from sale or transfer, until, as the case may be, either the Governor and Committee shall be satisfied that a final Bankruptcy is impossible, or until a Bankruptcy shall actually take place, and the Stock be disposed of by order of the Court of Chancery, or until the decision of the Court shall be obtained, on a Bill to be filed by the Trustees, to enforce the transfer of the Stock. Now, by either of the *two latter* processes, it is not for me to say *when* any part of this Stock may become available to the Creditors; and the only possible means of effecting the *former*, is to produce proof that every one of the Creditors has actually executed the Deed, or otherwise released me, so as to prevent any question about the possibility of a Bankruptcy; and if any of the Creditors should have been holding off, and waiting for the inducement of a Dividend being declared, before they execute the Deed, I beg to submit to their consideration the following brief view of the case, viz.

1*st*, No Dividend can be received from any funds in England, till the Hudson's-Bay Stock shall be disposed of.

2*nd*, The Hudson's-Bay Stock cannot be disposed of, until *all the Creditors* shall have executed the Deed.

3*rd*, Certain Creditors hesitate or delay to execute the Deed, until they are induced so to do by the payment of a Dividend;—and therefore,

4*th*, No Dividend can be expected, and no settlement can take place.

Until these matters shall be decided in some shape, any idea of *my* leaving England is out of the question. Whether it is to be my lot to surrender to a Commission of Bankruptcy, or, as the Attorney of my Trustees, to dispose of the Hudson's-Bay Stock, or to conduct a suit in Chancery to enforce the transfer thereof by the

THE NORTH WEST COMPANY

Hudson's-Bay Company, each and either of these duties is one which cannot be performed by deputy, and which in fact cannot be performed by any one but myself; so that whatever loss may arise, and much has already arisen, from delay in adjusting accounts and collecting debts in Canada, as well as in disposing to advantage of the real Estate in that Province, yet the Hudson's-Bay Stock and the question of Bankruptcy, are the main objects to which my attention must be directed; and I can assure the parties concerned, that it has entirely arisen from personal consideration *for me*, that the Stock pledged as security for money borrowed, has not long since been irrecoverably sacrificed, nor do I at all know how long I may be in a condition to preserve it, unless I am enabled to take some decided ground in regard to the Deed of Assignment.

The amount of Hudson's-Bay Stock *now* actually forthcoming out of my Estate—including the surplus of the amount so pledged for securities, as well as that standing in my Brother's name, and which is thus *impounded* by the Hudson's-Bay Company—has already been repeatedly stated; but as the Statement is of so much importance, I will introduce it here in a more detailed shape, as follows, viz.

My original Statement of the Hudson's-Bay Stock, (see Deed of Assignment, Schedule C, No. 3), shows that the sum originally "placed at the dis-"posal of, and belonging to Wm. M'Gillivray "and Simon M'Gillivray, (exclusive of certain "sums in trust)," was - - - - - £62,500 0 0
And that "there stood previously in my name "5900*l.*;" but the actual sum was - - - 5954 13 0

Total - - - - - - £68,454 13 4
Of which there has been transferred to S. Gerrard, Esq. and the Representatives of J. H. Dunn, Esq. - - - - - - - 9000 0 0

Balance remaining—Stock - - - - £59,454 13 4

Whereof the following is pledged for Loans, viz.
To Messrs. Smith, Payne and Smith, for £9500   5000 0 0
To Messrs. Overend, Gurney and Co. - 30,500   16,500 0 0

To the Hudson's-Bay Company - - 21,000	12,000	0 0
Loans - - - - -£61,000 on	£33,500	0 0
Carry forward - - - - -	£33,500	0 0
Brought forward - -	£33,500	0 0
Stock standing in the name of the late W. M'Gillivray, Esq. - - - - - - -	20,833	6 8
And of E. Ellice, Esq. against certain sums paid by him to M'Tavish, Fraser and Co. - - -	5121	6 8
Total remaining as above—Stock - -	£59,454	13 4
Subject to the payment of Loans for—Cash -	£61,000	0 0

Subject also to the payment of a Balance due to Mr. Ellice, on a Settlement of Accounts, in regard to which, a reference to the other Trustees may become necessary, but which, for the sake of an estimate, I shall suppose to be 10,000*l.*; thereby increasing the incumbrances to 71,000*l.*; and the *net value* of the Stock would be as follows, viz.

At 200 per cent. £118,909 6 8, less £71,000, is -	£47,909	6 8
At 225 — 133,773 0 0, less the same, is -	62,773	0 0
At 250 — 148,636 13 4, less the same, is -	77,636	13 4

And supposing Exchange at 8 per cent. premium, then

At 200 per cent. the surplus of £47,909 6 8 Sterling, would be—Currency - - - -	£57,491	4 0
At 225 per cent. the surplus of £62,773 0 0 Sterling, would be—Currency - - - -	75,327	12 0
At 250 per cent. the surplus of £77,636 13 4 Sterling, would be—Currency - - - -	93,164	0 0
The amount of the Debts, as already stated in page 5, is 230,000*l*. on which a Dividend of 5*s*. in the pound, would be - - - - - -	57,500	0 0
6*s*. 6*d*. -	74,750	0 0
and 8*s*. -	92,000	0 0

And *some one of* which Dividends, according to the price obtained for the Stock, might, but for the impediments which have arisen from the hostility of some and the supineness of other Creditors, have now been actually in course of payment; whereas, if these impediments are to wait for the decision of the Court of Chancery, so also must all hope of receiving the Dividends, until that decision shall have been given.

I do not know that I can say any thing to give additional weight to this statement, with any Creditors who will judge for themselves, and who will look coolly and dispassionately at their own interest. There are, however, some classes to which it is right to refer, both of Creditors who may have views and interests distinct from the general body, and of persons who are in fact Debtors, setting up claims as Creditors, and trying to put the *bonâ fide* Creditors on a false scent, in hopes to escape or evade the settlement of my claims, or rather those of my Creditors, against themselves.

The former class consists of Creditors who hold, or who may be advised that they hold, engagements constituting what are in Canada called *hypothecary claims* against the real Estate of my late Brother, or of Mr. Thain, in that Province, since it appears that all notarial engagements contracted in Canada, amount to hypothecary claims, or mortgages on the whole real Estate of the contracting party; and I have been informed, that the expectation of establishing such hypothecary claims, has prevented some Gentlemen who have verbally, and in writing, declared their assent to my arrangements, from actually executing the Deed. To these Gentlemen I have only to recommend the consideration of a Clause* in the Deed of Assignment, by which they may see that

*If any other of the said Creditors of the said late Honorable William M'Gillivray and Simon M'Gillivray, enumerated in the aforesaid Schedule marked A, do, or shall possess any hypothecary security for the whole or any part of their said Debts, then such Creditor or Creditors, at the time of signing these presents, or ratifying and confirming the same as aforesaid, shall state and produce such hypothecary claim; and the same, and the nature and particulars thereof, shall be entered, on a Schedule to be marked D, and to be signed by the party producing the same, and by the said Notaries, and to remain in the custody of one of the said Notaries; and in regard of such hypothecary claims so stated, and produced, and entered in the Schedule marked D, the Creditors holding the same, and who shall sign these presents, or ratify and confirm the same, shall not, such claims, if valid, may remain in force, notwithstanding their execution of the Deed; and if there should be any doubt about the real Estates in Canada paying the whole amount of such claims in full, then the parties entitled to the same, are, alike with the other Creditors, injuring their own best interests, by leaving in hazard the validity of the Assignment of my Estate for the payment of the House's debts. In short, they are really hazarding a substance to grasp at a shadow, since it is impossible for any of them, or for me, to ascertain by anticipation, what the amount of these hypothecary claims may be found to be.

The latter class consists of certain Partners and retired Partners of the different Firms and concerns of which I have been a Partner, and for the payment of whose Debts *I* have divested myself of the whole of my own Estate, as well as my Brother's, whilst these Gentlemen, instead of manifesting any disposition to follow my example, are even attempting to set up claims, as if, instead of being Debtors, they were Creditors of my Estate. The history of my connexion with these Gentlemen, and the financial difficulties in which the wasteful extravagance of some of them involved the Firm whereof they and I were mutually Partners, are sufficiently stated in Appendix, B, page 3, as also the fact of my having assigned to them certain shares of profit on the Trade of the Hudson's-Bay Company; in regard to which it is there stated, that "I consider "nearly the whole of *these Shares* still liable for the engagements "of the House, and that I may probably be enabled to retain them "for the benefit of the Creditors." And in a subsequent Statement, attached to my Deed of Assignment, as Schedule C, No. 4, it is further stated in explanation, that "these Shares are only "Annuities, payable to the Partners by Mr. Ellice and myself, "being in fact a charge upon our Hudson's-Bay Stock, and that "by *our* management, if the Deed of Trust shall give us sufficient "power, I think these means may be converted to the benefit of "the Creditors;" but it is added, that "we shall probably have "*questions to try* with these individuals, and it is only through *my*

by reason of any thing therein contained, lose any benefit or advantage from their respective hypothecs, nor be debarred from enforcing them, and all rights derived from them, but shall and may, notwithstanding these presents, avail themselves of their said hypothecs as fully, to all intents and purposes, as if these presents had not been made.

"*peculiar* Claims on them, that any part of this sum can be rendered "available to the Estate."

I now find these questions, which I anticipated, are attended with more difficulty than I at that time expected; but my opinion as to the merits of the case, remains unchanged, although those merits cannot be brought to issue until the point be decided, one way or another, as to the ratification of my Assignment by all the Creditors, or the resort to a Commission of Bankruptcy; and *these Gentlemen* availing themselves of this state of uncertainty, and of the forbearance of the Creditors in regard *to them*, are endeavouring to set up Claims against the House, as a pretext for the attempt to hold those *Shares* for their own benefit, instead of surrendering them for the benefit of the Creditors.

In order to shew the merits of this case, it is not needful that I should enter into any detailed Statement as to the Accounts of individual Partners. It is sufficient to refer to the facts already stated. None of these Gentlemen brought any Capital into the House. They have drawn out large sums, until at length the means were wanting to supply their continued demands. The large property surrendered by me, to pay engagements which were originally *theirs* more than *mine*, is still in existence, as a separate Estate, to a considerable amount, besides the heavy engagements which had previously been paid by my Brother and myself; and after absorbing *the whole of our* property, the Partnership Debts make the House *still* insolvent. How then can any Partner of the House have any claim on my Estate, or any right to withhold from the Creditors any separate property to which he might have been entitled, if the House had been solvent? This is the *plain* question, whatever attempts may be made to mystify it by these Gentlemen, or by their Lawyers; and the remedy is in the hands of the Creditors, to whom all other Partners are, or ought to be, as liable as I am, for the debts of the House.

Mr. Shaw is the only one of these Gentlemen who has yet been prosecuted by any of the Creditors; and being absent from Canada, he has hitherto been enabled, by the Law's delay, to resist the process. Mr. M'Leod, who is in Scotland, has assigned his Shares to his Brother-in-Law, Mr. Peter Burnett, who has served me with notice of this Assignment, and given me intimation, that he will require a settlement of Mr. M'Leod's claims before I leave

England; which I presume means, that he will apply to the Court of Chancery to impede my arrangements, in some shape, with a view to obtaining a settlement for Mr. M'Leod; and Mr. Henry Mackenzie has now given notice to the Trustees, of some objections on *his* part to my Assignment, and some imaginary complaints and claims, in virtue of alleged breaches of covenants by his Partners, in the Firm of M'Tavish, M'Gillivrays and Co.; whilst I have heard, that one of his Brothers, who is himself a retired Partner, has commenced some process, to establish an hypothecary claim against my Brother's Estate.

If any of these Gentlemen could discover a surplus of assets belonging to the Firm, and any attempt on my part, to retain for my own benefit more than my due share of the same, it would, I admit, afford just cause of complaint on their part against me; but it is quite impossible to object to my arrangements upon any such ground, or to maintain any claim on the part of these Gentlemen to any part of that property which I have assigned for the benefit of the Creditors. It seems almost needless to argue against such an absurdity, as that Partners of an Insolvent Firm should be Creditors of the same Firm; and yet such would be the effect of the claim which I understand is set up by Mr. Henry Mackenzie—but it is really a question in which *I* have no interest. I have assigned, so far as I was legally competent to assign, the whole of the Partnership Assets for the payment of the Partnership Debts; and those Assets, so far as I could find any in existence, being totally insufficient for the payment of these Debts, I have further assigned the whole of my own and my Brother's Estate, to make up the deficiency. How then can *any Partner* claim any part of those Assets which are totally insufficient for the payment of *the Creditors?*

But further, there are the *Hudson's-Bay Shares*, and some of these Gentlemen may perhaps expect, that, by setting up such imaginary claims, or preventing some Creditors from giving effect to my arrangements by the ratification of my Deed, they may induce the Trustees to consent to some compromise or discharge to themselves, without insisting upon the surrender of their property. Mr. Henry Mackenzie in particular, having no property to surrender, (since he has been insolvent in a Partnership into which he entered on the termination of his Partnership with me, and to enable him to form which, Mr. Thain and I, imprudently enough I admit, advanced him capital), but possibly expecting, that the interposition of impediments and delays, by which *he can lose nothing*, may have the effect of extorting some composition out of his claim on the Hudson's-Bay Share, which *I maintain* belongs to the Creditors—seems disposed to try the effect of *throwing a tub to the whale*, by impugning my arrangements, whilst his Brother's fraternal partiality may, as I am advised, by possibility engage *him* in proceedings rather hazardous to himself.

These differences *with Partners*, however, need not at all interfere with my arrangements, and the only object is, that the Deed should be ratified by the *real bonâ fide* Creditors. No Partners *can* establish any claim against me, nor can they even prosecute me; and the Creditors and the Trustees, if the Deed shall be completed, will have in their own discretion the most cogent arguments that can be addressed to refractory Partners. It must be evident, as I have already stated, that since I have relinquished the hope of any reversionary benefit from my own Estate, I have really no personal interest in these questions. I have surrendered all *my* right and title to *these Shares*, as well as to the rest of my property, and I have offered to do every thing in my power, to render them available to the Creditors; but if the Creditors shall think fit to relinquish *that*, or any other claim, for the benefit of Mr. Shaw, or Mr. M'Leod, or Mr. Mackenzie, *I* have no wish to interfere in the matter, provided only, that my own release is previously confirmed by all parties. In the event, however, of my having recourse to a Commission of Bankruptcy, the case will become very different; and until *that point* shall be finally ascertained, I shall resist any settlement, or compromise, or release, with, or to any of my Partners, or retired Partners; and such is the "glorious uncertainty of "the Law" on Partnership questions, and such is the intricacy of conflicting interests in these concerns, that I cannot presume to pronounce who may or may not, be found to be liable as Partners, although I think it very possible, that some Gentlemen, who have considered themselves, and whom I have considered Creditors, may find that they will not be admitted to rank as such before the Commissioners of Bankruptcy, and that they may even be held to be still Partners.

No further delay would have arisen on my part, in taking *the first step* to release *myself* at all hazards from these questions and difficulties, but that in the same Letters which apprize me of the determination of the Bank Proprietors, at their general meeting, to accept my Assignment, and assent to my release, the Trustees in Canada express to me their entire confidence, that the example will be followed by the other Creditors of the House; and they urge me in the most earnest terms, for the sake of my friends who are Creditors, and who have such deep interests at stake, to endure the state of suspense and uncertainty in which I am left, a little longer, and to refrain from seeking my release through the process of Bankruptcy, until, as *they* confidently expect, it may be obtained by the influence of reason and common sense. I am not by any means so sanguine in my own expectations, since I have too much experience of the lengths to which some men may be led by prejudice combined with ignorance, besides that I have suggested some sources of probable misrepresentation by parties interested in misleading the Creditors; and yet, in consideration of the request of the Trustees, and their representation of the ruinous consequences to so many of my friends, if my Estate is thrown into the Court of Chancery, I have determined to give them one more chance to carry through the arrangements under my Deed of Assignment, and therefore I shall wait a reasonable time for the result of this further and final appeal, which I shall beg permission to conclude with the following Extracts of Letters which I have at different times addressed to the Trustees, and which I now submit to the consideration of the Creditors, viz.

From Letter of 22d August, 1826.

"*Where*, I would ask, is the discrepancy, or the unexplained "difference, between my first voluntary Statement, and this my "Ultimatum?—*Where* is the point which any Creditor *has* gained, "or can *now* gain, by resisting my arrangements?—What advantage "could these arrangements ever afford *me*, unless they should first "pay every man 20*s*. in the pound?—Where is the value to me, "unless in point of feeling of that *confidence*, on which, by *some* "Gentlemen—not by those who bestowed it—so much stress has "been laid?—What course is *now* most advantageous to the "interests of the Creditors themselves, without reference to any "supposed interests or feelings of mine?—In answer to each and all

"of these questions, I will miantain without fear of contradiction,
"not only that I am entitled to all the confidence that I ever
"claimed, but further, that from the beginning, and throughout
"the whole of these transactions, I have been the person conferring
"most important benefits on the Creditors, instead of receiving
"any at their hands. How I have been requited, let my would-be
"persecutors* answer to the individuals and the families whom
"they are about to injure beyond remedy, in the attempt to oppress
"*me;* and *who*, let me ask, shall impute to me any blame, for resort-
"ing to the only protection within my reach, against such vindictive
"proceedings?"

From Letter of 30*th August*, 1826.

"In *my very first* proposal to the Creditors, I offered them
"more than, they now find, the utmost rigour of the Law can
"extort from me. I offered them my time and my labour, in
"addition to my property; and this I did, *not* ignorantly, but
"meaning to make every possible exertion for *their benefit*, without
"much thought of my own; and it is only when driven to it by
"most unjust and vindictive conduct in *some* of those whom I have
"thus sought to benefit, that I at length turn my attention to my
"own security, and to ulterior views; but being so *driven*, and after
"the question of becoming a Bankrupt, or not, has *to me* become
"almost matter of indifference, it cannot, I think, be reasonably
"expected that I should much longer remain at the mercy of the
"Gentlemen who have hitherto refused their assent to my Deed,
"and who, if they shall still persist in their pertinacity, will, I think,
"hereafter find to their cost, that their share of the injury which
"they may thus inflict upon other persons, will, of necessity attach
"to themselves."

From Letter of 21*st October*, 1826.

(After the information herein before given, see pages 15 and 16, in
regard to the transfer of Hudson's-Bay Stock, it proceeds):

"*This* I submit, as rather a cogent argument, *quoad* the interests
"of the Creditors; and if any interests or feelings *of mine* should at
"all be taken into consideration, I would only seek to refer to any
"Gentlemen among the Creditors themselves, whether it is reason-
"able to expect, that a man who has it in his power to obtain by a

*This alluded to the Majority of Bank Directors.

"certain process, a final discharge from claims which otherwise he
"can never hope to satisfy, shall, without obtaining such discharge,
"and with his eyes open, render himself again the slave of these
"concerns, remaining still at the mercy of those Creditors whose
"refusal to release him, sufficiently shows what he has to expect
"from them. On this subject I have nothing further to state.
"Those Creditors who, after the appeals which have been made to
"them, shall for any cause, or on any pretence, *delay* to accede to
"our arrangements, must be held to have *refused* so to do, and *to
"them* must be imputed the consequences, whatever these con-
"sequences may be."

From Letter of 14*th November*, 1826.

"I am getting more anxious every day for some prospect of a
"termination to these difficulties; and I look for something decisive
"from the Bank, after you shall have communicated to the Directors
"my Letter of the 22d of August. Through their Agents first, and
"themselves subsequently, all the time since my arrival in England,
"has been lost, as to any useful purpose for realizing the Estate, and
"the further continuance of this state of things ruins the Estate,
"wastes *my* time, and benefits *no* person. What do the Parties
"wish or expect from their pertinacity in this matter? They
"cannot *drag me* to Canada, and the worst injury they can inflict
"upon me, is the very thing to which I look as my ultimate relief—
"a Commission of Bankruptcy—only I am deterred from *yet* seeking
"that mode of relief, merely by consideration of the ruinous con-
"sequences in which it would involve those of the principal Creditors
"who are my personal Friends; but if any Gentlemen shall think
"that this, on my part, is a cry of "*loup! loup!*" I promise them
"they will speedily find themselves mistaken; for my endurance of
"this thing is very near a close, and the remedy is in my own hands."

From Letter of 28*th November*, 1826.
(On being informed that a Case had been submitted by the Bank
Directors to Counsel at Quebec).

"The case, altogether, therefore, appears to me so plain, as to
"require no opinion of Counsel for its elucidation; and if the facts
"have been *fairly stated* to Mr. Primrose, I cannot doubt as to
"what must have been his opinion and advice to the Bank; but

"people are sometimes apt to mis-state cases in which their own "interests or prejudices are engaged. The case in point, has from "the beginning been grossly mis-stated by the Agents of the Bank; "and if the Directors shall adopt their mis-statements, as they "began by adopting their compulsory process against me, then it "seems probable, that all which has been said and done, will not "suffice to keep this unfortnuate Estate from being wasted in legal "proceedings; and the time which has been devoted by you and by "me, to attempt its preservation for the benefit of the Creditors, "will have been very unprofitably employed.

"I consider it quite useless, under present circumstances, to "send you any further Statements of Accounts, or Opinions of "Counsel. I merely wait for decided intelligence, to take a step "which, instead of *opinions*, will require *decisions*, and which will "probably take the adjustment of accounts out of *your* hands, as "well as out of *mine*."

From Letter of 29*th November,* 1826.

"I inclose you a correspondence which has taken place between "T. Wilson and Co.'s Solicitor and mine; and you'll see by their "Queries, that they have taken up the matter with the true spirit "of litigation. I shall delay my answers to them, till I hear the "result of the questions sent to Mr. Primrose; but whatever my "answers may be, I see already it is quite hopeless to satisfy *them*. "They can always find some quibble on which to go to Counsel, "and Counsel and Solicitors may alike have a feeling towards "recommending an application to the Court. Now, if the Creditors "will not apply *their own* understanding to the consideration of "*their own* interest, but will thus be led by obstinate prejudices, "or by parties whose interest it may be to create difficulties, and "to incur charges, without regard to consequences—why *I* must "let them have their own way, and I think they will find the "result to be, that an Estate which, *but for their own conduct*, might "have promptly paid a very large Dividend, if not the full amount "of 20*s*. in the pound, will become—as I understand the Legal "Adviser of Mr.*** said last year at Montreal, that '*all Insolvent "Estates ought to become—the property of the Lawyers*,' leaving very "little for the Creditors, and *that* little, rather for their heirs, than "for the youngest of themselves.

"It is, however, quite useless *for me* to say any thing more on "the subject, which, after all, is in reality, Gentlemen, *your own* "affairs, and that of *the Creditors*, much more than *mine*. *I* have "done everything in my power to strengthen *your* hands, and to "make the means of the case clear to all who have any interest in it. "If *the Creditors* will not stir in their own cause, or if you and they "cannot surmount the obstacle started by a few men, who have "really very little interest in the question, why *so be it!* but I "entreat the decision may not be suffered to remain in a state of "interminable uncertainty."

These Extracts contain nearly all I could now say on the same subject, and no change has taken place either in my opinions or in my intentions, since the Letters referred to were written. I am merely induced to defer carrying those intentions into operation, until the Trustees shall have the opportunity which they so earnestly recommend me to allow *them*, for a further appeal to those Creditors who are still Dissentients; and I avail *myself* of the same opportunity, to offer to my Friends,—and to that portion of the Public to which my name and character may be known—as well as to the Creditors, this final explanation of transactions and proceedings, in which, however unfortunate may be the result, and however vexatious may be the details, to me, or to others, yet I have at least the satisfaction to be conscious, that no blame can justly be imputed to myself; but, on the contrary, that the more publicly my conduct may be scrutinized, throughout scenes of no ordinary difficulty, the more conducive ought the proceedings to be, to the success of my future prospects in life.

I remain, with due consideration,

SIR,

Your most obedient Servant,

SIMON M'GILLIVRAY

APPENDIX

A

Memorandum, No. 1, submitted by S. M'Gillivray to the Creditors of his House in December 1825.

THE cause, and the melancholy result of my late Brother's last unfortunate voyage to England, are sufficiently known. He went to seek relief from disease and suffering, and he has found it—in the grave. Mr. Thain also had been in bad health for some time before his departure, and besides that *his* voyage was connected with important arrangements in business, it was recommended by his physicians, as the only probable means of his restoration to health.

As a measure of necessity, upon *their* departure, *I* remained in Canada, and as a temporary substitute during the absence of Mr. Thain, I, for *the first time*, assumed the management of the concerns of the House in Montreal, with the details of which I had previously been very little acquainted.

My Brother's death, and Mr. Thain's protracted absence, in consequence of illness, having *now* left me to sustain alone the whole responsibility of these concerns, I have been endeavouring to investigate them; and I regret to be under the necessity of stating, that it is not in my power to produce any satisfactory result of my investigation.

The accounts of some of the most extensive and complicated transactions in which the House has been engaged, and of which accounts Mr. Thain has had the sole charge, have been left much in arrear, and many of the documents necessary for their elucidation, are locked up amongst a mass of *his* private papers; whilst the accounts themselves, and the statements to which I have access, appear to me to be in such a state of confusion, that it seems scarcely possible for any other man, except Mr. Thain himself, to clear them up satisfactorily.

My investigation, however, imperfect as it is, has sufficed to show, that notwithstanding very large sums of capital, which *my arrangements* have realized, and placed at the disposal of the House, within the last five years, yet that the engagements of the late Firm of M'Tavish, M'Gillivrays and Co. and those which have been entered into, *for that* concern, by the present Firm of M'Gillivrays, Thain and Co. are still very heavy; whilst *some* of the means which ought to be available for the payment of these engagements, are, from the state of the accounts, involved in obscurity, and *other means* which are well known to me, as they are of my own providing, are yet not within my immediate reach; neither are they at once convertible into resources to provide for the payment of immediate engagements.

By my Brother's last Will and Testament, executed a few days before his death, I am appointed his sole Executor, and sole Legatee and Devisee of all his Estate, real and personal; *the object* of which arrangement, was to enable me the more effectually to apply the whole of his property, if necessary, to the payment of these engagements of his House: but for this purpose, some time is necessarily required. To obtain possession of the property, the forms of law must be observed, both in England and in Canada; and it would ill become an Executor, in whom so much confidence has been placed, and it *might* even be ultimately injurious to the interests of the Creditors themselves, to sacrifice such property without allowing a reasonable time for the realization of its fair value.

Of the engagements of the House, a considerable portion consists of Promissory *Notes*, whereof several for large sums, are now nearly due; and under the circumstances in which I am placed, I do not feel myself justified in paying these notes, whilst there remains any uncertainty whether I could alike provide for other more remote engagements, and for the security of those Creditors who, on the faith of personal confidence, have placed their funds in the House at interest, and who would be the last to call for payment.

My *legal* responsibility for *all* these engagements is, unfortunately for myself, unquestionable; nor do I seek to evade it; but in justice to my own character, I cannot assume the responsibility of the accounts in their present state; neither can I reconcile it to myself, to ask, as personal favours, or on the ground of personal confidence, the renewal of engagements which the House may not ultimately be able to pay; nor yet to pay off these large engagements, at the risk, for ought I can tell, of satisfying *some* Creditors to the prejudice of others.

In justice therefore to all parties, and in the discharge of the unexpected and most painful duty which has devolved upon me, I see no alternative but to suspend the payments of the House, with a view to obtain time for the due investigation of the accounts, and for the advantageous conversion of the resources, and realizing of the property, by means of which I trust I may ultimately be enabled to make good all these engagements.

Those Gentlemen to whom this paper is addressed, are therefore requested to attend a private meeting at M'Gillivrays, Thain and Co.'s Compting-house, on Tuesday the 27th of December, at one, *p.m.* in order to take into consideration such measures as it may appear most advisable to adopt for the general benefit of the Creditors at large.

(Signed)   SIMON M'GILLIVRAY.

Montreal, December 1825.

B

Memorandum, No. 2, submitted by S. M'Gillivray to the Creditors of his House, on the 27*th December,* 1825.

In the notification submitted to the Creditors of M'Tavish, M'Gillivrays and Co., and M'Gillivrays, Thain and Co., I have alluded to the "very large sums of capital which *my arrangements* have realized "and placed at the disposal of the "House within the last five years." And in order that this allusion may be properly understood, and the circumstances to which it refers, duly appreciated, I think it due to myself, in my present position, to offer a detailed explanation upon the subject.

The embarrassment of our finances originated in the losses sustained, and the expenses incurred, during the contest in which the North-West Company was for some years engaged with the Earl of Selkirk and the Hudson's-Bay Company.

It is not necessary to my present purpose to enter into any discussion of the merits of that contest, further than to refer to the fact, now admitted by all parties,—that the *real object* in dispute all along, was the possession of the *Fur Trade*, and that, throughout the contest, the struggle on the part of the North-West Company, was merely to maintain possession of what they actually held, and to resist the attempts made to deprive them thereof; whilst, on the part of their opponents, the object was to deprive the North-West Company of that possession, which these opponents argued, was an intrusion upon *their* lawful and exclusive rights.

The merits of the question, as to legal rights, have never been decided; indeed it was found extremely difficult to bring them to any adjudication; and expensive competition in trade, and forcible seizures of property, appear to have been the means most relied on by the assailants, in the commencement of this contest. It is not, however, my present purpose to refer to the scenes of violence, the accusations, and the recriminations which ensued; but merely to show the necessity under which the Partners of the Firm of M'Tavish, M'Gillivrays and Co. were peculiarly placed, to resist, by all means in their power, those attacks upon interests which *they* considered themselves lawfully authorized to defend.

The whole capital of the House, together with a great deal of capital belonging to their friends, and which had been placed at interest in their hands, was all embarked in the trade of the North-West Company; and upon the *success* of that trade, and upon the *security* of the capital invested therein, did at all times depend the capability of the House to pay their engagements. Their resistance, therefore, of the powerful means brought into operation against them, was not only a necessary effort, on the principle of self-preservation, but was also the only means of preserving the interests of their Creditors.

Such having been the nature, and such the objects of the contest in question, it follows, that the charges and expenses attending the same, were actually unavoidable, whether the parties could afford them, or not; on the obvious principle of sacrificing *a part*, for the preservation of the *remainder*; but as it is not my present object, further to justify either the contest, or the expenses which it caused, I shall merely refer to the actual circumstances under which it was brought to a conclusion.

In the fall of the year 1820, the losses and expenses which had been incurred, had seriously impaired the means of sustaining a continuance of them; and as the weight of supplying these means fell chiefly, or I may with truth say, wholly upon me, since the resources of the House in Montreal always consisted of Bills of Exchange on London, which I was obliged to pay, *my credit*, which had previously been rather heavily taxed, was now seriously endangered; and if it had not been maintained, the whole fabric of the North-West Company, with all the capital embarked in it, whether belonging to Partners or to *Creditors*, would at once have crumbled into ruin.

This pressure on our finances was also far from being *the whole* of the difficulty in which the concern was placed. Many of our Partners in the North West, and almost all those at Montreal, were not only destitute of capital, but *some* had got deeply indebted to the House; and seeing no probability of sharing profits, by means of which to pay these debts, *some* became discouraged, and relaxed in their efforts for the common cause; others retired from the concern, in order to save their capital—which was done by almost all those of the North-West Partners who had realized *any* capital; *some* meditated a desertion of the cause, or rather, a change of sides in the contest; and by *these last*, delegates were sent to London, to open a negotiation with the Hudson's-Bay Company; whilst *some others*, apparently reckless of consequences, seemed only anxious to obtain the means of indulgence for the present day, and to waste, in heedless extravagance, as much as possible, of property which did not belong to them.

If it be asked, why Partners were permitted thus to squander the property of the concern, or of its Creditors? I will answer—*first, for myself*—that it was a matter into which I had neither time nor opportunity to inquire, and which it was not in my power to prevent. A man who, within the space of four years, crossed the Atlantic Ocean eight times,—voyaged to Lake Superior thrice, and once to the Red River,—upon whom devolved, at once, the duty of making the necessary arrangements, in times of extraordinary emergency, *in that country*, and of directing the conduct of legal proceedings, of no ordinary difficulty, in successive years, and terms, and in the different districts of *Upper Canada*,—who was also the organ, *in England*, of making to His Majesty's Government the representations necessary for defending his friends and associates, and maintaining their and his own rights and character, against the power of high rank, abundant wealth, extensive influence, and very uncommon talent and ingenuity, which were all united against them, and exerted with extraordinary pertinacity, and unsparing inveteracy, to effect their absolute destruction,—and who, at the same time, had to provide the means of paying the expenses of all these vexatious proceedings:—I submit that it was scarcely possible for a man, with these various avocations upon his hands, to attend, at the same time, to cash disbursements and current expenses at Montreal. The amount of these expenses was sure to come upon me at the end of the year; and it was a sufficient duty *for me*, and I often found it no easy task, during my winter visit to London, to organize resources for the payment of demands during my absence; and during the whole continuance of the contest, with the exception of these occasional and very needful visits to London, I scarcely remained *one month*, in *one place*, at any one time.

For my Brother, also, I beg to state, that, in some points, the contest bore more heavily on *his* time, on his person, and on his feelings, than even on my own; and the ordinary duties of superintending the details of general business, and of regulating current expenses at Montreal, devolved necessarily on other Partners; besides that, probably, the expenditure of individual Partners was less attended to in the midst of the bustle which prevailed, than it would have been under different circumstances.

Before the commencement of this unfortunate contest, the concern *had been* a profitable one. Large fortunes had *formerly* been made in the House; and, but for the competition of the Hudson's-Bay Company and Lord Selkirk, it was not doubted that the trade would continue to yield large profits. The effects of the impending contest were not duly appreciated; and the Partners had got too much into the habit of regulating their expenditure rather according to their own inclination and convenience, than to their actual income.

My Brother was considered a man of fortune; and he had been, in fact, originally the only capitalist amongst us; but *his Partners* also, seemed impatient to figure in the character of men of fortune; and some of them, who had not brought a shilling of capital into the House, had scarcely got their names admitted into the Firm, when they at once launched into all sorts of expenses;—got married, —set up establishment,—and gave entertainments,—without considering whether or not they could afford the means, and without regarding the limits to demands on the funds of the House, which were fixed by our articles of agreement. It is not my wish unnecessarily to drag forward the names, or to stigmatize the conduct of individuals; but, on the other hand, the circumstances in which I am placed, preclude my suppression of the truth, in deference to the feelings of *any* individuals; and if my statement is questioned, I have only to say, let the facts be investigated.

This system of extravagance became at last too serious to be overlooked, but it was not easy to interpose an effectual check, especially after things had gone a certain length; and those of us who were the most interested in interposing such check, were also the most occupied in the urgent and laborious duties connected with the contest, in which property, character, and personal feeling, were alike assailed, and alike to be defended; so that even the repression of the extravagance of Partners, came to be considered comparatively a secondary object. If it be said, that *all* were alike interested in preventing the waste of the House's means, I will answer, that at the time of which I speak, *some* Gentlemen had already drawn upon those means far beyond any share they could ever expect to derive from them; and when this system of extravagance was continued, in disregard alike of remonstrances, and of the repeated promises of the parties, as well as of the stipulations of our agreement; and when the peculiar situation of the House at the time, is taken into consideration, together with the danger at all times, of quarrelling with Partners, who have it in their power, if supplies are refused to them, to incur debts, which *must* be paid; it will be obvious that the case was one of some delicacy and difficulty. It was *our* misfortune to have too many of these Gentlemen Partners, supporting themselves and their *families*, upon *our* means; whilst of those amongst us, who provided the capital, and who performed all the important duties of the concern, *my Brother* was generally separated from *his* family; and Mr. Thain and I myself refrained from contracting engagements, to burthen ourselves with *families*, which, in the case of our Partners, we had found to be at once a cause of increased expense, and an excuse for neglect of duty.

It is however useless to pursue this subject; my present object being merely to show the circumstances in which the House was placed *five years ago*, and the consequent benefit which the Creditors have derived from *my* arrangements.

It was under the circumstances which I have thus described—with reduced means, with a losing trade, and with credit in jeopardy—with disunion in our councils, and defection among our Partners, if not direct treachery in our camp—

with *some* Partners of our House not only useless, but burthensome to us, and whom we yet feared to cast off, because they had the power to injure us—it was under these almost desperate circumstances, that in the month of December 1820, *I* opened a negotiation with the Hudson's-Bay Company, for a general arrangement upon a *new basis;* which, with the co-operation of my friend Mr. Ellice, was in three months concluded, and which in course of the following summer, I carried into effect throughout the interior country.

This arrangement has been a subject of much discussion, and amongst my Partners generally, of much discontent, which, if the case is fairly considered, will, I think, appear extremely unreasonable. It was effected just in time to save the whole concern from destruction; and our circumstances not being known to our opponents, and *they* also having their own reasons for wishing to terminate the contest, I obtained liberal, and even advantageous terms for all parties connected with the North-West Company, and yet *not one* was satisfied; and it even seemed as if those who had been the most anxious to abandon the ship, when they thought her sinking, was now fully entitled to participate in the salvage.

The Partners of the North-West Company consisted of *two* classes: *first*, those possessed of some capital, who had generally retired from the concern, as already mentioned, retaining, according to the agreement, a certain interest in the trade for a limited period, and leaving an adequate capital still at stake in the country; and *secondly*, the younger Partners, by whom the trade in the interior was actually conducted, in their respective wintering grounds, and who were generally indebted to the House at Montreal, for the capital furnished for their shares of the different outfits, as well as for advances made to them personally.

The arrangement with the Hudson's-Bay Company, which was thus a subject of discontent amongst these Gentlemen, has in fact saved the whole of them from serious, and by any other means inevitable, loss of property, and many of them from absolute ruin. It preserved the shares and the privileges of those who *remained* in the Indian country, who under its provisions have become chief factors and chief traders of the Hudson's-Bay Company, and who, if it had not been made, must have accepted any terms which the Hudson's-Bay Company, as conquerors in the contest, would have deigned to accord to them; and it realized at once the value of the property of those who had *retired;* which property, consisting as it did, of trading goods and stores at the different posts and stations occupied by the Company, from the Gulph of Saint Lawrence to the Pacific Ocean, it would have been extremely difficult to realize any value for, by any other means; and if the North-West Company had been compelled to give up the contest, or if the means of maintaining it had not been provided, it is certain that no value for this property would ever have been realized.

The realization of this property appeared to me to be a very important object, and I considered it peculiarly important and beneficial to those Gentlemen to whom I have last alluded; the greater number of whom, however, instead of being pleased or satisfied, actually complained, as if I had done them an injury, instead of a benefit; because, in addition to the preservation of their property, I had not created a fund to repay their *past* losses and expenses.

THE NORTH WEST COMPANY 373

The object most material to my *present* purpose, however, is to point out, that in thus realizing the value of *the inventories*, for account of those Partners who were *indebted to the House*, I so far converted into tangible means, *for the benefit* of the Creditors, debts which previously were scarce worth the paper upon which they were recorded; and the whole amount from those inventories so brought into the funds of the House, was three-fourths of 164,000*l.* or a sum of 123,000*l.* sterling.

This sum of 164,000*l.* and an equal sum, brought in by the Hudson's-Bay Company, was to form the Capital for carrying on the Fur Trade under the new arrangement; and it was agreed that one moiety of the 164,000*l.* should be supplied by my Brother and myself; in return for which, we were to hold certain shares in the trade. I was not at the time aware of the agreements of the House in Montreal, and in the distribution amongst the Partners thereof, of the shares so acquired under the new arrangement, I certainly meant to be *generous*; I *now* find to my cost, I was *profuse*; and still the case was the same as with the Partners of the North-West Company—*not one* was satisfied. For my Brother and myself I retained only of *present interest*, two shares and a half, as a compensation for the commissions which I had relinquished in London; and during the lives of both of us, two-thirds of eight shares, and one moiety of the same eight shares to the survivor; so that all to which *the survivor* would now be entitled, under that arrangement, would consist of *six shares and a half* of *present* interest, and a contingent interest in two shares and a half, upon which the dividends were to be retained in trust for certain purposes by the Hudson's-Bay Company. I also retained a reversionary interest in one moiety of all the shares acquired under the arrangement for Capitalists, distinct from the wintering or trading shares; but in consideration of providing one moiety of capital, and for the space of fourteen years, eight shares were given to certain Gentlemen, merely because they had been *our* Partners—who had no legal claim on us, beyond the termination of our Partnership in November 1822—of whom no capital was required, and, with the exception of Mr. Thain, no duty; and yet who all, with the same exception, appeared to be almost alike dissatisfied. It may, however, be satisfactory to the Creditors to know, that I consider nearly the whole, if not quite the whole, of *these shares*, still liable for the engagements of the House, and that I shall probably be enabled to retain them for the benefit of the Creditors; though I could not perhaps have done so for my Brother or myself. These shares have been valued at 5000*l.* sterling each, and I think they may be disposed of for that sum.

By a subsequent arrangement with the Hudson's-Bay Company, which, in conjunction with Mr. Ellice, I succeeded in effecting in the summer of 1824, and which is even *more* important and beneficial to *the Creditors* than the former one, I surrendered and assigned to the Hudson's-Bay Company our whole Capital, the moiety of 164,000*l.*, and the whole of my Brother's and my own shares and interest in the trade, *present, reversionary,* and *contingent,* and received in return a certain sum of *Hudson's-Bay Stock*, which is a saleable and transferable corporate security, convertible into money, and by which arrangement, if time shall be allowed to realize the stock at its full value, I have, at the sacrifice of the prospect of a large reversionary fortune to myself, brought into the funds now applicable to the payment of the engagements of the House, the whole value of the capital so given in, say 82,000*l*., and a further sum of clear profit, exceeding 100,000*l*. sterling.

This personal sacrifice of my reversionary interest, for the sake of immediate resources, I made, in consideration of my Brother's situation and feelings, though without his knowledge; for he was at the time in Canada, and did not even know the particulars of our negotiation.

I was also influenced, by having discovered, or rather, by having cause to suspect, that the engagements of the House in Montreal were larger than I had previously anticipated; although, even *then*, I had no doubt whatever of being enabled, by means of this last arrangement, at once to pay off all these engagements, which there was a manifest object in doing, because, in Canada, we paid interest at the rate of 6 per cent., while in England we received only 5 or 4.

It was publicly declared by me, both in London and in Canada, that the chief object of my voyage to America, in the beginning of the present year, was to settle all these engagements, and to bring all my concerns in this Province to a final close. It is of no use *here* to dwell upon my disappointment, and dismay, at finding these engagements so heavy, that all the means I had procured, by my arrangements and sacrifices, may possibly be insufficient for that purpose. My object is, neither to excite, nor to make any appeal to, sympathy or compassion; but merely as a matter of fact, to show the Creditors of the House, how much *they* have benefitted, by exertions on *my* part, which, it is now possible, may have little, if any surplus, *to myself*, but which, I submit, ought, at least, to give me some claim to *their* confidence and consideration.

Let it not be imputed to egotism, that I speak in the first personal singular, for I am perfectly entitled so to do. In these arrangements I had neither authority, nor instructions, nor assistance, from the North-West Company, or from M'Tavish, M'Gillivrays and Co., nor did I act on the behalf, or as the Representative, of either concern. I negotiated arrangements, and, as the Deeds will show, I executed Deeds, *in my own name and right*, and *on my own responsibility*; and when I executed the agreement with the Hudson's-Bay Company, I had not even a Power of Attorney from my Brother; although *for him* I had entered into stipulations; and the Company had no security beyond my personal engagement, that the arrangement should be carried into effect. I had, indeed, a moral confidence, that whatever I did, my Brother would support; and that our united influence would carry through any measure, which was right in itself; and neither in *this*, nor in any other point, did *he* ever deceive or disappoint me; but in justice to myself, I must declare, the arrangements were mine, and *he* merely aided me in carrying them into effect.

As to matters of separate personal interest, such as the division, betwixt ourselves, of the benefits thus acquired—the point never was made a subject of discussion. Our mutual object, and that for which each was at all times ready to make every sacrifice, was to maintain the character of the concern, and to support the credit of the House. Neither of us had any doubt as to the ultimate possession of a large fortune, between us; and every thing belonging to either of us, was considered so much in the light of common property, that we thought very little about the ultimate distribution of it. In *my* arrangements with third parties, I always placed my Brother's name before my own, and his interest on an equal footing; whilst, on the other hand, *he* always considered that this equality of interest should apply *only* to our *present* shares in the trade, and he always looked on the *contingent* and *reversionary* interests, which had been acquired *solely* by my arrangements, and which probably would not fall in during *his* life—to be *my* sole property.

In the first Deeds with the Hudson's-Bay Company, all the conditions and benefits were stipulated to be for the *survivors* and *survivor* of the contracting parties; and as the agreement was for a period of twenty-one years, *this* arrangement was made with a view to prevent any question about succession, in case of the death of any of the parties, but was not meant to affect the separate rights of any of those parties, or their representatives.

When subsequently it became necessary to make arrangements betwixt ourselves, for finding the Capital, which I had engaged we should supply, a Deed was executed in May 1822, by which it was agreed, that during both our lives, we should *jointly* provide the Capital, and *equally* divide our shares in the trade; and that in case of the death of either of us, during the twenty-one years, the responsibility of finding the whole Capital, and the whole of the reversionary and contingent interest, which I have mentioned, should devolve to the *survivor*. As the difference of age betwixt us was eighteen years, besides the impaired state of my Brother's constitution, the probable effect of this Deed was obvious, and it fully confirms what I have stated, as to *his* views in regard to the means acquired by my arrangements.

In my arrangement with the Hudson's Bay Company in 1824, this *reversionary and contingent interest* was, in common with our other rights and claims, given up, in consideration of receiving the Hudson's-Bay Stock; and it was taken as of more value than *all our present* shares of the trade under the general arrangement. It was, as the probable survivor, *my sole* and separate property; but I did not therefore make any difference betwixt my Brother and myself, in the distribution of the Stock obtained in exchange for it. On the contrary, an equal sum of that Stock was placed in the name of each of us; and as no part of that so transferred into my Brother's name, could be disposed of, without a *special* Power of Attorney from himself, and as a large sum of Stock was immediately required, to be pledged for sums of money which had been borrowed to meet the engagements of the House, the greatest portion of *my* Stock was at once transferred for that purpose, whilst the part nominally *his*, remained apparently unincumbered.

This was the state of matters when I left England in January last, and on my arrival here, *he* immediately executed Powers of Attorney, to ratify the Deeds into which I had entered on his behalf in England, and also for the transfer of the Stock placed in his name, if requisite. It was a part of the arrangement, under these Deeds, that the final account of the distribution of this Stock, and the payment of the money borrowed on the credit of it, should be adjusted in London *in June next;* and that adjustment still remains to take place, although *his* share of it now devolves upon *me*, in addition to my own.

It is scarcely necessary to point out how much it adds to the *security* of the

Creditors, that *he* carried, even *beyond the grave*, the feeling of reciprocal confidence which has always subsisted betwixt us, and which he has sufficiently manifested by appointing *me* his sole Executor, and his general Legatee, thereby enabling me at once to apply all this property to the payment of the House's debts.

These circumstances are all intimately known to my friend Mr. Ellice, who was in fact a party to all the Deeds which I have mentioned; and in allusion to the *last act* of my Brother's life, I cannot resist the impulse to quote here the following passage from Ellice's last Letter to me, dated on the 26th of October last, viz.

"His anxiety to place in your hands every means and assistance in his power, "to meet a situation which he foresaw would be attended with extreme difficulty "and embarrassment, and the wisdom and prudence of the last act of his life— "are all so many proofs (if proofs indeed were wanting to those who knew him) "of a mind gifted with no ordinary qualities of manliness, integrity, and the "highest principle."

This tribute indeed is justly due to his memory, and I could easily enlarge upon the subject; but that it is not my present purpose, either to indulge my own feelings, or to intrude upon those of others. I trust, however, I may be permitted to adduce this last act, of a man in the last stage of aggravated and protracted suffering which our nature is capable of sustaining—this anxiety for the interests of his Creditors, even when unable to think of the interests of his own Family—as an argument to weigh with those Creditors, in their measures towards his property, and towards his Family. I do not ask them to relinquish any part of their claims, but merely to allow time, to prevent my Brother's property and my own from being sacrificed. In the administration of the succession bequeathed to *me*, he knew well that I should consider myself as a Trustee, acting for the benefit of his Children; and in that character, it is my duty to make every possible exertion, to work out some surplus for *them*. It is also, obviously, on the principle of self-preservation, my duty, out of the wreck of these arrangements, by which, even at the commencement of the present year, I thought I had realized an independent fortune, to endeavour to save some surplus *for myself;* and since the debts must be paid, before either of these objects can be accomplished, I think it must be evident to the Creditors, that in this matter, *their* interests and *mine* are in fact the same.

Were I not—unfortunately for myself—liable, *as a Partner* of the Montreal House, for all its engagements, I should at this moment be its largest Creditor, *tenfold;* instead of seeing, as I now must see, the whole acquisitions of a life of no common exertion, and of exertion generally successful, swallowed up by the engagements of a concern, over the financial arrangements of which, in regard to the expenditure of money, I had no control; and from which I have never derived any benefit.

It was only in 1813, that I actually became a Partner of the House, and since that time no profits have been divided; therefore I have never shared in any profits of the *House in Montreal;* and from the trade or profits of the *North-West Company*, except my Commissions as a London Merchant, *previous to* 1813, I have never directly or indirectly received *one guinea*, which *fact* I am induced to mention, merely because it has been alleged by some of the *liberal* and *grateful* Partners of that concern, that I had enriched myself at *their* expense. *My* transactions and expenses, being now subject to investigation, will at least prove the falsity of any rumours imputing to me either selfish or illiberal conduct, towards any of my Partners or connexions; and in some cases, I must confess it might have been better for my Creditors, if I had been more studious of my own interest.

I have *here*, however, stated all matters as they really took place; I have set forth our arrangements as they were made; I have to the best of my knowledge, explained how our concerns came into their present state; and I trust I have shewn to the Creditors, that whatever disappointment *they* may feel at the suspension of our payments, and at the *delay*, or, as they may apprehend, the loss, likely to arise on the final settlement of our concerns—yet, that in these concerns, *I* am the principal sufferer; that if it had not been for *my* arrangements, *their* situation would have been very different from what it is likely to be; and finally, that it is *my interest*, as much as it is my wish, to make every exertion in my power, for the benefit of the Estate, and for *their* ultimate security.

(Signed)   SIMON M'GILLIVRAY.

Montreal, 27th Dec. 1825.

C

To the Creditors of the Firms of M'Tavish, M'Gillivrays and Co., and M'Gillivrays, Thain and Co., Parties to my Deed of Assignment.

London, 25th July, 1826.

GENTLEMEN,

I HAVE already so fully communicated to the Trustees to whom my property has been assigned, for the benefit of my Creditors generally, and of you amongst the number, all the circumstances which have occurred in regard to my unfortunate concerns, since my arrival in England, that it may seem unnecessary thus further to trespass upon your attention individually; but inasmuch as your own interests are deeply involved in the result of these concerns, and as the arrangements made for your benefit in regard to them, are now likely to be frustrated by circumstances over which I have no control, I think it incumbent upon me, in acknowledgment of the confidence and good feeling which induced you to become a party to my Deed of Assignment, to offer you an explanation of these circumstances, while it is yet possible that your own influence and interference may in some measure avail, to protect your own interests, and to prevent the final defeat of the arrangements which have been devised for your benefit.

It is not necessary that I should recapitulate the statements submitted to you last winter at Montreal. They were declared to be highly satisfactory, by all the Creditors who attended either of the three successive Meetings which took place, and they remain on record, in the possession of your Trustees. Neither is it becoming that a man should say too much on the subject of *his own* conduct or character, but, assailed as *I now am*,—conscious as I am, of having merited acknowledgment, rather than harshness, at the hands of my Creditors,—and confident as I am, that the more publicly and the more rigidly my transactions are scrutinized, the more evidently must appear the fairness and impartiality of my conduct towards my Creditors, to say the least of the matter;—I trust I may be excused for expressing my surprize, that any of them should refuse their assent to the arrangements which I voluntarily offered for their benefit, and which included every sacrifice of property and of time, that law or justice could require at the hands of any Debtor. Such conduct in Creditors, would tend to reduce to the same level, the man who promptly and unreservedly comes forward of his own accord, to declare insolvency, *not* imputable, be it remembered, to any thing done, or left undone by *himself*, to surrender his property for the payment of debts, *not* contracted by him, and to devote his time, to an extent which the law could not require, for the benefit of his Creditors: in short, it would tend to reduce the man of honour and probity to the level of him who, with culpable extravagance, has wasted the property which did not belong to him, or who, with fraudulent intentions, barely avoids the direct violation of the letter of the law; —but, happily, the law, and the administration of equity in England, gives to a man so unjustly treated, the right of appealing to authorities which can discriminate between misfortune and misconduct; and *my* chief regret, in contemplation of the appeal which it is likely that I may soon be under the necessity of making, arises from the consideration, that the unjust and vindictive proceedings which may reduce me to that necessity, can be resisted *only* by measures extremely injurious to *your* interests, as well as subversive to all my hopes of bringing these concerns to any satisfactory termination.

You will recollect, that it was early in the month of December last, that I received at Montreal the afflicting intelligence of the death of my late Brother, at the same time with the information in regard to the state of my own concerns and resources in England, which induced me to determine upon suspending the payments of our House, and at once declaring its situation to the Creditors. During the remaining part of the month of December, I had no payments of any importance to make; and some small deposits of money which I could not help receiving, were laid aside in my desk, and subsequently returned to the parties to whom they belonged. So soon as the conviction was forced upon me, that I could not meet all the engagements of the House, I acted on the ground that it was useless to put off the evil day, and that it would be wrong to make any payments which should have the effect of giving to any one set of Creditors a preference over others; but from this general principle I made two exceptions, and *not* out of any funds belonging to the House; but out of my own separate property, I made arrangements for securing about 12,000*l*. of public money, belonging to the Province of Upper Canada, and 11,000*l*. of Promissory Notes, indorsed for me by a Friend, and discounted at the Bank of Montreal. In regard to the public money, my arrangement in this matter has prevented proceedings which Government might otherwise have adopted, and which would have enforced the same result; and in regard to the Indorser of my Notes, I have only to say, that to provide *for his* security was *my* individual debt, because it was for *me*, and without any security or reciprocity from *the House*, that he had incurred this liability. I was about to make a sacrifice of a separate personal Estate of above 100,000*l.* for the payment of the debts of my Partners; and if, out of that sum, I secured the only separate personal debt I owed, I thought it was right, and I now find it was lawful, and that under the Bankrupt Laws of England, my separate Creditor was entitled to be paid in full out of my separate Estate, before it should become liable for the Partnership Debts. With these exceptions, I made no distinction between any other parties, but acted on the principle of "*felling the tree as it stood.*" My nearest friends and family connexions, who were Creditors of the House, are placed on the same footing with those whose names and claims were alike unknown to me when I arrived at Montreal; and whatever may be the result, I am prepared to prove, and I feel it due to myself to repeat the assertion, that no man ever met his Creditors more entitled to their approbation at least, if not their acknowledgment, than myself.

The arrangement for the security of Mr. Dunn and Mr. Gerrard, which I declared openly from the beginning, and which is as much on record as any of my other transactions, I have not indeed heard directly blamed; but I have heard that *other persons* are dissatisfied, because *they also* were not considered privileged Creditors; and from this dissatisfaction, and the proceedings to which it has led, has arisen the occasion for my troubling you with this Letter.

The first meeting of the Creditors took place on the 27th of December last, when every thing within my knowledge was declared, and the arrangement for the security of Mr. Dunn and Mr. Gerrard was particularly explained to them. At this meeting also, my voluntary offer to make an Assignment of the whole of my own and my Brother's Estate, for the payment of the House's debts, was received; with sympathy and applause. Few men are capable of more intense application than I devoted to the task of investigating accounts, and collecting and digesting information, preparatory to the second meeting on the 25th of January, at which the Deed of Assignment, and the statements therewith connected, were fully discussed; and at the third meeting, which took place on the 2d of February, the Deed was executed, having previously been modified to suit every condition and precaution suggested by any of the Creditors themselves, and in some of which, I confess, I thought they bore rather hard upon me; but I never anticipated that any Creditors could be so blind to their own interest, as to oppose, or to institute proceedings to set aside an arrangement so beneficial to themselves; and in the confidence that nothing of that kind could take place, and anxious to prevent the sacrifice of my funds in England, for which purpose my own presence and exertions were indispensably requisite, I hastened my departure from Canada, leaving my Deed signed by about one half in value of the whole of the Creditors.

The remote residence of many of the Creditors, rendered it impracticable within the time, to obtain their assent, or even to receive any communication from them. There were also other Creditors who held, or expected to establish, hypothecary or priviledged claims against my Brother's real Estate in Canada, under the local laws of that Province; and the only considerable Creditors at Montreal, who did not either sign, or declare their assent to the Deed, with the reservation of such hypothecary claims, were the Executors of the late Mr. David David, the debt to whom exceeds 18,000l., and the magnitude of whose claims, was, in my opinion, the best pledge of their ultimate assent to my arrangements; besides, that *two* of these Gentlemen had, for their own personal claims, become parties to the Deed, *a third* had attended the meetings, and expressed his assent to the principles of the arrangement, and *the fourth* was the only creditor who actually refused to execute the Deed; but even *he*, after giving instructions for commencing a prosecution against me, was induced, by the representations of one of my Trustees, to recall these instructions; so that, on leaving Montreal, without question or molestation, notice of my Assignment having been given in all the Newspapers, and my intended departure from the Province being publicly known, I really had every reason to consider my arrangements as virtually agreed to by all the Creditors.

It was at that time uncertain whether the Bank of Montreal would be among the Creditors, or not; and since it is from the Directors of that Institution, that the attempt now made to frustrate my arrangements proceeds, it is requisite that I should offer some explanation of the nature of *their* claims, and of the history of my transactions with the Bank.

It has already been stated by me officially, that the chief object of my voyage to America last year, was to settle all the engagements of the House in Canada, and to bring all my concerns in that Province to a final close; and enormous, beyond any previous knowledge or expectation of mine, as I found the Debts contracted by my Partners to be; yet still, my funds in England, had they not been depreciated in the general depreciation of all other funds, would have paid the whole. The intelligence of this depreciation, and at the same time, the news of my Brother's death, by which certain funds, on which I had previously relied, were locked up until I should be able to return to England—were the immediate cause of my determination to stop payment; but up to the time when that intelligence reached me, I had paid off every just demand brought against the House; and during the months of October and November last, I had provided in part the means of so doing, by selling to the Bank of Montreal, Bills of Exchange on the House of M'Tavish, Fraser and Co. of London, to the amount of about 29,000l. sterling. I had no cause to doubt, and I had no doubt whatever, about these Bills being duly honoured, since I had left what I considered ample funds for that purpose, in the hands of my friends in London. Edward Ellice and John Fraser, Esquires, had my Power of Attorney for the sale of 20,000l. Hudson's-Bay Stock, which at this time last year could have been sold for upwards of 50,000l. sterling; and Mr. Ellice was indebted to me, on an unsettled account of Capital, in a sum which I estimated at 18,000l., besides that there was a large sum of Hudson's-Bay Stock in my Brother's name, and he and myself being the principal Partners of the Firm on which the Bills were drawn, and which, under my own management in London, had always supported the highest character for credit and regularities, it was quite impossible for me to anticipate, nor did I anticipate, that any difficulty could have arisen in the payment of my

Bills. But in the mean time, the financial panic, the suspension of commercial credit, and the depreciation of all property, which have since produced such extensive distress in England, had already commenced; my Brother's state of health rendered him incapable of transacting any business after his arrival in London; and his death, without having transferred the Hudson's-Bay Stock standing in his name, locked up means which might have been derived from that resource, to a much greater amount than the whole of the Bills in question. Of the 20,000*l.* Hudson's-Bay Stock, which I had left in the hands of my Attorneys, Ellice and Fraser, an amount of 17,000*l.* had been by them pledged as security for 31,000*l.* which they borrowed to meet the engagements of M'Tavish, Fraser and Co. and the remaining sum of 3000*l.* was subsequently transferred to Mr. Ellice, in consideration of monies paid by him for the same purpose. My Partner, Mr. Fraser, had advanced, out of the funds so obtained, above 8000*l.* on unsuccessful Underwriting Accounts; and a further sum of above 10,000*l.* on *Shares* of *new* speculating or projected Public Companies, in which he had embarked after my departure from England, and without my knowledge, although for our joint account; so that, besides the depreciation, whereby my 20,000*l.* Hudson's-Bay Stock, instead of 50,000*l.*, produced only 37,000*l.* these transactions of my Partner deprived me of actual money to the amount of 18,000*l.*, and the funds in his hands being thus exhausted, the consequence was, that when my Bills from Canada, drawn on the 21st of October, were presented, they were suffered to be protested for non-acceptance.

The intelligence of my Bills being thus dishonoured was received by the Montreal Bank, and communicated to me by the Cashier on the 21st of January, four days before the second meeting of my Creditors, already mentioned. I had previously, on receiving the information which induced me to stop the payments of the House, written most earnestly and urgently to Mr. Ellice, to request that all my Bills should be paid out of any funds belonging to me, in possession or in expectancy; and so long as I retained the direction of my own concerns, I continued to urge the same request; but from the time that I agreed to make an Assignment of the whole of my remaining property for the general and equal benefit of all my Creditors, "*I considered myself precluded from taking any step* "*to change or improve the relative situation of the Bank, as compared with that of any* "*other Creditor,*" and I sent a written official intimation to the Cashier, *in these very words*, on the 23d of January; so that it is quite impossible for the Directors to allege any mis-statement or concealment on my part, as they had this intimation before them nine days before my Deed of Assignment was executed.

On my arrival in London, on the 1st of April, I found that about 11,000*l.* of my Bills had been accepted and paid by M'Tavish, Fraser and Co. by means of monies partly received at the Hudson's-Bay House, and partly from Mr. Ellice, and that Bills to the amount of 18,000*l.* were under protest for non-acceptance. It is a singular coincidence, that this amount was exactly the same with that of which I had been deprived by my Partner's transactions, as already explained; and M'Tavish, Fraser and Co. had no other funds wherewith to pay these Bills. All that remained of the Hudson's-Bay Stock, standing in my name, was only 7621*l.* 6*s.* 8*d.*; which sum I immediately transferred, in part of the 9000*l.* Stock which, according to the Deed and its Schedules, as well as by the proceedings of the Creditors, I was authorized to transfer, for the security of Messrs. Dunn and Gerrard, the Hudson's-Bay Stock standing in my Brother's name, and the eventual surplus of that Stock which had been pledged as security for borrowed money, or which is locked up in the different trusts specified in the Schedules to my Deed, were all equally locked up, out of my immediate reach, besides that I had already assigned my interest in them to the Trustees; and, as the Attorney of those Trustees, to have paid these Bills with monies raised on the faith of the funds thus assigned, would, even if it had been practicable, amount to a direct breach of trust on my part, to the Trustees, and to the other Creditors, a preference over whom would thus have been given to the Bank. I had *no other means* of paying these Bills, and Mr. Ellice refused to advance any funds for that purpose. I had therefore no choice, but to suffer them to be protested for non-payment, and they were taken up by the Bank Agents, Messrs. Thomas Wilson and Co. for the honour of the Bank.

The circumstances of the case were explained to Messrs. Wilson and Co., but the explanation was not satisfactory to them: an unfounded and injurious allegation of theirs, *that I had made representations in Canada, to mislead the Bank*, was indignantly denied; and the discussions which ensued, terminated in their bringing an Action against myself and Mr. Thain, for the sum of 16,000*l.* sterling, for which we are both held to bail, and thereby precluded from leaving this country, although it is of the utmost importance to the interests of the Creditors that both of us should speedily return to Canada, since by that means alone, can any satisfactory result of the Canadian accounts ever be reasonably expected. By the last advices from Montreal, I am apprized that the new Bank Directors have resolved to follow up this prosecution so commenced by their Agents; and the result of this proceeding on their part, is that to which I have now particularly to request your attention.

My Deed of Assignment gives me no defence, in law or in equity, against the Bank, or against any other Creditor who has not become a party thereto, and who may think fit to prosecute me; and having by that Assignment divested myself of all my property, I have no funds remaining, wherewith to pay such claims as may thus be prosecuted against me. Then what follows? After judgment shall have been obtained, since I cannot pay the debt, I must go to prison; and if I remain in prison twenty-one days, such imprisonment will constitute an act of Bankruptcy. The harshest part of this process, however, namely, the *imprisonment*, it rests with myself to avoid; and it would be a very useless sacrifice of one's feelings, to let matters go quite so far, for the sake of postponing that which it is now perfectly evident cannot be prevented, unless *all the Creditors* shall become parties to *my* Deed of Assignment. It has been my wish, undoubtedly, to avoid the *eclât* of a Commission of Bankruptcy; but if it becomes necessary, I can contemplate it with much less of painful feeling than I did my voluntary declaration of insolvency at Montreal in December last; and therefore unless, on re-consideration of the matter, the Bank Directors, or a general meeting of the Proprietors, shall quash the proceedings in this country, and assent to the Deed, and unless *all the other Creditors* shall also assent thereto, since it will be impossible, in such case, either for the Trustees or for me to act with any confidence or security; I shall have no alternative but to avail myself of the provision in the new Bankrupt Law, whereby a declaration of insolvency filed at the proper office, will at once place my *person* under the protection of the Commissioners of Bankruptcy, leaving the Trustees and the future Assignees to contend for my property.

Those Creditors whose prosecution may be the immediate cause of this catastrophe, will not thereby obtain any preference over others, but all alike must proceed as best they may, to establish their claims; and the difficulty, the complicated and protracted litigation, and the enormous expense which must necessarily ensue, will be ruinous to the Estate, and most destructive to the interests of all the parties concerned; excepting only the Lawyers, to whom it will yield a plentiful harvest of doubtful points and heavy fees. Amongst other questions which will immediately arise in regard to the *Hudson's-Bay Stock*, will be the following:—1st, Will my interest therein be vested in the Assignees to be appointed under the Commission of Bankriptcy? or can it be held and disposed of by the Trustees to whom I have assigned it?—2d, Will *you*, and the other Creditors who are parties to the Deed, relinquish your claim under it, in order to be admitted to prove your debts under the Commission?—*This* last question would probably depend upon the decision of the former, and whatever that decision might be, still, unless you *all* consent to such relinquishment, will not the Trustees for their own security, be obliged to maintain their title under the Deed, and to try the question with the Assignees? Further questions of extreme intricacy, and great uncertainty, will remain, as to the relative rights of the Creditors of the *three* Firms, of M'Tavish, M'Gillivrays and Co., M'Gillivrays, Thain and Co., and M'Tavish, Fraser and Co., as well as the claims on the separate Estates of the different Parties; and all these points must be discussed in the Court of Chancery. I would say *decided* in that Court, before any Dividend can be paid; but really I know not where or when to look for the *decision* of them; and if I may judge of the future by the past, and so estimate the time this matter will occupy in Court, by comparing it with the time which has been occupied by other causes of less intrinsic difficulty, then I shall be warranted in saying, that the *decision* is not to be expected during the remaining term of the Charter of the Bank of Montreal; and in the mean time, neither the Bank, nor any other Creditor, can receive one shilling of their claims, unless what may be recovered by hypothecary creditors proceeding against real Estate in Canada, under the local laws of that Province.

It is difficult, under such circumstances, to understand upon what principle any Creditors can determine to persist in the proceedings now adopted by the Directors of the Bank of Montreal, or what explanation these Directors will hereafter offer to their Constituents, for this ruinous waste of the property of the Bank, in common with that of the other Creditors. Do they expect to establish a claim as privileged Creditors? If so, they will find, when it may be too late to recede, how much they deceive themselves; and their present proceeding, which is one merely of personal annoyance by compulsory process, does not at all tend to the establishment of any privileged claim on my Estate. If the Directors should think, or should be advised, that they have any chance of establishing as claim as privileged Creditors, the rational course for them to pursue, would be to state the grounds of such claim to the Trustees, and to execute the Deed, subject to a reference of such claim to Barristers of eminence in the Court of Chancery; or they might resort to an amicable suit, so as to obtain from the Court itself a decision of the point on which they may rely; but the present proceeding is a personal Action at Law against Simon M'Gillivray and Thomas Thain, and that Action followed up, infallibly makes these Defendants Bankrupts; after which, no subsequent change of opinion, or admission of error, by any or by all the parties, will avail to prevent the ruinous consequences which have been sufficiently stated, and from which it manifestly results, that the decision now to be taken, whatever it may be, will be irrevocable.

I have perhaps no right to imagine, that in this matter these Directors can be actuated by any other feeling than a wish to promote the interests of their Stockholders; but evident as it is *to me*, and as I think I must have made it *to you*, that instead of promoting those interests, the proceedings in question will be most injurious to them, I am induced to suggest the consideration, whether this is not one of those cases, in which the Stockholders themselves would be the most competent judges of their own interests, especially if there should appear any cause to suppose that any feeling of irritation, or animosity, or old grudge operating on the mind of any individual, against me or my connexions, could have been mixed up in the recent resolutions of a majority of the Directors. A remarkable change of *opinion* appears to have taken place at the Board, as well as *other* recent changes, and *this* change certainly was unexpected by me. The late President and Vice-President of the Bank, the present President, and all those of the Directors who were Creditors of our House, are already parties to my Deed of Assignment. *This Letter* is addressed to these Gentlemen, in common with the other parties to the Deed, and I appeal to each of them, whether they have not individually expressed to me their entire approbation of my conduct in these unfortunate concerns, their conviction that my arrangements were the best which could be devised for the benefit of the Creditors, and their belief, that it was only by means of my own assistance and superintendence, that these complicated affairs could ever be brought to any satisfactory termination. The same sentiments were expressed by two other Directors, who were not Creditors, but to whom, as personal friends, I explained all my transactions; and I have not heard a difference of opinion from any person, whether Lawyer or Merchant, in Canada or in London, to whom the circumstances have been stated. It therefore seems rather extraordinary, that a majority of the present Directors should be the only individuals having cognizance of these arrangements, who seek, if they can, to overturn them, and thereby to ruin the interests of all the Creditors connected with them, not excepting those of their own Constituents; and under these extraordinary circumstances, I submit that it would be well for the Stockholders who have the largest interests at stake, to make some inquiry into the composition of this majority of Directors, and to consider what interest *they* individually may have in the Stock, and what grounds or feelings they may have acted upon in their recent decision, before that decision shall finally be carried into effect.

If any opinions or recommendations from London should have been amongst these grounds, then let the statements of facts therein contained be compared with mine, before any reliance is placed upon them, recollecting always, that *my* statement is that which I am prepared to maintain on oath in the Court of Chancery, whilst the statements of other persons in regard to my transactions, may be nothing more than mere surmise, such as assumed by Messrs. Thomas Wilson and Co. in their correspondence with me, as already stated. In short, let the Creditors and the Bank Stockholders look coolly at their own interests, and I really think the result cannot long be doubtful.

In the event, however, that prejudice, or the hope of obtaining some advantage over the other Creditors, should still lead the Bank, or any other Dissentient from the Deed, to persevere in withholding their assent from it; and in contemplation of the unavoidable consequence, whereby my arrangements for your benefit will be finally frustrated, it was my wish to have been enabled to point out to the Creditors who are parties to the Deed, that course of proceedings which would be most conducive to the protection of their interests under the administration of the future Commission of Bankruptcy, and on that point I have obtained, and transmitted to the Trustees, a special Opinion of Counsel, which they will be ready to communicate to you; but the point is involved in so much of doubt and difficulty, that in my present position I can scarce venture to offer you any specific advice. Any preconcerted measures, such as sending Powers of Attorney, or Affidavits of Debt, to this country, might be resisted, as collusive or fraudulent; and for *me*, the only safe course appears to be, to do nothing, but let matters take their course. By my Assignment, the Trustees are in possession of all my property, both in Canada and in England, and also of the Partnership Assets, so far as it was competent to me to assign the same; and it is the opinion of my Counsel, that the Trustees could maintain this possession against the Assignees under a Commission of Bankruptcy. The question, however, is doubtful; other Counsel may take a different view of the case, and I have at this moment before me, an Opinion dated this day, given to the Hudson's Bay Company by *their Counsel*, and whereby the Company is advised, in regard to the transfer of my Hudson's-Bay Stock, "*not to act otherwise than under the sanction of a Court of Equity.*" In this matter, it is easy enough for any party to bring all the rest into a *Court of Equity*. The difficulty is, to keep such complicated concerns out of that Court; and the absurdity is, that any party having important interests at stake, should force on a result so injurious to all parties, and which can benefit none. According to the principle of the Bankrupt Laws, all property recovered by Assignees, must, subject to the delays and expenses incident to the necessary proceedings, be ultimately divided amongst the Creditors who shall lawfully establish their claim; and *that result* is exactly what the Deed provides for, without delay, or expense, or litigation. The misfortune, however, is, that with such questions in the way of being mooted, the Trustees cannot venture to act, nor to part with a shilling of the property assigned to them; and any proceeding in the Court of Chancery, either by Assignees or Creditors, will lock up the whole of that property till these questions shall be disposed of; that is, possibly till another generation of mankind, or another constitution of the Court of Chancery, shall succeed to the present.

Upon the whole, I am inclined to be of opinion, that, in the event of a Bankruptcy, the only way of *ever arriving* at any settlement of the matter would be, that the Creditors who are parties to the Deed, should relinquish their rights under my Assignment, and prove their debts under the Commission; but if any one of them shall refuse to do this, the Trustees may be bound to maintain the rights of such party, under the Deed; and if it should be decided that those Creditors who are parties ot the Deed, have any vantage ground, I do not see on what principle of justice or of equity they can be expected to relinquish their rights, for the benefit of persons who, by refusing the choice now at their option, of executing the Deed, will be the immediate and the sole cause of such annoyance and expense to those who are now parties thereto. In grasping at the shadow of some imaginary advantage, the Creditors who have not executed the Deed, may throw away the substance of the arrangement now within their reach; and *any one* of them may involve himself and the Trustees in litigation, of which neither he nor I may live to see the result. Any one of them may thus prevent, for almost an indefinite time, the payment of any dividend from the Estate, and, in short, the payment of any thing except law charges; and where it is thus in the power of each and every class of the Creditors to inflict so much injury upon the rest, I would ask, is it *not* the common interest and the common duty of the whole, to unite in preventing expense and litigation, and in turning promptly to the best advantage, the assets which may immediately be realized for their benefit, by means of my arrangements?

In conclusion, I have only to observe, that as to any personal interest, or object of my own in this matter, it must be obvious, that from the moment at which I am compelled to relinquish the hope of some reversion remaining, after payment of all the Debts, the only rational object *for me* to pursue, is to get myself released from the unfortunate embarrassment in which I have been thus involved, and to be enabled to devote what may remain to me of life, capable of exertion, to some purpose useful to myself. In order to manifest every possible disposition to benefit the Creditors, and animated at the time by the hope of a reversionary benefit to myself, I voluntarily offered to devote to the settlement of these concerns, a great deal of time, and personal application, which no party had a right to exact from me; and so far as it may be an object to me to become once more master of my own time, I believe *that object* will be more speedily attained under a Commission of Bankruptcy, than under the covenant contained in my Deed of Assignment. Therefore, *this final appeal*, which I make for the benefit of the Creditors, and in order to bring the case distinctly before every one of them, is *to myself* really a matter of less importance than they may suppose. A man who has already divested himself of all his property, has nothing further to *give*, unless it be his time, and *that* also I have offered to give. And a man who is prepared to submit to Bankruptcy, has nothing further to *fear*, unless it be the consequent public investigation of character and conduct, from which it is at least some satisfaction to be able to say, that I do not shrink. It is, however, of some importance to *my ulterior views*, as well as to *your interests*, that the matter should be brought to as speedy an issue as possible; and after waiting a reasonable time for the result of the present communication, and unless, in the mean time, the Bank prosecution may have brought it to issue for me, then I may venture to promise you, that on my own part there shall be no delay.

I remain, respectfully,

GENTLEMEN,

Your most obedient Servant,

SIMON M'GILLIVRAY.

32: LETTER TO SIMON M'GILLIVRAY, ESQ. IN ANSWER TO ONE ADDRESSED BY HIM TO THE CREDITORS OF THE LATE FIRMS OF M'TAVISH, M'GILLIVRAYS & CO. AND M'GILLIVRAYS, THAIN & CO. DATED LONDON, 26TH OF FEBRUARY, 1826, BY HENRY MACKENZIE, LATE PARTNER OF THE FORMER FIRM.

Montreal, 19th June, 1827.

TO SIMON McGILLIVRAY, ESQUIRE,
LONDON,

SIR,

It is with extreme regret that I find myself under the necessity of endeavouring thus publicly, to correct the mis-statements and rebut the animadversions of a person whose interests were once intimately connected with my own. But I must either adopt this course or be content patiently to lie under the load of imputation cast upon my character and conduct, relative to the affairs of the late North West Company, in your last letter, addressed "to the "Creditors of the late firms of M'Tavish, M'Gillivrays & Co., and "M'Gillivrays, Thain & Co."—This is what I have not resignation enough to do; and if I had, a sense of duty to myself and my friends would compel me to vindicate myself even in the face of your formidable and well exercised epistolary attainments.

To those, then, whom you have so edified, I make my appeal, persuaded that when they shall have perused the plain statement of a plain man, they will do him that justice, which, it appears, he might vainly look for at your hands.

On the 1st of November, 1814, I entered into the association then formed under the continued title of M'Tavish, M'Gillivrays & Co., as co-agents, with the firm of Sir Alexander McKenzie & Co. for the North West Company. I did not obtain this distinction by dint of solicitation, but as a person who had enjoyed the entire confidence of the preceding firms of M'Tavish, Frobisher & Co. and their successors, M'Tavish, M'Gillivrays & Co., and whose experience and activity in the branch of commerce in which they had been engaged, seemed (if I may venture so to say) to render him an acquisition. In fact, I entered it on earnest invitation, abandoning other pursuits to which it would have perhaps been fortunate that I had adhered.—I am far, however, from meaning to say that I did not contemplate considerable advantage. I knew the fur trade to be very lucrative, as conducted by the old firms, (in whose employ I had been many years, and with whom I was afterwards connected for some years at Terrebonne, under the firm of M'Kenzie, Oldham & Co.,) and I had no reason to anticipate the reverse in the new. But I soon found myself mistaken. Shortly after I joined it, the conduct of my partners became wholly inconsistent, not only with the general principles of co-partnership, but with the very articles of our association. The books and accounts seemed confined to the examination of only a chosen few,—I was denied access to them on various pretences,—my partners entered into several transactions without either asking my advice, or afterwards communicating their existence,—and even a negociation with the late Earl of Selkirk was, in the winter of 1815-16, commenced and carried on, which was carefully concealed from me. Justly displeased at such circumstances, and aware of the fatal tendency of disunion, or even a want of mutual confidence, I, on the 1st of May, 1816, (Mr. M'Leod being then on the eve of his departure for the North West,) addressed a letter to the members of the House complaining of those improprieties, requesting that they should be discontinued, and at the same time, giving them notice, that as to all and every the past as well as the future transactions made and entered into without my knowledge and approbation, it should remain optional with me to abide by the result or not.—*See Appendix A.*

To this letter I received a satisfactory, though verbal, assurance, that those subjects of complaint should not recur. But, notwithstanding this assurance, I was obliged to reiterate my remonstrances, not only on their recurrence, but on the subject of a profusion and extravagance in the manner of conducting the business of the firm, which was wholly unjustifiable. Accordingly, I addressed to my partners a letter, I think in June 1819, submitting amongst other things to them, the necessity that I should be permitted immediately to take an active part in the Counting House, &c.—To this proposal they remained silent, until the 24th of November, 1819, when there occurred a more efficient opportunity of remonstrating a third time, which I did in writing as follows:—

"The signatures of the partners comprising the House of M'Tavish, M'Gillivrays & Co. being about to be required to sign the balance sheet of the books thereof closed on the 30th of November, 1818; and as such an act would infer an unqualified and unlimited acquiescence of the aforesaid individuals in every past circumstance that has occurred in the management of their concerns, Mr. Henry Mackenzie, before, by such signature-making admissions, not quite consonant to the impressions on his mind, thinks it fair as a man of honesty and candour, at the same time that he does full credit to the *intentions*, to explain wherein the *measures* of his esteemed friends and associates, have not, in his judgment, been altogether conducive to the interests of all, not in strict conformity to the articles of co-partnership.

1st—Each partner has not been furnished with an authenticated copy of the articles of co-partnership, nor had he at all times free access to the original, which, it is apprehended, should be, for such purpose, deposited in the vault, as well as all the other records and private documents of the firm.

2d—The concern in the Mackinac Company, to which Henry Mackenzie was a party, was closed before the agreement expired, without any intimation being given to him, or his consent asked.

3d—It appears that proposals were made to the Earl of Selkirk and the Hudson's Bay Company in the autumn of 1815, for a participation of the Indian trade, and although Henry Mackenzie was constantly in attendance at his post in Montreal, the other partners commenced and broke off that negociation without once consulting him on the subject, and therefore he does not feel himself liable for the consequences should the same prove prejudicial to his interest.

4th—By the agreement with his partners, Henry Mackenzie, amongst other things, was to carry on a general business for the concern in this country, by which he was induced to enter into the concern under the idea, not only of the general benefit expected to be thereby promoted for the facility of the operations of the firm, but also that thereby he might have had it in his power to attend occasionally to the outstanding dependencies of his former concern.

5th—Instead of availing himself of this clause, Henry Mackenzie was engaged for a considerable time in settling old accounts and estates—and was afterwards induced to consent to become the agent of the concern in relation to the disputes of the North West Company with the Earl of Selkirk, and he submits that these extra services have not been duly appreciated by his associates.

6th—The agents' (of the North West Company) office should be reduced to fewer expenses. The charges on merchandize-account exceed the annual expenditure nearly three times the sums expended by the old concerns for the same duty and labour, and which extra expenses, if continued, will, with interest, amount to nearly £30,000 at the end of the concern, by which, Henry Mackenzie apprehends, the whole of, and more than the emoluments, arising from the agency, are likely to be absorbed.

7th—In the articles of co-partnership there are certain remunerations stipulated, but others have been made since without the knowledge or consent of Henry Mackenzie. And such extra allowances, if not checked, will also amount, including interest, to about £20,000 at the end of the concern.

8th—Henry Mackenzie objects to the mode of transacting business at Fort William, on the part of the agents of the North West Company, as, in fact, he is at this moment ignorant of who are, or who are not, his partners in the North West Company, never having given, to the best of his recollection, his power to alter or amend the institutions of that concern.

9th—Henry Mackenzie is likewise further awakened to these observations, by proposals having been made, lately, at Fort William, to the North West Company, for a new association, without the same having been submitted, before or after, to the partners here.

10th—Henry Mackenzie objects also to the signing of Bills of Exchange by anticipation, and when the person so signing, is perhaps, absent from the country: though he finds no fault with the restriction of the signature to one individual, provided such person be on the spot, he thinks, moreover, that the restriction to one individual of signing checks or drafts on the Bank is attended at times, with great inconvenience, and is of opinion that this henceforward be exercised by any individual of the firm who may be present, and as the case may require.

11th—Henry Mackenzie declines signing the document in question until he is fully satisfied the same is according to the spirit of the agreement, which agreement, he feels himself called upon to say, has been neglected, and more particularly as respects the objects herein specified.

HENRY MACKENZIE.

Montreal, 24th November, 1819"

But these violations of agreement and improprieties, were not all I had to complain of—matters of far deeper interest were to be objected to in the conduct of yourself and brother.

Hitherto you had indeed shown a total disregard of the articles of copartnership and the general law of mercantile association, yet still had kept the firm entire; but on the 26th of March, 1821, you assumed higher powers, in conjunction with Edward Ellice, Esq., of London, representing yourselves as a sort of sovereigns of the North West Company, and of the firms their agents, and took upon yourselves wholly to dissolve the North West Company, one year and a half before the stipulated period of its termination (and notwithstanding an agreement, entered into in duplicate, at Fort William, in 1820, to which you were a party, to continue the North West Company till the returns of the outfit of the year 1832) and incorporated it with the Honorable Hudson's Bay Company, securing to yourselves, by the terms of the negociation, emoluments in the latter above all reasonable proportion to those which you possessed in the former—*see Appendix B.* In fact, that some extraordinary measure injurious to the interests of others (and which must be concealed lest it should be thwarted by those whom it was intended to affect) was in contemplation or progress became evident to me in the latter end of 1821, for on the 15th of November of that year, and frequently before, I observed that you, your brother, and Mr. Thain attended by counsel, and with locked doors, held deliberations to which I had no invitation, and from which I was in fact excluded. Towards the close of that day, however, I discovered that the following two advertisements had been sent to the offices of the Herald and Courant newspapers:—

NOTICE is hereby given that, in pursuance and performance of the conditions contained in a certain indenture, whereby it has been agreed that the Indian and Fur Trade, heretofore carried on by the *Governor and Company of Adventurers of England, trading into Hudson's Bay, and the North West Company of Montreal*, respectively, should henceforward under certain terms be carried on by and in the name of the said Governor and Company and their successors exclusively, the said indenture having been ratified and confirmed by the said North West Company, the functions of the Agents of the said North West Company, and also of the Agents of Sir Alexander Mackenzie and Company, have ceased and terminated.

M'TAVISH, M'GILLIVRAYS & CO.
THOMAS THAIN.   } *Agents of the North West Company.*
PIERRE DE ROCHEBLAVE.

Montreal, 15th November, 1821.

NOTICE is hereby given that the undersigned Archibald Norman M'Leod, Esquire, has retired from and ceased to be a Partner of the house or firm of M'Tavish, M'Gillivrays & Co.

M'TAVISH, M'GILLIVRAYS, & Co.
A. N. McLEOD.

Montreal, 15th November, 1821.

Having ascertained this fact, and before publication, I informed both Mr. Gray and Mr. Mower, the proprietors of those papers, that it was premature to publish them, as my consent had not been had, and that it was improper, because the contents were not true; upon which, they at that time abstained from publishing them. I then prepared an advertisement to accompany those just mentioned or to be published apart, which the partners on the 17th declined to do.—*See Appendix C.* On the following day, (the 16th November, 1821,) I addressed to you, and the other partners of the house, a letter which I inserted in the letter-book of the concern, and of which I handed each of you a copy signed by me, stating, that "common prudence had dictated to me the reiterated objections I had made against many transactions of our copartnership which had taken place without my knowledge or approbation, and that the recent, serious, and unwarrantable proceedings threatened to be carried into effect (at a period too when the books and accounts were not adjusted) determined me more than ever to resist such conduct, &c.—*See Appendix D.*

This declaration extracted, I presume, the resolutions of the secret meeting of the 15th, held by yourself, your brother, and Mr. Thain, therein calling yourselves the *majority* of the firm, which were signified to me, by the ministry of Griffin and Barron, Public Notaries,—intimating, amongst other things, "that it was expedient that you and your brother should proceed to England forthwith, and that Mr. Thomas Thain should, during your absence, be entrusted with the superintendance and management of the general business of the concern in addition to the finances and accounts, of which, since the retirement of John M'Tavish, he had had the charge under the general superintendance of your brother—that during your absence from this Province, Mr. Thain should be authorised to superintend and conduct the correspondence, the finances, and the general business of the firm, and to hold and possess the books, papers, and all the other property of the said house on behalf and in trust for all parties holding any just and lawful part, share, claim, or interest therein or any part thereof."—*See Appendix E.*

To this I promptly replied by the said notarial ministry, "that these arrangements, resolves, and other measures had been taken and entered into without my knowledge or consent, and even without any notice thereof to me proceedings which violated every sacred principle of reciprocity in agreements, and dissolved every social tie.—*See Appendix F.*

Having at length obtained, what I had hitherto asked for in vain, a copy of our articles of copartnership of the first of November, 1814, I made a second reply to those resolves, dated 21st of November, 1821, to which you and those who may read this are particularly referred.—*See Appendix G.* Notwithstanding which you and your brother soon after took your departure for England, leaving Mr. Thain in ample possession.

Your brother remained in England, but you returned the ensuing year; and on the 22d of November, 1822, our copartnership being near its termination, I again addressed you and Mr. Thain, stating, that the length of time which had elapsed since I had seen our books had effaced from my recollection many things recorded in them and left but a feeble impression of others;—that I was thus, at a time when the close of the concern was at hand, ignorant of the precise relation in which I stood with my partners, and without the means of forming a just estimate of my rights,—an acquaintance with which, it must be allowed, was necessary to place me upon a footing with you in any discussion to which the approaching settlement between us might give rise;—that I therefore requested to have immediate and free access to the books for the purpose of making such extracts as I might require; that our connexion being then so near a termination I thought it a duty I owed to myself to urge an immediate settlement of the accounts, to facilitate the accomplishment of which I would be prepared on a certain day to audit conjointly with you, all the books of account in which I had any concern.—*See Appendix H*.

To this letter, I, on the 23d of November, 1822, received your answer, stating, that you deemed it necessary in reply to my letter to refer to the tenth article of our deed of copartnership, and also to a certain deed bearing date the 6th of April, 1821;—that the outstanding adventures could not be realised nor even ascertained before the summer of 1824:—that therefore any investigation of the accounts at that time was premature, and, in fact, impracticable, —and that it would be inconvenient at that moment to produce the books for my proposed *audit;* that it was impossible to anticipate settlements depending on future contingencies, &c.—*See Appendix I*.

Not thinking your answers, to my just requests, satisfactory, I again wrote on the 25th, stating that your letter of the 23d, I was sorry to say, was no answer to mine; that you had either misapprehended its chief purpose, or, not choosing to comply with the request it contained, had evaded the question; that the lengthy statement you entered into established a point I never meant to deny, namely, that our books could not be finally closed, nor the affairs wound up till the outfits were realised; that my request embraced two objects,—*access to the books for the purpose of making extracts for my individual satisfaction, and an audit, or examination, or scrutiny, (if you please,) of the books as they then stood; an explanation of past transactions—not a premature settling of "contingencies" that depended on materials thereafter to be procured;*—I asked you if there was aught in our articles of copartnership to prohibit this?—to prohibit a copartner from seeing the books of the association to which he belonged? If there was such a clause, I called upon you to show it, and I required an explicit answer. As you had left town for St. Antoine, this letter was addressed to Mr. Thain, he being on the spot.—*See Appendix K.* On the 26th, I received Mr. Thain's reply, saying, that in answer to mine of the preceding day, which he had that morning communicated to you, he begged to inform me that the lengthy statement I alluded to was not written *with a view to evade my question;* that your letter had been written with the intention of explaining to me your reasons or rather your opinions why you did not consider it necessary to proceed to the *audit,* or inspection of the books I alluded to, and that you were still of the same opinion;—that no good could result to either party from such inspection at that time; but, that as I desired an explicit answer, he, Mr. Thain, begged leave to inform me that you could not agree to my request, and that I was well aware, *(independent of the state of the office,)* that his, (Mr. Thain's) time could be much more beneficially employed attending to other matters.—*See Appendix L.* After this, I had several interviews with Mr. Thain, who informed me that you had both come to the resolution of advancing me some money out of the concern in anticipation of the settlement of our accounts, to enable me, with my other means, to commence business on my own account. This offer I embraced, wearied with making fruitless remonstrances, and glad to separate myself from persons who had shown such a disregard to good faith, and on the 29th of November, 1822, I yielded to certain articles of agreement, in which, after several recitals, it was thus agreed:—

First—That notice, duly signed, should, by public advertisement, be given of the termination on the 30th of November, 1822, of our articles of copartnership of M'Tavish, M'Gillivrays and Co., dated first of November, 1814, and that it should also be notified that the said Thomas Thain was duly authorised to settle, collect, realize, and wind up all the outstanding engagements, debts, credits, and effects whatsoever of or belonging to the same.

Secondly,—That Thomas Thain should retain and hold the sole and exclusive possession, care, and custody of all books, accounts, vouchers, papers, and documents whatsoever of or belonging to our copartnership, until the 30th of November, 1825, in trust for the respective parties concerned or interested in the same.

Thirdly,—That the said Thomas Thain should make up, and on or before the 30th of November, 1825, exhibit just, true, and accurate accounts of all the business and transactions of our copartnership, and of all charges, profits, losses, or other contingencies, in any manner whatsoever affecting the same, but without prejudice to the right of any other of the said parties thereto, to impeach or object to any such part of such accounts as to them or either of them might appear unjust or objectionable.

Fourthly,—That in the event of any such objections or exceptions being made to the said accounts, the party making such objections or exceptions, and the party resisting them, should each name and appoint a disinterested and respectable merchant as an arbitrator, and that these two should nominate and appoint a third, who should also be a respectable and disinterested merchant, and these three arbitrators should, in such manner as they might deem necessary or requisite, examine and investigate such accounts, and such objections or exceptions as aforesaid, and in the premises, and in every point or particular regarding the same, and that the award of the said arbitrators or any two of them should be conclusive, and should be acquiesced in and submitted to by them and each and every of them the parties thereto.

Now, Sir, after these proceedings, in all which you had fully participated, if, indeed, they had not in many instances originated with you, it bespeaks contempt for the opinion of the world that you should treat mine as "imaginary complaints." Is it an "imaginary complaint," that the financial concerns of our house, which had been under the management of your late brother, were, and are still wholly concealed from me, and I have been even to this day denied (for what purpose I leave to the conjecture of my readers,) access to the partnership books of account? Is it merely an "imaginary" impropriety that negociations involving the existence of the house were commenced and broken off wholly without my knowledge? Is it merely an "imaginary" evil that profusion and extravagance reigned both in the domestic habits of the other partners of the firm here and abroad, and in the manner of conducting our business? Is it merely an "imaginary" evil that the North West Company was in a manner dissolved, and its capital (£164,000 sterling) and interests disposed of as the sole property of William M'Gillivray, yourself, and Edward Ellice, without even consulting me, or rendering any account to the parties interested, of whom I was and am one? Is it an "imaginary complaint," that you should declare the house of M'Tavish, M'Gillivrays and Co. insolvent, for whose engagements I *am* liable, and convey its assets to pay the debts of M'Gillivrays, Thain, and Co. for which I am *not* liable! or that finally I should refuse to ratify an assignment grounded on an alledged insolvency, which I, from my knowledge of the fur trade, could never have expected, and cannot account for, and the reality or causes of which I am, by the studious concealment of the books from me, wholly at a loss to ascertain. And yet, in a tone of triumph, you observe, that "it "seems almost needless to argue against such an absurdity, as that "partners of an insolvent firm should be creditors of the same firm." I argue not so, but I argue, that M'Tavish, M'Gillivrays and Co. may be *solvent* although M'Gillivrays, Thain & Co. may *not*; consequently that you may be a debtor to me, and it is my sincere belief that such will prove to be the case. In the mean time, however, you have the hardihood to lay claim to disinterestedness and a straight forward policy; but the world, Sir, will judge of the credit due to the claims and professions of a man who cannot only counsel and deliberately execute such monstrous acts of injustice, but even attempt to justify them with an air of affected indignation against those who have suffered by them and who venture to complain. That the late firm of M'Tavish, M'Gillivrays & Co. were insolvent on the 30th of November, 1822, is more than either you or I suspected *then*, and is what I firmly disbelieve *now*. I have already mentioned that I was denied access to the books; I, therefore, am unable to refer to their contents for proofs of the correctness of my opinion; but I am no less certain of it, from circumstances within my knowledge. Nay, by the very admission of the firm of M'Gillivrays, Thain & Co., which succeeded the former firm, and whose ostensible members then present, yourself, and Mr. Thain, were the partners who denied me access to the books, and reserved it altogether to yourselves, the preceding firm was solvent, otherwise M'Gillivrays, Thain & Co. would not, by a public advertisement inserted during many months in all the Canadian newspapers, and dated 30th of November, 1822, have "assumed, and declared "themselves liable to satisfy, all the engagements contracted by "the then late firm of M'Tavish, M'Gillivrays & Co." But, even if it were insolvent, not only am I free from the blame of such insolvency, but I am entitled to credit for strenuous exertions to avert it; and the fault must lie, not on mercantile misfortunes, of which the lucrative nature of the business forbids the supposition, but on the misconduct of individuals. I have already related the remonstrances I was compelled to make on the extravagant manner in which the business was conducted. To this must be added the profusion of some of the partners in their domestic expenditure both in Canada and London—a profusion wholly unsuitable to plain merchants, and affecting a style approaching to magnificence. This is notorious—and it is equally notorious that such profusion I by no means imitated. It is this profusion which probably caused Mr. Thain's debt to the several firms of M'Tavish, M'Gillivrays & Co. and to their successors, and to Sir Alexander M'Kenzie & Co., on the 30th of November, 1825, as I have learned from an authentic source, to amount to £96,018 4s. 8d.; the Honorable William M'Gillivray's, on the 20th of November, 1824, to £28,325 2s. 4d., including £22,000, advanced to him, to meet the demands on him of his former concern; and yours, Sir, on the 30th of November, 1824, to £42,190 10s. 6d., which on the corresponding day of the following year, I learn, encreased to £50,000 and upwards. Sums which, if forthcoming, would certainly set aside the question of insolvency. The first and last of which seem somewhat extraordinarily to have been incurred by such anti-matrimonial and self-denying personages as those respecting whom you have stated in your memorandum of the 27th of December, 1825, submitted to the creditors. "Mr. Thain and myself refrained from contracting "engagements to burthen ourselves with families, which in the case "of our partners we had found to be a cause of increased expense;" and may lead your creditors to inquire where was to be found the moiety of the £164,000 mentioned in the said letter as to be furnished by your brother and yourself as your shares of the capital to be joined to that of the Honorable Hudson's Bay Company, and what you mean when you speak of your and your brother's "estate," and your "capital," and "private fortune,"—and make them smile to hear of "plate" and "favorite pictures." Truly, Sir, I am ignorant of any estate except that in the Isle of Mull, which you, who are so anxious for the good of the creditors, state to be wholly out of their reach,—a circumstance the more to be regretted, as that estate belonged to your brother, the very person to whom, by the articles of our copartnership, the sole administration of the finance of our house was committed, and whose management of them may, without violent supposition, have had unfavorable influence on them. For some time indeed, during his absence in England, he substituted Mr. Thain, but this was contrary to the articles of our association, and, when viewed in relation to Mr. Thain's enormous debt, cannot be called an "imaginary complaint." And I am the more justified in supposing such mismanagement as a consciousness of it appears to be the only obvious reason for the extraordinary circumstance of denying to me access to the books of the firm of which I was a partner; and that on the very frivolous pretext that the accounts could not be finally closed till a year or two afterwards—was this any reason for concealing from me the state of *past* transactions? Certainly not; and, as its frivolity could not have escaped the ability, (which I acknowledge, more especially, Sir, yours; and which in fact cannot politely be refused to your frequent arrogations thereof in your correspondence with the creditors and trustees,) of those who refused, viz. yourself and Mr. Thain, it becomes a matter of serious inquiry, what it was that was so vigilantly concealed from the most active and economical partner of the firm.

In short, the position that I take is this:—that all the partners, debtors of the firm, should refund to it the amount of their respective debts, (or, in other words, equalize their debts with mine,) which would immediately stifle the pretension of insolvency, and that then the books should be exhibited, each partner's account current made out, and a balance struck—should this be done, I feel confident that a handsome sum of money would be at my disposal—over and above the sum you say, *you and Mr. Thain* "imprudently enough" advanced me. What imprudence there could be in this, I cannot conceive, unless you, Sir, consider it imprudent to introduce into your line of conduct the system of rendering to every one his due.

Indeed, you, in your last letter, would have it believed that I wish to divert my creditors from the pursuit of myself to the chase of "you," and you have illustrated this alledged attempt by an elegant simile; but after the facts I have stated, I trust it will be seen that far from throwing "*a tub to the whale*," my object is to direct the *harpooners to the whale*, which so ostentatiously *spouting* now, may afford hereafter a very competent quantity of *blubber*.

You, it is true, observe, "that if any of these gentlemen (mean-"ing me and others of the same opinion) could discover a surplus "of assets belonging to the firm, and any attempt, on my part, to "retain for my own benefit more than my due share of the same, "it would, I admit, afford just cause of complaint on their part "against me,"—which is certainly a very candid admission, and the more meritorious as the principle it contains is far from being obvious, since, without it, it never could have been conjectured that to commit a fraud would be improper. Now, Sir, I am at a loss to know what *due share* you have a right *to retain* of the assets of a firm you alledge to be insolvent. Neither can I accept your defiance to discover such "surplus of assets;" for, though it would be imprudent in me, without conclusive evidence, or at least strong grounds, to cast on you such imputation, yet I would generally and abstractedly observe, that such a challenge might be safely given, inasmuch as sums of money may be spent, especially in the speculative region of London, and be therefore no assets,—or property may be disposed of where it cannot easily be found—or money may be deposited where it may not be suspected to be, and which it may therefore be very difficult "to discover."

But you may take a more effectual manner of convincing your creditors, that all your property and that of the firm's have been fairly surrendered, than your reiterated assertions, and at once relieve yourself from your earnest anxiety to produce conviction on that head, by causing a commission of bankruptcy to be taken out against you, when your oath must satisfy the most incredulous, (if any there are who are not yet thoroughly convinced by your assertions,) that you have, at least, given up all the present assets, though the nature of your financial conduct before the dissolution of the firm must remain to me and others a secret, until the books, so long concealed from me, be exhibited. And, indeed, considering how often you have in your correspondence observed how much trouble you have had, and how much injudicious opposition you have experienced, and how ill-requited have been your efforts to settle the estate for the benefit of the creditors, and how a commission of bankruptcy would deliver you from those grievances, I feel somewhat surprised that you have not adopted it.

This suggestion, however, may be treated by you as a species of insolent insurrection against a sort of imperial authority with which you seem to have invested yourself, (the title to which I in vain seek to discover)—an authority which, exercised in a thousand minor instances, broke out with greater *eclât* in your refusal to me access to the books of a firm of which I was a partner, and reached its highest brilliancy in that unauthorised negociation whereby you procured for yourself and, with "*fraternal partiality*," for your brother, and sympathetic feeling with your bosom friend Mr. Ellice, those advantages which justly belonged to all the partners of the North West Company, of M'Tavish, M'Gillivrays & Co. and of Sir Alexander M'Kenzie and Co.—(the transaction having taken place during their copartnerships, and respecting their interests and property;) and you considered it no assumption to stipulate that, after the lapse of fourteen years, the share or interest you assigned to me in the Hudson's Bay Company, should revert to you and your brother, utterly forgetting that the shares acquired in that Company by you both, and Mr. Ellice, were procured by means of the undivided stock of the North West Company, (and of the other firms,) in which I had a proportionate permanent property, and in the improved value of which, when transferred to the Hudson's Bay Company, I had therefore a similar interest. And this you did, wholly disregarding the circumstance that I had largely participated in the toil, and contributed to the treasure that brought about the coalition, and that the shares which you reserved to yourself and brother and Mr. Ellice, as an indemnification for the cessation of commissions in the London Houses, M'Tavish, Fraser & Co., and Inglis, Ellice & Co., belonged to all those who had been concerned in those houses, and amongst others to me. And these advantages you procured by representing yourself and your brother the greatest capitalists in the North West Company, when, in fact, owing to the large sums you had drawn out, you had then no capital whatever, but on the contrary were largely indebted to the concern.

The tinsel curtain behind which you have placed your person and actions, I raise with reluctance, but I have been forced to it by your accusation that I, by setting up "imaginary claims," or preventing some creditors from giving effect to your arrangements, and by the interposition of impediments and delays, hope to "*extort*" some composition out of my claim on the Hudson's Bay share assigned to me, which you maintain belongs to the creditors, and which you have, without my authority, actually assigned over to your own creditors.

That that accusation is manifestly false must be evident from the consideration, that however guiltless I have been of the embarrassments of the firm, and however I may have exerted myself to avert them, yet I am responsible for all its debts, and therefore by no means stand in that commanding attitude that would countenance an attempt to "extort." No, the plain fact is this: I did every thing in my power to cause the business of the company to be conducted with propriety and economy—the fur trade was a prosperous one, and contained in it no seeds of insolvency. You have declared the firm insolvent four years after its dissolution! and after having, by the assumption of its debts impliedly acknowledged its solvency,—and being debarred from access to the books of account, (which this 19th day of June, 1827, has been again denied to me by your Trustees though notarially demanded,) I am prevented from fully demonstrating whether it is insolvent, or, if so, what have been the causes of its insolvency: whether, (which I cannot believe,) it arose from losses in the trade, or from the extravagance of any of the partners; or from employing its funds in speculations foreign to the business and unknown to any of the other partners; or from loans to support the sinking credit of other houses. I repeat, I cannot venture to say to which of these causes is due the alledged insolvency; but it will be allowed by every reasonable man that I have a right to suspect that there has been something culpable in the conduct of those partners who denied me access to the books; otherwise they would not have been concealed from me.

With a view then to the elucidation of those obscure transactions, I have instituted a suit at law, in the Court of King's Bench here, against the representations of such partners of the late firm of M'Tavish, M'Gillivrays & Co. as had assumed to themselves the direction of the finance, to compel them to render me that account which they have so long refused to my solicitations,—the result of which will, I feel confident, show to the world the real state of the affairs respecting which you have written so plausibly; and this I have done, fearless of that menace which has imprudently denounced my brother's proceedings in the same court as "rather hazardous to himself." But I trust, Sir, that my conduct will not suffer by a comparison with yours; for I have not let the creditors down by an imperceptible declivity from the hope of twenty shillings in the pound to an eager anxiety to procure twelve shillings and six-pence, nor have I called upon them to surrender their private judgment, and trust implicitly to me, arrogating to myself "intense application," giving shrewd hints that I am possessed of colossal ability, and finally menacing them "with a commission of bank-"ruptcy," "the Court of Chancery," the "glorious uncertainty of "the law on partnership questions," and "the intricacy of conflict-"ing interests in these concerns."

Thus far, Sir, a proper respect for my own character has compelled me reluctantly to animadvert upon your letter of the 26th of February last, addressed to the creditors of M'Tavish, M'Gillivrays & Co. and M'Gillivrays, Thain & Co. and rebut your calumnious imputation on me of an attempt to "extort"—an attempt that my conscience satisfies me I have never made, and which my fellow citizens, among whom I have so long resided, will require something more than your assertion to believe respecting,

Sir,

Your obedient Servant,

H. MACKENZIE.

APPENDIX

A

Montreal, 1st May, 1816.

Dear Sirs,

Before the departure of a leading partner (Mr. M'Leod) permit me briefly to state, that all transactions upon business since last autumn, by our absent partners, have not been duly known to me;—that in course of the winter, negociations were actually entered into with our opponents, (the Earl of Selkirk, &c.,) even through the medium of strangers, in which I had no voice;—that others were actually entered into and concluded with my own brother, Donald Mackenzie, without due notice; and I have reason to presume, that communications are now in forwardness to wintering partners to which I am not made privy. In short, gentlemen, it is obvious that many of the most important transactions of our establishment are, and have been, carried on without my knowledge, and likely so to continue;—with the intention, therefore, to avoid the rock upon which some of my predecessors split, (I allude to Sir Alexander M'Kenzie and Mr. Hallowell,) I do hereby give you due notice, that in all and every the past as well as the future transactions made and entered into without my knowledge and approbation it shall remain optional with me either to abide or not by the result.

I am,

Dear Sirs,

Your most obedient humble Servant,

H. MACKENZIE.

To Messrs. William M'Gillivray,
    Archd. Norman M'Leod,
    Thomas Thain, and
    John M'Tavish, } PRESENT.

B

EXTRACTS FROM THE COALITION ARTICLES OF COPARTNERSHIP BETWEEN THE HONORABLE HUDSON'S BAY COMPANY AND NORTH WEST COMPANY.

"This indenture made the 26th day of March, 1821, between the Governor "and Company of Adventurers of England, trading into the Hudson's Bay, of "the first part, and William M'Gillivray, of Montreal, in the Province of Lower, "Canada, Esquire, Simon M'Gillivray, of Suffolk Lane, in the City of London, "Merchant, and Edward Ellice, of Spring Gardens, in the County of Middlesex,

"of the second part. Whereas, the governor and company have for many years
"last past carried on a considerable trade in the purchasing and receiving by way
"of barter, furs, peltries, and other articles from the Indians in North America,
"as well within the territory granted by the charter of the said governor and
"company, as in other parts of North America. And whereas, under or by virtue
"of an agreement, bearing date the 5th day of November, 1804, and made or ex-
"pressed to be made between the several parties therein named and mentioned
"to be the parties then composing the company, or concern trading to the North
"West or Indian Country, and distinguished by the name of the Old North West
"company of the one part, and several persons therein named and mentioned to
"be the partners in the company then trading to the North West or Indian
"Country, distinguished by the name of the New North West Company of the
"other part. The said Old and New North West Companies became united, and
"in consequence of that union, the said parties hereto of the second part together
"with the other persons, are now engaged in copartnership in carrying on a trade
"in purchasing and receiving by way of barter, furs, peltries, and other articles
"from the Indians in Upper and Lower Canada, and in other parts of North
"America, in or under the name or firm of the North West Company. And
"whereas, in consequence of the conflicting interests of the said governor and
"company and the said North West Company, various disputes have arisen
"between them, tending to the manifest injury of both parties, and in order to
"avoid the occasion of such disputes, and for the purpose of promoting their
"mutual interests, it hath been agreed upon between the said parties hereto, that
"the said trade shall, from the period hereafter in that behalf mentioned, be
"carried on exclusively by and in the name of the said governor and company
"and their successors, for the time, and under the terms hereafter mentioned.
"And the said parties hereto of the *second part, who are the persons entitled to the
"greater part of the capital of the said North West Company, have agreed to enter
"into the covenants hereafter contained so and in such manner, as to be bound jointly
"and severally, as well for themselves as for all other persons who are concerned or
"interested in the said North West Company and the trade thereof*, and otherwise,
"as heretofore is mentioned in respect to the engagements hereby made with the
"said governor and company and their successors."

1st—That the trade with the Indians heretofore carried on by the governor and company and North West Company, shall, for the space of 21 years, commencing with the outfit of 1821, and ending with the outfit and returns of 1841, be carried on by the said governor and company exclusively.

3d—Capital stock and outfit to consist of the stock on hand of both companies, on 1st June, 1821, &c. &c.

16th—"That the clear gains and profits arising from the said concern shall
"be divided into 100 equal shares, and shall belong to the parties following, (that
"is to say,) 20 of the said shares shall belong to the said governor and company
"and their successors; 20 others of the said shares shall belong to the parties
"hereto of the second part, their executors and administrators; 40 others of the
"said shares shall belong to such persons as shall from time to time, be, by the
"said governor and company or their successors, appointed chief factors and

"chief traders for conducting the said trade in the interior of North America,
"and to such persons as shall hereafter be appointed to succeed them, it being the
"true intent and meaning of the parties hereto, that the said last mentioned shares
"shall always be appropriated as a remuneration to the persons actually em-
"ployed in conducting the trade in North America, or as a temporary provision
"for persons retiring from such actual employment. Provided that as often as
"there shall be any loss upon the returns of any one year, forty equal one hun-
"dredth shares of such loss shall be set off from and made good out of the said
"40 shares, so to be appropriated as aforesaid, the gains and profits arising from
"the trade of the said concern, in the ensuing year or years, until such 40 shares
"of total loss shall have fully been made good, and the appropriation of such 40
"shall be regulated according to the provisions intended to be contained in a
"Deed Poll already proposed and engrossed, and intended to bear even date with
"these presents, and to be under the common seal of the said governor and com-
"pany. Five shares of the said shares subject to a like proviso for setting off
"and making good thereout 5 equal one hundredth shares of such total loss as
"aforesaid, shall belong to the said governor and company or their successors, in
"order to carry into effect certain arrangements to be by them made with the
"representatives of the late Earl of Selkirk, deceased: 5 others of the said shares
"subject to a like proviso for setting off and making good thereout 5 equal one
"hundredth shares of such total loss as aforesaid, shall belong to the said Simon
"M'Gillivray and Edward Ellice, their executors and administrators, *as a com-
"pensation for the emoluments heretofore arising from the agency and commissions
"in London, on account of the said North West Company* which agency and
"commissions, will be lost by their respective commercial establishments, in con-
"sequence of this agreement—and for which 5 shares the receipts of the said
"Simon M'Gillivray, and of the survivor of them, and the executor or adminis-
"trator of such survivor, shall be from time to time effectual discharges to the
"said governor and company and their successors. And the remaining 10 of the
"said shares shall, as to the one moiety thereof, belong to the said governor and
"company and their successors; and as to the other moiety thereof, to the said
"parties of the second part, their executors or administrators, subject to the
"provisions hereafter contained, concerning the said remaining 10 shares.

"25th—That notwithstanding any thing heretofore contained, all interest
"which may be payable to the said parties hereto of the second part, their
"executors or administrators, under the provisions aforesaid, in respect of their
"shares of the capital, and also those 20 shares of the clear gains and profits,
"which it is herein before agreed, shall belong to the said parties hereto of the
"second part, their executors or administrators, generally, or any part of the
"said interests and shares may, from time to time, be retained and applied by the
"said governor and company or their successors, for the purpose of satisfying any
"deficiency which by reason of the previous losses or neglect to bring in one half
"such advance as aforesaid, or otherwise there may then be in the share of
"the said parties of the second part, their executors or administrators, in the
"capital stock of the said concern, together with any interest that may be pay-
"able in respect of such deficiency.

THE NORTH WEST COMPANY

"26th—That notwithstanding any thing heretofore contained, those 10 shares "of the said clear gains and profits which it is heretofore agreed, shall, as the one "moiety thereof, belong to the said governor and company and their successors, "and as to the other moiety thereof, to the said parties hereto of the second part, "their executors or administrators shall, from time to time, be invested by the "said governor and company and their successors, in their names, in the parlia- "mentary stocks or public funds of Great Britain, or upon government securities "in England, which may be varied from time to time, at their discretion, and the "said governor and company and their successors, shall stand possessed of such "stocks, funds and securities, and the dividends and annual produce shall be- "come due, to divide the same into two equal shares, and to retain one of such "shares for their own use, and to pay the other of such shares to the said parties "hereto of the second part, their executors or administrators. And upon further "trust, at the final winding up and closing of the said concern, to divide the said "stocks, funds, and securities, into two equal shares, and to retain one of such "shares for the use of the said governor and company or their successors, and to "transfer the other of such shares to the said parties hereto, of the second part, "their executors or administrators, provided, nevertheless, that the said governor "and company and their successors, shall, at any time or times during the con- "tinuance of the said concern, be at liberty to apply all or any part of the said "stocks, funds and securities, or of the dividends and annual produce thereof, in "the increase of the capital stock of the said concern, or in supplying any defi- "ciency thereof, to be occasioned by losses—provided also, that the share of the "said parties hereto, of the second part, their executors or administrators in the "said stocks, funds and securities, and the dividends and annual produce thereof "shall, from time to time, be liable to satisfy such deficiency and such interest, "for the satisfying of which, the said 20 shares of the said parties hereto, of the "second part, their executors and administrators of the said clear gains and "profits, together with interest, payable as aforesaid, and hereinbefore authorised "to be retained and applied as aforesaid. And shall, also, from time to time, be "liable to satisfy the said governor and company and their successors, all damages "to be occasioned to them by reason of the breach of any of the covenants herein "entered into by the said parties hereto, of the second part, and that such dis- "position may be made of the said stocks, funds and securities, dividends and "annual produce, as may be necessary or proper for answering the above purposes, "or any of them.

"37th—That in the event, and notwithstanding the death, bankruptcy or "insolvency of all or any of the said parties, hereto of the second part, and not. "withstanding any other cause, matter, or thing, whatsoever, neither the share "of the said parties hereto, of the second part, their executors or administrators "in the *capital stock*, *debts*, and effects of the said concern, or in the aforesaid "stocks, funds, and securities, nor any other monies or property which may be "payable or belong to the said parties, of the second part, their executors or ad- "ministrators, in respect of the said concern, nor any part of the said share, "monies or property respectively, other than such share of the said parties hereto, "of the second part, their executors or administrators, in the interest and in the "said gains and profits, and in the dividends and annual produce of the said "stocks, funds and securities, as is to be paid under the provisions aforesaid, "shall be drawn out of the said concern, during the continuance thereof.

42d—Parties of the second part, bound to save, defend, keep harmless, and indemnify the governor and company against all claims and demands, evils, damages and losses, occasioned by persons not concerned in present arrangements.

43d—And not oppose, dispute, or interfere with the rights and privileges conveyed by the H. B. charter, but concur and assent in any application for defining and securing the same.

C

Whereas William M'Gillivray, Simon M'Gillivray, Archibald Norman M'Leod, Thomas Thain, John M'Tavish, and Henry Mackenzie, did consent and agree to continue and carry on trade as copartners in the business heretofore carried on by the late firm of M'Tavish, M'Gillivrays & Co. in all matters in which they were in any wise interested or concerned:—And also in all other matters which the said parties thereto might thereafter see fit to undertake or to be concerned in during the period of nine years, commencing on the 1st day of December, 1813, under the firm of M'Tavish, M'Gillivrays & Co., and ending on the 30th day of November, 1822.

And whereas it was also agreed, amongst other stipulations set forth in the said agreement, that on or before the 30th day of November, 1820, the respective parties should require from the others a distinct and explicit avowal of their intention in regard of renewing and continuing the articles of copartnership, or winding up the concern, as the case might require.

And whereas, on the 26th day of March last past, the said William M'Gillivray and Simon M'Gillivray, conjointly with Edward Ellice of the city of London, merchant, did, without the knowledge of the undersigned, enter into an agreement with the Hudson's Bay Company, wherein they, upon their own responsibility, undertook to assign over to the said Hudson's Bay Company all the stock in the trade carried on by the said firm, and others concerned, in the Indian Territories, on the first day of June last past.

And whereas the said John M'Tavish did, in the autumn of the year 1818, retire from the said concern by mutual consent; and the said Archibald Norman M'Leod also retired therefrom in either the month of May or June last past; and the said William M'Gillivray and Thomas Thain entered into copartnership under the firm of Sweenys & Co., in the month of March last past, and into a variety of other concerns in their own names and on their own behalf; and thus the said parties have withdrawn themselves from our said firm save and except the said Henry Mackenzie. Now, therefore, public notice is hereby given, that the said copartnership will not, according to the articles thereof, cease and expire before the 30th day of November, 1822; and all persons having claims or demands on the said copartnership, or on the North West Company, or agents thereof, are hereby notified to make the same, on or before the aforesaid day of November, 1822, to receive and adjust which the undersigned will henceforth give his attendance at the counting-house of the said concerns every day from the hours of ten to three o'clock, Sundays and holidays excepted.

Montreal, 15th November, 9 P.M.   H. MACKENZIE.

D

GENTLEMEN,   Montreal, 16th November, 1821.

Common prudence dictated to me the reiterated objections occasionally made by me against many transactions of our partnership which took place without my previous knowledge and concurrence, and from the recent, actual, serious, and uncommon proceedings threatened to be carried into effect, (at a period too when the books and accounts are not adjusted,) I am now more than ever urged to inform you once for all, that I shall immediately and hereafter resist every extraordinary measure taken, or innovation made, regarding our partnership affairs, without my express sanction and authority first had and obtained,—and I hereby revoke and annul all and every power I may have given (since the articles of copartnership) to any of the partners jointly or severally to transact any part of the business.

I have the honor to be,
Gentlemen,
Your most obedient humble Servant,
H. MACKENZIE.

To the Honorable William M'Gillivray,
    Simon M'Gillivray
    Archd. Norman M'Leod, and
    Thomas Thain,
} Esquires.

E

PROTEST AT REQUEST OF THE HONORABLE WILLIAM M'GILLIVRAY, SIMON M'GILLIVRAY, AND THOMAS THAIN, ESQUIRES, AGAINST HENRY MACKENZIE, ESQUIRE.

Whereas, by certain articles of agreement made and entered into, and bearing date, at Montreal, the first day of November, one thousand eight hundred and fourteen, the Honorable William M'Gillivray, of Montreal, aforesaid, merchant, Simon M'Gillivray, of London, merchant, Archibald Norman M'Leod, Thomas Thain, John M'Tavish and Henry Mackenzie, all of Montreal, aforesaid, merchants, did enter into copartnership to carry on trade as merchants, and as agents for the North West Company, under certain stipulations and conditions, set forth in the said articles of agreement, which are hereby referred to, and among other things it was specially provided and agreed:—That the said William M'Gillivray should "conduct and manage the correspondence and Finance Department, and with such assistance as he might require from any of his said partners, should superintend the general business of the concern: and that the said William M'Gillivray reserved to himself the right in case he should at any time find that the affairs of the said concern would admit of his absence from Canada so to absent himself accordingly; and that save and except the said William M'Gillivray, and also the said Thomas Thain (who so long as he should continue to hold the situation of agent of Sir Alexander M'Kenzie and Co.) should not be required to assume the management of any department unless the same should be in some manner connected with the agency of the North West Company, it should be at the option and disposal of the majority of the said concern to employ any of the said partners, and also the said Thomas Thain, in the event of his relinquishing the said agency of the said Alexander M'Kenzie and Co. in any manner or in any business, which might be deemed most conducive to the general benefit of the said concern, and that certain of the said partners of the said concern or firm should be entitled to draw from out of the funds of the said concern, in each year, certain sums of money, and no more, in order to meet their several personal expenses."—And whereas, by an indenture, bearing date the twenty sixth day of March last past, and made between the Governor and Company of Adventurers of England, trading into Hudson's Bay, of the first part, and the said William M'Gillivray and Simon M'Gillivray, and Edward Ellice, of Spring Garden, in the County of Middlesex, Esquire, of the second part, it was amongst other things agreed and provided, that the trade heretofore carried on by the said Governor and Company and the said North West Company respectively, should, for the space of twenty one years, commencing with the outfit of the year one thousand eight hundred and twenty one, (but subject to the terms therein contained,) be carried on by and in the name of the said Governor and Company and their successors, exclusively.—And whereas, the said indenture and the terms and conditions therein contained, have been ratified and confirmed by the said North West Company, and also by the partners of the said concern or firm of M'Tavish, M'Gillivrays & Co., and the arrangements provided for by the said indenture, have in a great measure been carried into effect, and consequently the said North West Company has ceased to exist as a separate body, and the wintering partners thereof have, under the provisions contained in the said indenture, been appointed chief factors and chief traders, and as such, have become entitled to certain shares of the clear gains and profits arising from the said trade, so to be carried on as aforesaid, by and in the name of the said Governor and Company, and the said agency of the said North West Company and also the said agency of Sir Alexander M'Kenzie & Co., have ceased and determined, except as in so far as regards to settling and closing the accounts of the outfit of the said North West Company for the year one thousand eight hundred and twenty, which is the last outfit made or to be made by the said North West Company. And whereas, the business and transactions carried on by the said house or firm of M'Tavish, M'Gillivrays & Co., under their said articles of copartnership have principally depended upon and been confined to the said agency of the said North West Company, and the said agency having ceased and determined as aforesaid, the said business and transactions of the said house or firm as connected with the same, must also cease and determine with the close of the said accounts of the said outfit of the year one thousand eight hundred and twenty. And whereas, the said Archibald Norman M'Leod and the said John

M'Tavish have retired from the said firm or copartnership of M'Tavish, M'Gillivray & Co., and the undersigned, the majority of the remaining partners thereof, deem it necessary and requisite from henceforward until the termination of the said copartnership of M'Tavish, M'Gillivrays & Co. to confine their transactions solely to the completing and carrying into effect the said indenture and the said arrangements so made as aforesaid, with the said Governor and Company, and winding up, settling and realizing the accounts and affairs of the said firm or copartnership of M'Tavish, M'Gillivray & Co.; and for these purposes it is considered expedient that the said William M'Gillivray and the said Simon M'Gillivray should proceed to England forthwith, and that the said Thomas Thain shall, during their absence, be entrusted with the superintendence and management of the general business of the said concern or firm of M'Tavish, M'Gillivrays & Co., in addition to the finances and accounts, of which, since the retirement of the said John M'Tavish, he, the said Thomas Thain has had the charge, under the general superintendence of the said William M'Gillivray.

First—It is therefore accordingly agreed and resolved, that the said house or firm of M'Tavish, M'Gillivrays and Co. shall from henceforward, and until the termination of their said articles of copartnership, confine their transactions solely to completing and carrying into effect the said arrangements with the said Governor and Company, and to winding up, settling, and realizing the debts, effects, accounts, and property of the said firm, and that the said house or firm of M'Tavish, M'Gillivrays & Co. shall not, and that any individual partner thereof shall not be competent in the name, or on the behalf of the said house or firm of M'Tavish, M'Gillivrays & Co. to contract or enter into new transactions, purchases, engagements, or speculations whatsoever.

Second—That during the absence from this Province of the said William M'Gillivray, and the said Simon M'Gillivray, Thomas Thain be authorised, and he is hereby accordingly authorised to superintend and to conduct the correspondence, the finances, and the general business of the said house or firm of M'Tavish, M'Gillivrays & Co., and to hold and possess the books, papers, and all other property of the said house or firm, on behalf of and in trust for all parties holding any just and lawful part, share, claim, or interest therein, or any part thereof.

Third—That the said Thomas Thain shall be personally responsible for any future violation of the ninth article of the said copartnership agreement, being that which specifies and limits the sums of money to be drawn from the funds of the said copartnership or concern by the individual partners thereof to meet their several personal expenses.

In witness whereof, and of our consent and concurrence therein, we have hereunto set our hands and seals, at Montreal, this fifteenth day of November, one thousand eight hundred and twenty-one.

	WILLIAM M'GILLIVRAY,	(seal)
In presence of	SIMON M'GILLIVRAY,	(seal)
(Signed) C. TATE.	THOMAS THAIN.	(seal)
WILLIAM CASTLE.		

Duplicate referred to in the annexed Protest. H. GRIFFIN, N. P.

On this day, the seventeenth of November, in the year of our Lord one thousand eight hundred and twenty one, we, the undersigned Public Notaries duly commissioned, and sworn in and for the Province of Lower Canada, residing in the City of Montreal, at the special instance and request of the honorable William M'Gillivray, Simon M'Gillivray and Thomas Thain, Esquires, the majority of the partners in the house and firm of M'Tavish, M'Gillivrays and Company, in the said City of Montreal, merchants, did go to the house of Henry Mackenzie, Esquire, in Montreal aforesaid, one of the partners in the said house and firm, and there speaking to himself did signify unto him the annexed instrument of resolves made by the said majority of partners;—at the same time, at the request aforesaid, did declare to protest, as by these presents we do solemnly protest, against the said Henry Mackenzie for all costs, charges, losses, damages, and injuries, that may result by or from all or any act, or acts, of the said Henry Mackenzie should he go, act, or do contrary to the said resolved contained in the said annexed instrument, determined upon by the said William M'Gillivray, Simon M'Gillivray, and Thomas Thain, as the majority of the partners in the said house and firm of M'Tavish, M'Gillivrays & Company.

And to the end that the said Henry Mackenzie may not have cause to pretend ignorance in the premises, we, the said Notaries, at the same time delivered unto him a duplicate of the said instrument of resolves as well as a copy of these presents annexed.

Thus done and protested at the said City of Montreal, on the day, and month, and year, first above written.

(Signed) THOMAS BARRON, N. P. & H. GRIFFIN, N. P.

(*A true Copy.*)

One marginal note. Three words obliterated.

H. GRIFFIN, N. P.

F

SIGNIFICATION TO AND PROTEST AGAINST THE HONORABLE WILLIAM M'GILLIVRAY SIMON M'GILLIVRAY, AND THOMAS THAIN, ESQUIRES, AT THE REQUEST OF HENRY MACKENZIE, ESQUIRE.

Whereas on this day, the seventeenth day of November, one thousand eight hundred and twenty-one, I, Henry Mackenzie, one of the partners of M'Tavish, M'Gillivrays and Company, have received notice of divers transactions and arrangements said to be entered into by the said partnership, and particularly of the retiring of one of the partners—Archd. M'Leod, Esquire.

And whereas divers resolves are mentioned in the said notice to have been entered into by the said partnership. And whereas measures are said to have been adopted by the said partnership to wind up the affairs thereof. And whereas the absence of the Honorable William M'Gillivray and Simon M'Gillivray are said to be deemed necessary by the said partnership, and also that the said North West Company had ceased and determined. And whereas in the said notice it is particularly expressed by one of the resolves said to be made by the said partnership, that Thomas Thain, one of the partners, shall be hereafter responsible for any *future* violation of the ninth article of the copartnership agreement, being that which specifies and limits the sum of money to be drawn from the funds of the said copartnership or concern by the individual partners thereof to meet their several personal expenses. Now I, the said Henry Mackenzie, one of the partners aforesaid, do hereby declare and solemnly affirm that all the above arrangements, resolves, and other measures, said to be taken and adopted by the said partnership, have been made, taken, and entered into, without my knowledge and consent, and even without any notice thereof—which violates every sacred principle of reciprocity in agreements, and dissolves every social tie. And as to the second resolve said to be entered into by the said partnership—it is a conspiracy. And I further declare, that I object to the absence of any one of the partners, because they declare by the said pretended third resolve made by the said partnership, that Thomas Thain shall be personally responsible for any *future* violation of the ninth article of the said copartnership agreement without providing for any liability for the *past* violation of the same.

In witness whereof, I have hereunto set my hand and seal this seventeenth day of November, one thousand eight hundred and twenty-one.

(Signed)   H. MACKENZIE. (L. S.)

In presence of
(Signed)   C. JULIUS BROWN.
            H. GRIFFIN.
                        A true Copy.   H. GRIFFIN, N. P.

On this day, the seventeenth of November, in the year of our Lord one thousand eight hundred and twenty-one, WE, the undersigned Notaries Public, duly commissioned and sworn in and for the Province of Lower Canada, residing in the City of Montreal, at the special instance and request of Henry Mackenzie, Esquire, of the said city of Montreal, one of the partners in the house and firm of M'Tavish, M'Gillivrays & Company of Montreal aforesaid, merchanrs, did go to the house of Thomas Thain, Esquire, in the said city of Montreal, and there did signify unto the Honorable William M'Gillivray, Simon M'Gillivray, and Thomas Thain, Esquires, by speaking to the said Thomas Thain, the annexed declaration of (and signed and sealed by) the said Henry Mackenzie, at the same time, at the instance and request aforesaid, did declare to protest, as by these presents we do solemnly protest against the said William M'Gillivray, Simon M'Gillivray, and Thomas Thain, jointly and separately, and all and every other person and persons, whom it doth or may concern, for all costs, charges, damages, and injuries already suffered, or that can, shall, or may hereafter be suffered by the said Henry Mackenzie for and by reason of the resolves and determinations made by them, the said William M'Gillivray, Simon M'Gillivray, and Thomas Thain, signified this day upon the said Henry Mackenzie, and referred to in the said annexed declaration, and further for and by reason of all or any act or acts, thing or things, by them or either of them already done, or that may hereafter be done by them the said William M'Gillivray, Simon M'Gillivray, and Thomas Thain, or any or either of them, in virtue or in consequence of their said resolves and determinations, whereby the rights, prerogatives, or interests of the said Henry Mackenzie shall or may in any manner or way be prejudiced, hurt, or injured. And to the end that the said William M'Gillivray, Simon M'Gillivray, and Thomas Thain, or any or either of them, may not have cause to pretend ignorance in the premises, we, at the same time, delivered unto the said Thomas Thain a duplicate of the said declaration, signed and sealed as aforesaid, with a certified copy of these presents annexed.

This done and protested at Montreal aforesaid, on the day, month, and year first above written, in the afternoon.

(Signed) THOMAS BARRON, N. P. & H. GRIFFIN, N.P.

A true copy of the original minute.

H. GRIFFIN, N. P.

G

PROTEST BY HENRY MACKENZIE *versus* WILLIAM M'GILLIVRAY, SIMON M'GILLIVRAY, THOMAS THAIN, AND ARCHIBALD M'LEOD, ESQUIRES.

Whereas, by certain articles of agreement, bearing date the first day of November, one thousand eight hundred and fourteen, made and entered into by and between the Honourable William M'Gillivray, of Montreal, Simon M'Gillivray, of London, merchants, then present at Montreal, Archibald Norman M'Leod, Thomas Thain, John M'Tavish, and Henry Mackenzie, all of Montreal, aforesaid, merchants, (after reciting divers articles of agreement and other instruments,) they, the said parties did consent and agree to continue and carry on trade as copartners in the business theretofore carried on by the late house of M'Tavish, M'Gillivray & Co., and by the new house since the formation of the same, and all matters in which they were in any wise interested or concerned, and also in all other matters which the said parties thereto might see fit to undertake or be concerned in, for and during the term of nine years. And whereas, by the tenth article of the said agreement, it was expressly agreed that as it was considered desirable at some definite period before the close of the concern, arrangements should be made for continuing the business to be carried on thereby, or *for winding up the same and realizing the property and effects thereunto belonging at least two years* before the termination of the partnership, that is to say, on or before the thirtieth day of November, one thousand eight hundred and twenty, the respective parties thereto should be competent *to require each from the others a distinct and explicit avowal of their intention in regard to renewing and continuing articles of copartnership, or winding up the concern*, as the case might be—and in the event that the majority should enter into arrangements for the renewal thereof, the new concern were to be subject to certain engagements, and to enjoy such rights and privileges, and to observe and fulfil such regulations as were more particularly mentioned in the said article. And it was further agreed upon that in the event of a majority not entering into arrangements for a renewal thereof, and that it should become necessary to wind up and close the business and transactions of the said partnership, in that case it should be the duty of the partners employed in the agency of the North West Company to perform their usual duties in the summer following the termination of the said partnership. That it should be the duty of the London partner to receive and realize the return in the usual manner, and that it should be the duty of the partner employed in keeping the books to remain at his post, for which several duties the said respective partners should receive an adequate recompense—and that all other stock should be realized in such manner as a majority should see fit. And whereas, by the eleventh article of the said agreement, it was further stipulated and agreed upon by the said parties, that the death or retiring of any partner, or admission of any active partner or partners should not affect, determine or change the partnership thereby established, nor the period of its duration, but the same should nevertheless be continued and carried on under all the clauses, conditions, and stipulations therein contained, until the final conclusion and determination of the aforesaid term of nine years.. And whereas, on the seventeenth day of the present month of November, a certain writing or protest, with certain resolves thereunto annexed, signed and sealed by the Honorable William M'Gillivray, Simon M'Gillivray, and Thomas Thain, parties to the above recited agreement, was signified or served upon me, the said Henry Mackenzie one other of the said parties to the said recited agreement, in which said resolves were recited, certain articles of the said above recited agreement, and also certain indentures made between the Hudson's Bay Company and the Honorable William M'Gillivray, and others, and that the same had been ratified by the North West Company, and also by the partners of the house of M'Tavish, M'Gillivrays & Co., and that certain clauses therein mentioned had been carried into effect, and that the agency of the North West Company and the agency of Sir Alexander M'Kenzie & Co. had ceased, with the exception of the outfit one thousand eight hundred and twenty. And which said resolves further recited, that the business and transactions carried on by the said M'Tavish, M'Gillivrays & Co., had principally depended and been confined to the agency of the North West Company, and that the said agency having ceased, the business and transactions connected with the same had ceased; and further recited that John M'Tavish and Archibald Norman M'Leod had retired from the said copartnership—and that the undersigned majority of the remaining parties thereof, deemed it necessary and requisite from thenceforward, until the termination of the copartnership of M'Tavish, M'Gillivrays & Co., to confine their transactions to the completing and carrying into effect the said indenture and the said arrangements with the said Governor and Company, and winding up, settling, and realizing the accounts and affairs of the said M'Tavish, M'Gillivrays & Co. and for those purposes it was deemed expedient that the said William M'Gillivray and Simon M'Gillivray should proceed to England forthwith, and that the said Thomas Thain should, during their absence, be entrusted with the superintendance of the general business of M'Tavish, M'Gillivrays & Company, in addition to the finances and the accounts of which, since the retirement of the said John M'Tavish he had the charge. Wherefore it was agreed and resolved:—First, That the copartnership of M'Tavish, M'Gillivrays and Company should thenceforward, and until the termination thereof, confine their transactions solely to completing and carrying into effect the said arrangements with the said Governor and Company, and to winding up, settling, and realizing the debts and property of the said firm, and that the said house or firm of M'Tavish, M'Gillivrays & Company should not, and that any individual partner should not be competent *in the name or on the behalf* of the said firm of M'Tavish, M'Gillivrays and Company, to contract or enter into any new transactions, purchases, engagements, or speculations whatsoever. Secondly,—That during the absence of the said William M'Gillivray and Simon M'Gillivray, the said Thomas Thain should be authorised to superintend and to conduct the correspondence, the finances, and the general business of the said partnership, and should hold and possess the books, papers, and all other the property of the said house or firm on behalf of and in trust for all parties holding any just and lawful part or interest therein or any part thereof. And thirdly,— That the said Thomas Thain should be personally responsible for any future violation of the ninth article of the copartnership, being that which limits the amount to be taken out of the general funds by the individual partners for their personal expenses. Now I, the said Henry Mackenzie, one of the said parties to the above recited agreement, taking into due consideration all the clauses, stipulations, and conditions thereby entered into and agreed upon by and between all the parties thereto; and also having maturely and attentively considered the above recited resolves annexed to the said writing or protest so signified to me as aforesaid, do now for the preservation of all my rights and interests contained in the said recited articles of copartnership, solemnly protest against all the said resolves and the reasons contained in the recitals preceding the same, as being in direct contradiction to and violating the spirit and true intent and meaning of the above recited articles of copartnership entered into with me; and I hereby further protest against the said William M'Gillivray, Simon M'Gillivray, and Thomas Thain who have entered into the said resolves, and signed and sealed the same, for all costs, damages, interest, or injury which I have already suffered or hereafter may suffer by the same, either in property or character, and also against any act or acts which they or either of them may or do, or undertake to do, or cause to be done, under the pretended authority of the said resolves. And to the intent that they nor either of them may pretend cause of ignorance of the same, I hereby make known to them my lawful objections thereto.

First,—Because they the said William M'Gillivray, Simon M'Gillivray, and

Thomas Thain, (calling themselves a majority of partners, themselves only being present,) have assumed the right of altering and changing the essence or basis of the above recited articles of copartnership, whereas by the same, a majority of the partners can regulate only the departments or duties of the respective partners as therein specified.

Secondly,—Because it was stipulated and agreed upon by the above recited articles of copartnership, that the parties thereto should not only carry on the business formerly transacted by all the preceding partnerships therein mentioned, but also all other matters which they might see fit to undertake or to be concerned in—whereas, by their resolves, they limit and confine the transactions thereof solely to the completing and carrying into effect the arrangements with the Adventurers of the Hudson's Bay Company, and to the winding up, settling, and realizing the effects and debts of the said concern, and in restraining every individual partner thereof from contracting or entering into any engagement during the remainder of the term of the said agreement of copartnership, whereby the original intention of the association is totally frustrated and abridged, and which the power of no majority could alter or modify.

Thirdly,—Because the distinct and explicit avowal of the arrangements *for winding up, settling, and realizing the accounts and affairs* of the said partnership entered into by the majority, as expressed by the said resolves, was only notified to me on the seventeenth of the present month of November, one thousand eight hundred and twenty-one. Whereas by the tenth article it is expressly agreed upon, that at least two years before the expiration of the said partnership, viz. on or before the thirtieth day of November, one thousand eight hundred and twenty, a distinct and implicit avowal of the respective parties should be given to each other of their intention in regard to renewing and continuing articles of partnership or *winding up the concern*, as the case might be. And, in which said tenth article herein before particularly recited, a provision is made for winding up and settling the affairs of the said partnership, in case a determination or avowal, as agreed upon by the said articles of copartnership, should have been made.

Fourthly,—Because by the eleventh article herein before recited, it was expressly stipulated and agreed upon, that the death, or admission of any partner, should not affect, determine, or change the partnership thereby established, nor the duration thereof, but that the same should nevertheless be continued and carried on under all the clauses, conditions, and stipulations in the said agreement contained until the final conclusion. This special clause or article assures the inviolability of the agreement as to its duration and extent of business, for it was by the first article already agreed upon for the term of nine years, and by the said eleventh article it is ratified and renewed, with an assurance that events of death or innovation should not change nor lessen its duration, and that it should be continued under all the stipulations and conditions contained in the said agreement until its final determination—one of which stipulations was to carry on all business which might be entered into for nine years—whereas the first resolve herein before recited, entered into by the majority, the transactions of the said partnership are limited, by confining the same solely to the completing of the arrangements entered into with the Hudson's Bay Company, and to the winding up of the affairs of the said partnership of M'Tavish, M'Gillivrays & Company.

Fifthly,—Because by the fifth article of the said above recited agreement, it was stipulated, that the said Honorable William M'Gillivray should conduct and manage the correspondence and finance department, and with such assistance as he might require from any of his said partners, should superintend the general business of the concern—whereas in opposition thereto, by the second of the above recited resolves, the said Honorable William M'Gillivray has authorised the said Thomas Thain to superintend the general business of the said firm of M'Tavish, M'Gillivrays and Company—which superintendance of the general affairs could not be deputed by him to any one of the partners, as is plainly evinced and shown by the sixth article, which in the event of the death of the said William M'Gillivray, or his absence from the Province, expressly declares that the said Simon M'Gillivray should come to Montreal, and assume the management of the finance and correspondence departments only, leaving the authority, which such a power is supposed to give, equally to all the remaining partners.

Sixthly,—Because by the said above recited resolves it is attempted that I, the said Henry Mackenzie, should be left without any participation in the business of the said partnership, and thereby deprived of watching over my interests—which resolves, if carried into effect, will justify and demand as a duty from me every opposition in my power.

In witness whereof, I have hereunto set my hand, this twenty-first day of November, in the year one thousand eight hundred and twenty-one.

Twenty-five words being erased, three words interlined, and one marginal note.

H. MACKENZIE.

Montreal, 21st November, 1821.—We, the undersigned, do acknowledge to have received a true copy of the foregoing protest, and consider the same as valid as if the said protest had been made by a Notary Public.

WILLIAM M'GILLIVRAY.
SIMON M'GILLIVRAY,
THOMAS THAIN.

H

HENRY MACKENZIE TO SIMON M'GILLIVRAY AND THOMAS THAIN, ESQUIRES.

Montreal, 22d November, 1822.

Dear Sirs,

The length of time that has elapsed since I last saw the books of M'Tavish, M'Gillivrays & Co., and the agents of the North West Company, have effaced from my recollection many of the things recorded in them, and left but a feeble impression of others. I am thus, at a time when the close of the concern is at hand, ignorant of the precise relation in which I stand with my associates in business, and without the means of forming a just estimate of any rights which may belong to me as a person so connected; an acquaintance with which, you will, I dare say, allow, is necessary to place me upon a footing with you in any discussions to which the approaching settlement between us may give rise.

I therefore request that I may have immediate and free access to the abovementioned books, for the purpose of making such extracts from them as I may require. Further, our connexion being now so near a termination, I think it a duty I owe to myself to urge an immediate settlement of those books; to facilitate the accomplishment of which, I will be prepared, on Monday next, to audit in company with yourselves all the books of accounts in which I have any concern.

I trust, Gentlemen, that as I am conscious of having allowed no improper feeling to guide me in making these requests, so I trust they will be received in good part by you, and that you will suffer no unfounded suspicion of *latent* motives of action in me (which I am sorry to say I could perceive swayed decisions on former occasions) to stand in the way of acceding to what I think every man must call a reasonable request.

Be assured, Gentlemen, that in whichever way our matters may be finally arranged, I wish nothing to occur to interrupt, in the smallest degree, the offices of friendship which we have hitherto been disposed to extend to each other.

I am, with due regard,

Dear Sirs,

Your most obedient humble Servant,

H. MACKENZIE.

I

Montreal, 23d November, 1822,

Dear Sir,

In reply to your letter of yesterday, we deem it requisite to refer you to the partnership agreement of the firm of M'Tavish, M'Gillivrays & Co., the *tenth* article of which, in specifying the duties to be performed by the respective partners—"in the event that it shall become necessary to wind up and close the "business and transactions of this concern or partnership,"—provides, amongst others, that "it shall be the duty of the partner, employed in keeping the books "and accounts of this concern, to remain at his post, and to make up and exhibit "just, true, and accurate accounts of the *said returns*, (those spoken of are the "returns to be obtained for the outfit of the year,) "so to be realized, and all "other matters and transactions in which the concern may remain interested." Now that it *has* become necessary so to wind up and close the said business and transactions, is perfectly well known to you, and we have to inform you further, that by a resolution of the requisite majority* of the concern, Mr. Thain is authorised and appointed to perform the duty above specified.

That this duty should devolve upon Mr. Thain, almost necessarily follows, from the article quoted, since for the last four years *he* has been the partner employed in keeping the books and accounts of the concern, and as the realization of the returns, mentioned in the agreement, was necessarily to take place before the accounts depending upon them could be settled, and since you know, as well as we do, what time is required for realizing the returns of the outfit in question, it is quite unnecessary for us to point out to you what time must elapse before the production of the accounts specified in the agreement can be required.

We deem it requisite also to refer you to a certain deed, bearing date the 6th day of April, 1821, reciting and ratifying the recent arrangements with the Hudson's Bay Company, and of which you have recently received a copy. We refer you particularly to the stipulations for balancing inventories with the Hudson's Bay Company, of the first of June, 1823; and those for the payment to the firm of M'Tavish, M'Gillivrays & Co., of certain shares of profits on the outfits of 1821 and 1822, "in full discharge of all claims and demands of such house or firm, in respect of the "trade or concerns of the said North West Com- "pany, or in any wise relating thereto." These shares of profit on the outfit of 1822 cannot be realized, or even ascertained, before the summer of 1824 at the soonest; and the accounts of the agents of the North West Company cannot be brought to any settlement, as to the transfer of capital; until after the balance of inventories with the Hudson's Bay Company shall be adjusted in June next; nor probably as to the final results until after the settlement with retired partners, which is contingent upon the result of the outfits of 1821 and 1822. Therefore any investigation of these accounts, at this time, is premature, and, in fact, impracticable; and, for the very same reasons, such also is the case with the books of M'Tavish, M'Gillivrays & Co.—the settlement of which depends upon the previous result of the North West accounts; and this dependence is no new discovery to any of us, since it necessarily arises from the intrinsic nature of the business, and is manifestly contemplated by the articles of our partnership, and by every other instrument describing or referring to our transactions.

A statement of the probable result of these concerns was made out for your satisfaction last year,† and since that time, and since the resolution adopted and communicated to you, to enter into no new transaction during the remainder of the partnership, no further entries have been made in the books. Mr. Thain has merely kept temporary records of transactions which under the resolution in question he was authorised to superintend and conduct; therefore you would derive no benefit or information from the access which you seek to the books, and at this moment it would be inconvenient to produce them for your proposed *audit*.

*According to this principle, Articles of Copartnership would be nugatory, since they might always be violated by the majority.—H. M'K.

†If so, those who directed it must have changed their minds, for I never received it.—H. M'K.

From the statement in question, and the state of your private account, § it is very evident that you have drawn from the funds of the partnership much more money than by the articles of agreement you were entitled to draw,|| and more we fear than the probable amount of your share of the profits, even if they were now realized, instead of being, as you know they are, contingent upon the dependencies already stated; and as you brought no capital into the house,* it is only your share of profits that can come to balance the large sums of money heretofore advanced to you. We are as anxious as you can be to have all these matters brought to a point; and we trust it is unnecessary to declare that we have no wish or intention whatever to deprive you in the slightest degree of any right or advantage to which you may be justly or lawfully entitled; therefore every account in which you have any interest shall as speedily† as possible be settled, and submitted to such *audit* or examination as you may think requisite, but it is impossible to anticipate settlements depending on future contingencies.

We remain,

Dear Sir,

Your most obedient Servants,

SIMON M'GILLIVRAY
THOMAS THAIN.

K

Monday Evening, 8½ o'clock, 25th November, 1822.

Dear Sir,
Your and Mr. S. Gillivray's letter of the 23d, I received this evening, upon my return from Terrebonne. I am sorry to say it is no answer to mine to you. You have either misapprehended its chief purport, or not choosing to comply with

§I never received them.—H. M'K.
||I believe a considerable part was expended in the business of the firm.—H. M'K.
*This is not true:—I made over to the firm my stock in the concerns of "M'Kenzie, Oldham & Co." and "Henry Mackenzie and Jacob Oldham," of Terrebone, and gave Mr. M'Gillivray leave to realize it, while I was busily engaged here and elsewhere on the affairs of the North West Company in the contest with Lord Selkirk. If that stock has not been as productive as it would have been by my own exertions the blame lies on him who neglected it when it became a part of the capital of M'Tavish, M'Gillivrays & Co., and must be considered as a part of his administration of the finance of the latter firm.—H. M'K.
†This speed is excessively slow, and as yet has not equalled that of the snail.—H. M'K.

the request it contained, have evaded the question. The lengthy statement you have entered into establishes a point I never meant to deny, namely, that the books cannot be finally closed, nor the affairs wound up, till the outfits be realized. My request embraced two objects—Access to the books for the purpose of making extracts for my individual satisfaction, and an audit, or examination, or scrutiny, if you will, of them as they now stand; an explanation of *past* transactions, not a premature settling of "contingencies" that depend upon materials yet to be procured. Is there aught in the agreement to prohibit this!—to prohibit a partner from seeing the books of the association to which he belongs! If there be such a clause, show it. I must be permitted to say that I am very harshly, not to say unfairly, dealt with. This, I am convinced, must be the conclusion every unbiassed mind must come to on the subject.

Pray be explicit, and acquaint me whether you mean to deny my request as here explained.

I am, most truly yours,
H. MACKENZIE.

I must have an early answer to-morrow, if you please.   H. M.

THOMAS THAIN, Esq.

L

Montreal, 26th November, 1822, (Noon.)

Dear Sir,
In answer to your letter of yesterday evening, which I have this morning communicated to Mr. S. M'Gillivray, I beg leave to inform you that the lengthy statement you allude to was not written *with a view to evade your question*. Our letter was written with the intention of explaining to you our reasons, or rather our opinion, why we did not consider it necessary to proceed to the *audit* or inspection of the books you allude to, and we are still of the same opinion, that no good could result to either party from such inspection at present. But as you require an explicit answer, I beg leave to inform you, that we cannot agree to your request; and you are well aware (independent of the state of the office) that my time can be much more beneficially employed attending to other matters.

I remain,
Dear Sir,
Your most obedient Servant,
THOMAS THAIN.

H. MACKENZIE, Esq.

APPENDICES

APPENDIX A

A BIOGRAPHICAL DICTIONARY OF THE NOR' WESTERS

ASKIN, JOHN (1739?-1815) was born at Strabane, county Tyrone, Ireland, about 1739, the son of John Askin (or Erskine) and Alice Rea. He came to America in 1758, and served in the army during the later stages of the Seven Years' War. About 1761 he established himself in business as a merchant and fur-trader near Albany, New York; but having become a bankrupt, he went to Michilimackinac in 1765, and here he prospered in the fur-trade. In 1771 he was one of the group of traders who sent Thomas Corry (q.v.) to the Saskatchewan; and in 1772 he was described by the master of York Fort as carrying on "a large Trade, not less than 500 packs of Furs annually, when mustered from all parts". He was an agent for the North West Company in its initial stages; but in 1780 he moved his headquarters to Detroit, and henceforth he was interested especially in the south-west trade. When Detroit was handed over to the United States in 1802 he moved to Amherstburg, Upper Canada; and there he died in April, 1815. He married, first, an Indian woman, by whom he had three children; and, secondly, Archange Barthe, of Detroit, by whom he had nine children. His papers have been edited by Dr. M. M. Quaife, and published by the Detroit Library Commission (2 vols., Detroit, 1928-31).

BANNERMAN, JAMES (*fl.* 1775-1794) was a native of Scotland who was engaged in the fur-trade at Detroit and Michilimackinac as early as 1775. About 1776 he formed a partnership with Simon McTavish (q.v.); but this partnership was dissolved in 1779, and on October 28, 1779, Bannerman sailed for London. He was still living in Scotland in 1794.

BEIOLEY, JOSEPH (1785?-1859) was born about 1785, and entered the service of the Hudson's Bay Company in 1800. In 1819 he acted as governor of the Southern Department in the absence of Thomas Vincent (q.v.); and in 1821 he was made a chief factor. He retired from the service of the Company in 1843, and he died in 1859.

BELL, JOHN (1799-1868) was born in the Isle of Mull, Scotland, in 1799, and entered the service of the North West Company in 1818. He was taken over by the Hudson's Bay Company in 1821; and from 1821 to 1824 he was in the Winnipeg district. From 1824 to 1850, with the exception of the years 1847-8, when he was told off to assist in Arctic exploration, he was stationed in the Mackenzie River department. In 1851 he was at Oxford House; in 1852, at Cumberland House; from 1853 to 1856, at Fort Chipewyan; and from 1858-1860, in the Montreal department, at St. Maurice. He was promoted to be a chief trader in 1840; and he retired from the fur-trade in 1860, and died in 1868. He married a daughter of Peter Warren Dease (q.v.); and by her he had at least one daughter.

BETHUNE, ANGUS (1783-1858) was born at Carleton Island, in Lake Ontario, on September 9, 1783, the eldest son of the Rev. John Bethune and Veronica, daughter of Jean Etienne Wadden (q.v.). He entered the service of the North West Company, and in 1806 was a clerk at Lake Winnipeg. In 1813 he was transferred to the Columbia; and in 1814 he was made a partner of the North West Company. He was at Fort William in the summer of 1817, and again in the summer of 1820; and on the latter occasion he was appointed by the wintering partners as a delegate, with John McLoughlin, to go to London to open separate negotiations with the Hudson's Bay Company. He spent the winter of 1820-21 in London; and on the union of the North West and Hudson's Bay Companies in 1821, he was made a chief factor. He seems to have retired from the fur-trade before 1825; and he died in Toronto on November 13, 1858. He married Louisa, daughter of the Hon. Roderick McKenzie (q.v.), of Terrebonne; and by her he had five sons and one daughter. For an account of the Bethune family, see A. H. Young, *The Bethunes* (Ontario Historical Society, Papers and Records, vol. XXVII, 1931).

BIRD, GEORGE (d. 1856) was originally a clerk of the Hudson's Bay Company who entered its service in 1812. After the union of the Hudson's Bay and North West Companies in 1821, he was employed on the Saskatchewan. He retired from the Company's service in 1825, and settled at the Red River Settlement. Here he died on October 18, 1856.

BLACK, SAMUEL (d. 1841) was a native of Aberdeen, Scotland, and must have been born about 1785. He came to Canada in 1802 as a clerk in the XY Company, at the instance of Edward Ellice (q.v.); and in 1804 he was absorbed by the North West Company. In the struggle between the North West Company and the Hudson's Bay Company under Lord Selkirk, he took such an active part that, at the time of the union of 1821, he was deliberately excluded from employment by the Hudson's Bay Company. In 1823, however, Governor Simpson relented, and he was given a commission as chief trader. In 1824 he was employed in exploring the Finlay River. He was then transferred to the Columbia, where he was in charge, first, of Fort Walla Walla, and second, of Kamloops. He was promoted to be chief factor in 1837; and his career was cut short when he was murdered by an Indian on January 8, 1841, at a place near the mouth of the Columbia. Further details in regard to him will be found in J. N. Wallace, *The explorer of Finlay River in 1824* (Can. hist. rev., 1928, pp. 25-31).

BLEAKLEY, JOSIAH (*fl.* 1783-1816) was government storekeeper and clerk at Michilimackinac in 1783. He became a trader, and wintered on the Mississippi in 1785-6. He settled in Montreal in 1787, and was elected a member of the Beaver Club. In 1807 he was a partner in the South West Company; and in 1808 he was a member of the fur-trading brigade which was seized by the American government at Niagara. He was still living in Montreal in December, 1816. John Askin, Jr., refers to him in a letter (Wisconsin Historical Collections, XIX, 324) as "that poor simple man J. Bleakley".

BLONDEAU, BARTHÉLEMI (*fl.* 1743-1790) was born at Michilimackinac on August 24, 1743, the son of Thomas Blondeau and Marie-Josephte Celles-Duclos, and a first cousin of Maurice Régis Blondeau (q.v.). He was one of the first traders to reach the North-West after the British conquest. He was on the Red Deer River in 1772; and it is possible that he reached the Assiniboine as early as 1767 or 1769. In 1773 he was "up the Saskatchewan"; in 1774 he went "southwest, when a little above the Great Lake"; and in 1777-8 he was at Sturgeon River Fort, near what is now Prince Albert. He was not included in the original North West Company of 1779; and he seems thereafter to have turned his energies toward the Illinois country. He was at Michilimackinac in 1790; but after that I can find no trace of him.

BLONDEAU, MAURICE RÉGIS (1734-1809) was born in Montreal on June 23, 1834, the second son of Jean Baptiste Blondeau and Geneviève Lefebvre. Like others of his family, which had in it an early strain of Indian blood, he engaged in the fur-trade; and in 1772 he was one of the group of merchants that sent Thomas Corry (q.v.) to the West. On April 2, 1773, he was granted a seigniory on the west bank of the St. Lawrence, adjoining the Seigniory des Cèdres; and during his later years he appears to have taken little part in the fur-trade. He died at Montreal on July 20, 1809, aged 75 years.

BOYER, CHARLES (*fl.* 1778-1789) seems to have been a French Canadian, possibly a native of Michilimackinac. A Charles Boyer, son of Michel Boyer, appears in the Michilimackinac register as baptized in 1761; but this may have been a different person. The first definite reference to him is in a letter of John Askin (q.v.), dated May 18, 1778, in which he seems to figure as a clerk of Alexander Henry the elder (q.v.). In 1780 he was with William Bruce (q.v.) at Fort des Trembles on the Assiniboine River; and in the spring of 1781 they were attacked by the Indians, but saved the fort after a heroic defence. Later, Boyer went as a clerk of the North West Company to the Peace River, and he is said to have founded Fort Vermilion in 1787, near what is still known as Boyer River. In 1788 he was back at Lake Athabaska; and in 1789 he retired from the fur-trade and from the North West. What became of him after that, I have not been able to ascertain.

BRUCE, WILLIAM (d. 1781) was engaged in the fur-trade at La Baye, in Lake Michigan, as early as 1763. He first appears in the North-West in 1772, when Matthew Cocking met him at Basquia on the Saskatchewan. He told Cocking that "he had been a Trader among the Indians at Mississippi, where a difference happening between his Men and the Natives he had killed one of the latter, and was obliged to leave that part and entered into this Trade, being the first time of his being up". In 1773 he was near the Red Deer River; and in 1774, near Fort Dauphin. In 1778 he was described in a list of North West traders as "bad and rebel"; and he does not appear to have been included in the sixteen-share North West Company formed in 1779. In 1781 he made, with Charles Boyer (q.v.), a gallant defence of Fort des Trembles on the Saskatchewan, when it was attacked by the Indians; but shortly afterward he was carried off by the smallpox epidemic of 1781-2.

CADOT, JEAN BAPTISTE (*fl.* 1723-1803) was born at Batiscan, Canada, on December 5, 1723, the son of Jean Cadot and Marie-Joseph Proteau. He settled at Sault Ste. Marie before 1751, and he was left in charge of the French fort there when the French troops were withdrawn in 1758. Alexander Henry (q.v.) says that he was "the last governor of the French fort". After the British conquest, he entered in partnership with Alexander Henry; and during the Conspiracy of Pontiac he saved Henry's life from the Indians. Alexander Henry (q.v.) says that he was on the Saskatchewan in 1775; but his name was probably a mistake for that of Blondeau (q.v.). He continued to take part in the fur-trade at Sault Ste. Marie until 1796, when he handed over his business to his sons. He is said to have died about 1803; but there is some doubt about this, as there is evidence he was still alive at Sault Ste. Marie in 1812. In 1756 he had his marriage with Anastasia, a Nipissing woman, legitimized by the Church; and by her he had two daughters and two sons. An account of his life will be found in J. Tassé, *Les Canadiens de l'ouest* (2 vols., Montreal, 1878).

CADOT, JEAN BAPTISTE (1761-1818) was born at Sault Ste. Marie on October 25, 1761, the elder son of Jean Baptiste Cadot (q.v.) and his wife Anastasia, a Nipissing woman. He was educated in Lower Canada, and David Thompson, who met him in 1798 says that he "spoke fluently his native language, with Latin, French, and English". He entered the service of the North West Company, and in 1798-9 was a senior clerk in the Fond du Lac department. He was admitted a partner of the North West Company in 1801, but was expelled in 1803 for intemperance. From 1803 to 1813 he received an annual pension of £100 from the Company, but in the latter year this pension was discontinued, since about that time he had received an appointment as an interpreter in the Indian department in Upper Canada. He died about 1818. His wife was, like himself, a half-breed; and by her he had four children.

CADOT, MICHEL (*fl.* 1764-1804) was born at Sault Ste. Marie on July 22, 1764, the younger son of the elder Jean Baptiste Cadot (q.v.) and his wife Anastasia. He entered the employ of the North West Company, and in 1798 was in charge of a post on the River Tortue in the Fond du Lac department. In 1804 he is said to have been in charge of a North West Company post on the Montreal River, though he does not appear in the list of the Company's servants for this year printed in L. R. Masson, *Les bourgeois de la Cie. du Nord-Ouest*, vol. I (Quebec, 1889). In any case, he spent most of his life at La Pointe, Madelaine Island, in what is now Wisconsin; and here he died in 1836. He married the daughter of White Crane, a hereditary chief of the Chippewa tribe; and by her he had several daughters, two of whom married in 1821 two New England traders named Warren. Another daughter married Léon St. Germain (q.v.). See note on Michel Cadot in *Wisconsin Historical Collections*, vol. XIX, pp. 69-70.

CAMERON, ÆNEAS (1757?-1822) was born, probably in Scotland, about 1757. The first reference to him in the literature of the fur-trade, so far as I can find, is his signature to the North West Company's agreement of 1802, as a wintering partner. His name reappears in the agreement of 1804; but about 1805 he appears to have returned to Montreal, and to have been employed thereafter in a financial capacity in the headquarters of the Company. He was elected to the Beaver Club in 1807, and he continued an active member until 1815. In 1812 he was appointed paymaster to the Corps of Canadian Voyageurs raised by the North West Company in that year. He died at Montreal on August 18, 1822, aged 65 years; and in 1825 it appeared that the firm of McTavish, McGillivrays and Co. owed his estate £13,343.

CAMERON, ANGUS (1782?-1876) was born in Scotland about 1782, and when a young man entered the service of the North West Company. Most of his life seems to have been spent in the Timiskaming district. At the time of the union of the North West and Hudson's Bay Companies in 1821, he was appointed a chief trader; and in 1838 he was promoted to be chief factor. In 1844 he returned to Scotland; and he died at his residence of Firhall, near Nairn, on August 11, 1876, aged 94 years. He must be distinguished from Angus Cameron, jr, who joined the North West Company as a clerk in 1819, was employed in the Timiskaming district until 1823, and retired from the fur-trade in 1825.

CAMERON, DUNCAN (1764?-1848) was born at Glenmoriston, Inverness-shire, Scotland, about 1764, the son of Alexander Cameron and Margaret McDonell. His parents emigrated to America when he was a child, and settled at Schenectady in New York. During the American Revolution they came north to Canada, and settled at Williamstown, Glengarry. In 1784 Duncan Cameron entered the service of the North West Company as a clerk to Angus Shaw (q.v.), and for many years he was employed in the Nipigon department. He was elected a partner of the North West Company about 1800; and until 1807 he was proprietor in charge at Nipigon. From 1807 to 1811 he was stationed at Lake Winnipeg; and from 1811 to 1814, at Rainy Lake. In 1814, he was placed in charge of the Red River department; and it fell to him to deal with the situation created by the establishment of the Selkirk colony. He was taken prisoner by the officers of the Hudson's Bay Company in the attack on Fort Gibraltar in April, 1816, and was sent to England, by way of Hudson Bay, for trial. In England he was released, and obtained damages from the Hudson's Bay Company for false imprisonment. About 1820 he returned to Canada, and settled at Williamstown, Glengarry; and in 1824 he was elected to represent Glengarry in the Legislative Assembly of Upper Canada, but was unseated. He died at Williamstown on May 15, 1848, aged 84 years. In 1820 he married Margaret, daughter of Capt. McLeod of Hamer; and by her he had several children, one of whom later became Sir Roderick W. Cameron, of New York. Duncan Cameron's *Nipigon Journal* and his *Sketch of the customs of the natives of the Nipigon country* have been printed in L. R. Masson, *Les bourgeois de la Cie du Nord-Ouest* (2nd series, Quebec, 1890).

CAMERON, JOHN DUGALD (1777?-1857) was a brother of the Hon. Duncan Cameron (d. 1838), for many years secretary and registrar of Upper Canada, and was born about 1777. He entered the service of the North West Company about 1795; and for many years was a clerk in the Nipigon district. In 1811 he was placed in charge of the Lake Winnipeg district; and in 1813 he was made a partner of the North West Company. He took little part in the struggle between the North West Company and the Hudson's Bay Company; and on the union of the companies in 1821, he was appointed a chief factor. He became a great favourite with Sir George Simpson, who described him as "a happy fellow, nothing seems to concern him, and an excellent well-meaning man he is". Some glimpses of him may be obtained from the *Letters of Rev. James Evans*, edited by F. Landon (Ont. Hist. Soc., *Papers and Records*, XXVIII, 1932). He retired from the fur-trade in 1844, and settled at Grafton, near Cobourg, Upper Canada. Here he died on March 21, 1857, at the age of 80 years. By his Indian wife he had several children.

CAMERON, RONALD (*fl.* 1793-1817) first appears in the literature of the fur-trade as a clerk in the service of David and Peter Grant (q.v.) in their opposition to the North West Company in 1793-5. Later, he appears as a clerk of the North West Company at Nipigon in 1797, together with John Dugald Cameron (q.v.). In 1806 he was a clerk on the Montreal River; and in 1808 he was admitted a partner of the North West Company. From 1807 to 1815 he was proprietor at Lac des Isles; and in August, 1817, Ross Cox (q.v.) met him at Fort William. He died some time between 1817 and 1821.

CAMPBELL, COLIN (1787-1853) was born at River Beaudette, Lake St. Francis, in Glengarry, Canada, on November 25, 1787, the son of Alexander Campbell, a United Empire Loyalist, who represented Cornwall in the first legislature of Upper Canada, and his wife Magdalena Van Sice. He entered the service of the North West Company as a clerk in 1804, doubtless through the influence of his elder brother, John Duncan Campbell (q.v.). He spent most of his life in the Athabaska district. In 1813 Daniel Williams Harmon (q.v.) met him at Dunvegan; and he was described as an accountant in the Athabaska in 1816. He was taken over by the Hudson's Bay Company in 1821, and he remained in the Athabaska district until 1846. In 1828 he was promoted to be chief trader; but he never attained the rank of chief factor. After several years spent in charge of the Kenogamissee district he retired from the fur-trade on June 1, 1853; and a few months later he died, on November 9, 1853, at the Red River Settlement. He married Elizabeth, daughter of the Hon. John McGillivray (q.v.). For much of the information contained in this sketch, I am indebted to Mr. J. D. Campbell, of Cornwall, Ontario.

CAMPBELL, JOHN DUNCAN (1773-1835) was born at Scoharie, New York, on February 21, 1773, the son of Alexander Campbell and Magdalena Van Sice. His parents emigrated to Canada, as United Empire Loyalists, during the American Revolution, and settled ultimately at Cornwall, which Alexander Campbell represented in the first legislature of Upper Canada. John Duncan Campbell entered the employ of the North West Company as clerk some time before 1799, when he appears as a clerk at Upper Fort des Prairies. For most of his service he was stationed, however, in the English River department. He was admitted a partner of the North West Company in 1803, and from that date to 1819 he was in charge of this department. In 1809 he was elected a member of the Beaver Club. After the Selkirk troubles, he was arrested by officers of the Hudson's Bay Company at the Grand Rapid on June 18, 1819, was taken, with Benjamin Frobisher (q.v.), to Hudson Bay, was kept a prisoner for several months, and then brought down to Canada under guard, and released. (See S. H. Wilcocke, *The death of B. Frobisher*, in L. R. Masson, *Les bourgeois de la Cie. du Nord-Ouest*, 2nd series, Quebec, 1890.) On the union of the North West and Hudson's Bay Companies in 1821, he retired from the fur-trade, and settled in Cornwall, Upper Canada. Here he died on May 6, 1835. He married Elizabeth, daughter of John Macdonald of Garth (q.v.) and his Indian wife Nancy, daughter of Patrick Small (q.v.); and by her he had several children. For much of the above information I am indebted to one of his descendants, Mr. J. D. Campbell, of Cornwall, Ontario.

CAMPION, ETIENNE (1737-1795) was born in Montreal on January 15, 1737, the son of Etienne Campion. He became an Indian trader, and first wintered in the Indian country in 1753. With his younger brother Alexis, he engaged in the Illinois trade after the British conquest of Canada. He signed the agreement for a general store at Michilimackinac in 1779; and his name constantly appears in the Michilimackinac register between the years 1765 and 1794. He was a charter member of the Beaver Club in Montreal in 1787; and in his later years he was a member of the firm of Grant, Campion and Co. He died in Montreal in December, 1795. His will, which is dated December 19, 1795, and is witnessed by Richard Dobie (q.v.) and Samuel Gerrard (q.v.), is in the Montreal Court House.

CHABOILLEZ, CHARLES (1772-1812) was born in Montreal in 1772, the son of Charles Jean Baptiste Chaboillez (q.v.), and was educated at the College of Montreal. He entered the service of the North West Company about 1793, when his sister married Simon McTavish (q.v.); and he became a partner of the Company before 1799. For many years he was in the Red River and Assiniboine district; but from 1807 to 1809 he was at the Pic, on Lake Superior. He retired from the fur-trade in 1809, and was elected a member of the Beaver Club of Montreal. He died at St. Henri de Mascouche, Lower Canada, and was buried at Terrebonne, on December 29, 1812. He brought back with him from the West four half-breed children, who were baptized at Terrebonne in 1811; and the same year he married Jessy Dunbar Selby Bruyères, daughter of Capt. John Bruce, adjutant of the 10th Veteran Battalion, but he had by her no children. See E. Z. Massicotte, *Les Chaboillez* (Bull. rech. hist., vol. XXVIII, 1922).

CHABOILLEZ, CHARLES JEAN BAPTISTE (1736-1808) was born at or near Michilimackinac in 1736, the eldest son of Charles Chaboillez, a fur-trader, and Marie Anne, daughter of Jean Baptiste Chevalier. He engaged in the fur-trade, and his name occurs repeatedly in the fur-trade licences from 1769 to 1787. The statement has been repeatedly made that he became a partner in the North West Company; but I can find no evidence of this. It is clear that he has been hopelessly confused with his son Charles (q.v.). He died in Montreal on September 25, 1808. In 1769 he married Marguerite (d. 1798), daughter of Jacques Larchevêque *dit* La Promenade; and by her he had two sons and seven daughters. One of his daughters, Marie Marguerite, married in 1793 Simon McTavish (q.v.); another, Adelaide, married Joseph Bouchette; and a third, Marie Louise Rachel, married in 1803 the Hon. Roderick McKenzie (q.v.). For further details, see E. Z. Massicotte, *Les Chaboillez* (Bull. rech. hist., vol. XXVIII, 1922).

CLARKE, JOHN (1781-1852) was born in Montreal, Canada, in 1781, the son of Simon Clarke and Ann Waldorf. He entered the service of the North West Company as a clerk in 1800, and served successively on the Mackenzie River and on the Peace River. In 1810 he left the North West Company, and joined the Pacific Fur Company of John Jacob Astor, who appears to have been a relative of his mother. In 1811 he commanded the second expedition to Fort Astoria, and he was present in 1812 when the Fort was surrendered to the Nor' Westers. On his return to Canada in 1814 he took service with Lord Selkirk; and during the years 1815-19 he was the leader in the opposition which the Hudson's Bay Company offered the Nor' Westers along the Peace River. At the time of the union of the two companies, in 1821, he was made a chief factor. He retired from the fur-trade in 1830; and he spent the rest of his days in Montreal. Here he died in 1852. He was twice married, first, to a half-breed named Sapphira Spence, who died shortly afterwards; and second, in 1821, to Marian Tranclar, of Neufchâtel, Switzerland, by whom he had four sons and four daughters. For further details, see Adèle Clarke, *Old Montreal: John Clarke, his adventures, friends, and family* (Montreal, 1906), which must, however, be used with caution.

COLTMAN, WILLIAM BACHELER (d. 1826) was a merchant of Quebec who was appointed in 1812 a member of the Executive Council of Lower Canada. In 1816 he was made by Sir John Coape Sherbrooke, the governor, a commissioner to investigate the disturbances in the Indian countries; and in 1817 he visited the Red River Settlement. His report was printed in a blue-book entitled *Papers relating to the Red River Settlement* (London, 1819), and has been reprinted in the *Collections of the State Historical Society of North Dakota*, vol. IV (Fargo, N.D., 1913). He died on January 2, 1826.

CONOLLY, WILLIAM (1787?-1849) was born at Lachine, near Montreal, about 1787, and entered the service of the North West Company as a clerk about 1801. In the winter of 1803-4 he was at Rat River House. He was made a partner of the North West Company about 1818; and in 1819 he was in charge of Cumberland House, where he received Franklin on his first expedition to the Arctic. At the union of the North West and Hudson's Bay Companies in 1821, he was made a chief trader; and in 1825 he was promoted to the rank of chief factor. From 1824 to 1831 he was in charge of the district of New Caledonia; and in 1831 he retired from the fur-trade. He died at Montreal on June 3, 1849. In 1803 he married, "according to the custom of the country", a Cree woman named Susanne; and by her he had six children, one of whom became in 1828 the wife of James (afterwards Sir James) Douglas. In 1823, however, Conolly repudiated his Indian wife, having been advised by the Church that an Indian marriage was not valid, and married in Montreal his cousin, Julia Woolrich, the daughter of a wealthy Montreal merchant, by whom he had several children. His Indian wife was sent to a convent on the Red River, where she was supported, first by Conolly himself, and after his death by his white wife. On the death of the Indian wife, the eldest of Conolly's half breed sons, then a middle-aged man, brought suit in the courts to obtain his share of Conolly's estate. The Canadian courts ruled that the Indian marriage was valid; but the case was carried to the Judicial Committee of the Privy Council, and before judgment was given the case was settled out of court. An account of the litigation over Conolly's estate will be found in the *Lower Canada Jurist*, vol. 11, pp. 197 ff. Some account of Conolly's life will be found in Ross Cox, *Adventures on the Columbia*, p. 285.

CORRY, THOMAS (d. 1792) was one of the earliest fur-traders to penetrate to the valley of the Saskatchewan in the early days of British rule. He engaged in the fur-trade as early as 1767, when he obtained a licence to take two canoes to Kaministiquia, on Lake Superior. His guarantor was Isaac Todd (q.v.). He reached the Saskatchewan in 1771; and he spent the winters of 1771-2 and 1772-3 on the Saskatchewan. He did so well that he was able to retire with a competency. He settled first in Montreal, and then in L'Assomption, where he kept a shop from 1779 to 1785 or later. He died in Montreal on July 20, 1792, as appears from the Christ Church register. Between 1776 and 1785 there are noted in the Christ Church register the christenings of a number of Corry children, but whether these were the children of Thomas Corry is not certain.

COWIE, ROBERT (1795?-1859) was born about 1795 and entered the service of the North West Company about 1811. He was employed as a clerk and accountant, and was present at Fort William when it was captured by Lord Selkirk. He was clerk and accountant at Lachine from 1825 to 1829; and he was in charge of the affairs of McTavish, McGillivrays and Co. from 1825 to 1826, between the departure of Thomas Thain (q.v.) and the arrival of Sir George Simpson. He was appointed a chief trader in 1829, and he was employed consecutively at Portneuf, Fort Vancouver, and Moose Factory. He retired in 1846, and he died on June 6, 1859.

COX, ROSS (1793-1853) was born in Dublin, Ireland, in 1793, the son of Samuel Cox, of the Ordnance Office, and his wife Margaret Thorpe. He emigrated to America about 1811, and took service as a clerk in J. J. Astor's American Fur Company. He reached Astoria in the spring of 1812, and he was present at the surrender of Astoria to the North West Company in 1813. He then took service as a clerk with the North West Company; but he retired from the fur-trade in 1817, returning to Ireland by the overland route from the Columbia to Montreal. His *Adventures on the Columbia River* (London, 1831; 2nd ed., 1832; New York, 1832) is one of the most important documents relating to the later history of the North West Company. On his return to Dublin, he became the Irish correspondent of the London *Morning Herald* and a clerk in the Dublin Police Office. He died in Dublin in 1853. In 1819 he married in Dublin, Hannah Cumming; and by her he had a large family. For the above information, I am indebted largely to his grandchildren, the Rev. Samuel A. Cox, M.A. (T.C.D.), vicar of Great Coxwell, Faringdon, Berks., England, and Miss Thyrza Cox, of Melbourne, Australia.

CUMMING, CUTHBERT (1787-1870) was born in Banffshire, Scotland, in 1787, and
entered the service of the North West Company as a clerk at Fort Dauphin
in 1804. He was taken over as a clerk by the Hudson's Bay Company in
1821; and in 1827 he was promoted to be a chief trader. From 1821 to
1828 he was employed mainly in the Swan River department; in 1828 he
was moved to the Montreal department, and from 1831 to 1837 he was at
the Mingan Islands. From 1841 to 1843 he was at the Pic; and in 1843-4
he was back at Fort Pelly, in the Swan River district. In 1844 he resigned, and settled at Colborne, Ontario. Here he died on April 5, 1870,
aged 83 years. In 1842 he married at the Pic, Lake Superior, Jane,
daughter of Thomas McMurray (q.v.); and he was survived by his widow
and three sons.

DAVIS, JOHN (d. 1824) was a native of Clerkenwell, England, and entered the
service of the Hudson's Bay Company in 1801. He was made a chief
factor at the time of the union of 1821, and he returned to England on
furlough in 1822-3. In 1823-4 he was in charge at Lac Seul; and he was
drowned off the east point of Hannah Bay, in September, 1824, while on
his way from Moose Factory to take charge at Mistassini in the Rupert's
River district.

DEASE, CHARLES JOHNSON WATTS (*fl*. 1797-1826) was the youngest son of Dr.
John Dease, of the Indian department, a nephew of Sir William Johnson,
Bart., and was born at Côte des Neiges, near Montreal, on December 3,
1797. He entered the service of the North West Company as a clerk
in 1814, and was, after 1821, for several years a clerk in the Hudson's Bay
Company. In 1822-3 he was stationed in the Athabaska district; and
from 1824 to 1826 he was in the Mackenzie River district. In 1826 he
retired from the fur-trade, and returned to Canada.

DEASE, FRANCIS MICHAEL (1786-1864) was born at Niagara on August 10, 1786,
the third son of Dr. John Dease, of the Indian department, a nephew
of Sir William Johnson, Bart. During the War of 1812, he commanded
the Chippewas at the capture of Michilimackinac in July, 1812; and in
July, 1814, he took part in the engagement at Prairie-du-Chien as captain
commanding Dease's Mississippi Volunteers. On September 2, 1814, he
was appointed a captain in the Indian department; but in 1827 he entered
the service of the Hudson's Bay Company. In 1830 Sir George Simpson
reported in regard to him: "Has been in the service repeatedly, was a
clerk, but dull and unsteady, and placed as postmaster since he last
returned." He died at St. Boniface, on the Red River, on July 29,
1864. He was not married.

DEASE, JOHN WARREN (1783-1829) was born at Niagara on June 9, 1783, the
second son of Dr. John Dease, of the Indian department, a nephew of
Sir William Johnson, Bart. I have not been able to ascertain when he

entered the service of the North West Company, but in 1816 he was in charge of the important post of Rainy Lake. After the union of 1821 he was transferred to the Pacific slope, and was promoted to be a chief trader. He died at Fort Colville, in what is now the State of Washington, in December, 1829; and his will is on record at Hudson's Bay House, in London. He was elected a member of the Beaver Club in Montreal in 1815. He was twice married: first, to Mary Cadot, by whom he had two children, and secondly, to Jenny Benoist, by whom he had five children.

DEASE, PETER WARREN (1788-1863) was born at Michilimackinac on January 1, 1788, the fourth son of Dr. John Dease, of the Indian department, a nephew of Sir William Johnson, Bart. He was named after Sir Peter Warren, the captor of Louisbourg in 1745, who was an uncle of Sir William Johnson and of his grandmother. He entered the service of the XY Company in 1801; and for many years, after the XY and North West Companies were amalgamated, was stationed in the Mackenzie River district. At the time of the union of the Hudson's Bay and North West Companies in 1821, he was made a chief trader; and in 1826-7 he was in charge of the commissariat of Sir John Franklin's second expedition to the Arctic. In 1828 he was promoted to be chief factor; and in 1831 he was placed in charge of the district of New Caledonia. From 1836 to 1839 he was, with Thomas Simpson, in command of the expedition which explored the Arctic coast from the mouth of the Mackenzie River to Point Barrow; and for his services he is said to have been offered the honour of knighthood, but to have declined it. He retired from the fur-trade in 1842; and he is said to have received a pension of £100 a year from the British government. He settled on a farm at Côte Ste. Catherine, outside Montreal; and here he died on January 17, 1863. His son, Peter Warren Dease, jr., M.D., died at the same place on April 18, 1853. He was fond of music; and in the literature of the fur-trade there are several references to his violin, which he carried with him wherever he went. For some of the information contained in this sketch, I am indebted to Mr. F. J. Audet, of the Public Archives of Canada.

DOBIE, RICHARD (1731?-1805) was born in Scotland about 1731, and came to Canada about 1770. In 1785 he was described as "the principal merchant and inhabitant" of Montreal. He died in Montreal on March 25, 1805.

DOWIE, KENNETH (1798?-1866) was born about 1798, the youngest son of Capt. James Dowie, R.N., and Margaret Mackenzie, the younger sister of Sir Alexander Mackenzie (q.v.). He emigrated to Canada, and became ultimately a partner of the Hon. Peter McGill. He returned to England about 1825, and began business in Liverpool as a commission merchant. He died at 5 Southhill Road, Liverpool, on March 3, 1866, in his 69th year.

ELLICE, ALEXANDER (1743-1805) was born in 1743, and about 1765 emigrated to New York, where he purchased a partnership in a firm at Schenectady, later known as Phyn, Ellice and Co., which was interested in the fur-trade. In 1774 the headquarters of the firm were transferred to London and from 1774 to 1779 Alexander Ellice was the partner who looked after the affairs of the firm in Montreal. In 1779 he returned to London, leaving the Montreal office in charge of his younger brother Robert (q.v.); and he died in London on September 29, 1805, possessed of considerable wealth. His will is on file at Somerset House in London. He married a daughter of George Phyn, laird of the Corse of Monelly in Scotland, and thus became the brother-in-law of James Phyn (q.v.), and the uncle by marriage of the Hon. John Forsyth (q.v.) and the Hon. John Richardson (q.v.). For an account of the history of the firm of Phyn, Ellice and Co., see R. H. Fleming, *Phyn, Ellice and Company of Schenectady* (Contributions to Canadian Economics, 1932).

ELLICE, EDWARD (1781-1863) was born in 1781, the third son of Alexander Ellice (q.v.). He was educated at Marischall College, Aberdeen (B.A., 1797; M.A., 1800); and he became a partner in the firm of Phyn, Ellices and Inglis, which had become interested in the XY Company in Canada. He was sent to Canada about 1803, and in 1804 became a party to the union of the XY and North West Companies. He became a partner in the North West Company, and during the struggle with Lord Selkirk he played a not unimportant part. He was the anonymous author of *The communications of Mercator* (Montreal, 1817), in which the claims of the North West Company were upheld. In 1820-21, he was, with William and Simon McGillivray (q.v.), active in bringing about the union of the North West and the Hudson's Bay Companies; and it was actually with him and the McGillivrays that the union was negotiated. On the death of William McGillivray (q.v.) and the failure of the firm of McTavish, McGillivrays, and Co. in 1825, he became the only member of the trio who stood between the Hudson's Bay Company and the claims of the discontented members of the North West Company; and he became involved in a series of litigations which lasted for a quarter of a century. He was made a member of the Committee of the Hudson's Bay Company, however, and a fund, known as The North West Partners' Trust Fund, was set aside to satisfy the claims of those who had just claims on the North West Company. It has frequently been said that he became a deputy-governor of the Hudson's Bay Company, but this is a mistake. It was his son Edward who occupied this position; and it was the son who became in 1857 a member of the committee of the British House of Commons appointed to inquire into the affairs of the Hudson's Bay Company. But the father came to play a conspicuous part in English politics. From 1818 to 1826, and from 1830 to 1863, he represented Coventry in the House of Commons; and from 1830 to 1832 he was Secretary to the Treasury in Earl Grey's government, and from 1832 to 1834 Secretary of

War. He died at Ardochy, on his estate in Glengarry, Scotland, on September 17, 1863. He was known as "Bear" Ellice, probably from his connection with the Canadian fur-trade. In 1809 he married Lady Hannah Altheah Bettesworth (d. 1832), widow of Captain Bettesworth, R.N., and youngest sister of the second Earl Grey, and by her he had one son, Edward. In 1843 he married secondly Lady Leicester, widow of the first Earl of Leicester; and she died in 1844.

ELLICE, JAMES (d. 1787) was a younger brother of Alexander Ellice (q.v.) who was left in Schenectady, in charge of the affairs of Phyn, Ellice and Company in 1775, after the headquarters of the firm were transferred to London. After suffering "heavy suspicion" and "close confinement", he was allowed to take the oath of allegiance to the State of New York in 1779. He remained for several years in charge of the declining affairs of the Schenectady office of the firm, until his death in Montreal on October 15, 1787. For further details, see R. H. Fleming, *Phyn, Ellice and Company of Schenectady* (Contributions to Canadian Economics, 1932).

ELLICE, ROBERT (d. 1790) was a younger brother of Alexander Ellice (q.v.) who was taken into the firm of Phyn, Ellice and Co. in Schenectady in 1768. From 1779 to 1790 he was in charge of the Montreal office of the firm, which was known as Robert Ellice and Co., and in 1787 he became a partner in the London firm of Phyn, Ellices, and Inglis. He died in 1790. For further details, see R. H. Fleming, *Phyn, Ellice and Company of Schenectady* (Contributions to Canadirn Economics, 1932).

ERMATINGER, CHARLES OAKES (1780?-1853) was born about 1780, a son of Lawrence Ermatinger (q.v.) and Jemima Oakes (d. 1809), a sister of Forrest Oakes (q.v.). He became an Indian trader, and lived for many years at Sault Ste. Marie. In 1805 he was admitted a partner of the North West Company, to begin with the outfit of 1808; and he acted as an agent of the North West Company at Sault Ste. Marie for several years. His later days were spent on the island of Montreal, where he bought a property at Elmwood, Long Point; and here he died on September 4, 1853. He married an Indian woman, named Charlotte Kallawabide, who died at Philipsburgh on July 9, 1850, aged 65 years; and by her he had three snos, Charles Oakes, William, and James, and four daughters, Frances, Jemima, Jane, and Ann. His eldest son, Capt. Charles Oakes Ermatinger, died at Montreal on January 14, 1857, aged 55 years.

ERMATINGER, EDWARD (1797-1876) was born on the island of Elba, in the Mediterranean Sea, in February, 1797, the son of Lawrence Edward Ermatinger, the eldest son of Lawrence Ermatinger (q.v.). His father was employed in the commissariat of the British Army, under the patronage of his relative, Sir Hildebrand Oakes (see *Dict. Nat. Biog.*). Edward Ermatinger was educated in England, and in 1818 he was, with his brother Francis (q.v.) apprenticed to the Hudson's Bay Company. He remained in the service of the Company for ten years; but in 1830 he retired from the fur-trade, and settled at St. Thomas, Upper Canada. Here he died in 1876. He was the author of a *Life of Colonel Talbot* (St. Thomas, C. W., 1859); and his *York Factory express journal* has been edited by his son, Judge C. O. Ermatinger (Trans. Roy. Soc. Can., 1912).

ERMATINGER, FRANCIS (1798-1858) was born in Lisbon, Portugal, in 1798, the son of Lawrence Edward Ermatinger. He was educated in England, and, with his brother Edward (q.v.) was apprenticed to the Hudson's Bay Company in 1818. He spent between thirty and forty years in the service of the Company, mostly on the Pacific coast; and was promoted to the rank of chief trader in 1841. He was described by Sir George Simpson (q.v.) in 1830 as "a bustling, active, boisterous fellow". He retired from the Company in 1853; and he died at St. Thomas, Canada West, on August 12, 1868.

ERMATINGER, LAWRENCE (d. 1789) was a Swiss merchant who appears to have made his way from London to Canada in the early days of British rule. An Ermatinger child (Ann Mary) was born in Montreal in 1766. In 1770 Lawrence Ermatinger was declared a bankrupt in London; but he evidently succeeded in re-establishing himself in Canada, for his name appears in the fur-trade licences as trading to Grand Portage between 1779 and 1783. He died in Montreal on October 6, 1789. He married Jemima Oakes (d. 1809), the sister of Forrest Oakes (q.v.); and by her he had several children.

FARIES, HUGH (1779-1852) was born in Montreal in 1779, the son of Hugh Faries and Mary Warfinger. He entered the service of the North West Company as a clerk, and in 1804-6 was at Rainy Lake. He was one of the first officers of the Company to cross the Rocky Mountains, and in 1807 was the first master of Fort George in New Caledonia. Later, from 1812 to 1817, he was at Cumberland House on the Saskatchewan. At the union of the North West and Hudson's Bay Companies in 1821, he was made a chief trader; and from 1821 to 1826 he was employed in the Peace River district. In 1827 he was proposed as a member of the Beaver Club in Montreal. From 1827 to 1837 he was stationed in the Kenogamissie district; and he was promoted to the rank of chief factor in 1838. He retired from the fur-trade in 1840; and he died at Berthier, Canada East, on March 23, 1852. His Rainy Lake journal for 1804-5 has been published, with annotations, in C. M. Gates (ed.), *Five fur-traders of the Northwest* (Minneapolis, 1933).

FINLAY, JACO (d. 1828) was a half-breed son of James Finlay, sr. (q.v.). He became a clerk of the North West Company, and in 1806 was in charge of an outpost of Rocky Mountain House, on the Kootenay Plain. In 1810 or 1811 he built Spokane House on the Spokane River. He died at Spokane in May, 1828.

FINLAY, JAMES (d. 1797) was a native of Scotland who came to Canada in the early days of British rule. Here he engaged in the fur-trade, and the date on the medal given him by the Beaver Club of Montreal, of which he became a charter member in 1785, shows him to have wintered in the Indian country as early as 1766. He was the first of the "Old Subjects" to reach the valley of the Saskatchewan, and in 1768 he built what was known as Finlay's House near Neepawin. Later, he entered into partnership with a young Englishman named John Gregory (q.v.); and from 1773 to 1783 the firm of Finlay and Gregory appears in the fur-trade licences as sending canoes to the West. It was in the service of this firm that Sir Alexander Mackenzie (q.v.) served his apprenticeship in the fur-trade. In 1783, James Finlay retired from the fur-trade; and in his later years he was inspector of chimneys in Montreal. He died in Montreal in 1797. He married in Montreal, apparently, about 1765, Christiana Youel; and by her he had two sons, James (q.v.) and John (q.v.), and two daughters, Anne and Christy, the latter of whom became the wife of Capt. Edward Townsend Jones of the 34th Foot.

FINLAY, JAMES (1766-1830) was born in Montreal in 1766, the son of James Finlay (q.v.) and Christiana Youel. He entered the service of the "Little Company", in opposition to the North West Company, as an apprentice clerk, in 1784, at the same time as the Hon. Roderick Mackenzie (q.v.). He became a clerk of the North West Company in 1787, and in 1792 he was made a wintering partner of the Company, in charge of Fort de l'Isle, on the Saskatchewan. He relinquished his two shares in the Company in 1805, and in 1814 he was a merchant at Belœil on the River Chambly, in Lower Canada. From 1814 to 1817 he was store-keeper of the Indian department at Lachine, and in 1817 he petitioned for the position formerly held by his father as inspector of chimneys at Montreal. He died at Montreal on January 3, 1830. In 1798 he married Elizabeth Grant, daughter of John Grant (q.v.), and granddaughter of Richard Dobie (q.v.); and by her he had "a large family". His daughter Elizabeth married on March 26, 1835, Frederick, son of Sir John Chetwode, Bart., of Oakley Park, Cheshire.

FINLAY, JOHN (1774-1833) was born in Montreal in 1774, the son of James Finlay (q.v.) and Christiana Youel. He became a clerk of the North West Company in 1789, and in 1792 was with Alexander Mackenzie (q.v.) on the Peace River. By 1799 he had been admitted to partnership in the Company, and was proprietor in charge of Lake Athabaska. He signed the agreement of 1802; but he retired from the fur-trade in 1804, and in 1805 he relinquished one of his two shares in the Company. In 1807 he was elected a member of the Beaver Club in Montreal; and in 1827 he presided over the last meeting of the Club. He obtained an appointment as deputy assistant commissary-general at Montreal; and he died at Montreal on December 19, 1833, aged 59 years.

OF THE NOR' WESTERS

FINLAYSON, DUNCAN (1795-1862) was born at Dingwall, Scotland, in 1795, the son of John Finlayson, later of Montreal, and younger brother of Nicol Finlayson (q.v.). He entered the service of the Hudson's Bay Company in 1815. He was promoted to the rank of chief factor in 1831, and was in that year in charge at Red River. From 1833 to 1837 he was on the Columbia; from 1839 to 1844 he was governor of Assiniboia; and in 1844 he succeeded James Keith (q.v.) in charge at Lachine. He retired from the Company in 1855, but was reappointed, and retired finally only in 1859. He died in London, England, on July 25, 1862. He was a brother-in-law of Lady Simpson, the wife of Sir George Simpson.

FINLAYSON, NICOL (1794-1877) was born at Foderty, Rossshire, Scotland, in 1794, the son of John Finlayson, later of Montreal, and elder brother of Duncan Finlayson (q.v.). He entered the service of the Hudson's Bay Company in 1815. He was promoted to the rank of chief trader in 1833, and to that of chief factor in 1846. He retired from the Company in 1855, and he died in 1877.

FINLAYSON, RODERICK (1818-1892) was born in the parish of Lochalsh, Rossshire, Scotland, on March 16, 1818, and was probably a relative of Duncan Finlayson (q.v.). He came to America in 1837, and entered the service of the Hudson's Bay Company as a clerk. In 1839 he was sent across the Rocky Mountains to the Pacific slope; and here he spent most of the rest of his life. He was at Fort Simpson, on the Mackenzie River, in 1842; but in 1843 he returned to the Pacific coast, and he took part in the founding of Fort Victoria. For many years he was in charge of this post, and may be described as "the founder of Victoria". He was promoted to the rank of chief trader in 1850, and to that of chief factor in 1859. From 1851 to 1863 he was a member of the Legislative Council of Victoria Island. He retired from the Company's service in 1872; and he died at Victoria, British Columbia, on January 30, 1892. His unpublished autobiography, covering the years from 1837 to 1851, is in the Provincial Archives of British Columbia.

FISHER, ALEXANDER (1783?-1847) was born about 1783, and was possibly the son of Alexander Fisher, the first judge of the Midland district of Upper Canada. In any case, he appears from his will, which is preserved in Hudson's Bay House in London, to have come from the neighbourhood of Kingston, Upper Canada. He entered the service of the North West Company as a clerk some years before the union of 1821, and he was taken over as a clerk by the Hudson's Bay Company in that year. In 1823 he was promoted to the rank of chief trader; and he retired from the Company's service in 1845. He died on April 2, 1847. He is not to be confused with another Alexander Fisher, who entered the service of the North West Company in 1815, and was taken over by the Hudson's Bay Company in 1821, but retired from the fur trade in 1824.

FLETCHER, JOHN (1787-1844) was born in England in 1787, and was called to the English bar. He came to Canada in 1810, and began the practice of law in Quebec. In 1816 he was appointed a commissioner, with the Hon. W. B. Coltman (q.v.), for the purpose of investigating the disturbances in the Indian country; but he did not go farther west than Fort William. In 1823 he was appointed provincial judge of the district of St. Francis; and he died at Sherbrooke, in the Eastern Townships, on October 11, 1844. A fuller sketch of his life will be found in the *Church*, October 25, 1844.

FORSYTH, GEORGE (1755-1806) was the eldest son of William Forsyth, of Huntly, Scotland, and Jean, daughter of George Phyn, laird of the Corse of Monelly, Aberdeenshire, and was born in Scotland on April 2, 1855. He came to Canada; and was a merchant at Niagara. He died at Niagara on September 15, 1806. He married a wife named Tenbroeck, who died at Niagara in 1817; and by her he had a daughter, Mary Ann, who lived later at Brechin, Scotland, and who died, unmarried, about 1862.

FORSYTH, JAMES (1759-1843) was born in Scotland on June 23, 1759, the fourth son of William Forsyth and Jean Phyn, of Huntly. He was in Canada for a short time, in the firm of Forsyth, Richardson and Co., but returned to England, and became a member of Lloyds. He died in 1843.

FORSYTH, JOHN (1762-1837) was born in Scotland on December 8, 1762, the sixth son of William Forsyth, of Huntly, and Jean, daughter of George Phyn, laird of the Corse of Monelly. His mother's sister married Alexander Ellice (q.v.); her brother George married the sister of Edward Ellice (q.v.); another brother, James (q.v.), became the head of the firm of Phyn, Inglis, and Ellice, in London; and another sister was the mother of the Hon. John Richardson (q.v.). John Forsyth emigrated to Canada in 1779, and about 1790 he became the head of the firm of Forsyth, Richardson and Co., which was one of the firms behind the so-called XY Company, and which acquired an interest in the North West Company in 1804. In 1827 he was appointed a member of the Legislative Council of Lower Canada, and he continued a legislative councillor of the province until his death in London on December 29, 1837. He died at Morley's Hotel, which used to stand at the south-west corner of Trafalgar Square; and he was buried in Kensal Green. He married Margaret, the daughter of Charles Grant (q.v.); and by her he had two sons and one daughter. The elder son, William, married his cousin, Eweretta Jane, daughter of Joseph Forsyth (q.v.), and later assumed the name of Forsyth-Grant. The younger, John Blackwood, married Mary, daughter of Samuel Gerrard (q.v.); and the daughter, Jane Prescott, married George Gregory, the son of John Gregory (q.v.). For the above information I am indebted to Capt. Forsyth-Grant, M.C., of Ecclesgreig, near Montrose, Scotland.

FORSYTH, JOSEPH (1764-1813) was the seventh son of William Forsyth of Huntly and Jean Phyn, and was born on January 24, 1764. He came to Canada about 1784, and became a merchant in Kingston, Upper Canada. He died in Kingston in September, 1813. He married, first, the daughter of one Bell, by whom he had a son, William, who died unmarried; and second, he married in Kingston, Alicia, daughter of James Robins, by whom he had three sons and three daughters, descendants of some of whom are still living. For this information I am indebted to Capt. Forsyth-Grant of Ecclesgreig, near Montrose, Scotland.

FORSYTH, THOMAS (1761-1832) was the fifth son of William Forsyth of Huntly and his wife Jean Phyn, and was born on March 2, 1761. He came to Canada before 1784, and became a partner in the firm of Forsyth, Richardson and Co. About 1804 he returned to England, and he died there, unmarried, on March 19, 1832.

FRANCHÈRE, GABRIEL (1786-1863) was born at Montreal, Canada, on November 3, 1786, the son of Gabriel Franchère, a merchant. In 1810 he took service with the Pacific Fur Company of John Jacob Astor; and in 1811 he took part in the founding of Astoria. After the surrender of Astoria to the North West Company in 1813, he entered the service of the North West Company, but only long enough to enable him to return overland to Montreal in 1814. In 1820 he published his *Relation d'un voyage à la côte du nordouest de l'Amérique septentrionale dans les années 1810, 11, 12, 13, et 14* (Montreal, 1820; Eng. trans. by J. V. Huntington, New York, 1854). In his later years, he lived, successively, at Sault Ste. Marie, at St. Louis, and at New York. He died on April 12, 1863, at St. Paul, Minnesota. In 1815 he married Sophie (d. 1837), daughter of J. B. Routhier; and by her he had several children.

FRASER, ALEXANDER (1761?-1837) was born at Murray Bay, Canada, about 1761, the eldest son of Malcolm Fraser, the seignior of Murray Bay, and Marie Allaire. He entered the service of the North West Company as a clerk prior to 1789, possibly through the influence of Simon Fraser, sr., a merchant of Quebec, known as "the Bonhomme", who was his father's financial agent, and was a cousin of Simon McTavish (q.v.). He seems to have been employed mainly in the English River district. In 1789-90 he wintered at the Côte des Serpents; in 1797 he was in charge of the post to which David Thompson (q.v.) came, when he transferred from the service of the Hudson's Bay Company to that of the North West Company; and in 1799 he is described as "proprietor, Lower English River". He must, therefore, have become a partner of the North West Company before 1799. In 1801 he went to Montreal on leave; and in 1802-3 he was "employed as a partner assisting the Company's concerns in the King's Posts and Hudson's Bay". In 1804 he returned to the North West; but he retired from the fur-trade about 1806, and settled at Rivière-du-Loup. He had bought the seigniory of Rivière-du-Loup-en-Bas in 1802; and he lived here until his death on June 14, 1837. He married in the Indian country an Indian wife, known as Angélique Meadows (d. 1833); and by her he had one son and three daughters. After settling down at Rivière-du-Loup, and while his Indian wife was living, in Indian fashion, at the Point at Rivière-du-Loup, he married, secondly, Pauline Michaud, and by her he had seven children. On his death a prolonged litigation over his estate took place between the children of his white and his Indian wife; and this was terminated only when in 1884 the courts adjudged his marriage to his Indian wife valid. For further details about his family, see W. S. Wallace, *Notes on the family of Malcolm Fraser of Murray Bay* (Bull. rech. hist., XXXIX, 267-71).

FRASER, PAUL (d. 1855) was a brother of Colonel the Hon. Alexander Fraser of Fraserfield, Glengarry, Upper Canada, and entered the service of the North West Company in 1819. He was taken over as a clerk by the Hudson's Bay Company in 1821; and from 1822 to 1824 he was stationed on Lesser Slave Lake. From 1825 to 1832 he was in the Athabaska department, latterly in charge of Fort Vermilion; and in 1832 he was transferred to New Caledonia, and he spent the rest of his life there. He was promoted to the rank of chief trader in 1843; and he died on July 29, 1855. His will is preserved in Hudson's Bay House in London.

FRASER, RICHARD DUNCAN (1783?-1857) was born about 1783, the son of Capt. Thomas Fraser, a United Empire Loyalist. He entered the service of the North West Company when a young man, and in 1805 was a clerk at Lake Nipigon. He seems to have left the service of the Company, however, before 1812; and he died at Frasersfield, Edwardsburgh, Canada West, on April 1, 1857, aged 75 years. He married Mary Macdonell, who died at Brockville, Ont., on October 27, 1871, in her 80th year; and by her he had several children.

FRASER, SIMON (*fl.* 1766-1804), known as Simon Fraser, Sr., or "Bonhomme" Fraser, was born in Scotland, the cousin of Simon McTavish (q.v.). He came to Canada prior to 1766, and became a merchant in Quebec. He seems to have been for a time the Quebec agent of the North West Company, and certainly he had close business relations with the Company. But, after the death of his son Simon (q.v.), he returned to Scotland; and he was living in Perth in 1805. In 1804 Simon McTavish left him in his will an annuity.

FRASER, SIMON (d. 1796), known as Simon Fraser, jr., was the son of Simon Fraser, sr. (q.v.), of Quebec. About 1795 he appears to have become a partner in the North West Company; but he died in London, England, "at the house of Mr. Young, New Street, Bishopsgate", on April 11, 1796. He may have been the Simon Fraser who married Geneviève Lefebvre in Montreal in 1770. In any case, he left behind him two orphaned daughters.

FRASER, SIMON (1760?-1839) was born about 1760, probably in the parish of Boleskine, Stratherrick, Invernessshire, Scotland, the son of Capt. Alexander Fraser. He came to Canada, and entered the fur-trade prior to the year 1789, when he and Toussaint Lesieur (q.v.) took the posts of Rivière des Trembles and Portage de l'Isle on a sort of lease from the North West Company. He appears to have become a partner of the North West Company about 1795; and in 1797 he was in charge at Grand Portage. He retired from the fur-trade about 1800; and in 1805 he relinquished his two shares in the North West Company. He was elected a member of the Beaver Club in Montreal in 1803, and he continued an active member until 1816. In 1807 he purchased from John Gregory (q.v.) the fief Bellevue, on the Lake of Two Mountains; and he lived here until the house in which he lived was burned in 1820, when he bought a property at Ste. Anne's on the island of Montreal, where he lived until his death at Ste. Anne's, on May 6, 1839. In 1804 he married Catherine (d. 1846), daughter of Donald McKay, and sister of William, Alexander, and Donald McKay (q.v.); and by her he had five sons and three daughters. In his obituary notice in the *Quebec Gazette*, he is described as "formerly a partner of the North West Company, and subsequently one of the firm of Fraser, Caldwell, and Co., of Albany". He would appear to have been a connection of Simon McTavish (q.v.), for McTavish came from the same locality in Scotland, signed his marriage register, and was a trustee in his marriage contract, while he witnessed in 1804 McTavish's will. For much of the information contained in this sketch, I am indebted to his grand-daughter, Mrs. M. S. Blaiklock, of Montreal.

FRASER, SIMON (1776-1862) was born at Bennington, New York, in 1776, the youngest son of Capt. Simon Fraser of Guisachan and Isabella Grant, daughter of the laird of Daldreggan. His father, who joined the Loyalist forces during the American Revolution, was captured by the revolutionists, and died in prison at Albany. His mother came to Canada, and ultimately settled near Cornwall. Simon Fraser, the son, was educated at Montreal, where his uncle, John Fraser, was a judge of the Court of Common Pleas; and in 1792 he was apprenticed to the North West Company. He was employed in the Athabaska department as early as 1799; and he continued to be attached to this department until 1805. In 1801 he was elected a partner of the North West Company; and in 1805 he was placed in charge of the Company's operations beyond the Rocky Mountains. In 1808 he explored to its mouth the river that bears his name; and the journal of his exploration has been published in L. R. Masson, *Les bourgeois de la Cie. du Nord-Ouest*, vol. I (Quebec, 1889). In 1816 he took charge of the Red River department; and in 1817 he was one of those arrested by Lord Selkirk as an accessory to the massacre at Seven Oaks. He retired from the North West Company before 1820, and settled at St. Andrew's, near Cornwall, Upper Canada. Here he died on April 19, 1862, aged 86 years. He was a Roman Catholic, whereas most of the other Frasers in the fur-trade were Protestants. After he returned from the West, he married a daughter of Allan Macdonell, at Matilda, Upper Canada. An account of his life will be found in W. N. Sage, *Simon Fraser, explorer and fur-trader* (Proceedings of the Pacific Coast Branch of the Amer. Hist. Assoc., 1929).

FROBISHER, BENJAMIN (1742?-1787) was born in Yorkshire, England, about 1742. He emigrated to Canada, and embarked in the fur-trade as early as 1765, in partnership with John Welles; and he was later associated in turn with James McGill (q.v.), Richard Dobie (q.v.), and his brothers Joseph (q.v.) and Thomas (q.v.). So far as I can discover, he never went west of Grand Portage; but looked after the Montreal end of the business of Frobisher and Co., in which his brothers were partners with him. He died at Montreal on April 14, 1787.

FROBISHER, BENJAMIN (1782-1819) was born in Montreal in 1782, the son of Joseph Frobisher (q.v.). He entered the service of the North West Company in 1799, and in that year was a clerk at Lake Winnipeg. From 1804 to 1808 he represented the county of Montreal in the Legislative Assembly of Lower Canada. In 1819, during the Selkirk troubles, he was captured by the Hudson's Bay men, was carried to York Factory, and perished from exhaustion at Cedar Lake in an attempt to escape to a North West Company post. An account of his death is to be found in S. H. Wilcocke, "Death of B. Frobisher", in L. R. Masson, *Les bourgeois de la Compagnie du Nord-Ouest* (2 vols., Quebec, 1889-90).

FROBISHER, JOSEPH (1740-1810) was born in Halifax, Yorkshire, England, on April 15, 1740. He appears to have followed his brother Benjamin (q.v.) to Canada, and to have first gone to the West in 1768. It is known that he made an attempt to pass beyond Grand Portage in 1769, but was turned back by the Indians. The statement is made in the McDonell Diary, under date of September 4, 1793, that he wintered on the Red River in 1770-71; but this statement is open to doubt. Certainly he reached the Saskatchewan in 1773, with his brother Thomas (q.v.); and spent the winter near the site of what afterwards became Fort Cumberland. In 1774-5 he wintered on the Churchill River, in the hope of cutting off the fur-trade from Fort Churchill, and nearly perished of starvation. He was an original member of the North West Company in 1779; and he became one of its great figures. On the death of his brother Benjamin in 1787, he joined forces with Simon McTavish (q.v.), to form McTavish, Frobisher and Co., which was for many years the virtual directorate of the North West Company. He retired from business in 1798, and lived at his place, Beaver Hall, in Montreal. He represented the East Ward of Montreal in the Legislative Assembly of Lower Canada from 1792 to 1796; and he died in Montreal on September 12, 1810. In 1779 he married Charlotte Joubert, of Montreal. His letter-book and his "Diary of my dinners" are preserved in the Library of McGill University.

FROBISHER, THOMAS (1744-1788) was born in Yorkshire, England, in 1744, the brother of Benjamin and Joseph Frobisher (q.v.). He came to Canada about 1769, and engaged in the fur-trade with his brothers. He was on the Saskatchewan in 1773 and on the Churchill River in 1774; and in 1776 he founded the first post at Isle à la Crosse. Though a good man in the bush, he apparently lacked the business capacity of his brothers. He died at Montreal on September 12, 1788.

GERRARD, SAMUEL (1767-1857) was born in Ireland in 1767, and came to Canada about 1787. He entered business in Montreal, and became a partner in the firm of Parker, Gerrard, and Ogilvy, later Gerrard, Gillespie and Co. This was one of the firms which financed the XY Company between the years 1797 and 1804; and through it Samuel Gerrard acquired after 1804 an indirect interest in the North West Compnay. When the firm of McTavish, McGillivrays and Co. failed in 1825, Samuel Gerrard was appointed one of the trustees; and it largely fell to him to unravel the tangled finances of the North West Company. His papers, which are now in the Sulpician Library in Montreal, naturally contain a vast amount of material of interest to the historian of the fur-trade. Gerrard died in Montreal on March 24, 1857, aged 90 years; and his wife, Ann Grant, who was the granddaughter of Richard Dobie (q.v.), died in Montreal on October 18, 1854, aged 81 years. Their only surviving child, Samuel Henry Gerrard, died in Germany in 1858. For further details, see Charles Drisard, *L'honorable Samuel Gerrard* (Bull. des rech. hist., 1928, pp. 63-64).

GIASSON, JACQUES (1747-1808) was born in Montreal in 1747, the son of Jacques Giasson and Marie Angélique Hubert. Following his father, who had been a fur-trader at Green Bay in the French period, he was engaged all his life in the South-West trade. He was elected a member of the Beaver Club of Montreal in 1791; and he died at Montreal on January 30, 1808.

GILLESPIE, GEORGE (1772-1842) was born in Scotland in 1772, one of a family of fourteen children. He came to Canada about 1790, and seems to have been for a time in the service of the North West Company. In 1798 he was in charge of the house of the North West Company at St. Joseph's; and in 1799 he was elected a member of the Beaver Club, of Montreal. He became a partner in the firm of Parker, Gerrard, Ogilvy, and Co., later Gillespie, Moffatt, and Co.; and for a number of years represented this firm at Michilimackinac. He returned to Scotland shortly after 1812; and he spent the remainder of his life at Biggar Park, Lanarkshire. Here he died in 1842. For much of this information I am indebted to his grandson, Mr. Walter Gillespie, of the Toronto Mortgage Company, Toronto.

GILLESPIE, ROBERT (1785-1863) was born in Scotland in 1785, a younger brother of George Gillespie (q.v.). He came to Canada about the year 1800; and ultimately became a partner in the firm of Gillespie, Moffatt, and Co.

He returned to England in 1822; and was until 1856 at the head of the English branch of Gillespie, Moffatt, and Co. He died in 1863. He married (1) Anna Agnes, daughter of Dr. Robert Kerr, formerly surgeon of Sir John Johnson's "Royal Greens", by whom he had at least one son, Sir Robert Gillespie (1818-1901); and (2) Caroline Matilda (d. 1879), second daughter of Dr. Daniel Arnoldi, of Montreal.

GRANT, CHARLES (*fl.* 1780-84) was a son of James Grant, laird of Kincorth, and a cousin of Robert Grant the Nor' Wester (q.v.). I have in my notes the following statement by a grandson of Charles Grant: "I find a letter to my father, from Mr. J. P. Grant, dated Kincorth, Forres, 11 Nov., 1845, in which he says that he learns from Mrs. Grant of Kincorth, an old lady who was, I think, his mother-in-law, that 'Mr. Grant residing in Glenbeg in the parish of Cromdale, Strathspey, was father of James Grant, a brother of Robert Grant of Lethendry in that parish. The said James Grant was father of Charles Grant, Esq., of Quebec in America.... Portraits of Mr. Grant of Glenbeg and of Mr. Robert Grant of Lethendry are still preserved at Castle Grant, the seat of Lord Seafield, in Strathspey.'" Charles Grant became a merchant of Quebec, and in 1780 he made to General Haldimand the report on the fur-trade which is printed on pp. 62-6. He married Jane Holmes, and had by her two sons and two daughters. One of the sons was Charles Grant the younger (q.v.), and the other was Frederick, who was a merchant in Quebec, and afterwards purchased the estate of Ecclesgreig in Scotland, where the Forsyth-Grants still live. One daughter, Jane, married Capt. Kenelm Conner Chandler, of the 60th Regiment, seignior of Nicolet; and the other, Margaret, married the Hon. John Forsyth (q.v.). Charles Grant died at Quebec in December, 1784; and in 1793 his widow married in Quebec the Hon. John Blackwood. Mr. A. St. L. Trigge, a descendant of Capt. Chandler, tells me that there is a family tradition that Charles Grant was connected with the family of William Grant of St. Roch (q.v.), who married the Baroness de Longueuil.

GRANT, CHARLES (1784-1843) was born, probably in Quebec, about September, 1784, the younger son of Charles Grant of Quebec (q.v.). He entered the service of the North West Company as a clerk; and in 1816 he was stationed at Rainy Lake. He was at Grand Portage in 1821, but seems to have retired from the fur-trade at that time. In 1815 he was elected a member of the Beaver Club, and in 1827 he was its acting secretary. He acquired the ownership of the fief Bruyères; and during his later years he lived on a farm at Côte Ste. Catherine (now Outremont), near Montreal. About 1828 he married Amelia Williams; and by her he had four sons and five daughters, several of whom have left descendants. His sister Margaret (d. 1818) married the Hon. John Forsyth; and her son William, on succeeding to the estate of his maternal uncle, Frederick Grant, in Scotland, assumed the name of Forsyth-Grant. He died on May 21, 1843, aged 58 years and 9 months. For much of this information I am indebted to Mr. A. St. L. Trigge, of Melbourne, Quebec.

GRANT, CUTHBERT (d. 1799) was probably the son of David Grant of Lethendry, in the parish of Cromdale, Strathspey, Scotland, and his wife Margaret, third daughter of Robert Grant of Glenbeg, and a younger brother of Robert Grant (q.v.). Certainly Robert Grant had a younger brother named Cuthbert who was a "merchant in Canada". The difficulty is that there was another Cuthbert Grant, a merchant of Quebec, who died in Quebec in 1792. At any rate, the Cuthbert Grant who was a fur-trader appears in the North West as early as 1786 when, with Laurent Leroux (q.v.) in opposition, he led the way to the Great Slave Lake. In 1787-88 he was with Alexander Mackenzie (q.v.) in the Athabaska department; but his later years were spent chiefly on the Assiniboine, where his "favourite residence" appears to have been at River Tremblante. He was made a partner of the North West Company about 1795; and he died in the North West in 1799. His shares in the North West Company lapsed in 1805.

GRANT, CUTHBERT (1796?-1854) was a half-breed son of Cuthbert Grant (q.v.), and was born in the North West about 1796. He was baptized in the Scotch Presbyterian Church in Montreal in 1798, and was educated in Montreal. He returned to the North West about 1815, and in 1816 he was one of the leaders of the *Bois-Brulés* in the affair at Sevenoaks. In 1817 he was arrested by Lord Selkirk; but in 1818 he escaped from prison in Montreal. In 1823-24 he was employed as a clerk by the Hudson's Bay Company, but was discharged. In 1828 he was given the nominal post of "Warden of the Plains", and he retained this until 1848. He died at White Horse Plain, Manitoba, on July 15, 1854. He was survived by his wife, Mary McGillis. See M. Complin, *The warden of the plains* (Canadian Geographical Journal, August, 1934).

GRANT, DAVID (d. 1797?) is a somewhat nebulous person. What relation he bore to the other Grants in the fur-trade, I have not been able to ascertain. A David Grant, possibly the same, was married in Montreal to Jane Beaty in February, 1776, as appears from the Christ Church register. Prior to 1787 he was apparently a clerk in the employ of the Frobishers. Our next reference to him in the West is in 1789, when Angus Shaw (q.v.) writes that "David Grant would not accept of £100, for which reason our friend Cuthbert was sent in his place". In 1791 John Macdonald of Garth (q.v.) was in opposition to him at Sturgeon River, on the Lower Saskatchewan, and describes him as "an old experienced trader". He appears in a list of "Gentlemen of the North West" in 1793, as contributing toward the building fund of the Scotch Presbyterian Church in Montreal; and in 1794 he figures in the *Journal* of Duncan McGillivray (edited by A. S. Morton, Toronto, 1929) as the leader of an opposition to the North West Company on the Saskatchewan, which was backed by other Grants. This opposition ended disastrously for "the Grants", and in 1796 David Grant was back in Montreal, as appears from an entry in the register of the Scotch Presbyterian Church, where he is described as "an Indian trader". He appears to have died in Montreal in 1797, for the death of a David Grant is noted in the register of the Scotch Church for that year.

GRANT, JAMES (d. 1798?) appears first in the fur-trade licences in 1777, as trading to Lake Timiskaming. From that date to 1783 he is associated with John Porteous and then Daniel Sutherland (q.v.) in the Timiskaming trade. In 1782 he is a partner of George McBeath (q.v.) at Michilimackinac; and in 1783 Perrault (*Mich. Hist. Coll.*, X, 672) mentions him at Cahokia. In 1785 the firm of Sutherland and Grant sent six canoes to Timiskaming and ten canoes to Michilimackinac, and in 1786 sixteen canoes to Michilimackinac. In 1791 James Grant was back at Lake Timiskaming; and he was dead by 1799, as appears from McTavish, Frobisher and Co.'s agreement of 1799, where he is described as "the late". A "J. Grant" died in Montreal on December 26, 1798, and this may have been James Grant.

GRANT, JAMES (*fl.* 1805-1827) was a clerk of the North West Company at Fond du Lac in 1805, and continued in charge of this post until 1813. From 1814 to 1815 he was at the Pic, on Lake Superior, but in 1816 he was back at Fond du Lac, as he was there arrested by Lord Selkirk. He was made a partner of the North West Company in 1816, and in 1817 Ross Cox (q.v.) met him at Fort William. He retired from the fur-trade in 1821, and in 1827 he was the guest of Charles Grant, jr. (q.v.) at the Beaver Club in Montreal. After that, he disappears from view. In 1798 a half-breed son of Cuthbert Grant (q.v.), named James, was baptized in the Scotch Presbyterian Church in Montreal, aged seven years; but this would appear to be a different person, unless the North West Company appointed clerks at the age of fourteen years.

GRANT, JOHN, of Lachine (1749-1817), was born in Glenmoriston, near Inverness, Scotland, in 1749. He came to Canada in 1771, and established himself at Lachine, where he engaged in the business of forwarding. In the fur-trade licences, his name appears as trading to Oswegatchie, Cataraqui, Niagara, and Detroit between 1777 and 1785. In 1804 he was an agent of Quetton de St. George at York (Toronto). The Rev. R. Campbell, in his *History of the Scotch Presbyterian Church, St. Gabriel Street, Montreal* (Montreal, 1887), p. 230, says, on what authority I do not know, that he was "agent for the North West Company, and attended to the forwarding of their supplies from Montreal". On July 30, 1777, he married in Montreal Margaret Beattie; and one of his daughters married in Lachine in 1806 Thomas Blackwood. His son, James C. Grant, became a prominent member of the Lower Canada bar. He died at Lachine on August 23, 1817. He does not appear to have been related to the other Grants in the fur-trade, but was more probably connected with Commodore Alexander Grant, administrator of the province of Upper Canada in 1805-6, who also came from Glenmoriston.

GRANT, JOHN, of Montreal (d. 1809), was apparently a brother of William Grant of St. Roch (q.v.). He appears to have come to Canada in the early days of British rule, for he married before 1774 Anne Freeman, the illegitimate daughter of Richard Dobie (q.v.). By her he had at least five daughters, one of whom, Anne, married Samuel Gerrard (q.v.), and another, Elizabeth, married in 1798 James Finlay, jr. (q.v.). From 1779 to 1785 John Grant was engaged, in company with Gabriel Cotté and Maurice Blondeau (q.v.), in trading to Lake Superior, but in 1798 he is described as "at present absent from this province". He died in 1809, and his will is in the Montreal Court House.

GRANT, PETER (1764-1848) was born, apparently in Scotland, in 1764. He came to Canada, and entered the service of the North West Company in 1784, at the same time as Edward Umfreville (q.v.). In 1789 he was at Lac Rouge; in 1793 he was at the forks of the River Qu'Appelle, in opposition to the North West Company, but he rejoined it in 1795; he was met by David Thompson (q.v.) near Grand Portage in July, 1797; and in 1799 he was proprietor of the post at Rainy Lake. He was made a partner of the North West Company after 1795, and was for several years in charge of the Red River department. In 1802 he was sent as an agent of the North West Company to deal with the military authorities at Sault Ste. Marie. He relinquished one of his shares in the Company in 1805, but was still apparently a partner in 1808, when William McGillivray (q.v.) signed for him at Fort William. He seems to have retired from the fur-trade before 1807, when he was made a member of the Beaver Club at Montreal; and he settled at Ste. Anne, Bout de l'Isle. He died at Lachine on July 20, 1848, aged 85 years. Though not a son, he would appear to have been a relative of John Grant of Lachine. He had at least one daughter, named Mary, who appears from a photograph of her in my possession to have been born of an Indian mother.

GRANT, RICHARD (1793-1862) was born in Montreal in 1793, the son of William Grant of Three Rivers (q.v.). He entered the service of the North West Company in 1816, and in 1821, when the North West Company was merged with the Hudson's Bay Company, was stationed on the Saskatchewan. He became a clerk in the Hudson's Bay Company, and in 1836 he was promoted to the rank of chief trader. He retired in 1853, and he died in 1862.

GRANT, ROBERT (1752-1801) was born in 1752, the grandson of Donald Grant of Easter Lethendry, in the parish of Cromdale, Strathspey, Scotland, and the second son of David Grant of Lethendry and Margaret, third daughter of Robert Grant of Glenbeg, in the same parish. He came to Canada, and entered the fur-trade. In 1778 John Askin (q.v.) noted that he and his partner, William Holmes (q.v.), whom he described as "deserving young men", were embarking in the North West trade. In

1779 Holmes and Grant appear as one of the partnerships in the original sixteen-share North West Company of that year; and they appear also in the twenty-share Company of 1783. Robert Grant seems to have spent most of his time in the West in the Red River district. Roderick McKenzie in his *Reminiscences* says that he wintered on the Red River in 1785-6, and he was again there in 1790. In 1787, he is reputed to have founded Fort Espérance on the Qu'Appelle River. His partner Holmes sold out in 1790; and in 1793 Robert Grant retired, and returned to Scotland. On December 5, 1795, he married Anne, second daughter of the Rev. Lewis Grant of Cromdale; and by her he had two sons and two daughters, the youngest of whom, Davina, married on November 9, 1819, Frederick Grant, a son of Charles Grant the elder (q.v.), who purchased the estate of Mount Cyrus or Ecclesgreig, near Montrose, where the Forsyth-Grant family still lives. In 1797 Robert Grant acquired the estate of Kincorth, and there he lived until his death on August 16, 1801. For much of the information in this sketch I am indebted to Capt. Forsyth-Grant, M.C., of Ecclesgreig, and to Miss Evelyn Grant of Nairn, Scotland, who is the last of the Lethendry line. She tells me that the tombstone of Robert Grant in Cromdale churchyard describes him as "an original member of the North West Company of Canada".

GRANT, WILLIAM, of St. Roch (1741-1805), was born in Scotland in 1741, and came to Canada in 1763, as a partner in the London firm of Robert Grant and Co., which had engaged in the trade with Canada. In 1763 he purchased from the Marquis de Vaudreuil a grant of the fur-trading rights in La Baye, Lake Michigan; but this grant was voided, and William Grant appears, so far as I can discover, to have taken no direct part subsequently in the fur-trade. But most of the Grants who embarked in the fur-trade appear to have been related to him, though the exact relationship is difficult to determine. He himself concentrated his energies about Quebec and the lower St. Lawrence. In 1777 he was appointed deputy receiver-general of Quebec; and in 1778 he was appointed a member of the Legislative Council of the province. In 1784 he was relieved of his duties as deputy receiver-general, because of serious deficiencies in his accounts; and he was not appointed to the Legislative Council of Lower Canada on its creation in 1791. From 1792 to his death, however, he represented the upper town of Quebec in the Legislative Assembly of Lower Canada. He purchased a large number of seigniories along the banks of the St. Lawrence, and he had extensive interests in Quebec, near which, at St. Roch, he had a large house. But he evidently died insolvent, for after his death his seigniories were put up to auction. He died at Quebec on October 5, 1805. In 1770 he married the widow of Charles Jacques Le Moyne, third Baron de Longueuil; and his nephew, Capt. David Alexander Grant, married her daughter, who was heiress to the title.

GRANT, WILLIAM, of Three Rivers (d. 1801?), first appears in the fur-trade in 1777, when he goes security for five canoes sent to Nipigon. In 1778 he was at Michilimackinac; and from that date until 1788 he appears to have been associated with George McBeath (q.v.) in the firm of McBeath, Grant, and Co., in sending canoes to Michilimackinac. His business associates, to judge from the fur-trade licences, were Richard Dobie (q.v.), John Grant of Montreal (q.v.), Etienne Campion (q.v.), and R. Griffin. He was at Michilimackinac as late as 1790; and it may be surmised that he was one of the Grants who backed David Grant (q.v.) in his disastrous opposition to the North West Company in 1794. Certainly, the firm of Grant, Campion and Co., of which he was a partner, appears to have dissolved about that year. In 1788 he purchased a property in Three Rivers, and thenceforward he was known as William Grant of Three Rivers. He appears to have died in Montreal in October, 1801; but his widow was still living at Three Rivers in 1845.

GREGORY, JOHN (1751?-1817) was a native of England who came to Canada about 1773. He may have been connected with the London firm of Mark and Thomas Gregory, which was engaged in the trade with Canada in the early days of British rule. He entered into partnership with James Finlay (q.v.), and from 1773 to 1783 the firm of Finlay and Gregory continued to send canoes to the West. On Finlay's retirement in 1784, Gregory took into partnership Normand McLeod, and the firm of Gregory and McLeod was the backbone of the opposition to the North West Company in 1783-7. In 1787 he became a partner in the North West Company, and later a member of the firm of McTavish, Frobisher and Co. In 1791 he was elected a member of the Beaver Club. He retired from the firm of McTavish, Frobisher and Co. on May 31, 1806; and he died in Montreal on February 22, 1817. In 1779 he married Isabella Ferguson; and by her he had several children. His son George (d. 1850) married a daughter of the Hon. John Forsyth (q.v.); and his youngest daughter married, in 1806, David Mitchell. He had a brother George who lived for many years in Quebec.

HALDANE, JOHN (d. 1857) was a native of Scotland who entered the service of the XY Company about 1798; and he was one of the six members of the XY Company who became wintering partners in 1804. In 1804 he was at Red Lake and Lac Seul; from 1806 to 1812 he was at Monontagué, from 1812 to 1813 at the Pic; from 1813 to 1814 on the Athabaska River, and from 1814 to 1815 on the Churchill River. In 1817 Ross Cox (q.v.) met him at Fort William. In 1821, on the union of the North West and Hudson's Bay Companies, he was made a chief factor, and was placed in charge of the Columbia district, to which he had already been transferred. In 1823 he was brought east to take charge of the Lake Superior district, and he remained in charge of this district until his retirement from the fur-trade in 1827. He died in Edinburgh, Scotland, on October 11, 1857; and his will is on file in Hudson's Bay House in London.

HALLETT, HENRY (1772?-1844) was born in England about 1772, and was a nephew of Philip Turnor. He entered the service of the Hudson's Bay

Company as a writer in 1793, but was dismissed from the Company's service in 1810 because of his "atrocious cowardly murder of an Indian". He then entered the service of the North West Company as a clerk; and he was taken over as a clerk by the Hudson's Bay Company at the union of 1821. He retired from the fur-trade in 1822, and he lived at the Red River until 1843. He died in March, 1844.

HALLOWELL, JAMES (1748?-1830) was born in England about 1748. He was a relative, and probably a cousin of the Benjamin Hallowell who died in York, Upper Canada, in 1799, and after whom Hallowell (now Picton) was named. He came to Canada about 1780; and in 1787 he became a partner in the firm of McTavish, Frobisher and Co. He continued to be a partner in this firm, and consequently a member of the North West Company, until 1795, when he withdrew in favour of his son William (q.v.). He died at Bedford, England, on April 20, 1830, at the age of 82. He had seven children, all of whom died young, except two, William (q.v.) and James (q.v.).

HALLOWELL, JAMES (1778-1816) was the second son of James Hallowell (q.v.), and was born in 1778, probably in England. He came to Canada with his parents as an infant; and became connected, like his father and elder brother William (q.v.), with the firm of McTavish, Frobisher and Co. He died at Brooklyn, Long Island, in the United States, on November 29, 1816. He married a daughter of Daniel Sutherland (q.v.); and William Hallowell, M.D. (1814-1863), of Toronto, of whom there is a sketch in William Canniff, *The medical profession in Upper Canada* (Toronto, 1894), would appear to have been his son.

HALLOWELL, WILLIAM (1771-1838) was the eldest son of James Hallowell (q.v.) and was born, probably in England, on August 17, 1771. He came to Canada with his parents about 1780; and in 1802 he became a junior partner in the firm of McTavish, McGillivrays and Co., and a partner in the North West Company. About 1814, he had, with his father, a disagreement with his partners in McTavish McGillivrays and Co., and withdrew from the fur-trade. He died in Montreal in September, 1838. He married in Albany, New York, on February 8, 1798, Martha Henry; and by her he had three sons and two daughters. His eldest son, James (1796-1858), became a member of the Montreal bar, and practised law at Sherbrooke, in the Eastern Townships; and his elder daughter, Elizabeth (1799-1866), married the Rev. John Bethune, dean of Montreal, and brother of Angus Bethune (q.v.). For much of the above information I am indebted to Mrs. Cecil Bowen, of Sherbrooke, a great-granddaughter of William Hallowell, in whose possession is William Hallowell's family Bible.

HARGRAVE, JAMES (1798-1865) was born in Roxburghshire, Scotland, in 1798. He entered the service of the North West Company in 1820, and was taken over by the Hudson's Bay Company in 1821 as a clerk. He was promoted to the rank of chief trader in 1833, and to that of chief factor in 1844. Most of his service was spent at York Factory. He retired from the service of the Company in 1859, and he died at Burnside House, Brockville, Upper Canada, on or about May 16, 1865. In 1840 he married Letitia McTavish (d. 1854), a niece of John George McTavish (q.v.), and a sister of William McTavish, governor of Rupertsland from 1864 to 1870; and after her death he married, secondly, Margaret Alcock. His son, Joseph James Hargrave (d. 1894), who was also a servant of the Hudson's Bay Company, published a volume entitled *Red River* (Montreal, 1871), in which he made use of the copious papers which his father had preserved, and which are described in George Bryce, *The remarkable history of the Hudson's Bay Company* (London, 1900). These papers are now in the possession of The Champlain Society.

HARMON, DANIEL WILLIAMS (1778-1845) was born in Vermont in 1778. He entered the service of the North West Company as a clerk in 1800; and was employed, successively, on the Saskatchewan and in the Athabaska district. In 1810 he was transferred to New Caledonia. Here he remained for over eight years; but in 1819 he returned to Montreal, and retired from the fur-trade. He brought back with him his fur-trade journals; and these were edited and published by the Rev. Daniel Haskel, of Andover, Massachusetts, under the title *Journal of voyages and travels in the interior of North America* (Andover, 1820). In his later years, he settled on the shores of Lake Champlain; and he died in 1845. In 1805 he married in the West a French half-breed; and by her he had fourteen children.

HARRIOTT, JOHN EDWARD (1797-1877) was born in London, England, in 1797, and entered the service of the Hudson's Bay Company in 1809. He was promoted to the rank of chief trader in 1829, and to that of chief factor in 1846. He died in Montreal in 1877.

HENEY, HUGH (1789-1844) was born on September 9, 1789. He was educated at Montreal, and became for a short time a clerk in the service of the North West Company. In 1804 he was stationed on the upper Red River, and in 1805 he accompanied F. A. Larocque (q.v.) to the Mandan country. He returned to the East about 1807; and in 1811 he was called to the bar of Lower Canada. In 1818 he translated into French and published in Montreal both Halkett's *Statement respecting the Earl of Selkirk's settlement at Kildonan* (London, 1817) and Wilcocke's *A narrative of occurrences in the Indian countries of North America* (London, 1817). From 1820 to 1830 he was a member of the Legislative Assembly of Lower Canada for Montreal East; and in the Assembly he opposed the extremists under Papineau. In 1833 he was appointed a member of the Executive Council of Lower Canada, and he continued a member until 1841. In

1842 he was appointed a commissioner for the revision of the Statutes of Lower Canada; but he died, before the completion of this work, at Three Rivers, Lower Canada, on January 15, 1844. He was the author of a *Commentaire sur l'Acte constitutionel du Haut et du Bas-Canada* (Montreal, 1832).

HENRY, ALEXANDER (1739-1824) was born in New Jersey in August, 1739. He was one of the first English traders to reach Michilimackinac after the British conquest of Canada; and he narrowly escaped being murdered by the Indians during Pontiac's Conspiracy in 1763. From that date to 1780 he was one of the pioneers of the Canadian fur-trade. For several years he was a trader on Lake Superior; but on October 14, 1775, he reached Cumberland House, in the valley of the Saskatchewan; and he wintered on Beaver Lake. He was not included in the original North West Company in 1779; and in 1781 he settled in Montreal as a general merchant. Some time after 1787, however, he sold out his interests in the Indian country to the North West Company, and became (according to a statement made in the biography of him in the *Canadian Magazine* for April and May, 1824) "a dormant partner in that firm, where he continued until 1796". In 1796 he and Alexander Henry, jr., sold their shares to William Hallowell. He died at Montreal on April 4, 1824. The story of his career as a fur-trader is told in his *Travels and adventures in Canada and the Indian countries* (New York, 1809; new ed., by James Bain, Toronto, 1901).

HENRY, ALEXANDER (d. 1814) was a nephew of Alexander Henry the elder (q.v.), the author of *Travels and adventures*. He entered the service of the North West Company as a clerk about 1792; and during the next twenty-two years he travelled all over the North West, from the Great Lakes to the Pacific. His journals, which he kept from day to day, have been published by Elliott Coues under the title, *New light on the early history of the greater North-West* (3 vols., New York, 1897). He became a partner of the North West Company between 1799 and 1802; and he was drowned off Fort George, on the Pacific coast, on May 22, 1814.

HENRY, ALEXANDER (d. 1813?) was the second son of Alexander Henry the elder (q.v.), the author of *Travels and adventures*. He was born after 1785, and became a clerk in the North West Company. He was murdered by the Indians at Fort Nelson, on the Liard River, in the Mackenzie River department, either at the end of 1812 or the beginning of 1813.

HENRY, ROBERT (1778?-1859) was an adopted nephew of Alexander Henry the elder (q.v.), and was born about 1778. He entered the service of the North West Company as a clerk, and became a partner of the Company in 1810. From 1810 to 1811 he was on the Churchill River, and from 1811 to 1815 he was in the Athabaska department. He "went down" on rotation in 1815; and in that year he was elected a member of the Beaver Club in Montreal. In 1817 he retired from the fur-trade, and settled in Cobourg, Upper Canada. Here he pursued for many years the business of banking; and here he died on May 10, 1859, aged 81 years. On November 2, 1817, he married Christine, daughter of the Rev. John Bethune, and sister of Angus Bethune (q.v.); and by her he had two daughters.

HENRY, ROBERT (*fl*. 1813-1824) entered the service of the North West Company as a clerk in 1813, and was taken over by the Hudson's Bay Company at the time of the union of 1821. In 1822 he was employed on the Churchill River; and in 1823 in the Athabaska department. In 1824 he retired to Canada; and henceforth disappears from view. He would appear to have been a son, possibly a half-breed son, of Alexander Henry the younger (q.v.), the author of the Henry *Journals*.

HENRY, WILLIAM (1783?-1864?) was the eldest son of Alexander Henry the elder (q.v.), and was born about 1783. He entered the service of the North West Company as a clerk in 1801; and from 1801 to 1809 he was employed in the Red River district. In 1810 he was at Cumberland House; and in 1811 he was on the Athabaska River. In 1812 he was transferred to the Columbia department, and until 1816 he was in charge of a post on the Willamette River. In 1817 he returned to Fort William; and he was then sent to Lesser Slave Lake. He was retained as a clerk in this district on the union of the North West and Hudson's Bay Companies in 1821; but in 1823 he appears to have retired to Canada. Here he became a surveyor and civil engineer. About 1848 he settled in Newmarket, Upper Canada; and here he died about 1864. In Montreal, after 1823, he married the sister of John Felton, who had been the signal midshipman on Nelson's flagship, the *Victory*, at the battle of Trafalgar; and by her he had several children. One of his sons, Charles, died, after a most adventurous career, in Barrie, Ontario, in June, 1897.

HERON, FRANCIS (d. 1840) was a native of county Donegal, Ireland, and was a brother of James Heron (q.v.). He entered the service of the Hudson's Bay Company in 1812; and in 1814 was the steward at York Factory. From 1815 to 1818 he was at Fort Cumberland; from 1818 to 1821, at Fort Edmonton; from 1821 to 1822, at Fort Cumberland; from 1822 to 1823, on the South Branch expedition; from 1823 to 1824, in the Mackenzie River district; from 1824 to 1828, at Fort Garry; from 1828 to 1829 at Brandon House; from 1829 to 1835 at Fort Colville, in the Columbia district; and from 1835 to 1839 he was in Europe on furlough. He was promoted to the rank of chief trader in 1828; and he retired from the Company's service in 1839. He died in April, 1840.

HERON, JAMES (*fl*. 1812-1832) was a native of Rathmelon, county Donegal, Ireland, and was a brother of Francis Heron (q.v.). He entered the service of the Hudson's Bay Company in 1812; and was first stationed in the Winnipeg district. In 1815 he deserted to the North West Company, "because of bad treatment"; and in 1817 Ross Cox (q.v.) met him at Fort Alexander. From 1821 to 1827 he was on the Churchill River, and from 1828 to 1831 at Fort Chipewyan. In 1832, however, he was discharged from the Company's service, and retired to Canada. He settled at what came to be known as Heron's Isle, in the parish of St. Martin, Lower Canada; but the date of his death I have not ascertained. He married Fanny, the eldest daughter of George Keith (q.v.); and she died on Heron's Isle on December 30, 1850.

HOLMES, WILLIAM (d. 1792) was a native of Ireland, and was probably a brother of the Jane Holmes who married Charles Grant (q.v.), and a half-brother of John King (d. 1806), of the firm of King and McCord, of Montreal. He came to Canada a few years after the British conquest, and engaged in the fur-trade. He was on the Saskatchewan in 1774, and again in 1776; and in 1778 he formed a partnership with Robert Grant (q.v.). He became an original member of the North West Company in 1779. He was at Sturgeon River Fort on the Saskatchewan in 1779-80, and on the Red Deer River in 1782-3; and he was at Cumberland House in May, 1784, on his way to Grand Portage. He was on the North Saskatchewan again in 1787-8; but in 1790 he sold his share in the North West Company to John Gregory (q.v.), and retired from the fur-trade. He died at Montreal on August 17, 1792.

HOWARD, JOSEPH (d. 1797) was a merchant who came to Canada, and settled in Montreal, in the early days of British rule. He was prominent in attempting to break in on the monopoly of the trade at the King's Posts acquired by Gray and Dunn in 1765; and in 1766 he was one of those arrested on suspicion of having been concerned in the assault on Thomas Walker. He was prominent in the fur-trade at Michilimackinac about 1778, but was not included in the North West Company in 1779. In his later years he was a merchant at Berthier; and here he died in December, 1797.

HUGHES, JAMES (1772-1853) was born in Montreal on October 3, 1772, probably the son of Capt. James Hughes (1738-1825), town major of Montreal. He entered the service of the North West Company about 1791, and in 1793 was a clerk at Fort de l'Isle on the Saskatchewan. From 1798 to 1817 he was almost continuously in the Fort des Prairies department; and he was made a partner in the North West Company between 1799 and 1802. He retired from the fur-trade in 1821; but during the next nine years he ran through his savings, and in 1830 he was engaged as a clerk by the Hudson's Bay Company, when nearly sixty years of age. He retired to Canada again in 1833; and he was in his later years an officer of the Indian department, with the rank of major. He was killed near Lachine, on the island of Montreal, on July 13, 1853, when his horse bolted into a

OF THE NOR' WESTERS 459

Grand Trunk Railway train; and his widow obtained £500 damages from the railway company. John Macdonald of Garth (q.v.) described him as being "as brave a fellow as ever treaded the earth".

HUGHES, GUY (d. 1824) was probably a son of James Hughes (q.v.). He entered the service of the North West Company in 1814, and was taken over as a clerk by the Hudson's Bay Company at the time of the union in 1821. In 1823, he was murdered, with four other servants of the Company, at Fort St. John.

INGLIS, JOHN (d. 1822) was a native of Scotland who was prior to 1787 employed by the firm of Phyn and Ellice in London. In 1787 he was made a member of the firm of Phyn, Ellices, and Inglis. He signed the North West Company agreement of 1804 by attorney, and became a partner in the Company. He died in London in 1822; and his will is filed in Somerset House, London.

KEITH, GEORGE (d. 1859) was a native of Scotland who entered the service of the North West Company between 1799 and 1806, when he appears as a clerk in the Athabaska department. From 1806 to 1815 he was in the Mackenzie River department; and in 1813 he was made a partner of the North West Company. From 1817 to 1821 he was in charge of the Athabaska department; and at the union of 1821 he was made a chief factor of the Hudson's Bay Company. For several years after 1821 he was in charge of the English River department. He went on furlough to England, with his brother James (q.v.), in 1843; and he retired from the service of the Hudson's Bay Company in 1845. He died in Aberdeen, Scotland, on January 22, 1859.

KEITH, JAMES (d. 1851) was a younger brother of George Keith (q.v.). He entered the service of the North West Company about the beginning of the nineteenth century; and became a partner in 1814. From 1813 to 1816 he was on the Columbia. In 1821 he was made a chief factor of the Hudson's Bay Company, and was placed in charge of the English River department. Later he was transferred to Fort Chipewyan. In 1826 he was placed in charge of the Montreal department, with headquarters at Lachine; and here he remained until 1843. He was then granted furlough, returned to Scotland, and retired from the service of the Hudson's Bay Company in 1845. He died at 101 Crown Street, Aberdeen, Scotland, on January 27, 1851. He was a brother-in-law of Sir George Simpson, having married a sister of Lady Simpson.

LANE, WILLIAM FLETCHER (*fl.* 1820-1863) was a native of Ireland who entered the service of the North West Company as a constable in 1820. At the union of 1821 he became a clerk of the Hudson's Bay Company; and he was employed first on the Ottawa River, and later in New Caledonia.

He retired from the service of the Company, still with the rank of clerk, in 1863, and was granted a pension of £50 per annum. He married a daughter of Simon McGillivray, jr. (q.v.).

LAROCQUE, FRANÇOIS ANTOINE (*fl.* 1801-1815) was a brother of Joseph Larocque (q.v.). He entered the service of the XY Company as a clerk in 1801 and was stationed successively on the Churchill River, at Fort des Prairies, and on the Red River. He was a clerk on the Red River when the union of the XY and the North West Companies took place in 1804; and in the autumn of that year he made, with Charles Mackenzie, a journey to the Mandans. His journal for this expedition has been printed in L. R. Masson, *Les bourgeois de la Cie. du Nord-ouest*, vol. 1 (Quebec, 1889); and a journal of a subsequent expedition has been edited, with introduction and notes, by L. J. Burpee, under the title *Journal of Larocque from the Assiniboine to the Yellowstone* (Publications of the Canadian Archives, No. 3, Ottawa, 1910). He retired from the fur-trade before 1815, and settled in Montreal, where he was elected a member of the Beaver Club. He spent his last days, at an advanced age, in the convent of the Grey Nuns at St. Hyacinthe, Lower Canada. He married a daughter of Gabriel Cotté, a merchant of Michilimackinac; and by her he had one son.

LAROCQUE, JOSEPH (1787?-1866) was born in Canada about 1787, the younger brother of François Antoine Larocque (q.v.). He entered the service of the XY Company in 1801, and in 1804 he was a clerk of the North West Company on the Churchill River. Later he was transferred to the Pacific slope; and in 1813 he was with John George McTavish (q.v.) when the latter received the surrender of Astoria. He remained for several years on the Pacific slope, where Ross Cox (q.v.) frequently met him; but he was back at Fort William in the summer of 1817. Between 1817 and 1820 he was made a partner of the North West Company; and at the time of the union of 1821, he became a chief trader in the Hudson's Bay Company. In 1825 he left the West; and for several years he was in charge at Mingan, on the lower St. Lawrence. He resigned from the service of the Company about 1830; and in 1833 he married Archange Guillon (d. 1863). From 1837 to 1851 he lived in France; then he spent several years at Montreal; and in 1857 he went to spend his last years with the Grey Nuns in Ottawa. Here he died on December 1, 1866. A fuller account of his life will be found in J. Tassé, *Les Canadiens de l'Ouest* (2 vols., Montreal, 1878).

LEITH, JAMES (1777-1838) was born in August, 1777, in Aberdeenshire, Scotland, the son of Alexander Leith, a graduate of King's College, Aberdeen. He emigrated to Canada about 1800, at the instance of Edward Ellice (q.v.), and in 1798 entered the service of the XY Company. He appears to have been a relative of George Leith (d. 1801), senior partner in the Montreal firm of Leith, Jamieson and Co. He was one of the six wintering partners of the XY Company absorbed as wintering partners by the North West Company in 1804; and at the time of the union of the North West and

Hudson's Bay Companies in 1821, he was made a chief factor. From 1806 to 1807 he was at Folle Avoine; from 1807 to 1810, at Michipicoten; from 1810 to 1811, at Rainy Lake; from 1811 to 1812, at the Red River; from 1812 to 1815, at Monontagué and Lake Nipigon; in 1816 at Rainy Lake; and in 1817 he was sent to the Red River to arrest some of Selkirk's men. In 1821 he was in charge of the Athabaska district; and from 1822 to 1829 he was in charge of the Cumberland House district. He retired from the Company's service in 1830; and he died at Torquay, England, unmarried, on June 19, 1838. By his will he left half his estate for the propagation of the Protestant religion among the Indians. For some of the above information, I am indebted to Mr. James Leith Ross, of Toronto.

LEROUX, LAURENT (1758?-1855) was born in Canada about 1758, and first appears in the fur-trade as a clerk in the service of Gregory, McLeod and Co. in 1784. On the union of Gregory, McLeod and Co. in 1787, he became a clerk in the service of the North West Company, and was chiefly employed in the Athabaska district. In 1786 he was employed on the Great Slave Lake. He returned to Canada in 1796, and settled at L'Assomption. From 1827 to 1830 he represented the constituency of Leinster in the Legislative Assembly of Lower Canada. He died in 1855, aged 97 years. After 1796, he married Esther Loiselle.

LESIEUR, TOUSSAINT (*fl.* 1784-1799) was a native of New France who became a clerk in the service of Gregory, McLeod and Co. about 1784. In 1787 he was in opposition to Cuthbert Grant (q.v.) in the Athabaska district. In 1789 he was in partnership with Simon Fraser, of St. Anne's (q.v.), in charge of a post at Rivière des Trembles and Portage de l'Isle. This partnership apparently continued until Simon Fraser became a partner of the North West Company, and Lesieur returned to Canada. According to the accounts of McTavish, Frobisher and Co., he was still living in 1799.

McBEAN, JOHN (d. 1854?) was born about 1778, and entered the North West Company prior to 1804, when he was clerk and interpreter at Fond du Lac. He became a partner of the North West Company about 1816; and on the union of the North West and Hudson Bay Companies in 1821, he was made a chief factor of the Hudson's Bay Company. From 1821 to 1836 he was in charge of the Lake Huron district; and in 1837 he retired to Canada. Sir George Simpson described him in 1832 as "an ignorant, illiterate, common kind of fellow ... has been a tolerable bruiser, and was at one time a tolerable snow-shoe walker." He settled at Berthier, Lower Canada, in a house called "North West Hall"; and he married the widow of Alexander Mackenzie (q.v.), by whom he had two children. He died at Berthier about 1854.

McBEATH, GEORGE (1740?-1812) was born in Scotland about 1740, and came to Canada soon after the British conquest. He engaged in the fur-trade, and spent his first winter in the Indian country in 1766-7. He was interested in some of the earliest ventures to the North-West, and in 1775 was in partnership with Simon McTavish (q.v.). In 1779 he was one of the partners in the original sixteen-share North West Company; and he retained his two shares in the North West Company of 1783. In 1787 he sold one of his shares to McTavish, Frobisher and Co.; and in 1792 he sold the second share to Alexander (later Sir Alexander) Mackenzie (q.v.). In 1785 he was one of the founders of the Beaver Club of Montreal. In his later years he was a victim of financial reverses; and in 1785 he went to live at L'Assomption. From 1793 to 1796 he represented Leinster in the first legislature of Lower Canada. He died at Montreal on December 3, 1812. He was, apparently, twice married. By his first wife, Jane Graham, who died in 1787, he had one son and one daughter; and in 1801 he married secondly, at Pointe-aux-Trembles, Erie Smyth, widow of David McCrae, of L'Assomption. For fuller details about his life, see the Hon. E. Fabre-Surveyer, *George McBeath* (La Presse, 1927).

McCORMICK, CHARLES (d. 1790) was a trader who was on the Saskachewan from 1777 to 1779. E. M. Chadwick (*Ontarian families*, I, 120) identifies him with the Lieut. McCormick who was with Major Robert Rogers when he took possession of the Western Posts in 1760; but this is doubtful. William Tomison, the Hudson's Bay officer at Cumberland House, described him, on March 15, 1779, as "going about sword in hand threatening the Natives to make them trade with him"; and he was not included in the North West partnership of 1779. He died at St. Laurent, near Montreal, in 1790, and his will, which is preserved in the Court House at Montreal, and is in French, describes him as "cydevant marchand". In October, 1779, he married in Christ Church, Montreal, Marguerite (d. 1854), daughter of John Peter Arnoldi of Montreal; and by her he had two sons, the elder of whom, John Johnson Dease, died young, and the second of whom, Thomas, became for many years manager of the Bank of Upper Canada at Niagara. Sir John Johnson, bart., was named tutor of his son, in case his wife remarried. Some account of his descendants will be found in E. M. Chadwick, *Ontarian families* (Toronto, 1894).

McDONALD, ARCHIBALD (1790-1853) was born at Leechkentium, Glenco Appin, Argylshire, Scotland, on February 3, 1790, and came out to the Red River in 1813, in charge of a party of Lord Selkirk's colonists. He was deputy governor of the Red River Settlement under Miles Macdonell (q.v.). He wrote a *Narrative respecting the destruction of the Earl of Selkirk's settlement upon the Red River in 1815* (Montreal, 1816) and a *Reply to the letter recently addressed to the Earl of Selkirk by the Hon. and Rev. J. Strachan* (Montreal, 1816). After the Red River troubles, he entered the service of the Hudson's Bay Company; and shortly after the union of the Hudson's Bay and North West Companies in 1821, he was sent to the Columbia. In 1828 he accompanied Governor Simpson (q.v.) on a journey from York Factory to the Columbia; and his diary of this journey has been published by Malcolm McLeod, under the title, *Peace River* (Ottawa, 1872). He was promoted to the rank of chief trader in 1828; and from 1828 to 1833 he was in charge at Fort Langley. From 1834 to 1844 he was in charge at Fort Colville; and in 1842 he was made a chief factor. When he retired from the Company's service, he settled at St. Andrew's, Lower Canada; and here he died on January 15, 1853. In 1823 he married a daughter of Chief Comcomly, of the Chinook tribe; and by her he had one son, Ranald McDonald, whose reminiscences have been edited by W. S. Lewis and N. Murakami, under the title *Ranald MacDonald* (Spokane, Wash., 1923).

McDONALD, FINAN (1782-1851) was born in Aberdeenshire, Scotland, in 1782, the son of Angus Ban McDonald and Nelly McDonell, and the younger brother of John McDonald le Borgne (q.v.). He entered the service of the North West Company in 1804; and was with David Thompson on the Columbia from 1807 to 1812. In 1813 Ross Cox (q.v.) met him among the Flat-Heads. He was taken over as a clerk by the Hudson's Bay Company in 1821; and he remained in the Columbia department until his retirement in 1827, when he settled in Upper Canada. He was at Williamstown in 1835, and at Lancaster in 1843. He died at Charlottenburg, Glengarry, Upper Canada, on December 3, 1851, and is buried in the Roman Catholic cemetery in St. Raphael's, Ontario. He married a Spokane wife, and by her had two children. In his later years he became involved in litigation over his brother's estate; and in May, 1849, he was in jail in Toronto, possibly in connection with the administration of the estate. For much of the above information, I am indebted to Mr. F. D. McLennan, of Cornwall, Ont. For further details, see J. A. Meyers, *Finan McDonald* (Washington Historical Quarterly, XIII, 1922).

McDONALD, JOHN (1770-1828), known as "McDonald le Borgne", was born in 1770 at Munial Farm, at the east end of Loch Hourne, Invernessshire, Scotland, the son of Angus Ban McDonald. With his father and mother and brothers and sisters, he emigrated to Glengarry, Canada, in 1786. He was a clerk at Lachine in 1791, and in 1798 he became a wintering partner in the XY Company. He was one of the six wintering partners of the XY Company who became partners of the North West Company in 1804; and in 1806 he was stationed in the Fort des Prairies district. He was distinguished by the letters "A McK Co" after his name, whereas John McDonald of Garth (q.v.) was described as "John McDonald N.W." In 1816 he was one of the partners arrested by Lord Selkirk at Fort William, and he afterwards stood trial at York (Toronto), but was acquitted. In 1821, on the union of the North West and Hudson's Bay Companies, he was made a chief factor. From 1821 to 1822 he was in charge of the upper Red River; and from 1823 to 1826, of the Winnipeg

River district at Fort Alexander. He was granted furlough in 1827; and he died in February, 1828, and was buried in the Church of England cemetery at Newmarket, Upper Canada. He married a half-breed, Marie Poitras; and by her he had at least one daughter, who married Angus Grant, and some of whose descendants are said to be still living at Midland, Ontario. About 1825 he bought a property on the north side of Kempenfeldt Bay on Lake Simcoe; and it is probable that he died here.

McDONALD, JOHN (1782-1834), known as "McDonald le Grand", was born in Inverness-shire, Scotland, in 1782, and entered the service of the North West Company in 1801. Ross Cox (q.v.) met him in New Caledonia in 1814; and he seems to have spent most of his service as a clerk in this department. From 1831 to 1833 he was stationed at Great Slave Lake; and he retired from the Company's service in 1834. He died at St. St. Andrew's, Lower Canada, on December 1, 1834; and his will is filed in Hudson's Bay House in London.

McDONALD OF GARTH, JOHN (1774?-1860), was born in Scotland about 1774, and was a relative of Patrick Small (q.v.). Through the influence of General John Small, he was apprenticed to the North West Company as a clerk in 1791; and his sister married William McGillivray (q.v.), the nephew of Simon McTavish (q.v.). By 1800 he had become a partner in the Company; and in 1799 he built Rocky Mountain House. He was in charge at Fort des Prairies in 1806-8, at Upper Red River in 1809-11, and on the Columbia in 1811-12 and 1813-14. In 1813 he received the surrender of Astoria. He retired from the fur-trade in 1815; and he settled at Gray's Creek, Glengarry, Upper Canada. From the fact that he had a withered arm, he was known among the *voyageurs* as *Le Bras Croche*. He died at Gray's Creek, Glengarry, in 1860. His "Autobiographical Notes" have been published, in a somewhat mutilated form, in L. R. Masson, *Les bourgeois de la Compagnie du Nord-Ouest*, vol. 2 (Quebec, 1890).

MACDONELL, ÆNEAS (d. 1809) was a clerk in the service of the North West Company who was shot by a servant of the Hudson's Bay Company named Mowat at Eagle Lake, in the Nipigon department, on September 16, 1809. He would appear to have been an older brother of Alexander Macdonell (q.v.), and he had been at Lac Seul since 1803.

MACDONELL, ALEXANDER (d. 1835) was the sixth son of Alexander Macdonell of Greenfield, and a second cousin of John Macdonell (q.v.) and Miles Macdonell (q.v.). He entered the service of the North West Company, and in 1808 was a clerk in the Red River department, under John McDonald of Garth (q.v.). He was made a partner of the North West Company in 1814, was placed in charge of the Red River department, and played a prominent part in the Selkirk troubles of the years immediately following. In 1820 he was in charge of the English River department;

but at the union of the North West and Hudson's Bay Companies, he retired from the fur-trade. He was elected to represent the county of Glengarry in the Legislative Assembly of Upper Canada in 1821; and for a number of years he was sheriff of the Ottawa district. In 1834 he was elected to represent Prescott and Russell in the Legislative Assembly of Upper Canada; and he died in Toronto, in February, 1835, while attending the first session of the Assembly. He was the author of a *Narrative of the transactions in the Red River country, from the commencement of the operations of the Earl of Selkirk till the summer of 1816* (London, 1819).

MACDONELL, ALLAN (*fl.* 1799-1843) entered the service of the XY Company in 1799; and in 1804 he is listed as a clerk in the North West Company at Fort Dauphin. He was for many years employed in the Swan River or Red River departments; and in 1806 took part in an expedition to the Mandans. He took a prominent part in the Selkirk troubles; and was one of the officers of the North West Company arrested by Lord Selkirk in 1816, and tried at York (Toronto) in 1818. In 1816 he was made a partner of the North West Company; and at the union of 1821 he became a chief trader of the Hudson's Bay Company. From 1821 to 1826 he was in charge of the Swan River department, with headquarters, first, at Fort Dauphin, and, secondly, at Fort Pelly; and from 1826 to 1834 he was in charge of the Timiskaming district. He was promoted to the rank of chief factor in 1828. From 1835 to 1841 he was in charge of the Rainy Lake district; and in 1839 he was made a councillor of Rupert's Land. He was granted furlough in 1841; and he retired from the service of the Hudson's Bay Company in 1843.

MACDONELL, JOHN (1768-1850) was born in Scotland on November 30, 1768, the eldest son of John Macdonell of Scothouse, commonly known as "Spanish John", and the elder brother of Miles Macdonell (q.v.). He came to America with his father in 1773; and at the close of the American Revolution came to Canada. Between 1788, when he was gazetted an ensign in the militia battalion of Cornwall and Osnabruck, and 1793, when he first appears in the West, he became a clerk in the service of the North West Company. His journal for the years 1793-7 has been printed in L. R. Masson, *Les bourgeois de la Compagnie du Nord-Ouest*, vol. I (Quebec, 1889). He was made a partner of the North West Company about 1796; and in 1799 he was in charge of the Upper Red River department. He was employed in this department almost continuously until 1809, when he was placed in charge of the Athabaska River department. In 1808 he was elected a member of the Beaver Club of Montreal. He retired as a partner of the North West Company in 1812, and returned to Canada. He settled at Point Fortune, on the Ottawa River; and here he opened a store, and for many years ran a boat service on the Ottawa River. He died at Point Fortune on April 17, 1850, and was buried in the Roman Catholic cemetery at St. Andrews, P.Q. He married Magdeleine Poitras

(d. 1871); and by her he had six sons and two daughters. He is described by John McDonald of Garth (q.v.) as "Big McDonell... an easy man of no exertion"; and he was sometimes known, because of his piety, as "Macdonell le prêtre". Some account of him will be found in the Rev. A. G. Morice, *Miles Macdonell and his brothers* (Can. hist. rev., 1929).

MACDONELL, MILES (1769-1828) was born in Scotland in 1769, the second son of John Macdonell of Scothouse, otherwise known as "Spanish John", and the younger brother of John Macdonell *le prêtre* (q.v.). He came to America with his father in 1773; and about 1783 he settled with his father and a number of his relatives at Rivière aux Raisins, on the upper St. Lawrence, in Canada. In 1794 he was gazetted a lieutenant, and in 1796 a captain, in the Royal Canadian Volunteers; and in 1800 he was an unsuccessful candidate for election to the Legislative Assembly of Upper Canada for the county of Glengarry. In 1811 Lord Selkirk made him his agent in the establishment of the Red River colony; and he was appointed by the Hudson's Bay Company the first governor of Assiniboia. He came into conflict with the Nor' Westers, was arrested by them, and was carried a prisoner to Montreal in 1815. He returned to the Red River with Selkirk in 1817, but only for a short time; and his later years were spent mainly on his farm at Osnaburgh, Upper Canada. He died at the house of his brother, John Macdonell, at Point Fortune, on the Ottawa River, on June 28, 1828.

McDOUGALL, ALEXANDER (*fl.* 1799-1814) became a partner of the North West Company prior to 1799. He signed the agreements of 1802 and 1804 by attorney; and he does not appear to have been ever at Grand Portage or Fort William. Probably he was in charge of some district, such as the Timiskaming or Abitibi district, dependent on Montreal. A "Mr. M'gdougle" is said by J. B. Perrault (q.v.) to have been in charge of a fort at the lower end of Lake Abitibi in 1812. He seems to have retired from the fur-trade about 1813; and in 1814 he was elected a member of the Beaver Club of Montreal. He was dead by 1825.

McDOUGALL, DUNCAN (*fl.* 1810-1817) joined the Pacific Fur Company of J. J. Astor as a partner in 1810, and took part in the founding of Fort Astoria in 1811. He is said to have been a former clerk of the North West Company; but I can find no proof of this. He was in charge at Fort Astoria when it was handed over to the Nor' Westers in 1813; and he then entered the service of the North West Company, apparently as a partner. He remained on the Pacific coast until 1817, when he went east to Fort William, and when Ross Cox (q.v.) met him on his way to his winter quarters. Franchère (q.v.) says that he died "a miserable death" at Bas de la Rivière, Lake Winnipeg; but does not say when. He married in 1813 a daughter of Comcomly, chief of the Chinooks.

McDougall, George (fl. 1815-1843) was a brother of James McDougall (q.v.). D. W. Harmon (q.v.), who met him in New Caledonia in 1816, says that he had come out to the Peace River in 1815, as a clerk in the Hudson's Bay Company party commanded by John Clarke (q.v.). He left the Hudson's Bay Company at Fort Vermilion, and crossed the mountains to visit his brother James (q.v.). At Stuart's Lake, in 1816, he took service with the North West Company; and he remained in New Caledonia until after 1825. He was taken over as a clerk by the Hudson's Bay Company in 1821; and most of his later service was at Lesser Slave Lake. He was still a clerk in 1843.

McDougall, James (1783-1851) was born about 1783, and entered the service of the North West Company in 1798. He was a clerk in the Athabaska department in 1799; and from 1808 to 1816 he was employed either in New Caledonia or on the Peace River. He was taken over as a clerk by the Hudson's Bay Company in 1821; and the rest of his service was spent entirely in New Caledonia. He was "superannuated" in 1832; and John McLean described him as, in 1841, "still struggling with adversity". He died at Montreal, on August 17, 1851, aged 67 years.

McGill, Andrew (1756-1805) was born in Glasgow, Scotland, in 1756, the fifth son of James McGill, a merchant of Glasgow, and a younger brother of James McGill (q.v.) of Montreal. He matriculated into Glasgow University in 1765, at the early age of ten years. He joined his brothers James and John (p.v.) in Montreal about 1775, and became a junior partner in the firm of Todd and McGill. He died in Montreal on August 1, 1805, aged 49 years. He married Anne, daughter of Dr. Wood of Cornwall; and she married in 1807 the Rev. John Strachan, afterwards first bishop of Toronto.

McGill, James (1744-1813) was born in Glasgow, Scotland, on October 6, 1744, the eldest son of James McGill, a merchant of Glasgow. He matriculated into Glasgow University in 1756, but it does not appear that he graduated from the University. He emigrated to the American colonies, and engaged in the fur-trade. He later became a charter member of the Beaver Club of Montreal; and the date on his Beaver Club medal reveals the fact that he first wintered in the Indian country in 1766. He spent the winter of 1771 at Crow Wing River, west of Fond du Lac. He made Montreal his headquarters about 1774; and he was a party to the joint stock arrangement of the Western traders in 1775. He entered into partnership with Isaac Todd (q.v.), and played for many years a foremost part in the Canadian fur-trade. He was never, as has been sometimes stated, a member of the North West Company; but after 1781 confined himself to the south-west trade. From 1792 to 1796, and from 1800 to 1804, he represented the West Ward of Montreal in the Legislative Assembly of Lower Canada; and in 1793 he was appointed a member of the Executive

Council of the province. He died at Montreal on December 12, 1813; and a large part of his estate was left by will to found McGill University. In 1776 he married Charlotte, daughter of Guillaume Guillemin, and widow of François des Rivières.

McGILL, JOHN (1746-1797) was born in 1746, a son of James McGill, a merchant of Glasgow, Scotland, and a younger brother of James McGill (q.v.), of Montreal. He came to Canada as early as 1770, for his name appears in the fur-trade licences of that date; and the date on his Beaver Club medal reveals the fact that he wintered in the Indian country in 1770. In 1773 he appears in the fur-trade licences as a partner of his brother James, and in 1774 as a partner of Charles Paterson (q.v.). He became a member of the firm of Todd and McGill, and he died in Montreal on December 1, 1797.

McGILLIS, ANGUS (d. 1811) was the second son of Donald McGillis, a United Empire Loyalist who settled in Charlottenburg, Glengarry, Upper Canada, and his wife Mary, daughter of Ranald McDonell, Lundy. He entered the service of the North West Company and was a clerk at Fort Dauphin in 1805. He died in 1811; and his will is preserved in the Sulpician Library at Montreal. He married an Indian wife, and by her had four children. One of these was probably the Angus McGillis who was a clerk at the time of the union of the North West and Hudson's Bay Companies in 1821, and who died at the Red River on January 23, 1843. Another was a daughter who married one Grant, and lived afterwards in St. Paul, Minnesota.

McGILLIS, HUGH (1767?-1848) was born at Muneraghie, Inverness-shire, Scotland, about 1767, the fifth son of Donald McGillis, afterwards a United Empire Loyalist, who settled in Charlottenburgh, Upper Canada, and his wife Mary, daughter of Ranald McDonell, Lundy. He came to America with his parents in 1773, and after the American Revolution came north with them to Glengarry, Upper Canada. He entered the service of the North West Company as a clerk in 1790; and in 1801 he became a partner of the Company. He was at Fort Dauphin in 1799; and in 1802 he succeeded Archibald Norman McLeod (q.v.) in charge at this post. From 1806 to 1812 he was at Fond du Lac; from 1812 to 1813, at Fort William; from 1813 to 1814 at Michipicoten; and from 1814 to 1815 at the Lesser Slave Lake. In 1816 he was one of the partners of the North West Company arrested by Lord Selkirk at Fort William, and he was afterwards tried at York (Toronto), but acquitted. He retired from the fur-trade in 1816; and in 1818 he purchased Sir John Johnson's property at Williamstown, Upper Canada. Here he resided until his death, at Williamstown, on July 23, 1848, aged 81. There is a tablet to his memory in the Roman Catholic church at Williamstown. He married in the West an Indian woman, by whom he had seven children, and whom he sent back to the

West after he settled in Williamstown. All his children died without issue; and he left his property to his nephew, John McGillis, son of his brother Duncan. Another son of Duncan McGillis, Dr. Donald McGillis, died at his house in Williamstown in 1830. For most of the above information, I am indebted to Mr. F. D. McLennan, of Cornwall, Ont., whose grandmother was a first cousin of Hugh McGillis.

McGILLIS, DONALD (*fl.* 1786-1817) was a son of John McGillis, the eldest brother of Hugh McGillis (q.v.), and was probably born in Cape Breton in 1786, but afterwards came to Glengarry, Upper Canada. In 1811 he went out on the *Tonquin* with the expedition of J. J. Astor that founded Astoria. When Astoria was captured by the Nor' Westers in 1813, he took service with the North West Company. He did not, however, remain long in the Company's service, for in 1817 Ross Cox (q.v.) found him living on the Ottawa River. Later, he lived in Alexandria, Upper Canada, where he was for a time deputy registrar of deeds for Glengarry. He married Ruby Rutherford, of Middleboro, Vermont. For much of the above information, I am indebted to Mr. F. D. McLennan, of Cornwall, Ont., a grand-nephew of Donald McGillis.

McGILLIVRAY, ARCHIBALD (*fl.* 1803-1816) was probably a son of the Hon. William McGillivray (q.v.). He entered the service of the North West Company in 1803, and in 1808 D. W. Harmon (q.v.) went with him to the Athabaska district. He was in the Athabaska district, at Fort Vermilion, in 1815 and 1816; and he was at Fort William in the summer of 1816. He seems to have died or disappeared between 1816 and 1821.

McGILLIVRAY, DUNCAN (d. 1808) was the second son of Donald McGillivray, "a small tenant of the Lovat Estate in Inverness-shire", and his wife, Anne McTavish, a sister of Simon McTavish (q.v.). He entered the service of the North West Company some time prior to 1793, and in 1793-5 he was stationed in the Upper Fort des Prairies department. His *Journal* for 1794-5 has been published, with valuable notes and introduction, by A. S. Morton (Toronto, 1929). He remained in this department until 1799, when he returned to Montreal, was elected a member of the Beaver Club, and became a partner in the firm of McTavish, Frobisher, and Co. As such, he returned to the West in 1800, and made an attempt, only partially successful, to cross the Rocky Mountains. He left the West finally in 1802; and from 1802 to 1807 he was one of the agents of the North West Company at Fort William. He died, unmarried, in Montreal on April 9, 1808.

McGILLIVRAY, JOHN (1777?-1855) was born near Inverness, Scotland, about the year 1777, the second son of Farquhar McGillivray, who is reputed to have led the remnant of the Clan Chattan from the field of Culloden. With his elder brother Duncan, he came to Canada and entered the service of the North West Company about 1796. His brother (who must be distinguished from the Duncan McGillivray who was a brother of the Hon. William McGillivray) died soon afterwards; but John McGillivray rose rapidly in the service of the North West Company. He was made a partner of the Company in 1801; and he was in charge at Athabaska River from 1806 to 1810, and at Dunvegan from 1810 to 1815. He was one of the partners of the Company arrested by Lord Selkirk in 1816, and tried at York (Toronto) in 1817. He retired from the fur-trade in 1818, and settled at Williamstown, Upper Canada. From 1839 to 1841 he was a member of the Legislative Council of Upper Canada; and in 1852 he fell heir to the estate of Dunmaglass, near Inverness, Scotland, the home of the head of the clan. He never himself came into possession of the estate, for there was prolonged litigation over it; and he died at Williamstown, Upper Canada, in October, 1855. In 1819 he married at St. Andrews, Upper Canada, Isabelle, daughter of Colonel the Hon. Neil McLean; and by her he had four sons, Neil, Farquhar, William, and George.

McGILLIVRAY, JOSEPH (1790?-1832) was born about 1790, a son of the Hon. William McGillivray (q.v.). He was made a partner of the North West Company in 1813, and from 1813 to 1817 was at Fort Okanogan. He was at Fort William in the summer of 1817; but evidently returned to the Columbia department, where he remained until 1828. In 1821 he was promoted to the rank of chef trader. In 1828 he was transferred to New Caledonia; and he retired from the fur-trade in 1831. He died at Montreal on April 22, 1832, aged 42. He was a friend and correspondent of Ross Cox (q.v.), from whose book further details about him may be derived.

McGILLIVRAY, SIMON (1783-1840) was born in Stratherrick in Inverness-shire Scotland, in 1783, the youngest son of Donald McGillivray and Anne McTavish, a sister of Simon McTavish (q.v.). He was educated at his uncle's expense; but lameness precluded him from entering the fur-trade, like his brothers William and Duncan (q.v.). In 1805 he became a partner in the London firm of McTavish, Fraser and Co.; and in 1813 he became also a partner in the Montreal house of McTavish, McGillivrays and Co. He played a leading part in bringing about the union of the Hudson's Bay and North West Companies in 1821, and in the summer of 1821 he made a journey to Fort William to oversee the details of the union. In 1822 he became a member of the new firm of McGillivrays Thain, and Co.; and from 1821 to 1824 he was one of the special joint committee for the oversight of the fur-trade. In 1824, he and his brother William accepted stock in the Hudson's Bay Company in lieu of their rights; but in 1825 the firms of McTavish, McGillivrays, and Co. and McGillivrays, Thain, and Co. were declared insolvent, and Simon McGillivray was forced to go to Montreal to attempt to straighten out their tangled finances. In this, however, he was unsuccessful; and in 1829 he accepted an appointment as one of the commissioners appointed by the United Mexican Silver Mining Company to reorganize the management of their silver mines. He was in Mexico from 1830 to 1835. On his return to London, he became one of the proprietors of the *Morning Chronicle*; and in 1837 he married the eldest daughter of Sir John Easthope, his fellow-proprietor. He died at his residence, Dartmouth Row, Blackheath, London; and was buried in Norwood cemetery, near London. He was survived by his widow, and one daughter, Mary, who afterwards married Rear-Admiral Richard Dawkins. From 1822 to 1840 he was grand master of the second Provincial Grand Lodge of Upper Canada; and fuller details about him may be found in J. Ross Robertson, *The history of freemasonry in Canada* (2 vols., Toronto, 1899).

McGILLIVRAY, SIMON, JR. (d. 1840) was a son of the Hon. William McGillivray (q.v.), and a younger brother of Joseph McGillivray (q.v.). He entered the service of the North West Company as a clerk about 1803. He was for a number of years employed in the Athabaska department; and he was made a partner of the North West Company before the union of 1821. He was made a chief trader of the Hudson's Bay Company in 1821; and he spent most of the rest of his life at Hamilton Inlet, on the Labrador coast. In 1839, however, he was ordered to return to the Athabaska district; and he died, on his way thither, in the summer of 1840. His will is on file at Somerset House, in London. He married Theresa Roy; and by her he had four sons, Edward, Montrose, Napoleon Buonaparte, and Frederick, and five daughters, Cecilia, Mary, Anne Auldjo, Susan, and Theresa. Montrose entered the service of the Hudson's Bay Company in 1838, at the age of 16, and died in 1850. Cecilia married William Fletcher Lane (q.v.), and Mary married James Isbester, a postmaster or interpreter in the service of the Hudson's Bay Company. McGillivray had also a natural son, named John, who lived at Berthier, Lower Canada.

McGILLIVRAY, WILLIAM (1764?-1825) was born about 1764 in Scotland, probably in Stratherrick, Inverness-shire, and was the son of Donald McGillivray and Anne McTavish, sister of Simon McTavish (q.v.). He was educated at his uncle's expense; and in 1784 he came to Canada, and entered the service of the North West Company as a clerk. In 1785-6 he was in the Red River department; and in 1786-7 he was in charge of the post at Lac des Serpents, and, with Roderick McKenzie (q.v.) was mainly responsible for bringing about the union of the North West Company and the Gregory, McLeod Company in 1787. He became a partner in the North West Company in 1790, and a member of the firm of McTavish, Frobisher and Co. in 1793; and on the death of his uncle, Simon McTavish (q.v.) in 1804, he became the chief director of the North West Company. Fort William was named after him in 1807. He directed the policy of the North

West Company in regard to the Selkirk settlement at the Red River; and in 1816 he was arrested by Lord Selkirk at Fort William and sent down to Canada for trial. With his brother Simon (q.v.), he helped to negotiate the union of the North West Company and the Hudson's Bay Company in 1821; and after the union he became one of the joint board for consulting and advising on the management of the fur-trade. He bought the estate of Peine-au-Ghael, in the Isle of Mull, Scotland; but does not appear to have lived there. He died at St. John's Wood, London, on October 16, 1825, aged 61. He married in 1800 Magdeleine (d. 1810), the daughter of Capt. John McDonald of Garth and Magdeleine Small, and the sister of John McDonald of Garth (q.v.); and by her had two daughters. By an Indian woman, he had before this two sons, Joseph (q.v.) and Simon (q.v.), and a daughter, Elizabeth, who married one Jourdain, of Berthier, Lower Canada.

McGILLIVRAY, WILLIAM (1800-1832) was a half-breed, born in 1800, probably the son of Duncan McGillivray (q.v.). He entered the service of the North West Company in 1814. From 1821 to 1828 he was a clerk of the Hudson's Bay Company in the Athabaska department; and in 1828 he was transferred to New Caledonia. Here he was drowned on January 31, 1832. He was described by Sir George Simpson as "a perfect Indian in nature and character".

McINTOSH, ANGUS (1756?-1833) was born near Inverness, Scotland, about 1756, the son of the head of the McIntosh clan. He emigrated to Canada as a young man, and settled in Detroit prior to 1788. In 1796, on the American occupation of Detroit, he removed to Sandwich, Upper Canada. He was, for a number of years, agent for the North West Company at Detroit and Sandwich, though he never became a partner in the Company. In 1820 he was appointed a member of the Legislative Council of Upper Canada; but in 1831 he returned to Scotland to take possession of his ancestral estate at Moy Hall, Inverness-shire; and he died at Inverness, on January 25, 1833. He married in 1788 Mary (d. 1827), daughter of Jacques Baudry dit Desbuttes dit St. Martin; and by her he had several sons, who returned with him to Scotland.

McINTOSH, DONALD (1773?-1845) was born about 1773, and entered the service of the North West Company. He was in charge at Michipicoten in 1816, when he was arrested by Lord Selkirk (q.v.). He was appointed a chief trader in 1821; and he spent the remainder of his service in the Lake Superior district. From 1830 to 1838 he was in charge at Fort William; and in 1840 he retired, and settled at St. Polycarpe, near Montreal. Here he died on November 15, 1845, aged 72 years.

McINTOSH or MACKINTOSH, WILLIAM (1782-1842) was born in 1782, and entered the service of the North West Company. He was stationed at Lesser

Slave Lake in 1803. In 1805 he was transferred to the Peace River; and in 1815 he made a successful defence of Fort Vermilion against the Hudson's Bay men under John Clarke (q.v.). He was made a partner of the North West Company in 1816; and in 1819 he was one of the Nor' Westers arrested by William Williams (q.v.). At the time of the union of 1821, he was made a chief trader; and he was promoted to the rank of chief factor in 1823. From 1825 to 1829 he was in charge at Nelson House; from 1829 to 1832, at Cumberland House; and from 1832 to 1834, at Dunvegan. He retired from the fur-trade in 1837, and he died on February 16, 1842. His son, Duncan, was married at Lachine, near Montreal, in 1850.

McKay, Alexander (d. 1811) was the son of Donald McKay and Elspeth Kennedy, United Empire Loyalists who settled in the township of Charlottenburg, Glengarry county, Upper Canada. He entered the service of the North West Company before 1791, and accompanied Sir Alexander Mackenzie (q.v.) on his overland journey to the Pacific Ocean in 1793. He was at Portage la Prairie in 1794-5, and he was made a partner of the North West Company in 1799. He was in charge at Lake Winnipeg in 1806; and he retired from the North West Company in 1808. In 1807 he was elected a member of the Beaver Club of Montreal. In 1810 he became a partner in the Pacific Fur Company of J. J. Astor, and sailed to Astoria with Gabriel Franchère (q.v.). He was murdered by the Indians on the Tonquin, near Nootka, in the summer of 1811. He married a half-breed, by whom he had at least one son, Thomas (q.v.); and his widow afterwards married Dr. John McLoughlin (q.v.). His sister Catherine married in 1804 Simon Fraser (q.v.), of Ste. Anne's, Bout de l'Isle.

McKay, Donald (*fl.* 1786-1810) was a brother of Alexander and William McKay (q.v.). He entered the service of the North West Company, and was on the Saskatchewan in 1786, when he passed Cumberland House. He entered the service of the Hudson's Bay Company in 1790. He was stationed at Osnaburgh House in 1792, and on the Red River in 1794. In 1799 he left York Factory for England, on board the *King George*; and he died, according to a record in the possession of the McKay family, in 1810. He was known as "Mad McKay". Another Donald McKay, possibly a half-breed son of the older Donald, entered the service of the Hudson's Bay Company as a clerk in 1806, retired from the service in 1836, and died in Canada in 1838.

McKay, Thomas (*fl.* 1798-1848) was born in the Indian country about 1798, the half-breed son of Alexander McKay (q.v.), and was baptized in the Scotch Presbyterian Church at Williamstown, Glengarry, on November 9, 1804, aged 6 years. He entered the service of the Pacific Fur Company in 1810, and accompanied his father to Astoria. On the capture of Astoria in 1813 he took service with the North West Company; and he remained a clerk in the Columbia department, first with the North West Company and, after 1821, with the Hudson's Bay Company, almost continuously for about twenty-five years. He seems to have left the service of the latter between 1836 and 1839; and in 1839 Townsend met him near the Great Salt Lake, Utah. He appears to have settled on a farm in Oregon, to have become a citizen of the United States, and to have taken part in the Cayuse War of 1848.

McKay, William (1772-1832) was born in 1772, the son of Donald McKay and Elspeth Kennedy, and was a brother of Alexander McKay (q.v.). He entered the service of the North West Company in 1790, and was made a partner in 1796, Alexander Mackenzie relinquishing 1/46 share in his favour. He was in charge at Lake Winnipeg in 1799, and in 1805 was at Portage la Prairie. He retired from the fur-trade in 1807, and was elected a member of the Beaver Club of Montreal. In the War of 1812 he commanded the British force which captured Prairie-du-chien; and after the war he became an officer of the Indian department, with the rank of lieut.-colonel. He died in Montreal in 1832. In 1808 he married Eliza, daughter of the Hon. Mr. Justice Davidson; and by her he had a son, Robert, who became a judge of the Superior Court of Quebec. McKay Street, in Montreal, is called after him.

Mackenzie, Sir Alexander (1764-1820) was born near Stornoway, in the Island of Lewis, the second son of Kenneth Mackenzie and Isabella Maciver. In 1774, he emigrated with his father and two of his maternal aunts to New York, where his maternal uncle, John Maciver, known as "Ready Money John", was established in business. On the outbreak of the American Revolution, Kenneth Mackenzie, with his older brother John, obtained commissions in Sir John Johnson's Royal Greens; and the young Alexander was sent north, later, to school in Montreal. Kenneth Mackenzie died on service in 1780 at Carleton Island, in Lake Ontario; but his brother John, who probably became Alexander's guardian, settled in 1784 in Glengarry, and died, unmarried, in 1795. The young Alexander entered about 1779 the service of the firm of Finlay, Gregory and Co., afterwards Gregory, McLeod, and Co., as a clerk; and in 1784 he was sent to Detroit. In 1785 he was sent to the West, as a wintering partner of the firm; and when the firm was absorbed by the North West Company in 1787 he became a partner of this Company. In 1788 he was placed in charge of Fort Chipewyan on Lake Athabaska; and in 1789 he made from this post the expedition to the Arctic Ocean which has given his name to the Mackenzie River. In 1793 he followed this with his epoch-making journey to the Pacific Ocean. In 1799, because of disagreements with Simon McTavish (q.v.) and William McGillivray (q.v), he announced his intention of severing his connection with the North West Company, and went to England. Here he published his *Voyages* (London, 1801), and in 1802 received the honour of knight bachelor. He returned to Canada in 1802; and became the leading partner in the XY Company. On the union of the XY and North West Companies in 1804, he again acquired an interest in the North West Company, but was "excluded from any interference", and organized the firm of Sir Alexander Mackenzie and Co. to look after his interests in the North West Company. In 1805 he was elected a member of the Legislative Assembly of Lower Canada for the county of Huntingdon; but in 1808 he returned to Scotland, and there he spent his remaining years. In 1812 he married Geddes, the daughter of George Mackenzie of Avoch, a merchant of Tower Hill, London, by whom he had two sons and one daughter; and the same year he purchased her father's estate of Avoch, in Ross-shire. He died in a wayside inn on his way from Edinburgh to Avoch, on March 12, 1820. For many years he had received nothing from his interest in the North West Company; and on the failure of McTavish, McGillivrays and Co. in 1825, his estate was a heavy creditor of this firm. In 1830, after some litigation, Lady Mackenzie received from Edward Ellice (q.v.), one of those who had brought about the union of the North West and Hudson's Bay Companies in 1821, the sum of £10,000. There are several biographies of Mackenzie; but the latest and most authoritative is M. S. Wade, *Mackenzie of Canada* (Edinburgh, 1927).

McKenzie, Alexander (1767?-1830) was a nephew of Sir Alexander Mackenzie (q.v.), and was born, probably in Scotland, about 1767. From 1790 to 1796 he was a trader near Detroit; and in 1798 he entered the service of the XY Company as a wintering partner. He became a partner of the North West Company on the union of the two companies in 1804; and from 1804 to 1808 he was in charge of the Athabaska department. From 1809 to 1810 he was at the Pic, on Lake Superior; and from 1811 to 1812 he was agent of the Company at Fort William. He was one of the North West partners arrested by Lord Selkirk (q.v.) in 1816, and was tried at the assizes in York in 1818, but was acquitted. He appears to have become a retired partner about this time; but he was at Fort William in the summer of 1821, as an agent of McTavish, McGillivrays, and Co. He died in Montreal on July 23, 1830; and his will is on file at the Court House in Montreal. He married Isabella Latour; and by her he had two children, John George McKenzie, who was born at Long Lake, and died at Berthier, Lower Canada, on January 17, 1838, and Ann (Nancy), who was born at Grand Portage, and married in 1829 William Cowie at Sault Ste. Marie. His widow married John McBean (q.v.). On the Athabaska he was known by the nickname "The Emperor"; and in his obituary notice in the *Canadian Courant* he is described as a "Major on the staff of the militia of this province".

McKenzie, Alexander (1794-1828) was born at Inverness, Scotland, in 1794, the son of John Mackenzie, and entered the service of the North West

Company as an apprentice clerk in 1812. At the union of 1821 he became a clerk in the Hudson's Bay Company, and was stationed in the Columbia district. He was murdered by the Indians at Hood's Canal, on the Columbia, in 1828.

McKenzie, Andrew (d. 1809) was a half-breed son of Sir Alexander Mackenzie (q.v.). He was employed as a clerk of the North West Company in the Athabaska district as early as 1806; and he died at Fort Vermilion on March 1, 1809.

McKenzie, Charles (1774-1855) was born at Farintosh, in Scotland, in 1774, and was probably a relative of the Hon. Roderick McKenzie (q.v.). He entered the service of the North West Company in 1803; and in 1804 he was a clerk on the Assiniboine. His account of the Missouri Indians, to whom he made four trading expeditions in the years 1804 to 1806, has been published by L. R. Masson, in his *Bourgeois de la Compagnie du Nord-Ouest*, I (Quebec, 1889). In 1807 he was transferred to the region between Rainy Lake and Albany; and here he spent most of the rest of his service. He was taken over as a clerk by the Hudson's Bay Company in 1821; and he was still a clerk when he retired from the service in 1854. He died at the Red River Settlement on March 3, 1855; and his will is on record at Hudson's Bay House in London. He married an Indian woman; and by her he had one son, Hector, and three daughters.

McKenzie, Daniel (1769?-1832) was born, probably in Scotland, about 1769. He entered the service of the North West Company about 1790, and in 1791 was at Fort Chipewyan, on Lake Athabaska. He was at Upper Fort des Prairies and Rocky Mountains in 1799; and he became a partner of the North West Company in 1796, Alexander Mackenzie relinquishing 1/46 share in his favour. In 1806 he was in charge of the Athabaska district; from 1808 to 1809 he was on the Lower Red River; from 1809 to 1812 he was in the English River department; and from 1813 to 1815 he was at Fond-du-Lac. He was one of the North West Company partners arrested by Lord Selkirk in 1816, but was released, and was at Ste. Anne's, in the island of Montreal, in 1817. In 1818 he published *A letter to the Rt. Hon. the Earl of Selkirk in answer to a pamphlet entitled "A postscript in answer to the Statement respecting the Earl of Selkirk's settlement on the Red River in North America"*, which was written, but not printed, at Sandwich, Upper Canada, and is one of the rarest items in the literature relating to the Selkirk controversy. He retired from the fur-trade about this time; and, because of his intemperate habits, a trust fund was established for his support. He died at Brockville, Upper Canada, on May 8, 1832, aged 63 years, and is described in his obituary notice as "of Augusta, North Carolina". His half-breed son Roderick (q.v.) was a clerk in the Southern Department in 1821.

McKenzie, Donald (1783-1851) was born in Scotland in 1783, and was a younger brother of the Hon. Roderick McKenzie (q.v.). He emigrated to Canada in 1800, and entered the service of the North West Company as a clerk. In 1809 he entered the service of J. J. Astor's American Fur Company; and in 1811 he made the overland journey to Astoria. Here he remained until the purchase of Astoria by the Nor' Westers in 1813, when he re-entered the service of the North West Company. He became a partner of the North West Company; and at the union of 1821 he became a chief factor of the Hudson's Bay Company. In 1822 he was appointed a member of the Council of the North West Territories; and from 1825 to 1833 governor of Assiniboia. He then retired from the fur-trade, and settled in Mayville, Chatauqua County, New York. Here he died on January 20, 1851.

McKenzie, Henry (1781?-1832) was born in Scotland about 1781, and was a younger brother of the Hon. Roderick McKenzie (q.v.). He came to Canada about 1800, and in 1803 was at Kaministiquia (Fort William). On the death of Simon McTavish (q.v.), he was appointed to manage his seigniory and mills at Terrebonne; and when Sir Alexander Mackenzie left Canada in 1808, he was appointed to manage his affairs in Canada. In 1814 he became a member of the firm of McTavish, McGillivrays and Co. of Montreal; and during the Selkirk controversy of 1814-18 he was particularly charged with the publicity campaign of the North West Company. After the union of 1821, however, his relations with his partners in the firm of McTavish, McGillivrays and Co. became strained, and he was denied access to the books of the Company. After the failure of the Company in 1825 he published a *Letter to Simon McGillivray* (Montreal, 1827), which is a review of his relations with it. In 1815 he was elected a member of the Beaver Club of Montreal, and in 1819 he became an elder, and afterwards clerk of session, in the St. Gabriel's Street Presbyterian Church in Montreal. He died of cholera in Montreal on June 28, 1832. In 1815 he married Anne, youngest daughter of the Rev. John Bethune, and sister of Angus Bethune (q.v.), and by her he had two children who were still living in 1887, Mrs. Stow, of Parkdale, Toronto, and Simon McTavish McKenzie, of Montreal.

McKenzie, James (d. 1849) was a younger brother of the Hon. Roderick McKenzie (q.v.), and entered the service of the North West Company as a clerk in 1794. He was in the Athabaska department in 1795, and remained here until 1806. In 1802 he became a partner of the North West Company; and in 1806 he was appointed to the King's Posts in the Lower St. Lawrence. His Athabaska journal of 1799-1800 and his account of the King's Posts in 1808 have been published by Masson in his *Bourgeois de la Compagnie du Nord-Ouest*, vol. 2 (Quebec, 1890). He seems to have retired from the management of the King's Posts prior to the union of 1821, for at that time they were managed by James C. McTavish (q.v.);

but he evidently retained some connection with them, for in the notice of his death, which took place at Quebec on July 18, 1849, "of the prevailing malady", he is described as "agent of the Hudson's Bay Company". His wife died at Quebec on October 19, 1850. He had two sons and two daughters. One of the sons, Keith, was a servant of the Hudson's Bay Company, and was living in 1889; one of the daughters became Mrs. Patrick, and the other was in 1889 the widow of Lt. Col. McDougall of Kingston.

McKenzie, Kenneth (d. 1817) would appear to have been a relative of the Hon. Roderick McKenzie (q.v.), since his will is preserved among the Masson papers in the Canadian Archives, which came from the Hon. Roderick McKenzie's estate. He entered the service of the North West Company, at a date not ascertained. He was made a partner in 1805; and from 1806 to 1816 he was in charge at Fort William. In 1813 he was elected a member of the Beaver Club in Montreal; and in 1816 he was, with William McGillivray (q.v.), one of the agents of the North West Company at Fort William. He was arrested by Lord Selkirk at Fort William in 1816; and he was drowned, while still a prisoner, on Lake Superior in 1817. He is to be distinguished from the Kenneth Mackenzie (1801-1861), who is described as a relative of Sir Alexander Mackenzie (q.v.), who was a clerk in the service of the North West Company in 1820, and whose later career in the American fur-trade is described in H. M. Chittenden, *History of the fur-trade of the far west* (3 vols., New York, 1902).

McKenzie, Roderick (d. 1844) was a first cousin of Sir Alexander Mackenzie, and came to Canada in 1784. He entered the service of Gregory, McLeod and Co., and in 1785 was sent to the West as a clerk. In 1788 he built Fort Chipewyan, on Lake Athabaska; and in 1789 and 1792 he was in charge at this post during his cousin's expeditions to the Arctic and Pacific Oceans. He declined to follow his cousin when he left the North West Company; and the relations between them were strained for many years. He was made a partner of McTavish, Frobisher and Co. in 1800; and was one of the agents of the Company at Grand Portage in that year. He retired from active participation in the fur-trade in 1801, resigning one of his two shares in the Company; and he resigned the other share in 1805. He continued, however, to be a dormant partner in the firm of McTavish, Frobisher and Co. (later McTavish, McGillivrays and Co.) until its failure in 1825; and in 1827 he brought action against the trustees appointed by Simon McGillivray (q.v.) to recover his share of the assets of the firm. In 1804 he purchased from the estate of Simon McTavish (q.v.) the seigniory of Terrebonne; and here he lived till his death on August 15, 1844. In his later years he devoted himself to gathering materials for the history of the fur-trade; and much of this material was afterwards published by his son-in-law, the Hon. L. R.

Masson, in his *Bourgeois de la Compagnie du Nord-Ouest* (2 vols., Quebec 1889-90). From 1817 to 1838 he was a member of the Legislative Council of Lower Canada. In 1803 he married Marie Louise Rachel, daughter of Charles Jean Baptiste Chaboillez (q.v.); and by her he had several children.

McKenzie, Roderick (1772?-1859) was born in Scotland, about 1772, and entered the service of the Hudson's Bay Company. He was a clerk at Fort Wedderburn, on Lake Athabaska, during the Selkirk troubles of 1816-17. In 1821 he was made a chief trader; and in 1830 he was promoted to the rank of chief factor. From 1830 to 1843 he was in charge of the English River department at Isle à la Crosse; but he must have retired soon after this date. He died, on January 2, 1859, at Caberleigh Cottage, Red River Settlement, aged 87 years. He was usually known as "Roderick McKenzie, senior".

McKenzie, Roderick (fl. 1804-1821) was a clerk of the North West Company who was for many years employed in the Lake Nipigon district. He was a clerk at Lake Nipigon in 1804; he was in charge at Fort Duncan, Lake Nipigon, in 1807-8; and Ross Cox (q.v.), who met him at Fort William in 1817, and who calls him "Captain Roderick McKenzie", says that he was at that time nearly 50 years of age, and had been 25 years in the Indian country. He was made a chief trader at the time of the union of 1821; and he seems to have died or retired about 1829.

McKenzie, Roderick (d. 1830) was a half-breed, possibly a son of Capt. Roderick McKenzie (q.v.), who entered the service of the North West Company, and was taken over by the Hudson's Bay Company in 1821, when he was a clerk at Lake Nipigon. He was referred to in the records of the Company as Roderick McKenzie "A". In 1827 he was discharged from the service, but he re-entered it in 1829, and he died on February 25, 1830.

McKenzie, Roderick (fl. 1818-1860) was a half-breed who entered the service of the North West Company in 1818, and was taken over by the Hudson's Bay Company in 1821. He was known as Roderick McKenzie "B". He was discharged from the service in 1845, but re-entered it in 1847; and he was still a clerk in 1860.

McLellan, Archibald (d. 1820) entered the service of the North West Company in 1792, and in 1795 he appears as a clerk at Bas de la Rivière House, having arrived there from his winter quarters. He was at Rainy Lake in 1799, and he seems to have remained there until 1810. He was admitted a partner of the North West Company in 1805, to begin with the outfit of 1808. Between 1810 and 1815 he was at Michipocoten; and in 1815 he was sent to Lake Athabaska. He took a prominent part in the Selkirk troubles; and in 1818 he was, with Charles de Reinhard, tried at Quebec for murder, but was acquitted. For an account of the trial, see S. H. Wilcocke (ed.), *Report of the trials of Charles de Reinhard and Archibald McLellan for murder* (Montreal, 1818). He retired from the fur-trade in 1819; and he died in Glengarry, Upper Canada, on January 15, 1820.

McLEOD, ALEXANDER (d. 1809) was a native of the parish of Deurinish in Scotland, and was a nephew of Normand McLeod (q.v.), of Gregory, McLeod and Co. He entered the service of the North West Company before 1787, and in 1791 was at Fort Chipewyan, on Lake Athabaska. He became a wintering partner of the Company in 1795; but he left the Peace River district, where he had been stationed, in 1799, and in 1802 he was at Grand Portage. He retired from the fur-trade about this time, and in 1805 he relinquished his two shares in the Company. He settled in Montreal, and here he died in 1809. He had a natural daughter, Ann, born in the Indian country, who was brought up by the Rev. John Bethune in Glengarry, Upper Canada, and who married "Squire" Alexander Mackenzie of Williamstown, Upper Canada. By Mary McGillis he had two natural sons, Alexander and John, and one natural daughter, Margaret (Peggy). Alexander married in 1825 Mary Chisholm of Charlottenburgh Upper Canada, was a school-teacher in Prescott, and lived to an advanced age. John died young. Margaret married Duncan McIntyre, a farmer near Williamstown; and had several children. For much of this information, I am indebted to Mr. F. D. McLennan, of Cornwall, Ontario. Alexander McLeod's will is preserved in the Court House at Montreal.

McLEOD, ALEXANDER RODERICK (d. 1840) entered the service of the North West Company in 1802, and was a clerk on the Peace River in 1806. His journal for 1806 has been printed by J. N. Wallace, in his *Wintering partners on the Peace River* (Ottawa, 1929). In 1809 he was at Rocky Mountain House, and again in 1811. He was at Grand Portage in the summer of 1821, and was made a chief trader in the Hudson's Bay Company. From 1821 to 1823 he was stationed in the Athabaska district; from 1823 to 1825, in the Mackenzie River district; in 1825, at Fort Vancouver; from 1831 to 1833, at Fort Simpson; in 1833 to 1835, with Back's expedition; from 1835 to 1836, at Great Slave Lake; and from 1838 to 1839, at Fort Dunvegan. In 1839 he went to Canada on furlough; and he died on June 11, 1840.

McLEOD, ARCHIBALD NORMAN (*fl.* 1796-1837) entered the service of the North West Company prior to 1796, for D. W. Harmon (q.v.) says that Alexander McLeod, a half-breed son by a Rapid River woman, was in his fifth year in July, 1801. It is probable that he was a relative of Normand McLeod (q.v.), of Gregory, McLeod, and Co.; but what the relationship was, I have not been able to discover. He was made a partner of the North West Company before 1799, when he was "proprietor at Fort Dauphin". He went to the Athabaska country in 1802, and he remained there until

1808. He became a partner in McTavish, McGillivrays and Co., and a member of the Beaver Club in 1808; and in 1809 he retired as a wintering partner of the North West Company. He took a prominent part in the Selkirk troubles of 1815-18, and he was at Fort William in 1821; but on the union of the North West Company and the Hudson's Bay Company in that year, he withdrew from the fur-trade, and went to live in Scotland. In 1826 he was described as living "at Sunnybank, in the county of Aberdeen"; and in 1837 he was barrack-master at Belfast, Ireland. I have not discovered the date of his death, but it occurred between 1837 and 1845, since his widow died at Coley Parsonage, Halifax, Yorkshire, on March 12, 1845. Possibly he died in 1838, as a new barrack-master at Belfast was appointed in that year. The diary kept by him at Fort Alexandria in 1800-1 has been printed, with annotations, in C. M. Gates (ed.), *Five fur-traders of the Northwest* (Minneapolis, 1933).

McLeod, John (1788-1849) was born at Stornoway, Scotland, in 1788, and entered the service of the Hudson's Bay Company in 1811. In 1814 he was in charge of the post at the forks of the Red River, and his diary describing his defence of the post against the Nor' Westers has been printed in the *Collections of the State Historical Society of North Dakota*, vol. 2 (Bismarck, N.D., 1908). He played a prominent part in the Selkirk troubles; and in 1821 he was promoted to the rank of chief trader. From 1822 to 1826 he was in the Columbia department. He retired from the service of the Hudson's Bay Company in 1848; and he died at Hochelaga, Lower Canada, on July 24, 1849. He married a daughter of John Peter Pruden (q.v.); and his son, Malcolm McLeod, was the editor of Archibald McDonald's *Peace River* (Ottawa, 1872).

McLeod, John (*fl.* 1821-1840) was a native of Scotland, and entered the service of the North West Company prior to 1821, when he was a clerk on the Churchill River. From 1824 to 1830 he was in the Mackenzie River district; and later he was employed on the Columbia. He was promoted to the rank of chief trader in 1834, and he retired from the fur-trade in 1842. Sir George Simpson described him as "a fine, active fellow".

McLeod, John (*fl.* 1821-1824) was a son of Archibald Norman McLeod (q.v.), "a poor, deformed lad" who was employed as a clerk at Fort Dauphin in 1821. In 1824 he was "permitted to retire".

McLeod, Normand (d. 1796) was a native of the Island of Skye, Scotland. In a letter dated Detroit, January 6, 1780, to Capt. Mathews, he refers to "faithful services from the beginning of the year 1747 in Holland, Brabant, and North America, to the end of the year 1764" (*Mich. Pion. Coll.*, X, 374-5); and it is probable that he was the Captain Normand McLeod who was a friend and correspondent of Sir William Johnson (see *The Johnson Papers*, 8 vols., Albany, N.Y., 1921—). He was for a time an officer of the Indian department, but by 1776 he was established as a trader in Detroit. In 1777 he was appointed town major of Detroit; but there was some difficulty about his appointment, and in 1780 he declined to accept pay. He was in Detroit as late as July, 1782; and in December, 1782, he was at Mackinac. In 1783 he became a partner of John Gregory (q.v.), in the firm of Gregory, McLeod, and Co., which succeeded to that of Finlay, Gregory and Co. In 1787, when Gregory, McLeod and Co. were absorbed in the North West Company, he became a dormant partner. He sold out his interest in the Company in 1790, and he died in Montreal in 1796. He married, probably in Detroit, Cécile Robert; but he seems to have had no children. His will is on record in the Court House at Montreal.

McLoughlin, John (1784-1857) was born at Rivière du Loup, Canada, on October 19, 1784, the son of John McLoughlin and Angélique, eldest daughter of Malcolm Fraser of Murray Bay. He studied medicine at Edinburgh, and became a qualified physician. On his return to Canada about 1806, he entered the service of the North West Company, probably through the influence of his uncle, Alexander Fraser (q.v.); and in the summer of 1807 he was at Sturgeon Lake in the Nipigon department, when D. W. Harmon (q.v.) was sent to him for medical attention. The following winter he was at Vermilion Lake, near Rainy Lake; and he seems to have been employed in the Rainy Lake district for a number of years. In 1814, when he was made a partner of the North West Company, he was placed in charge of the Rainy Lake district. In 1820 he went, with Angus Bethune (q.v.), to London as a representative of the wintering partners, to arrange a union with the North West Company; but the Hudson's Bay Company declined to negotiate separately with Bethune and himself, and the union was concluded with the McGillivrays (q.v.) and Edward Ellice (q.v.). McLoughlin was very much discontented with the terms of the union of the North West Company and the Hudson's Bay Company in 1821; but accepted a commission in the Hudson's Bay Company as chief factor. In 1823 he was sent to the Columbia department; and in 1824 he was in charge at Fort George (Astoria), but in 1826 he removed his headquarters to Fort Vancouver, which he built. Here he remained until 1846. He then resigned from the Hudson's Bay Company, and during his last years he kept a general store in Oregon City. He came to be known as "the father of Oregon". He died at Oregon City on September 3, 1857. He married the widow of Alexander McKay (q.v.); and by her he had two sons and two daughters. For his biography, see F. V. Holman, *Dr. John McLoughlin* (Cleveland, 1907).

McMillan, James (d. 1858) was born in Scotland, and entered the service of the North West Company prior to 1804, when he appears as a clerk at Fort des Prairies. With David Thompson (q.v.), he was one of the pioneers of the fur-trade with the Columbia. Ross Cox (q.v.) met him on the Spokane River in 1813. In 1821 he became a chief trader of the Hudson's Bay Company; and in 1827 he was promoted to the rank of chief factor. He explored the lower part of the Fraser River in 1824, and he built Fort Langley at the mouth of the Fraser in 1827. He left the Columbia department in 1829; and from 1830 to 1834 he was placed in charge of the Experimental Farm at the Red River Settlement. He was granted furlough in 1837, and he retired from the Company's service in 1839. He died in 1858.

McMurray, Thomas (1779?-1849) would appear to have been a younger son of Thomas McMurray (d. 1795), and to have been born in Montreal in 1779. He entered the service of the XY Company, and in 1803-4 was in charge of the XY post at Fort Dauphin. On the union of the XY and the North West Companies, he was sent as a clerk to Rainy Lake. In 1817 Ross Cox (q.v.) met him at Isle à la Crosse, and it was at Isle à la Crosse that he was arrested by John Clarke (q.v.) in 1820. He was elected a member of the Beaver Club of Montreal in 1815, and he was made a partner of the North West Company in 1816. At the time of the union of 1821, he was made a chief trader. In 1821, he was stationed at the Winnipeg River; in 1823, at Fort Dauphin; in 1824, at Rainy Lake; from 1825 to 1831 at the Lake of the Woods; and from 1831 to 1834 at the Pic. He was granted furlough in 1841, and he retired from the Company's service in 1843. He died near Brighton, in the township of Cramahé, Upper Canada, on January 15, 1849. He was married; and had at least two sons, William (afterwards a chief factor of the Hudson's Bay Company, after whom Fort McMurray was named in 1870) and Samuel.

McMurray, Thomas (d. 1795) was a trader who settled in Montreal about 1772. He appears to have been at Michilimackinac between 1769 and 1772. His name occurs in the fur-trade licences for 1778, and that of his son Samuel (d. 1795) for 1790. He died in the early part of 1795, apparently at the same time as his son. In September, 1772, he married, first, Jane (d. 1778), widow of Tobias Izenhoult; and in January, 1782, he married, secondly, Helen Peacock, of Montreal-

McPherson, Murdock (1796?-1863) was born at Gairloch, Ross-shire, Scotland, about 1796, and entered the service of the North West Company in 1816. Ross Cox (q.v.) met him when he was *en route* for the Athabaska district in 1817. He was taken over as a clerk by the Hudson's Bay Company at the union of 1821; and in 1823 he was transferred to the Mackenzie River department. He remained here until 1848, with the exception of the years 1840-3, which he spent on furlough and at Tadoussac. He was promoted to be a chief trader in 1834, and a chief factor in 1847. He was granted two years' furlough in 1849, and he retired in 1851. He died in 1863.

McTavish, Alexander (1784?-1832) was born about 1784, and was probably a relative of Donald McTavish (q.v.). He came out to Astoria on the *Isaac Todd* in 1813, as a clerk in the service of the North West Company. In 1817 he was at Fort William, and in 1821, when he was taken over as a clerk by the Hudson's Bay Company, he was stationed at the Pic, on Lake Superior. From 1824 to 1832 he was in charge at Lake Nipigon; and in 1828 he was promoted to the rank of chief trader. He died at Lake Nipigon on December 9, 1832, of apoplexy, aged about 48 years. In 1822 Sir George Simpson described him as "a very respectable and deserving man, a good clerk and trader"; but by 1832 he had changed his opinion, as he described him in his confidential book of "Servants' Characters" as "a sly, sneaking, plausible fellow ... was a recruiting sergeant, but more likely to show off on the parade than in the field".

McTavish, Donald (d. 1814) was born in Stratherrick, Inverness-shire, Scotland, and was a son of Alexander McTavish, and a first cousin of Simon McTavish (q.v.). He must have entered the service of the North West Company as a clerk prior to 1790, since his obituary notice in the *Quebec Gazette*, of December 14, 1815, describes him as having been employed in the West upwards of twenty-five years. He was made a partner of the North West Company prior to 1799, for in that year he was "proprietor" on the Upper English River. He was in charge of the English River department until 1808; and from 1808 to 1811 he was in charge at Fort Dunvegan, in the Athabaska department. He returned to Great Britain in 1812; and in 1813 he commanded the expedition which sailed on the *Isaac Todd* for Fort Astoria. He was drowned near the mouth of the Columbia on May 22, 1814. In 1814, before the news of his death reached Montreal, he was made a partner in the firm of McTavish, McGillivrays, and Co.

McTavish, Dugald (1817-1871) was born at Kilchrist, Argyllshire, Scotland, in 1817, and was a nephew of John George McTavish (q.v.). He entered the service of the Hudson's Bay Company as an apprentice clerk at Moose Factory in 1833. In 1836 he was at Michipocoten, and in 1837 at Lachine; but in 1839 he was transferred to the Columbia; and here, except for a period spent in the Sandwich Islands about 1847, he remained until 1859. He was promoted to the rank of chief trader in 1851; and he died at Montreal, of heart disease, on May 24, 1871.

McTavish, James Chisholm (d. 1827) was probably a relative of Donald McTavish (q.v.), and sailed with him for Astoria in the *Isaac Todd* in 1813. He was at Fort William, when that place was captured by Lord Selkirk in 1816. Prior to 1821, he was employed in the management of the King's Posts, on the Lower St. Lawrence; and he was continued in that capacity, after the union of the North West and Hudson's Bay Companies, until 1827, when he was dismissed from the service. He died, shortly afterwards, on the Island of Orleans, Lower Canada, on December 16, 1827.

McTavish, John (d. 1852) was born in Scotland, a son of Alexander McTavish, and a nephew of Simon McTavish (q.v.). He came to Canada about 1808; and in 1814 he became a partner in McTavish, McGillivrays, and Co., in charge of the accounting department. He did not prove a success in this capacity, however, and in 1816 he went to the United States. There he married, in 1816, Emily, youngest daughter of Richard Caton, of Doughoregon Manor House, near Baltimore, Maryland, who was connected with the Carrols of Carrolltown. In 1834 he was appointed British consul at Baltimore; and he died on June 21, 1852.

McTavish, John George (d. 1847) was the second son of the chief of the Clan Tavish, and was introduced into the fur-trade in Canada through the friendship of Simon McTavish (q.v.) with his father. From a letter in my possession, it is clear that Simon McTavish, while in Scotland, introduced himself to the head of the clan, somewhat dazzled him with his wealth, persuaded him to have his arms registered (as well as those of Simon McTavish himself, as a distant kinsman), and in 1798 took his son John George into the North West Company as a clerk. The latter was at Grand Portage in 1802; he was stationed in the Athabaska district in 1808; and he was with John McDonald of Garth (q.v.) when he went to the relief of David Thompson (q.v.) in 1811. In 1913 he was on the Columbia, and received the surrender of Fort Astoria. He was made a partner of the North West Company in 1813; and in 1819 he was arrested by William Williams (q.v.), of the Hudson's Bay Company, in connection with the Selkirk troubles. He was sent to England for trial; but was released in 1821, and was appointed a chief factor of the Hudson's Bay Company. He was in charge at York Factory from 1821 to 1828, and at Moose Factory from 1831 to 1834. From 1836 to 1847 he was in charge at the Lake of Two Mountains, near Montreal. He retired from the Company early in 1847; and he died on July 20, 1847. His wife died at the Lake of Two Mountains on October 8, 1841.

McTavish, Simon (1750-1804) was born in 1750, probably in Stratherrick, Inverness-shire. He belonged to a branch of the Clan Tavish which had fled from Argyllshire, and settled in Inverness-shire several generations before he was born. He emigrated to America before 1772, and engaged in the fur-trade from Albany. He was in Detroit as early as 1772; and in 1775 he transferred his headquarters to Montreal. He was trading at Grand Portage in 1776, in partnership with James Bannerman (q.v.); and in 1779 he was one of the partners in the original sixteen-share North West Company of that year. He seems to have been one of the prime movers in bringing about the renewed agreement of 1783; and in 1787 he formed a partnership with Joseph Frobisher, known as McTavish,

Frobisher and Co., which became the supply house and virtual directorate of the North West Company. As the head of this house, he became in fact, if not in name, the general manager of the Company; and for many years he visited Grand Portage in the summer to superintend the trade. There is no evidence that he ever wintered in the Indian country; and it is significant that he was never a member of the Beaver Club of Montreal. He became perhaps the richest man in Montreal. In 1793 Sir Alured Clarke recommended that he should be appointed a member of the Legislative Council; but for some reason this recommendation was never acted on. In 1800 he purchased the estate of Dunardarie in Argyllshire, which was the home of the chief of Clan Tavish, and which had recently come into the market; and in 1803 he commenced the building of a mansion on the side of the mountain in Montreal. This house was not yet completed when he died in Montreal, on July 6, 1804. His will, which is on file in Somerset House, London, is printed in this volume, and throws a flood of light, not only on his relationships, but on the history of the North West Company. On February 27, 1793, he married Marguerite, daughter of Charles Jean Baptiste Chaboillez (q.v.), "a handsome young lady with a *plum*"; and by her he had two sons, William and Simon, jr., and two daughters, Ann and Mary. William died at Strand-on-the-Green, London, England, on May 4, 1816, aged 21; Simon, jr., at Ramsgate, England, on October 9, 1828, aged 25; Ann, at Bridport, England, on May 22, 1819, aged 19; and Mary, at Sidmouth, England, on June 9, 1819, aged 21. A monument to these four children is still to be seen in Chiswick Parish Church, London. The widow married, a few years after McTavish's death, William Smith Plenderleath, an officer in the British army. Over McTavish's will a good deal of litigation resulted; and the final distribution did not take place until 1839. His Montreal property, on which he was buried, finally reverted to his eldest nephew, John McTavish (q.v.), whose executors sold it. Before it was sold, however, one of the executors had Simon McTavish's tomb covered with a mound of earth, to prevent vandals breaking in.

MALHIOT, FRANÇOIS VICTOR (1776-1840) was born in 1776, and entered the service of the North West Company as a clerk about 1791. He was a cousin of Jacques Porlier (q.v.). From 1796 to 1804 he was in the Upper Red River department; and from 1804 to 1807 he was in charge of a post at Lac aux Flambeaux. His journal for 1804-5 has been printed in the *Wisconsin Historical Collections*, XIX, 1910. In 1807 he retired from the fur-trade, and settled at Contrecoeur, Lower Canada, with his half-breed son. Here he died in 1840. D. W. Harmon (q.v.) describes his marriage to an Indian woman on August 8, 1800, at Fort Alexandria.

MILES, ROBERT SEABORN (1795?-1870) was born about 1795 at Fairford, Oxfordshire, England. He entered the service of the Hudson's Bay Company as an accountant and writer; and from 1821 to 1833 he was accountant at York Factory. He was promoted to the rank of chief trader in 1828, and to that of chief factor in 1844. From 1844 to 1857, he was in charge at Moose Factory; and from 1858 to 1860, in the Lake Huron district. He retired in 1861; and he died at Horning Toft, near Brockville, Ontario, on May 3, 1870, aged 74 years. In 1868 his daughter Harriett married at Brockville Adam Hudspeth, of Lindsay, Ontario.

MITCHELL, DAVID, Jr. (d. 1809) was a son of Dr. David Mitchell, of the Indian department, and a Chippewa woman. In 1806 he was one of the agents and attornies of the Michilimackinac Company; and he was a member of the Beaver Club of Montreal. According to the minutes of the Beaver Club, he died at Montreal on April 11, 1809.

MOFFATT, GEORGE (1787-1865) was born at Sidehead, Durham, England, on August 13, 1787, and came to Canada in 1801. He entered the service of the XY Company; and Thomas Verchères de Boucherville, who met him on Lake Superior in 1803, describes him as a nephew of Sir Alexander Mackenzie (q.v.), though I can find no confirmation of this. He appears to have remained in the western country, as a clerk, first of the XY Company, and then of the North West Company, until about 1810. In 1811 he appears in Montreal, in partnership with a young merchant named Dowie, who was almost certainly a nephew of Sir Alexander Mackenzie (q.v.). Shortly afterwards he entered the firm of Parker, Gerrard, and Ogilvy, which had been the supply house of the XY Company, and had an interest in the North West Company; and in time he acquired a controlling interest in this firm, which came to be known as Gerrard, Gillespie, Moffatt, and Co., and then as Gillespie, Moffatt, and Co. He was elected a member of the Beaver Club in 1814. In 1830 he was called to the Legislative Council of Lower Canada; and in 1839 he was sworn of the Executive Council. On the union of Upper and Lower Canada in 1841, he was elected to represent Montreal in the Legislative Assembly of Canada; and he held this seat until 1847, when he withdrew from active politics. He died at Montreal on February 25, 1865. In 1809, while in the Indian country, he had born to him a son, Lewis, afterwards a merchant in Toronto; but in 1816 he married Sophia, daughter of David McCrae, of St. John's, who was himself an old Indian trader, and a member of the Beaver Club. By her he had three sons, George, John Ogilvy, and Kenneth Mackenzie. For a fuller account of his life, see Adam Shortt, *The Honourable George Moffatt* (Journal of the Canadian Bankers' Association, XXXII).

MONTOUR, NICOLAS (d. 1808), was a French Canadian who went to the West, apparently, in 1777, as clerk to Barthélemi Blondeau. Later, in 1782, he was described as "clerk to the Messrs. Frobisher". He became a partner in the North West Company in 1784, when he was given, apparently, two shares in the sixteen-share concern of that year. He seems to have spent most of his time on the Saskatchewan. In 1788 he was at "Finlay's old fort of Rivière au Pas". He retired from the fur-trade about 1792; and in 1795 he bought the seigniory of La Pointe-du-Lac, Lower Canada, where he built a manor-house which has been likened to "the Châteaux of the Middle Ages". He was elected a member of the Beaver Club in 1790; and from 1796 to 1800 he represented the county of St. Maurice in the Legislative Assembly of Lower Canada, when he voted generally with the English party. He died "at his manor of Woodlands" on August 6, 1808; and he was buried "in the new cemetery of Three Rivers" (*Quebec Gazette*, August 25, 1808). He left behind him in the West a half-breed son, also named Nicholas Montour, who was a clerk at Fort des Prairies in 1804-6, was stationed in the Kootenay country in 1813, and was discharged on the Saskatchewan by Simpson in 1823. After his return to Lower Canada, the elder Montour married Geneviève Wills, who died on April 2, 1832, aged 64 years; and by her he had three daughters. See Soeur Marie du Rédempteur, *La Pointe-du-Lac aux 19e et 18e siècles* (Bulletin des recherches historiques, 1932).

MORRISON, WILLIAM (1785-1866) was born in Montreal in 1785, the son of Alan Morrison and Josepha, the daughter of Jean Etienne Wadden (q.v.). He entered the service of the XY Company about 1802; and for a number of years after the union of 1804 he was a clerk in the service of the North West Company in the Fond du Lac and Nipigon departments, where he encountered Jean Baptiste Perrault (q.v.). In 1816 he entered the service of the South West Company, and was for many years in charge of the Fond du Lac department. He retired from the fur-trade about 1826, and settled at Morrison's Island, near Berthier, Lower Canada. He died at Morrison's Island on August 7, 1866. He married an Indian wife; and one of his sons accompanied J. C. Fremont on one of his exploring expeditions.

MUNRO, HENRY (1770?-1854) was a son of the Hon. John Munro, one of the members of the first Legislative Council of Upper Canada, and became a surgeon in the service of the North West Company in 1796. For several years he was stationed at, or near, Grand Portage. In 1805, he was sent to succeed J. B. Perrault (q.v.) at the Pic, on Lake Superior; and in 1812 he was appointed surgeon's mate in the Corps of Canadian Voyageurs raised by the North West Company. He died at Lachenaie, Lower Canada, on August 20, 1854, and was buried in the old Protestant cemetery at Mascouche.

MURE, JOHN (d. 1823) was a merchant of Quebec who became in 1798 one of the partners in the XY Company; and on the union of the XY and North West Companies in 1804, he became a partner in Sir Alexander Mackenzie and Co., which controlled a quarter interest in the new organization. From 1804 to 1810 he represented the county of York in the Legislative

Assembly of Lower Canada, and from 1810 to 1814, the lower town of Quebec; and in 1812 he was appointed a member of the Executive Council of the province. He died on January 17, 1823.

NOLIN, JEAN BAPTISTE (1777-1819) was an Indian trader, who settled at Sault Ste. Marie, and acted there in some capacity for the North West Company for many years. As early as 1777, he was in partnership with Venant St. Germain (q.v.), and purchased from Alexander Henry (q.v.) the fort at Michipicoten, on Lake Superior. In his later years he appears to have been a merchant at Sault Ste. Marie; and in 1819 he sold out his interests there to C. O. Ermatinger (q.v.), and went to live at Pembina, on the Red River. His son, François, was a clerk in the service of the North West Company at Fort Dauphin in 1799 and again in 1804.

OAKES, FORREST (d. 1783) was an English merchant who came to Canada in the earliest days of British rule. He was a partner in the firm of Mackenzie and Oakes in Quebec in 1761; and he was in Montreal in February, 1762, when he ran foul of the soldiers, during the period of military rule, and was tried by court-martial. He is said to have been a son of Sir Hildebrand Oakes (see *Dict. Nat. Biog.*); but this is impossible. It is certain, however, that there was some relationship between them, though what it was I have not been able to determine. He engaged in the Indian trade; and his name appears in the fur-trade licences between 1769 and 1782. In 1779 he became one of the parties to the formation of the original North West Company; but his firm was not included in the agreement of 1783-4, for he died in Montreal in 1783. His will, dated April 17, 1783, which is preserved in the Court House at Montreal, was witnessed by William Dummer Powell, John McGill (q.v.), and Richard Dobie (q.v.); and it reveals the fact that he left property in the parish of Handsworth, Staffordshire, England. He left one son, John Meticamish Oakes, evidently a half-breed, who was a minor, and two sisters, Jemima (d. 1809), the wife of Lawrence Ermatinger (q.v.), and Margaret, who had married in 1767 Edward William Gray, afterwards sheriff of Montreal. Another sister, who would appear to have predeceased him, married in 1770 Edward Chinn, an early Indian trader at Michilimackinac.

OGDEN, PETER SKENE (1794-1854) was born in Quebec, Lower Canada, in 1794, the son of the Hon. Isaac Ogden, a judge of the Admiralty Court, and Sarah Hanson. He entered the service of the North West Company as a clerk in 1811; and from 1811 to 1818 he was stationed at Isle à la Crosse. He was transferred to the Columbia department in 1818; and in 1820 he was made a partner of the Company. In 1823, after the union of 1821 he was given rank as a chief trader in the Hudson's Bay Company, and in 1835 he became a chief factor. He spent most of his life, after 1818, on the Pacific slope; and he died near Oregon City on September 27, 1854. It has been said that he was the anonymous author of *Traits of*

American Indian life and character (London, 1853); but this is doubtful. For a fuller account of his life, see T. C. Elliott, *Peter Skene Ogden* (Quarterly of the Oregon Historical Society, 1910).

OGILVY, JOHN (1769?-1819) was born in Scotland about 1769. He came to Canada about 1790, and became a partner in the firm of Parker, Gerrard and Ogilvy. This was the firm that joined with Forsyth, Richardson, and Co. to form the XY Company; and John Macdonald of Garth (q.v.) says in his autobiography that in 1798 John Ogilvy was "at the head of the XY Co." He signed the agreement of 1804, by which the XY and North West Companies were amalgamated; and thus acquired in the North West Company an indirect interest. In 1817 he was appointed a commissioner, under the Treaty of Ghent, for determining the boundaries of British North America; and he died, while engaged in this capacity, at Sandwich, Upper Canada, on September 28, 1819, in his 51st year.

PAMBRUN, PIERRE CHRYSOLOGUE (1792-1841) was born at L'Islet, below Quebec, Lower Canada, on December 17, 1792, the son of André Dominique Pambrun. He served in the Canadian *Voltigeurs* under Salaberry in the War of 1812, and took part in the battle of Châteauguay. After the war, in 1815, he entered the service of the Hudson's Bay Company; and in 1816 he was taken prisoner by the Bois-Brulés of the North West Company on the Qu'Appelle River. In 1821 he was stationed at Cumberland House; and in 1824 he was transferred to the Pacific slope. Here he spent the remainder of his life. He died at Fort Walla Walla, in the Oregon country, in 1841, as the result of injuries received when breaking in a wild horse. Just before his death, in 1840, he had been promoted to the rank of chief trader. About 1821, at Cumberland House, he married the half-breed daughter of Edward Umfreville (q.v.); and she was still living, in the state of Washington, in 1878. One of his sons, Pierre Chrysologue, entered the service of the Hudson's Bay Company, and was met by Lord Milton and Dr. Cheadle in the foothills of the Rocky Mountains in 1868. An account of the life of the elder Pierre Chrysologue Pambrun will be found in J. Tassé, *Les Canadiens de l'Ouest* (Montreal, 1878).

PANGMAN, PETER (1744?-1819) was born in New England, of German descent, about 1744. He engaged in the fur-trade; and in 1767 his name appears in the Michilimackinac licences as trading to the Mississippi. In 1774 he transferred his energies to the Saskatchewan; and he was engaged in the fur-trade on the Saskatchewan almost continuously until 1790. In 1783 he joined Gregory, McLeod, and Co.; and in 1787, when this firm was absorbed by the North West Company, he became a partner in the North West Company. He retired from the fur-trade about 1794; and in that year he purchased the seigniory of Lachenaie, in Lower Canada; and here he died on August 28, 1819. He had a half-breed son, commonly known as "Bastonnais Pangman", who was prominent in the Seven Oaks affair on the Red River in 1816; and in 1796 he married Grace MacTier, by whom he had one son and one daughter. The son, John Pangman, became in 1837 a member of the Legislative Council of Lower Canada.

PARKER, WILLIAM (1760?-1831) was born about 1760 in Kilmarnock, Scotland, and came to Canada before 1787. He became the senior partner of Parker, Gerrard, Ogilvy, and Co., which was one of the supply firms of the XY Company. He returned to Great Britain at an early date; and he died in London, England, at his house in John Street, America Square, on June 18, 1831, aged 71 years. In his obituary notice he is described as "one of the oldest Canada merchants in London".

PATERSON, CHARLES (d. 1788) was a trader from Montreal whose name first appears in the fur-trade licences in 1770. He appears on the Saskatchewan in 1774, and in the winter of 1775-6 he made, with Alexander Henry (q.v.) and William Holmes (q.v.) an overland journey to the Assiniboine. He formed a partnership with John McGill (q.v.), and the firm of McGill and Paterson held two shares in the sixteen-share North West Company formed in 1779. About 1783, however, he withdrew from the North West trade, for his name is not found among the partners of the North West Company of that year; and shortly afterward he became the director for the trade of the Michilimackinac Company in Lake Michigan. He was drowned in Lake Michigan, off a point still known as Paterson's Point, on September 10, 1788; and a vivid account of his death has been left us by J. B. Perrault (q.v.), who was an eyewitness. He had a brother, Allan, who was in partnership with him after 1780, but who retired from the fur-trade after his death, and who married in 1784 Cornelia, the daughter of Capt. John Munro, of Matilda. Patrick Campbell, in his *Travels* (Edinburgh, 1793) has left an account of a conversation with Allan Paterson, in which the latter told how he and his brother Charles had, during the first three years of their partnership, lost £3000, but how in the two subsequent years they had had a profit of twice that sum.

PERRAULT, JEAN BAPTISTE (1761-1844) was born at Three Rivers, Canada, in 1761, the son of Jean Baptiste Perrault and Marie LeMaitre. He was educated at Quebec, and entered the fur-trade about 1783. For ten years he was a trader in the Illinois country; but in 1793 he entered the service of the North West Company as a clerk. He was stationed in the Fond du Lac department until 1799; and from 1799 to 1805 he was in charge at the Pic, on Lake Superior. From 1805 to 1806 he was on the St. Maurice and Ottawa Rivers; and in 1806 he left the employ of the North West Company. He was subsequently employed by the Pacific Fur Company, by an independent trader, and by the Hudson's Bay Company; but he retired from the service of the Hudson's Bay Company in 1821, and settled at Sault Ste. Marie. Here he died in 1844. He married an

Indian woman; and by her he had at least nine children. His *Narrative*, a translation of which has been published in the *Michigan Pioneer and Historical Collections*, vol. 37, 1909-10, is one of the most interesting and valuable documents to the history of the fur-trade.

PHYN, JAMES (*fl.* 1763-1804) was a son of George Phyn, of the Corse of Monelly, in Scotland, and his wife Janet Simpson. He was thus an uncle of the Hon. John Forsyth (q.v.) and his brothers, and of the Hon. John Richardson (q.v.). He came to America before 1763, for in that year he became a partner of John Duncan, an Indian trader of Schenectady, in a firm which came to be known in 1767 as Phyn, Ellice, and Co. In 1774 he left for England, to found in London the firm of Phyn, Ellice, and Co., which was destined to play for many years an important rôle in the history of the Canadian fur-trade. It was a party to the formation of the XY Company in 1798; and on the union of the XY and North West Companies in 1804, it became one of the regular supply houses of the North West Company. I have not been able to ascertain the date of James Phyn's death; but it seems to have occurred not long after 1804. About 1768 he married in Schenectady the daughter of Dr. John Constable, a friend of Sir William Johnson; and by her he had at least two sons. Some account of his life in America will be found in R. H. Fleming, *Phyn, Ellice and Company of Schenectady* (Contributions to Canadian Economics, IV, 1932).

POND, PETER (1740-1807?) was born in Milford, Connecticut, on January 18, 1740. After serving as a soldier in the French and Indian wars, he became a fur-trader at Detroit, and was for ten years or more engaged in the fur-trade on the upper Mississippi. In 1775 he made his first expedition to the Canadian North West; and in the development of the fur-trade here he played an important part. In 1778 he established the first post in the Athabaska country; and he appears to have reached later Great Slave Lake. In 1783 he became one of the partners in the North West Company; but the murder of John Ross (q.v.) by some of his men in 1787, being the second murder with which he had been connected in the West, brought about his retirement from the fur-trade, and in 1790 he sold his share in the Company to William McGillivray (q.v.). He returned to the United States, and became for a time a special agent of the American government in its dealings with the Indians. In his later years, he returned to New England, and he died about 1807 a poverty-stricken and forgotten old man. The maps which he drew of his explorations in the North West were among the first which exercised an influence over future events. A full account of his life and work is to be found in H. A. Innis, *Peter Pond, fur-trader and adventurer* (Toronto, 1930). The most recent edition of the fragment of his *Narrative* which has come down to us is in C. M. Gates (ed.), *Five fur-traders of the North West* (Minneapolis, 1933).

OF THE NOR' WESTERS

PORLIER, JACQUES (1765-1839) was born in Montreal in 1765, and was educated there. He went to Green Bay, on Lake Michigan, and engaged in the fur-trade about 1791. He was elected a member of the Beaver Club of Montreal in 1801; and he became a partner of the South West Company. He died at Green Bay on July 12, 1839. Further details about him will be found in J. Tassé, *Les Canadiens de l'Ouest*, vol. I (Montreal, 1878).

PRITCHARD, JOHN (1777-1856), was born in Shropshire, England, in 1777. He went to Canada about 1800, and became a clerk in the XY Company. In 1804 he was stationed at Lake Nipigon. He became a clerk in the North West Company in 1805, and from 1808 to 1814 he was in charge of the Souris River post. In 1815 he took service with Lord Selkirk, and was appointed a councillor of Assiniboia. He was present at the affair of Seven Oaks in 1816, and was made a prisoner by the half-breeds. Taken to Montreal, he gave evidence in the Selkirk trials. Afterwards he settled on the Red River, and in 1822 he organized the Buffalo Wool Company. He died at the Red River Settlement in 1856.

PRUDEN, JOHN PETER (1778?-1870?) was born at Edmonton, Middlesex, England, about 1778. He entered the service of the Hudson's Bay Company in 1791, as an apprentice, and later as a writer, at York Factory. From 1795 to 1808 he was on the Saskatchewan; and from 1809 to 1824 he was in charge of Carlton House. In 1821 he was made a chief trader. He was in charge at Norway House in 1825-6, but later returned to command at Carlton House. He was promoted to the rank of chief factor in 1836; and he retired from the Company's service in 1837. After his retirement, he lived at the Red River; and here he died about 1870. His daughter married Chief Trader John McLeod (q.v.).

QUESNEL, JULES MAURICE (1786-1842) was born in Montreal in 1786, the second son of Joseph Quesnel and Marie Josephte Deslandes. He entered the service of the North West Company as a clerk, and in 1804 was stationed at Edmonton. In 1806 he accompanied Simon Fraser (q.v.) in his exploration of the Fraser River. He left the service of the North West Company in 1811, and returned to Canada. In 1838 he was appointed a member of the Special Council of Lower Canada; and in 1841, a member of the Legislative Council of United Canada. He died at Montreal on May 20, 1842.

RICHARDSON, JOHN (1755?-1831) was born at Portsoy, Banffshire, Scotland, about 1755, the son of John Richardson and a daughter of George Phyn, of the Corse of Monelly. He was thus a nephew of James Phyn (q.v.) and a cousin of John Forsyth (q.v.) and Edward Ellice (q.v.). He came to America in 1773, and entered the employ of Phyn and Ellice at Schenectady. During the American Revolution he saw service on a privateer. In 1787 he removed to Canada, and entered the employ of Robert Ellice and Co.

This firm, however, was dissolved in 1790; and Richardson became a partner in its successor, which was known as Forsyth, Richardson, and Co. This firm became one of the firms that supplied the XY Company; and on the union of the XY and North West Companies in 1804, its members became partners in the North West Company. He represented Montreal in the Legislative Assembly of Lower Canada from 1792 to 1796, and from 1804 to 1808; in 1804 he was appointed a member of the Executive Council of the province; and in 1816, a member of the Legislative Council. In 1817 he was one of the founders of the Bank of Montreal. He died at Montreal on May 18, 1831. For a fuller account of his life, see Adam Shortt, *The Hon. John Richardson* (Journal of the Canadian Bankers' Association XXIX, 1921). Some of his letters have been published by E. Cruikshank in the *Papers and Records* of the Ontario Historical Society, 1905.

ROBERTSON, COLIN (1779?-1842) was born about 1779, and entered the service of the North West Company as a clerk prior to 1804. He was employed mainly in the English River department; but in September, 1809, he was dismissed from the service by John McDonald of Garth (q.v.). In 1812 he entered the employ of Lord Selkirk and the Hudson's Bay Company; and in 1818 he was the chief officer of the Hudson's Bay Company in the Athabaska district. In 1819 he was arrested by the Nor' Westers, but escaped, it was said, by breaking his parole. In 1820, he went to England, and was in London when the negotiations in regard to the union of the North West and Hudson's Bay Companies were in progress; and his letters, preserved in Hudson's Bay House, are one of our chief sources for the history of these negotiations. In 1821 he was made a chief factor of the Hudson's Bay Company, and was placed in charge at Norway House. In 1824 he was transferred to Fort Churchill; in 1826, to Island Lake; and in 1830, to Swan River. He had leave of absence from 1832 to 1837; but from 1837 to 1839 he had charge of the New Brunswick district. He retired in 1840, with a pension of £100. In 1841 he was elected to represent the Lake of Two Mountains in the first Legislative Assembly of United Canada; but he died at Montreal on February 3, 1842, from the effects of being thrown from his cariole the preceding day. His eldest son, Colin Robertson, jr., died at Montreal on November 29, 1844, aged 23.

ROCHEBLAVE, PIERRE RASTEL DE (1764?-1840) was born about 1764, the son of Philippe François Rastel de Rocheblave, British governor of Illinois, who was captured by George Rogers Clark in 1778. He became a wintering partner of the XY Company in 1798; and in 1802 was in opposition to John McDonald of Garth (q.v.) at Fort Augustus. On the union of the XY and North West Companies in 1804, he became a wintering partner of the North West Company, and was placed in charge of the Assiniboine district. From 1807 to 1810 he was again in the Athabaska department; from 1810 to 1812 he was in charge of the Pic, on Lake Superior; and in 1814 he was appointed agent of the North West Company in regard to the South-West trade. In 1816 he became a partner in McTavish, McGillivrays, and Co.; and from 1816 to 1821 he was one of the agents of the North West Company at the annual meetings at Fort William. In 1821 he retired from the fur-trade; but on the failure of McTavish, McGillivrays, and Co. in 1825, and the subsequent return of Simon McGillivray (q.v.), he was placed in temporary charge of the Montreal office, until the Hudson's Bay Company took charge of it. From 1824 to 1827 he represented Montreal West in the Legislative Assembly of Lower Canada; in 1832 he was appointed a member of the Legislative Council of Lower Canada, and in 1838 of the Special Council; and from 1838 to his death he was a member of the Executive Council of the province. He died in Montreal on October 5, 1840. In 1819 he married Elmire (d. 1886), daughter of Jean Bouthillier; and by her he had two daughters. One of these was still living, unmarried, in Montreal in 1908.

Ross, Alexander (1783-1856) was born in Nairnshire, Scotland, on May 9, 1783. He emigrated to Canada in 1805, and for several years he taught school in Glengarry, Upper Canada. In 1810 he entered the service of the Pacific Fur Company, and he took part in the founding of Fort Astoria. In 1813, when Astoria was handed over to the Nor' Westers, he became a a clerk in the North West Company; and he remained on the Pacific slope until after the union of the North West and Hudson's Bay Companies in 1821. He retired from the fur-trade in 1825, and settled in the Red River district. He became sheriff of Assiniboia; and from 1835 to 1850 he was a member of the council of Assiniboia. He died at the Red River Settlement on October 23, 1856. He was the author of *Adventures of the first settlers on the Oregon or Columbia River* (London, 1849), *The fur-hunters of the far West* (2 vols., London, 1855), and *The Red River settlement* (London, 1856). Some of his letters have been published in *Transaction No. 63* of the Manitoba Historical and Scientific Society.

Ross, Charles (d. 1844) was a native of Scotland who entered the service of the North West Company as a clerk in 1818. The statement is made in N. de B. Lugrin, *The pioneer women of Vancouver Island* (Victoria, B.C., 1928) that, "according to Bishop Ridge, he was the son of a Scottish nobleman". He was stationed at Rainy Lake in 1822; and here, apparently, he married his wife, whose name was Isabella Melville (or Merilia). In 1824 he was transferred to New Caledonia, and he was made a chief trader in 1831. He was in charge of the building of Fort Victoria in 1843; and he died there on June 28, 1844. His family settled at Ross Bay, Vancouver Island; and it is said that some of his descendants still live there. He must be distinguished from the Charles Ross who was in charge at Fort Vermilion in 1833, was afterwards transferred to the Columbia department, and was commissioned a chief trader in 1843.

Ross, Donald (d. 1852), entered the service of the Hudson's Bay Company in 1816. He was at Cumberland House as a clerk in 1822, and in 1824-6 was at York Factory. He was appointed a chief trader in 1829, and for many years was in charge at Norway House. In his later years he retired to the Red River Settlement, and here he died on November 18, 1852.

Ross, John (d. 1787) was a trader who first appears in the fur-trade licences in 1779. In 1780 he was in partnership with Peter Pangman (q.v.). He became a partner in the venture organized by Gregory, McLeod, and Co. in 1783, and was placed in charge of the Athabaska district. In the spring of 1787 he was killed in a scuffle with some of the men of Peter Pond (q.v.), the North West Company partner who was opposed to him. Patrick Campbell says in his *Travels* (Edinburgh, 1793) that in 1791 he met at Lachine "a Mr. Ross" who was "a partner of the North West Company"; but this statement cannot be accurate.

Ross, William (1780?-1855) was born in Ross-shire, Scotland, about 1780. For several years he served as an ensign in the 11th Regiment of Foot. Then he entered the service of the Hudson's Bay Company, and was successively in charge at Oxford House, at Nelson House, and at Fort Churchill. After his retirement, he lived at Ottawa, Canada West; and there he died on January 12, 1855, aged 76 years.

Rowand, John (1787-1854) was born in Montreal, Canada, in 1787, the son of an assistant surgeon in the Montreal General Hospital. He entered the service of the North West Company as an apprentice clerk, and was stationed in 1804 and 1805 at Fort des Prairies, and in 1806 on the Lower Red River. In 1807 he returned to the Saskatchewan; and in 1808 he built a fort on the site of what is now the city of Edmonton. Here he remained, with brief intervals, for most of the rest of his life. He was made a partner of the North West Company shortly before the union of 1821; and in 1821 he became a chief trader in the Hudson's Bay Company. In 1823 he was placed in charge at Fort Edmonton; and in 1826 he was promoted to the rank of chief factor. He died at Fort Pitt on the Saskatchewan on June 1, 1854. He married an Indian girl who saved his life when he was thrown from his horse on the prairies in his early days in the West; and by her he had several children. One of his sons entered the service of the North West Company; and another, who was educated at Edinburgh University, became a successful physician at Quebec.

St. Germain, Venant (or Venance) Lemaire (1751-1821) was born at the Lake of Two Mountains on May 18, 1751, the son of Bernardin Lemaire *dit* St. Germain and Marie-Josephte Lefebvre. His name appears as trading to Grand Portage as early as 1777; and in 1784 he was second-in-command under Edward Umfreville (q.v.) in the journey of exploration from Lake Nipigon to Lake Winnipeg. In 1790 he was at Rainy Lake; and in 1791 he made an agreement with the North West Company to take the post at Rivière la à Biche for five years, on condition that if the profits did not reach £200 per annum, the Company would make up the deficiency He seems to have retired from the fur-trade about 1795, for in November of that year he was married at Repentigny, Lower Canada, and in 1796 he purchased the seigniory of the Bouchard Isles. He became a merchant at Repentigny, Lower Canada; and here he died in 1821. He married at Repentigny, Catherine, daughter of Pierre Pichet; and by her he had several children. He is not to be confused with his nephew, Venant St. Germain, who was killed at Pembina in 1804.

SAYER, JOHN (1750?-1818) was born about 1750, and first appears in the fur-trade in 1780, when he was granted a licence to send one canoe to Michilimackinac. He engaged in the fur-trade in the Fond-du-Lac district; and as early as 1793 he was described by J. B. Perrault (q.v.) as "an agent of the [North West] Company" in this region. In 1799 he was "proprietor" in charge of the Fond du Lac department; but he retired from the fur-trade about 1806, and went to live at St. Anne's, on the island of Montreal. In 1810 he was elected a member of the Beaver Club of Montreal, though he does not appear to have attended any of its meetings. Ross Cox (q.v.) met him at St. Anne's in September, 1817; and he died here on October 2, 1818, aged 68 years. He was apparently married to a French-Canadian half-breed; for he had a half-breed son, named Guillaume Sayer, who was the leader of a half-breed rising on the Red River in 1844. John Charles Sayer, who was a clerk and interpreter in the service of the North West Company in 1815, and was concerned in the Selkirk troubles of that year, would appear to have been another son.

SHARP, GEORGE (d. 1800) was a prominent trader of Detroit and the North West in the period subsequent to the American Revolution. In 1798 he became one of the original partners of the XY Company; but he died at Montreal on January 17, 1800.

SHAW, ANGUS (d. 1832) was a native of Scotland who entered the service of the North West Company as a clerk prior to 1787. In 1789 he was at Fort L'Orignal, on Moose Hill Lake; and in 1790 he was again "at Moose Hill Lake, up the Beaver River, from Isle à la Crosse". In 1791 he was back at Fort L'Orignal; and in 1792 he was at Fort George. He became a partner in the North West Company between 1795 and 1799; in 1797 he was elected a member of the Beaver Club of Montreal; and in 1799 he was proprietor in charge of the Upper English River district. In 1802 he was appointed agent in charge of the King's Posts, with headquarters at Quebec; and in 1808 he became a member of McTavish, McGillivrays, and Co. He was one of the agents of the North West Company at Fort William in 1810 and 1811; but thereafter he took little part in the fur-trade, until the struggle with Lord Selkirk reached its height, when he was one of the partners of the North West Company arrested by the Hudson's Bay men in 1819. He continued to be a partner in McTavish, McGillivrays, and Co. after the union of 1821, when they were made Montreal agents of the Hudson's Bay Company; and his estate, which was involved in the failure of that firm in 1825, was not settled until 1847. He became a victim of pulmonary tuberculosis; and he died at New Brunswick, New Jersey, on July 25, 1832, two days after his arrival at that place. He married a sister of the Hon. William McGillivray; and she died in London, England, on March 27, 1820. But before his marriage he had a daughter, named Anna, who was born of "an Indian woman", and who was baptized in Montreal in 1797, aged 9 years.

SIVERIGHT, JOHN (1779?-1856) was born in Scotland about 1779, and entered the service of the XY Company in 1799, and that of the North West Company in 1805. Sir George Simpson wrote in 1832 that he "was promoted to the rank of clerk from being a gentleman's body servant". In 1815 he was at Portage la Prairie, and he became implicated in the Selkirk trials. From 1813 to 1823 he was in charge at Sault Ste. Marie; and from 1824 to 1847 he was in charge at Fort Coulonge on the Ottawa, and at Lake Timiskaming. He was promoted to the rank of chief trader in the Hudson's Bay Company in 1828; and to that of chief factor in 1846. He went on furlough in 1847; and he retired from the Company's service in 1849. He died at Edinburgh, Scotland, on September 4, 1856.

SMALL, PATRICK (d. 1810?) was probably born near Perth, Scotland, the son of John Small, and the grand-nephew of General John Small (1730-1796) lieutenant-governor of Guernsey. Through the influence of General Small, who had been an officer in the British army at the battle of Bunker's Hill, who had later been stationed in Nova Scotia, and who was a friend of Simon McTavish (q.v.), he, like his relative, John McDonald of Garth (q.v.), became a clerk in the service of the North West Company. He first appears in the West in 1779, when he wintered on the Churchill River. For a number of years he was in charge at Isle à la Crosse. He became a partner in the North West Company in 1783; but he retired from the fur-trade in 1791, and returned to Great Britain. In 1794 he was "residing in Wood Street, London", and he is described in the London directory of that year as a partner of the firm of Small and Young, "Scotch factors". In 1794 he was adopted by his grand-uncle, General Small, and in 1796, at the latter's death, he was left by his will, which is to be seen in Somerset House, London, a large part of his estate, including his property in Nova Scotia. He seems to have died about 1810, since, in the minutes of the Beaver Club of Montreal (of which he became a member in 1789), he is described as among the members "in England" in 1809-10, but disappears in the list for 1810-11. By a Cree woman at Isle à la Crosse he had one son, Patrick (q.v.), and at least two daughters, one of whom, Charlotte, married David Thompson (q.v.), and the other of whom, Nancy, was the "Indian wife" of John McDonald of Garth.

SMALL, PATRICK (1785?-1846) was born, probably at Fort Isle à la Crosse, about 1785, the son of Patrick Small (q.v.) and a woman of the Cree tribe. He entered the service of the North West Company as a clerk in 1804, and was taken over as a clerk by the Hudson's Bay Company in 1821. From 1822 to 1830 he was on the Saskatchewan. He died in the West on January 18, 1846; and his will is preserved in Hudson's Bay House in London. Sir George Simpson (q.v.) described him as "deficient in education, but a good trader, kept sober by the dread of being turned out of the service only".

SMITH, EDWARD (d. 1849) entered the service of the North West Company prior to 1806, when he appears as a clerk in the Athabaska department. He was employed for many years in the Athabaska and Mackenzie River departments; and in 1814 he was made a partner of the North West Company. At the union of 1821, he was made a chief factor of the Hudson's Bay Company; and from 1821 to 1823 he was in charge at Fort Chipewyan, from 1823 to 1832 at Fort Simpson, and from 1834 to 1837 again at Fort Chipewyan. He was granted furlough in 1837, and shortly afterwards retired from the Company's service. He died in 1849.

STEWART, ALEXANDER (*fl.* 1796-1840) entered the service of the North West Company as an apprentice clerk in 1796. In 1806 D. W. Harmon (q.v.) met him at Fort des Prairies. Later, he was placed in charge of a post on Lesser Slave Lake; and in 1812, though still a clerk, he was placed in charge of the Athabaska River department. He was made a partner of the North West Company in 1813; and was transferred to the Columbia, where he was present at the capture of Fort Astoria. In 1815 he returned to Lesser Slave Lake, and there he remained for several years. At the time of the union of 1821, he was made a chief factor of the Hudson's Bay Company. From 1821 to 1823 he was in charge at Fort William; from 1823 to 1826, at Island Lake; from 1826 to 1830, at Fort Chipewyan; and from 1831 to 1832, at Moose Factory. He was granted furlough in 1832; and he retired from the Company's service in 1833. He died in May, 1840. His name is frequently misspelled "Stuart".

STEWART, ANDREW (1789?-1822) was born in Glasgow, Scotland, about 1789, entered the service of the Hudson's Bay Company in 1811, as a writer at Moose Factory. In 1814-15 he was the master at Moose, and in 1815-16 at Missakami Lake. In 1816-17 he was at Kenogamissee; and from 1817 to 1821 he was at Michipicoten. He was promoted to the rank of chief trader in 1821; and he died at Osnaburgh House on May 24, 1822.

STUART, DAVID (1765?-1853) was born in Callander, Perthshire, Scotland, about 1765. He is said to have been the son of that Alexander Stuart who was the successful opponent of the famous Rob Roy; and he was a cousin of John Stuart (q.v.) of the North West Company. He emigrated to Canada, and lived in Montreal before the close of the eighteenth century. His obituary notice in the *Detroit Daily Advertiser*, October 19, 1853, is authority for the statement that "for a time he was an agent of the Hudson Bay Company on the Atlantic Coast, in Nova Scotia, and elsewhere"; but this is almost certainly a mistake, for the Hudson's Bay Company had no posts in these districts at that time. It is possible that he was employed by the North West Company at the King's Posts or in the maritime provinces. (A David Stuart of Quebec was elected a member of the Beaver Club of Montreal in 1816; but it is doubtful if this was the same person.) In 1810, however, he became a partner in John Jacob Astor's American Fur Company; and he was one of the founders of Astoria. He remained with the American Fur Company for many years; but he retired from the fur-trade about 1833, and went to live with his nephew, Robert Stuart (q.v.), in Detroit, Michigan. Here he died, at the house of his nephew's widow, on October 18, 1853, aged 88 years. For much of the information contained in this sketch, I am indebted to Dr. M. M. Quaife, secretary of the Burton Historical Collection, of Detroit.

STUART, JOHN (1779-1847) was born in Strathspey, Scotland, in 1779, the son of Donald Stuart of Leanchoil. His sister Barbara was the mother of the first Lord Strathcona. He entered the service of the North West Company in 1799, and was sent to the Peace River district. In 1806 he accompanied Simon Fraser (q.v.) on his descent of the Fraser River to the Pacific. He was placed in charge of New Caledonia in 1809; and in 1813 he became a partner of the North West Company. At the union of 1821, he was commissioned a chief factor of the Hudson's Bay Company; and he remained in charge in New Caledonia until 1824. He retired from the service of the Hudson's Bay Company in 1839, and returned to Scotland. He died at his place, Springfield House, near Forres, Scotland, on January 14, 1847. His will is on file at Hudson's Bay House, in London. Stuart Lake, in British Columbia, is called after him.

STUART, ROBERT (1785-1848) was born in Callander, Perthshire, Scotland, on February 19, 1785, the nephew of David Stuart (q.v.). He emigrated to Canada in 1807, and in 1810 he joined John Jacob Astor's Pacific Fur Company. He was one of the founders of Astoria; and in 1812-13 he made the overland journey back from Astoria to St. Louis. In 1819 he went to Michilimackinac, as the agent of the American Fur Company; and he remained there until 1834. He then retired from the fur-trade, and settled in Detroit, Michigan. He died at Chicago, Illinois, on October 28, 1848. His son, David, born at Brooklyn, New York, in 1816, became a member of Congress for Detroit, and commanded a brigade under General W. T. Sherman in the American Civil War.

SUTHERLAND, DANIEL (1756?-1832) was born, probably in Scotland, about 1756, and came to Canada prior to 1778, when his name first appears in the fur-trade licences. With James Grant (q.v.) he was engaged for a number of years in the Timiskaming fur-trade; and in 1790 he became, apparently through his friendship with Simon McTavish (q.v.), a partner in the North West Company. He appears to have disposed of his share in the Company in 1795; and he became a partner in the XY Company in 1798. At the union of the North West and XY Companies in 1804, his interest was allowed to expire; and he took thenceforth little part in the fur-trade. In 1812 he was appointed postmaster at Montreal; and in 1817 he became deputy postmaster-general for British North America, with headquarters at Quebec. From 1818 to 1824 he was also cashier of the Bank of Montreal at Quebec. He retired from the office of deputy postmaster-general in 1828; and he died at Quebec, of cholera, on August 19, 1832, aged 76 years. In 1781 he married in Montreal Margaret Robertson; and by her he had several children. His daughter Louisa married in 1817 T. A. Stayner, who succeeded him in 1828 as deputy postmaster-general. Some account of his life, with his portrait, will be found in *Journal of the Canadian Antiquarian and Numismatic Society*, 3rd series, III, 174-80.

SUTHERLAND, JAMES (1777?-1844) was born at Ronaldshay, in the Orkney Islands, about 1777, and entered the service of the Hudson's Bay Company in 1797. He was first employed as a writer at York Factory. From 1808 to 1813 he was master at Cumberland House; and in 1816 he was made a prisoner by the Nor' Westers, during the Selkirk troubles. From 1819 to 1821 he was in charge of the Swan River district; and he was promoted to the rank of chief factor in 1821. He retired from the Company's services in 1827; and he died at the Red River Settlement on September 30, 1844. He is to be distinguished from an earlier servant of the Hudson's Bay Company, named James Sutherland, who died while in charge of Brandon House in 1797.

THAIN, THOMAS (d. 1832) was born in Scotland, the son of a sister of the Hon. John Richardson (q.v.). Through his mother (who died at Aberdeen, Scotland, on January 16, 1824), he was related to the Phyns, the Ellices, and the Forsyths. He came to Canada prior to 1804, for in that year Thomas Verchères de Boucherville met him on Lake Superior, evidently as a clerk in the employ of the XY Company. In 1804 he was appointed, with John Ogilvy (q.v.), an agent to represent at Grand Portage the interests of Sir Alexander Mackenzie and Co. in the reorganized North West Company; and in 1813 he became a partner in the firm of McTavish, McGillivrays, and Co. In 1822 he became also a partner in the firm of McGillivrays, Thain, and Co., which was formed to wind up the affairs of McTavish, McGillivrays, and Co. From 1821, when McTavish, McGillivrays, and Co. became the Montreal agents of the Hudson's Bay Company, he was the virtual manager of the Montreal office and head of the Montreal department. Shortly before McTavish, McGillivrays, and Co. and McGillivrays, Thain, and Co. were forced into insolvency in 1825, he left Canada suddenly, in ill health, leaving the accounts of these firms in great confusion; and soon afterwards he was reported as being "confined as a lunatic in an asylum in Scotland". He died at Aberdeen, Scotland, on January 6, 1832. His brother, Alexander Thain, of Montreal, died at Liverpool, England, on April 1, 1825, as he was about to board a vessel for Canada, possibly in order to come to his brother's assistance. Another brother, John Richardson Thain, of Edinburgh, acknowledged on January 20, 1835, the receipt of moneys received from Samuel Gerrard (q.v.) and George Gregory, "trustees to the estate of McGillivrays, Thain, and Co.", advanced by him for account of his "late brother", Thomas Thain. John McLean in his *Notes of a twenty-five years' service* described him as "a man of rather eccentric character, but possessed of a heart that glowed with the best feelings of humanity".

THOMPSON, DAVID (1770-1857) was born in the parish of St. John the Evangelist, Westminster, England, on April 30, 1770, the son of David Thompson. In 1784 he was apprenticed to the Hudson's Bay Company; and he spent the years 1784-97 in the service of this Company, partly at the posts on Hudson Bay, and partly in the interior. He took service as a clerk with the North West Company in 1797; and in 1804 he became a partner. He was employed by the North West Company as a geographer and explorer; and in 1811 he was the first white man to explore the Columbia River from its source to its mouth. He traversed a large part of the fur-trade country, making traverses of his course and observing for longitude and latitude wherever he went; and when he retired from the fur-trade in 1812, he pepared a map of the Canadian North West which has been the basis of all subsequent maps. He settled at Terrebonne, Lower Canada, and later at Williamstown, Upper Canada. From 1816 to 1826 he was employed in surveying the boundary line between Canada and the United States; and later he was employed in other surveys. He died, in extreme penury, at Longueuil, near Montreal, on February 10, 1857. In 1799 he married, at Isle à la Crosse, Charlotte, half-breed daughter of Patrick Small (q.v.); and by her he had sixteen children. His *Narrative of his explorations* has been edited, with introduction and notes, by J. B. Tyrrell (Toronto, Champlain Society, 1916).

THOMSON, JOHN (d. 1828) was of Scottish origin. Possibly he was a son of John Thomson, the first postmaster of Montreal. He entered the service of the North West Company before 1789, for from that year to 1791 he was in charge of a post "near the lower part of Grass River in the Port Nelson track". In 1798 he was on the Peace River; in 1799, on Lake Athabaska;

and in 1800 he built "Old Rocky Mountain House" on the Mackenzie River. He was stationed in the Athabaska department from 1806 to 1810, and in the English River department from 1811 to 1821. In 1804 he became a partner of the North West Company; and at the union of 1821 he became a chief factor of the Hudson's Bay Company. He retired from the service, however, on June 1, 1821; and he died on January 8, 1828, probably in the parish of Ste. Magdeleine de Rigaud, Lower Canada, where he lived after his retirement. He married Françoise Boucher, and he had by her seven children.

THOMSON, ROBERT (d. 1795?) was probably a brother of John Thomson (q.v.). In 1793 he had been for several years stationed in the lower Churchill district; and he was killed here in a quarrel with the Indians in the winter of 1794-5.

THORBURN, WILLIAM (*fl.* 1789-1805) was a native of Scotland who entered the employ of the North West Company prior to 1789, when he was left in charge of "Finlay's old fort" on the Saskatchewan. He had become a partner of the North West Company by 1795, but had ceased to be a wintering partner before 1799. He relinquished his shares in the Company in 1805. He was in Scotland in the winter of 1793-4; and I can find no evidence that he ever returned. But there is no partner of the North West Company about whom less information seems available.

TODD, ISAAC (1743?-1819), came to Canada in the early days of British rule, and was a merchant in Montreal in 1770. He was one of those who outfitted Thomas Corry (q.v.) in 1771; and he later formed a partnership with James McGill (q.v.). He was one of the original partners of the North West Company in 1779; but in 1784 the firm of Todd and McGill withdrew from the North West trade, and devoted their attention to the Mississippi and Lake Michigan trade. In 1795 he was elected a member of the Beaver Club. He exerted his influence to bring about the union of the North West and XY Companies in 1804; but did not himself enter the amalgamated company. After the death of James McGill in 1813, he retired from business, and went to live at Bath, England. Here he died, on May 22, 1819.

UMFREVILLE, EDWARD (*fl.* 1771-1790) was a writer in the service of the Hudson's Bay Company from 1771 to 1782. He was captured by the French under La Pérouse in 1782, and on his release in 1783 went to Canada, where he entered the service of the North West Company as a clerk. In 1784 he was employed to discover a new route from Lake Superior to Lake Winnipeg; and his journal of this exploration has been edited by R. Douglas, under the title *Nipigon to Winnipeg* (Ottawa, 1929). He spent the years 1784-8 on the north branch of the Saskatchewan, but left the North West Company's service in 1788, and returned to England by way of New

York. It appears from the records of the Hudson's Bay Company that he applied to be taken back into the service of this company in 1789, but failed to obtain satisfactory terms. He then published a book, entitled *The present state of Hudson Bay* (London, 1790), which was in part an attack on the Hudson's Bay Company. What happened to him after this, I have not been able to discover.

VINCENT, THOMAS (1776?-1832) was born in England about 1776, and entered the service of the Hudson's Bay Company as a writer at Albany in 1790. In 1814 he was governor of Moose Factory and the Southern Department; and in 1821 he was made a chief factor. He retired from the service of the Hudson's Bay Company, and returned to England, in 1826; and he died in 1832.

WADDEN (WADEN, WADIN, or WADDENS), JEAN ETIENNE (*fl.* 1761-1782) was a Swiss Protestant, the son of Adam Samuel Waddens (or Vaudin) and Bernardine Ermon, of La Tour-de-Paix, in the canton of Berne. His father is said to have been a professor at the University of Geneva; but I can find no corroboration of this. The son would appear to have come to Canada with the British army, and to have settled in Canada as a merchant and trader. On November 23, 1761, he married at St. Laurent, near Montreal, Marie-Joseph Deguire (b. 1739); and there is in the register of Christ Church, Montreal, the record of the christening of a number of Wadden children after this date. On January 27, 1768, "Capt. Woden" appears in a list of signatories in the "Minutes of a general meeting of the proprietors of Canada bills", held in London, England; and in 1772 his name first appears in the fur-trade licences as trading to Grand Portage. About 1779 he formed a partnership with Venant St. Germain (q.v.); and he was one of the partners in the original sixteen-share North West Company in that year. In the winter of 1781-82, while at Lac la Ronge, he was killed in an altercation with Peter Pond (q.v.). One of his daughters, Veronica (d. 1846), married in 1782 the Rev. John Bethune; and her son, Angus Bethune (q.v.), became a partner of the North West Company. Another daughter, Josepha, married in Montreal in April, 1780, Alan Morrison, and her son William Morrison (q.v.) became a clerk in the XY and North West Companies.

WALKER, THOMAS (*fl.* 1752-1785), was born in England, possibly in 1718. He emigrated to Boston, Massachusetts, in 1752; and he settled in Montreal in 1763. Here he engaged in the fur-trade; and he was one of the merchants who outfitted Thomas Corry (q.v.) in 1771. In 1764 he was appointed a justice of the peace, and shortly afterwards he was the victim of an assault by the military, in which one of his ears was cut off. The incident greatly embittered feeling in the colony, and Walker became the centre of a violent agitation. In 1774, when the Americans invaded the province, Walker threw in his lot with them; and he left the province with them in 1776. In 1786 Pierre du Calvet met him in London, England, but after that he passes from view. See A. L. Burt, *The mystery of Walker's ear* (Canadian historical review, 1922).

WENTZEL, WILLARD FERDINAND (*fl.* 1799-1832) was probably the son of Adam Wentzel, a Norwegian merchant in Montreal, and Endimia Grout, who were married in Montreal in 1779. He entered the service of the North West Company in 1799; and for many years he was a clerk in the Athabaska country. He was taken over as a clerk by the Hudson's Bay Company at the time of the union of 1821; but he retired to Canada in 1825. He re-entered the Hudson's Bay Company's service in 1827, and for two years was a clerk at Mingan, on the Lower St. Lawrence, but in 1829 he retired a second time, and he fell a victim to the cholera epidemic of 1832.

WILLIAMS, WILLIAM (d. 1837) was appointed resident governor of the Hudson's Bay Company's territories, with headquarters at York Factory, at the height of the Selkirk troubles in 1818. In 1819, in consequence of the aggressions of the North West Company, he took an expedition to the Grand Rapids at the mouth of the Saskatchewan, and arrested a number of partners and clerks of the North West Company, some of whom were sent to England for trial, and one of whom, Benjamin Frobisher (q.v.), died while trying to escape. A warrant was issued for the arrest of Williams; and George (afterwards Sir George) Simpson was sent out to hold his position in case he was removed from the territories over which he was governor. At the union of 1821, he was appointed joint governor with Simpson; and in 1822 he was placed in charge of the Southern Department. He returned to England in 1826; and he died in 1837.

WILLS, JOHN (d. 1814?) became a partner of the XY company shortly after 1798, and was one of the six wintering partners of the XY Company who became partners of the North West Company in 1804. Soon after 1804 he built Fort Gibraltar at the junction of the Red and Assiniboine Rivers; and he remained in charge of the Red River district until 1806, when he was transferred to Rat River. He returned to the Red River, however, in 1809; and he remained in charge of this department until he was relieved, because of ill-health, by J. D. Cameron (q.v.) in the summer of 1814. He died at Fort Gibraltar, either in the latter part of 1814, or in the beginning of 1815. He was elected a member of the Beaver Club of Montreal in 1807.

YALE, JAMES MURRAY (1801-1871) was born at Lachine, Lower Canada, in 1801. He entered the service of the North West Company about 1820, and was taken over as a clerk by the Hudson's Bay Company in 1821. He was sent to New Caledonia in 1821. He remained on the Pacific slope for the rest of his life; and he died at Saanich, British Columbia, on May 17, 1871. Fort Yale was named after him.

APPENDIX B

A SELECT BIBLIOGRAPHY RELATING TO THE HISTORY OF THE NORTH WEST COMPANY

AMOS, ANDREW. *Report of trials in the courts of Canada, relative to the destruction of the Earl of Selkirk's settlement on the Red River; with observations.* London: John Murray. 1820. Pp. iv, 388.

BATHURST, HENRY BATHURST, 3rd Earl, and HALKETT, J. *Correspondence in the years 1817, 1818, and 1819 between Earl Bathurst and J. Halkett, on the subject of Lord Selkirk's settlement at the Red River, in North America.* London: Printed by J. Brettell. 1819. Pp. 180.

BOUCHER, FRANÇOIS FIRMIN. *Relation donnée par lui-même des évènements qui ont eu lieu sur le territoire des sauvages depuis le mois d'octobre 1815, jusqu'au 19 juin 1816, époque de la mort de Mr. Semple, avec les détails de son long emprisonnement, jusqu'à son jugement.* Montreal. 1819.

BOUCHERVILLE, THOMAS VERCHÈRES DE. *Journal... dans ses voyages aux pays d'en haut, et durant la dernière guerre avec les Americains.* Canadian Antiquarian and Numismatic Journal, 3rd series, v. III, pp. 1-167.
 Reminiscences of a clerk in the service of the X Y Company during the years 1803-4.

BURPEE, LAWRENCE J. *The search for the western sea.* Toronto: Musson Book Co. 1908. Pp. lx, 651; illus. and fold. maps.

Copy of the deed poll under the seal of the Governor and Company of Adventurers of England, trading into Hudson's Bay, bearing date the twenty-sixth day of March, 1821, stating the appropriation of the forty shares reserved by the principal deed for chief factors and chief traders, with their duties; the regulations relating thereto, and for carrying on the trade. London: H. K. Causton. 1821. Pp. 22.

COUES, ELLIOTT (ed.). *New light on the early history of the Greater Northwest. The manuscript journals of Alexander Henry, fur-trader of the North West Company, and of David Thompson, official geographer and explorer of the same Company.* 3 vols. New York, 1897. Pp. xxviii, 446; vi, 447-916; 917-1027.

COX, ROSS. *Adventures on the Columbia River, including the narrative of a residence of six years on the western side of the Rocky Mountains, among various tribes of Indians hitherto unknown; together with a journey across the American continent.* London: Henry Colburn and Richard Bentley. 1831. 2 vols. Pp. xxiv, 358; viii, 400.

A SELECT BIBLIOGRAPHY

  A second edition was published in London in 1832; and an American edition, in one volume, in New York in 1832.

DAVIDSON, GORDON CHARLES. *The North West Company.* (University of California Publications in History, Vol. VII.) Berkeley: University of California Press. 1918. Pp. xii, 349; maps.

DOUGLAS, R. (ed.). *Nipigon to Winnipeg: A canoe voyage through western Ontario by Edward Umfreville in 1784, with extracts from the writings of other early travellers through the region.* Ottawa: R. Douglas. 1929. Pp. 63.

[ELLICE, EDWARD.] *The communications of Mercator upon the contest between the Earl of Selkirk, and the Hudson's Bay Company on one side, and the North West Company on the other.* Montreal: W. Gray. 1817. Pp. 111.
  Republished from the Montreal Herald.

[FAUCHE, G. A.] *Account of the transactions at Fort William on Lake Superior, in August, 1816, by Mr. Fauche, late lieutenant of the Regiment de Meuron, who accompanied the Earl of Selkirk to settle at Red River colony in North America.* Westminster. 1817. Pp. 8.

FLEMING, R. HARVEY. *McTavish, Frobisher and Company, of Montreal.* Canadian Historical Review, June, 1929, pp. 136-152.

FLEMING, R. HARVEY. *Phyn, Ellice and Company of Schenectady.* Contributions to Canadian Economics, IV, 1932, pp. 7-41.

FLEMING, R. HARVEY. *The origin of "Sir Alexander Mackenzie and Company".* Canadian Historical Review, June, 1928, pp. 137-155.

FRANCHÈRE, GABRIEL. *Relation d'un voyage à la côte du nord-ouest de l'Amérique septentrionale, dans les années 1910, 11, 12, 13, et 14.* Montreal: C. B. Pasteur. 1820. Pp. 284.
  An English translation by J. V. Huntingdon was published in New York in 1854 (pp. 376; front., plates.)

FRANKLIN, Sir JOHN. *Narrative of a journey to the shores of the polar sea, in the years 1819, 20, 21, and 22.* With an appendix on various subjects relating to science and natural history. London: John Murray, 1823. Pp. xvi; 768; front.; illus.; plates; port. fold. maps.
  A second edition in 2 vols. was published in 1824, and also a third edition in 2 vols. in the same year.

FRASER, SIMON. *First journal . . . from April 12th to July 18th, 1806.* Canadian Archives Report for 1929 (Ottawa, 1930), Appendix B, pp. 109-45.

FRASER, SIMON. *Letters from the Rocky Mountains from August 1st, 1806, to February 10th, 1807.* Canadian Archives Report for 1929 (Ottawa, 1930), Appendix C, pp. 147-59.

[GALE, SAMUEL.] *Notices on the claims of the Hudson's Bay Company and the conduct of its adversaries.* Montreal: William Gray. 1817. Pp. 161.

What appears to be a reprint of this was published in London in 1819.

GARRY, FRANCIS N. A. (ed.). *Diary of Nicholas Garry, deputy-governor of the Hudson's Bay Company from 1822-35: a detailed narrative of his travels in the North-West Territories of North America in 1821.* Transactions of the Royal Society of Canada, 2nd series, v. vi (1900), sect. ii, 73-204; with illustrations.

GATES, CHARLES M. (ed.). *Five fur-traders of the northwest: Being the narrative of Peter Pond and the diaries of John Macdonell, Archibald N. McLeod, Hugh Faries, and Thomas Connor.* With an introduction by GRACE LEE NUTE. The University of Minnesota Press: Published for the Minnesota Society of the Colonial Dames of America. 1933. Pp. 298.

Great Britain. Colonial Office. Hudson's Bay Company; *return to an address of the Honorable the House of Commons, dated 26 May, 1842, for copy of the existing charter or grant by the Crown to the Hudson's Bay Company, together with copies or extracts of the correspondence which took place at the last renewal of the charter between the government and the Company, or of individuals on behalf of the Company, also the dates of all former charters or grants to that Company.* London: Ordered by the House of Commons to be printed. 1842. Pp. 32.

[HALKETT, JOHN.] *Postscript to the Statement respecting the Earl of Selkirk's settlement upon the Red River.* [Montreal.] 1818. Pp. 195-222.

[HALKETT, JOHN.] *Statement respecting the Earl of Selkirk's settlement of Kildonan, upon the Red River in North America, is destruction in the years 1815 and 1816, and the massacre of Governor Semple and his party.* London: J. Brettell. 1817. Pp. 125, lxxxix; fold. map.

Printed for private circulation only in January 1817. A new, revised, and enlarged edition, with *Observations upon a recent publication entitled "A narrative of occurrences in the Indian countries", &c.*, was published in London in June, 1817, by John Murray (Pp. viii, 194, cii; map). An American edition of this was issued in New York in 1818; and a French translation, by Hugh Heney, was published in Montreal in 1818 by James Lane, under the title, *Précis touchant la colonie du Lord Selkirk sur la Rivière Rouge.*

HARGRAVE, JOSEPH JAMES. *Red River.* Montreal: Printed for the author by John Lovell. 1871. Pp. 506.

Appendix B contains a fragment of a journal kept by John Clarke at Isle à la Crosse in 1819.

A SELECT BIBLIOGRAPHY 509

HARMON, DANIEL WILLIAMS. *A journal of voyages and travels in the interior of North America.* Andover: Printed by Flagg and Gould. 1820. Pp. xxiii, 432; front. and map.
    Reprinted in New York in 1903 and 1922, and in Toronto in 1911.

HENRY, ALEXANDER. *Travels and adventures in Canada and the Indian territories, between the years 1760 and 1776.* New York: J. Riley. 1809. Pp. vii, 331; front. (port.).
    New ed., with introduction and notes, by J. Bain (Toronto, 1901).

[HENRY, JOHN.] *On the origin and progress of the North-West Company of Canada, with a history of the fur trade as connected with that concern, and observations on the political importance of the company's intercourse with and influence over the Indians or savage nations of the interior.* London: Cox, Son and Baylis. 1811. Pp. 38.

INNIS, HAROLD ADAMS. *Peter Pond, fur-trader and adventurer.* Toronto. 1930. Pp. xi, 153; map.

INNIS, HAROLD ADAMS. *The North West Company.* Canadian Historical Review, December, 1927. Pp. 308-321.

INNIS, HAROLD ADAMS. *The fur-trade in Canada; an introduction to Canadian economic history.* With a preface by R. M. MacIver. New Haven: Yale University Press. London: H. Milford, Oxford University Press. 1930. Pp. 444; plates; map.

JACKSON, MARJORIE GORDON. *The beginnings of British trade at Michilimackinac.* Minnesota History, September, 1930. Pp. 231-70.

KEATING, WILLIAM HYPOLITUS (comp.). *Narrative of an expedition to the source of St. Peter's River, Lake Winnepeek, Lake of the Woods, etc., performed in the year 1823, by order of the Hon. J. C. Calhoun, Secretary of War, under the command of Stephen H. Long, U.S.T.E.* Comp. from the notes of Major Long, Messrs. Say, Keating & Calhoun. 2 vols. London: George B. Whittaker. 1825. Pp. xiii, 458; 248, 156; front. illus.

LAROCQUE, FRANÇOIS ANTOINE. *Journal of Larocque from the Assiniboine to the Yellowstone, 1805.* Edited with notes by L. J. Burpee. Ottawa: Government Printing Office. 1910. Pp. 82. (Canada, Public Archives, Publication No. 3.)

MCADAM, ADAM (pseud.). *Communications from Adam McAdam, originally published in the Montreal Herald, in reply to the letters inserted therein under the signature of Archibald Macdonald, respecting Lord Selkirk's Red River Colony.* Montreal: W. Gray. Pp. 57.

MACDONALD, ARCHIBALD. *Narrative respecting the destruction of the Earl of Selkirk's settlement upon Red River in . . . 1815.* London: Printed by J. Brettell. 1816. Pp. 14.

MACDONALD, ARCHIBALD. *Reply to the letter, lately addressed to the Earl of Selkirk, by the Hon. and Rev. John Strachan, D.D. &c. Being four letters (reprinted from the Montreal Hearld), concerning the settlement on Red River, in the district of Ossiniboia, territory of the Hudson's Bay Company, properly called Rupert's Land.* Montreal (Lower Canada): Printed by W. Gray. 1816. Pp. 50.

According to Gagnon (vol. II., p. 437), one "Arch. McDonnell" replied to Strachan in *La Gazette de Québec*, May 30, 1816.

MACDONALD, ALEXANDER GREENFIELD. *A narrative of transactions in the Red River country; from the commencement of the operations of the Earl of Selkirk, till the summer of the year 1816.* London: B. McMillan, 1819. Pp. xix; 85; front. (fold. map).

[McGILLIVRAY, DUNCAN.] *Some account of the trade carried on by the North West Company.* Canadian Archives Report for 1928 (Ottawa, 1929), Appendix E, pp. 56-73.

This document was the basis of John Henry's *On the origin and progress of the North West Company of Canada* (London, 1811).

MACKENZIE, Sir ALEXANDER. *Voyages from Montreal, on the River St. Lawrence, through the continent of North America, to the Frozen and Pacific Oceans; in the years 1789 and 1793. With a preliminary account of the rise, progress, and present state of the fur-trade of that country.* London: Printed . . . by R. Noble, Old-Bailey. 1801. Pp. cxxxii, 412; front. and maps.

The introduction, which is entitled "A general history of the fur-trade from Canada to the North West" is valuable, but when it deals with matters outside the author's personal knowledge, not always accurate. The volume was translated into French (Paris, 1802), and has been many times reprinted in English, but generally without the maps.

McKENZIE, DANIEL. *A letter to the Rt. Hon. the Earl of Selkirk in answer to a pamphlet entitled "A postscript in answer to the statement respecting the Earl of Selkirk's settlement on the Red River in North America."* [Sandwich]. 1818. Pp. 8.

A rare pamphlet which appears to be a reprint from a newspaper.

MARTIN, CHESTER (ed.). *Red River settlement, papers in the Canadian Archives relating to the pioneers.* [Ottawa:] Archives Branch. 1910. Pp. 27.

MASSON, L. R. (ed.). *Les bourgeois de la Compagnie du Nord-Ouest.* 2 vols. Quebec, 1889-90. Pp. x, 415; vi, 499; maps.

A SELECT BIBLIOGRAPHY 511

MORTON, ARTHUR S. (ed.). *The journal of Duncan McGillivray of the North West, Company at Fort George on the Saskatchewan, 1794-5, with introduction notes, and appendix.* Toronto: The Macmillan Company. 1929. Pp. lxxviii, 79; 24; 6; maps.

O'NEIL, MARION. *The maritime activities of the North West Company, 1813 to 1821.* Washington Historical Quarterly, October, 1930, pp. 243-67.

Papers relating to the Red River settlement: Viz.: Return to an address from the honourable house of commons to his royal highness the prince regent dated 24th June 1819; for copies or extracts of official communications which may may have taken place between the secretary of state and the provincial government of Upper or Lower Canada, or to any complaints made of those proceedings by Lord Selkirk or the agents of the Hudson's Bay or the North-West Companies; also for copies or extracts of the reports made by the commissioners of special inquiry, appointed to inquire into the offences committed in the Indian territory so far as can be made public without prejudice to the public service, or to judicial proceedings now pending in Canada. Ordered by the house of commons to be printed, 12 July 1819. [London.] Pp. 287; 3 maps.
  That part of this blue-book which contains the Coltman report has been reprinted in the *Collections* of the State Historical Society of North Dakota, IV, 1913, 449-63.

PERRAULT, JEAN BAPTISTE. *Narrative of the travels and adventures of a merchant voyageur in the savage countries of northern America, leaving Montreal the 20th of May 1783 (to 1820).* Edited, with introduction and notes by JOHN SHARPLESS FOX. Michigan Pioneer and Historical Collections, V. 37 (1909-10). Pp. 508-619.

POND, PETER. *Journal of "Sir" Peter Pond, born in Milford Connecticut in 1740.* [Hartford.] n.d. Pp. 23; illus.

PRITCHARD, JOHN. *Glimpses of the past in the Red River Settlement, from letters of Mr. John Pritchard, 1805-1836.* Notes by Rev. Dr. Bryce. Middle Church: Rupert's Land Indian Industrial School Press. 1892. Pp. 25.

PRITCHARD, JOHN et al. *Narratives of John Pritchard, Pierre Chrysologue Pambrun, and Frederick Damien Heurter respecting the aggressions of the North-West Company, against the Earl of Selkirk's settlement upon Red River.* London: John Murray. 1819. Pp. 91.

ROSS, ALEXANDER. *Adventures of the first settlers on the Oregon or Columbia River; being a narrative of the expedition fitted out by John Jacob Astor to establish the "Pacific Fur Company", with an account of some Indian tribes on the coast of the Pacific.* London: Smith, Elder & Co. 1849. Pp. xvi, 352; front.; fold. map.

Ross, Alexander. *The fur hunters of the far West; a narrative of adventures in the Oregon and Rocky Mountains.* London: Smith, Elder & Co., 1855. 2 vols. Pp. xv, 333; viii, 262; front.

Selkirk, Thomas Douglas, 5th Earl of. *A letter to the Earl of Liverpool from the Earl of Selkirk, accompanied by a correspondence with the colonial department (in the years 1817, 1818, and 1819), on the subject of the Red River Settlement in North America.* [London.] 1819. Pp. 224.
Printed for private distribution.

Selkirk, Thomas Douglas, 5th Earl of. *Memorial presented to His Royal Highness the Prince Regent in Council relating to the North West Company.* London: Printed by J. Brettell. [1819.] Pp. 5.

Selkirk, Thomas Douglas, 5th Earl of. *Sketch of the British fur-trade in North America, with observations relative to the North-West Company of Montreal.* London: James Ridgeway. 1816. Pp. 130.
A second edition was published in New York in 1818; and a French translation by Hugh Heney was printed by James Brown in Montreal in 1819, under the title, *Esquisse du commerce de pelletries des Anglais dans l'Amérique septentrionale avec des observations relatives à la Compagnie du Nord-Ouest de Montreal.*

Simpson, William S. *Report at large on the trial of Charles de Reinhard for murder (Committed in the Indian Countries), at a court of Oyer and Terminer held at Quebec, May 1818, to which is annexed a summary of Archibald McLellan's indicted as an accessory.* Montreal. Printed for the reporter. Pp. xii, 340.

Stevens, Wayne Edson. *The northwest fur-trade, 1763-1800.* (University of Illinois Studies in the Social Sciences, Vol. xiv, no. 3.) Urbana: The University of Illinois. 1928. Pp. 204.

Strachan, John. *A letter to the Right Honourable the Earl of Selkirk on his settlement at the Red River near Hudson's Bay.* London: Printed for Longman, Hurst, Rees, Orme and Brown. 1816. Pp. 76.

Tanner, John. *A narrative of the captivity and adventures of John Tanner (U.S. interpreter at the Saut de Ste. Marie), during thirty years residence among the Indians in the interior of North America.* Prepared for the press by Edwin James. New York: G. & C. & H. Carvill. 1830. Pp. 426; front. (port.); illus.

Tyrrell, James Burr (ed.). *David Thompson's Narrative of his explorations in Western America, 1784-1812.* Toronto: The Champlain Society. 1916. Pp. xcviii, 582; maps and illus.

Tyrrell, James Burr (ed.). *Journals of Samuel Hearne and Philip Turnor.* Toronto: The Champlain Society. 1934. Pp. xviii, 611; maps.

A SELECT BIBLIOGRAPHY

WADE, M. A. *Mackenzie of Canada: The life and adventures of Alexander Mackenzie, discoverer.* Edinburgh and London: William Blackwood & Sons. 1927. Pp. xii, 332; illus. and sketch maps.

    The most authoritative account of the life of Sir Alexander Mackenzie.

WALLACE, J. N. *The wintering partners on Peace River from the earliest records to the Union of 1821, with a summary of the Dunvegan journal, 1806.* Ottawa: Thorburn and Abbott. 1929. Pp. 139; map.

WALLACE, WILLIAM STEWART. *The pedlars from Quebec.* Canadian Historical Review, December, 1932, pp. 387-402.

[WILCOCKE, SAMUEL HULL.] *A narrative of occurrences in the Indian countries of North America, since the connexion of the Right Hon. the Earl of Selkirk with the Hudson's Bay Company, and his attempt to establish a colony on the Red River; with a detailed account of his lordship's military expedition to, and subsequent proceedings at Fort William in Upper Canada.* London: Printed by B. McMillan, Bow Street, Covent Garden. Pp. xiv, 152, 87.

    A second edition, revised, was published at Montreal by Nahum Mower, in 1818; and two editions of a French translation by Hugh Heney, were printed in Montreal by James Brown in 1818, under the title, *Récit des évènements qui ont eu lieu sur le territoire des sauvages dans l'Amérique septentrionale.*

[WILCOCKE, SAMUEL HULL (ed.)]. *Report of proceedings at a Court of Oyer and Terminer, appointed for the investigation of cases from the Indian territories, held by adjournment at Quebec, in Lower Canada, 21st October, 1819, at which the following gentlemen partners of and connected with the North West Company . . . Archd. N. McLeod, James Leith, Hugh McGillis, Simon Fraser, Alexr. Macdonnell, Archd. McLellan, and John Siveright, who were under accusation by the Earl of Selkirk . . . made their appearance.* Montreal: William Gray. 1819. Pp. vi, 120.

[WILCOCKE, SAMUEL HULL (ed.).] *Report of the proceedings connected with the disputes between the Earl of Selkirk and the North West Company, at the assizes held in York in Upper Canada, October 1818.* From minutes taken in court. Montreal: Printed by James Lane and Nahum Mower. 1819. Pp. xxiii, 200, 218, 55, 4, xlviii.

    Another edition was published in London in 1818 by B. McMillan.

[WILCOCKE, SAMUEL HULL (ed.)]. *Report of the trials of Charles de Reinhard and Archibald McLellan for murder at a court of Oyer and Terminer, held at Quebec, May, 1818.* From minutes taken in shorthand under the sanction of the court. Montreal: Printed by James Lane and Nahum Mower. Pp. xxiv, 4, 652, 52, 159.

WILLIAMS, MEADE C[REIGHTON]. *Early Mackinac; a sketch historical and descriptive.* New edition, revised and enlarged. New York: Duffield and Co., 1912. Pp. 184; front.; map; illus.; ports.

INDEX

ABBOTT, James, 52, 61
Adhémar, Jacques, 221
Allaire, Marie, 443
America, Adventure per, 105
American Fur Co., 239-45
Amos, Andrew, *Report of trials*, 506
Andrews, Colin, 57
Andrews, Michel, 219
Angelica, 50
Arnoldi, *Dr.* Daniel, 448
Arnoldi, John Peter, 462
Askin, John, at Emissions, 4; quoted, 5; mentioned, 40-1; biography, 425
Astor, John Jacob, 22, 239-45, 266, 268, 432
Athabaska district, invaded by Hudson's Bay Co., 27
Azure, Joseph, 220

BABY COLLECTION, 170, 295
Bank of Montreal, 336, 340, 342-51, 380-5
Bannerman, James, partner of Simon McTavish, 7, 10; letters of, 51-62; biography, 425
Barber, *Capt.* C., 62
Barnett, Jean, 221
Barr, Richard William, witness, 94
Barron, Thomas, notary public, 134, 412, 414
Bathurst, Henry Bathurst, 3rd *Earl*, appeals to Edward Ellice, 29; *Correspondence*, 506
Batt, Isaac, 42
Baxter, Alexander, 69-70
Beaubien, François, 158
Beaudrie, B., 221
Beek, notary public, 84
Beioley, Joseph, biography, 425
Bell, John, biography, 425
Belleau, Pierre, 105
Berens, J., jr., member of Hudson's Bay Co. committee, 31
Bethune, Angus, sent as delegate to London, 29; mentioned, 220, 290, 318, 319, 321, 454, 457, 477, 504; biography, 426

Bethune, Anne, 477
Bethune, Christine, 457
Bethune, *Rev.* John (1751-1815), 426, 480
Bethune, *Rev.* John, dean of Montreal, 454
Bibliography, 506-13.
Bird, George, biography, 426
Black, Samuel, 219; biography, 426
Blackwood, *Hon.* John, of Quebec, 76, 294, 448
Blackwood, John, of Montreal, 76*n*
Blackwood, Thomas, 450
Bleakley, Josiah, 224; biography, 426
Blondeau, Barthélemi, 3; biography, 427
Blondeau, Maurice Régis, 4, 40, 451; biography, 427
Blondin, Pierre, 219
Boucher, F., 221
Boucher, François Firmin, *Relation*, 506
Boucher, Françoise, 503
Boucher, Paul, 219
Boucherville, Thomas Verchères de, *Journal*, 506
Bouchette, Joseph, 432
Bourguignon, Isaac, 220
Bouthillier, Jean, 495
Bove, a Canadian, 43
Boyd, Errol, 104
Boyer, Charles, 80, 81; biography, 427
Brevoort, *Mr.*, of New York, 343, 346
Brickwood, Pattle, and Co., 80
Brousseau, L., 219
Brown, C. Julius, witness, 413
Bruce, Charles, 220
Bruce, William, 3, 45, 53, 427; biography, 428
Brunosh, J. B., 219
Bryce, George, *The remarkable history of the Hudson's Bay Co.*, cited, 455
Burnett, Peter, 347, 359
Burns and Woolsey, 105
Burt, A. L., *The mystery of Walker's ear*, cited, 505

INDEX

CADOT, Jean Baptiste (*fl.* 1723-1803), biography, 428
Cadot, Jean Baptiste (1761-1818), documents relating to, 90-4; mentioned, 109, 171, 173, 174, 175, 179, 183-6, 198, 267-8; biography, 428
Cadot, Mary, 436
Cadot, Michel, agreement with North West Co., 176-8; mentioned, 221, 226; biography, 429
Caldwell, James, merchant in Montreal, 96, 105
Caldwell, James, clerk in North West Co., 220
Caldwell, Sir John, *Bart.*, 319-20
Caldwell, Fraser and Co., 96, 105
Cameron, Æneas, 104, 109, 110, 144, 157, 174, 175, 188, 216, 231, 232; biography, 429
Cameron, Angus, biography, 429
Cameron, Duncan, 109, 110, 144, 156, 174, 175, 179, 182, 188, 195, 204, 207, 209, 210, 211, 216, 220, 223, 224, 231, 232, 238, 246, 250, 254, 257, 258, 259, 261, 264, 269, 270, 275, 276, 280, 288; biography, 430
Cameron, John Dugald, 220, 269, 270, 275, 279, 288; biography, 430
Cameron, Ronald, 205, 221, 235-7, 246, 254, 257, 259, 261, 264, 269, 270, 275, 276, 280, 288; biography, 430.
Campbell, Alexander, 220, 431
Campbell, Colin, 219, 264; biography, 431
Campbell, D., 220
Campbell, John Duncan, 144, 156, 189-93, 195, 204, 207, 210, 219, 224, 231, 232, 238, 246, 254, 259, 260, 261, 264, 269, 270, 274, 277, 280, 288, 318; biography, 431
Campbell, Patrick, *Travels*, cited, 491, 496
Campbell, Richard, 264
Campion, Alexis, 431
Campion, Etienne, biography, 431-2
Capois, François, 220
Cardinal, Joachim, 219
Cardinal, Joseph, 220
Carrière, *Abbé*, 319
Carroll, Charles, of Maryland, 343, 346
Cartier, Joseph, 219
Cartwright, Richard, 104
Castle, William, witness, 411
Caton, Emily, 485
Chaboillez, Charles, 106, 108, 110, 144, 156, 171, 175, 179, 188, 195, 204, 207, 208, 209, 210, 216, 220, 232, 238, 246, 254, 258, 259, 261; biography, 432

Chaboillez, Charles Jean Baptiste, 138; biography, 432
Chaboillez, Charlotte, 139
Chaboillez, Marguerite (Margaret), wife of Simon McTavish, 135, 486
Chaboillez, Marie Louise Rachel, 138, 479
Chadwick, E. M., *Ontarian families*, cited, 462.
Chaguamigan, 176
Chaloux, Charles, 221
Chandler, *Capt.* Kenelm Conner, 448
Charles, Lewis, witness, 143
Chatelain, Louis, 80, 81, 105, 220
Chénier, Léon, 221
Chicoine, Pierre, 221
Chinn, Edward, 489
Chisholm, Donald, 220
Chittenden, H. M., *History of the fur-trade of the far west*, cited, 478
Church, Joseph, 139
Clark, Alexander, 221
Clarke, Adèle, *Old Montreal*, cited, 433
Clarke, John, in service of the Hudson's Bay Co., 26; journal, 508; biography, 432-3
Clarke, Simon, 432
Cocking, Matthew, quoted, 4; sent inland, 43; extracts from journal, 44-7.
Cole, John, 40-3
Collin, Joseph, 220
Coltman, William Bacheler, biography, 433
Colville, A., member of Hudson's Bay Co. committee, 31, 319
Comcomly, chief of the Chinook tribe, 463, 466
Conolly, William, 220; biography, 433-4
Constable, *Dr.* John, 492
Corbin, J. B., 221
Corry, Thomas, on the Saskatchewan, 3; spearhead of a group of traders, 4; mentioned, 220; biography, 434
Cotté, Gabriel, 451, 460
Cotté, P., 221
Cotterell, M., 220
Cowie, Robert, biography, 434
Cowie, William, 475
Cox, Ross, biography, 434
Cruickshank, Robert, 84, 105
Cumming, Cuthbert, 220; biography, 435

DAVID, David, 380
Davidson, Eliza, 474
Davis, John, biography, 435

INDEX

Dawkins, *Rear-Admiral* Richard, 471
Dease, Charles Johnson Watts, biography, 435
Dease, Francis Michael, biography, 435
Dease, *Dr.* John, 435-6
Dease, John Warren, 221; biography, 435-6
Dease, Peter Warren, 219, 426; biography, 436
Dease, Peter Warren, jr., 436
Decoigne, ——, 290
Deguire, Marie-Joseph, 504
Delisle, John, 104
Delorme, ——, in opposition to the North West Company, 23, 221, 232
Delorme, Pierre, 219
Desmarrais, Jean Baptiste, 105
Des Rivières, François, 468.
Dobie, Richard, 82-4, 104, 432, 440, 446, 447, 457, 489; biography, 436
Donovan, Richard, 105
Dorion, Louis, 220
Doty, *Madame*, 139
Douglas, *Sir* James, 433
Dowie, Alexander, 169, 231, 237
Dowie, Kenneth, biography, 436
Du Calvet, Pierre, 505
Ducharme, Dominique, 220
Ducharme, Nicholas, 220
Dufaux, Joseph, 104
Dumas, Pierre, 220
Dunardry, in Argyleshire, Scotland, 140-42, 486
Duncan, François, 220
Duncan, John, 492
Dunn, J. H., 338, 339, 346, 355, 379
Duplessis, A., 220
Dupuis, Louis, 220
Durand, Louis, 220
Durocher, Amable, 221
Durocher, Joseph, 220
Dyer, Allan, and Co., 80

Easthope, *Sir* John, 47
Edgar, William, letters to, 47-62
Edwards, Edward, 104
Ellice, Alexander, 54, 144, 155, 159, 169, 231, 232; biography, 437
Ellice, Edward, brings about union of Hudson's Bay and North West Cos., 29; member of advisory board on fur-trade, 31; receives stock in Hudson's Bay Co., 32; on committee of Hudson's Bay Co., 32; involved in litigation over North West Co. Partners' Trust, 34; mentioned, 319, 320, 321, 324, 327, 344, 353, 356, 372, 373, 376, 380, 382, 391, 397, 401; biography, 437-8.
Ellice, James, biography, 438
Elliott, T. C., *Peter Skene Ogden*, cited, 490
Ermatinger, Charles Oakes, 205, 220, 254, 489; biography, 438
Ermatinger, Edward, biography, 438-9
Ermatinger, Frederick William, 157
Ermatinger, Francis, biography, 439
Ermatinger, Lawrence, quoted, 5; partner of Forrest Oakes, 7; biography, 439
Ermatinger, Lawrence Edward, 438, 439
Evans, James, letters of, 430

Faries, Hugh, 221; biography, 439
Farquharson, Alexander, 220
Fauche, G. A., *Account of the transactions*, 507
Felicity, 49, 51, 52, 54
Ferguson, Isabella, 453
Finlay, Hugh, 104
Finlay, Jaco, biography, 439
Finlay, James (d. 1797), winters on the Saskatchewan, 3; partner of John Gregory, 11; mentioned, 105; biography, 440
Finlay, James (1766-1830), 105, 206, 451; biography, 440
Finlay, John, 105, 109, 110, 144, 156, 171, 175, 179, 206, 208, 209, 231, 232; biography, 440
Finlayson, Duncan, biography, 441
Finlayson, Nicol, biography, 441
Finlayson, Roderick, biography, 441
Fisher, Alexander, biography, 441
Fisher, Duncan, 104
Fleming, R. H., *Phyn, Ellice and Co.*, cited, 492
Fleming, ——, 52, 54, 55, 62
Fletcher, John, biography, 442
Forbes, *Capt.*, at Oswegatchie, 50
Forbes, John, 219
Forsyth, George, biography, 442
Forsyth, James, 144, 155, 157, 169, 231, 232; biography, 442
Forsyth, John, 144, 155, 157, 169, 231-2, 448; biography, 442
Forsyth, Joseph, biography, 442-3
Forsyth, Thomas, 144, 155, 157, 169, 231, 232; biography, 443
Forsyth-Grant, William, 442, 448
Forsyth, Richardson and Co., 16, 17, 144, 149, 157, 164
Fort Astoria, founded, 22

INDEX

Fort William, 2, 20, 23; seized by Selkirk, 25; last meeting of North West Company partners, 31; meetings at, 170; name adopted, 249-50
Fournier, Pierre, 139
Franceway, in the West, 3; is retired, 45
Franchère, Gabriel, biography, 443
François. *See* Franceway
Franklin, Sir John, *Narrative*, 507
Fraser, Alexander, sent on expedition to Hudson bay, 19; mentioned, 104, 109, 110, 144, 157, 175, 179, 188, 195, 204, 207, 208, 210, 216, 232, 258, 282; biography, 443-4
Fraser, *Capt.* Alexander, 445
Fraser, *Hon.* Alexander, of Fraserfield, 444
Fraser, Hugh, of Brightmoney, 137, 138, 142
Fraser, John (d. 1795), 445
Fraser, John, of London, 31, 97-8, 137, 142, 143, 299-300, 380-81
Fraser, John, jr., of London, 137, 295, 299-300
Fraser, Malcolm, 443, 444, 482
Fraser, Paul, biography, 444
Fraser, Peter, 219
Fraser, Richard Duncan, 220; biography, 444
Fraser, *Capt.* Simon, of Guisachan, 445
Fraser, Simon, of Albany, 96
Fraser, Simon, of Farraline, 137
Fraser, Simon (*fl.* 1766-1804), 104, 139, 443; biography, 445
Fraser, Simon (d. 1796), 105; biography, 444
Fraser, Simon (1760?-1839), 104, 143, 144, 156, 206; biography, 445
Fraser, Simon (1776-1862), explores Fraser river, 22; mentioned, 109, 110, 171, 175, 179, 182, 188, 209, 210, 216, 219, 224, 231, 232, 246, 254, 258, 259, 261, 264, 269, 270, 274, 280, 288; *Journal* and *Letters*, 507; biography, 445-6
Fraser, *Capt.* Thomas, 105, 444
Fraser, William, 105
Fraser's Highlanders (78th Regiment), 35
Frobisher, Benjamin (1742?-1787), 4; partner of Joseph Frobisher, 6; partner in the N.W. Co. of 1783, 8; death of, 13; mentioned, 58; letters of, 66-75; biography, 446
Frobisher, Benjamin (1782-1819), mentioned, 220, 300; biography, 446
Frobisher, Joseph, reaches the West, 3; partner of Benjamin Frobisher, 6; partner in the North West Co. of 1783, 8; partner of Simon McTavish, 13-14; retires, 21; agreement with Simon McTavish, 77-81; mentioned, 84, 95, 105, 108, 137, 139, 142, 300; biography, 446
Frobisher, Joseph, jr., 137
Frobisher, Thomas, reaches the West, 3; biography, 447
Fulloh, John, 296, 298-9

GALE, Samuel, *Notices on the claims of the Hudson's Bay Co.*, 508
Galliard, Louis, 221
Garry, Nicholas, member of Hudson's Bay Co. committee, 31; *Diary*, cited, 31, 508
Gauthier, Charles, 221
Gérome, Pierre, 220
Gerrard, Samuel, 125, 127, 134, 170n, 338, 341, 346, 349, 350, 379, 432, 442, 451; biography, 447
Gerrard, Samuel Henry, 447
Gerrard, Gillespie and Co. *See* Parker, Gerrard, and Ogilvy
Giasson, Jacques, 224; biography, 447
Gibb, Benaiah, 104
Gillespie, George, 125, 127, 134, 224; biography, 447
Gillespie, John, 125, 127, 134
Gillespie, Robert, biography, 447-8
Gillespie, Sir Robert, 448
Gillespie, Moffatt, and Co. *See* Parker, Gerrard, and Ogilvy
Gilmour, William, witness, 143
Goddard, ——, 49, 50
Goddard, *Mrs.*, 105
Goedeke, Frederick, 219
Graham, Andrew, master at York Fort, letter from, 39
Graham, Jane, 462
Grand Portage, 74, 88, 147, 170
Grant, *Commodore* Alexander, 450
Grant, Alexander, son of *Commodore* Grant, 139
Grant, Charles (d. 1784), report on fur-trade, 6, 62-5; mentioned, 442; biography, 448
Grant, Charles (1784-1843), 219, 318; biography, 448
Grant, Cuthbert (d. 1792), 449
Grant, Cuthbert (d. 1799), 91, 104, 106, 108, 206; biography, 449
Grant, Cuthbert (1796?-1854), biography, 449
Grant, David, 16, 80, 453; biography, 449-50
Grant, *Capt.* David Alexander, 452

INDEX

Grant, Frederick, 448, 452
Grant, James (d. 1798?), 105, biography, 450
Grant, James (*fl.* 1805-1827), 104, 221, 270, 271, 288; biography, 450.
Grant, John, of Kingston, 105
Grant, John, of Lachine, 104; biography, 450
Grant, John, of Montreal; biography, 451
Grant, Margaret, 448
Grant, Peter, 16, 104, 109, 110, 144, 157, 171, 174, 175, 179, 188, 206, 208, 209, 231, 233; biography, 451
Grant, *Rev.* Peter, 137
Grant, Richard; biography, 451
Grant, Robert, 3; partner of William Holmes, 7; partner in the North West Co., 8, 14; retired, 16; mentioned, 84-9; biography, 451-2
Grant, William, of St. Roch, biography, 452
Grant, William, of Three Rivers, biography, 452-3
Gray, Edward William, 82-4, 157, 489
Gray, Jonathan Abraham, notary-public, 134
Gray, William, 392
Graves, Booty, 3, 53
Gregory, George, of Quebec, 453, 502
Gregory, George (d. 1850), 453
Gregory, John, partner of James Finlay, and later of Normand McLeod, 11; partner in the North West Co., 13; partner of McTavish, Frobisher and Co., 15; retired, 21; mentioned, 75, 82-4, 90, 94-103, 105, 107, 108, 139, 143, 156, 199, 295, 296, 442, 445; biography, 453
Gregory, McLeod, and Co., history of, 11-13; deed of assignment, 82-4
Griffin, H., 411, 412, 413, 414
Guillon, Archange, 460
Guillemin, Guillaume, 468
Guimond, Louis, 221

Halcro, Joseph, 220
Haldane, John, 144, 155, 157, 165, 169, 204, 210, 211, 216, 221, 224, 232, 238, 246, 250, 254, 259, 260, 261, 264, 269, 270, 274, 275, 280, 288; biography, 453
Halkett, John, *Correspondence*, 506; *Statement*, 508
Hallett, Henry, biography, 453
Hallowell, Benjamin, 454
Hallowell, James (1748?-1830), partner in McTavish, Frobisher and Co., 21; mentioned, 81, 95, 103, 105; biography, 454
Hallowell, James (1778-1816), forced out of McTavish, McGillivrays and Co., 21; mentioned, 103, 104, 292, 297, 301; biography, 454
Hallowell, James (1796-1858), 454
Hallowell, William (1771-1838), forced out of McTavish, McGillivrays, and Co., 21; mentioned, 94-103, 105, 107, 139, 143, 156, 179, 224, 232, 292, 295, 302, 316, 404; biography, 454
Hallowell, William (1814-1863), 454
Hamilton, Charles, 220
Hamilton, W., 220
Hanson, Sarah, 489
Hardenbrook, David, witness, 245
Hargrave, James, biography, 454-5
Hargrave, Joseph James, 455; author of *Red River*, 508
Harmon, Daniel Williams, 220; biography, 455; *Journal*, 509
Harriott, John Edward, biography, 455
Harris, William, 221
Harrison, E., 221
Hawes, Jasper, 219
Hearne, Samuel, quoted, 3; mentioned, 43; *Journals*, 512
Heney, Hugh, biography, 455-6
Henry, Alexander (1739-1824), makes his first appearance in the West, 3; quoted, 4, 5; mentioned, 52, 84, 104; biography, 456
Henry, Alexander (d. 1813?), 219; biography, 456
Henry, Alexander (d. 1814), 109, 144, 156, 171, 173, 174, 175, 179, 188, 195, 204, 207, 209, 210, 216, 220, 223, 224, 232, 246, 254, 258, 259, 260, 263-4, 269, 270, 274, 277, 280; biography, 456
Henry, John, *On the origin and progress of the North West Co.*, 509
Henry, Martha, 454
Henry, Robert (1778?-1859), 219, 249, 264, 269, 270, 274, 280, 288; biography, 456-7
Henry, Robert (*fl.* 1813-24); biography, 457
Henry, William, 220; biography, 457
Heron, Francis, biography, 457
Heron, James, biography, 457-8
Heurter, Frederick Damien, *Narrative*, 511
Holman, F. V., *Dr. John McLoughlin*, cited, 482
Holmes, D., 219
Holmes, Jane, 448, 458

INDEX

Holmes, William, 3; partner of Robert Grant, 7; partner in the North West Co., 8, 14; mentioned, 89; biography, 458
Holmes and Grant, a partnership in the North West Company (1779), 6, 7
Howard, Joseph, biography, 458
Hudson's Bay Company, competition of, 1; absorbs North West Company, 2; monopoly attacked, 19; relations with North West Co., 24-31; union of 1821 with North West Co., 30-31; agreement of 1821, 321-7; articles of coalition, 404-8; references to, 148, 203-4, 266-7, 289, 290, 328, 353-6, 370, 372-5, 391
Hudspeth, Adam, 487
Hughes, Guy, biography, 459
Hughes, *Capt.* James (1738-1825), 458
Hughes, James, 109, 110, 144, 156, 175, 179, 188, 195, 209, 210, 211, 216, 220, 231, 232, 238, 246, 254, 258, 259, 260, 264, 267, 269, 274, 280, 288, 318; biography, 458-9
Hutchins, Thomas, 43

INGLIS, Ellice & Co., 242, 401. *See also* Phyn, Ellice and Co.
Innis, Harold Adams, cited, 8, 492
Invincible, 271, 275
Ireland, William, 169, 170
Irving, Washington, quoted, 2
Isbester, James, 471
Izenhoult, Tobias, 483

JOHNSON, Sir John, bart., 462
Johnson, Sir William, bart., 481, 492
Johnston, John, 226
Joubert, Charlotte, 446

KAY, William, 138
Keith, Fanny, 458
Keith, George, 219, 274, 279, 280, 288, 458; biography, 459
Keith, James, 219, 274, 290; biography, 459
Kerr, *Dr.* Robert, 448
Keshew, brother of Maurice Blondeau, 40
King, John, 458
King's posts, lease acquired by the North West Co., 19; mentioned in documents, 139, 209, 212, 248, 255
Kittson, George, 105

LACROIX, Paul, 220
LaFleur, J. B., jr., 219

LaFleur, J. B., sr., 219
La France, François, 81
La Garde, Joseph, 221
La Mar, S., 221
La Marche, Charles, 220
Lamisette, F., 219
Landry, Nicholas, 221
Lane, William Fletcher, biography, 459
La Prise, J. B., 219
Larocque, François Antoine, 220; biography, 460
Larocque, Joseph, 219; biography, 460
Laronde, Toussaint, 221
Latour, Isabella, 475
Laurent, Pierre, 80, 81
Laurie, Peter, 104
Laverdière, Joseph, 221
LeClaire, Charles, 220
Lees, John, of Quebec, 47
Leith, Alexander, 460
Leith, George, 460
Leith, James, partner in New North West Co., 18; mentioned, 144, 156, 157, 165, 169, 204, 210, 211, 216, 221, 224, 232, 238, 246, 254, 259, 260, 261, 264, 270, 272, 275, 280, 288; biography, 460-1.
Leith, Jamieson and Co., partners in the New North West Co., 17; mentioned, 144, 146, 157, 159, 163-4.
Leroux, Laurent, biography, 461
Lesieur, Toussaint, 104; biography, 461
Leslie, James, 345, 348
Lewis, Philo, 221
Lindsay, William, 105
Logan, Robert, 221, 262, 269, 270
Loiselle, Esther, 461
Longmore, Robert, 46
Lorin, Joseph, 220
Lugrin, N. de B., *The pioneer women of Vancouver Island*, cited, 495
Lyons, ——, 48, 51, 56

MABANE, Adam, 66*n*

MCADAM, Adam (pseud.), *Communications*, 509
McAulay, Aulay, 221
McBean, John, 221, 275, 288; biography, 461
McBeath, George, 4; partner of Peter Pond, 7; partner in the North West Co. of 1783, 8; mentioned, 40, 51, 56, 76, 89, 450, 453; biography, 461-2
McCormick Charles, 3; biography, 462
McCormick, John Johnson Dease, 462
McCormick, Thomas, 462
McCrae, David, 138, 462, 487

INDEX

McCrae, William, 221
McDonald, Angus Ban, 463
McDonald, Angus Grant, 464
McDonald, Archibald (*fl.* 1799), 105
McDonald, Archibald (1790-1853), biography, 462-3
McDonald, Finan, 220; biography, 463
McDonald, John (1770-1828), 144, 165, 169, 175, 182, 188, 195, 204, 207, 208, 209, 211, 216, 220, 223, 224, 231, 232, 238, 246, 254, 258, 259, 260, 261, 264, 269, 272, 275, 279, 288; biography, 463-4
McDonald, John (1774?-1860), of Garth, 106, 108, 110, 144, 156, 170, 175, 216, 220, 232, 238, 246, 254, 259, 261, 264, 269, 270, 280, 288, 431; biography, 464
McDonald, John (1782-1834), biography, 464
McDonald, Magdeleine, 472
McDonald, Ranald, 463
Macdonell, Æneas, 221; biography, 464
Macdonell, Alexander, 105, 221, 288, 290, 327; biography, 464-5
Macdonell, Allan, 220, 446; biography, 465
McDonell, James, 219
Macdonell, John, 106, 108, 110, 156, 157, 171, 174, 179, 188, 204, 207, 208, 210, 211, 216, 220, 223, 224, 238, 246, 254, 259, 260, 264, 269, 270, 464; biography, 465-6
Macdonell, Mary, 444
Macdonell, Miles, 290-1; biography, 466
McDougall, Alexander, 105, 109, 110, 144, 156, 179, 188, 216, 232; biography, 466
McDougall, Duncan, 283; biography, 466
McDougall, George, biography, 467
McDougall, James, biography, 467
McGill, Andrew, biography, 467
McGill, James, 3, 4; partner in Todd and McGill, 6; disappears from North West Co., 9; mentioned, 446; biography, 467-8
McGill, John, partner of Charles Paterson, 6; drops out of North West Co. (1783), 9; mentioned, 489, 491; biography, 468
McGill, *Hon.* Peter, 436
McGill and Paterson, a partnership in the North West Co. (1779), 6; disappears (1783), 9
McGillis, Angus, 220; biography, 468
McGillis, Donald, biography, 469

McGillis, *Dr.* Donald, 469
McGillis, Hugh, 109, 110, 144, 156, 171, 173, 175, 179, 188, 195, 204, 209, 210, 211, 216, 221, 223, 224, 231, 232, 238, 254, 258, 259, 261, 264, 269, 270, 275, 280, 285, 288; biography, 468-9
McGillis, John, 469
McGillis, Mary, 449, 480
McGillivray, Archibald, 219; biography, 469
McGillivray, Donald, 469
McGillivray, Duncan, tries to open trade on Pacific slope, 19; partner in McTavish, Frobisher and Co., 21; orders opposition from Grand Portage, 23; mentioned, 94-103, 104, 107, 137, 138, 140, 142-4, 148-9, 156, 175, 178, 179, 182, 188, 207, 211, 216, 219, 224, 246n, 250, 293, 295, 298; biography, 469; author of *Some account of the trade*, 510, *Journal*, 511
McGillivray, Farquhar, 469
McGillivray, John, 109, 110, 144, 156, 171, 173, 175, 179, 188, 195, 204, 209, 210, 219, 224, 231, 232, 246, 254, 256, 258, 259, 260, 264, 269, 270, 271, 274, 280, 288, 431; biography, 469-70
McGillivray, Joseph, 219; biography, 470
McGillivray, Magdalene, wife of William McGillivray, 137
McGillivray, Montrose, 471
McGillivray, Simon (1783-1840), partner in McTavish, McGillivrays and Co., 21; receives advances, 28; negotiates union with Hudson's Bay Co., 29-30; member of advisory-board on fur-trade, 31; receives stock in Hudson's Bay Co., 31; tries to wind up affairs of McTavish, McGillivrays and Co., 33-4; appointed gold commissioner in South America, 34; memoranda from, 367-77; letters from, 335-66, 377-87; letter of Henry McKenzie to, 387-422; explanation of accounts, 329-33; mentioned, 137, 139, 140, 142, 292-5, 299, 301, 304, 306, 310, 315, 319-21, 324, 327, 329, 334, 408; biography, 471
McGillivray, Simon (d. 1840), 219, 460; biography, 471
McGillivray, William (1764-1825), 12; purchases share of Peter Pond, 14; agent at Grand Portage, 15; succeeds Simon McTavish as chief director of

INDEX

North West Co., 21; receives advances, 28; negotiates union with Hudson's Bay Co., 29-30; member of advisory board on fur trade, 31; death of, 33; letters from, 317-18, 327-9; mentioned, 84-9, 91, 94-103, 105, 107, 108, 137, 138, 140, 142, 143, 156, 170, 174, 178, 179, 182, 188, 195, 207, 211, 224, 231, 232, 238, 239-45, 246*n*, 257, 263, 282, 291, 292, 295, 301, 303, 306, 310, 315, 321, 327, 356, 367, 397, 398, 464, 469, 498; biography, 471-2.

McGillivray, William (1800-1832), biography, 472

McGillivrays, Thain and Co., formed, 28, 170*n*, 335

McIntosh, Angus, agent of the North West Co. at Sandwich, 105, 152; biography, 472

McIntosh, Donald, 221; biography, 472

McIntosh, Duncan, 473

McIntosh, William, 219; biography, 472-3

Maciver, John, 474

McKay, Alexander, 23, 109, 110, 144, 156, 175, 179, 188, 204, 207, 209, 210, 211, 216, 221, 223, 224, 232, 238, 246, 248, 255, 258, 259, 445; biography, 473

McKay, Catherine, 445, 473

McKay, Donald, 445; biography, 473

McKay, Robert, 474

McKay, Thomas, 473

McKay, William, 104, 108, 144, 156, 170, 175, 179, 182, 188, 195, 204, 207, 208, 209, 210, 211, 216, 220, 223, 224, 231, 232, 238, 256, 259, 445; biography, 474

Mackenzie, *Sir* Alexander (1764-1820), quoted, 6, 12; enters fur-trade, 11; partner in North West Co., 13-14; agent at Grand Portage, 15; explorations, 16; joins New North West Co., 17-18; "excluded from interference" in the fur-trade, 20; creditor of North West Co., 28; mentioned, 84-9, 91, 95 6, 101, 105, 108, 125, 128, 134, 144, 155, 157, 164, 169, 232, 320, 404, 436, 462; biography, 474-5; author of *Voyages*, 510

McKenzie, Alexander (1767?-1830), 144, 155, 157, 165, 169, 210, 216, 219, 224, 231, 232, 254, 259, 260, 261, 267, 269, 461; biography, 475

McKenzie, Alexander (1794-1828), biography, 475-6

Mackenzie, "*Squire*" Alexander, 480

McKenzie, Andrew, 219, 234; biography, 476

McKenzie, Ann (Nancy), 475

McKenzie, Charles, 220; biography, 476

McKenzie, Daniel, quoted, 28; mentioned, 104, 108, 144, 156, 170, 175, 204, 208, 209, 210, 216, 219, 223, 224, 231, 232, 246, 254, 259, 260, 261, 269, 270, 275, 280; biography, 476; author of *Letter to the Earl of Selkirk*, 510

McKenzie, Donald, 221, 288, 404; biography, 477

Mackenzie, Geddes, 475

Mackenzie, George, of Avoch, 475

McKenzie, Hector, 476

McKenzie, Henry, partner of McTavish, McGillivrays and Co., 32-3; letter to Simon McGillivray, 387-422; mentioned, 105, 139, 173, 175, 176, 178, 190, 193, 294, 295, 301, 304, 305, 316, 359-61; biography, 477

Mackenzie, J. C., 182

Mackenzie, John (d. 1795), 474

McKenzie, John, witness, 294

McKenzie, John George, 475

McKenzie, Keith, 478

Mackenzie, Kenneth (d. 1780), 474

McKenzie, Kenneth (d. 1817), 229-31; 235, 238, 246, 249, 254, 259, 261, 264, 267, 269, 270, 275, 288; biography, 478

Mackenzie, Kenneth (1801-1861), 478

McKenzie, N., 221

McKenzie, Rachel. *See* Chaboillez, Marie Louise Rachel

McKenzie, Roderick (d. 1844), 12; partner in McTavish, Frobisher and Co., 21; mentioned, 102-3, 105, 108, 143, 156, 170, 173, 179, 195, 204, 206, 207, 208, 211, 216, 224, 232, 250, 257, 292, 295, 302, 426, 432; biography, 478-9

McKenzie, Roderick (1772?-1859), biography, 479

McKenzie, Roderick (*fl.* 1804-21), 220, 261, 269, 270, 275; biography, 479

McKenzie, Roderick (d. 1830), biography, 479

McKenzie, Roderick (*fl.* 1818-60), biography, 479

McKenzie, Simon McTavish, 477

Mackenzie, Oldham, and Co., 309, 388, 421

Mackinac Company. *See* Michilimackinac Company

INDEX

McLean, John, *Notes of a twenty-five years' service*, cited, 23, 502
McLean, *Hon.* Neil, 470
McLellan, Archibald, 205, 221, 232-4, 235, 246, 254, 259, 261, 264, 269, 270, 271, 275, 280, 288; biography, 479-80
McLeod, A. M., 219
McLeod, Alexander, 104, 108, 110, 170, 174, 189, 206, 208; biography, 480
McLeod, Alexander Roderick, biography, 480
McLeod, Ann, 480
McLeod, Archibald Norman, partner in McTavish, McGillivrays and Co., 21; witness, 94; mentioned, 104, 109, 144, 156, 171, 174, 175, 179, 182, 188, 195, 204, 207, 208, 209, 210, 211, 216, 219, 223, 224, 231, 232, 246, 254, 258, 259, 270, 292, 293, 295, 298, 301, 304, 318, 359, 388, 392, 404, 408; biography, 480-1
McLeod, John (*fl.* 1821-40), biography, 481
McLeod, John (1788-1849), biography, 481
McLeod, John (*fl.* 1821-1824), biography, 481
McLeod, Malcolm, *Peace River*, cited, 463
McLeod, Normand, partner of John Gregory, 11; partner in North West Co. (1787), 13; witness, 94; mentioned, 82-4, 89, 453, 480; biography, 481-2
McLoughlin, *Dr.* John, sent as delegate to London, 29; mentioned, 221, 288, 290, 317, 318-21, 473; biography, 482
McMillan, James, 220; biography, 482-3
McMurray, Samuel, 483
McMurray, Thomas (d. 1795), biography, 483
McMurray, Thomas (1779?-1849), 221; biography, 483
McMurray, William, 483
Macomb, ——, 51, 52, 55
McPhail, John, 220
McPherson, Murdock, biography, 483
McQuhae, James, witness, 294
McTavish, Alexander, nephew of Simon McTavish, 142
McTavish, Alexander, brother of Simon McTavish, 136
McTavish, Alexander (1784?-1832), biography, 484
McTavish, Anne, sister of Simon McTavish, 469, 470, 471

McTavish, Anne, daughter of Simon McTavish, 136, 140, 486
McTavish, Donald, 105, 108, 110, 137, 156, 170, 174, 179, 188, 195, 208, 209, 210, 211, 216, 219, 223, 224, 231, 238, 246, 253, 254, 258, 259, 260, 264, 269, 271, 280, 302, 304, 309, 317, 484; biography, 484
McTavish, Dugald, biography, 484
McTavish, James Chisholm, biography, 484
McTavish, John, 139, 140, 142, 294, 295, 301, 304, 305, 316, 393, 404, 408, 416; biography, 485
McTavish, John George, 175, 176, 182, 234, 270, 272, 279, 280, 317, 455; biography, 485
McTavish, Letitia, 455
McTavish, Marjory, sister of Simon McTavish, 138
McTavish, Mary, daughter of Simon McTavish, 136, 140, 486
McTavish, Simon (1750-1804), partner of James Bannerman, and later Patrick Small, 7; guiding spirit of the N.W. Co., 10; enters partnership with Joseph Frobisher, 13-14; death of, 19; letters of, 47-60; letter to J. Frobisher, 75-7; agreement with J. Frobisher, 77-81; last will and testament, 134-43; mentioned, 86, 94-103, 105, 107, 108, 170, 179, 199, 295, 320, 432, 445, 462, 485; biography, 485-6
McTavish, Simon (d. 1828), 136, 140, 486
McTavish, William, son of Simon McTavish, 140, 486
McTavish, William, governor of Rupertsland (1864-70), 455
McTavish, Fraser and Co., 21, 95, 97-8, 105, 107, 242, 292, 296, 299, 315, 356, 380-81, 401
McTavish, Frobisher and Co., formed, 14; position in the North West Co., 15; continues to conduct business of North West Co., 20; reorganized as McTavish, McGillivray, and Co., 21; agreement of 1799, 94-103; accounts, 104-7; mentioned, 82-3, 84-9, 149, 173, 206, 296. *See also* McTavish, McGillivrays and Co.
McTavish, McGillivrays and Co., organized, 21; becomes merely headquarters of Montreal district, 30; becomes insolvent, 33-4; agreement of 1811, 292-5; agreement of 1814, 295-304; mentioned, 170*n*, 297, 302-17, 329-33, 335-66, 397

523

INDEX

MacTier, Grace, 491
Malcolm, Neil, 140
Malhiot, François Victor, biography, 486
Martel, G., 221
Martin, Charles, 219
Massicotte, E. Z., *Les Chaboillez*, cited, 432
Masson papers, 108n, 143
Meldrum, George, 52, 61
Michilimackinac, trade of, 64
Michilimackinac (Mackinac) Company, 9, 224-9, 240, 263, 389
Miles, Robert Seaborn, biography, 486-7
Mille Vaches, seigniory, 173
Miln, John, 104
Minecker, Louis, 220
Mitchell, David, 224; biography, 487
Moffatt, George, enters Parker, Gerrard, and Ogilvy, 18; witness, 23; mentioned, 237, 346, 347, 348, 350; biography, 487
Moffatt, John Ogilvy, 487
Moffatt, Kenneth Mackenzie, 487
Moffatt, Lewis, 487
Monin, Joseph, 219, 220
Monk, G. H., 221
Montour, Nicholas, 3; partner in the N.W. Co. of 1783, 8, 14; retires, 16; mentioned, 76, 80, 81, 84-9, 105; biography, 487-8
Montour, Richard, 219
Montreal Michilimackinac Co., 239-45
Morice, Rev. A. G., *Miles Macdonell and his brothers*, cited, 466
Morisseau, Antoine, 220
Morrison, Alan, 488, 504
Morrison, Charles, 60
Morrison, Roderick, 220
Morrison, William, 221; biography, 488
Mower, Nahum, 392
Munro, Cornelia, 491
Munro, Henry, 221; biography, 488
Munro, J., 220
Munro, *Hon.* John, 488, 491
Mure, John, partner in the New North West Co., 17; mentioned, 125, 127, 128, 144, 155, 158, 164, 169, 231, 232; biography, 488-9

NANCY, schooner, 152
Nelson, George, 220
New North West Company, formed, 17; history of, 18-19; unites with North West Co., 19-20; references, 145-55, 158-70, 301
Noel and Shorts, 104

Nolin, François, 489
Nolin, Jean Baptiste, 226; biography, 489

OAKES, Forrest, partner of Lawrence Ermatinger, 7, 9; biography, 489
Oakes, *Sir* Hildebrand, 438, 489
Oakes, Jemima, 439, 489
Oakes, John Meticamish, 489
Oakes, Margaret, 489
Ogden, *Hon.* Isaac, 489
Ogden, Peter Skene, biography, 489
Ogilvy, John, becomes partner in the New North West Co., 17; mentioned, 125, 127, 128, 134, 144, 151, 155, 157, 158, 161, 164, 165, 169, 224, 231, 232; biography, 490
Overend, Gurney, and Co., 355

PACIFIC FUR COMPANY, founds Astoria, 22; mentioned, 282
Pambrun, Pierre Chrysologue, *Narrative*, 511
Pangman, Bastonnais, 491
Pangman, John, 491
Pangman, Peter, 3; at variance with other pedlars, 4; partner in Gregory McLeod and Co., 11; partner in the N.W. Co. (1787), 13; retires, 16; mentioned, 84-9, 496; biography, 490-91
Parker, William, 125, 127, 134; biography, 491
Parker, Gerrard, and Ogilvy, later Gerrard, Gillespie and Co., and Gillespie, Moffatt, and Co., 17
Paterson, Allan, 53, 76, 491
Paterson, Charles, 3; partner of John McGill, 6; drop out of N.W. Co., 9; director of the trade of the upper Mississippi, 9; mentioned, 76; biography, 491
Patterson, R., 347
Paul, Joseph M., 219
Peacock, Helen, 483
Pelly, J. H., member of Hudson's Bay Co. committee, 31
Perrault, Jean Baptiste, *Narrative*, 511; biography, 491-2
Perriauger, the, 51, 53
Perry, John, witness, 295
Phyn, George, 492
Phyn, James, biography, 492
Phyn, Ellice and Co., later Inglis, Ellice and Co., 16, 144, 157, 164, 166-7
Pichet, Catherine, 497

INDEX

Pichet, Pierre, 497
Pickel, John, jr., 178, 195, 202
Plenderleath, William Smith, 486
Poitras, Magdeleine, 465
Poitras, Marie, 464
Pond, Peter, makes his first appearance in the West, 3; partner of George McBeath, 7; partner in the N.W. Co. of 1783, 8; concerned in murder of Ross, 12; sells his share to William McGillivray, 14; mentioned, 53; biography, 492; *Journal*, 511
Porlier, Jacques, 486; biography, 493
Porteous, John, 56, 58, 450
Porteous, John, jr., 347, 348
Pothier, Toussaint, 105, 224
Powell, Wm. Dummer, 489
Prickets, Richard, 221
Primeau, Joseph, 220
Primeau, Louis, 42
Primrose, ——, 364, 365
Pritchard, John, 220; biography, 493; *Glimpses of the Past*, 511; *Narrative*, 511
Pruden, John Peter, biography, 493

QUEBEC ACT, 10
Quesnel, Jules Maurice, 220; biography, 493

RANKIN (Rinken or Renken), James, 48, 59, 61, 62
Raphael, Jacques, 220
Rasicotte, R., 221
Red River colony, 25
Reid, *Hon.* James, 139, 142, 229
Reinhard, Charles de, 479
Rhéaume, Pierre, 51
Richard, François, jr., 220
Richard, François, sr., 220
Richardson, John, 82-4, 144, 155, 157, 169, 231, 501; biography, 493-4
Robert, Cécile, 482
Robertson, Colin, in the service of the Hudson's Bay Co., 26; sails for London, 29; 219; letters of, 318-21; biography, 494
Robertson, John, 221
Robertson, Margaret, 501
Robertson, William, 105
Robillard, J. B., 220
Rocheblave, Philippe François Rastel de, 494
Rocheblave, Pierre Rastel de, in charge of Montreal office, 34; mentioned, 144, 155, 157, 165, 210, 211, 224, 231, 232, 246, 254, 258, 259, 260, 264, 267, 269, 270, 274, 280, 288, 292, 334-5, 392; biography, 494-5

Rocque, Joseph, 220
Rogers, *Major* Robert, 462
Ross, Alexander, biography, 495
Ross, Charles, biography, 495
Ross, David, witness, 229
Ross, Donald, biography, 496
Ross, John, 7; becomes a free trader, 9; partner in Gregory, McLeod and Co., 11-12; murdered, 12; biography, 496
Ross, Malcolm, 46
Ross, William, biography, 496
Roussain, E., 221
Rousseau, Dominic, in opposition to North West Co., 22-3
Rowand, John, 220; biography, 496
Roy, Theresa, 471
Roy, Vincent, 221
Rutherford, Ruby, 469

SAGE, W. N., *Simon Fraser*, cited, 446
St. Germain, B., 221
St. Germain, Joseph, 104, 221
St. Germain, Léon, 221
St. Germain, Venant Lemaire, 3; partner of Jean Etienne Wadden, 7; becomes an employee, 9; mentioned, 72, 80, 81, 104; biography, 496-7
Sansregret, J. B., 220
Sauvé, J. B., 220
Sayer, Guillaume, 497
Sayer, John, 104, 109, 110, 144, 157, 171, 174, 175, 179, 182, 204, 207, 208, 210, 216, 232, 235-7, 247-8, 258; biography, 497
Sayer, John Charles, 221, 497
Selby, George, 105, 138
Selby, William, 138
Selkirk, Thomas Douglas, *Earl of*, 1; quoted, 22; struggle with North West Co., 25-6; death of, 26; his influence on the fur-trade, 35-6; mentioned, 324, 369, 370, 388, 389, 390, 406, 421; publications of, 512
Semple, Robert, killed, 25
Seton, Maitland and Co., 105
Seven Oaks, battle at, 25
Sharp, George, 158; biography, 497
Shaw, Angus, partner in McTavish, McGillivrays and Co., 21; mentioned, 105, 108, 137, 144, 156, 170, 173, 174, 179, 208, 212, 231, 232, 246n, 254-5, 256, 269, 292, 293, 297-8, 302, 304, 317, 359; biography, 497-8
Shaw, Anna, 498
Shortt, Adam, *The Hon. George Moffatt*, cited, 487; *The Hon. John Richardson*, cited, 494

INDEX

Simpson, *Sir* George, letter from, 334-5; mentioned, 32, 441, 459
Simpson, Janet, 492
Simpson, Thomas, 436
Sinclair, Patrick, lieutenant-governor at Michilimackinac, quoted, 5
Sir Alexander Mackenzie and Co., the name applied after 1803 to the reorganized New North West Co., 18, 20; agreement of 1804, 157-69; references to, 126, 158-70, 267, 301, 329-30, 334, 398
Sieveright, John, 221; biography, 498
Small, Charlotte, 499, 502
Small, *General* John, 7, 464, 498
Small, Magdeleine, 472
Small, Nancy, 499
Small, Patrick (d. 1810?), 3; partner of Simon McTavish, 7; partner in N.W. Co., 9, 14; retires, 16; mentioned, 76, 84-9, 104, 431, 464; biography, 498-9.
Small, Patrick (1785?-1846), 219; biography, 499
Smith, Edward, 219, 288, 290; biography, 499
Smith, W., 220
Smith, Payne, and Smith, 355
Smyth, Erie, 462
Solomon, Ezekiel, 53, 55
South West Fur Co., 245, 266-7, 268, 281
South West trade, 9
Stayner, T. A., 501
Stedman, John, 58, 59
Stewart, Alexander, 219, 270, 274, 279, 280; biography, 499
Stewart, Andrew, biography, 499
Stewart, J. C., 104; witness, 125, 171, 172, 173, 176, 182, 186, 188, 190, 193, 195, 202
Stewart, John, 219
Strachan, *Rev.* John, 327, 467; *Letter to the Earl of Selkirk*, 512
Stuart, David, biography, 500
Stuart, John, 271-2, 279, 280, 288, 317; biography, 500
Stuart, Peter, 174
Stuart, Robert, biography, 500
Sutherland, Daniel, partner in North West Co., 15; mentioned, 84-9, 139, 158, 162, 450, 454; biography, 501
Sutherland, James, biography, 501
Sutherland, Louisa, 501
Sweenys and Co., 408
Symes, Henry Richard, 105

Tait, James, 221
Tanner, John, *Narrative*, 512
Tassé, J., *Les Canadiens de l'ouest*, cited, 428, 460, 493
Tate, C., witness, 411
Thain, Alexander, 502
Thain, John Richardson, 502
Thain, Thomas, partner of McTavish, McGillivrays and Co., 28; leaves Montreal, 33; extract of letter from, 334; mentioned, 144, 151, 157, 161, 162, 165, 169, 204, 211, 216, 224, 231, 232, 238, 246n, 250, 257, 264, 295, 304-6, 332-4, 343, 357, 361, 367, 371, 382, 392-9, 409-12, 416, 419-22, 434; biography, 501
Thomas Wilson and Co., 343-5, 382, 385
Thompson, David, crosses Rockies, 22; mentioned, 144, 156, 182, 195, 196-202, 210, 211, 216, 220, 231, 232, 246, 254, 259, 260, 264, 266, 269, 270, 272; biography, 502
Thomson, John, 144, 156, 210, 216, 219, 232, 246, 254, 259, 260, 264, 269, 270, 274, 277, 280, 288; biography, 502-3
Thomson, Robert, 104; biography, 503
Thorburn, William, 16, 104, 108, 174, 206; biography, 503
Todd, Isaac, 3, 4; partner in Todd and McGill, 6; drops out of N.W. Co., 9; 40, 47, 57, 105, 142; biography, 503
Todd and McGill, a partnership in the North West Co. (1779), 6; disappears (1783), 9; backs the Mackinac Company, 9; mentioned, 71
Tomison, William, quoted, 462
Tranquil, Paul, 220
Turner, Thomas A., witness, 169, 170
Turnor, Philip, *Journals*, 512
Tute, James, 3

Umfreville, Edward, 72, 80, 81; biography, 503-4

Vallé, Antoine, 221
Vallé, Louis, 221
Veaudrie, Toussaint, 220
Versailles, Louis, 219
Vincent, Thomas, biography, 504
Voyageurs Fund, 104, 256, 268

Wadden, Jean Etienne, partner of Venant St. Germain, 7; murder of, 8; mentioned, 426, 488; biography, 504

INDEX

Wadden, Josepha, 504
Wadden, Veronica, 504
Wade, M. S., *Mackenzie of Canada*, cited, 475
Waldorf, Ann, 432
Walker, Thomas, 4, 41, 104; biography, 504-5
Wallace, J. N., *The explorer of Finlay river*, cited, 426
Wappenassew, 40
Warren, *Sir* Peter, 436
Watson, John, 105
Welles, John, 91, 102, 104, 446
Welles, John K., 125; witness, 182, 186, 188
Wentzel, Willard Ferdinand, 219; biography, 505
Wilcocke, Samuel Hull, publications, 513

Wilkie, Alexander, 220
Williams, William, biography, 505
Wills, Geneviève, 488
Wills, John, 144, 156, 157, 165, 169, 210, 220, 224, 232, 238, 246, 254, 259, 260, 261, 264, 269, 270, 275, 280, 281; biography, 505
Woolrich, James, 104
Woolrich, Julia, 433

XY Company, agreement of 1803, 125. *See also* New North West Company

Yale, James Murray, biography, 505
Yeoward, Thomas, 125, 127, 134
Young, A. H., *The Bethunes*, cited, 426
Young, John, 105